Exploring Philosophy

An Introductory Anthology

SIXTH EDITION

Edited By

STEVEN M. CAHN

New York   Oxford

OXFORD UNIVERSITY PRESS

Oxford University Press is a department of the University of Oxford. It furthers the University's objective of excellence in research, scholarship, and education by publishing worldwide. Oxford is a registered trade mark of Oxford University Press in the UK and certain other countries.

Published in the United States of America by Oxford University Press
198 Madison Avenue, New York, NY 10016, United States of America.

© 2018, 2015, 2012, 2009, 2004, 1999 by Oxford University Press

Library of Congress Cataloging-in-Publication Data

Names: Cahn, Steven M., editor.
Title: Exploring philosophy : an introductory anthology / edited by Steven M. Cahn.
Description: Six edition. | New York : Oxford University Press, [2017] | Includes index.
Identifiers: LCCN 2017029791 | ISBN 9780190674335 (pbk.)
Subjects: LCSH: Philosophy—Textbooks.
Classification: LCC BD21 .E96 2017 | DDC 100—dc23
LC record available at https://lccn.loc.gov/2017029791

Printing number: 9 8 7 6 5 4 3
Printed by LSC Communications, Inc.

To the memory of my mother,
Evelyn Baum Cahn

CONTENTS

PREFACE

Those who begin the study of philosophy may easily become discouraged. Many classic texts are daunting in their complexity, and much contemporary writing is intended primarily for a professional audience.

A few prominent philosophers of our day write in a style understandable by all, but nonspecialists are often left unaware of this work. They may never realize that serious discussion of central problems of philosophy can proceed without arcane terminology, unexplained references, or convoluted arguments.

The guiding principle of this book is that reading clear, concise essays by recent philosophers offers an inviting avenue to understanding philosophical inquiry. While some of the articles are reprinted in their entirety, many are shortened to sharpen their focus and increase their accessibility.

For readers who wish to understand the development of philosophical inquiry over the centuries, I have included a substantial number of historical sources, including without abridgement Plato's *Defence of Socrates* and *Crito*, as well as substantial segments from his *Republic*, Descartes' *Meditations on First Philosophy*, and Hume's *An Enquiry Concerning Human Understanding* and his *Dialogues Concerning Natural Religion*. Most of these are identified by the name of the work from which the selection is drawn, while with regard to some of the recent essays, I have taken the liberty of developing short, descriptive titles.

NEW TO THIS EDITION

- A section devoted to Asian Outlooks.
- New essays on reasoning, egoism, virtue ethics, world hunger, aesthetic concepts, interpretation, Buddhism, Confucianism, Taoism, and Zen Buddhism.
- An expansion of Christine Vitrano's essay on meaningful lives.
- Over one-quarter of the contemporary essays are authored by women.

READINGS ADDED TO THE NEW EDITION

Steven M. Cahn, Patricia Kitcher, and George Sher, "The Elements of Argument"
Ray Billington, "The Tao"
Julia Driver, "Virtue Ethics"
Christopher W. Gowans, "The Buddha's Message"
Sallie McFague, "Speaking in Parables"
James Rachels, "Egoism and Moral Skepticism"
Henry Rosemont, Jr., "The Confucian Way"
Frank Sibley, "Aesthetic Concepts"
Travis Timmerman, "A Reply to Singer"
Twelve Zen Stories

Omitted after inclusion in the previous edition are selections by Scott F. Aikin and Robert B. Talisse, Gillian Barker and Philip Kitcher, Morris R. Cohen and Ernest Nagel, Carl Cohen, Marcia M. Eaton, Philippa Foot, Harry G. Frankurt, Karen Hanson, Grace M. Jantzen, David Lewis, Bernard Mayo, Robert McKim, Anne C. Minas, Terence Penelhum, Wesley C. Salmon, Amartya Sen, L. Susan Stebbing, Eleonore Stump, Laurence Thomas, Susan Wolf, Celia Wolf-Devine, Iris Marion Young, two by Charles L. Stevenson, and one by the editor.

INSTRUCTOR'S MANUAL AND COMPANION WEBSITE

An Instructor's Manual and Companion Website (www.oup.com/us/cahn) for both Instructors and Students accompany *Exploring Philosophy*. The Instructor's Manual features PowerPoint lecture outlines, reading summaries, a glossary, and a Test Bank of objective and essay questions. A link to the instructor materials can be found on the Companion Website along with student resources such as self-test questions with answers, suggested readings, and helpful web links.

ACKNOWLEDGMENTS

I am grateful to my editor, Robert Miller, for his continuing support and sound advice. I also wish to thank associate editor Alyssa Palazzo and production editor Marianne Paul for their generous help, as well as numerous other members of the staff at Oxford University Press for their thoughtful assistance throughout production.

In planning this new edition I have been guided in part by suggestions from reviewers chosen by the Press. I would like to thank them individually:

Carol Enns, *College of the Sequoias*
Carey Ford, *Navarro College, Corsicana*
Brent Franklin, *Rowan College at Burlington County*

Justin Garson, *Hunter College, CUNY*
Samuel LiPuma, *Cuyahoga Community College*
Joel E. Mann, *St. Norbert College*
Matthew Pianalto, *Eastern Kentucky University*
Timothy Torgerson, *University of Wisconsin, Superior*
Sandra Woien, *Arizona State University*

My editorial commentary reflects, as usual, stylistic pointers offered by my brother, Victor L. Cahn, playwright, critic, and Professor Emeritus of English at Skidmore College. The title of this book was originally proposed by my wife, Marilyn Ross, MD, to whom I owe so much more.

NOTE

Some of the materials throughout the book were written when the custom was to use the noun "man" and the pronoun "he" to refer to all persons, regardless of sex, and I have retained the author's original wording. With this proviso, let us embark on exploring philosophy.

PART 1

Introduction

What Is Philosophy?

MONROE C. BEARDSLEY AND ELIZABETH LANE BEARDSLEY

The study of philosophy is unlike the study of any other subject. No dates, formulas, or rules need be memorized. No field work is necessary, and no technical equipment required. The only prerequisite is an inquiring mind.

About what do philosophers inquire? The word *philosophy* is of Greek origin and literally means "the love of wisdom." But what sort of wisdom do philosophers love?

The answer is provided in our first selection. Its authors are Elizabeth Lane Beardsley (1914–1990), who taught at Lincoln University and then Temple University, and her husband, Monroe C. Beardsley (1915–1985), who taught at Swarthmore College and then Temple University.

While the best way to understand the nature of philosophical inquiry is to consider some specific philosophical issues, an overview of the subject is helpful, and that is what the Beardsleys provide.

Philosophical questions grow out of a kind of thinking that is familiar to all of us: the thinking that we do when we ask ourselves whether something that we believe is reasonable to believe. "Reasonable" has a broad, but definite, meaning here: a reasonable belief is simply a belief for which a good reason can be given. Reasonable beliefs are logically justifiable. It would seem that a belief that is reasonable stands a better chance of being true than one that is not, so anyone who is interested in the truth of his beliefs should be concerned about their reasonableness.

All of us have known, long before we approached the systematic study of philosophy, what it is like to want to make a belief reasonable, and also what it is like not to care whether a belief is reasonable or not. We have all had the experience of accepting beliefs without worrying about their logical justification, for we have all been children. We absorbed the beliefs of our parents, or the opinions current in our society or culture, without thinking about them very much or looking at them with a critical eye. We may not even have been fully aware that we had them; we may have acted on them without ever having put them into words. As long as our own experience did not seem to conflict with those early beliefs, or those beliefs did not seem to clash with one another, it did not occur to us to question them or to inquire into the reasons that could be given for them.

But a growing individual cannot grow for very long without sometimes wondering whether his most cherished beliefs have any foundation. This experience, too, dates back to childhood. When, for example, a child notices that the Santa Claus on the street corner is about as tall as his father, while the one in the department store is a good deal taller, and is moved to ask questions about Santa's location and stature, he is looking critically at a belief and inquiring into its reasons.

As we emerge from childhood, we continue to have experiences of this kind and to acquire further beliefs. Some beliefs we go on accepting without checking up on their reasonableness; other beliefs we do question, some of them very seriously. But two things happen to many of us. First, the questioned beliefs increase in proportion to the unquestioned beliefs. And second, the questioning process, once begun, is carried on for longer and longer times before it is allowed to end. The child who is told that the department store Santa is "really" Santa Claus, while those in the street are merely trusted helpers, may be satisfied for a time, but at some later stage he will probably ask himself what reason there is for believing *this* to be true, especially if he compares notes with his cousin from another city, who has been provided with a different candidate for the "real Santa Claus." The junior high school student who has been told he should accept what his science teacher says because the latter knows his subject may wonder why the teacher is judged to be a qualified authority in this field. If provided with satisfactory assurances, he will call a halt to his questioning process at that stage; but later on, perhaps in college, he may be moved to ask why we should ever accept anything told us by "authorities," no matter how well qualified. Should we not rely entirely on our own firsthand experience? Is anything else really *knowledge?*

The search for good reasons for our beliefs, and for good reasons for the reasons, can be carried as far as we wish. If it is carried far enough, the searcher finds himself confronted by questions of a peculiar kind: the questions of philosophy. Among these questions you will find some that you have already thought about, as well as others that will be unfamiliar to you. Many of them, however, originally came to be asked because someone undertook a critical examination of his ordinary beliefs.

PHILOSOPHICAL QUESTIONS

As our first example, let us trace the origin of a few philosophical questions that arise out of the moral aspects of life. People sometimes say, "He ought to be put in jail for that." Sometimes this is only an exclamation of anger at some instance of meanness or brutality; sometimes it leads to action, however, for juries do put people in jail because (if the jurors are conscientious) they believe that this punishment is just. Suppose you hear a friend remark, about the recent conviction of someone who has violated the law—a holdup man, a venal judge, an industrialist who has conspired to fix prices, a civil rights demonstrator who has blocked a construction site—that the jail sentence is deserved. After you hear all the relevant details, you may agree with him. But even so, you might still wonder whether you are right, and—not because you plan to do anything about the case, but merely because you would like to be sure you *are* right—you may begin to ask further, more searching, questions.

Why does the man deserve to be sent to jail? Because he committed a crime, of course. Yes, but why should he be sent to jail for committing a crime? Because to disobey the laws of the state is wrong. But *why?* Just because certain people you don't even know, perhaps people who died years before you were born, passed a law against, let us say, spitting in the subway or disorderly conduct, how does that obligate you to obey the law? This line of questioning, as we can foresee, will, if carried far, lead into some perplexing questions about the moral basis of the law, the tests of right and wrong, and the purposes of government and society. For example, we may discover that in approving the jail sentence we are assuming that the existence of a government is so important to maintain that governments have the right, under certain conditions, to deprive any citizen of his liberties. This assumption is a philosophical belief. And when we ask whether or not it is true, we are asking a philosophical question.

But consider how the questioning might turn into a different channel. Granted that the act was illegal, there still remains the question whether the man should be punished. Sometimes people do wrong things because they are feeble-minded or mentally ill, and we do not regard them as punishable. Well, in this case, it might be said, the man is responsible for his action. Why responsible? Because he was free when he committed it—free to commit the act or to refrain from committing it. He had, some would say, free will. Indeed, all men have free will—though they do not always exercise it. Then what reason is there to believe that this, in turn, is true? How do we know there is such a thing as free will? Again, we seem to have uncovered an underlying belief that lies deeper than the lawyer's or the juror's immediate problems, something they do not themselves discuss, but (according to one theory) take for granted. We have reached another belief that can be called philosophical, and exposed another philosophical question: do human beings have free will?

Let us see what it is about these questions that makes them philosophical. One of the first things that might be noticed about them is that they are highly *general.* One question is more general than another if it is about a broader class of things: about brown cows rather than about Farmer Jones's brown cow Bessie, or about cows rather than about brown cows, or about animals rather than about cows. A question about everything there is would be the most general of all—we shall be trying in due course to answer such questions. Most philosophical questions are highly general: Are all right actions those that promote human happiness? Is all knowledge based on sense experience? Or—to recall those that turned up in our example—do all human beings have free will? Do all citizens owe certain obligations to their governments? Those who specialize in subjects other than philosophy may be interested in particular things or events, such as individual crimes or criminals.

Or they may be interested in things or events of certain limited kinds, such as the psychological or sociological causes of crime. The philosopher goes into action when questions are raised about much larger classes, such as the class of human beings or of knowledge. Those who limit their investigations are entirely justified in doing so, for human knowledge could scarcely develop otherwise. Courts would never get their work done if every judge felt called upon to solve wide-ranging questions about guilt and responsibility before he could get down to the business of trying a particular case. But somebody, sometime, must ask those broad questions and try to answer them. That is the job of the philosopher.

Some questions count as philosophical because of a second, and even more important, quality: they are highly *fundamental.* The beliefs that a particular person has at a particular time constitute a more or less orderly system, depending on the extent to which they are logically interconnected, some being reasons for others, some of the others being in turn reasons for still others, etc. When you are pressed for your reason for predicting rain, if you reply that you observe dark clouds, then in your thinking at that time the second belief is more fundamental than the first. Of course a belief that is very fundamental in one person's thinking may not be at all fundamental in another's; that is one reason why each person comes at philosophy a little differently from everyone else. But there are some beliefs that are pretty sure to be fundamental in the thinking of anyone who holds them at all, and it is these that we have in mind when we speak of fundamental beliefs and fundamental questions without mentioning any particular believer.

When one belief supports another, but is not itself supported by it, it is logically more fundamental; there is more to it, so to speak, and therefore, in principle at least, it is capable of supporting a wider range of other beliefs. Thus, of two beliefs, the more fundamental one is probably the one that underlies and supports more of your other beliefs. If you should discover that you were mistaken about a particular fact, you would probably not have to revise many of your other beliefs to accommodate this change. But, for example, a belief in the immortality of the soul may be tied up with many other beliefs about morality, religion, education, and science. A highly fundamental question is a question about the truth of a highly fundamental belief. And such questions are philosophical ones. The more general a question is, the more fundamental it is likely to be, because it will range over a larger area. But this is not necessarily true. For example, the question, "Are all men selfish?" and the question, "Do all men wear shoes?" are equally general, since they are about all men; but they are not equally fundamental, since the former has important consequences for our beliefs about the nature of moral obligation (which includes a host of beliefs about particular obligations), while little seems to depend upon the latter. On the other hand, the philosophical question, "Does God exist?" does not seem to be general at all, for it is about a single being. Nevertheless, this question is fundamental for many people, since many other beliefs about human beings and the physical universe may depend upon the answer to it—and some of these beliefs are themselves highly general.

We do not know how to set up any rules telling exactly how general or how fundamental a question must be in order for it to be considered a philosophical one. Philosophers themselves might not all agree on the proper classification of every question you can think of. But if the demand for good reasons is pressed, beginning with any belief, it will gradually pass beyond the scope of various special fields of knowledge and investigation, and at some point it will bring to light a question that many philosophers would be interested in and would recognize—perhaps with joy, and perhaps, if it is a very tough one, with uneasiness—as their very own.

PHILOSOPHICAL EXAMINATION

Any thinking that concerns the truth of a philosophical belief is *philosophical thinking*. It may take the form of accepting a belief as true and investigating its logical connections with other beliefs; this may be called *exploring* the belief. Or it may take the form of questioning the belief and attempting to determine whether it is based on good reasons; this may be called *examining* the belief. Professional philosophers are those who have made philosophical thinking their vocation, but they have no monopoly on that activity. It is pursued by specialists in other fields—by scientists, historians, literary critics—whenever they inquire into the fundamental questions about their own disciplines. And it is pursued by all intelligent human beings who want to understand themselves and their world. Professional philosophers who genuinely respect their subject do not erect "No Trespassing" signs around philosophical questions.

In order to illustrate a little more fully what is involved in the process of examining a belief philosophically, let us take an example from history—let us begin with the belief that such and such a culture flourished hundreds of years before the Christian era in Central Africa or Nigeria. When the historian tells us this, we believe him. But if we have some intellectual curiosity, we might wonder how he knows it. Since the culture had no written language, he cannot rely on documents. And since their thatched houses and all the organic materials they once used in their daily life (wood, hide, cloth) would long ago have disintegrated in the tropical climate, the African historian has less to go on than his colleagues in other areas.[1] The usual methods developed by archaeologists are seldom available to him. It is hard to find organic materials on which to use the carbon-14 dating method (based on the constant rate of decay of this isotope in living organisms), though some artifacts have been dated in this way. Because of the rapid decay of dead wood and the eccentricities of seasonal growth, he cannot make much use of dendrochronology (dating by tree rings). But suppose the historian answers our challenge by using another method, thermoluminescence. In pottery there are uranium impurities that radiate naturally, but this radiation is trapped until the pottery is heated to a very high temperature. When the radiation rate for a particular substance is known, it is possible to determine how long ago the pottery was baked by measuring the amount of radiation built up in it.

Now we began with a question asked by the historian, "When did this culture flourish?" and the historian gave his answer. But when we ask him for his reasons, he appeals to principles of physics: for example, that the radiation rate of this kind of pottery is always such and such. If we ask him, "How do you know this?" he will, of course, conduct us to the physicist and advise us to direct our question to him—he is the expert on radiation. Suppose we do so. Presumably the physicist's answer will be something of this sort: "We have tested various samples in our laboratory under controlled conditions and have found that the radiation rate is constant." Now, "constant" here means that it holds not only for last week's laboratory samples, but for the same substance a thousand years ago and a thousand years hence.

Our historical curiosity is satisfied, and we would ordinarily be content to accept the physicist's conclusion, too. But, however irritating it may be, let us continue to press our question ruthlessly. "Why do you say," we ask the physicist, "that just because the radiation rate was constant all last week, it must have been the same thousands of years ago?" At first he may not quite know what we are after. "Well," he might say, hoping to appease us, "my experiments have shown that the radiation rate is independent of various environmental conditions, such as moisture, and I have reason to believe that the *relevant* conditions were the same in the past as they are now." If we are astute as well as doggedly persistent, we can point out something to him in return: "But you seem to be assuming a general proposition that whenever the same conditions exist, the same effects will occur—'Like causes, like effects,' or something of the sort."

Granted that if this general principle holds true, the physicist's particular law about the constancy of radiation rate can be justified—but again we can ask, "How do we know that like causes produce like effects? How do we know that an event always has certain relevant causal conditions and that whenever these conditions recur, the effect must recur, too?" Now we have left the physicist behind, too, and crossed over into the mysterious territory of philosophy. For we have asked a highly general question—since it is about all events, without exception, including everything that has happened or ever will happen. And it seems to be a highly fundamental question, since the assumption that every event has a cause, if it is true, must underlie an enormous number of other beliefs, not only in history and physics but in the common affairs of ordinary life.

Indeed, at this point we seem to have left everyone behind but the philosopher. And that is one of the peculiarities of this subject. When Harry Truman was President, he had a sign over his desk that said, "The buck stops here." The philosopher does his intellectual work under a similar sign, for there is no one to whom he can pass on a question with the plea that it is too general or too fundamental for him to deal with. The philosopher—and with him anyone else who is doing philosophical thinking—stands at the end of the line.

Here are two more samples of thinking that begin with a nonphilosophical belief but lead gradually but directly into philosophy. We present them in the form of brief dialogues.

Dialogue I

A: You ought to have written to your parents last Sunday.

B: Why?

A: Because you promised you would write every Sunday.

B: I know I did, but I've been awfully busy. Why was it so important to keep my promise?

A: Not just *that* promise—*any* promise. It's wrong ever to break a promise.

B: Well, I used to think that, but now I'm not sure. What makes you think it's always wrong to break promises?

A: My reason is simply that most people in our society disapprove of it. You know perfectly well that they do.

B: Of course I know that most people in our society disapprove of breaking promises, but does that prove it really is always wrong to do it? The majority opinion in our society could be mistaken, couldn't it? I don't see why it should be taken for granted that what most Americans *think* is wrong and what really *is* wrong should always coincide. What's the connection between the two?

Dialogue II

A: In my paper for political science I had to define "democracy." "Democracy" means "government by the people collectively."

B: What made you choose that definition?

A: I looked up the word in the dictionary, of course.

B: How do you know your dictionary is right? My dictionary doesn't always give the same definitions as yours.

A: Oh, but mine is larger and more recent, so it's bound to be more reliable.

B: Yes, but language is constantly changing, and words like "democracy" are used in lots of different ways. I think one shouldn't feel bound by any dictionary definition. Every writer should feel free to define any word as he wishes.

A: But that would be chaotic. Besides, you wouldn't really have definitions at all, in that case.

B: Why wouldn't you have definitions? There's no such thing as *the* "one true meaning" of a word, is there? Words mean whatever people make them mean, so why shouldn't I select my own meanings and put them in definitions of my own?

Very different topics are discussed in these brief conversations, but they follow a similar pattern. In each case, speaker A makes an opening remark of a fairly specific sort, speaker B asks A to give a good reason for his opening statement, and A does provide what, on the level of ordinary common-sense thinking, would be regarded as a satisfactory reason. Many conversations would end at this stage; but B is disposed to probe more deeply, to uncover the assumptions underlying A's reasons, and to ask whether these more basic assumptions, in turn, are reasonable. Notice how the beliefs being questioned become more general and more fundamental as the questioning goes on. In each of the little dialogues, B pushes A over the brink into philosophy. At the end of each, he raises a question concerning the truth of a philosophical belief—and there the matter is left, for the time being.

But you may not be content to leave it at that. If you feel some frustration or impatience with the way A and B are arguing, you are on the verge of doing some philosophical thinking yourself. Wouldn't you like to ask B some searching questions—for example, about the way in which he is using some of his key words? This would all be a lot clearer, you may have said to yourself while you were reading Dialogue I, if we were sure just what the word "wrong" means here. Maybe it means simply "disapproved by a majority of people in one's own society." In that case, what happens to B's final question? Isn't he confused? But *does* "wrong" mean only this? And take the term "free will," which was used in one of the other examples of philosophical thinking discussed above. How can we decide whether it is reasonable to believe that human beings have this mysterious thing without saying precisely what it is?

If you have been thinking for yourself along these lines, or (even if you haven't) if you can now see the sense in raising these questions about the meaning of key words, you will be able to sympathize with a good deal of what contemporary philosophers have been doing. Philosophers at all periods have been concerned to analyze the meaning of basic philosophical terms, but this task has received more attention from twentieth-century philosophers—or from many of them, at least—than ever before. By "key words" in philosophy we mean simply those words that are used in statements of beliefs that are highly general and fundamental, and in questions about these beliefs. A question about the meaning of such a word, such as the question, "What does 'cause' mean?" is itself highly fundamental, since the notion of causality plays a pervasive part in our thinking, and much might depend upon being clear about it. And we can see how it is that questions about the meaning of particular terms have led philosophers very naturally to still more fundamental questions about meaning itself, along with other basic characteristics of language. This further stage of interest in language is displayed in Dialogue II, in which speaker B is not content to accept A's remarks about the definition of the word "democracy" without questioning his assumptions about the very process of definition itself. Here B reveals a conviction (which we all can share) that we ought to be as clear as possible about the words in which we express our beliefs.

Increased clearness in your own beliefs is, then, one of the three chief benefits you can derive from a study of philosophy—if, as we hope, you are not content merely to learn about the theories and arguments of the great philosophers (interesting and valuable as that is), but will make this study an active exercise in philosophical thinking.

The second benefit, partly dependent on the first, is increased assurance that your beliefs are reasonable. A belief whose reasons have been examined deeply enough to reach the level of philosophical questioning rests on a firmer foundation than one that has been examined less thoroughly. This does not mean that everyone should become a professional philosopher (though we cannot help hoping that some readers of this book will ultimately make that choice). Admittedly, the philosopher's desire to base his beliefs on good reasons is unusually persistent and intense: the philosopher would not only rather be right than President—he would rather be right than anything. But all of us who want assurance that our beliefs are well grounded should do some philosophical thinking about some of them, at least, in order to secure the firmest possible grounds.

The third benefit which the study of philosophy can confer upon our beliefs is increased consistency. For philosophical thinking forces each of us to see whether his fundamental beliefs in different areas of experience form a logically coherent whole. We have already encountered . . . a pair of philosophical beliefs that seem in danger of clashing head-on in a contradiction. You will recall how we found that the philosophical examination of a belief about an African culture seemed to uncover an underlying assumption that every event happens under such conditions that when they are repeated, the same sort of event must happen again—in other words, that every event happens in accordance with a law of nature. And when we examined the assumptions underlying punishment we found that these seem to include the assumption that human beings have free will. To have free will is to be able to act in two different ways under precisely the same conditions. But if it is ever true that a man could have acted differently under the same conditions— i.e., that the conditions did not completely determine his action—then here is *one event* (namely the action) that did *not* happen in accordance with any law of nature. Perhaps further examination would clear things up, but it looks as if we have here a contradiction in beliefs. Philosophical thinking has diagnosed it, and further philosophical thinking is the only thing that will provide a cure.

The three values we have cited—clarity, reasonableness, and consistency—are basic intellectual values. But perhaps you are saying to yourself something like this: "I can see that studying philosophy may help me improve my beliefs, but, after all, there is more to life than thinking and believing. What I most want from my education is to improve my *actions*. How can philosophical thinking help me to *live* better?"

Part of our answer here is that we must beware of drawing too sharp a line between beliefs and actions. Our beliefs—including philosophical beliefs—have a considerable influence on our actions. This influence can be seen most directly in one area of philosophy, where we are concerned with questions of value, but answers to some other basic philosophical questions may also possess some power to affect, however indirectly, the way we live. Although knowledge may be valuable for its own sake, as well as for its practical consequences, it is not wrong to expect philosophy to have its effects. It would be wrong, however, to ask every philosophical belief to show a direct and simple connection with human action. Perhaps the growing appreciation of the importance of basic research in science may foster an appreciation of the quest for answers to other highly fundamental questions, without insistence on immediate practical results.

In saying that beliefs influence actions, we do not mean to lose sight of the effect of emotions on human conduct. Temporary emotions, as well as more enduring emotional attitudes, are often powerful enough to make us behave in ways counter to what we believe intellectually. Philosophical thinking can do a great deal to clarify and harmonize our beliefs at all levels, and to strengthen their foundations. But the philosopher is no substitute for the psychiatrist, or for the parents and teachers of our early years who help create our emotional make-up. Yet many philosophers have claimed that the experience of thinking about philosophical questions can affect our emotional attitudes as well as our beliefs.

When we detach our minds from immediate practical matters and from the limited boundaries of particular fields of specialization, we experience a kind of release from petty and provincial concerns. The experience of thinking as human beings who are trying to understand themselves and their universe may produce a serenity and breadth of mind that can in time become enduring attitudes.

NOTE

1. For this example, and the details concerning it, we are indebted to Harrison M. Wright, "Tropical Africa: The Historian's Dilemma," *Swarthmore Alumni Magazine* (October, 1963).

STUDY QUESTIONS

1. According to the Beardsleys, what is a philosophical question?
2. Construct a brief dialogue of your own, like Dialogues I and II, that illustrates how a philosophical issue can arise in the course of an ordinary conversation.
3. According to the Beardsleys, what are the three chief benefits to be derived from the study of philosophy?
4. Present an example of a philosophical belief that has influenced action.

The Value of Philosophy

BERTRAND RUSSELL

As we begin the study of philosophy, you may wonder whether the value of the subject can be explained briefly. Here is an insightful, inspirational statement from Bertrand Russell (1872–1970), the English philosopher, mathematician, and social activist, winner of the 1950 Nobel Prize for Literature, and one of the most prominent figures of the twentieth century.

. . . [I]t will be well to consider . . . what is the value of philosophy and why it ought to be studied. It is the more necessary to consider this question, in view of the fact that many men, under the influence of science or of practical affairs, are inclined to doubt whether philosophy is anything better than innocent but useless trifling, hair-splitting distinctions, and controversies on matters concerning which knowledge is impossible.

This view of philosophy appears to result, partly from a wrong conception of the ends of life, partly from a wrong conception of the kind of goods which philosophy strives to achieve. Physical science, through the medium of inventions, is useful to innumerable people who are wholly ignorant of it; thus the study of physical science is to be recommended, not only, or primarily, because of the effect on the student, but rather because of the effect on mankind in general. Thus utility does not belong to philosophy. If the study of philosophy has any value at all for others than students of philosophy, it must be only indirectly, through its effects upon the lives of those who study it. It is in these effects, therefore, if anywhere, that the value of philosophy must be primarily sought.

But further, if we are not to fail in our endeavour to determine the value of philosophy, we must first free our minds from the prejudices of what are wrongly called "practical" men. The "practical" man, as this word is often used, is one who recognizes only material needs, who realizes that men must have food for the body, but is oblivious of the necessity of providing food for the mind. If all men were well off, if poverty and disease had been reduced to their lowest possible point, there would still remain much to be done to produce a valuable society; and even in the existing world the goods of the mind are at least as important as the goods of the body. It is exclusively among the goods of the mind that the value of philosophy is to be found; and only those who are not indifferent to these goods can be persuaded that the study of philosophy is not a waste of time.

Philosophy, like all other studies, aims primarily at knowledge. The knowledge it aims at is the kind of knowledge which gives unity and system to the body of the sciences, and the kind which results from a critical examination of the grounds of our convictions, prejudices, and beliefs. But it cannot be maintained that philosophy has had any very great measure of success in its attempts to provide definite answers to its questions. If you ask a mathematician, a mineralogist, a historian, or any other man of learning, what definite body of truths has been ascertained by his science, his answer will last as long as you are willing to listen. But if you put the same question to a philosopher, he will, if he is candid, have to confess that his study has not achieved positive results such as have been achieved by other sciences. It is true that this is partly accounted for by the fact that, as soon as definite knowledge concerning any subject becomes possible, this subject ceases to be called philosophy and becomes a separate science. The whole study of the heavens, which now belongs to astronomy, was once included in philosophy; Newton's great work was called "the mathematical principles of natural philosophy." Similarly, the study of the human mind, which was a part of philosophy, has now been separated from philosophy and has become the science of psychology. Thus, to a great extent, the uncertainty of philosophy is more apparent than real: those questions which are already capable of definite answers are placed in the sciences, while those only to which, at present, no definite answer can be given will remain to form the residue which is called philosophy.

This is, however, only a part of the truth concerning the uncertainty of philosophy. There are many questions—and among them those that are of the profoundest interest to our spiritual life—which, so far as we can see, must remain insoluble to the human intellect unless its powers become of quite a different order from what they are now. Has the universe any unity of plan or purpose, or is it a fortuitous concourse of atoms? Is consciousness a permanent part of the universe, giving hope of indefinite growth in wisdom, or is it a transitory accident on a small planet on which life must ultimately become impossible? Are good and evil of importance to the universe or only to man? Such questions are asked by philosophy, and variously answered by various philosophers. But it would seem that, whether answers be otherwise discoverable or not, the answers suggested by philosophy are none of them demonstrably true. Yet, however slight may be the hope of discovering an answer, it is part of the business of philosophy to continue the consideration of such questions, to make us aware of their importance, to examine all the approaches to them, and to keep alive that speculative interest in the universe which is apt to be killed by confining ourselves to definitely ascertainable knowledge. . . .

The value of philosophy is, in fact, to be sought largely in its very uncertainty. The man who has no tincture of philosophy goes through life imprisoned in the prejudices derived from common sense, from the habitual beliefs of his age or his nation, and from convictions which have grown up in his mind without the co-operation or consent of his deliberate reason. To such a man the world tends to become definite, finite, obvious; common objects rouse no questions, and unfamiliar possibilities are contemptuously rejected. As soon as we begin to philosophize, on the contrary, we find . . . that even the most everyday things lead to problems to which only very incomplete answers can be given. Philosophy, though unable to tell us with certainty what is the true answer to the doubts which it raises, is able to suggest many possibilities which enlarge our thoughts and free them from the tyranny of custom. Thus, while diminishing our feeling of certainty as to what things are, it greatly increases our knowledge as to what they may be; it removes the somewhat arrogant dogmatism of those who have never travelled into the region of liberating doubt, and it keeps alive our sense of wonder by showing familiar things in an unfamiliar aspect.

Apart from its utility in showing unsuspected possibilities, philosophy has a value—perhaps its chief value—through the greatness of the objects which it contemplates and through the freedom from narrow and personal aims resulting from this contemplation. The life of the instinctive man is shut up within the circle of his private interests: Family and friends may be included, but the outer world is not regarded except as it may help or hinder what comes within the circle of instinctive wishes. In such a life there is something feverish and confined, in comparison with which the philosophic life is calm and free. The private world of instinctive interests is a small one, set in the midst of a great and powerful world which must, sooner or later, lay our private world in ruins. Unless we can so enlarge our interests as to include the whole outer world, we remain like a garrison in a beleagured fortress, knowing that the enemy prevents escape and that ultimate surrender is inevitable. In such a life there is no peace, but a constant strife between the insistence of desire and the powerlessness of will. In one way or another, if our life is to be great and free, we must escape this prison and this strife. . . .

Thus, to sum up our discussion of the value of philosophy: Philosophy is to be studied, not for the sake of any definite answers to its questions, since no definite answers can, as a rule, be known to be true, but rather for the sake of the questions themselves; because these questions enlarge our conception of what is possible, enrich our intellectual imagination and diminish the dogmatic assurance which closes the mind against speculation; but above all because, through the greatness of the universe which philosophy contemplates, the mind also is rendered great, and becomes capable of that union with the universe which constitutes its highest good.

STUDY QUESTIONS

1. Do you agree with Russell that the goods of the mind are at least as important as the goods of the body?
2. According to Russell, who are wrongly called "practical men"?
3. What value does Russell find in uncertainty?
4. According to Russell, what is the mind's highest good?

Defence of Socrates

PLATO

Philosophers build on the work of their predecessors, and the intellectual links that form the chain of the history of philosophy extend back to ancient Greece, more than five centuries before the Christian era. While only tantalizing fragments remain from the writings of the earliest philosophers, three men made such enormous contributions to the development of the subject that their overwhelming impact is widely acknowledged: Socrates (c. 470–399 B.C.E.), Plato (c. 429–347 B.C.E.), and Aristotle (384–322 B.C.E.).

Their relationship is unusual. Socrates wrote nothing, but in conversation was able to befuddle the most powerful minds of his day. Plato, his devoted student, responded to Socratic teaching not, as one might suppose, by being intimidated but by becoming the greatest of philosophical writers, whose *Dialogues,* mostly featuring the character Socrates, form the foundation of all subsequent Western philosophy. Such a towering figure as Plato could have been expected to produce mere disciples, but, after studying with Plato for more than two decades, Aristotle developed his own comprehensive philosophical system, opposed in many respects to that of Plato, and so powerful in its own right that throughout history its impact has rivaled that of Plato. Surely Socrates and Plato were remarkable teachers as well as philosophers.

The *Defence of Socrates* (or *Apology* as it is sometimes titled) is an account of the trial of Socrates, who, after having been found guilty of impiety, was put to death by the Athenian democracy. Socrates' speech to the jury, as related by Plato, has come down through the ages as an eloquent defense of not only Socrates' life but also philosophy itself.

Are the words actually those Socrates spoke? Scholars disagree, but a plausible answer is provided by David Gallop, Professor Emeritus of Philosophy at Trent University in Ontario, Canada, the author of the translation from the Greek that we are using:

> [I]t is inconceivable that any speaker could have improvised before a real court such an artfully structured, nuanced, and polished composition as Plato's *Defence of Socrates.* That is not to say that the work falsifies any biographical facts about Socrates, still less that its content is wholly invented. For we all know to the contrary, it may even in some places faithfully

From *Defence of Socrates, Euthyphro, and Crito,* translated by David Gallop. Copyright © 1997 by Oxford University Press. Reprinted by permission of the publisher and translator.

reproduce what Socrates said in court. But whatever blend of fact and fiction it contains, the speech as a whole is a philosophical memoir, intended to convey a sense of Socrates' mission and the supreme injustice of his conviction. It remains, above all, an exhortation to the practice of philosophy. No less than Plato's dramatic dialogues, it is designed to draw its readers into philosophical reflection, so that they may recover for themselves the truths to which the master had borne witness.

If that is the chief aim of the *Defence,* its fidelity to fact becomes a secondary issue.

To assist you in reading the *Defence,* Notes and an Index of Names prepared by the translator are provided at the end.

....

I don't know[1] how you, fellow Athenians, have been affected by my accusers, but for my part I felt myself almost transported by them, so persuasively did they speak. And yet hardly a word they have said is true. Among their many falsehoods, one especially astonished me: their warning that you must be careful not to be taken in by me, because I am a clever speaker. It seemed to me the height of impudence on their part not to be embarrassed at being refuted straight away by the facts, once it became apparent that I was not a clever speaker at all—unless indeed they call a "clever" speaker one who speaks the truth. If that is what they mean, then I would admit to being an orator, although not on a par with them.

As I said, then, my accusers have said little or nothing true; whereas from me you shall hear the whole truth, though not, I assure you, fellow Athenians, in language adorned with fine words and phrases or dressed up, as theirs was: you shall hear my points made spontaneously in whatever words occur to me— persuaded as I am that my case is just. None of you should expect anything to be put differently, because it would not, of course, be at all fitting at my age, gentlemen, to come before you with artificial speeches, such as might be composed by a young lad.

One thing, moreover, I would earnestly beg of you, fellow Athenians. If you hear me defending myself with the same arguments I normally use at the bankers' tables in the market-place (where many of you have heard me) and elsewhere, please do not be surprised or protest on that account. You see, here is the reason: This is the first time I have ever appeared before a court of law, although I am over 70; so I am literally a stranger to the diction of this place. And if I really were a foreigner, you would naturally excuse me, were I to speak in the dialect and style in which I had been brought up; so in the present case as well I ask you, in all fairness as I think, to disregard my manner of speaking—it may not be as good, or it may be better—but to consider and attend simply to the question whether or not my case is just; because that is the duty of a judge, as it is an orator's duty to speak the truth.

To begin with, fellow Athenians, it is fair that I should defend myself against the first set of charges falsely brought against me by my first accusers, and then turn to the later charges and the more recent ones. You see, I have been accused before you by many people for a long time now, for many years in fact, by people who spoke not a word of truth. It is those people I fear more than Anytus and his crowd, though they too are dangerous. But those others are more so, gentlemen: they have taken hold of most of you since childhood, and made persuasive accusations against me, yet without an ounce more truth in them. They say that there is one Socrates, a "wise man," who ponders what is above the earth and investigates everything beneath it, and turns the weaker argument into the stronger.[2]

Those accusers who have spread such rumour about me, fellow Athenians, are the dangerous ones, because their audience believes that people who inquire into those matters also fail to acknowledge the gods. Moreover, those accusers are numerous, and have been denouncing me for a long time now, and they also spoke to you at an age at which you would be most likely to believe them, when some of you were children or young lads; and their accusations simply went by default for lack of any defence. But the most absurd thing of all is that one cannot even get to know their names or say who they were—except perhaps one who happens to be a comic playwright.[3] The ones who have persuaded you by malicious slander, and also some who persuade others because they have been persuaded themselves, are all very hard to deal with: one cannot put any of them on the stand here in court, or cross-examine anybody, but one must literally engage in a sort of shadow-boxing to defend oneself, and cross-examine without anyone to answer. You too, then, should allow, as I just said, that I have two sets of accusers: one set who have accused me recently, and the other of long standing to whom I was just referring. And please grant that I need to defend myself against the latter first, since you too heard them accusing me earlier, and you heard far more from them than from these recent critics here.

Very well, then. I must defend myself, fellow Athenians, and in so short a time[4] must try to dispel the slander which you have had so long to absorb. That is the outcome I would wish for, should it be of any benefit to you and to me, and I should like to succeed in my defence—though I believe the task to be a difficult one, and am well aware of its nature. But let that turn out as God wills: I have to obey the law and present my defence.

Let us examine, from the beginning, the charge that has given rise to the slander against me—which was just what Meletus relied upon when he drew up this indictment. Very well then, what were my slanderers actually saying when they slandered me? Let me read out their deposition, as if they were my legal accusers:

"Socrates is guilty of being a busybody, in that he inquires into what is beneath the earth and in the sky, turns the weaker argument into the stronger, and teaches others to do the same."

The charges would run something like that. Indeed, you can see them for yourselves, enacted in Aristophanes' comedy: in that play, a character called "Socrates" swings around, claims to be walking on air,[5] and talks a lot of other nonsense on subjects of which I have no understanding, great or small.

Not that I mean to belittle knowledge of that sort, if anyone really is learned in such matters—no matter how many of Meletus' lawsuits I might have to defend myself against—but the fact is, fellow Athenians, those subjects are not my concern at all. I call most of you to witness yourselves, and I ask you to make that quite clear to one another, if you have ever heard me in discussion (as many of you have). Tell one another, then, whether any of you has ever heard me discussing such subjects, either briefly or at length; and as a result you will realize that the other things said about me by the public are equally baseless.

In any event, there is no truth in those charges. Moreover, if you have heard from anyone that I undertake to educate people and charge fees, there is no truth in that either—though for that matter I do think it also a fine thing if anyone *is* able to educate people, as Gorgias of Leontini, Prodicus of Ceos, and Hippias of Elis profess to. Each of them can visit any city, gentlemen, and persuade its young people, who may associate free of charge with any of their own citizens they wish, to leave those associations, and to join with them instead, paying fees and being grateful into the bargain.

On that topic, there is at present another expert here, a gentleman from Paros; I heard of his visit, because I happened to run into a man who has spent more money on sophists[6] than everyone else put together—Callias, the son of Hipponicus. So I questioned him, since he has two sons himself.

"Callias," I said, "if your two sons had been born as colts or calves, we could find and engage a tutor who could make them both excel superbly in the required qualities—and he'd be some sort of expert in horse-rearing or agriculture. But seeing that they are actually human, whom do you intend to engage as their tutor? Who has knowledge of the required human and civic qualities? I ask, because I assume you've given thought to the matter, having sons yourself. Is there such a person," I asked, "or not?"

"Certainly," he replied.

"Who is he?" I said; "Where does he come from, and what does he charge for tuition?"

"His name is Evenus, Socrates," he replied; "He comes from Paros, and he charges 5 minas."[7]

I thought Evenus was to be congratulated, if he really did possess that skill and imparted it for such a modest charge. I, at any rate, would certainly be giving myself fine airs and graces if I possessed that knowledge. But the fact is, fellow Athenians, I do not.

Now perhaps one of you will interject: "Well then, Socrates, what is the difficulty in your case? What is the source of these slanders against you? If you are not engaged in something out of the ordinary, why ever has so much rumour and talk arisen about you? It would surely never have arisen, unless you were up to something different from most people. Tell us what it is, then, so that we don't jump to conclusions about you."

That speaker makes a fair point, I think; and so I will try to show you just what it is that has earned me my reputation and notoriety. Please hear me out. Some of you will perhaps think I am joking, but I assure you that I shall be telling you the whole truth.

You see, fellow Athenians, I have gained this reputation on account of nothing but a certain sort of wisdom. And what sort of wisdom is that? It is a human kind of wisdom, perhaps, since it might just be true that I have wisdom of that sort. Maybe the people I just mentioned possess wisdom of a superhuman kind; otherwise I cannot explain it. For my part, I certainly do not possess that knowledge; and whoever says I do is lying and speaking with a view to slandering me.

Now please do not protest, fellow Athenians, even if I should sound to you rather boastful. I am not myself the source of the story I am about to tell you, but I shall refer you to a trustworthy authority. As evidence of my wisdom, if such it actually be, and of its nature, I shall call to witness before you the god at Delphi.[8]

You remember Chaerephon, of course. He was a friend of mine from youth, and also a comrade in your party, who shared your recent exile and restoration.[9] You recall too what sort of man Chaerephon was, how impetuous he was in any undertaking. Well, on one occasion he actually went to the Delphic oracle, and had the audacity to put the following question to it—as I said, please do not make a disturbance, gentlemen—he went and asked if there was anyone wiser than myself, to which the Pythia responded that there was no one. His brother here will testify to the court about that story, since Chaerephon himself is deceased.

Now keep in mind why I have been telling you this: it is because I am going to explain to you the origin of the slander against me. When I heard the story, I thought to myself: "What ever is the god saying? What can his riddle mean? Since I am all too conscious of not being wise in any matter, great or small, what ever can he mean by pronouncing me to be the wisest? Surely he cannot be lying: For him that would be out of the question."

So for a long time I was perplexed about what he could possibly mean. But then, with great reluctance, I proceeded to investigate the matter somewhat as follows. I went to one of the people who had a reputation for wisdom, thinking there, if anywhere, to disprove the oracle's utterance and declare to it: "Here is someone wiser than I am, and yet you said that I was the wisest."

So I interviewed this person—I need not mention his name, but he was someone in public life; and when I examined him, my experience went something like this, fellow Athenians: in conversing with him, I formed the opinion that, although the man was thought to be wise by many other people, and especially by himself, yet in reality he was not. So I then tried to show him that he thought himself wise without being so. I thereby earned his dislike, and that of many people present; but still, as I went away, I thought to myself: "I am wiser than that fellow, anyhow. Because neither of us, I dare say, knows anything of great value; but he thinks he knows a thing when he doesn't; whereas I neither know it in fact, nor think that I do. At any rate, it appears that I am wiser than he in just this one small respect: if I do not know something, I do not think that I do."

Next, I went to someone else, among people thought to be even wiser than the previous man, and I came to the same conclusion again; and so I was disliked by that man too, as well as by many others.

Well, after that I went on to visit one person after another. I realized, with dismay and alarm, that I was making enemies; but even so, I thought it my duty to attach the highest importance to the god's business; and therefore, in seeking the oracle's meaning, I had to go on to examine all those with any reputation for knowledge. And upon my word,[10] fellow Athenians—because I am obliged to speak the truth before the court—I truly did experience something like this: As I pursued the god's inquiry, I found those held in the highest esteem were practically the most defective, whereas men who were supposed to be their inferiors were much better off in respect of understanding.

Let me, then, outline my wanderings for you, the various "labours" I kept undertaking,[11] only to find that the oracle proved completely irrefutable. After I had done with the politicians, I turned to the poets—including tragedians, dithyrambic poets,[12] and the rest—thinking that in their company I would be shown up as more ignorant than they were. So I picked up the poems over which I thought they had taken the most trouble, and questioned them about their meaning, so that I might also learn something from them in the process.

Now I'm embarrassed to tell you the truth, gentlemen, but it has to be said. Practically everyone else present could speak better than the poets themselves about their very own compositions. And so, once more, I soon realized this truth about them too: it was not from wisdom that they composed their works, but from a certain natural aptitude and inspiration, like that of seers and sooth-sayers—because those people too utter many fine words, yet know nothing of the matters on which they pronounce. It was obvious to me that the poets were in much the same situation; yet at the same time I realized that because of their compositions they thought themselves the wisest people in other matters as well, when they were not. So I left, believing that I was ahead of them in the same way as I was ahead of the politicians.

Then, finally, I went to the craftsmen, because I was conscious of knowing almost nothing myself, but felt sure that amongst them, at least, I would find much valuable knowledge. And in that expectation I was not disappointed: They did have knowledge in fields where I had none, and in that respect they were wiser than I. And yet, fellow Athenians, those able craftsmen seemed to me to suffer from the same failing as the poets: because of their excellence at their own trade, each claimed to be a great expert also on matters of the utmost importance; and this arrogance of theirs seemed to eclipse their wisdom. So I began to ask myself, on the oracle's behalf, whether I should prefer to be as I am, neither wise as they are wise, nor ignorant as they are ignorant, or to possess both their attributes; and in reply, I told myself and the oracle that I was better off as I was.

The effect of this questioning, fellow Athenians, was to earn me much hostility of a very vexing and trying sort, which has given rise to numerous slanders, including this reputation I have for being "wise"—because those present on each occasion imagine me to be wise regarding the matters on which I examine others. But in fact, gentlemen, it would appear that it is only the god who is truly wise; and that he is saying to us, through this oracle, that human wisdom is worth little or nothing. It seems that when he says "Socrates," he makes use of my name, merely taking me as an example—as if to say, "The wisest amongst you, human beings, is anyone like Socrates who has recognized that with respect to wisdom he is truly worthless."

That is why, even to this day, I still go about seeking out and searching into anyone I believe to be wise, citizen or foreigner, in obedience to the god. Then, as soon as I find that someone is not wise, I assist the god by proving that he is not. Because of this occupation, I have had no time at all for any activity to speak of, either in public affairs or in my family life; indeed, because of my service to the god, I live in extreme poverty.

In addition, the young people who follow me around of their own accord, the ones who have plenty of leisure because their parents are wealthiest, enjoy listening to people being cross-examined. Often, too, they copy my example themselves, and so attempt to cross-examine others. And I imagine that they find a great abundance of people who suppose themselves to possess some knowledge, but really know little or nothing. Consequently, the people they question are angry with me, though not with themselves, and say that there is a nasty pestilence abroad called "Socrates," who is corrupting the young.

Then, when asked just what he is doing or teaching, they have nothing to say, because they have no idea what he does; yet, rather than seem at a loss, they resort to the stock charges against all who pursue intellectual inquiry, trotting out "things in the sky and beneath the earth," "failing to acknowledge the gods," and "turning the weaker argument into the stronger." They would, I imagine, be loath to admit the truth, which is that their pretensions to knowledge have been exposed, and they are totally ignorant. So because these people have reputations to protect, I suppose, and are also both passionate and numerous, and have been speaking about me in a vigorous and persuasive style, they have long been filling your ears with vicious slander. It is on the strength of all this that Meletus, along with Anytus and Lycon, has proceeded against me: Meletus is aggrieved for the poets, Anytus for the craftsmen and politicians, and Lycon for the orators. And so, as I began by saying, I should be surprised if I could rid your minds of this slander in so short a time, when so much of it has accumulated.

There is the truth for you, fellow Athenians. I have spoken it without concealing anything from you, major or minor, and without glossing over anything. And yet I am virtually certain that it is my very candour that makes enemies for me—which goes to show that I am right: The slander against me is to that effect, and such is its explanation. And whether you look for one now or later, that is what you will find.

So much for my defence before you against the charges brought by my first group of accusers. Next, I shall try to defend myself against Meletus, good patriot that he claims to be, and against my more recent critics. So once again, as if they were a fresh set of accusers, let me in turn review their deposition. It runs something like this:

"Socrates is guilty of corrupting the young, and of failing to acknowledge the gods acknowledged by the city, but introducing new spiritual beings instead."

Such is the charge: let us examine each item within it.

Meletus says, then, that I am guilty of corrupting the young. Well I reply, fellow Athenians, that Meletus is guilty of trifling in a serious matter, in that he brings people to trial on frivolous grounds, and professes grave concern about matters for which he has never cared at all. I shall now try to prove to you too that that is so.

Step forward, Meletus, and answer me. It is your chief concern, is it not, that our younger people shall be as good as possible?

—It is.

Very well, will you please tell the judges who influences them for the better— because you must obviously know, seeing that you care? Having discovered me, as you allege, to be the one who is corrupting them, you bring me before the judges here and accuse me. So speak up, and tell the court who has an improving influence.

You see, Meletus, you remain silent and have no answer. Yet doesn't that strike you as shameful, and as proof in itself of exactly what I say—that you have never cared about these matters at all? Come then, good fellow, tell us who influences them for the better.

—The laws.

Yes, but that is not what I'm asking, excellent fellow. I mean, which *person*, who already knows the laws to begin with?

—These gentlemen, the judges, Socrates.

What are you saying, Meletus? Can these people educate the young, and do they have an improving influence?

—Most certainly.

All of them, or some but not others?

—All of them.

My goodness, what welcome news, and what a generous supply of benefactors you speak of! And how about the audience here in court? Do they too have an improving influence, or not?

—Yes, they do too.

And how about members of the Council?[13]

—Yes, the Councillors too.

But in that case, how about people in the Assembly, its individual members, Meletus? They won't be corrupting their youngers, will they? Won't they all be good influences as well?

—Yes, they will too.

So every person in Athens, it would appear, has an excellent influence on them except for me, whereas I alone am corrupting them. Is that what you're saying?

—That is emphatically what I'm saying.

Then I find myself, if we are to believe you, in a most awkward predicament. Now answer me this. Do you think the same is true of horses? Is it everybody who improves them, while a single person spoils them? Or isn't the opposite true: A single person, or at least very few people, namely the horse-trainers, can improve them; while lay people spoil them, don't they, if they have to do with horses and make use of them? Isn't that true of horses as of all other animals, Meletus? Of course it is, whether you and Anytus deny it or not. In fact, I dare say our young people are extremely lucky if only one person is corrupting them, while everyone else is doing them good.

All right, Meletus. Enough has been said to prove that you never were concerned about the young. You betray your irresponsibility plainly, because you have not cared at all about the charges on which you bring me before this court.

Furthermore, Meletus, tell us, in God's name, whether it is better to live among good fellow citizens or bad ones. Come sir, answer: I am not asking a hard question. Bad people have a harmful impact upon their closest companions at any given time, don't they, whereas good people have a good one?

—Yes.

Well, is there anyone who wants to be harmed by his companions rather than benefited?—Be a good fellow and keep on answering, as the law requires you to. Is there anyone who wants to be harmed?

—Of course not.

Now tell me this. In bringing me here, do you claim that I am corrupting and depraving the young intentionally or unintentionally?

—Intentionally, so I maintain.

Really, Meletus? Are you so much smarter at your age than I at mine as to realize that the bad have a harmful impact upon their closest companions at any given time, whereas the good have a beneficial effect? Am I, by contrast, so far gone in my stupidity as not to realize that if I make one of my companions vicious, I risk incurring harm at his hands? And am I, therefore, as you allege, doing so much damage intentionally?

That I cannot accept from you, Meletus, and neither could anyone else, I imagine. Either I am not corrupting them—or if I am, I am doing so unintentionally;[14] so either way your charge is false. But if I am corrupting them unintentionally, the law does not require me to be brought to court for such mistakes, but rather to be taken aside for private instruction and admonition—since I shall obviously stop doing unintentional damage, if I learn better. But you avoided association with me and were unwilling to instruct me. Instead you bring me to court, where the law requires you to bring people who need punishment rather than enlightenment.

Very well, fellow Athenians. That part of my case is now proven: Meletus never cared about these matters, either a lot or a little. Nevertheless, Meletus, please tell us in what way you claim that I am corrupting our younger people. That is quite obvious, isn't it, from the indictment you drew up? It is by teaching them not to acknowledge the gods acknowledged by the city, but to accept new spiritual beings instead? You mean, don't you, that I am corrupting them by teaching them that?

—I most emphatically do.

Then, Meletus, in the name of those very gods we are now discussing, please clarify the matter further for me, and for the jury here. You see, I cannot make out what you mean. Is it that I am teaching people to acknowledge that some gods exist—in which case it follows that I do acknowledge their existence myself as well and am not a complete atheist, hence am not guilty on that count—and yet that those gods are not the ones acknowledged by the city, but different ones? Is that your charge against me—namely, that they are different? Or are you saying that I acknowledge no gods at all myself and teach the same to others?

—I am saying the latter: you acknowledge no gods at all.

What ever makes you say that, Meletus, you strange fellow? Do I not even acknowledge, then, with the rest of mankind, that the sun and the moon are gods?[15]

—By God, he does not, members of the jury, since he claims that the sun is made of rock, and the moon of earth!

My dear Meletus, do you imagine that it is Anaxagoras you are accusing?[16] Do you have such contempt for the jury, and imagine them so illiterate as not to know that books by Anaxagoras of Clazomenae are crammed with such assertions? What's more, are the young learning those things from me when they can acquire them at the bookstalls, now and then, for a drachma at most, and so ridicule Socrates if he claims those ideas for his own, especially when they are so bizarre? In God's name, do you really think me as crazy as that? Do I acknowledge the existence of no god at all?

—By God no, none whatever.

I can't believe you, Meletus—nor, I think, can you believe yourself. To my mind, fellow Athenians, this fellow is an impudent scoundrel who has framed this indictment out of sheer wanton impudence and insolence. He seems to have devised a sort of riddle in order to try me out: "Will Socrates the Wise tumble to my nice self-contradiction?[17] Or shall I fool him along with my other listeners?" You see, he seems to me to be contradicting himself in the indictment. It's as if he were saying: "Socrates is guilty of not acknowledging gods, but of acknowledging gods"; and yet that is sheer tomfoolery.

I ask you to examine with me, gentlemen, just how that appears to be his meaning. Answer for us, Meletus; and the rest of you, please remember my initial request not to protest if I conduct the argument in my usual manner.

Is there anyone in the world, Meletus, who acknowledges that human phenomena exist, yet does not acknowledge human beings?—Require him to answer, gentlemen, and not to raise all kinds of confused objections. Is there anyone who does not acknowledge horses, yet does acknowledge equestrian phenomena? Or who does not acknowledge that musicians exist, yet does acknowledge musical phenomena?

There is no one, excellent fellow: if you don't wish to answer, I must answer for you, and for the jurors here. But at least answer my next question yourself. Is there anyone who acknowledges that spiritual phenomena exist, yet does not acknowledge spirits?

—No.

How good of you to answer—albeit reluctantly and under compulsion from the jury. Well now, you say that I acknowledge spiritual beings and teach others to do so. Whether they actually be new or old is no matter: I do at any rate, by your account, acknowledge spiritual beings, which you have also mentioned in your sworn deposition. But if I acknowledge spiritual beings, then surely it follows quite inevitably that I must acknowledge spirits. Is that not so?—Yes, it is so: I assume your agreement, since you don't answer. But we regard spirits, don't we, as either gods or children of gods? Yes or no?

—Yes.

Then given that I do believe in spirits, as you say, if spirits are gods of some sort, this is precisely what I claim when I say that you are presenting us with a riddle and making fun of us: you are saying that I do not believe in gods, and yet again that I do believe in gods, seeing that I believe in spirits.

On the other hand, if spirits are children of gods,[18] some sort of bastard offspring from nymphs—or from whomever they are traditionally said, in each case, to be born—then who in the world could ever believe that there were children of gods, yet no gods? That would be just as absurd as accepting the existence of children of horses and asses—namely, mules—yet rejecting the existence of horses or asses!

In short, Meletus, you can only have drafted this either by way of trying us out, or because you were at a loss how to charge me with a genuine offense. How could you possibly persuade anyone with even the slightest intelligence that someone who accepts spiritual beings does not also accept divine ones, and again that the same person also accepts neither spirits nor gods nor heroes? There is no conceivable way.

But enough, fellow Athenians. It needs no long defence, I think, to show that I am not guilty of the charges in Meletus' indictment; the foregoing will suffice. You may be sure, though, that what I was saying earlier is true: I have earned great hostility among many people. And that is what will convict me, if I am convicted: not Meletus or Anytus, but the slander and malice of the crowd. They have certainly convicted many other good men as well, and I imagine they will do so again; there is no risk of their stopping with me.

Now someone may perhaps say: "Well then, are you not ashamed, Socrates, to have pursued a way of life which has now put you at risk of death?"

But it may be fair for me to answer him as follows: "You are sadly mistaken, fellow, if you suppose that a man with even a grain of self-respect should reckon up the risks of living or dying, rather than simply consider, whenever he does something, whether his actions are just or unjust, the deeds of a good man or a bad one." By your principles, presumably, all those demigods who died in the plain of Troy[19] were inferior creatures—yes, even the son of Thetis,[20] who showed so much scorn for danger, when the alternative was to endure dishonour. Thus, when he was eager to slay Hector, his mother, goddess that she was, spoke to him— something like this, I fancy:

> My child, if thou dost avenge the murder of thy friend, Patroclus,
> And dost slay Hector, then straightway [so runs the poem]
> Shalt thou die thyself, since doom is prepared for thee
> Next after Hector's.

But though he heard that, he made light of death and danger, since he feared far more to live as a base man, and to fail to avenge his dear ones. The poem goes on:

> Then straightway let me die, once I have given the wrongdoer
> His deserts, lest I remain here by the beak-prowed ships,
> An object of derision, and a burden upon the earth.

Can you suppose that he gave any thought to death or danger?

You see, here is the truth of the matter, fellow Athenians. Wherever a man has taken up a position because he considers it best, or has been posted there by his commander, that is where I believe he should remain, steadfast in danger, taking no account at all of death or of anything else rather than dishonour. I would therefore have been acting absurdly, fellow Athenians, if, when assigned to a post at Potidaea, Amphipolis, or Delium[21] by the superiors you had elected to command me, I remained where I was posted on those occasions at the risk of death, if ever any man did; whereas now that the god assigns me, as I became completely convinced, to the duty of leading the philosophical life by examining myself and others, I desert that post from fear of death or anything else. Yes, that would be unthinkable; and then I truly should deserve to be brought to court for failing to acknowledge the gods' existence, in that I was disobedient to the oracle, was afraid of death, and thought I was wise when I was not.

After all, gentlemen, the fear of death amounts simply to thinking one is wise when one is not: it is thinking one knows something one does not know. No one knows, you see, whether death may not in fact prove the greatest of all blessings for mankind; but people fear it as if they knew it for certain to be the greatest of evils. And yet to think that one knows what one does not know must surely be the kind of folly which is reprehensible.

On this matter especially, gentlemen, that may be the nature of my own advantage over most people. If I really were to claim to be wiser than anyone in any respect, it would consist simply in this: just as I do not possess adequate knowledge of life in Hades, so I also realize that I do not possess it; whereas acting unjustly in disobedience to one's betters, whether god or human being, is something I *know* to be evil and shameful. Hence I shall never fear or flee from something which may indeed be a good for all I know, rather than from things I know to be evils.

Suppose, therefore, that you pay no heed to Anytus, but are prepared to let me go. He said I need never have been brought to court in the first place; but that once I had been, your only option was to put me to death. He declared before you that, if I got away from you this time, your sons would all be utterly corrupted by practising Socrates' teachings. Suppose, in the face of that, you were to say to me:

"Socrates, we will not listen to Anytus this time. We are prepared to let you go—but only on this condition: you are to pursue that quest of yours and practise philosophy no longer; and if you are caught doing it any more, you shall be put to death."

Well, as I just said, if you were prepared to let me go on those terms, I should reply to you as follows:

"I have the greatest fondness and affection for you, fellow Athenians, but I will obey my god rather than you; and so long as I draw breath and am able, I shall never give up practising philosophy, or exhorting and showing the way to any of you whom I ever encounter, by giving my usual sort of message. 'Excellent friend,' I shall say; 'You are an Athenian. Your city is the most important and renowned for its wisdom and power; so are you not ashamed that, while you take care to acquire as much wealth as possible, with honour and glory as well, yet you take no care or thought for understanding or truth, or for the best possible state of your soul?'

"And should any of you dispute that, and claim that he does take such care, I will not let him go straight away nor leave him, but I will question and examine and put him to the test; and if I do not think he has acquired goodness, though he says he has, I shall say, 'Shame on you, for setting the lowest value upon the most precious things, and for rating inferior ones more highly!' That I shall do for anyone I encounter, young or old, alien or fellow citizen; but all the more for the latter, since your kinship with me is closer."

Those are my orders from my god, I do assure you. Indeed, I believe that no greater good has ever befallen you in our city than my service to my god; because all I do is to go about persuading you, young and old alike, not to care for your bodies or for your wealth so intensely as for the greatest possible well-being of your souls. "It is not wealth," I tell you, "that produces goodness; rather, it is from goodness that wealth, and all other benefits for human beings, accrue to them in their private and public life."

If, in fact, I am corrupting the young by those assertions, you may call them harmful. But if anyone claims that I say anything different, he is talking nonsense. In the face of that I should like to say: "Fellow Athenians, you may listen to Anytus or not, as you please; and you may let me go or not, as you please, because there is no chance of my acting otherwise, even if I have to die many times over."

Stop protesting, fellow Athenians! Please abide by my request that you not protest against what I say, but hear me out; in fact, it will be in your interest, so I believe, to do so. You see, I am going to say some further things to you which may make you shout out—although I beg you not to.

You may be assured that if you put to death the sort of man I just said I was, you will not harm me more than you harm yourselves. Meletus or Anytus would not harm me at all; nor, in fact, could they do so, since I believe it is out of the question for a better man to be harmed by his inferior. The latter may, of course, inflict death or banishment or disenfranchisement; and my accuser here, along with others no doubt, believes those to be great evils. But I do not. Rather, I believe it a far greater evil to try to kill a man unjustly, as he does now.

At this point, therefore, fellow Athenians, so far from pleading on my own behalf, as might be supposed, I am pleading on yours, in case by condemning me you should mistreat the gift which God has bestowed upon you—because if you put me to death, you will not easily find another like me. The fact is, if I may put the point in a somewhat comical way, that I have been literally attached by God to our city, as if to a horse—a large thoroughbred, which is a bit sluggish because of its size, and needs to be aroused by some sort of gadfly. Yes, in me, I believe, God has attached to our city just such a creature—the kind which is constantly alighting everywhere on you, all day long, arousing, cajoling, or reproaching each and every one of you. You will not easily acquire another such gadfly, gentlemen; rather, if you take my advice, you will spare my life. I dare say, though, that you will get angry, like people who are awakened from their doze. Perhaps you will heed Anytus and give me a swat: you could happily finish me off, and then spend the rest of your life asleep—unless God, in his compassion for you, were to send you someone else.

That I am, in fact, just the sort of gift that God would send to our city, you may recognize from this: it would not seem to be in human nature for me to have neglected all my own affairs, and put up with the neglect of my family for all these years, but constantly minded your interests, by visiting each of you in private like a father or an elder brother, urging you to be concerned about goodness. Of course, if I were gaining anything from that, or were being paid to urge that course upon you, my actions could be explained. But in fact you can see for yourselves that my accusers, who so shamelessly level all those other charges against me, could not muster the impudence to call evidence that I ever once obtained payment or asked for any. It is I who can call evidence sufficient, I think, to show that I am speaking the truth—namely, my poverty.

Now it may perhaps seem peculiar that, as some say, I give this counsel by going around and dealing with others' concerns in private, yet do not venture to appear before the Assembly, and counsel the city about your business in public. But the reason for that is one you have frequently heard me give in many places: it is a certain divine or spiritual sign[22] which comes to me, the very thing to which Meletus made mocking allusion in his indictment. It has been happening to me ever since childhood: a voice of some sort which comes and which always—whenever it does come—restrains me from what I am about to do, yet never gives positive direction. That is what opposes my engaging in politics—and its opposition is an excellent thing, to my mind; because you may be quite sure, fellow Athenians, that if I had tried to engage in politics, I should have perished long since and should have been of no use either to you or to myself.

And please do not get angry if I tell you the truth. The fact is that there is no person on earth whose life will be spared by you or by any other majority, if he is genuinely opposed to many injustices and unlawful acts and tries to prevent their occurrence in our city. Rather, anyone who truly fights for what is just, if he is going to survive for even a short time, must act in a private capacity rather than a public one.

I will offer you conclusive evidence of that—not just words, but the sort of evidence that you respect, namely, actions. Just hear me tell my experiences, so that you may know that I would not submit to a single person for fear of death, contrary to what is just; nor would I do so, even if I were to lose my life on the spot. I shall mention things to you which are vulgar commonplaces of the courts, yet they are true.

Although I have never held any other public office in our city, fellow Athenians, I have served on its Council. My own tribe, Antiochis, happened to be the presiding commission[23] on the occasion when you wanted a collective trial for the ten generals who had failed to rescue the survivors from the naval battle.[24] That was illegal, as you all later recognized. At the time I was the only commissioner opposed to your acting illegally, and I voted against the motion. And though its advocates were prepared to lay information against me and have me arrested, while you were urging them on by shouting, I believed that I should face danger in siding with law and justice, rather than take your side for fear of imprisonment or death, when your proposals were contrary to justice.

Those events took place while our city was still under democratic rule. But on a subsequent occasion, after the oligarchy had come to power, the Thirty summoned me and four others to the round chamber,[25] with orders to arrest Leon the Salaminian and fetch him from Salamis[26] for execution; they were constantly issuing such orders, of course, to many others, in their wish to implicate as many as possible in their crimes. On that occasion, however, I showed, once again not just by words but by my actions, that I couldn't care less about death—if that would not be putting it rather crudely—but that my one and only care was to avoid doing anything sinful or unjust. Thus, powerful as it was, that regime did not frighten me into unjust action: when we emerged from the round chamber, the other four went off to Salamis and arrested Leon, whereas I left them and went off home. For that I might easily have been put to death, had the regime not collapsed shortly afterwards. There are many witnesses who will testify before you about those events.

Do you imagine, then, that I would have survived all these years if I had been regularly active in public life and had championed what was right in a manner worthy of a brave man, and valued that above all else, as was my duty? Far from it, fellow Athenians: I would not, and nor would any other man. But in any public undertaking, that is the sort of person that I, for my part, shall prove to have been throughout my life; and likewise in my private life, because I have never been guilty of unjust association with anyone, including those whom my slanderers allege to have been my students.[27]

I never, in fact, was anyone's instructor[28] at any time. But if a person wanted to hear me talking, while I was engaging in my own business, I never grudged that to anyone, young or old; nor do I hold conversation only when I receive payment, and not otherwise. Rather, I offer myself for questioning to wealthy and poor alike, and to anyone who may wish to answer in response to questions from me. Whether any of those people acquires a good character or not, I cannot fairly be held responsible, when I never at any time promised any of them that they would learn anything from me, nor gave them instruction. And if anyone claims that he ever learnt anything from me, or has heard privately something that everyone else did not hear as well, you may be sure that what he says is untrue.

Why then, you may ask, do some people enjoy spending so much time in my company? You have already heard, fellow Athenians: I have told you the whole truth—which is that my listeners enjoy the examination of those who think themselves wise but are not, since the process is not unamusing. But for me, I must tell you, it is a mission which I have been bidden to undertake by the god, through oracles and dreams[29] and through every means whereby a divine injunction to perform any task has ever been laid upon a human being.

That is not only true, fellow Athenians, but is easily verified—because if I do corrupt any of our young people, or have corrupted others in the past, then presumably, when they grew older, should any of them have realized that I had at any time given them bad advice in their youth, they ought now to have appeared here themselves to accuse me and obtain redress. Or else, if they were unwilling to come in person, members of their families—fathers, brothers, or other relations— had their relatives suffered any harm at my hands, ought now to put it on record and obtain redress.

In any case, many of those people are present, whom I can see: first there is Crito, my contemporary and fellow demesman, father of Critobulus here; then Lysanias of Sphettus, father of Aeschines here; next, Epigenes' father, Antiphon from Cephisia, is present; then again, there are others here whose brothers have spent time with me in these studies: Nicostratus, son of Theozotides, brother of Theodotus—Theodotus himself, incidentally, is deceased, so Nicostratus could not have come at his brother's urging; and Paralius here, son of Demodocus, whose brother was Theages; also present is Ariston's son, Adimantus, whose brother is Plato here; and Aeantodorus, whose brother is Apollodorus here.

There are many others I could mention to you, from whom Meletus should surely have called some testimony during his own speech. However, if he forgot to do so then, let him call it now—I yield the floor to him—and if he has any such evidence, let him produce it. But quite the opposite is true, gentlemen: you will find that they are all prepared to support me, their corruptor, the one who is, according to Meletus and Anytus, doing their relatives mischief. Support for me from the actual victims of corruption might perhaps be explained; but what of the uncorrupted—older men by now, and relatives of my victims? What reason would they have to support me, apart from the right and proper one, which is that they know very well that Meletus is lying, whereas I am telling the truth?

There it is, then, gentlemen. That, and perhaps more of the same, is about all I have to say in my defence. But perhaps, among your number, there may be someone who will harbour resentment when he recalls a case of his own: he may have faced a less serious trial than this one, yet begged and implored the jury, weeping copiously, and producing his children here, along with many other relatives and loved ones, to gain as much sympathy as possible. By contrast, I shall do none of those things, even though I am running what might be considered the ultimate risk. Perhaps someone with those thoughts will harden his heart against me; and enraged by those same thoughts, he may cast his vote against me in anger. Well, if any of you are so inclined—not that I expect it of you, but if anyone *should* be—I think it fair to answer him as follows:

"I naturally do have relatives, my excellent friend, because—in Homer's own words—I too was 'not born of oak nor of rock,' but of human parents; and so I do have relatives—including my sons,[30] fellow Athenians. There are three of them: one is now a youth, while two are still children. Nevertheless, I shall not produce any of them here, and then entreat you to vote for my acquittal."

And why, you may ask, will I do no such thing? Not out of contempt or disrespect for you, fellow Athenians—whether or not I am facing death boldly is a different issue. The point is that with our reputations in mind—yours and our whole city's, as well as my own—I believe that any such behaviour would be ignominious, at my age and with the reputation I possess; that reputation may or may not, in fact, be deserved, but at least it is believed that Socrates stands out in some way from the run of human beings. Well, if those of you who are believed to be preeminent in wisdom, courage, or any other form of goodness are going to behave like that, it would be demeaning.

I have frequently seen such men when they face judgment: they have significant reputations, yet they put on astonishing performances, apparently in the belief that by dying they will suffer something unheard of—as if they would be immune from death, so long as you did not kill them! They seem to me to put our city to shame: they could give any foreigner the impression that men preeminent among Athenians in goodness, whom they select from their own number to govern and hold other positions, are no better than women.[31] I say this, fellow Athenians, because none of us who has even the slightest reputation should behave like that; nor should you put up with us if we try to do so. Rather, you should make one thing clear: you will be far more inclined to convict one who stages those pathetic charades and makes our city an object of derision than one who keeps his composure.

But leaving reputation aside, gentlemen, I do not think it right to entreat the jury, nor to win acquittal in that way, instead of by informing and persuading them. A juror does not sit to dispense justice as a favour, but to determine where it lies. And he has sworn, not that he will favour whomever he pleases, but that he will try the case according to law. We should not, then, accustom you to transgress your oath, nor should you become accustomed to doing so: neither of us would be showing respect towards the gods. And therefore, fellow Athenians, do not require behaviour from me towards you which I consider neither proper nor right nor pious—more especially now, for God's sake, when I stand charged by Meletus here with impiety: because if I tried to persuade and coerce you with entreaties in spite of your oath, I clearly *would* be teaching you not to believe in gods; and I would stand literally self-convicted, by my defence, of failing to acknowledge them. But that is far from the truth: I do acknowledge them, fellow Athenians, as none of my accusers do; and I trust to you, and to God, to judge my case as shall be best for me and for yourselves.

For many reasons, fellow Athenians, I am not dismayed by this outcome[32]—your convicting me, I mean—and especially because the outcome has come as no surprise to me. I wonder far more at the number of votes cast on each side, because I did not think the margin would be so narrow. Yet it seems, in fact, that if a mere thirty votes had gone the other way, I should have been acquitted.[33] Or rather, even as things stand, I consider that I have been cleared of Meletus' charges. Not only that, but one thing is obvious to everyone: if Anytus had not come forward with Lycon to accuse me, Meletus would have forfeited 1,000 drachmas, since he would not have gained one-fifth of the votes cast.

But anyhow, this gentleman demands the death penalty for me. Very well, then: what alternative penalty[34] shall I suggest to you, fellow Athenians? Clearly, it must be one I deserve. So what do I deserve to incur or to pay, for having taken it into my head not to lead an inactive life? Instead, I have neglected the things that concern most people—making money, managing an estate, gaining military or civic honours, or other positions of power, or joining political clubs and parties which have formed in our city. I thought myself, in truth, too honest to survive if I engaged in those things. I did not pursue a course, therefore, in which I would be of no use to you or to myself. Instead, by going to each individual privately, I tried to render a service for you which is—so I maintain—the highest service of all. Therefore that was the course I followed: I tried to persuade each of you not to care for any of his possessions rather than care for himself, striving for the utmost excellence and understanding; and not to care for our city's possessions rather than for the city itself; and to care about other things in the same way.

So what treatment do I deserve for being such a benefactor? If I am to make a proposal truly in keeping with my deserts, fellow Athenians, it should be some benefit; and moreover, the sort of benefit that would be fitting for me. Well then, what *is* fitting for a poor man who is a benefactor, and who needs time free for exhorting you? Nothing could be more fitting, fellow Athenians, than to give such a man regular free meals in the Prytaneum;[35] indeed, that is far more fitting for him than for any of you who may have won an Olympic race with a pair or a team of horses: that victory brings you only the appearance of success, whereas I bring you the reality; besides, he is not in want of sustenance, whereas I am. So if, as justice demands, I am to make a proposal in keeping with my deserts, that is what I suggest: free meals in the Prytaneum.

Now, in proposing this, I may seem to you, as when I talked about appeals for sympathy, to be speaking from sheer effrontery. But actually I have no such motive, fellow Athenians. My point is rather this: I am convinced that I do not treat any human being unjustly, at least intentionally—but I cannot make you share that conviction, because we have conversed together so briefly. I say this, because if it were the law here, as in other jurisdictions, that a capital case must not be tried in a single day, but over several,[36] I think you could have been convinced; but as things stand, it is not easy to clear oneself of such grave allegations in a short time.

Since, therefore, I am persuaded, for my part, that I have treated no one unjustly, I have no intention whatever of so treating myself, nor of denouncing myself as deserving ill, or proposing any such treatment for myself. Why should I do that? For fear of the penalty Meletus demands for me, when I say that I don't know if that is a good thing or a bad one? In preference to that, am I then to choose one of the things I know very well to be bad, and demand that instead? Imprisonment, for instance? Why should I live in prison, in servitude to the annually appointed prison commissioners? Well then, a fine, with imprisonment until I pay? That would amount to what I just mentioned, since I haven't the means to pay it.

Well then, should I propose banishment? Perhaps that is what you would propose for me. Yet I must surely be obsessed with survival, fellow Athenians, if I am so illogical as that. You, my fellow citizens, were unable to put up with my discourses and arguments, but they were so irksome and odious to you that you now seek to be rid of them. Could I not draw the inference, in that case, that others will hardly take kindly to them? Far from it, fellow Athenians. A fine life it would be for a person of my age to go into exile, and spend his days continually exchanging one city for another, and being repeatedly expelled—because I know very well that wherever I go, the young will come to hear me speaking, as they do here. And if I repel them, they will expel me themselves, by persuading their elders; while if I do not repel them, their fathers and relatives will expel me on their account.

Now, perhaps someone may say: "Socrates, could you not be so kind as to keep quiet and remain inactive, while living in exile?" This is the hardest point of all of which to convince some of you. Why? Because, if I tell you that that would mean disobeying my god, and that is why I cannot remain inactive, you will disbelieve me and think that I am practising a sly evasion. Again, if I said that it really is the greatest benefit for a person to converse every day about goodness, and about the other subjects you have heard me discussing when examining myself and others—and that an unexamined life is no life for a human being to live—then you would believe me still less when I made those assertions. But the facts, gentlemen, are just as I claim them to be, though it is not easy to convince you of them. At the same time, I am not accustomed to think of myself as deserving anything bad. If I had money, I would have proposed a fine of as much as I could afford: that would have done me no harm at all. But the fact is that I have none—unless you wish to fix the penalty at a sum I could pay. I could afford to pay you 1 mina, I suppose, so I suggest a fine of that amount—

One moment, fellow Athenians. Plato here, along with Crito, Critobulus, and Apollodorus, is urging me to propose 30 minas,[37] and they are saying they will stand surety for that sum. So I propose a fine of that amount, and these people shall be your sufficient guarantors of its payment.

For the sake of a slight gain in time, fellow Athenians, you will incur infamy and blame from those who would denigrate our city, for putting Socrates to death[38]—a "wise man"—because those who wish to malign you will say I am wise, even if I am not; in any case, had you waited only a short time, you would have obtained that outcome automatically. You can see, of course, that I am now well advanced in life, and death is not far off. I address that not to all of you, but to those who condemned me to death; and to those same people I would add something further.

Perhaps you imagine, gentlemen, that I have been convicted for lack of arguments of the sort I could have used to convince you, had I believed that I should do or say anything to gain acquittal. But that is far from true. I have been convicted, not for lack of arguments, but for lack of brazen impudence and willingness to address you in such terms as you would most like to be addressed in—that is to say, by weeping and wailing, and doing and saying much else that I claim to be unworthy of me—the sorts of thing that you are so used to hearing from others. But just as I did not think during my defence that I should do anything unworthy of a free man because I was in danger, so now I have no regrets about defending myself as I did; I should far rather present such a defence and die than live by defending myself in that other fashion.

In court, as in warfare, neither I nor anyone else should contrive to escape death at any cost. On the battlefield too, it often becomes obvious that one could avoid death by throwing down one's arms and flinging oneself upon the mercy of one's pursuers. And in every sort of danger there are many other means of escaping death, if one is shameless enough to do or to say anything. I suggest that it is not death that is hard to avoid, gentlemen, but wickedness is far harder, since it is fleeter of foot than death. Thus, slow and elderly as I am, I have now been overtaken by the slower runner; while my accusers, adroit and quick-witted as they are, have been overtaken by the faster, which is wickedness. And so I take my leave, condemned to death by your judgment, whereas they stand for ever condemned to depravity and injustice as judged by Truth. And just as I accept my penalty, so must they. Things were bound to turn out this way, I suppose, and I imagine it is for the best.

In the next place, to those of you who voted against me, I wish to utter a prophecy. Indeed, I have now reached a point at which people are most given to prophesying—that is, when they are on the point of death. I warn you, my executioners, that as soon as I am dead retribution will come upon you—far more severe, I swear, than the sentence you have passed upon me. You have tried to kill me for now, in the belief that you will be relieved from giving an account of your lives. But in fact, I can tell you, you will face just the opposite outcome. There will be more critics to call you to account, people whom I have restrained for the time being though you were unaware of my doing so. They will be all the harder on you since they are younger, and you will rue it all the more—because if you imagine that by putting people to death you will prevent anyone from reviling you for not living rightly, you are badly mistaken. That way of escape is neither feasible nor honourable. Rather, the most honourable and easiest way is not the silencing of others, but striving to make oneself as good a person as possible. So with that prophecy to those of you who voted against me, I take my leave.

As for those who voted for my acquittal, I should like to discuss the outcome of this case while the officials are occupied, and I am not yet on the way to the place where I must die. Please bear with me, gentlemen, just for this short time: there is no reason why we should not have a word with one another while that is still permitted.

Since I regard you as my friends, I am willing to show you the significance of what has just befallen me. You see, gentlemen of the jury—and in applying that term to you, I probably use it correctly—something wonderful has just happened to me. Hitherto, the usual prophetic voice from my spiritual sign was continually active, and frequently opposed me even on trivial matters, if I was about to do anything amiss. But now something has befallen me, as you can see for yourselves, which one certainly might consider—and is generally held—to be the very worst of evils. Yet the sign from God did not oppose me, either when I left home this morning, or when I appeared here in court, or at any point when I was about to say anything during my speech; and yet in other discussions it has very often stopped me in mid-sentence. This time, though, it has not opposed me at any moment in anything I said or did in this whole business.

Now, what do I take to be the explanation for that? I will tell you: I suspect that what has befallen me is a blessing, and that those of us who suppose death to be an evil cannot be making a correct assumption. I have gained every ground for that suspicion, because my usual sign could not have failed to oppose me, unless I were going to incur some good result.

And let us also reflect upon how good a reason there is to hope that death is a good thing. It is, you see, one or other of two things: either to be dead is to be nonexistent, as it were, and a dead person has no awareness whatever of anything at all; or else, as we are told, the soul undergoes some sort of transformation, or exchanging of this present world for another. Now if there is, in fact, no awareness in death, but it is like sleep—the kind in which the sleeper does not even dream at all—then death would be a marvellous gain. Why, imagine that someone had to pick the night in which he slept so soundly that he did not even dream, and to compare all the other nights and days of his life with that one; suppose he had to say, upon consideration, how many days or nights in his life he had spent better and more agreeably than that night; in that case, I think he would find them easy to count compared with his other days and nights—even if he were the Great King of Persia,[39] let alone an ordinary person. Well, if death is like that, then for my part I call it a gain; because on that assumption the whole of time would seem no longer than a single night.

On the other hand, if death is like taking a trip from here to another place, and if it is true, as we are told, that all of the dead do indeed exist in that other place, why then, gentlemen of the jury, what could be a greater blessing than that? If upon arriving in Hades, and being rid of these people who profess to be "jurors," one is going to find those who are truly judges, and who are also said to sit in judgment there[40]—Minos, Rhadamanthys, Aeacus, Triptolemus, and all other demigods who were righteous in their own lives—would that be a disappointing journey?

Or again, what would any of you not give to share the company of Orpheus and Musaeus, of Hesiod and Homer? I say "you," since I personally would be willing to die many times over, if those tales are true. Why? Because my own sojourn there would be wonderful, if I could meet Palamedes, or Ajax, son of Telamon, or anyone else of old who met their death through an unjust verdict. Whenever I met them, I could compare my own experiences with theirs—which would be not unamusing, I fancy—and best of all, I could spend time questioning and probing people there, just as I do here, to find out who among them is truly wise, and who thinks he is without being so.

What would one not give, gentlemen of the jury, to be able to question the leader of the great expedition against Troy,[41] or Odysseus, or Sisyphus, or countless other men and women one could mention? Would it not be unspeakable good fortune to converse with them there, to mingle with them and question them? At least that isn't a reason, presumably, for people in that world to put you to death—because amongst other ways in which people there are more fortunate than those in our world, they have become immune from death for the rest of time, if what we are told is actually true.

Moreover, you too, gentlemen of the jury, should be of good hope in the face of death, and fix your minds upon this single truth: nothing can harm a good man, either in life or in death; nor are his fortunes neglected by the gods. In fact, what has befallen me has come about by no mere accident; rather, it is clear to me that it was better I should die now and be rid of my troubles. That is also the reason why the divine sign at no point turned me back; and for my part, I bear those who condemned me, and my accusers, no ill will at all—though, to be sure, it was not with that intent that they were condemning and accusing me, but with intent to harm me—and they are culpable for that. Still, this much I ask of them. When my sons come of age, gentlemen, punish them: give them the same sort of trouble that I used to give you, if you think they care for money or anything else more than for goodness, and if they think highly of themselves when they are of no value. Reprove them, as I reproved you, for failing to care for the things they should and for thinking highly of themselves when they are worthless. If you will do that, then I shall have received my own just deserts from you, as will my sons.

But enough. It is now time to leave—for me to die, and for you to live—though which of us has the better destiny is unclear to everyone, save only to God.

NOTES

1. It is striking that the *Defence of Socrates* begins, as it ends, with a disavowal of knowledge.
2. Socrates' reputation for skill in argument enabled Aristophanes to caricature him as an instructor in logical trickery. Cf. *Clouds* (112–15).
3. The reference is to Aristophanes.

4. Speeches in Athenian lawcourts were timed.

5. This describes Socrates' first appearance in the *Clouds* (223–5), where he is swung around in a basket in the air, and he says he is walking on air and thinking about the sun.

6. Professional educators who offered instruction in many subjects.

7. A mina equalled 100 silver drachmas. At the end of the fifth century a drachma was roughly equivalent to one day's pay for a man employed in public works. Evenus' fees were therefore not as "modest" as Socrates pretends.

8. The god Apollo, though nowhere named in the *Defence,* is the deity whose servant Socrates claims to be. In what follows, however, when he speaks of "the god," it is not always clear whether he means Apollo or a personal God distinct from any deity of traditional Greek religion.

9. Politicians of the democratic party had fled from Athens during the regime of the Thirty Tyrants. They returned under an amnesty in 403 B.C. when the Thirty were overthrown.

10. Literally, "by the dog," a favourite Socratic oath, which may have originated as a euphemism.

11. Socrates alludes to the labours of Heracles, twelve tasks of prodigious difficulty imposed upon a hero of legendary strength and courage.

12. The dithyramb was an emotionally powerful lyric poem, performed by a chorus of singers and dancers.

13. The Athenian Council was a body of 500, with fifty members from each of the ten tribes, elected annually by lot from citizens over the age of 30. In conjunction with the magistrates, it carried on state business and prepared an agenda for the Assembly.

14. Socrates' denial that he corrupts the young intentionally relies upon the principle that human beings never intentionally follow a course of action which they know or believe to be harmful to themselves. Since, in Socrates' view, all wrongdoing is harmful to the agent, it follows that all wrongdoing is unintentional and is curable by the removal of ignorance. This doctrine, one of the so-called Socratic Paradoxes, is often summarized in the slogan "Virtue Is Knowledge." It is elaborated in the *Meno.*

15. The sun and moon, even though not the objects of an official cult at Athens, were widely believed to be divine.

16. According to one tradition, Anaxagoras had been prosecuted for heresies regarding the composition of the sun and moon.

17. The "riddle" which Socrates attributes to Meletus consists in the self-contradictory statement "Socrates acknowledges gods and does not acknowledge gods." Greek riddles often take the form of paradoxes generated by apparent self-contradiction.

18. Spirits were sometimes begotten by gods through union with nymphs or mortals.

19. Site of the legendary war between the Greeks and Trojans, which is the context of Homer's *Iliad.*

20. Achilles, heroic Greek warrior in the Trojan War. As the offspring of a goddess mother by a mortal father, he is referred to as a "demigod."

21. Potidaea, in Thrace, was the scene of a campaign in 432 B.C.

22. Socrates here confirms that his well-known mysterious "sign" had been used to substantiate the charge of "introducing new spiritual realities."

23. Fifty representatives from each of the ten tribes who made up the Council took turns during the year to provide an executive for the entire body.

24. In 406 B.C., after a sea battle off the Ionian coast at Arginusae, several Athenian commanders were charged for their failure to rescue the shipwrecked survivors and recover

the dead. A motion to try them collectively was endorsed by the Council and referred to the Assembly. Although a collective trial was unconstitutional, the motion was passed by the Assembly after a stormy debate, and six surviving commanders were convicted and executed.

25. A building also called the "sun-shade" from its shape. It was commandeered as a seat of government by the Thirty.

26. An island separated by a narrow channel from the coast of Africa.

27. Socrates is probably alluding, especially, to two of his former associates who had become notorious enemies of the Athenian democracy, Alcibiades and Critias. The former was a brilliant but wayward politician, who had turned against Athens and helped her enemies. The latter was an unscrupulous oligarch, who had become a leading member of the Thirty Tyrants.

28. Socrates here, in effect, contrasts himself with the sophists, in that he did not set himself up as a professional teacher.

29. For example, the Delphic oracle, whose answer had led Socrates to undertake his mission. Dreams had long been believed to be a source of divine communication with human beings, and are often so treated by Plato.

30. At the time of the trial Socrates had two little boys, Sophroniscus and Menexenus, and an older son, Lamprocles.

31. This is one of many disparaging remarks in Plato about women. Open displays of emotion, especially grief, are regarded as distinctively female, an indulgence of the "female side" of our nature.

32. The verdict was "Guilty." Socrates here begins his second speech, proposing an alternative to the death penalty demanded by the prosecution.

33. With a jury of 500, this implies that the vote was 280–220, since at the time of Socrates' trial an evenly split vote (250–250) would have secured his acquittal.

34. The court had to decide between the penalty demanded by the prosecution and a counter-penalty proposed by the defence, with no option of substituting a different one.

35. The Prytaneum was the building on the north-east slope of the Acropolis, in which hospitality was given to honoured guests of the state as well as to Olympic victors and other sports heroes.

36. This was the law at Sparta, because of the irrevocability of capital punishment.

37. This seems to have been a normal amount for a fine and was a considerable sum.

38. The jury has now voted for the death penalty, and Socrates begins his final speech.

39. This monarch embodied the popular ideal of happiness.

40. It is not clear whether Socrates envisages them merely as judging disputes among the dead, or as passing judgment upon the earthly life of those who enter Hades.

41. Agamemnon, chief of the Greek forces in the Trojan War.

INDEX OF NAMES

Ajax: Greek hero of the Trojan War, mentioned as a victim of an "unjust verdict." This refers to the award of Achilles' armour to ODYSSEUS in a contest with Ajax. The latter's resulting madness and suicide are the subject of *Ajax,* one of the extant tragedies by Sophocles.

Anaxagoras: Presocratic philosopher, originally from Clazomenae in Ionia. Important fragments of his work are extant. He spent many years in Athens and was prominent in Athenian intellectual life.

Antiphon: from Cephisia, father of EPIGENES and supporter of Socrates at his trial, but not otherwise known.

Anytus: leading Athenian democratic politician and accuser of Socrates as well as the main instigator of the prosecution.

Apollodorus: ardent devotee of Socrates, notorious for his emotional volatility.

Ariston: Athenian of distinguished lineage and father of Plato.

Aristophanes: *c.* 450–385. The most famous playwright of Athenian Old Comedy. Eleven of his plays and many fragments are extant.

Callias: wealthy Athenian patron of sophistic culture.

Cebes: citizen of Thebes in Boeotia, who had studied there with the Pythagorean philosopher Philolaus. A disciple of Socrates.

Chaerephon: long-time faithful follower of Socrates. Expelled from Athens in 404 during the regime of the Thirty Tyrants, he returned when the democracy was restored in the following year. The comic poets nicknamed him "the bat" from his squeaky voice.

Crito: Socrates' contemporary, fellow demesman, and one of his closest friends.

Critobulus: son of CRITO and member of the Socratic circle, who was present at Socrates' trial and death.

Cronus: mythical son of URANUS (Heaven) and Gaea (Earth), father of ZEUS, and his predecessor as chief among the gods. He mutilated his father, married his sister Rhea, and devoured his children, except for Zeus, who overthrew him.

Daedalus: legendary artist, craftsman, and inventor. His many marvellous works included the labyrinth for the Minotaur in the palace of King Minos of Crete, along with wings for himself and his son, Icarus. He was also believed to have made statues that could open their eyes, walk, and move their arms.

Demodocus: father of THEAGES.

Epigenes: an associate of Socrates. He was present at Socrates' death.

Euthyphro: self-proclaimed expert on religious law. Since Plato portrays him as somewhat eccentric, it is a nice irony that his name should mean "Straight-Thinker" or "Right-Mind."

Evenus: a professional teacher of human excellence, or "sophist."

Gorgias: *c.* 480–376, from Leontini in Sicily; commonly but perhaps wrongly classified as a "sophist." He cultivated an artificial but influential prose style and gave lessons in rhetoric, or effective public speaking.

Hades: the underworld inhabited by the dead. The name belongs, properly, to the mythical king of that realm, who was the brother of ZEUS and Poseidon.

Hector: son of Priam, and leading Trojan hero in the war between Greece and Troy. In HOMER's *Iliad* he kills PATROCLUS, squire of Achilles, who in turn avenges his friend's death by slaying Hector.

Hephaestus: lame god of fire and of the forge. He is associated with volcanoes in Greek mythology and was cast out of heaven by his mother HERA because he was deformed.

In revenge he sent her a golden throne to which she was chained with invisible bonds when she sat upon it.

Hera: daughter of CRONUS, wife and sister of ZEUS, and mother of HEPHAESTUS.

Hesiod: one of the earliest extant Greek poets. His *Theogony* contains an account of the origin of the traditional gods. His *Works and Days* is a didactic poem giving moral and practical precepts about rural life.

Hippias: itinerant teacher or "sophist," probably a close contemporary of Socrates, who claimed expertise in many subjects.

Hipponicus: member of wealthy Athenian family and the father of CALLIAS.

Homer: greatest epic poet of Greece and composer of the *Iliad* and the *Odyssey.* The *Iliad* contains episodes from the legendary Trojan War, while the *Odyssey* recounts the travels and adventures of the hero ODYSSEUS during his journey home after the war.

Leon: resident of Salamis, unjustly arrested and murdered by the Thirty Tyrants in 404.

Lycon: Athenian politician and co-accuser of Socrates with MELETUS and ANYTUS.

Lysanias: of Sphettus, father of AESCHINES, but otherwise unknown.

Meletus: youthful co-accuser of Socrates with ANYTUS and LYCON. He drew up the indictment against Socrates, but was evidently a mere tool of Anytus.

Minos: legendary king of Crete and also a traditional judge in the underworld.

Musaeus: mythical bard or singer, closely connected with ORPHEUS.

Nicostratus: supporter of Socrates, present at his trial but otherwise unknown.

Odysseus: legendary hero in HOMER's *Iliad* and also a central figure in the *Odyssey,* which recounts his wanderings after the Trojan War.

Orpheus: legendary bard and founder of the archaic mystical or religious movement known as "Orphism."

Palamedes: Greek hero of the Trojan War, credited with invention of the alphabet.

Paralius: supporter of Socrates who was present at his trial but is not otherwise known.

Patroclus: squire and close friend of Achilles in HOMER's *Iliad,* slain by HECTOR and avenged by Achilles.

Prodicus: itinerant teacher from Ceos and also one of the sophists.

Proteus: mythical "old man of the sea," who eluded all attempts at capture by constantly changing his form.

Rhadamanthys: with AEACUS and MINOS one of the three traditional judges in the underworld.

Simmias: citizen of Thebes and follower of Socrates. He was prepared to finance Socrates' escape.

Sisyphus: mythical wrongdoer, famous for his endless punishment in the underworld. His task was to push a boulder up to the top of a hill, from which it always rolled down again.

Tantalus: mythical king of Phrygia, possessing proverbial wealth. In one tradition he tried to make himself immortal by stealing the food of the gods. For this he was punished by being made to stand in water which receded as soon as he stooped to drink, and to stretch out for fruit which the wind always blew away from his grasp.

Telamon: legendary king of Salamis and father of AJAX.

Theages: disciple of Socrates, whose brother PARALIUS was present at the trial, though Theages himself was already dead.

Theodotus: associate of Socrates who died before his trial but is not otherwise known.

Theozotides: father of NICOSTRATUS and THEODOTUS. Though deceased by the time of Socrates' trial, he is known to have introduced two important democratic measures after the fall of the Thirty Tyrants. Plato may therefore have mentioned him to counter suspicion that Socrates had antidemocratic leanings.

Thetis: sea-nymph or goddess, given in marriage to the mortal Peleus. Achilles was her only child.

Triptolemus: mythical agricultural hero from Eleusis, as well as a central figure in its mystery cults.

Uranus: heaven or the sky, conceived in mythology as child and husband of Gaea (earth). Chief deity before his son CRONUS.

Zeus: son of CRONUS, as well as chief among the Olympian gods.

STUDY QUESTIONS

1. According to Socrates, why did the Delphic oracle declare that no one was wiser than Socrates?
2. According to Socrates, what mistake is involved in the fear of death?
3. Why is Socrates unwilling to give up the study of philosophy?
4. According to Socrates, what is far harder to avoid than death?

PART 2

Reasoning

The Elements of Argument

STEVEN M. CAHN, PATRICIA KITCHER, AND GEORGE SHER

To assert a belief is simple; defending it is far more difficult. Yet if a belief is not defended adequately, why accept it?

Saying something is true does not make it true. Suppose Smith says that both Charles Darwin, who developed the theory of evolution, and Abraham Lincoln were born on February 12, 1809. Jones denies this claim. If saying something is true proves it true, then what Smith says is true and what Jones says is also true— which is impossible, because one of them denies exactly what the other affirms. Their statements are contradictory, and asserting both of them amounts to saying nothing at all. (Incidentally, Smith is correct.)

To reason effectively, we need to avoid contradiction and accept beliefs that are adequately defended. But what are the appropriate standards by which we can determine if our beliefs are consistent with each other and well-confirmed by the available evidence? Logic is the subject that offers answers to these questions, and the scope of logic is explained in the following essay by Patricia Kitcher, Professor of Philosophy at Columbia University; George Sher, Professor of Philosophy at Rice University; and myself. At one time we were colleagues in the Department of Philosophy at the University of Vermont.

....

We reason every day of our lives. All of us argue for our own points of view, whether the topic be politics, the value or burden of religion, the best route to drive between Boston and New York, or any of a myriad of other subjects. We are constantly barraged by the arguments of others, seeking to convince us that they know how to build a better computer, or how to prevent a serious illness, or whatever.

ARGUMENTS

In ordinary parlance, an argument is a verbal dispute carried out with greater or less ferocity. The technical, philosophical notion is quite different. An argument is a collection of sentences consisting of one or more *premises* and a *conclusion.*

This essay is a condensed version of Steven M. Cahn, Patricia Kitcher, and George Sher, "The Uses of Argument," in *Philosophical Horizons: Introductory Readings*, second edition, eds. Steven M. Cahn and Maureen Eckert. Copyright © 2012. Reprinted by permission of Wadsworth/Cengage Learning.

It is sometimes said that a true philosopher never assumes anything; every claim must be proved. Taken literally, this cannot be right. For if you are going to construct an argument at all, you must take some claim (or claims) as your premise(s). It would obviously be backwards to assume the truth of a very controversial claim in order to argue for something that is obvious to everyone. The direction of argumentation must always be, as above, from the more obvious to the less obvious. Ideally a reasoner will assume, as premises, claims that are very uncontroversial and argue that a much more controversial, perhaps even surprising, conclusion follows from those unproblematic assumptions.

A chain of argumentation is exactly as solid as the arguments it contains. If any link is weak, then the entire chain will break down. From a logical point of view, the crucial aspect of arguments is the relationship between the premises and the conclusion. Logic is the branch of philosophy that studies the inferential relations between premises and conclusion. The task of logic is to establish rules or guidelines about which claims can be inferred from other claims. This task has been carried out with great success for *deductive inference.*

DEDUCTIVE ARGUMENTS

The central concept of deductive logic is *validity.* An argument is valid if and only if the following relation holds between its premises and its conclusion: *It is impossible for the conclusion to be false if the premises are true.* Alternatively, in a valid argument, if the premises are true, this guarantees that the conclusion is also true. It is important to realize that logicians are not concerned with truth itself. Logicians will certify an argument as valid whether or not the premises are true. Their concern is only with the relation between the premises and the conclusion. Regardless of whether the premises are true, an argument is valid if, *if* the premises *happen* to be true, then the conclusion *must* be true. If all the arguments in a chain of argumentation are valid, then the entire chain will also be valid. Valid arguments are ideal, because if you start from true premises, true conclusions are guaranteed. Like a trolley car that is bound to follow the tracks, if you start with the truth and make only valid inferences, you will never veer away from the truth.

It is somewhat unfortunate that, in ordinary English, "valid" and "true" are often used as synonyms. Their technical, philosophical meanings are quite distinct. In the primary philosophical use of "valid," it makes no sense to say that a statement is "valid," for validity is a *relation among statements.* Statements can be true, but not valid; arguments can be valid, but not true. "True" and "valid" have distinct meanings, and truth and validity are independent properties; that is, each property can occur without the other. Arguments whose premises are all true can still be invalid and valid arguments can have false premises. Thus, a valid argument can have (a) true premises and a true conclusion, as in (1) below; (b) one or more false premises and a false conclusion, as in (2); or (c) one or more false premises and a true conclusion, as in (3). The only possibility ruled out by validity is that the argument have true premises and a false conclusion.

(1) P_1 Wombats belong to the order of marsupials.
     P_2 Koalas belong to the order of marsupials.
     C   Wombats and koalas belong to the same order.
(2) P_1 All philosophers lived in Ancient Greece. (false)
     P_2 Bertrand Russell was a philosopher.
     C   Bertrand Russell lived in Ancient Greece. (false)
(3) P_1 All canaries are polar bears. (false)
     P_2 All polar bears have feathers. (false)
     C   All canaries have feathers.

Finally, an argument can have true premises and a true conclusion and still be invalid, as in (4).

(4) P_1 Some roses are red.
     P_2 Some violets are blue.
     C   Some flowers give some people hay fever.

The problem with argument (4) is that, while all the claims are true, the fact that P_1 and P_2 are true gives us no reason whatsoever to believe that C is true.

So far, we have been assuming that the reader can simply "see" when an argument is valid or invalid. But how can we actually test for deductive validity? In one sense, the test for validity comes right out of the definition of validity: A valid argument is one whose conclusion cannot be false if its premises are true. To test for validity, try negating the conclusion while assuming the truth of the premises.

(5) P_1 All Englishmen love the Queen. (false)
     P_2 Henry is English.
     C   Henry loves the Queen.

In (5) we would negate the conclusion, yielding "Henry does not love the Queen." Now the question is, can we still maintain the truth of the premises? Obviously not, for if we try to claim that Henry does *not* love the Queen, while holding to the truth of P_2, "Henry is English," then we shall have to give up the truth of P_1, "All Englishmen love the Queen." Conversely, if we claim that Henry does not love the Queen and try to maintain P_1 as well, then we will have to give up P_2. Since we cannot maintain the truth of both (or all) premises while negating the conclusion, this argument is valid. If it is possible to preserve the truth of the premises, while denying the conclusion, as in (6), then the argument is invalid.

(6) P_1 Only U.S. citizens vote in American elections.
     P_2 Jones is a U.S. citizen.
     C   Jones votes in American elections.

Even though P_1 and P_2 are true, C could be false, if Jones is one of the citizens who does not bother to vote. . . .

A compelling deductive argument should be valid. Otherwise, the premises should not lead us to accept the conclusion. However, validity is not enough. Even if the truth of a conclusion may be validly inferred from the truth of certain premises, that gives us no reason at all to accept the conclusion, unless we have good reason to believe that the premises are, in fact, true. Unfortunately, there is no magical device we can use to determine truth. For philosophers, as for anyone else, establishing the truth of claims is often a complex, difficult, and uncertain project. Still, through their explicit study of argumentation, philosophers have recognized that there is a general method that can be used to assess the worth of premises, even in the absence of a test of truth.

In analyzing arguments, philosophers noticed that the key terms in some premises were either so vague or so ambiguous that the premise ought to be rejected out of hand. For example,

(7) P_1 The Constitution requires that public education be theologically neutral.
    P_2 The theory of evolution is really just a religious doctrine.
    C   Therefore, since evolution is taught in schools, the biblical account of creation should also be taught in order to ensure theological neutrality.

While P_2 is also highly questionable, we will just consider the terminology employed in P_1 and the conclusion. What is the key expression "theologically neutral" supposed to mean? Given a standard interpretation of the Constitutional doctrine of the separation of Church and State, if P_1 is to be true, then "theologically neutral" must be read as something like "devoid of theology." Notice, however, that this cannot be the intended reading of "theologically neutral" in the conclusion, or the conclusion would be self-contradictory, asserting that the way to make public education devoid of theology is to start teaching the biblical account of creation. There, "theologically neutral" must be interpreted to mean something like "theologically balanced." In this example, the ambiguous terminology completely vitiates the argument. The only reason the premises even appear to support the conclusion is that the same phrase occurs in both P_1 and C. That connection is illusory, however, because the phrase is used ambiguously. In cases like this, the arguments may be dismissed without trying to determine the *truth* of the premises. In fact, when a key term in a premise is either ambiguous or vague, there is no way to figure out whether the premise is true or not. For if we are unsure about what the premise asserts, we are in no position to find out whether what the premise asserts is true. . . .

NONDEDUCTIVE ARGUMENTS

We have looked briefly at one type of inferential relation between premises and conclusions—the relation of deductive validity. . . . [W]e must try to deal with nondeductive reasoning, because there are many good, but nondeductive inferences that we encounter in everyday and scientific discussions. Suppose, for example, that a particular drug is given a hundred thousand trials across a wide variety of people and it never produces serious side effects. Even the most scrupulous researcher would conclude that the drug is safe. Still, this conclusion cannot be validly inferred from the data.

(8) P₁   In 100,000 trials, drug X produced no serious side effects.
$\quad$ C   Drug X does not have any serious side effects.

We can use our regular method of testing validity to show that this argument is invalid. Assuming the negation of the conclusion—drug X *has* a serious side effect—can we preserve the truth of premise P₁? It could turn out that a serious side effect only shows up on the 100,001st trial. Thus the premise, P₁, could be true, even though C is false, so the argument is invalid.

There are many more good, but invalid, arguments. Here is a mundane example.

(9) P₁   The dining room window is shattered.
$\quad$ P₂   There is a baseball lying in the middle of the glass on the dining room floor.
$\quad$ P₃   There is a baseball bat lying on the ground in the yard outside the dining room.
$\quad$ C   The dining room window was shattered by being hit with a baseball. . . .

If we cling to the standard of deductive validity, then . . . the previous arguments—and all other arguments like these—will have to be dismissed as bad reasoning. That constraint on argumentation is unacceptable for three reasons. First, these arguments appear to be perfectly reasonable, at least at first glance. Second, it is hard to see how we could get by without engaging in the sorts of reasoning represented by these examples. Finally, and perhaps most critically, it seems unreasonable to demand that the truth of the premises must *guarantee* the truth of the conclusion. Very often it is reasonable to believe something that is merely very probable, given the evidence. To take a different example, given the number of traffic lights in Manhattan, it is reasonable to believe that, if you drive the entire length of the island in normal traffic, you will have to stop at some traffic light or other (and probably at several). At least, we would be willing to make a small wager on this point.

Logic has, therefore, a second task. It needs to provide criteria for evaluating good, but nondeductive, inferences. . . .

INDUCTION

Without any detailed knowledge of combustion, we know that if we place a dry piece of paper into the flame of a candle, the paper will burn. We know this because we have witnessed or heard about many similar events in the past. In the past, the paper has always burned, so we infer that the paper will burn in the present case. This common type of reasoning is called *induction*. In induction, one relies on similar, observed cases, to infer that the same event or property will recur in as yet unobserved cases. We reason that since paper has always burned when placed in a flame, the same thing will happen in the present case. . . .

For different cases, we will have different amounts of evidence on which to draw. If only ten instances of a disease have been observed, then we will have much less confidence in predicting the course of the disease than if we had observed ten thousand occurrences. Philosophers usually describe our "confidence" in a claim as our "strength of belief" in that claim. The obvious suggestion is that our strength of belief in a claim should vary with the amount of evidence supporting the claim. More precisely, our strength of belief should increase with the number of positive instances of the claim. In other words, the degree of *rational* belief *does* increase as positive instances increase. So, for example, if you arrive in a new town and notice that all the buses you see on your first day are green, then as the days pass and you continue to observe nothing but green buses, the degree of your rational belief in the claim that all the buses in town are green will continually go up. Each new instance of a green bus is said to "confirm" the generalization that all the buses are green. Another way to state this relationship is that the degree of rational belief in an inductive generalization should vary with the amount of confirmation that the generalization has received.

Positive instances gradually confirm an inductive generalization, making it more and more reasonable to accept the generalization. By contrast, a negative instance defeats the generalization in a single stroke. To take a dramatic twentieth-century example, with the splitting of the first atom, the long-standing claim that atoms are indivisible particles of matter had to be given up. Besides the sheer number of positive instances, another criterion for good inductive reasoning is that the evidence be varied. If you have observed buses in many different parts of town, then you are more justified in claiming that the town's buses are all green than if you only considered the buses on your street.

HYPOTHESIS TESTING

It is a commonplace that people—most notably scientists and detectives—test hypotheses and accept those hypotheses that pass the tests they have devised. The process of *hypothesis testing* (with consequent acceptance or rejection) is very similar to the process of inductive reasoning. For example, imagine that a problem has developed in a small rural town. Residents are falling sick, complaining of severe nausea, abdominal pains, and other symptoms. The local doctor hypothesizes that the trouble has been caused by the opening of a new chemical plant that is emptying waste within a mile of one of the lakes that yield the town's supply of drinking water. The hypothesis can be tested in a number of different ways. The residents might check the consequences of only drinking water from lakes that are not close to the chemical plant. Or they might examine the effects on laboratory animals of drinking water obtained shortly after large amounts of waste had been ejected from the plant. It is relatively easy to see how the doctor's hypothesis might fail such tests. The residents might find that using water from different lakes achieved nothing, and that the sickness continued to spread. Equally, it is evident how the hypothesis could pass the tests. One might discover, for example, that the health of laboratory animals was dramatically affected by providing them with water obtained shortly after an episode of waste disposal.

The case just described indicates the general way in which a hypothesis might be tested. Frequently we advance a claim—a hypothesis—whose truth or falsity we are unable to ascertain by relatively direct observation. We cannot just look and see what causes the sickness in the rural town (or what causes various forms of cancer); we cannot just look and see if the earth moves, or if the continents were once part of a single land mass, or if the butler committed the crime. In evaluating such hypotheses, we consider what things we would expect to observe if the hypothesis were true. Then we investigate to see if these expectations are or are not borne out. If they are, then the hypothesis passes the test, and its success counts in its favor. If they are not, then the failure counts against the hypothesis. . . .

INFERENCE TO THE BEST EXPLANATION

Another common and indispensable type of nondeductive inference should be familiar to readers of both scientific essays and detective stories. Sherlock Holmes uses this type of reasoning in his first encounter with Dr. Watson in *A Study in Scarlet*:

> "*I knew* you came from Afghanistan. From long habit the train of thoughts ran so swiftly through my mind that I arrived at the conclusion without being conscious of intermediate steps. There were such steps, however. The train of reasoning ran, 'Here is a gentleman of a medical type, but with the air of a military man. Clearly an army doctor, then. He has just come from the tropics, for his face is dark, and that is not the natural tint of his skin, for his wrists are fair. He has undergone hardship and sickness, as his haggard face says clearly. His left arm has been injured. He holds it in a stiff and unnatural manner. Where in the tropics could an English army doctor have seen much hardship and got his arm wounded? Clearly in Afghanistan.' The whole train of thought did not occupy a second. I then remarked that you came from Afghanistan, and you were astonished."[1]

It is no help to students of reasoning that Sir Arthur Conan Doyle consistently misdescribes Holmes' reasoning as "deduction." Holmes' argument is obviously invalid. Even though Watson has a deep tan and a wounded arm, it is still entirely possible that he has never been in Afghanistan. He could have obtained the tan in Florida and the wound in a knife fight in Peru. Still, Holmes's argument does provide considerable support for his claim that Watson had been in Afghanistan. This is the way Holmes' reasoning (here and in most other places) actually works. He lists a number of facts: the military bearing, the medical bag, the tan, the wounded arm. Then he uses those facts to infer a conclusion, *on the grounds that the claim made by the conclusion would explain all the facts presented*. In this case, if Watson is, in fact, a military doctor who has just returned from active service in Afghanistan, that would explain why he has a medical bag, a tan, and so forth. The correct, if clumsy, name for this type of reasoning is *argument by inference to the best explanation*.

Inference to the best explanation is related to hypothesis testing. In hypothesis testing, a hypothesis is supported when observations which can be deduced from that hypothesis are borne out by observation. In inference to the best explanation, the relation between the conclusion—the explanation—and the observed facts is looser. For example, the fact that Watson was in Afghanistan does not deductively imply that his face was tanned. (He could have worn a large hat to protect his face from the sun.) Still, the conclusion, that he was in Afghanistan, makes it likely that, other things being equal, he would be deeply tanned. So, in argument by inference to the best explanation, the premises support the conclusion because, if the conclusions were true, that would give us good reason to expect that the premises would be true, and the premises are true. . . .

ARGUMENT ANALYSIS

We have examined various types of inference. Now we will consider how this information may be used in analyzing reasoning. The basic task of argument analysis is to provide a clear formulation of the chain of argumentation presented in a piece of prose. It is important to realize that arguments do not come neatly packaged, with labels clearly identifying the premises and the conclusion. A critic needs to be careful and sympathetic. The best critic works hard at finding the optimal version of the argumentation contained in a passage before evaluating it.

While it may seem surprising, the first step in evaluating a piece of reasoning is to find the conclusion. The conclusion may occur at the beginning, or at the end, or in the middle of the passage. Often the conclusion will not be stated at all! To find the conclusion, you need to ask yourself, What is the author trying to get us to believe?

After locating the conclusion, the next step in analyzing an argument is to list the stated premises. To find the stated premises of an argument, you need to ask about the author's starting place. What claims is the author assuming, without argument? Once you have found the conclusion and found the stated premises (and eliminated any other apparent claims as rhetorical fluff), then you are ready to move to the most difficult stage in argument analysis. You need to trace a plausible route from the premises to the conclusion. This stage is frequently the most difficult. Authors do not tell us what kinds of arguments they are making, nor (obviously) do they tell us their unstated assumptions. Often it will be necessary to try several alternative reconstructions before you are satisfied that you have found the argument buried in the prose. Besides adding needed unstated assumptions and deleting any unnecessary rhetorical flourishes, you will often have to clarify the meanings of key terms, as we noted above. Once you have reconstructed the argument, so that you know how it is supposed to work, then you can appraise its success or failure. This step employs the criteria for evaluating different types of inferences, some of which are presented above.

Evaluating reasoning is a complex task, because human language is rich and fluid, and because we are able to see a large number of subtle connections among the facts we confront. While the task is difficult, the alternative is unacceptable. For if we give up trying to understand reasoning, then we must either naively accept the arguments of others, as if we were children, or play the cynic and forswear the possibility of learning from the insights of others.

NOTE

1. "A Study in Scarlet," in Arthur Conan Doyle, *The Complete Sherlock Holmes* (Garden City, N.Y.: Doubleday, n.d.), p. 24.

STUDY QUESTIONS

1. Can a valid deductive argument have true premises and a false conclusion?
2. Can a valid deductive argument have false premises and a true conclusion?
3. Give your own example of hypothesis testing.
4. Give your own example of arguing by inference to the best explanation.

Improving Your Thinking

Stephen F. Barker

Effective reasoning calls for avoiding fallacious arguments and clarifying ambiguous terms. Our next selection, written by Stephen F. Barker, Professor Emeritus of Philosophy at Johns Hopkins University, addresses both these issues.

You can strengthen your own thinking by being alert to some commonly used words that are so notoriously vague that their appearance in any argument signals trouble. Here are some examples: subjective, natural, relative, pragmatic, diverse. Next time you hear someone use one of these terms, ask what it means. Everyone will benefit from the clarification.

....

1. FALLACIES

If we want to become more skillful at playing chess, or football, or any other game, it is a good idea to study not only the shrewd moves that experts make, but also the poor moves that less experienced players make—we can learn from their mistakes. Similarly, as we try to improve our ability to reason logically, we should not confine our attention to specimens of good reasoning; we should also consider plenty of tempting examples of bad reasoning. By becoming more aware of how these bad arguments are bad, we strengthen our ability to distinguish between good and bad reasoning.

From *The Elements of Logic*, 5th edition, by Stephen F. Barker. Copyright © 1989 by McGraw-Hill, Inc. Reprinted by permission of the publisher.

In ordinary talk the term "fallacy" is often loosely applied to any sort of mistaken belief or untrue sentence. "It's a fallacy to believe that handling a toad causes warts," people say. Here the thing being called a fallacy is just a belief, not a piece of reasoning. But in logic the term "fallacy" is restricted to mistakes in reasoning: a *fallacy* is a logical mistake in reasoning, especially one that it is tempting to make. There is a logical fallacy only when there are premises and a conclusion which is erroneously thought to be proved by them.

Many types of fallacies have been given special names, especially those types that are rather tempting and likely to deceive people. . . .

An argument is called a *petitio principii* (or begging of the question) if the argument fails to prove anything because it somehow takes for granted what it is supposed to prove. Suppose a man says "Jones is insane, you know," and we reply "Really? Are you sure?" and he responds, "Certainly, I can prove it. Jones is demented; therefore he is insane." This is a valid argument in the sense that if the premise is true, the conclusion must be true too; but the argument is unsatisfactory, for it does not really prove anything. The premise is merely another statement of the conclusion, so that practically anyone who doubts the truth of the conclusion ought to be equally doubtful about the truth of the premise, and the argument is useless for the purpose of convincing us of the truth of the conclusion. Thus the argument takes for granted just what it is supposed to prove; it begs the question.

Consider a longer chain of reasoning:

"We must not drink liquor."
"Why do you say that?"
"Drinking is against the will of Allah."
"How do you know?"
"The Koran says so."
"But how do you know that the Koran is right?"
"Everything said in the Koran is right."
"How do you know that?"
"Why, it's all divinely inspired."
"But how do you know that?"
"Why, the Koran itself declares that it is divinely inspired."
"But why believe that?"
"You've got to believe the Koran, because everything in the Koran is right."

This chain of reasoning is a more extended case of begging the question; the speaker is reasoning in a large circle, taking for granted one of the things that is supposed to be proved.

One specific form of *petitio principii*, or begging of the question, has a special name of its own: the fallacy of *complex question*. This is the fallacy of framing a question so as to take for granted something controversial that ought to be proved.

Suppose Mr. White is trying to prove that Mr. Green has a bad character, and White asks Green the famous question "Have you stopped beating your wife yet?" If Green answers "Yes" to this question, White will argue that Green is admitting to having been a wife-beater; if he answers "No," then White will argue that Green is admitting to still being a wife-beater. The questioner has framed his question in such a way as to take for granted that Green has a wife whom he has been beating. The fallacy is that this is a controversial proposition that is at least as doubtful as is the conclusion (that Green has a bad character) supposedly being established. It is not proper in this debate to take for granted this controversial proposition; it needs to be proved if White is to make use of it at all. . . .

One important type of fallacy . . . is the *ad hominem* fallacy. An argument is *ad hominem* (Latin: "to the man") if it is directed at an opponent in a controversy rather than being directly relevant to proving the conclusion under discussion. Such arguments are often, but not always, fallacious. For example, suppose someone argues: "Of course Karl Marx must have been mistaken in maintaining that capitalism is an evil form of economic and social organization. Why, he was a miserable failure of a man who couldn't even earn enough money to support his family." This is an *ad hominem* argument, for it attacks Marx the man instead of offering direct reasons why his views are incorrect. . . .

Another quite different fallacy of irrelevance is the appeal to unsuitable authority. . . . We commit this fallacy when we appeal to some admired or famous person as if that person were an authority on the matter being discussed—but when we have no good reason for thinking that the person is a genuine authority on it. Of course it is not always fallacious to appeal to authorities, but we are not entitled to appeal to persons as authorities unless there are good reasons for believing them to be authorities, and we should not trust an authority outside his or her special proven field of competence. A famous guitarist may be an expert on one type of music, but this does not make her an authority on philosophy of life. A movie star may be an authority on how to look attractive to the opposite sex, but is not likely to be an authority on which pain reliever is most healthful or which toothpaste tastes best. . . .

We conclude with . . . the fallacy of *black-and-white* thinking. A wife may say to her husband "So you think the soup is too cold, do you? Well, I suppose you would like to have had it scalding hot then, instead." The second remark is presented as if it followed logically from the first, and yet there is no logical connection whatever. But people find it very easy to fall into this sort of thinking in extremes, especially in the heat of controversy.

2. DEFINITIONS

When we encounter words that cause confusion because their meanings are ambiguous, it is often helpful to define them. . . .

Definitions that are useful in preventing ambiguity may be subdivided into two types. Some of them serve the purpose of describing the meaning that a word already has in language. We might call these *analytical* definitions. In giving this kind of definition of a word, the speaker does not aim to change its meaning; he aims only to characterize the meaning it already has. Dictionary definitions are of this type. When a definition has this purpose, we can properly ask whether the definition is correct or incorrect.

In order to be correct in its description of the meaning of a word, an analytical definition must not be *too broad;* that is, it must not embrace things that do not really belong. (To define "pneumonia" as "disease of the lungs" would be too broad, for there are many lung diseases besides pneumonia.) Also, in order to be correct in its description of the meaning of a word, an analytical definition must not be *too narrow;* that is, it must not exclude things that really belong. (To define "psychosis" as "schizophrenia" would be too narrow, for there are other kinds of psychoses. . . .)

Finally, a definition cannot serve much useful purpose if it is circular. . . . For example, to define "straight line" as "the line along which a ray of light travels when it goes straight" is circular and uninformative. . . .

A second type of definition useful in preventing ambiguity is the *stipulative* definition, whose purpose is to declare how a speaker intends that a certain word, phrase, or symbol shall be understood ("Let 'S' mean 'Samoans'"; "Let 'heavy truck' mean 'truck that can carry a load of 5 tons or more'"; etc.). Perhaps the expression being defined is one that previously had no meaning, or perhaps it had a different or a vaguer meaning. At any rate, the point of the stipulative definition is that the expression now is deliberately endowed with a particular meaning. Obviously, a stipulative definition cannot be of much use if it is unclear or circular. However, we do not have to worry about whether it is too broad or too narrow, for that sort of correctness cannot pertain to stipulative definitions. A stipulative definition is arbitrary, in that it expresses only the speaker's intention to use the word in the stipulated manner, and the speaker is, after all, entitled to use it in any desired way, so long as it does not cause confusion.

In order to avoid causing confusion, however, a stipulative definition should not assign to a word that already has an established meaning some new meaning that is likely to be confused with it. Consider the following dialogue:

> SMITH: General Green is insane, you know. He ought to be dismissed.
> JONES: He is? I agree that we should not have insane persons serving in the Army. But how do you know he's insane?
> SMITH: It's obvious. He says he believes in extrasensory perception, and according to my definition—surely I'm entitled to use words as I please— anyone who does that is insane.

Here the stipulative definition is used to promote ambiguity rather than to prevent it. In the ordinary sense of the term "insane," Jones agrees with Smith that insane persons ought not to be generals. But Smith offers no evidence that General Green is insane in this sense. All that Smith shows is that the general is "insane" in a special, idiosyncratic sense of the word. From that, nothing follows about whether he ought to be dismissed. Smith is causing confusion by failing to keep distinct these two very different senses of the word; this happens because he fails to recognize the difference here between a stipulative and an analytical definition. . . .

The two kinds of definitions mentioned so far both aim to inform us about verbal usage. . . . It would be a mistake, however, to suppose that everything called a definition belongs to one of these two kinds. In fact, the profoundest and most valuable definitions usually do not fit tidily into either kind. When Newton defined force as the product of mass times acceleration, when Einstein defined simultaneity of distant events in terms of the transmission of light rays . . . [w]hat these definitions did was to propose new verbal usages growing out of the previously established usages. It was felt that these new usages perfected tendencies of thought implicit in the old usages and offered more insight into the subject matter being treated.

We might give the name *revelatory* definitions to definitions like these, which do not fit into either of the two categories of stipulative and analytical. Revelatory definitions constitute a third category. Further examples of revelatory definitions can be found in other, diverse fields. For example, when a nineteenth-century writer defined architecture as frozen music, he was not trying to describe how the word "architecture" is used in our language. (He took it for granted that his readers would know what kinds of constructions are considered architecture.) Nor was he proposing some arbitrary new usage. We should not censure his definition on the ground that it is unhelpful for the purpose of preventing ambiguity; that is not the purpose of this kind of definition. This definition is a metaphor, and it suggests a new way of looking at architecture, comparing the structural organization of the parts of a building with the structural organization of the parts of a musical composition. In trying to decide whether the definition is a good one or not, we must reflect about the extent and validity of this comparison between music and buildings; the definition is a good one if and only if the comparison is revealing. . . .

How frequently are definitions needed? People sometimes think that one always should define one's terms at the beginning of any discussion. But this idea becomes absurd if carried too far. Suppose that we as speakers did undertake to define all our terms in noncircular ways. However far we proceeded, we would always still have . . . undefined terms; therefore this task is an impossible one to complete. Moreover, we do have a fairly adequate understanding of the meanings of many words that we have never bothered to define and also of many words that we would not know how to define satisfactorily even if we tried. Thus, it would be foolish to try indiscriminately to define all or even most of our terms before proceeding with our thinking. What we should do at the beginning of a discussion is seek definitions of those particular words which are especially likely to make trouble in the discussion because they are harmfully ambiguous, obscure, or vague.

This is especially true with regard to discussions in which confusion is caused by failure to notice the different meanings of a term. A *verbal dispute* is a dispute arising solely from the fact that some word is being used with different meanings; this kind of dispute can be settled merely by giving the definitions that clarify the situation (though this is not to say that such disputes always are *easy* to settle).

The American philosopher William James gives a classic example of such a verbal dispute. . . . Suppose there is a squirrel on the trunk of a tree, and a man walks around the tree. The squirrel moves around the tree trunk so as to stay out of sight, always facing the man but keeping the tree between them. Has the man gone around the squirrel or not? Some of James's friends disputed hotly for a long time about this question. Here is a purely verbal dispute; it can be settled by pointing out that in one sense the man has gone "around" the squirrel, for he has moved from the north to the west and then to the south and east of the squirrel's location, but in another sense the man has not gone "around" the squirrel, for the squirrel has always been facing him. Once we have pointed out these two different senses of the word, we have done all that can reasonably be done; there is nothing more worth discussing (though this does not ensure that discussion will cease). With a verbal dispute like this, giving definitions is the way to resolve the dispute. But it would be utterly wrong to assume that all disputes are verbal in this way. There are many serious problems for the settling of which definitions are not needed, and there are many other problems where if definitions help, they mark only the beginning of the thinking needed to resolve the issue.

STUDY QUESTIONS

1. Give an example of an argument that begs the question.
2. Give your own example of an *ad hominem* argument.
3. Explain the danger involved in offering a stipulative definition that uses an ordinary word in an idiosyncratic manner.
4. Give your own example of a purely verbal dispute.

Necessary and Sufficient Conditions

Steven M. Cahn

One key to effective thinking is understanding the concepts of necessary and sufficient conditions. In the next selection I explain their proper and improper uses.

One state of affairs, A, is a necessary condition for another state of affairs, B, if B cannot occur without A occurring. For instance, in the United States a person must be at least eighteen years old before being entitled to vote. In other words, being eighteen is a necessary condition for being entitled to vote.

One state of affairs, A, is a sufficient condition for another state of affairs, B, if the occurrence of A ensures the occurrence of B. For instance, in an American presidential election for a candidate to receive 300 electoral votes ensures that candidate's election. In other words, receiving 300 electoral votes is a sufficient condition for winning the election.

Note that even if A is a necessary condition for B, A need not be a sufficient condition for B. For instance, even if you need to be eighteen to vote, you also need to be a citizen of the United States. Thus being eighteen is necessary but not sufficient for voting.

Similarly, even if A is a sufficient condition for B, A need not be a necessary condition for B. For instance, if a presidential candidate receives 300 electoral votes, then that candidate is elected, but receiving 300 electoral votes, while sufficient for election, is not necessary, because a candidate who receives 299 votes is also elected.

Confusing necessary and sufficient conditions is a common mistake in reasoning. If one individual argues that extensive prior experience in Washington, DC, is required for a person to be a worthy presidential candidate, that claim is not refuted by pointing out that many candidates with such experience have not been worthy. To refute the claim that experience is necessary for worthiness requires demonstrating not that many with experience have been unworthy but that a person without experience *has* been worthy. After all, the original claim was that experience is necessary, not sufficient.

Suppose A is both necessary and sufficient for B. For example, being a rectangle with all four sides equal is necessary and sufficient for being a square. In other words, a geometric figure cannot be a square unless it is a rectangle with all four sides equal, and if a rectangle has all four sides equal, then it is a square. Thus a satisfactory definition of "square" is "rectangle with all four sides equal."

Now here is an additional twist that may be surprising. What is the difference between asserting that A is a necessary condition for B and that B is a sufficient condition for A? Nothing. These are two ways of saying that the occurrence of B ensures the occurrence of A. Furthermore, what is the difference between asserting that A is a sufficient condition for B and that B is a necessary condition for A? Again, nothing. These are two ways of saying that the occurrence of A ensures the occurrence of B.

The critical mistake is thinking that if A is necessary for B, then A is sufficient for B. Or that if A is sufficient for B, then A is necessary for B. These are fallacies.

Hence the next time you hear someone say, for example, that you can be well educated without knowing any logic, because some people who know logic are not well educated, you can point out that the speaker has confused necessary and sufficient conditions. Just because some people who know logic are not well educated does not prove that you can be well educated without knowing logic. That conclusion would only follow if some people who don't know logic are nevertheless well educated.

If you're on the lookout for this fallacy, you'll find it committed far more often than you might suppose.

STUDY QUESTIONS

1. If A is a necessary condition for B, is B always a necessary condition for A?
2. If A is a necessary condition for B, is B always a sufficient condition for A?
3. Is the claim that the study of philosophy is necessary for happiness undermined by presenting cases of unhappy people who have studied philosophy?
4. Present your own example of the fallacy of confusing necessary and sufficient conditions.

Scientific Inquiry

CARL G. HEMPEL

The scientific method of explanation involves formulating a hypothesis and testing it, then accepting, rejecting, or modifying it in light of the experimental results. But how do we test a hypothesis? That is the subject of the following selection by the celebrated philosopher of science Carl G. Hempel (1905–1997), who was Professor of Philosophy at Princeton University.

As you read about hypothesis testing, you may wonder how hypotheses are developed. What is their source? No mechanical procedures are available; the answer lies in creative imagination. While giving free rein to ingenuity, however, scientific method requires that our intuitions be accepted only if they pass the rigors of careful testing.

1. A CASE HISTORY AS AN EXAMPLE

As a simple illustration of some important aspects of scientific inquiry, let us consider Semmelweis' work on childbed fever. Ignaz Semmelweis, a physician of Hungarian birth, did this work during the years from 1844 to 1848 at the

Vienna General Hospital. As a member of the medical staff of the First Maternity Division in the hospital, Semmelweis was distressed to find that a large proportion of the women who were delivered of their babies in that division contracted a serious and often fatal illness known as puerperal fever or childbed fever. In 1844, as many as 260 out of 3,157 mothers in the First Division, or 8.2 per cent, died of the disease; for 1845, the death rate was 6.8 per cent, and for 1846, it was 11.4 per cent. These figures were all the more alarming because in the adjacent Second Maternity Division of the same hospital, which accommodated almost as many women as the First, the death toll from childbed fever was much lower: 2.3, 2.0, and 2.7 per cent for the same years. In a book that he wrote later on the causation and the prevention of childbed fever, Semmelweis describes his efforts to resolve the dreadful puzzle.[1]

He began by considering various explanations that were current at the time; some of these he rejected out of hand as incompatible with well-established facts; others he subjected to specific tests.

One widely accepted view attributed the ravages of puerperal fever to "epidemic influences," which were vaguely described as "atmospheric–cosmic–telluric changes" spreading over whole districts and causing childbed fever in women in confinement. But how, Semmelweis reasons, could such influences have plagued the First Division for years and yet spared the Second? And how could this view be reconciled with the fact that while the fever was raging in the hospital, hardly a case occurred in the city of Vienna or in its surroundings: a genuine epidemic, such as cholera, would not be so selective. Finally, Semmelweis notes that some of the women admitted to the First Division, living far from the hospital, had been overcome by labor on their way and had given birth in the street: yet despite these adverse conditions, the death rate from childbed fever among these cases of "street birth" was lower than the average for the First Division.

On another view, overcrowding was a cause of mortality in the First Division. But Semmelweis points out that in fact the crowding was heavier in the Second Division, partly as a result of the desperate efforts of patients to avoid assignment to the notorious First Division. He also rejects two similar conjectures that were current, by noting that there were no differences between the two Divisions in regard to diet or general care of the patients.

In 1846, a commission that had been appointed to investigate the matter attributed the prevalence of illness in the First Division to injuries resulting from rough examination by the medical students, all of whom received their obstetrical training in the First Division. Semmelweis notes in refutation of this view that (a) the injuries resulting naturally from the process of birth are much more extensive than those that might be caused by rough examination; (b) the midwives who received their training in the Second Division examined their patients in much the same manner but without the same ill effects; (c) when, in response to the commission's report, the number of medical students was halved and their examinations of the women were reduced to a minimum, the mortality, after a brief decline, rose to higher levels than ever before.

Various psychological explanations were attempted. One of them noted that the First Division was so arranged that a priest bearing the last sacrament to a dying woman had to pass through five wards before reaching the sickroom beyond: the appearance of the priest, preceded by an attendant ringing a bell, was held to have a terrifying and debilitating effect upon the patients in the wards and thus to make them more likely victims of childbed fever. In the Second Division, this adverse factor was absent, since the priest had direct access to the sickroom. Semmelweis decided to test this conjecture. He persuaded the priest to come by a roundabout route and without ringing of the bell, in order to reach the sick chamber silently and unobserved. But the mortality in the First Division did not decrease.

A new idea was suggested to Semmelweis by the observation that in the First Division the women were delivered lying on their backs; in the Second Division, on their sides. Though he thought it unlikely, he decided "like a drowning man clutching at a straw," to test whether this difference in procedure was significant. He introduced the use of the lateral position in the First Division, but again, the mortality remained unaffected.

At last, early in 1847, an accident gave Semmelweis the decisive clue for his solution of the problem. A colleague of his, Kolletschka, received a puncture wound in the finger, from the scalpel of a student with whom he was performing an autopsy, and died after an agonizing illness during which he displayed the same symptoms that Semmelweis had observed in the victims of childbed fever. Although the role of microorganisms in such infections had not yet been recognized at the time, Semmelweis realized that "cadaveric matter" which the student's scalpel had introduced into Kolletschka's blood stream had caused his colleague's fatal illness. And the similarities between the course of Kolletschka's disease and that of the women in his clinic led Semmelweis to the conclusion that his patients had died of the same kind of blood poisoning: he, his colleagues, and the medical students had been the carriers of the infectious material, for he and his associates used to come to the wards directly from performing dissections in the autopsy room, and examine the women in labor after only superficially washing their hands, which often retained a characteristic foul odor.

Again, Semmelweis put his idea to a test. He reasoned that if he were right, then childbed fever could be prevented by chemically destroying the infectious material adhering to the hands. He therefore issued an order requiring all medical students to wash their hands in a solution of chlorinated lime before making an examination. The mortality from childbed fever promptly began to decrease, and for the year 1848 it fell to 1.27 per cent in the First Division, compared to 1.33 in the Second.

In further support of his idea, or of his hypothesis, as we will also say, Semmelweis notes that it accounts for the fact that the mortality in the Second Division consistently was so much lower: the patients there were attended by midwives, whose training did not include anatomical instruction by dissection of cadavers.

The hypothesis also explained the lower mortality among "street births": women who arrived with babies in arms were rarely examined after admission and thus had a better chance of escaping infection.

Similarly, the hypothesis accounted for the fact that the victims of childbed fever among the newborn babies were all among those whose mothers had contracted the disease during labor; for then the infection could be transmitted to the baby before birth, through the common bloodstream of mother and child, whereas this was impossible when the mother remained healthy.

Further clinical experiences soon led Semmelweis to broaden his hypothesis. On one occasion, for example, he and his associates, having carefully disinfected their hands, examined first a woman in labor who was suffering from a festering cervical cancer; then they proceeded to examine twelve other women in the same room, after only routine washing without renewed disinfection. Eleven of the twelve patients died of puerperal fever. Semmelweis concluded that childbed fever can be caused not only by cadaveric material, but also by "putrid matter derived from living organisms."

2. BASIC STEPS IN TESTING A HYPOTHESIS

We have seen how, in his search for the cause of childbed fever, Semmelweis examined various hypotheses that had been suggested as possible answers. . . . [L]et us examine how a hypothesis, once proposed, is tested.

Sometimes, the procedure is quite direct. Consider the conjectures that differences in crowding, or in diet, or in general care account for the difference in mortality between the two divisions. As Semmelweis points out, these conflict with readily observable facts. There are no such differences between the divisions; the hypotheses are therefore rejected as false.

But usually the test will be less simple and straightforward. Take the hypothesis attributing the high mortality in the First Division to the dread evoked by the appearance of the priest with his attendant. The intensity of that dread, and especially its effect upon childbed fever, are not as directly ascertainable as are differences in crowding or in diet, and Semmelweis uses an indirect method of testing. He asks himself: Are there any readily observable effects that should occur if the hypothesis were true? And he reasons: If the hypothesis were true, *then* an appropriate change in the priest's procedure should be followed by a decline in fatalities. He checks this implication by a simple experiment and finds it false, and he therefore rejects the hypothesis.

Similarly, to test his conjecture about the position of the women during delivery, he reasons: If this conjecture should be true, *then* adoption of the lateral position in the First Division will reduce the mortality. Again, the implication is shown false by his experiment, and the conjecture is discarded.

In the last two cases, the test is based on an argument to the effect that *if* the contemplated hypothesis, say *H*, is true, *then* certain observable events (e.g., decline in mortality) should occur under specified circumstances (e.g., if the priest refrains from walking through the wards, or if the women are delivered in lateral position); or briefly, if *H* is true, then so is *I*, where *I* is a statement describing the observable occurrences to be expected. For convenience, let us say that *I* is inferred from, or implied by, *H*; and let us call *I* a *test implication of the hypothesis H*. . . .

In our last two examples, experiments show the test implication to be false, and the hypothesis is accordingly rejected. The reasoning that leads to the rejection may be schematized as follows:

> (2*a*)   If *H* is true, then so is *I*.
> But (as the evidence shows) *I* is not true.
> *H* is not true.

Any argument of this form, called *modus tollens* in logic, is deductively valid; that is, if its premises (the sentences above the horizontal line) are true, then its conclusion (the sentence below the horizontal line) is unfailingly true as well. Hence, if the premises of (2*a*) are properly established, the hypothesis *H* that is being tested must indeed be rejected.

Next, let us consider the case where observation or experiment bears out the test implication *I*. From his hypothesis that childbed fever is blood poisoning produced by cadaveric matter, Semmelweis infers that suitable antiseptic measures will reduce fatalities from the disease. This time, experiment shows the test implication to be true. But this favorable outcome does not conclusively prove the hypothesis true, for the underlying argument would have the form

> (2*b*)   If *H* is true, then so is *I*.
> (As the evidence shows) *I* is true.
> *H* is true.

And this mode of reasoning, which is referred to as the *fallacy of affirming the consequent*, is deductively invalid, that is, its conclusion may be false even if its premises are true. This is in fact illustrated by Semmelweis' own experience. The initial version of his account of childbed fever as a form of blood poisoning presented infection with cadaveric matter essentially as the one and only source of the disease; and he was right in reasoning that if this hypothesis should be true, then destruction of cadaveric particles by antiseptic washing should reduce the mortality. Furthermore, his experiment did show the test implication to be true. Hence, in this case, the premises of (2*b*) were both true. Yet, his hypothesis was false, for as he later discovered, putrid material from living organisms, too, could produce childbed fever.

Thus, the favorable outcome of a test, that is, the fact that a test implication inferred from a hypothesis is found to be true, does not prove the hypothesis to be true. Even if many implications of a hypothesis have been borne out by careful tests, the hypothesis may still be false. The following argument still commits the fallacy of affirming the consequent:

(2c)   If H is true, then so are $I_1, I_2, \ldots, I_n$.
(As the evidence shows) $I_1, I_2, \ldots, I_n$ are all true.

H is true.

This, too, can be illustrated by reference to Semmelweis' final hypothesis in its first version. As we noted earlier, his hypothesis also yields the test implications that among cases of street births admitted to the First Division, mortality from puerperal fever should be below the average for the Division, and that infants of mothers who escape the illness do not contract childbed fever; and these implications, too, were borne out by the evidence—even though the first version of the final hypothesis was false.

But the observation that a favorable outcome of however many tests does not afford conclusive proof for a hypothesis should not lead us to think that if we have subjected a hypothesis to a number of tests and all of them have had a favorable outcome, we are no better off than if we had not tested the hypothesis at all. For each of our tests might conceivably have had an unfavorable outcome and might have led to the rejection of the hypothesis. A set of favorable results obtained by testing different test implications, $I_1, I_2, \ldots, I_n$, of a hypothesis shows that as far as these particular implications are concerned, the hypothesis has been borne out; and while this result does not afford a complete proof of the hypothesis, it provides at least some support, some partial corroboration or confirmation for it.

NOTE

1. The story of Semmelweis' work and of the difficulties he encountered forms a fascinating page in the history of medicine. A detailed account, which includes translations and paraphrases of large portions of Semmelweis' writings, is given in W. J. Sinclair, *Semmelweis: His Life and His Doctrine* (Manchester, England: Manchester University Press, 1909). Brief quoted phrases in this chapter are taken from this work. The highlights of Semmelweis' career are recounted in the first chapter of P. de Kruif, *Men Against Death* (New York: Harcourt, Brace & World, Inc., 1932).

STUDY QUESTIONS

1. Give your own example of testing a hypothesis by use of scientific method.
2. Give your own example of an argument in the form of *modus tollens*.
3. If an implication inferred from a hypothesis is found to be true, is the hypothesis thereby proven to be true?
4. What is the value of a partial confirmation of a hypothesis?

PART 3

Knowledge

Caring and Epistemic Demands

Linda Zagzebski

We now turn to a fundamental field of philosophy: the theory of knowledge, or, as philosophers often refer to it, "epistemology," from the Greek word epistēmē, meaning "knowledge." Why should we care whether we hold true beliefs? An answer is provided in the next selection by Linda Zagzebski, Professor of Philosophy at the University of Oklahoma.

....

We all care about a lot of things. Even if it were possible not to care about anything, we would not have a good life if we did not care. Caring about many things is not only natural, but is part of any life we would care to live. But if we care about anything, we must care about having true beliefs in the domains we care about. If I care about my children's lives and I am minimally rational, I must care about having true beliefs about my children's lives. If I care about football, I must care about having true beliefs about football. I'll call a belief that is governed by a concern for truth a *conscientiously* held belief. I assume that conscientiousness is something that comes in degrees, and I propose that (with some qualifications) the more we care about something, the more conscientious we must be.

I think that caring imposes a demand for conscientious belief on us in two ways. First, there is a demand to be conscientious in whatever beliefs we have in that domain, and second, there is a demand to acquire conscientious beliefs in the domain. The first demand is no doubt stronger than the second because our ability to care probably extends beyond our ability to form beliefs, although our inability to form beliefs in some domain probably limits our ability to care. For example, we may care about the personal well-being of all the victims of a hurricane, but since there are so many of them, none of us can acquire beliefs about very many of those people. I suspect that this limits our ability to care about them individually. What we tend to do is get beliefs about them as a class, and if that is all we have, then I suspect that we can only care about them as a class. That is probably why photojournalists try to put a face on disastrous events; it aids us in caring about the victims as individuals.

I am suggesting, then, that not only do we commit ourselves to conscientiously getting beliefs about those things we care about, but if we don't or can't do it, that tends to weaken our caring. And if we need to care about many things to

From Linda Zagzebski, *On Epistemology*, Wadsworth/CENGAGE Learning, 2009. Reprinted by permission of the publisher.

have a good life, the limitations of our ability to form beliefs conscientiously limit the desirability of our lives.

There are some qualifications on the demand to acquire beliefs in the domains we care about. Sometimes having beliefs in a domain we care about conflicts with something else we care about. Even if you care about your friends' personal happiness, if you also care about their privacy, you will not care about having beliefs about the most personal aspects of their lives, at least not many detailed beliefs. So there are exceptions to the demand to conscientiously acquire beliefs in the domains of what we care about, but the exceptions also arise from something we care about, such as the privacy of other people. (This is one reason why curiosity can be a vice.)

Another qualification is that the desire to acquire beliefs about what we care about can sometimes be counterproductive. For example, health is clearly an important component of a desirable life, but obsession with one's health can detract from the desirability of one's life because getting too much information about health can impair your health. But aside from these qualifications, I think that in general, if we care about something, merely being conscientious in whatever beliefs we happen to have in that domain is not enough. We also need to get beliefs in those domains.

So we care about many things, and caring about anything imposes a demand on us to care about true belief in the domains of what we care about, and that includes a demand to acquire beliefs conscientiously in those domains. But the logic of caring demands something more than conscientious belief for a variety of reasons. For one thing, we are often agents in the domains of what we care about. We want beliefs that can serve as the ground of action, and that requires not only true beliefs, but confidence that the particular beliefs we are acting upon are true. The degree of confidence needed varies with the context. Acting involves time, usually effort, and sometimes risk or sacrifice, and it is not rational to engage in action without a degree of confidence in the truth of the beliefs upon which we act that is high enough to make the time, effort, and risk involved in acting worthwhile. Sometimes the degree of confidence we need amounts to certainty, but usually it does not.

We also know that we have false beliefs, if for no other reason than that we sometimes have beliefs that conflict, and since we do not want false beliefs in the domains of what we care about, we want mechanisms to sort out the false beliefs from the true ones. Imagine you are digging for a precious substance such as gold. (Ignore the fact that these days you are not likely to find any.) Suppose that as you dig for gold, you find lots of gold nuggets, but you also find lots of Fool's Gold, which we will imagine is hard to distinguish from real gold. Imagine also that you discover that some of the nuggets you have kept in the past are actually Fool's Gold, so even though you are pretty sure that you have lots of real gold, you are not sure which is which. Even though you have some valuable gold, it is not very helpful to have it if it is mixed up with Fool's Gold. You not only want gold, but you also want to distinguish the real gold from the fake gold. Similarly, we not only want true beliefs, but we also want to distinguish the true beliefs from the false ones. It diminishes the value of our true beliefs if they are mixed up with too many false beliefs.

Among the things we care about is caring that others care about what we care about, which means that we care about their having true beliefs about what we care about, and we also care to some extent about what they care about. So we care about being good informants to others. We want the ability to convey true beliefs and not false beliefs to others.

Conscientiousness requires self-trust. Being conscientious is all I can do to get true beliefs, but there is no guarantee that being conscientious gives me the truth. I can be careful, be thorough in seeking and evaluating evidence, be open-minded, listen to those with a contrary view, and so forth, but there are no guarantees. So I need trust that there is a close connection between conscientious belief and true belief. If I did not trust, and my lack of trust led me to have fewer conscientious beliefs in the domains I care about, I would care less about what I care about and that would give me a less desirable life, a life I would not care to have. Furthermore, since I depend upon other people for most of my beliefs, I need another sort of trust. I am not often in a position to confirm that other people are conscientious, so I need to trust that they are. And again, if I don't trust them, I will have fewer beliefs about what I care about and that will give me a less desirable life.

The logic of caring requires that we live in a community of epistemic trust, the importance of which is dramatically described in the Greek legend of Cassandra. According to that myth, Apollo gave Cassandra the gift of prophecy as part of a scheme to seduce her. When she rebuffed him, he did not take back his gift, but did something much worse. He allowed her to continue to see the future, but she was fated never to be believed. Cassandra's curse meant that her warning that the Trojan horse was a trick went unheeded, with disastrous results for the Trojans, but its effect on her was terrible in a different way. She was the ultimate voiceless woman. Aeschylus tells us it drove her mad.

Cassandra was disbelieved only in her predictions about the future, but imagine what it would be like to be disbelieved about everything you say. You would be epistemically isolated in such an extreme way that you would probably be isolated in every other way as well. Every attempt at communication would be futile, so there would be no point in trying to talk with anybody about anything. You could not make plans with others, successfully express your feelings to them, or even do the minimum that it takes to carry on practical life. We need trust, but trust breaks down when people are thought to be untrust*worthy*. Living in a community of epistemically trusting and trustworthy people is an important requirement of any worthwhile life.

Another thing we care about is not being surprised at what happens next. We want to be able to predict the way the world will be tomorrow. We probably want that anyway, but we certainly want to be able to predict the way the world will be in ways that impinge on what we care about. That is one reason science has so much status. It allows us to explain the future as well as the past.

I have mentioned a series of epistemic values that we have because we care about many things and caring about things is part of living a life we would care to live. These values include true belief, the ability to distinguish true from false belief, certainty or at least confidence in our beliefs, credibility, trust and trustworthiness, and predictability. Each of these things is desirable within a domain of what we care about because we care about that domain. Caring imposes these demands on us, which means we impose these demands on ourselves by caring. Some of these values may be components of knowledge, but knowledge might be something else. In any case, knowledge also is something we want in the domains of what we care about, and we might also want knowledge for its own sake.

STUDY QUESTIONS

1. According to Zagzebski, in what two ways does caring impose a demand for conscientious belief?
2. What does Zagzebski mean by "a community of epistemic trust"?
3. What lesson does Zagzebski draw from the legend of Cassandra?
4. If some of your beliefs turned out to be false, would you care, and, if so, why?

What Is Knowledge?

A. J. AYER

A traditional definition of knowledge is that you know that something is the case if (1) you are sure of it, (2) what you are sure of is true, and (3) you have a right to be sure. In our next selection A. J. Ayer (1910–1989), who was Professor of Philosophy at the University of Oxford and one of the most eminent philosophers of the twentieth century, explains the reasoning behind these three conditions.

The first requirement [of knowing that something is the case] is that what is known should be true, but this is not sufficient; not even if we add to it the further condition that one must be completely sure of what one knows. For it is possible to be completely sure of something which is in fact true, but yet not to know it. The circumstances may be such that one is not entitled to be sure. For instance, a superstitious person who had inadvertently walked under a ladder might be convinced as a result that he was about to suffer some misfortune; and he might in fact be right. But it would not be correct to say that he knew that this was going to be so. He arrived at his belief by a process of reasoning which would not be generally reliable; so, although his prediction came true, it was not a case of knowledge.

Again, if someone were fully persuaded of a mathematical proposition by a proof which could be shown to be invalid, he would not, without further evidence, be said to know the proposition, even though it was true. But while it is not hard to find examples of true and fully confident beliefs which in some ways fail to meet the standards required for knowledge, it is not at all easy to determine exactly what these standards are.

One way of trying to discover them would be to consider what would count as satisfactory answers to the question, How do you know? Thus people may be credited with knowing truths of mathematics or logic if they are able to give a valid proof of them, or even if, without themselves being able to set out such a proof, they have obtained this information from someone who can. Claims to know empirical statements may be upheld by a reference to perception, or to memory, or to testimony, or to historical records, or to scientific laws. But such backing is not always strong enough for knowledge. Whether it is so or not depends upon the circumstances of the particular case. If I were asked how I knew that a physical object of a certain sort was in such and such a place, it would, in general, be a sufficient answer for me to say that I could see it; but if my eyesight were bad and the light were dim, this answer might not be sufficient. Even though I was right, it might still be said that I did not really know that the object was there. If I have a poor memory and the event which I claim to remember is remote, my memory of it may still not amount to knowledge, even though in this instance it does not fail me. If a witness is unreliable, his unsupported evidence may not enable us to know that what he says is true, even in a case where we completely trust him and he is not in fact deceiving us. In a given instance it is possible to decide whether the backing is strong enough to justify a claim to knowledge. But to say in general how strong it has to be would require our drawing up a list of the conditions under which perception, or memory, or testimony, or other forms of evidence are reliable. And this would be a very complicated matter, if indeed it could be done at all.

Moreover, we cannot assume that, even in particular instances, an answer to the question, How do you know? will always be forthcoming. There may very well be cases in which one knows that something is so without its being possible to say how one knows it. . . . Suppose that someone were consistently successful in predicting events of a certain kind, events, let us say, which are not ordinarily thought to be predictable, like the results of a lottery. If his run of successes were sufficiently impressive, we might very well come to say that he knew which number would win, even though he did not reach this conclusion by any rational method, or indeed by any method at all. We might say that he knew it by intuition, but this would be to assert no more than that he did know it but that we could not say how. In the same way, if someone were consistently successful in reading the minds of others without having any of the usual sort of evidence, we might say that he knew these things telepathically. But in default of any further explanation, this would come down to saying merely that he did know them, but not by any ordinary means. Words like "intuition" and "telepathy" are brought in just to disguise the fact that no explanation has been found.

But if we allow this sort of knowledge to be even theoretically possible, what becomes of the distinction between knowledge and true belief? How does our man who knows what the results of the lottery will differ from one who only makes a series of lucky guesses? The answer is that, so far as the man himself is concerned, there need not be any difference. His procedure and his state of mind, when he is said to know what will happen, may be exactly the same as when it is said that he is only guessing. The difference is that to say that he knows is to concede to him the right to be sure, while to say that he is only guessing is to withhold it. Whether we make this concession will depend upon the view which we take of his performance. Normally we do not say that people know things unless they have followed one of the accredited routes to knowledge. If someone reaches a true conclusion without appearing to have any adequate basis for it, we are likely to say that he does not really know it. But if he were repeatedly successful in a given domain, we might very well come to say that he knew the facts in question, even though we could not explain how he knew them. We should grant him the right to be sure, simply on the basis of his success. . . .

I conclude then that the necessary and sufficient conditions for knowing that something is the case are first that what one is said to know be true, secondly that one be sure of it, and thirdly that one should have the right to be sure.

STUDY QUESTIONS

1. Can you be sure of something, yet not know it?
2. Can you know something without being able to say how you know it?
3. How does knowledge differ from true belief?
4. Give an example of a situation in which you believe a claim to be true, it is true, and you have the right to be sure it is true.

Is Justified True Belief Knowledge?

Edmund L. Gettier

Ayer's definition of knowledge may appear unexceptionable, but a type of counterexample is offered in a much-discussed article by Edmund L. Gettier, Professor Emeritus of Philosophy at the University of Massachusetts at Amherst. Here for your consideration is a case he presents.

From Edmund L. Gettier, *Analysis,* 23 (1963). Reprinted by permission of the author.

Ayer has stated the necessary and sufficient condition for [S knows that P] as follows:

(i) P is true,
(ii) S is sure that P is true, and
(iii) S has the right to be sure that P is true.

I shall argue that the conditions stated therein do not constitute a *sufficient* condition for the truth of the proposition that S knows that P. . . .

Suppose that Smith and Jones have applied for a certain job. And suppose that Smith has strong evidence for the following conjunctive proposition:

(d) Jones is the man who will get the job, and Jones has ten coins in his pocket.

Smith's evidence for (d) might be that the president of the company assured him that Jones would in the end be selected, and that he, Smith, had counted the coins in Jones's pocket ten minutes ago. Proposition (d) entails:

(e) The man who will get the job has ten coins in his pocket.

Let us suppose that Smith sees the entailment from (d) to (e), and accepts (e) on the grounds of (d), for which he has strong evidence. In this case, Smith is clearly justified in believing that (e) is true.

But imagine, further, that unknown to Smith, he himself, not Jones, will get the job. And, also, unknown to Smith, he himself has ten coins in his pocket. Proposition (e) is then true, though proposition (d), from which Smith inferred (e), is false. In our example, then, all of the following are true: (*i*) (e) is true, (*ii*) Smith believes that (e) is true, and (*iii*) Smith is justified in believing that (e) is true. But it is equally clear that Smith does not *know* that (e) is true; for (e) is true in virtue of the number of coins in Smith's pocket, while Smith does not know how many coins are in Smith's pocket, and bases his belief in (e) on a count of the coins in Jones's pocket, whom he falsely believes to be the man who will get the job.

STUDY QUESTIONS

1. What is the point of Gettier's example?
2. Is Smith justified in believing that the man who will get the job has ten coins in his pocket?
3. Does Smith know that Jones will get the job?
4. Can you develop your own example along the same lines as Gettier's case?

Conditions for Knowledge

ROBERT NOZICK

Many philosophers have proposed revised definitions of knowledge in an effort to deal with cases like the one Gettier presents. An intriguing suggestion is developed by Robert Nozick (1938–2002), who was Professor of Philosophy at Harvard University.

....

In knowledge, a belief is linked somehow to the fact believed; without this linkage there may be true belief but there will not be knowledge. Plato first made the point that knowledge is not simply a belief that is true, if someone knowing nothing about the matter separately tells you and me contradictory things, getting one of us to believe p while the other believes not-p, although one of us will have a belief that happens to be true, neither of us will have knowledge. Something more is needed for a person S to know that p, to go alongside

(1) p is true.
(2) S believes that p.

This something more, I think, is not simply an additional fact, but a way that 1 and 2 are linked. . . .

Our task is to formulate further conditions to go alongside

(1) p is true.
(2) S believes that p.

We would like each condition to be necessary for knowledge, so any case that fails to satisfy it will not be an instance of knowledge. Furthermore, we would like the conditions to be jointly sufficient for knowledge, so any case that satisfies all of them will be an instance of knowledge. . . .

Let us consider. . . .

(3) If p weren't true, S wouldn't believe that p.

The subjunctive condition 3 serves to exclude cases of the sort first described by Edmund Gettier, such as the following. Two other people are in my office and I am justified on the basis of much evidence in believing the first owns a Ford car; though he (now) does not, the second person (a stranger to me) owns one. I believe truly and justifiably that someone (or other) in my office owns a Ford car, but I do not know someone does. Concluded Gettier, knowledge is not simply justified true belief.

The following subjunctive, which specifies condition 3 for this Gettier case, is not satisfied: if no one in my office owned a Ford car, I wouldn't believe that someone did. The situation that would obtain if no one in my office owned a Ford is one where the stranger does not (or where he is not in the office); and in that situation I still would believe, as before, that someone in my office does own a Ford, namely, the first person. So the subjunctive condition 3 excludes this Gettier case as a case of knowledge. . . .

Despite the power and intuitive force of the condition that if p weren't true the person would not believe it, this condition does not (in conjunction with the first two conditions) rule out every problem case. There remains, for example, the case of the person in [a] tank who is brought to believe, by direct electrical and chemical stimulation of his brain, that he is in the tank and is being brought to believe things in this way; he does not know this is true. However, the subjunctive condition is satisfied: if he weren't floating in the tank, he wouldn't believe he was.

The person in the tank does not know he is there, because his belief is not sensitive to the truth. Although it is caused by the fact that is its content, it is not sensitive to that fact. The operators of the tank could have produced any belief, including the false belief that he wasn't in the tank; if they had, he would have believed that. Perfect sensitivity would involve beliefs and facts varying together. We already have one portion of that variation, subjunctively at least: if p were false, he wouldn't believe it. This sensitivity as specified by a subjunctive does not have the belief vary with the truth or falsity of p in all possible situations, merely in the ones that would or might obtain if p were false.

The subjunctive condition 3 . . . tells us only half the story about how his belief is sensitive to the truth-value of p. It tells us how his belief state is sensitive to p's falsity, but not how it is sensitive to p's truth; it tells us what his belief state would be if p were false, but not what it would be if p were true.

To be sure, conditions 1 and 2 tell us that p is true and he does believe it, but it does not follow that his believing p is sensitive to p's being true. This additional sensitivity is given to us by a further subjunctive: if p were true, he would believe it.

(4) If p were true, S would believe that p.

A person knows that p when he not only does truly believe it, but . . . if it weren't true he wouldn't believe it, and if it were true he would believe it. To know that p is to be someone who would believe it if it were true, and who wouldn't believe it if it were false.

It will be useful to have a term for this situation when a person's belief is thus subjunctively connected to the fact. Let us say of a person who believes that p, which is true, that when 3 and 4 hold, his belief *tracks* the truth that p. To know is to have a belief that tracks the truth. Knowledge is a particular way of being connected to the world, having a specific real factual connection to the world: tracking it.

STUDY QUESTIONS

1. What task does Nozick set for himself?
2. What two subjunctive conditions for knowledge does he offer?
3. Are both conditions needed to exclude Gettier's case?
4. What does Nozick mean by "a belief that tracks the truth"?

Appearance and Reality

BERTRAND RUSSELL

An ancient philosophical question is whether we know the world as it is or only as we experience it from a limited perspective. The relation between what appears to be the case and what is the case, between appearance and reality, is the theme of our next selection. Its author is Bertrand Russell, whose work we read previously.

Is there any knowledge in the world which is so certain that no reasonable man could doubt it? This question, which at first sight might not seem difficult, is really one of the most difficult that can be asked. When we have realized the obstacles in the way of a straightforward and confident answer, we shall be well launched on the study of philosophy—for philosophy is merely the attempt to answer such ultimate questions, not carelessly and dogmatically, as we do in ordinary life and even in the sciences, but critically, after exploring all that makes such questions puzzling, and after realizing all the vagueness and confusion that underlie our ordinary ideas.

In daily life, we assume as certain many things which, on a closer scrutiny, are found to be so full of apparent contradictions that only a great amount of thought enables us to know what it is that we really may believe. In the search for certainty, it is natural to begin with our present experiences, and in some sense, no doubt, knowledge is to be derived from them. But any statement as to what it is that our immediate experiences make us know is very likely to be wrong. It seems to me that I am now sitting in a chair, at a table of a certain shape, on which I see sheets of paper with writing or print. By turning my head I see out of the window buildings and clouds and the sun. I believe that the sun is about ninety-three million miles from the earth; that it is a hot globe many times bigger than the earth; that, owing to the earth's rotation, it rises every morning, and will continue to do so for an indefinite time in the future. I believe that, if any other normal person comes into my room, he will see the same chairs and tables and books and papers as I see, and that the table which I see is the same as the table which I feel pressing against my arm. All this seems to be so evident as to be hardly worth stating, except in answer to a man who doubts whether I know anything. Yet all this may be reasonably doubted, and all of it requires much careful discussion before we can be sure that we have stated it in a form that is wholly true.

To make our difficulties plain, let us concentrate attention on the table. To the eye it is oblong, brown and shiny, to the touch it is smooth and cool and hard; when I tap it, it gives out a wooden sound. Any one else who sees and feels and hears the table will agree with this description, so that it might seem as if no difficulty would arise; but as soon as we try to be more precise our troubles begin. Although I believe that the table is "really" of the same colour all over, the parts that reflect the light look much brighter than the other parts, and some parts look white because of reflected light. I know that, if I move, the parts that reflect the light will be different, so that the apparent distribution of colours on the table will change. It follows that if several people are looking at the table at the same moment, no two of them will see exactly the same distribution of colours, because no two can see it from exactly the same point of view, and any change in the point of view makes some change in the way the light is reflected.

For most practical purposes these differences are unimportant, but to the painter they are all-important: the painter has to unlearn the habit of thinking that things seem to have the colour which common sense says they "really" have, and to learn the habit of seeing things as they appear. Here we have already the beginning of one of the distinctions that cause most trouble in philosophy—the distinction between "appearance" and "reality," between what things seem to be and what they are. The painter wants to know what things seem to be, the practical man and the philosopher want to know what they are; but the philosopher's wish to know this is stronger than the practical man's, and is more troubled by knowledge as to the difficulties of answering the question.

To return to the table. It is evident from what we have found, that there is no colour which preeminently appears to be *the* colour of the table, or even of any one particular part of the table—it appears to be of different colours from different points of view, and there is no reason for regarding some of these as more really its colour than others. And we know that even from a given point of view the colour will seem different by artificial light, or to a colour-blind man, or to a man wearing blue spectacles, while in the dark there will be no colour at all, though to touch and hearing the table will be unchanged. This colour is not something which is inherent in the table, but something depending upon the table and the spectator and the way the light falls on the table. When, in ordinary life, we speak of *the* colour of the table, we only mean the sort of colour which it will seem to have to a normal spectator from an ordinary point of view under usual conditions of light. But the other colours which appear under other conditions have just as good a right to be considered real; and therefore, to avoid favouritism, we are compelled to deny that, in itself, the table has any one particular colour.

The same thing applies to the texture. With the naked eye one can see the grain, but otherwise the table looks smooth and even. If we looked at it through a microscope, we should see roughnesses and hills and valleys, and all sorts of differences that are imperceptible to the naked eye. Which of these is the "real" table? We are naturally tempted to say that what we see through the microscope is more real, but that in turn would be changed by a still more powerful microscope. If, then, we cannot trust what we see with the naked eye, why should we trust what we see through a microscope? Thus, again, the confidence in our senses with which we began deserts us.

The *shape* of the table is no better. We are all in the habit of judging as to the "real" shapes of things, and we do this so unreflectingly that we come to think we actually see the real shapes. But, in fact, as we all have to learn if we try to draw, a given thing looks different in shape from every different point of view. If our table is "really" rectangular, it will look, from almost all points of view, as if it had two acute angles and two obtuse angles. If opposite sides are parallel, they will look as if they converged to a point away from the spectator; if they are of equal length, they will look as if the nearer side were longer. All these things are not commonly noticed in looking at a table, because experience has taught us to construct the "real" shape from the apparent shape, and the "real" shape is what interests us as practical men. But the "real" shape is not what we see; it is something inferred from what we see. And what we see is constantly changing in shape as we move about the room; so that here again the senses seem not to give us the truth about the table itself, but only about the appearance of the table.

Similar difficulties arise when we consider the sense of touch. It is true that the table always gives us a sensation of hardness, and we feel that it resists pressure. But the sensation we obtain depends upon how hard we press the table and also upon what part of the body we press with; thus the various sensations due to various pressures or various parts of the body cannot be supposed to reveal *directly* any definite property of the table, but at most to be *signs* of some property which perhaps *causes* all the sensations, but is not actually apparent in any of them. And the same applies still more obviously to the sounds which can be elicited by rapping the table.

Thus it becomes evident that the real table, if there is one, is not the same as what we immediately experience by sight or touch or hearing. The real table, if there is one, is not *immediately* known to us at all, but must be an inference from what is immediately known. Hence, two very difficult questions at once arise; namely, (1) Is there a real table at all? (2) If so, what sort of object can it be?

It will help us in considering these questions to have a few simple terms of which the meaning is definite and clear. Let us give the name of "sense-data" to the things that are immediately known in sensation: such things as colours, sounds, smells, hardnesses, roughnesses, and so on. We shall give the name "sensation" to the experience of being immediately aware of these things. Thus, whenever we see a colour, we have a sensation *of* the colour, but the colour itself is a sense-datum, not a sensation. The colour is that *of* which we are immediately aware, and the awareness itself is the sensation. It is plain that if we are to know anything about the table, it must be by means of the sense-data—brown colour, oblong shape, smoothness, etc.—which we associate with the table; but, for the reasons which have been given, we cannot say that the table *is* the sense-data, or even that the sense-data are directly properties of the table. Thus a problem arises as to the relation of the sense-data to the real table, supposing there is such a thing. . . .

In fact, almost all philosophers seem to be agreed that there is a real table: they almost all agree that, however much our sense-data—colour, shape, smoothness, etc.—may depend upon us, yet their occurrence is a sign of something existing independently of us, something differing, perhaps, completely from our sense-data, and yet to be regarded as causing those sense-data whenever we are in a suitable relation to the real table. . . .

[I]t will be well to consider for a moment what it is that we have discovered so far. It has appeared that, if we take any common object of the sort that is supposed to be known by the senses, what the senses *immediately* tell us is not the truth about the object as it is apart from us, but only the truth about certain sense-data which, so far as we can see, depend upon the relations between us and the object. Thus what we directly see and feel is merely "appearance," which we believe to be a sign of some "reality" behind. But if the reality is not what appears, have we any means of knowing whether there is any reality at all? And if so, have we any means of finding out what it is like?

Such questions are bewildering, and it is difficult to know that even the strangest hypotheses may not be true. Thus our familiar table, which has roused but the slightest thoughts in us hitherto, has become a problem full of surprising possibilities. The one thing we know about it is that it is not what it seems.

STUDY QUESTIONS

1. By what reasoning does Russell reach the conclusion that the table has no particular color?
2. By what reasoning does Russell reach the conclusion that the table has no particular shape?
3. What does Russell mean by "sense-data"?
4. Has Russell proven that the table is not what it seems?

What Can I Know?

D. Z. Phillips

Philosophers often test fundamental beliefs by raising doubts about them, then considering possible ways of resolving the doubts. The previous selection, by Bertrand Russell, raised doubts about the evidence of the senses and concluded that a familiar table is not what it seems. Our next article, authored by D. Z. Phillips (1934–2006), who was Professor of Philosophy at the University of Wales, Swansea, maintains that Russell's doubts can be answered and that we do know the table as it is.

Here is a typical instance of philosophers disagreeing. Which, if either, is correct? Just as each member of a jury at a trial needs to make a decision and defend a view after considering all the relevant evidence, so each philosophical inquirer needs to make a decision and defend a view after considering all the relevant arguments. The challenge and excitement of philosophy is that, after taking account of the work others have done, the responsibility for reaching conclusions is your own.

What is philosophy about? Before I went to university, but knowing that philosophy was going to be one of the subjects I was to study there, I read a well-known introduction to philosophy in the hope of answering that question. My first impression was that the philosopher is an ultra-cautious person. Philosophers do not rush into saying that we know this or that, as most people do. They step back and think about things. Although we say we know all sorts of things, strictly speaking—philosophers conclude—we do not.

Given this view of philosophy, it seemed to me that the usefulness of philosophy was evident. Philosophy is a way of sharpening our thinking. It teaches us to be cautious, and not to be over-hasty in reaching our conclusions. By imposing its strict demands, philosophy tightens up our standards of knowledge. Our day-to-day assumptions are shot through with contradictions and inconsistencies. A great deal of reflection is necessary before we can arrive at what we really know. Philosophy is an indispensable guide in this reflection. This view of the usefulness of philosophy was reflected in the views of many educationalists, and this is still the case. They favour introductory classes in philosophy even for those whose primary intentions are to study other subjects. The pencil needs to be sharpened before it can write with sufficient care about other topics.

This straightforward view of philosophy was given a severe jolt, however, when I read further and discovered the kinds of things that many philosophers were prepared to doubt.[1] They doubt things that we ordinarily would not doubt. The list that I read in the introduction to philosophy was surprising, to say the least. The philosopher told me that it seemed to him, at a certain moment, that he was sitting in a chair at a table which had a certain shape, on which he saw sheets of paper with writing or print on them. By turning his head he could see buildings, clouds, and the sun through the window. He believed that the sun is about ninety-three million miles away from the Earth and that, owing to the Earth's rotation, it rises every morning and will continue to do so for an indefinite time in the future. He believed that if any other normal person came into the room, that person would see the same chairs, tables, books, and papers as he saw. Further, he believed that the table he saw was the same table as he felt pressing against his arm.

What puzzled me was this: on the one hand, the philosopher wrote that all these things seemed so evident as to be hardly worth stating; but on the other hand, he said that all these facts could be reasonably doubted and that much reflection is needed before we can arrive at a description of the situation which would be wholly true. Of course, he was quite prepared to admit that most people would not bother to question these facts. They would see no point in doing so. My initial reaction was to think that the majority were correct on this issue. Suddenly, in view of what the philosopher was prepared to doubt, philosophy, so far from appearing to be a useful subject, now appeared to be a complete waste of time. The philosophical doubt seemed to be, not a tightening up of standards, but a trivial game; the kind of game which irritates parents when, on the first visit home after commencing the subject, budding philosophers confront them with the question, "So you think there's a table here, do you?" Recently, some philosophers have reacted in the same way to philosophers' doubts. They have asked why philosophers should give young people doubts that they would never have had in the first place if the philosophers had not opened their mouths. On this view, philosophy does not clarify our confusions—it creates them.

My new reaction, however, simply led to a new puzzle. Why should we doubt what seems so evident as to not need stating? Surely, it is not enough simply to accuse philosophers of indulging in trivial pursuits. They take their doubts seriously. I felt there was something wrong about these doubts, but did not know why. Whether we like it or not, people have always been puzzled about the doubts that philosophers discuss. I felt it was insufficient to say to someone who has doubts about whether we *know* something, "Well, we *do,* so that's that." Even if we feel that there is something odd about the philosophical doubts, that response will not help the doubter. The doubter is not going to accept the answer on authority. If the doubt is misplaced, we have to show the route by which it is reached. Unless we show the road to confusion, there is no road back from it. . . .

How do I come to know anything? Before I know anything, my mind must have been like an empty receptacle, waiting to receive knowledge. Where is this knowledge to come from? Surely, from something outside myself, something which will furnish my mind with knowledge. How else am I to become acquainted with "yellow," "red," "hardness," "softness," "hot," "cold," "sweetness," "bitterness," and so on? These are experiences that I receive as a result of my interaction with the external world. I call the experiences that I have "ideas," "impressions," or "sensations." These are the furnishings of my mind, the data on which any knowledge I have relies.

But, now, a sceptical worry surfaces. If the sensory experiences of my mind are my necessary starting-point in my search for knowledge, how do I ever get beyond them? I say that these experiences come from an external world, but how do I know this? If my mind is acquainted only with its own ideas, how do I know—how can I know—whether these ideas refer to anything? How can I know that they refer to an external world? The very *possibility* of knowledge of an external world seems thrown into question.

Consider "seeing" as an example; seeing a table, let us say. I want to say that this experience came about as a result of something external to itself, namely, the table. But how can I ever know that? How do I get from my experience, my idea of the table, to the real table? If I have an experience called "seeing a table," I have an obvious interest in knowing whether it refers to a table. My experience may have been caused by some other object, or by no object at all. Light conditions may create the illusion that I am seeing a table. But how can I find out whether my experience does refer to a table, or to some other object, or whether it is illusory? If I want to know what causes the bulge in my sock, I can take out the object causing the bulge, a golf ball, let us say, and find out by doing so. In this example I have an independent access to the cause of the bulge in my sock. But when I want to know the cause of the ideas in my mind, I can have no independent access to their cause. But in that case, how do I know that they are caused by anything or refer to anything? I seem to be locked in the circle of my own ideas.

Let us suppose that my mental experience takes the form of an image of an apple. How can I know whether I am seeing an apple or imagining an apple? If I am imagining an apple, my experience makes no contact with a real apple. But, once again, I can only check this if I have independent access to the apple, the very access which seems to be denied to me. How on Earth am I going to get out of this predicament? . . .

Perhaps we ought to question the initial starting point of the challenge, the assumption that all I am acquainted with are the ideas of my own mind. What is it that makes this assumption attractive? Think of examples such as hearing a car in the distance. It may be said that to say I hear a car is to say more than I know, strictly speaking. I am going beyond the immediate datum of my experience. That immediate datum is a sound. That is what I can be said to know. In saying that it is the sound of a car, I am interpreting the sound, perhaps by association with other occasions, and so on.

For examples such as these, the illegitimate assumption is made that *all* our experiences are based on minimal, immediate data. Thus, although there is nothing wrong in saying that I see a book, I am told that this is a very complex claim. What I experience immediately, it is said, is not a book, but a certain diversity of light and colour. These immediate data are self-authenticating. We cannot be mistaken about them. They are called *sense-data*. When we say that we see tables and chairs we are clearly going beyond our immediate experience of sense-data. The sceptical challenge can now be reformulated in these terms: What is the relation between our experience of sense-data and our claim to experience an external world? How can we ever get from sense-data to knowledge of the external world? Claims about the external world always stand in need of evidence. Sense-data, on the other hand, provide the evidence. But the problem is that sense-data can never provide sufficient justification for saying that we are in contact with an external world. Let us see why.

What qualifies as an example of an indubitable immediate experience? "I hear a car" clearly does not qualify, since that is a claim that I could be mistaken about. But "I hear a purring engine-like noise" will not qualify either, since I could be mistaken about that too. I may have forgotten that I have cotton-wool in my ears, and the noise may, in fact, be quite a loud one. Will "I hear a noise" qualify as a minimal, immediate experience? No, because I may be mistaken about that too. What I am hearing is simply noises in my head. And so we arrive at a minimal sense-datum: "It seems to me now as if I were hearing a noise."

The outcome of our quest for an example of a minimal sense-experience is not encouraging. We must not forget that the purpose of locating such data was to provide evidence for claims concerning the external world. We were supposed to be enabled to *advance* from such data to statements concerning the external world. But the location of such data constitutes not an advance to, but a retreat from, any claims about the external world. In terms of our example, the retreat takes the following form: "I hear a car"—"I seem to hear a car"—"It seems to *me* I hear a car"—"It seems to me *now* that I hear a purring noise"—"It seems to me now as though I were hearing a purring noise."

Why did we go in search of minimal sense-data in the first place? We did so because we felt that any statement about an external world can always be doubted, and thus stands in need of evidence. What we know immediately are minimal sense-data. But is this true? . . . [W]e doubt in circumstances that we call unfavourable. But what of favourable circumstances? Can I doubt that I hear a car in these? The car may be coming directly towards me. I may be sitting in the car or driving it. There may be no room for doubt at all. It would be absurd to suggest that there is always room for doubt because I may have forgotten that I had cotton-wool in my ears. It would be odd to say that any kind of judgement or verdict on the basis of sense-data is necessary when, in favourable circumstances, we hear a car. Verdicts are needed, for the most part, when we are not in a position to hear or see things clearly. But if I am sitting at a table, leaning on it, and so on, I am not giving a verdict on anything. My sitting at a table is not a claim which stands in need of evidence. It is not a claim at all. When I see a book, select it, pick it up, turn its pages, and read it, I am not verifying anything. I am simply seeing, selecting, picking up, turning the pages, and reading a book.

Whether a statement stands in need of evidence depends on the circumstances in which it is made. Once this is admitted, we can see that there is no absolute distinction between two kinds of statement—one kind of statement which always stands in need of evidence, and another kind of statement which always provides evidence. So we cannot say that any statement about the external world stands in need of evidence and that it is the function of statements about sense-data to provide such evidence. But once this absolute distinction is rejected, we reject the terms of the sceptical challenge at the same time. It can no longer be said that we *must* show how knowledge of an external world can be arrived at on the basis of the immediate data of our experience. Indeed, when circumstances are favourable, the onus is not on us to say when we can stop doubting and be able to assert "I see a book." The onus is on the sceptic to tell us why we should have started to doubt in the first place. . . .

[W]e are sometimes mistaken about what we think we perceive. I see a stick partly immersed in water and think it is bent. Later I find out that I was mistaken. The stick was not bent. But what I saw was bent. What, then, did I see? It is tempting to reply, "Not the stick, but the appearance of the stick." What "appears," the sense-datum, does not guarantee any reference to what is really the case. By such an argument, experiences become a "something" between me and objects in the external world. In the case of illusions the "something" that I experience does not refer to anything, whereas in the case of perceptions it does.

But this conception of a sense-datum, the necessary object of my experience, is a confused one. If I think I see a bent stick which later turns out to be straight, I do not need to postulate anything other than the stick to account for my mistake. I do not see "the appearance" of the stick. It is the stick that looks bent. It is the *same* thing, namely, the stick, which—in certain conditions—appears to be bent when it is not. The phenomenon of deception does not necessitate the postulation of two realms, one of sense-data and the other of physical objects. That being so, we are not faced with the task of showing how we move from the first realm to the second.

NOTE

1. [S]ee Russell, *The Problems of Philosophy,* one of the most famous introductions to philosophy.

STUDY QUESTIONS

1. How do you know whether you are seeing an apple or imagining an apple?
2. According to Phillips, are you acquainted with more than the contents of your own mind?
3. According to Phillips, does every statement about the external world stand in need of evidence?
4. According to Phillips, why is "sense-datum" a confused notion?

The Problem of Induction

Bertrand Russell

We now return to the writings of Bertrand Russell and consider a different problem about knowledge. This one is raised by reflecting on our common practice of assuming that the laws of nature that have held in the past will continue to hold in the future.

We have learned that bread nourishes us; stones do not. But do we have good reason to believe that the laws of nature will remain constant? Starting tomorrow, might stones nourish us and bread be inedible? That is the question Russell challenges us to answer.

He is not urging that we change our basic beliefs but that we seek to understand their justification. In other words, he asks that we engage in philosophical inquiry.

....

It is obvious that if we are asked why we believe that the sun will rise tomorrow, we shall naturally answer, "Because it always has risen every day." We have a firm belief that it will rise in the future, because it has risen in the past. If we are challenged as to why we believe that it will continue to rise as heretofore, we may appeal to the laws of motion: the earth, we shall say, is a freely rotating body, and such bodies do not cease to rotate unless something interferes from outside, and there is nothing outside to interfere with the earth between now and tomorrow. Of course it might be doubted whether we are quite certain that there is nothing outside to interfere, but this is not the interesting doubt. The interesting doubt is as to whether the laws of motion will remain in operation until tomorrow. If this doubt is raised, we find ourselves in the same position as when the doubt about the sunrise was first raised.

The *only* reason for believing that the laws of motion will remain in operation is that they have operated hitherto, so far as our knowledge of the past enables us to judge. It is true that we have a greater body of evidence from the past in favour of the laws of motion than we have in favour of the sunrise, because the sunrise is merely a particular case of fulfilment of the laws of motion, and there are countless other particular cases. But the real question is: Do *any* number of cases of a law being fulfilled in the past afford evidence that it will be fulfilled in the future? If not, it becomes plain that we have no ground whatever for expecting the sun to rise tomorrow, or for expecting the bread we shall eat at our next meal not to poison us, or for any of the other scarcely conscious expectations that control our daily lives. It is to be observed that all such expectations are only *probable;* thus we have not to seek for a proof that they *must* be fulfilled, but only for some reason in favour of the view that they are *likely* to be fulfilled.

Now in dealing with this question we must, to begin with, make an important distinction, without which we should soon become involved in hopeless confusions. Experience has shown us that, hitherto, the frequent repetition of some uniform succession or coexistence has been a *cause* of our expecting the same succession or coexistence on the next occasion. Food that has a certain appearance generally has a certain taste, and it is a severe shock to our expectations when the familiar appearance is found to be associated with an unusual taste. Things which we see become associated, by habit, with certain tactile sensations which we expect if we touch them; one of the horrors of a ghost (in many ghost stories) is that it fails to give us any sensations of touch. Uneducated people who go abroad for the first time are so surprised as to be incredulous when they find their native language not understood.

And this kind of association is not confined to men; in animals also it is very strong. A horse which has been often driven along a certain road resists the attempt to drive him in a different direction. Domestic animals expect food when they see the person who usually feeds them. We know that all these rather crude expectations of uniformity are liable to be misleading. The man who has fed the chicken every day throughout its life at last wrings its neck instead, showing that more refined views as to the uniformity of nature would have been useful to the chicken.

But in spite of the misleadingness of such expectations, they nevertheless exist. The mere fact that something has happened a certain number of times causes animals and men to expect that it will happen again. Thus our instincts certainly cause us to believe that the sun will rise tomorrow, but we may be in no better a position than the chicken which unexpectedly has its neck wrung. We have therefore to distinguish the fact that past uniformities *cause* expectations as to the future, from the question whether there is any reasonable ground for giving weight to such expectations after the question of their validity has been raised.

The problem we have to discuss is whether there is any reason for believing in what is called "the uniformity of nature." The belief in the uniformity of nature is the belief that everything that has happened or will happen is an instance of some general law to which there are *no* exceptions. The crude expectations which we have been considering are all subject to exceptions, and therefore liable to disappoint those who entertain them. But science habitually assumes, at least as a working hypothesis, that general rules which have exceptions can be replaced by general rules which have no exceptions. "Unsupported bodies in air fall" is a general rule to which balloons and airplanes are exceptions. But the laws of motion and the law of gravitation, which account for the fact that most bodies fall, also account for the fact that balloons and airplanes can rise; thus the laws of motion and the law of gravitation are not subject to these exceptions.

The belief that the sun will rise tomorrow might be falsified if the earth came suddenly into contact with a large body which destroyed its rotation; but the laws of motion and the law of gravitation would not be infringed by such an event. The business of science is to find uniformities, such as the laws of motion and the law of gravitation, to which, so far as our experience extends, there are no exceptions. In this search, science has been remarkably successful, and it may be conceded that such uniformities have held hitherto. This brings us back to the question: Have we any reason, assuming that they have always held in the past, to suppose that they will hold in the future?

It has been argued that we have reason to know that the future will resemble the past, because what was the future has constantly become the past, and has always been found to resemble the past, so that we really have experience of the future, namely of times which were formerly future, which we may call past futures. But such an argument really begs the very question at issue. We have experience of past futures, but not of future futures, and the question is: Will future futures resemble past futures? This question is not to be answered by an argument which starts from past futures alone. We have therefore still to seek for some principle which shall enable us to know that the future will follow the same laws as the past.

STUDY QUESTIONS

1. Do we have good reason to expect the sun to rise tomorrow?
2. What is "the uniformity of nature"?
3. Does our belief that the sun will rise tomorrow depend on our believing in the uniformity of nature?
4. Do we have any alternative to relying on inductive reasoning?

Induction Without a Problem

P. F. Strawson

In response to Russell, P. F. Strawson (1919–2006), who taught at the University of Oxford, argues that seeking a justification for induction is not sensible, because any successful method of finding things out necessarily has inductive support.

From *Introduction to Logical Theory*, by P. F. Strawson. Copyright © 1952 by Methuen & Co. Reprinted by permission of the publisher.

I want to point out that there is something a little odd about talking of "the inductive method," or even "the inductive policy," as if it were just one possible method among others of arguing from the observed to the unobserved, from the available evidence to the facts in question. If one asked a meteorologist what method or methods he used to forecast the weather, one would be surprised if he answered: "Oh, just the inductive method." If one asked a doctor by what means he diagnosed a certain disease, the answer "By induction" would be felt as an impatient evasion, a joke, or a rebuke. The answer one hopes for is an account of the tests made, the signs taken account of, the rules and recipes and general laws applied. When such a specific method of prediction or diagnosis is in question, one can ask whether the method is justified in practice; and here again one is asking whether its employment is inductively justified, whether it commonly gives correct results. This question would normally seem an admissible one. One might be tempted to conclude that, while there are many different specific methods of prediction, diagnosis, &c., appropriate to different subjects of inquiry, all such methods could properly be called "inductive" in the sense that their employment rested on inductive support; and that, hence, the phrase "non-inductive method of finding out about what lies deductively beyond the evidence" was a description without meaning, a phrase to which no sense had been given; so that there could be no question of justifying our selection of one method, called "the inductive," of doing this.

However, someone might object: "Surely it is possible, though it might be foolish, to use methods utterly different from accredited scientific ones. Suppose a man, whenever he wanted to form an opinion about what lay beyond his observation or the observation of available witnesses, simply shut his eyes, asked himself the appropriate question, and accepted the first answer that came into his head. Wouldn't this be a non-inductive method?" Well, let us suppose this. The man is asked: "Do you usually get the right answer by your method?" He might answer: "You've mentioned one of its drawbacks; I never do get the right answer; but it's an extremely easy method." One might then be inclined to think that it was not a method of finding things out at all. But suppose he answered: Yes, it's usually (always) the right answer. Then we might be willing to call it a method of finding out, though a strange one. But, then, by the very fact of its success, it would be an inductively supported method. For each application of the method would be an application of the general rule, "The first answer that comes into my head is generally (always) the right one"; and for the truth of this generalization there would be the inductive evidence of a long run of favourable instances with no unfavourable ones (if it were "always"), or of a sustained high proportion of successes to trials (if it were "generally").

So every successful method or recipe for finding out about the unobserved must be one which has inductive support; for to say that a recipe is successful is to say that it has been repeatedly applied with success; and repeated successful application of a recipe constitutes just what we mean by inductive evidence in its favour. Pointing out this fact must not be confused with saying that "the inductive method" is justified by its success, justified because it works. This is a mistake, and an important one. I am not seeking to "justify the inductive method," for no meaning has been given to this phrase. *A fortiori*, I am not saying that induction is justified by its success in finding out about the unobserved. I am saying, rather, that any successful method of finding out about the unobserved is necessarily justified by induction. . . . The phrase "successful method of finding things out which has no inductive support" is self-contradictory. Having, or acquiring, inductive support is a necessary condition of the success of a method.

STUDY QUESTIONS

1. According to Strawson, why is it "a little odd" to talk about the inductive method?
2. Why would anyone decide not to use inductive reasoning?
3. According to Strawson, what mistake is involved in claiming that the inductive method is justified by its success?
4. Do you agree with Strawson that every successful method of finding out about the unobserved must have inductive support?

Puzzling Out Knowledge

Susan Haack

Susan Haack is Professor of Philosophy and of Law at the University of Miami. She draws an analogy between enhancing knowledge and solving crossword puzzles.

....

Evidence is complex and ramifying, often confusing, ambiguous, or misleading. Think of the controversy over that four-billion-year-old meteorite discovered in 1984 Antarctica, thought to have come from Mars about eleven thousand years ago, and containing what might possibly be fossilized bacteria droppings. Some space scientists thought this was evidence of bacterial life on Mars; others thought the bacterial traces might have been picked while the meteorite was in Antarctica; and others again believed that what look like fossilized bacteria

From Susan Haack, *Putting Philosophy to Work: Essays on Science, Religion, Law, Literature, and Life*, Prometheus Books, 2013. Reprinted by permission of the publisher.

droppings might be merely artifacts of the instrumentation. How did they know that giving off these gases when heated indicates that the meteorite comes from Mars? that the meteorite is about four billion years old? that this is what fossilized bacteria droppings look like?—like crossword entries, reasons ramify in all directions.

How reasonable a crossword entry is depends on how well it is supported by its clue and any already completed intersecting entries; how reasonable those other entries are, independent of the entry in question; and how much of the crossword has been completed. How justified a belief is, similarly, depends on how well it is supported by experiential evidence and by reasons, i.e., background beliefs; how justified those background beliefs are, independent of the belief in question; and how much of the relevant evidence the evidence includes.

The quality of the evidence for a claim is objective, depending on how supportive it is of the claim in question, how comprehensive, and how independently secure. A person's judgments of the quality of evidence, however, are perspectival, depending on his background beliefs. Suppose you and I are working on the same crossword puzzle, but have filled in some long, much-intersected entry differently; you think a correct intersecting entry must have an "F" in the middle, while I think it must have a "D" there. Suppose you and I are on the same appointments committee, but you believe in graphology, while I think it's bunk; you think how the candidate writes his gs is relevant to whether he can be trusted, while I scoff at your "evidence." Or, to take a real example: in 1944, when Oswald Avery published his results, even he hedged over the conclusion to which they pointed, that DNA is the genetic material; for the then-accepted wisdom was that DNA is composed of the four nucleotides in regular order, and so is too stupid, too monotonous, a molecule to carry the necessary information. But by 1952, when Hershey and Chase published their results, the tetranucleotide hypothesis had been discredited; and then it could be seen that Avery already had good evidence in 1944 that DNA, not protein, is the genetic material.

Inquiry can be difficult and demanding, and we very often go wrong. Sometimes the obstacle is a failure of will; we don't really want to know the answer badly enough to go to all the trouble of finding out, or we really *don't* want to know, and go to a lot of trouble *not* to find out. I think of the detective who doesn't really want to know who committed the crime, just to collect enough evidence to get a conviction; of the academic who cares less about discovering the causes of racial disharmony than about getting a large grant to investigate the matter—and of my own disinclination to rush to the library to check out the article that might oblige me to redo months of work.

Other things being equal, inquiry goes better when the will and the intellect, instead of pulling in different directions, work together; that's why intellectual integrity is valuable. But even with the best will in the world, even when we really want to find out, we often fail. Our senses, imaginations, and intellects are limited;

we can't always see, or guess, or reason, well enough. With ingenuity, we can devise ways of overcoming our natural limitations, from cupping our ears to hear better, through tying knots in rope or cutting notches in sticks to keep count, to highly sophisticated electron microscopes and techniques of computer modelling. Of course, our ingenuity is limited too.

Everyone who looks into how some part or aspect of the world is—the physicist and the detective, the historian and the entomologist, the quantum chemist and the investigative journalist, the literary scholar and the X-ray crystallographer—works on part of a part of the same vast crossword. Since they all investigate the same world, sometimes their entries intersect: a medical researcher relies on an amateur historian's family tree in his search for the defective gene responsible for a rare hereditary form of pancreatitis; ancient historians use a technique devised for the detection of breast cancer to decipher traces on the lead "postcards" on which Roman soldiers wrote home. . . .

Progress in the sciences is ragged and uneven, and each step, like each crossword entry, is fallible and revisable. But each genuine advance potentially enables others, as a robust crossword entry does; "nothing succeeds like success" is the phrase that comes to mind. . . .

Just about every inquirer, in the most mundane of everyday inquiries, depends on others; otherwise, each would have to start on his part of the crossword alone and from scratch. Natural-scientific inquiry is no exception; in fact, it is more so—the work, cooperative and competitive, of a vast intergenerational community of inquirers, a deeply and unavoidably social enterprise.

STUDY QUESTIONS

1. According to Haack, in what ways is enhancing knowledge akin to solving a crossword puzzle?
2. Can you present your own example of how you enhanced your knowledge in a manner akin to solving a crossword puzzle?
3. What does Haack mean by "intellectual integrity"?
4. Do we sometimes not want knowledge?

Meditations on First Philosophy

RENÉ DESCARTES

The Frenchman René Descartes (1596–1650), mathematician, scientist, and phi-losopher, wrote one of the most influential of all philosophical works, his *Medita-tions on First Philosophy,* published in Latin in 1641. Its combination of personal narrative and rigorous argument is highly unusual.

Descartes is driven by his desire to place philosophy on an unshakable foun-dation. He searches for a starting point that can withstand all doubt. Because the evidence of our senses sometimes misleads us, it does not provide a secure basis for knowledge. Furthermore, we cannot be certain that we are awake and not dream-ing. Nor can we be sure that we are not being systematically fooled by an evil genius who wishes to deceive us. Given such possibilities, can we be sure of any truth?

The *Meditations* is universally regarded as a philosophical classic, even by the many who do not accept all the steps in Descartes' argument. What continues to fascinate philosophers is the provocative manner in which Descartes formulated and pursued such crucial issues. To meditate along with him is as good a way as any to come to an understanding of philosophical inquiry.

What follows is the first of Descartes' six meditations. We shall return to the second meditation in the next section of the book.

FIRST MEDITATION

What Can Be Called into Doubt

Some years ago I was struck by the large number of falsehoods that I had accepted as true in my childhood, and by the highly doubtful nature of the whole edifice that I had subsequently based on them. I realized that it was necessary, once in the course of my life, to demolish everything completely and start again right from the foundations if I wanted to establish anything at all in the sciences that was stable and likely to last. But the task looked an enormous one, and I began to wait until I should reach a mature enough age to ensure that no subsequent time of life would be more suitable for tackling such inquiries. This led me to put the project off for so long that I would now be to blame if by pondering over it any further I wasted the time still left for carrying it out. So today I have expressly rid my mind of all worries and arranged for myself a clear stretch of free time. I am here quite alone, and at last I will devote myself sincerely and without reservation to the general demolition of my opinions.

But to accomplish this, it will not be necessary for me to show that all my opinions are false, which is something I could perhaps never manage. Reason now leads me to think that I should hold back my assent from opinions which are not completely certain and indubitable just as carefully as I do from those which are patently false. So, for the purpose of rejecting all my opinions, it will be enough if I find in each of them at least some reason for doubt. And to do this I will not need to run through them all individually, which would be an endless task. Once the foundations of a building are undermined, anything built on them collapses of its own accord; so I will go straight for the basic principles on which all my former beliefs rested.

Whatever I have up till now accepted as most true I have acquired either from the senses or through the senses. But from time to time I have found that the senses deceive, and it is prudent never to trust completely those who have deceived us even once.

Yet although the senses occasionally deceive us with respect to objects which are very small or in the distance, there are many other beliefs about which doubt is quite impossible, even though they are derived from the senses—for example, that I am here, sitting by the fire, wearing a winter dressing-gown, holding this piece of paper in my hands, and so on. Again, how could it be denied that these hands or this whole body are mine? Unless perhaps I were to liken myself to madmen, whose brains are so damaged by the persistent vapours of melancholia that they firmly maintain they are kings when they are paupers, or say they are dressed in purple when they are naked, or that their heads are made of earthenware, or that they are pumpkins, or made of glass. But such people are insane, and I would be thought equally mad if I took anything from them as a model for myself.

A brilliant piece of reasoning! As if I were not a man who sleeps at night, and regularly has all the same experiences while asleep as madmen do when awake—indeed sometimes even more improbable ones. How often, asleep at night, am I convinced of just such familiar events—that I am here in my dressing-gown, sitting by the fire—when in fact I am lying undressed in bed! Yet at the moment my eyes are certainly wide awake when I look at this piece of paper; I shake my head and it is not asleep; as I stretch out and feel my hand I do so deliberately, and I know what I am doing. All this would not happen with such distinctness to someone asleep. Indeed! As if I did not remember other occasions when I have been tricked by exactly similar thoughts while asleep! As I think about this more carefully, I see plainly that there are never any sure signs by means of which being awake can be distinguished from being asleep. The result is that I begin to feel dazed, and this very feeling only reinforces the notion that I may be asleep.

Suppose then that I am dreaming, and that these particulars—that my eyes are open, that I am moving my head and stretching out my hands—are not true. Perhaps, indeed, I do not even have such hands or such a body at all. Nonetheless, it must surely be admitted that the visions which come in sleep are like paintings, which must have been fashioned in the likeness of things that are real, and hence that at least these general kinds of things—eyes, head, hands, and the body as a whole—are things which are not imaginary but are real and exist. For even when painters try to create sirens and satyrs with the most extraordinary bodies, they cannot give them natures which are new in all respects; they simply jumble up the limbs of different animals. Or if perhaps they manage to think up something so new that nothing remotely similar has ever been seen before—something which is therefore completely fictitious and unreal—at least the colours used in the composition must be real. By similar reasoning, although these general kinds of things— eyes, head, hands and so on—could be imaginary, it must at least be admitted that certain other even simpler and more universal things are real. These are as it were the real colours from which we form all the images of things, whether true or false, that occur in our thought.

This class appears to include corporeal nature in general, and its extension; the shape of extended things; the quantity, or size and number of these things; the place in which they may exist, the time through which they may endure, and so on.

So a reasonable conclusion from this might be that physics, astronomy, medicine, and all other disciplines which depend on the study of composite things are doubtful; while arithmetic, geometry, and other subjects of this kind, which deal only with the simplest and most general things, regardless of whether they really exist in nature or not, contain something certain and indubitable. For whether I am awake or asleep, two and three added together are five, and a square has no more than four sides. It seems impossible that such transparent truths should incur any suspicion of being false.

And yet firmly rooted in my mind is the long-standing opinion that there is an omnipotent God who made me the kind of creature that I am. How do I know that he has not brought it about that there is no earth, no sky, no extended thing, no shape, no size, no place, while at the same time ensuring that all these things appear to me to exist just as they do now? What is more, just as I consider that others sometimes go astray in cases where they think they have the most perfect knowledge, how do I know that God has not brought it about that I too go wrong every time I add two and three or count the sides of a square, or in some even simpler matter, if that is imaginable? But perhaps God would not have allowed me to be deceived in this way, since he is said to be supremely good. But if it were inconsistent with his goodness to have created me such that I am deceived all the time, it would seem equally foreign to his goodness to allow me to be deceived even occasionally; yet this last assertion cannot be made.

Perhaps there may be some who would prefer to deny the existence of so powerful a God rather than believe that everything else is uncertain. Let us not argue with them, but grant them that everything said about God is a fiction. According to their supposition, then, I have arrived at my present state by fate or chance or a continuous chain of events, or by some other means; yet since deception and error seem to be imperfections, the less powerful they make my original cause, the more likely it is that I am so imperfect as to be deceived all the time. I have no answer to these arguments, but am finally compelled to admit that there is not one of my former beliefs about which a doubt may not properly be raised; and this is not a flippant or ill-considered conclusion, but is based on powerful and well thought-out reasons. So in the future I must withhold my assent from these former beliefs just as carefully as I would from obvious falsehoods, if I want to discover any certainty.

But it is not enough merely to have noticed this; I must make an effort to remember it. My habitual opinions keep coming back, and, despite my wishes, they capture my belief, which is as it were bound over to them as a result of long occupation and the law of custom. I shall never get out of the habit of confidently assenting to these opinions, so long as I suppose them to be what in fact they are, namely, highly probable opinions—opinions which, despite the fact that they are in a sense doubtful, as has just been shown, it is still much more reasonable to believe than to deny. In view of this, I think it will be a good plan to turn my will in completely the opposite direction and deceive myself, by pretending for a time that these former opinions are utterly false and imaginary. I shall do this until the weight of preconceived opinion is counter-balanced and the distorting influence of habit no longer prevents my judgement from perceiving things correctly. In the meantime, I know that no danger or error will result from my plan, and that I cannot possibly go too far in my distrustful attitude. This is because the task now in hand does not involve action but merely the acquisition of knowledge.

I will suppose therefore that not God, who is supremely good and the source of truth, but rather some malicious demon of the utmost power and cunning has employed all his energies in order to deceive me. I shall think that the sky, the air, the earth, colours, shapes, sounds, and all external things are merely the delusions of dreams which he has devised to ensnare my judgement. I shall consider myself as not having hands or eyes, or flesh, or blood or senses, but as falsely believing that I have all these things. I shall stubbornly and firmly persist in this meditation; and, even if it is not in my power to know any truth, I shall at least do what is in my power, that is, resolutely guard against assenting to any falsehoods, so that the deceiver, however powerful and cunning he may be, will be unable to impose on me in the slightest degree. But this is an arduous undertaking, and a kind of laziness brings me back to normal life. I am like a prisoner who is enjoying an imaginary freedom while asleep; as he begins to suspect that he is asleep, he dreads being woken up, and goes along with the pleasant illusion as long as he can. In the same way, I happily slide back into my old opinions and dread being shaken out of them, for fear that my peaceful sleep may be followed by hard labour when I wake, and that I shall have to toil not in the light, but amid the inextricable darkness of the problems I have now raised.

STUDY QUESTIONS

1. Can you ever be sure your senses are not deceiving you?
2. How can you tell that you are not now asleep?
3. Why does Descartes introduce the possibility of a malicious demon?
4. Can you doubt all your beliefs at once?

An Essay Concerning Human Understanding

JOHN LOCKE

Philosophers like Descartes, who base knowledge on reason alone rather than sense experience, are known as "rationalists." Those who base knowledge on sense experience rather than pure reason are known as "empiricists," and the leading historical exponents of empiricism are John Locke, George Berkeley, and David Hume.

Locke (1632–1704) argues that we can be mistaken in our beliefs about the external world; they fall short of Descartes' standard of absolute certainty. Nevertheless, our understanding of physical objects is a paradigm of knowledge, thus demonstrating that Descartes was mistaken in the standard he set.

Locke claims that all our ideas can be traced to two sources: sensation (i.e., sense perception) and reflection (i.e., awareness of the operations of our mind). Our knowledge of the world has its source in sensation. For example, I know a solid brown table is in front of me, and the basis for my knowledge is the evidence of my senses.

Locke draws a distinction between an object's primary and secondary qualities. The primary qualities are those inseparable from an object, such as its solidity, size, or velocity. The secondary qualities are powers in an object to produce sensations in us, for example, color, taste, and odor. So the solid brown table I see in front of me is in itself solid but only perceived as brown. If I looked at it in a different light, it would still be solid but might look black or some other color.

CONCERNING OUR SIMPLE IDEAS OF SENSATION

7. To discover the nature of our ideas the better, and to discourse of them intelligibly, it will be convenient to distinguish them as they are ideas or perceptions in our

From *An Essay Concerning Human Understanding* by John Locke (1690), Book II, Chapter VIII and Book IV, Chapter XI.

minds, and as they are modifications of matter in the bodies that cause such perceptions in us, that so we may not think (as perhaps usually is done) that they are exactly the images and resemblances of something inherent in the subject; most of those of sensation being in the mind no more the likeness of something existing without us, than the names that stand for them are the likeness of our ideas, which yet upon hearing they are apt to excite in us.

8. Whatsoever the mind perceives in itself, or is the immediate object of perception, thought, or understanding, that I call idea; and the power to produce any idea in our mind, I call quality of the subject wherein that power is. Thus a snowball having the power to produce in us the ideas of white, cold, and round, the power to produce those ideas in us, as they are in the snowball, I call qualities; and as they are sensations or perceptions in our understandings, I call them ideas; which ideas, if I speak of sometimes as in the things themselves, I would be understood to mean those qualities in the objects which produce them in us.

9. Qualities thus considered in bodies are, first, such as are utterly inseparable from the body, in what state soever it be; such as in all the alterations and changes it suffers, all the force can be used upon it, it constantly keeps; and such as sense constantly finds in every particle of matter which has bulk enough to be perceived and the mind finds inseparable from every particle of matter, though less than to make itself singly be perceived by our senses, e.g., take a grain of wheat, divide it into two parts, each part has still solidity, extension, figure, and mobility; divide it again, and it retains still the same qualities; and so divide it on till the parts become insensible, they must retain still each of them all those qualities. For division (which is all that a mill, or pestle, or any other body, does upon another, in reducing it to insensible parts) can never take away either solidity, extension, figure, or mobility from any body, but only makes two or more distinct separate masses of matter, of that which was but one before; all which distinct masses, reckoned as so many distinct bodies, after division, make a certain number. These I call original or primary qualities of body, which I think we may observe to produce simple ideas in us, viz., solidity, extension, figure, motion or rest, and number.

10. Secondly, such qualities which in truth are nothing in the objects themselves, but powers to produce various sensations in us by their primary qualities, i.e., by the bulk, figure, texture, and motion of their insensible parts, as colours, sounds, tastes, etc., these I call secondary qualities. To these might be added a third sort, which are allowed to be barely powers, though they are as much real qualities in the subject, as those which I, to comply with the common way of speaking, call qualities, but for distinction, secondary qualities. For the power in fire to produce a new colour or consistency in wax or clay, by its primary qualities, is as much a quality in fire as the power it has to produce in me a new idea or sensation of warmth or burning, which I felt not before, by the same primary qualities, viz., the bulk, texture, and motion of its insensible parts.

11. The next thing to be considered is, how bodies produce ideas in us; and that is manifestly by impulse, the only way which we can conceive bodies to operate in.

12. If then external objects be not united to our minds when they produce ideas therein, and yet we perceive these original qualities in such of them as singly fall under our senses, it is evident that some motion must be thence continued by our nerves or animal spirits, by some parts of our bodies, to the brain, or the seat of sensation, there to produce in our minds the particular ideas we have of them. And since the extension, figure, number, and motion of bodies of an observable bigness may be perceived at a distance by the sight, it is evident some singly imperceptible bodies must come from them to the eyes, and thereby convey to the brain some motion, which produces these ideas which we have of them in us.

13. After the same manner that the ideas of these original qualities are produced in us, we may conceive that the ideas of secondary qualities are also produced, viz., by the operations of insensible particles on our senses. For it being manifest that there are bodies and good store of bodies, each whereof are so small, that we cannot by any of our senses discover either their bulk, figure, or motion, as is evident in the particles of the air and water, and others extremely smaller than those, perhaps as much smaller than the particles of air and water, as the particles of air and water are smaller than peas or hailstones; let us suppose that the different motions and figures, bulk and number, of such particles, affecting the several organs of our senses, produce in us those different sensations which we have from the colours and smells of bodies; e.g., that a violet, by the impulse of such insensible particles of matter of peculiar figures and bulks, and in different degrees and modifications of their motions, causes the ideas of the blue colour and sweet scent of that flower to be produced in our minds; it being no more impossible to conceive that God should annex such ideas to such motions, with which they have no similitude, than that he should annex the idea of pain to the motion of a piece of steel dividing our flesh, with which that idea has no resemblance.

14. What I have said concerning colours and smells may be understood also of tastes and sounds, and other the like sensible qualities; which, whatever reality we by mistake attribute to them, are in truth nothing in the objects themselves, but powers to produce various sensations in us, and depend on those primary qualities, viz., bulk, figure, texture, and motion of parts, as I have said.

15. From whence I think it easy to draw this observation, that the ideas of primary qualities of bodies are resemblances of them, and their patterns do really exist in the bodies themselves; but the ideas produced in us by these secondary qualities have no resemblance of them at all. There is nothing like our ideas existing in the bodies themselves. They are in the bodies we denominate from them, only a power to produce those sensations in us; and what is sweet, blue, or warm in idea, is but the certain bulk, figure, and motion of the insensible parts in the bodies themselves, which we call so.

16. Flame is denominated hot and light; snow, white and cold; and manna, white and sweet, from the ideas they produce in us; which qualities are commonly thought to be the same in those bodies that those ideas are in us, the one the perfect resemblance of the other, as they are in a mirror; and it would by most men be judged very extravagant if one should say otherwise. And yet he that will consider

that the same fire that at one distance produces in us the sensation of warmth, does at a nearer approach produce in us the far different sensation of pain, ought to bethink himself what reason he has to say that this idea of warmth, which was produced in him by the fire, is actually in the fire; and his idea of pain, which the same fire produced in him the same way, is not in the fire. Why are whiteness and coldness in snow, and pain not, when it produces the one and the other idea in us; and can do neither, but by the bulk, figure, number, and motion of its solid parts?

17. The particular bulk, number, figure, and motion of the parts of fire or snow are really in them, whether anyone's senses perceive them or not, and therefore they may be called real qualities, because they really exist in those bodies; but light, heat, whiteness, or coldness, are no more really in them than sickness or pain is in manna. Take away the sensation of them; let not the eyes see light or colours, nor the ears hear sounds; let the palate not taste, nor the nose smell; and the colours, tastes, odours, and sounds, as they are such particular ideas, vanish and cease, and are reduced to their causes, i.e., bulk, figure, and motion of parts.

18. A piece of manna of a sensible bulk is able to produce in us the idea of a round or square figure; and by being removed from one place to another, the idea of motion. This idea of motion represents it as it really is in the manna moving: a circle or square are the same, whether in idea or existence, in the mind or in the manna; and this both motion and figure are really in the manna, whether we take notice of them or not: this everybody is ready to agree to. Besides, manna, by the bulk, figure, texture, and motion of its parts, has a power to produce the sensations of sickness, and sometimes of acute pains or gripings in us. That these ideas of sickness and pain are not in the manna, but effects of its operations on us, and are nowhere when we feel them not, this also everyone readily agrees to. And yet men are hardly to be brought to think that sweetness and whiteness are not really in manna, which are but the effects of the operations of manna, by the motion, size, and figure of its particles on the eyes and palate; as the pain and sickness caused by manna are confessedly nothing but the effects of its operations on the stomach and guts, by the size, motion, and figure of its insensible parts (for by nothing else can a body operate, as has been proved); as if it could not operate on the eyes and palate, and thereby produce in the mind particular distinct ideas, which in itself it has not, as well as we allow it can operate on the guts and stomach, and thereby produce distinct ideas, which in itself it has not. These ideas being all effects of the operations of manna on several parts of our bodies, by the size, figure, number, and motion of its parts; why those produced by the eyes and palate should rather be thought to be really in the manna than those produced by the stomach and guts; or why the pain and sickness, ideas that are the effect of manna, should be thought to be nowhere when they are not felt; and yet the sweetness and whiteness, effects of the same manna on other parts of the body, by ways equally as unknown, should be thought to exist in the manna, when they are not seen or tasted, would need some reason to explain.

19. Let us consider the red and white colours in porphyry: hinder light from striking on it, and its colours vanish, it no longer produces any such ideas

in us; upon the return of light it produces these appearances on us again. Can any one think any real alterations are made in the porphyry by the presence or absence of light, and that those ideas of whiteness and redness are really in porphyry in the light, when it is plain it has no colour in the dark? It has, indeed, such a configuration of particles, both night and day, as are apt, by the rays of light rebounding from some parts of that hard stone, to produce in us the idea of redness, and from others the idea of whiteness; but whiteness or redness are not in it at any time, but such a texture that has the power to produce such a sensation in us.

23. The qualities, then, that are in bodies, rightly considered, are of three sorts.

First, the bulk, figure, number, situation, and motion or rest of their solid parts; those are in them, whether we perceive them or not; and when they are of that size that we can discover them, we have by these an idea of the thing as it is in itself, as is plain in artificial things. These I call primary qualities.

Secondly, the power that is in any body, by reason of its insensible primary qualities, to operate after a peculiar manner on any of our senses, and thereby produce in us the different ideas of several colours, sounds, smells, tastes, etc. These are usually called sensible qualities.

Thirdly, the power that is in any body, by reason of the particular constitution of its primary qualities, to make such a change in the bulk, figure, texture, and motion of another body, as to make it operate on our senses differently from what it did before. Thus the sun has a power to make wax white, and fire to make lead fluid. These are usually called powers.

The first of these, as has been said, I think may be properly called real, original, or primary qualities, because they are in the things themselves, whether they are perceived or not; and upon their different modifications it is that the secondary qualities depend.

The other two are only powers to act differently upon other things, which powers result from the different modifications of those primary qualities.

OF OUR KNOWLEDGE OF THE EXISTENCE OF OTHER THINGS

1. The knowledge of our own being we have by intuition. The existence of a God reason clearly makes known to us. . . .

The knowledge of the existence of any other thing we can have only by sensation: for there being no necessary connection of real existence with any idea a man has in his memory; nor of any other existence but that of God with the existence of any particular man: no particular man can know the existence of any other being, but only when, by actually operating upon him, it makes itself perceived by him. For the having the idea of anything in our mind no more proves the existence of that thing than the picture of a man evidences his being in the world, or the visions of a dream make thereby a true history.

2. It is therefore the actual receiving of ideas from without that gives us notice of the existence of other things, and makes us know that something does exist at that time without us which causes that idea in us, though perhaps we neither know nor consider how it does it. For it takes not from the certainty of our senses, and the ideas we receive by them, that we know not the manner wherein they are produced: e.g., while I write this, I have, by the paper affecting my eyes, that idea produced in my mind, which whatever object causes, I call white; by which I know that that quality or accident (i.e., whose appearance before my eyes always causes that idea) does really exist, and has a being without me. And of this, the greatest assurance I can possibly have, and to which my faculties can attain, is the testimony of my eyes, which are the proper and sole judges of this thing; whose testimony I have reason to rely on as so certain, that I can no more doubt, whilst I write this, that I see white and black, and that something really exists that causes that sensation in me, than that I write or move my hand; which is a certainty as great as human nature is capable of, concerning the existence of anything but a man's self alone, and of God.

3. The notice we have by our senses of the existing of things without us, though it be not altogether so certain as our intuitive knowledge, or the deductions of our reason employed about the clear abstract ideas of our own minds; yet it is an assurance that deserves the name of *knowledge*. If we persuade ourselves that our faculties act and inform us right concerning the existence of those objects that affect them, it cannot pass for an ill-grounded confidence: for I think nobody can, in earnest, be so sceptical as to be uncertain of the existence of those things which he sees and feels. At least, he that can doubt so far (whatever he may have with his own thoughts) will never have any controversy with me; since he can never be sure I say anything contrary to his opinion. As to myself, I think God has given me assurance enough of the existence of things without me; since by their different application I can produce in myself both pleasure and pain, which is one great concern of my present state. This is certain, the confidence that our faculties do not herein deceive us is the greatest assurance we are capable of concerning the existence of material beings. For we cannot act anything but by our faculties, nor talk of knowledge itself, but by the help of those faculties which are fitted to apprehend even what knowledge is. But besides the assurance we have from our senses themselves, that they do not err in the information they give us of the existence of things without us, when they are affected by them, we are farther confirmed in this assurance by other concurrent reasons.

4. First, It is plain those perceptions are produced in us by exterior causes affecting our senses, because those that want the organs of any sense never can have the ideas belonging to that sense produced in their minds. The organs themselves, it is plain, do not produce them; for then the eyes of a man in the dark would produce colours, and his nose smell roses in the winter: but we see nobody gets the relish of a pineapple till he goes to the Indies where it is, and tastes it.

5. Secondly, Because sometimes I find that I cannot avoid the having those ideas produced in my mind. For though when my eyes are shut, or windows fast,

I can at pleasure recall to my mind the ideas of light or the sun, which former sensations had lodged in my memory; so I can at pleasure lay by that idea, and take into my view that of the smell of a rose, or taste of sugar. But if I turn my eyes at noon towards the sun, I cannot avoid the ideas which the light or sun then produces in me. So that there is a manifest difference between the ideas laid up in my memory, and those which force themselves upon me, and I cannot avoid having. And therefore it must be some exterior cause, and the brisk acting of some objects without me, whose efficacy I cannot resist, that produces those ideas in my mind, whether I will or not. Besides, there is nobody who does not perceive the difference in himself between contemplating the sun as he has the idea of it in his memory, and actually looking upon it: of which two, his perception is so distinct, that few of his ideas are more distinguishable one from another. And therefore he has certain knowledge that they are not both memory, or the actions of his mind, and fancies only within him; but that actual seeing has a cause without. . . .

7. Fourthly, Our senses, in many cases, bear witness to the truth of each other's report concerning the existence of sensible things without us. He that sees a fire may, if he doubt whether it be anything more than a bare fancy, feel it too, and be convinced by putting his hand in it; which certainly could never be put into such exquisite pain by a bare idea or phantom, unless that the pain be a fancy too; which yet he cannot, when the burn is well, by raising the idea of it, bring upon himself again.

Thus I see, while I write this, I can change the appearance of the paper; and by designing the letters, tell beforehand what new idea it shall exhibit the very next moment, barely by drawing my pen over it: which will neither appear (let me fancy as much as I will) if my hand stand still, or though I move my pen, if my eyes be shut: nor, when those characters are once made on the paper, can I choose afterwards but see them as they are; that is, have the ideas of such letters as I have made. Whence it is manifest that they are not barely the sport and play of my own imagination, when I find that the characters that were made at the pleasure of my own thoughts do not obey them; nor yet cease to be, whenever I shall fancy it, but continue to affect my senses constantly and regularly, according to the figures I made them. To which if we will add, that the sight of those shall, from another man, draw such sounds as I beforehand design they shall stand for, there will be little reason left to doubt that those words I write do really exist without me, when they cause a long series of regular sounds to affect my ears, which could not be the effect of my imagination, nor could my memory retain them in that order.

8. But yet, if after all this anyone will be so sceptical as to distrust his senses, and to affirm that all we see and hear, feel and taste, think and do, during our whole being, is but the series and deluding appearances of a long dream whereof there is no reality; and therefore will question the existence of all things or our knowledge of anything: I must desire him to consider, that if all be a dream, then he does but dream that he makes the question; and so it is not much matter that a waking man should answer him. But yet, if he pleases, he may dream that I make him this answer, that the certainty of things existing *in rerum natura* when we

have the testimony of our senses for it, is not only as great as our frame can attain to, but as our condition needs. For our faculties being suited not to the full extent of being; nor to a perfect, clear, comprehensive knowledge of things free from all doubt and scruple; but to the preservation of us, in whom they are; and accommodated to the use of life: they serve to our purpose well enough, if they will but give us certain notice of those things which are convenient or inconvenient to us. For he that sees a candle burning, and has experimented the force of its flame by putting his finger in it, will little doubt that this is something existing without him, which does him harm and puts him to great pain. And if our dreamer pleases to try whether the glowing heat of a glass furnace be barely a wandering imagination in a drowsy man's fancy, by putting his hand into it, he may perhaps be awakened into a certainty, greater than he could wish, that it is something more than bare imagination. So that this evidence is as great as we can desire, being as certain to us as our pleasure or pain, i.e., happiness or misery; beyond which we have no concern, either of knowing or being. Such an assurance of the existence of things without us is sufficient to direct us in the attaining the good and avoiding the evil which is caused by them, which is the important concern we have of being made acquainted with them.

STUDY QUESTIONS

1. How does Locke distinguish primary from secondary qualities?
2. How can you decide if a quality is primary or secondary?
3. According to Locke, how do we know of a world outside ourselves?
4. How does Locke reply to those who would doubt that they have knowledge of the material world?

A Treatise Concerning the Principles of Human Knowledge

GEORGE BERKELEY

George Berkeley (1685–1753), born in Ireland, published his most important works during his twenties. At one time he lived in Rhode Island, then returned to his homeland to become bishop of Cloyne.

From *A Treatise Concerning the Principles of Human Knowledge* by George Berkeley (1710).

Berkeley accepts Locke's view of secondary qualities as mind-dependent and extends Locke's position to primary qualities, arguing that they too are mind-dependent. For example, an object that appears solid to one perceiver may not appear solid to another (the basis for many magic tricks).

But if both the primary and secondary qualities are mind-dependent, what remains of the material object? Berkeley's startling answer is: nothing. Physical objects exist but only as ideas in the minds of perceivers, who are themselves immaterial spirits. Does a table go out of existence when not being perceived by us? No, for it is being perceived by the "governing Spirit" we call God. He sends us our sensations in an orderly manner, thus giving rise to a world of sensations exhibiting the laws of nature.

Berkeley, after all, was a clergyman. So his epistemological and theological views are in harmony. Berkeley's idealism, his position that reality is fundamentally mental in nature, may not persuade many readers, but finding errors in his reasoning is no easy matter.

PART 1

1. It is evident to anyone who takes a survey of the objects of human knowledge, that they are either ideas actually imprinted on the senses, or else such as are perceived by attending to the passions and operations of the mind, or lastly ideas formed by help of memory and imagination, either compounding, dividing, or barely representing those originally perceived in the aforesaid ways. By sight I have the ideas of light and colours with their several degrees and variations. By touch I perceive, for example, hard and soft, heat and cold, motion and resistance, and of all these more and less either as to quantity or degree. Smelling furnishes me with odours; the palate with tastes, and hearing conveys sounds to the mind in all their variety of tone and composition. And as several of these are observed to accompany each other, they come to be marked by one name, and so to be reputed as one thing. Thus, for example, a certain colour, taste, smell, figure and consistence having been observed to go together, are accounted one distinct thing, signified by the name *apple*. Other collections of ideas constitute a stone, a tree, a book, and the like sensible things; which, as they are pleasing or disagreeable, excite the passions of love, hatred, joy, grief, and so forth.

2. But besides all that endless variety of ideas or objects of knowledge, there is likewise something which knows or perceives them, and exercises divers operations, as willing, imagining, remembering about them. This perceiving, active being is what I call *mind, spirit, soul* or *myself.* By which words I do not denote any one of my ideas, but a thing entirely distinct from them, wherein they exist, or, which is the same thing, whereby they are perceived; for the existence of an idea consists in being perceived.

3. That neither our thoughts, nor passions, nor ideas formed by the imagination exist without the mind is what everybody will allow. And it seems no less evident that the various sensations or ideas imprinted on the sense, however

blended or combined together (that is, whatever objects they compose), cannot exist otherwise than in a mind perceiving them. I think an intuitive knowledge may be obtained of this, by anyone that shall attend to what is meant by the term *exist* when applied to sensible things. The table I write on, I say, exists, that is, I see and feel it; and if I were out of my study I should say it existed, meaning thereby that if I was in my study I might perceive it, or that some other spirit actually does perceive it. There was an odour, that is, it was smelled; there was a sound, that is to say, it was heard; a colour or figure, and it was perceived by sight or touch. This is all that I can understand by these and the like expressions. For as to what is said of the absolute existence of unthinking things without any relation to their being perceived, that seems perfectly unintelligible. Their *esse* is *percipi*, nor is it possible they should have any existence, out of the minds or thinking things which perceive them.

4. It is indeed an opinion strangely prevailing amongst men that houses, mountains, rivers, and in a word all sensible objects have an existence natural or real, distinct from their being perceived by the understanding. But with how great an assurance and acquiescence soever this principle may be entertained in the world; yet whoever shall find in his heart to call it in question, may, if I mistake not, perceive it to involve a manifest contradiction. For what are the forementioned objects but the things we perceive by sense, and what do we perceive besides our own ideas or sensations; and is it not plainly repugnant that any one of these or any combination of them should exist unperceived?

5. If we thoroughly examine this tenet, it will, perhaps, be found at bottom to depend on the doctrine of *abstract ideas*. For can there be a nicer strain of abstraction than to distinguish the existence of sensible objects from their being perceived, so as to conceive them existing unperceived? Light and colours, heat and cold, extension and figures, in a word the things we see and feel, what are they but so many sensations, notions, ideas or impressions on the sense; and is it possible to separate, even in thought, any of these from perception? For my part I might as easily divide a thing from itself. I may indeed divide in my thoughts or conceive apart from each other those things which, perhaps, I never perceived by sense so divided. Thus I imagine the trunk of a human body without the limbs, or conceive the smell of a rose without thinking on the rose itself. So far I will not deny I can abstract, if that may properly be called *abstraction*, which extends only to the conceiving separately such objects, as it is possible may really exist or be actually perceived asunder. But my conceiving or imagining power does not extend beyond the possibility of real existence or perception. Hence as it is impossible for me to see or feel anything without an actual sensation of that thing, so is it impossible for me to conceive in my thoughts any sensible thing or object distinct from the sensation or perception of it.

6. Some truths there are so near and obvious to the mind that a man need only open his eyes to see them. Such I take this important one to be, to wit, that all the choir of heaven and furniture of the earth, in a word all those bodies which compose the mighty frame of the world, have not any subsistence, without a mind,

that their being is to be perceived or known; that consequently so long as they are not actually perceived by me, or do not exist in my mind or that of any other created spirit, they must either have no existence at all, or else subsist in the mind of some eternal spirit: it being perfectly unintelligible and involving all the absurdity of abstraction, to attribute to any single part of them an existence independent of a spirit. To be convinced of which, the reader need only reflect and try to separate in his own thoughts the being of a sensible thing from its being perceived.

7. From what has been said, it follows, there is not any other substance than *spirit*, or that which perceives. But for the fuller proof of this point, let it be considered, the sensible qualities are colour, figure, motion, smell, taste, and such like, that is, the ideas perceived by sense. Now for an idea to exist in an unperceiving thing, is a manifest contradiction; for to have an idea is all one as to perceive; that therefore wherein colour, figure, and the like qualities exist, must perceive them; hence it is clear there can be no unthinking substance or *substratum* of those ideas.

8. But say you, though the ideas themselves do not exist without the mind, yet there may be things like them whereof they are copies or resemblances, which things exist without the mind, in an unthinking substance. I answer, an idea can be like nothing but an idea; a colour or figure can be like nothing but another colour or figure. If we look but ever so little into our thoughts, we shall find it impossible for us to conceive a likeness except only between our ideas. Again, I ask whether these supposed originals or external things, of which our ideas are the pictures or representations, be themselves perceivable or no? If they are, then they are ideas, and we have gained our point; but if you say they are not, I appeal to anyone whether it be sense, to assert a colour is like something which is invisible, hard or soft, like something which is intangible; and so of the rest.

9. Some there are who make a distinction betwixt *primary* and *secondary* qualities: by the former, they mean extension, figure, motion, rest, solidity or impenetrability and number: by the latter they denote all other sensible qualities, as colours, sounds, tastes, and so forth. The ideas we have of these they acknowledge not to be the resemblances of anything existing without the mind or unperceived; but they will have our ideas of the primary qualities to be patterns or images of things which exist without the mind, in an unthinking substance which they call *matter*. By matter therefore we are to understand an inert, senseless substance, in which extension, figure, and motion, do actually subsist. But it is evident from what we have already shewn, that extension, figure and motion are only ideas existing in the mind, and that an idea can be like nothing but another idea, and that consequently neither they nor their archetypes can exist in an unperceiving substance. Hence it is plain that the very notion of what is called *matter* or *corporeal substance* involves a contradiction in it.

10. They who assert that figure, motion, and the rest of the primary or original qualities do exist without the mind, in unthinking substances, do at the same time acknowledge that colours, sounds, heat, cold, and such like secondary qualities, do not, which they tell us are sensations existing in the mind alone, that

depend on and are occasioned by the different size, texture and motion of the minute particles of matter. This they take for an undoubted truth, which they can demonstrate beyond all exception. Now if it be certain that those original qualities are inseparably united with the other sensible qualities, and not, even in thought, capable of being abstracted from them, it plainly follows that they exist only in the mind. But I desire anyone to reflect and try, whether he can by any abstraction of thought, conceive the extension and motion of a body, without all other sensible qualities. For my own part, I see evidently that it is not in my power to frame an idea of a body extended and moved, but I must withal give it some colour or other sensible quality which is acknowledged to exist only in the mind. In short, exten-sion, figure, and motion, abstracted from all other qualities, are inconceivable. Where therefore the other sensible qualities are, there must these be also, to wit, in the mind and nowhere else.

14. I shall farther add that after the same manner, as modern philosophers prove certain sensible qualities to have no existence in matter, or without the mind, the same thing may be likewise proved of all other sensible qualities what-soever. Thus, for instance, it is said that heat and cold are affections only of the mind, and not at all patterns of real beings, existing in the corporeal substances which excite them, for that the same body which appears cold to one hand seems warm to another. Now why may we not as well argue that figure and extension are not patterns or resemblances of qualities existing in matter, because to the same eye at different stations, or eyes of a different texture at the same station, they appear various, and cannot therefore be the images of anything settled and determinate without the mind? Again, it is proved that sweetness is not really in the sapid thing because the thing remaining unaltered the sweetness is changed into bitter, as in case of a fever or otherwise vitiated palate. Is it not as reasonable to say that motion is not without the mind, since if the succession of ideas in the mind become swifter, the motion, it is acknowledged, shall appear slower without any alteration in any external object.

15. In short, let anyone consider those arguments, which are thought mani-festly to prove that colours and tastes exist only in the mind, and he shall find they may with equal force, be brought to prove the same thing of extension, figure, and motion? Though it must be confessed this method of arguing doth not so much prove that there is no extension or colour in an outward object, as that we do not know by sense which is the true extension or colour of the object. But the argu-ments foregoing plainly shew it to be impossible that any colour or extension at all, or other sensible quality whatsoever, should exist in an unthinking subject without the mind, or in truth, that there should be any such thing as an outward object.

16. But let us examine a little the received opinion. It is said extension is a mode or accident of matter, and that matter is the *substratum* that supports it. Now I desire that you would explain what is meant by matter's *supporting* extension: say you, I have no idea of matter, and therefore cannot explain it. I answer, though you have no positive, yet if you have any meaning at all, you must at least have a relative idea of matter; though you know not what it is, yet you must be supposed to know

what relation it bears to accidents, and what is meant by its supporting them. It is evident *support* cannot here be taken in its usual or literal sense, as when we say that pillars support a building: in what sense therefore must it be taken?

17. If we inquire into what the most accurate philosophers declare themselves to mean by *material substance;* we shall find them acknowledge, they have no other meaning annexed to those sounds, but the idea of being in general, together with the relative notion of its supporting accidents. The general idea of being appeareth to me the most abstract and incomprehensible of all other; and as for its supporting accidents, this, as we have just now observed, cannot be understood in the common sense of those words; it must therefore be taken in some other sense, but what that is they do not explain. So that when I consider the two parts or branches which make the signification of the words *material substance*, I am convinced there is no distinct meaning annexed to them. But why should we trouble ourselves any farther, in discussing this material *substratum* or support of figure and motion, and other sensible qualities? Does it not suppose they have an existence without the mind? And is not this a direct repugnancy, and altogether inconceivable?

18. But though it were possible that solid, figured, moveable substances may exist without the mind, corresponding to the ideas we have of bodies, yet how is it possible for us to know this? Either we must know it by sense, or by reason. As for our senses, by them we have the knowledge only of our sensations, ideas, or those things that are immediately perceived by sense, call them what you will: but they do not inform us that things exist without the mind, or unperceived, like to those which are perceived. This the materials themselves acknowledge. It remains therefore that if we have any knowledge at all of external things, it must be by reason, inferring their existence from what is immediately perceived by sense. But what reason can induce us to believe the existence of bodies without the mind, from what we perceive, since the very patrons of matter themselves do not pretend there is any necessary connexion betwixt them and our ideas? I say it is granted on all hands (and what happens in dreams, phrensies, and the like, puts it beyond dispute) that it is possible we might be affected with all the ideas we have now, though no bodies existed without resembling them. Hence it is evident the supposition of external bodies is not necessary for the producing our ideas: since it is granted they are produced sometimes, and might possibly be produced always in the same order we see them in at present, without their concurrence.

19. But though we might possibly have all our sensations without them, yet perhaps it may be thought easier to conceive and explain the manner of their production, by supposing external bodies in their likeness rather than otherwise; and so it might be at least probable there are such things as bodies that excite their ideas in our minds. But neither can this be said; for though we give the materialists their external bodies, they by their own confession are never the nearer knowing how our ideas are produced; since they own themselves unable to comprehend in what manner body can act upon spirit, or how it is possible it should imprint any idea in the mind. Hence it is evident the production of ideas or sensations in our minds can be no reason why we should suppose matter or corporeal substances,

since that is acknowledged to remain equally inexplicable with or without this supposition. If therefore it were possible for bodies to exist without the mind, yet to hold they do so, must needs be a very precarious opinion; since it is to suppose, without any reason at all, that God has created innumerable beings that are entirely useless, and serve to no manner of purpose.

22. I am afraid I have given cause to think me needlessly prolix in handling this subject. For to what purpose is it to dilate on that which may be demonstrated with the utmost evidence in a line or two, to anyone that is capable of the least reflexion? It is but looking into your own thoughts, and so trying whether you can conceive it possible for a sound, or figure, or motion, or colour, to exist without the mind, or unperceived. This easy trial may make you see that what you contend for is a downright contradiction. Insomuch that I am content to put the whole upon this issue; if you can but conceive it possible for one extended moveable substance, or in general, for any one idea or anything like an idea, to exist otherwise than in a mind perceiving it, I shall readily give up the cause: and as for all that *compages* of external bodies which you contend for, I shall grant you its existence, though you cannot either give me any reason why you believe it exists, or assign any use to it when it is supposed to exist. I say, the bare possibility of your opinion's being true shall pass for an argument that it is so.

23. But you say, surely there is nothing easier than to imagine trees, for instance, in a park, or books existing in a closet, and nobody by to perceive them. I answer, you may so, there is no difficulty in it: but what is all this, I beseech you, more then framing in your mind certain ideas which you call *books* and *trees*, and at the same time omitting to frame the idea of anyone that may perceive them? But do not you yourself perceive or think of them all the while? This therefore is nothing to the purpose: it only shows you have the power of imagining or forming ideas in your mind; but it doth not shew that you can conceive it possible, the objects of your thought may exist without the mind: to make out this, it is necessary that you conceive them existing unconceived or unthought of, which is a manifest repugnancy. When we do our utmost to conceive the existence of external bodies, we are all the while only contemplating our own ideas. But the mind taking no notice of itself, is deluded to think it can and doth conceive bodies existing unthought of or without the mind; though at the same time they are apprehended by or exist in itself. A little attention will discover to anyone the truth and evidence of what is here said, and make it unnecessary to insist on any other proofs against the existence of material substance.

25. All our ideas, sensations, or the thing which we perceive, by whatsoever names they may be distinguished, are visibly inactive, there is nothing of power or agency included in them. So that one idea or object of thought cannot produce, or make any alteration in another. To be satisfied of the truth of this, there is nothing else requisite but a bare observation of our ideas. For since they and every part of them exist only in the mind, it follows that there is nothing in them but what is perceived. But whoever shall attend to his ideas, whether of sense or reflexion, will not perceive in them any power or activity; there is therefore no such thing contained

in them. A little attention will discover to us that the very being of an idea implies passiveness and inertness in it, insomuch that it is impossible for an idea to do anything, or, strictly speaking, to be the cause of anything: neither can it be the resemblance or pattern of any active being, as is evident from *Sect.* 8. Whence it plainly follows that extension, figure and motion, cannot be the cause of our sensations. To say therefore, that these are the effects of powers resulting from the configuration, number, motion, and size of corpuscles, must certainly be false.

26. We perceive a continual succession of ideas, some are a new excited, others are changed or totally disappear. There is therefore some cause of these ideas whereon they depend, and which produces and changes them. That this cause cannot be any quality or idea or combination of ideas is clear from the preceding section. It must therefore be a substance; but it has been shewn that there is no corporeal or material substance; it remains therefore that the cause of ideas is an incorporeal active substance or spirit.

27. A spirit is one simple, undivided, active being: as it perceives ideas, it is called the *understanding*, and as it produces or otherwise operates about them, it is called the *will*. Hence there can be no idea formed of a soul or spirit: for all ideas whatever, being passive and inert, *vide Sect.* 25, they cannot represent unto us, by way of image or likeness, that which acts. A little attention will make it plain to anyone that to have an idea which shall be like that active principle of motion and change of ideas is absolutely impossible. Such is the nature of *spirit* or that which acts that it cannot be of itself perceived, but only by the effects which it produceth. If any man shall doubt of the truth of what is here delivered, let him but reflect and try if he can frame the idea of any power or active being; and whether he hath ideas of two principal powers, marked by the names *will* and *understanding*, distinct from each other as well as from a third idea of substance or being in general, with a relative notion of its supporting or being the subject of the aforesaid powers, which is signified by the name *soul* or *spirit*. This is what some hold; but so far as I can see, the words *will, soul, spirit* do not stand for different ideas, or in truth, for any idea at all, but for something which is very different from ideas, and which being an agent cannot be like unto, or represented by, any idea whatsoever. Though it must be owned at the same time that we have some notion of soul, spirit, and the operations of the mind, such as willing loving, hating, in as much as we know or understand the meaning of those words.

28. I find I can excite ideas in my mind at pleasure, and vary and shift the scene as oft as I think fit. It is no more than willing, and straightway this or that idea arises in my fancy: and by the same power it is obliterated and makes way for another. This making and unmaking of ideas doth very properly denominate the mind active. Thus much is certain, and grounded on experience: but when we talk of unthinking agents, or of exciting ideas exclusive of volition, we only amuse ourselves with words.

29. But whatever power I may have over my own thoughts, I find the ideas actually perceived by sense have not a like dependence on my will. When in broad day-light I open my eyes, it is not in my power to choose whether I shall see or no, or

to determine what particular objects shall present themselves to my view; and so likewise as to the hearing and other senses, the ideas imprinted on them are not creatures of my will. There is therefore some other will or spirit that produces them.

30. The ideas of sense are more strong, lively, and distinct than those of the imagination; they have likewise a steadiness, order, and coherence, and are not excited at random, as those which are the effects of human wills often are, but in a regular train or series, the admirable connexion whereof sufficiently testifies the wisdom and benevolence of its Author. Now the set rules or established methods, wherein the mind we depend on excites in us the ideas of sense, are called the *Laws of Nature*: and these we learn by experience, which teaches us that such and such ideas are attended with such and such other ideas, in the ordinary course of things.

31. This gives us a sort of foresight, which enables us to regulate our actions for the benefit of the life. And without this we should be eternally at a loss: we could not know how to act anything that might procure us the least pleasure, or remove the least pain of sense. That food nourishes, sleep refreshes, and fire warms us; that to sow in the seed-time is the way to reap in the harvest, and, in general, that to obtain such or such ends, such or such means are conducive, all this we know, not by discovering any necessary connexion between our ideas, but only by the observation of the settled Laws of Nature, without which we should be all in uncertainty and confusion, and a grown man no more knows how to manage himself in the affairs of life than an infant just born.

32. And yet this consistent uniform working, which so evidently displays the goodness and wisdom of that governing spirit whose will constitutes the Laws of Nature, is so far from leading our thoughts to him that it rather sends them a wandering after second causes. For when we perceive certain ideas of sense constantly followed by other ideas, and we know this is not of our doing, we forthwith attribute power and agency to the ideas themselves and make one the cause of another, than which nothing can be more absurd and unintelligible. Thus, for example, having observed that when we perceive by sight a certain round luminous figure, we at the same time perceive by touch the idea of sensation called *heat,* we do from thence conclude the sun to be the cause of heat. And in like manner perceiving the motion and collision of bodies to be attended with sound, we are inclined to think the latter an effect of the former.

33. The ideas imprinted on the senses by the Author of Nature are called *real things:* and those excited in the imagination being less regular, vivid and constant, are more properly termed *ideas,* or *images of things*, which they copy and represent. But then our sensations, be they never so vivid and distinct, are nevertheless *ideas,* that is, they exist in the mind, or are perceived by it, as truly as the ideas of its own framing. The ideas of sense are allowed to have more reality in them, that is, to be more strong, orderly, and coherent than the creatures of the mind; but this is no argument that they exist without the mind. They are also less dependent on the spirit, or thinking substance which perceives them, in that they are excited by the will of another and more powerful spirit: yet still they are *ideas,* and certainly no *idea,* whether faint or strong, can exist otherwise than in a mind perceiving it.

145. From what has been said it is plain that we cannot know the existence of other spirits otherwise than by their operations, or the ideas by them excited in us. I perceive several motions, changes, and combinations of ideas that inform me there are certain particular agents, like myself, which accompany them and concur in their production. Hence, the knowledge I have of other spirits is not immediate, as is the knowledge of my ideas, but depending on the intervention of ideas, by me referred to agents or spirits distinct from myself, as effects or concomitant signs.

146. But though there be some things which convince us human agents are concerned in producing them, yet it is evident to everyone that those things which are called "the works of nature," that is, the far greater part of the ideas or sensations perceived by us, are not produced by, or dependent on, the wills of men. There is therefore some other spirit that causes them; since it is repugnant that they should subsist by themselves. See sec. 29. But, if we attentively consider the constant regularity, order, and concatenation of natural things, the surprising magnificence, beauty, and perfection of the larger, and the exquisite contrivance of the smaller parts of the creation, together with the exact harmony and correspondence of the whole, but above all the never-enough-admired laws of pain and pleasure, and the instincts or natural inclinations, appetites, and passions of animals; I say if we consider all these things, and at the same time attend to the meaning and import of the attributes: one, eternal, infinitely wise, good, and perfect, we shall clearly perceive that they belong to the aforesaid spirit, "who works all in all," and "by whom all things consist."

147. Hence it is evident that God is known as certainly and immediately as any other mind or spirit whatsoever distinct from ourselves. We may even assert that the existence of God is far more evidently perceived than the existence of men; because the effects of nature are infinitely more numerous and considerable than those ascribed to human agents. There is not any one mark that denotes a man, or effect produced by him, which does not more strongly evince the being of that spirit who is the Author of Nature. For it is evident that in affecting other persons the will of man has no other object than barely the motion of the limbs of his body; but that such a motion should be attended by, or excite any idea in the mind of another, depends wholly on the will of the Creator. He alone it is who, "upholding all things by the word of his power," maintains that intercourse between spirits whereby they are able to perceive the existence of each other. And yet this pure and clear light which enlightens everyone is itself invisible.

STUDY QUESTIONS

1. Do you believe that Berkeley succeeds in his attack on Locke's distinction between primary and secondary qualities?
2. How does Berkeley reply to the claim that nothing is easier to imagine than trees in a park with nobody there to perceive them?
3. How does Berkeley distinguish real things and images of things?
4. Why does Berkeley believe that the existence of God is evident?

An Enquiry Concerning Human Understanding

DAVID HUME

The Scotsman David Hume (1711–1776), essayist, historian, and philosopher, developed one of the most influential of all philosophical systems. He presented it first in his monumental *Treatise of Human Nature*, published when he was twenty-eight years old. Later he reworked the material to make it more accessible, and the selection that follows is from *An Enquiry Concerning Human Understanding*, which appeared in 1748.

The fundamental principle of Hume's philosophy is that our knowledge of the world depends entirely on the evidence provided by our senses. While this premise may appear uncontroversial, as developed by Hume it has startling consequences.

To use an example he offers, suppose you see one billiard ball hit a second, and then the second ball moves. You would say the first made the second move. Hume points out, however, that all you see is one event followed by another; you do not actually see any connection between them. You assume the connection, but the force of Hume's argument is that your assumption violates the principle that our knowledge rests only on the evidence of our senses, for you did not sense any necessary connection between the two events, but presumed it anyway.

Hume extends this reasoning and argues that, so far as we know, the world consists of entirely separate events, some regularly following others but all unconnected. He concludes that our beliefs about the necessity of causation are instinctive, not rational.

Hume's arguments are among the most challenging in the history of philosophy, and in a later section we shall read more of his work.

....

OF THE ORIGIN OF IDEAS

Everyone will readily allow that there is a considerable difference between the perceptions of the mind, when a man feels the pain of excessive heat, or the pleasure of moderate warmth, and when he afterwards recalls to his memory this sensation, or anticipates it by his imagination. These faculties may mimic or copy the perceptions of the senses; but they never can entirely reach the force and vivacity of the original sentiment. The utmost we say of them, even when they

From *An Enquiry Concerning Human Understanding* by David Hume (1748).

operate with greatest vigor, is that they represent their object in so lively a manner that we could *almost* say we feel or see it: But, except the mind be disordered by disease or madness, they never can arrive at such a pitch of vivacity, as to render these perceptions altogether undistinguishable. All the colors of poetry, however splendid, can never paint natural objects in such a manner as to make the description be taken for a real landscape. The most lively thought is still inferior to the dullest sensation.

We may observe a like distinction to run through all the other perceptions of the mind. A man in a fit of anger is actuated in a very different manner from one who only thinks of that emotion. If you tell me that any person is in love, I easily understand your meaning and form a just conception of his situation; but never can mistake that conception for the real disorders and agitations of the passion. When we reflect on our past sentiments and affections, our thought is a faithful mirror and copies its objects truly; but the colors which it employs are faint and dull in comparison of those in which our original perceptions were clothed. It requires no nice discernment or metaphysical head to mark the distinction between them.

Here therefore we may divide all the perceptions of the mind into two classes or species, which are distinguished by their different degrees of force and vivacity. The less forcible and lively are commonly denominated *thoughts* or *ideas.* The other species want a name in our language, and in most others; I suppose, because it was not requisite for any but philosophical purposes to rank them under a general term or appellation. Let us, therefore, use a little freedom and call them *impressions;* employing that word in a sense somewhat different from the usual. By the term *impression,* then, I mean all our more lively perceptions, when we hear, or see, or feel, or love, or hate, or desire, or will. And impressions are distinguished from ideas, which are the less lively perceptions, of which we are conscious, when we reflect on any of those sensations or movements above mentioned.

Nothing, at first view, may seem more unbounded than the thought of man, which not only escapes all human power and authority, but is not even restrained within the limits of nature and reality. To form monsters, and join incongruous shapes and appearances, costs the imagination no more trouble than to conceive the most natural and familiar objects. And while the body is confined to one planet, along which it creeps with pain and difficulty; the thought can in an instant transport us into the most distant regions of the universe; or even beyond the universe, into the unbounded chaos, where nature is supposed to lie in total confusion. What never was seen, or heard of, may yet be conceived; nor is anything beyond the power of thought, except what implies an absolute contradiction.

But though our thought seems to possess this unbounded liberty, we shall find, upon a nearer examination, that it is really confined within very narrow limits and that all this creative power of the mind amounts to no more than the faculty of compounding, transposing, augmenting, or diminishing the materials afforded us by the senses and experience. When we think of a golden mountain, we only join two consistent ideas, *gold*, and *mountain*, with which we were formerly acquainted. A virtuous horse we can conceive; because, from our own feeling, we can conceive virtue; and this we may unite to the figure and shape of a horse, which is an animal familiar to us. In short, all the materials of thinking are derived either from our outward or inward sentiment: the mixture and composition of these belongs alone to the mind and will. Or, to express myself in philosophical language, all our ideas or more feeble perceptions are copies of our impressions or more lively ones.

To prove this, the two following arguments will, I hope, be sufficient. First, when we analyze our thoughts or ideas, however compounded or sublime, we always find that they resolve themselves into such simple ideas as were copied from a precedent feeling or sentiment. Even those ideas, which, at first view, seem the most wide of this origin, are found, upon a nearer scrutiny, to be derived from it. The idea of God, as meaning an infinitely intelligent, wise, and good Being, arises from reflecting on the operations of our own mind, and augmenting, without limit, those qualities of goodness and wisdom. We may prosecute this inquiry to what length we please; where we shall always find that every idea which we examine is copied from a similar impression. Those who would assert that this position is not universally true nor without exception have only one, and that an easy method of refuting it; by producing that idea, which, in their opinion, is not derived from this source. It will then be incumbent on us, if we would maintain our doctrine, to produce the impression, or lively perception, which corresponds to it.

Secondly. If it happens, from a defect of the organ, that a man is not susceptible of any species of sensation, we always find that he is as little susceptible of the correspondent ideas. A blind man can form no notion of colors; a deaf man of sounds. Restore either of them that sense in which he is deficient; by opening this new inlet for his sensations, you also open an inlet for the ideas; and he finds no difficulty in conceiving these objects. . . . When we entertain, therefore, any suspicion that a philosophical term is employed without any meaning or idea (as is but too frequent), we need but inquire, *from what impression is that supposed idea derived?* And if it be impossible to assign any, this will serve to confirm our suspicion. By bringing ideas into so clear a light we may reasonably hope to remove all dispute which may arise concerning their nature and reality. . . .

SCEPTICAL DOUBTS CONCERNING THE OPERATIONS OF THE UNDERSTANDING

Part I

All the objects of human reason or inquiry may naturally be divided into two kinds, to wit, *relations of ideas,* and *matters of fact.* Of the first kind are the sciences of geometry, algebra, and arithmetic; and in short, every affirmation which is either intuitively or demonstratively certain. *That the square of the hypothenuse is equal to the squares of the two sides* is a proposition which expresses a relation between these figures. *That three times five is equal to the half of thirty* expresses a relation between these numbers. Propositions of this kind are discoverable by the mere operation of thought, without dependence on what is anywhere existent in the universe. Though there never was a circle or triangle in nature, the truths demonstrated by Euclid would forever retain their certainty and evidence.

Matters of fact, which are the second objects of human reason, are not ascertained in the same manner; nor is our evidence of their truth, however great, of a like nature with the foregoing. The contrary of every matter of fact is still possible; because it can never imply a contradiction, and is conceived by the mind with the same facility and distinctness, as if ever so conformable to reality. *That the sun will not rise tomorrow* is no less intelligible a proposition, and implies no more contradiction than the affirmation, *that it will rise.* We should in vain, therefore, attempt to demonstrate its falsehood. Were it demonstratively false, it would imply a contradiction and could never be distinctly conceived by the mind.

It may, therefore, be a subject worthy of curiosity to inquire what is the nature of that evidence which assures us of any real existence and matter of fact, beyond the present testimony of our senses or the records of our memory. This part of philosophy, it is observable, has been little cultivated, either by the ancients or moderns; and therefore our doubts and errors, in the prosecution of so important an inquiry, may be the more excusable; while we march through such difficult paths without any guide or direction. They may even prove useful, by exciting curiosity and destroying that implicit faith and security, which is the bane of all reasoning and free inquiry. The discovery of defects in the common philosophy, if any such there be, will not, I presume, be a discouragement, but rather an incitement, as is usual, to attempt something more full and satisfactory than has yet been proposed to the public.

All reasonings concerning matter of fact seem to be founded on the relation of *cause and effect.* By means of that relation alone, we can go beyond the evidence of our memory and senses. If you were to ask a man why he believes any matter of fact, which is absent; for instance, that his friend is in the country, or in France; he would give you a reason; and this reason would be some other fact; as a letter received from him, or the knowledge of his former resolutions and promises. A man finding a watch or any other machine in a desert island would conclude that there had once been men in that island. All our reasonings concerning fact are of the same nature. And here it is constantly supposed that there is a connection between the present fact and that which is inferred from it. Were there nothing to bind them together, the inference would be entirely precarious. The hearing of an articulate voice and rational discourse in the dark assures us of the presence of some person: Why? because these are the effects of the human make and fabric, and closely connected with it. If we anatomize all the other reasonings of this nature, we shall find that they are founded on the relation of cause and effect, and that this relation is either near or remote, direct or collateral. Heat and light are collateral effects of fire, and the one effect may justly be inferred from the other.

If we would satisfy ourselves, therefore, concerning the nature of that evidence, which assures us of matters of fact, we must inquire how we arrive at the knowledge of cause and effect.

I shall venture to affirm, as a general proposition, which admits of no exception, that the knowledge of this relation is not, in any instance, attained by reasonings a priori; but arises entirely from experience, when we find that any particular objects are constantly conjoined with each other. Let an object be presented to a man of ever so strong natural reason and abilities; if that object be entirely new to him, he will not be able, by the most accurate examination of its sensible qualities, to discover any of its causes or effects. Adam, though his rational faculties be supposed, at the very first, entirely perfect, could not have inferred from the fluidity and transparency of water that it would suffocate him, or from the light and warmth of fire that it would consume him. No object ever discovers, by the qualities which appear to the senses, either the causes which produced it, or the effects which will arise from it; nor can our reason, unassisted by experience, ever draw any inference concerning real existence and matter of fact.

This proposition, *that causes and effects are discoverable, not by reason but by experience,* will readily be admitted with regard to such objects, as we remember to have once been altogether unknown to us; since we must be conscious of the utter inability, which we then lay under, of foretelling what would arise from them. Present two smooth pieces of marble to a man who has no tincture of natural philosophy; he will never discover that they will adhere together in such a manner as to require great force to separate them in a direct line, while they make so small a resistance to a lateral pressure. Such events, as bear little analogy to the common course of nature, are also readily confessed to be known only by experience; nor does any man imagine that the explosion of gunpowder, or the attraction of a loadstone, could ever be discovered by arguments a priori. In like manner, when an effect is supposed to depend upon an intricate machinery or secret structure of parts, we make no difficulty in attributing all our knowledge of it to experience. Who will assert that he can give the ultimate reason why milk or bread is proper nourishment for a man, not for a lion or a tiger?

But the same truth may not appear, at first sight, to have the same evidence with regard to events, which have become familiar to us from our first appearance in the world, which bear a close analogy to the whole course of nature, and which are supposed to depend on the simple qualities of objects, without any secret structure of parts. We are apt to imagine that we could discover these effects by the mere operation of our reason, without experience. We fancy that were we brought a sudden into this world, we could at first have inferred that one billiard ball would communicate motion to another upon impulse; and that we needed not to have waited for the event in order to pronounce with certainty concerning it. Such is the influence of custom, that, where it is strongest, it not only covers our natural ignorance, but even conceals itself, and seems not to take place, merely because it is found in the highest degree.

But to convince us that all the laws of nature, and all the operations of bodies without exception, are known only by experience, the following reflections may, perhaps, suffice. Were any object presented to us, and were we required to pronounce concerning the effect, which will result from it, without consulting past observation; after what manner, I beseech you, must the mind proceed in this operation? It must invent or imagine some event, which it ascribes to the object as its effect; and it is plain that this invention must be entirely arbitrary. The mind can never possibly find the effect in the supposed cause, by the most accurate scrutiny and examination. For the effect is totally different from the cause, and consequently can never be discovered in it. Motion in the second billiard ball is a quite distinct event from motion in the first: nor is there anything in the one to suggest the smallest hint of the other. A stone or piece of metal raised into the air, and left without any support, immediately falls: but to consider the matter a priori, is there anything we discover in this situation which can beget the idea of a downward, rather than an upward, or any other motion, in the stone or metal?

And as the first imagination or invention of a particular effect, in all natural operations, is arbitrary, where we consult not experience, so must we also esteem the supposed tie or connection between the cause and effect, which binds them together and renders it impossible that any other effect could result from the operation of that cause. When I see, for instance, a billiard ball moving in a straight line towards another; even suppose motion in the second ball should by accident be suggested to me, as the result of their contact or impulse; may I not conceive that a hundred different events might as well follow from that cause? May not both these balls remain at absolute rest? May not the first ball return in a straight line, or leap off from the second in any line or direction? All these suppositions are consistent and conceivable. Why then should we give the preference to one, which is no more consistent or conceivable than the rest? All our reasonings a priori will never be able to show us any foundation for this preference.

In a word, then, every effect is a distinct event from its cause. It could not, therefore, be discovered in the cause, and the first invention or conception of it, a priori, must be entirely arbitrary. And even after it is suggested, the conjunction of it with the cause must appear equally arbitrary, since there are always many other effects, which, to reason, must seem fully as consistent and natural. In vain, therefore, should we pretend to determine any single event, or infer any cause or effect, without the assistance of observation and experience. . . .

Part II

But we have not yet attained any tolerable satisfaction with regard to the question first proposed. Each solution still gives rise to a new question as difficult as the foregoing, and leads us on to farther inquiries. When it is asked, *What is the nature of all our reasonings concerning matter of fact?* the proper answer seems to be that they are founded on the relation of cause and effect. When again it is asked, *What is the foundation of all our reasonings and conclusions concerning that relation?* it may be replied in one word, *experience.* But if we still carry on our sifting humor, and ask, *What is the foundation of all conclusions from experience?* this implies a new question, which may be of more difficult solution and explication. Philosophers, that give themselves airs of superior wisdom and sufficiency, have a hard task when they encounter persons of inquisitive dispositions, who push them from every corner to which they retreat, and who are sure at last to bring them to some dangerous dilemma. The best expedient to prevent this confusion is to be modest in our pretensions, and even to discover the difficulty ourselves before it is objected to us. By this means, we may make a kind of merit of our very ignorance.

I shall content myself, in this section, with an easy task and shall pretend only to give a negative answer to the question here proposed. I say then that, even after we have experience of the operations of cause and effect, our conclusions from that experience are *not* founded on reasoning, or any process of the understanding. This answer we must endeavor both to explain and to defend.

It must certainly be allowed that nature has kept us at a great distance from all her secrets and has afforded us only the knowledge of a few superficial qualities of objects, while she conceals from us those powers and principles on which the influence of those objects entirely depends. Our senses inform us of the color, weight, and consistence of bread; but neither sense nor reason can ever inform us of those qualities which fit it for the nourishment and support of a human body. Sight or feeling conveys an idea of the actual motion of bodies; but as to that wonderful force or power, which would carry on a moving body forever in a continued change of place, and which bodies never lose but by communicating it to others; of this we cannot form the most distant conception. But notwithstanding this ignorance of natural powers and principles, we always presume, when we see like sensible qualities, that they have like secret powers and expect that effects, similar to those which we have experienced, will follow from them. If a body of like color and consistence with that bread, which we have formerly eat, be presented to us, we make no scruple of repeating the experiment, and foresee, with certainty, like nourishment and support. Now this is a process of the mind or thought, of which I would willingly know the foundation. It is allowed on all hands that there is no known connection between the sensible qualities and the secret powers; and consequently, that the mind is not led to form such a conclusion concerning their constant and regular conjunction, by anything which it knows of their nature. As to past *experience,* it can be allowed to give *direct* and *certain* information of those precise objects only, and that precise period of time, which fell under its cognizance: but why this experience should be extended to future times, and to other objects, which, for aught we know, may be only in appearance similar; this is the main question on which I would insist. The bread, which I formerly eat, nourished me; that is, a body of such sensible qualities was, at that time, endued with such secret powers: but does it follow that other bread must also nourish me at another time and that like sensible qualities must always be attended with like secret powers? The consequence seems no wise necessary. At least, it must be acknowledged that there is here a consequence drawn by the mind; that there is a certain step taken, a process of thought, and an inference, which wants to be explained. These two propositions are far from being the same, *I have found that such an object has always been attended with such an effect,* and *I foresee that other objects, which are, in appearance, similar, will be attended with similar effects.* I shall allow, if you please, that the one proposition may justly be inferred from the other; I know, in fact, that it always is inferred. But if you insist that the inference is made by a chain of reasoning, I desire you to produce that reasoning. . . .

To say it is experimental is begging the question. For all inferences from experience suppose, as their foundation, that the future will resemble the past and that similar powers will be conjoined with similar sensible qualities. If there be any suspicion that the course of nature may change, and that the past may be no rule for the future, all experience becomes useless and can give rise to no inference or conclusion. It is impossible, therefore, that any arguments from experience can prove this resemblance of the past to the future, since all these arguments are founded on the supposition of that resemblance. Let the course of things be allowed hitherto ever so regular; that alone, without some new argument or inference, proves not that, for the future, it will continue so. In vain do you pretend to have learned the nature of bodies from your past experience? Their secret nature, and consequently all their effects and influence, may change, without any change in their sensible qualities. This happens sometimes, and with regard to some objects: Why may it not happen always, and with regard to all objects? What logic, what process of argument secures you against this supposition? My practice, you say, refutes my doubts. But you mistake the purport of my question. As an agent, I am quite satisfied in the point; but as a philosopher, who has some share of curiosity, I will not say scepticism, I want to learn the foundation of this inference. No reading, no inquiry has yet been able to remove my difficulty, or give me satisfaction in a matter of such importance. Can I do better than propose the difficulty to the public, even though, perhaps, I have small hopes of obtaining a solution? We shall, at least, by this means, be sensible of our ignorance, if we do not augment our knowledge. . . .

SCEPTICAL SOLUTION OF THESE DOUBTS

. . . Suppose a person, though endowed with the strongest faculties of reason and reflection, to be brought on a sudden into this world; he would, indeed, immediately observe a continual succession of objects, and one event following another; but he would not be able to discover anything farther. He would not, at first, by any reasoning, be able to reach the idea of cause and effect; since the particular powers, by which all natural operations are performed, never appear to the senses; nor is it reasonable to conclude, merely because one event, in one instance, precedes another, that therefore the one is the cause, the other the effect. Their conjunction may be arbitrary and casual. There may be no reason to infer the existence of one from the appearance of the other. And in a word, such a person, without more experience, could never employ his conjecture or reasoning concerning any matter of fact, or be assured of anything beyond what was immediately present to his memory and senses.

Suppose, again, that he has acquired more experience, and has lived so long in the world as to have observed familiar objects or events to be constantly conjoined together; what is the consequence of this experience? He immediately infers the existence of one object from the appearance of the other. Yet he has not, by all his experience, acquired any idea or knowledge of the secret power by which the one object produces the other; nor is it, by any process of reasoning, he is engaged to draw this inference. But still he finds himself determined to draw it: And though he should be convinced that his understanding has no part in the operation, he would nevertheless continue in the same course of thinking. There is some other principle which determines him to form such a conclusion.

This principle is *custom* or *habit*. For wherever the repetition of any particular act or operation produces a propensity to renew the same act or operation, without being impelled by any reasoning or process of the understanding, we always say that this propensity is the effect of *custom*. By employing that word, we pretend not to have given the ultimate reason of such a propensity. We only point out a principle of human nature, which is universally acknowledged and which is well known by its effects. Perhaps we can push our inquiries no farther, or pretend to give the cause of this cause, but must rest contented with it as the ultimate principle, which we can assign, of all our conclusions from experience. . . .

Custom, then, is the great guide of human life. It is that principle alone which renders our experience useful to us and makes us expect, for the future, a similar train of events with those which have appeared in the past. Without the influence of custom, we should be entirely ignorant of every matter of fact beyond what is immediately present to the memory and senses. We should never know how to adjust means to ends, or to employ our natural powers in the production of any effect. There would be an end at once of all action, as well as of the chief part of speculation. . . .

What, then, is the conclusion of the whole matter? A simple one; though, it must be confessed, pretty remote from the common theories of philosophy. All belief of matter of fact or real existence is derived merely from some object, present to the memory or senses, and a customary conjunction between that and some other object. Or in other words; having found, in many instances, that any two kinds of objects—flame and heat, snow and cold—have always been conjoined together; if flame or snow be presented anew to the senses, the mind is carried by custom to expect heat or cold and to *believe* that such a quality does exist, and will discover itself upon a nearer approach. This belief is the necessary result of placing the mind in such circumstances. It is an operation of the soul, when we are so situated, as unavoidable as to feel the passion of love, when we receive benefits; or hatred, when we meet with injuries. All these operations are a species of natural instincts, which no reasoning or process of the thought and understanding is able either to produce or to prevent.

STUDY QUESTIONS

1. Explain Hume's distinction between "relations of ideas" and "matters of fact."
2. According to Hume, what is the foundation for all reasonings concerning matters of fact?
3. What does Hume mean by "custom"?
4. According to Hume, why is custom "the great guide of human life"?

Critique of Pure Reason

IMMANUEL KANT

Immanuel Kant (1724–1804), who lived his entire life in the Prussian town of Königsberg, is a preeminent figure in the history of philosophy, having made groundbreaking contributions in virtually every area of the subject. Kant seeks to show that the laws of nature are based in human reason. First, he distinguishes between analytic and synthetic propositions. An analytic proposition, such as "all bachelors are unmarried," is true because its subject, "bachelor," contains its predicate, "unmarried"; in a synthetic proposition, such as "all bachelors are happy," the subject does not contain the predicate. Kant also distinguishes between *a posteriori* propositions, the truth of which can be determined only by the evidence of experience, and *a priori* propositions, the truth of which can be determined without such evidence.

Are any synthetic propositions true *a priori*? Kant thought so and maintained that, for example, "every event has a cause" is such a synthetic *a priori* proposition, an informative statement known to be true without appeal to the evidence of experience. Thus does Kant develop a strategy for responding to Hume's skepticism about human knowledge.

I. THE DISTINCTION BETWEEN PURE AND EMPIRICAL KNOWLEDGE

There can be no doubt that all our knowledge begins with experience. For how should our faculty of knowledge be awakened into action did not objects affecting our senses partly of themselves produce representations, partly arouse the activity

From *The Critique of Pure Reason* by Immanuel Kant, translated by Norman Kemp Smith, 1929. Reprinted by permission of the publishers: Macmillan & Company, Ltd., London, and St. Martin's Press, Inc., New York.

of our understanding to compare these representations, and, by combining or separating them, work up the raw material of the sensible impressions into that knowledge of objects which is entitled experience? In the order of time, therefore, we have no knowledge antecedent to experience, and with experience all our knowledge begins.

But though all our knowledge begins with experience, it does not follow that it all arises out of experience. For it may well be that even our empirical knowledge is made up of what we receive through impressions and of what our own faculty of knowledge (sensible impressions serving merely as the occasion) supplies from itself. If our faculty of knowledge makes any such addition, it may be that we are not in a position to distinguish it from the raw material, until with long practice of attention we have become skilled in separating it.

This, then, is a question which at least calls for closer examination and does not allow of any off-hand answer:—whether there is any knowledge that is thus independent of experience and even of all impressions of the senses. Such knowledge is entitled *a priori*, and distinguished from the *empirical*, which has its sources *a posteriori*, that is, in experience.

The expression "*a priori*" does not, however, indicate with sufficient precision the full meaning of our question. For it has been customary to say, even of much knowledge that is derived from empirical sources, that we have it or are capable of having it *a priori*, meaning thereby that we do not derive it immediately from experience, but from a universal rule—a rule which is itself, however, borrowed by us from experience. Thus we would say of a man who undermined the foundations of his house, that he might have known *a priori* that it would fall, that is, that he need not have waited for the experience of its actual falling. But still he could not know this completely *a priori*. For he had first to learn through experience that bodies are heavy, and therefore fall when their supports are withdrawn.

In what follows, therefore, we shall understand by *a priori* knowledge, not knowledge independent of this or that experience, but knowledge absolutely independent of all experience. Opposed to it is empirical knowledge, which is knowledge possible only *a posteriori*, that is, through experience. *A priori* modes of knowledge are entitled pure when there is no admixture of anything empirical. Thus, for instance, the proposition, "every alteration has its cause," while an *a priori* proposition, is not a pure proposition, because alteration is a concept which can be derived only from experience.

II. WE ARE IN POSSESSION OF CERTAIN MODES OF *A PRIORI* KNOWLEDGE, AND EVEN THE COMMON UNDERSTANDING IS NEVER WITHOUT THEM

What we here require is a criterion by which to distinguish with certainty between pure and empirical knowledge. Experience teaches us that a thing is so and so, but not that it cannot be otherwise. First, then, if we have a proposition which in being thought is thought as *necessary*, it is an *a priori* judgement; and if, besides, it is not derived from any proposition except one which also has the validity of a necessary judgement, it is an absolutely *a priori* judgement. Secondly, experience never confers on its judgements true or strict, but only assumed and comparative *universality*, through induction. We can properly only say, therefore, that, so far as we have hitherto observed, there is no exception to this or that rule. If, then, a judgement is thought with strict universality, that is, in such manner that no exception is allowed as possible, it is not derived from experience, but is valid absolutely *a priori*. Empirical universality is only an arbitrary extension of a validity holding in most cases to one which holds in all, for instance, in the proposition, "all bodies are heavy." When, on the other hand, strict universality is essential to a judgement, this indicates a special source of knowledge, namely, a faculty of *a priori* knowledge. Necessity and strict universality are thus sure criteria of *a priori* knowledge and are inseparable from one another. But since in the employment of these criteria the contingency of judgements is sometimes more easily shown than their empirical limitation, or, as sometimes also happens, their unlimited universality can be more convincingly proved than their necessity, it is advisable to use the two criteria separately, each by itself being infallible.

Now it is easy to show that there actually are in human knowledge judgements which are necessary and in the strictest sense universal, and which are therefore pure *a priori* judgements. If an example from the sciences be desired, we have only to look to any of the propositions of mathematics; if we seek an example from the understanding in its quite ordinary employment, the proposition, "every alteration must have a cause," will serve our purpose. In the latter case, indeed, the very concept of a cause so manifestly contains the concept of a necessity of connection with an effect and of the strict universality of the rule, that the concept would be altogether lost if we attempted to derive it, as Hume has done, from a repeated association of that which happens with that which precedes, and from a custom of connecting representations, a custom originating in this repeated association, and constituting therefore a merely subjective necessity. Even without appealing to such examples, it is possible to show that pure *a priori* principles are indispensable for the possibility of experience, and so to prove their existence *a priori*. For whence could experience derive its certainty, if all the rules, according to which it proceeds, were always themselves empirical, and therefore contingent? Such rules could hardly be regarded as first principles. At present, however, we may be content to have established the fact that our faculty of knowledge does have a pure employment, and to have shown what are the criteria of such an employment.

Such *a priori* origin is manifest in certain concepts, no less than in judgements. If we remove from our empirical concept of a body, one by one, every feature in it which is [merely] empirical, the colour, the hardness or softness, the weight, even the impenetrability, there still remains the space which the body (now entirely vanished) occupied, and this cannot be removed. Again, if we remove from our empirical concept of any object, corporeal or incorporeal, all properties which experience has taught us, we yet cannot take away that property through which the object is thought as substance or as inhering in a substance (although this concept of substance is more determinate than that of an object in general). Owing, therefore, to the necessity with which this concept of substance forces itself upon us, we have no option save to admit that it has its seat in our faculty of *a priori* knowledge.

III. PHILOSOPHY STANDS IN NEED OF A SCIENCE WHICH SHALL DETERMINE THE POSSIBILITY, THE PRINCIPLES, AND THE EXTENT OF ALL *A PRIORI* KNOWLEDGE

But what is still more extraordinary than all the preceding is this, that certain modes of knowledge leave the field of all possible experiences and have the appearance of extending the scope of our judgements beyond all limits of experience, and this by means of concepts to which no corresponding object can ever be given in experience.

It is precisely by means of the latter modes of knowledge, in a realm beyond the world of the senses, where experience can yield neither guidance nor correction, that our reason carries on those enquiries which owing to their importance we consider to be far more excellent, and in their purpose far more lofty, than all that the understanding can learn in the field of appearances. Indeed we prefer to run every risk of error rather than desist from such urgent enquiries, on the ground of their dubious character, or from disdain and indifference. These unavoidable problems set by pure reason itself are *God, freedom,* and *immortality.* The science which, with all its preparations, is in its final intention directed solely to their solution is metaphysics; and its procedure is at first dogmatic, that is, it confidently sets itself to this task without any previous examination of the capacity or incapacity of reason for so great an undertaking.

Now it does indeed seem natural that, as soon as we have left the ground of experience, we should, through careful enquiries, assure ourselves as to the foundations of any building that we propose to erect, not making use of any knowledge that we possess without first determining whence it has come, and not trusting to principles without knowing their origin. It is natural, that is to say, that the question should first be considered, how the understanding can arrive at all this knowledge *a priori,* and what extent, validity, and worth it may have. Nothing, indeed, could be more natural, if by the term "natural" we signify what fittingly and reasonably ought to happen. But if we mean by "natural" what ordinarily happens, then on the contrary nothing is more natural and more intelligible than the fact that this enquiry has been so long neglected. For one part of this knowledge, the mathematical, has long been of established reliability, and so gives rise to a favourable presumption as regards the other part, which may yet be of quite different nature. Besides, once we are outside the circle of experience, we can be sure of not being *contradicted* by experience. The charm of extending our knowledge is so great that nothing short of encountering a direct contradiction can suffice to arrest us in our course; and this can be avoided, if we are careful in our fabrications—which nonetheless will still remain fabrications. Mathematics gives us a shining example of how far, independently of experience, we can progress in *a priori* knowledge. It does, indeed, occupy itself with objects and with knowledge solely insofar as they allow of being exhibited in intuition. But this circumstance is easily overlooked, since this intuition can itself be given *a priori* and is therefore hardly to be distinguished from a bare and pure concept. Misled by such a proof of the power of reason, the demand for the extension of knowledge recognises no limits. The light dove, cleaving the air in her free flight, and feeling its resistance, might imagine that its flight would be still easier in empty space. It was thus that Plato left the world of the senses, as setting too narrow limits to the understanding, and ventured out beyond it on the wings of the ideas, in the empty space of the pure understanding. He did not observe that with all his efforts he made no advance—meeting no resistance that might, as it were, serve as a support upon which he could take a stand, to which he could apply his powers, and so set his understanding in motion. It is, indeed, the common fate of human reason to complete its speculative structures as speedily as may be, and only afterwards to enquire whether the foundations are reliable. All sorts of excuses will then be appealed to, in order to reassure us of their solidity, or rather indeed to enable us to dispense altogether with so late and so dangerous an enquiry. But what keeps us, during the actual building, free from all apprehension and suspicion, and flatters us with a seeming thoroughness, is this other circumstance, namely, that a great, perhaps the greatest, part of the business of our reason consists in analysis of the concepts which we already have of objects. This analysis supplies us with a considerable body of knowledge, which, while nothing but explanation or elucidation of what has already been thought in our concepts, though in a confused manner, is yet prized as being, at least as regards its form, new insight. But so far as the matter or content is concerned, there has been no extension of our previously possessed concepts, but only an analysis of them. Since this procedure yields real knowledge *a priori*, which progresses in an assured and useful fashion, reason is so far misled as surreptitiously to introduce, without itself being aware of so doing, assertions of an entirely different order, in which it attaches to given concepts others completely foreign to them, and moreover attaches them *a priori*. And yet it is not known how reason can be in position to do this. Such a question is never so much as thought of. I shall therefore at once proceed to deal with the difference between these two kinds of knowledge.

IV. THE DISTINCTION BETWEEN ANALYTIC AND SYNTHETIC JUDGEMENTS

In all judgements in which the relation of a subject to the predicate is thought (I take into consideration affirmative judgements only, the subsequent application to negative judgements being easily made), this relation is possible in two different ways. Either the predicate B belongs to the subject A, as something which is (covertly) contained in this concept A; or B lies outside the concept A, although it does indeed stand in connection with it. In the one case I entitle the judgement analytic, in the other synthetic. Analytic judgements (affirmative) are therefore those in which the connection of the predicate with the subject is thought through identity; those in which this connection is thought without identity should be entitled synthetic. The former, as adding nothing through the predicate to the concept of the subject, but merely breaking it up into those constituent concepts that have all along been thought in it, although confusedly, can also be entitled explicative. The latter, on the other hand, add to the concept of the subject a predicate which has not been in any wise thought in it, and which no analysis could possibly extract from it; and they may therefore be entitled ampliative. If I say, for instance, "All bodies are extended," this is an analytic judgement. For I do not require to go beyond the concept which I connect with "body" in order to find extension as bound up with it. To meet with this predicate, I have merely to analyse the concept, that is, to become conscious to myself of the manifold which I always think in that concept: The judgement is therefore analytic. But when I say, "All bodies are heavy," the predicate is something quite different from anything that I think in the mere concept of body in general; and the addition of such a predicate therefore yields a synthetic judgement.

Judgements of experience, as such, are one and all synthetic. For it would be absurd to found an analytic judgement on experience. Since, in framing the judgement, I must not go outside my concept, there is no need to appeal to the testimony of experience in its support. That a body is extended is a proposition that holds *a priori* and is not empirical. For, before appealing to experience, I have already in the concept of body all the conditions required for my judgement. I have only to extract from it, in accordance with the principle of contradiction, the required predicate, and in so doing can at the same time become conscious of the necessity of the judgement—and that is what experience could never have taught me. On the other hand, though I do not include in the concept of a body in general the predicate "weight," nonetheless this concept indicates an object of experience through one of its parts, and I can add to that part other parts of this same experience, as in this way belonging together with the concept. From the start I can apprehend the concept of body analytically through the characters of extension, impenetrability, figure, etc., all of which are thought in the concept. Now, however, looking back on the experience from which I have derived this concept of body, and finding weight to be invariably connected with the above characters, I attach it as a predicate to the concept; and in doing so I attach it synthetically, and am therefore extending my knowledge. The possibility of the synthesis of the predicate "weight" with the concept of "body" thus rests upon experience. While the one concept is not contained in the other, they yet belong to one another, though only contingently, as parts of a whole, namely, of an experience which is itself a synthetic combination of intuitions.

But in *a priori* synthetic judgements this help is entirely lacking [I do not here have the advantage of looking around in the field of experience.] Upon what, then, am I to rely, when I seek to go beyond the concept A, and to know that another concept B is connected with it? Through what is the synthesis made possible? Let us take the proposition, "Everything which happens has its cause." In the concept of "something which happens," I do indeed think an existence which is preceded by a time, etc., and from this concept analytic judgements may be obtained. But the concept of a "cause" lies entirely outside the other concept, and signifies something different from "that which happens," and is not therefore in any way contained in this latter representation. How come I then to predicate of that which happens something quite different, and to apprehend that the concept of cause, though not contained in it, yet belongs, and indeed necessarily belongs, to it? What is here the unknown = X which gives support to the understanding when it believes that it can discover outside the concept A a predicate B foreign to this concept, which it yet at the same time considers to be connected with it? It cannot be experience, because the suggested principle has connected the second representation with the first, not only with greater universality, but also with the character of necessity, and therefore completely *a priori* and on the basis of mere concepts. Upon such synthetic, that is, ampliative principles, all our *a priori* speculative knowledge must ultimately rest; analytic judgements are very important, and indeed necessary, but only for obtaining that clearness in the concepts which is requisite for such a sure and wide synthesis as will lead to a genuinely new addition to all previous knowledge.

STUDY QUESTIONS

1. Explain Kant's distinction between knowledge *a priori* and knowledge *a posteriori*.
2. Explain Kant's distinction between analytic and synthetic judgments.
3. According to Kant, why are analytic propositions important?
4. Do you agree with Kant that some propositions might be synthetic but known *a priori*?

PART 4

Mind

The Ghost in the Machine

GILBERT RYLE

Philosophers sometimes consider questions about the fundamental nature of the world. Does every event have a cause? Do human beings possess free will? Does each person consist of a soul connected to a body? Such issues belong to the field of philosophy known as "metaphysics," a Greek term meaning "after physics," so called because when Aristotle's works were first catalogued more than two millennia ago, the treatise in which he discussed such matters was placed after his treatise on physics.

One of the central issues in metaphysics is commonly referred to by philosophers as "the mind–body problem." Are you identical with your body, your mind, or some combination of the two? If you are a combination, how are the mind and body connected so as to form one person?

An influential writer on these matters is Gilbert Ryle (1900–1976), who was Professor of Philosophy at the University of Oxford. He argues that it is a mistake to suppose that the mind is something inside the body, a "ghost in the machine." Such a misconception Ryle calls a "category mistake," the sort of error that would be committed by one who, having been shown a college's classrooms, offices, playing fields, and libraries, would then ask, "But where is the university?" The university, of course, is not a separate building that one can see, and Ryle believes that the mind is not a separate entity that one can sense.

THE OFFICIAL DOCTRINE

There is a doctrine about the nature and place of minds which is so prevalent among theorists and even among laymen that it deserves to be described as the official theory. Most philosophers, psychologists and religious teachers subscribe, with minor reservations, to its main articles and, although they admit certain theoretical difficulties in it, they tend to assume that these can be overcome without serious modifications being made to the architecture of the theory. It will be argued here that the central principles of the doctrine are unsound and conflict with the whole body of what we know about minds when we are not speculating about them.

The official doctrine, which hails chiefly from Descartes, is something like this. With the doubtful exceptions of idiots and infants in arms, every human being

From *The Concept of Mind,* by Gilbert Ryle, Hutchinson and Co., 1949. Reprinted by permission of Taylor & Francis Books UK and the Principal, Fellows and Scholars of Hertford College at Oxford University.

has both a body and a mind. Some would prefer to say that every human being is both a body and a mind. His body and his mind are ordinarily harnessed together, but after the death of the body his mind may continue to exist and function.

Human bodies are in space and are subject to the mechanical laws which govern all other bodies in space. Bodily processes and states can be inspected by external observers. So a man's bodily life is as much a public affair as are the lives of animals and reptiles and even as the careers of trees, crystals and planets.

But minds are not in space, nor are their operations subject to mechanical laws. The workings of one mind are not witnessable by other observers; its career is private. Only I can take direct cognisance of the states and processes of my own mind. A person therefore lives through two collateral histories, one consisting of what happens in and to his body, the other consisting of what happens in and to his mind. The first is public, the second private. The events in the first history are events in the physical world, those in the second are events in the mental world.

It has been disputed whether a person does or can directly monitor all or only some of the episodes of his own private history; but, according to the official doctrine, of at least some of these episodes he has direct and unchallengeable cognisance. In consciousness, self-consciousness and introspection he is directly and authentically apprised of the present states and operations of his mind. He may have great or small uncertainties about concurrent and adjacent episodes in the physical world, but he can have none about at least part of what is momentarily occupying his mind.

It is customary to express this bifurcation of his two lives and of his two worlds by saying that the things and events which belong to the physical world, including his own body, are external, while the workings of his own mind are internal. This antithesis of outer and inner is of course meant to be construed as a metaphor, since minds, not being in space, could not be described as being spatially inside anything else, or as having things going on spatially inside themselves. But relapses from this good intention are common and theorists are found speculating how stimuli, the physical sources of which are yards or miles outside a person's skin, can generate mental responses inside his skull, or how decisions framed inside his cranium can set going movements of his extremities.

Even when "inner" and "outer" are construed as metaphors, the problem how a person's mind and body influence one another is notoriously charged with theoretical difficulties. What the mind wills, the legs, arms and the tongue execute; what affects the ear and the eye has something to do with what the mind perceives; grimaces and smiles betray the mind's moods; and bodily castigations lead, it is hoped, to moral improvement. But the actual transactions between the episodes of the private history and those of the public history remain mysterious, since by definition they can belong to neither series. They could not be reported among the happenings described in a person's autobiography of his inner life, but nor could they be reported among those described in someone else's biography of that person's overt career. They can be inspected neither by introspection nor by laboratory experiment. They are theoretical shuttlecocks which are forever being bandied from the physiologist back to the psychologist and from the psychologist back to the physiologist.

Underlying this partly metaphorical representation of the bifurcation of a person's two lives there is a seemingly more profound and philosophical assumption. It is assumed that there are two different kinds of existence or status. What exists or happens may have the status of physical existence, or it may have the status of mental existence. Somewhat as the faces of coins are either heads or tails, or somewhat as living creatures are either male or female, so, it is supposed, some existing is physical existing, other existing is mental existing. It is a necessary feature of what has physical existence that it is in space and time; it is a necessary feature of what has mental existence that it is in time but not in space. What has physical existence is composed of matter, or else is a function of matter; what has mental existence consists of consciousness, or else is a function of consciousness.

There is thus a polar opposition between mind and matter, an opposition which is often brought out as follows. Material objects are situated in a common field, known as "space," and what happens to one body in one part of space is mechanically connected with what happens to other bodies in other parts of space. But mental happenings occur in insulated fields, known as "minds," and there is, apart maybe from telepathy, no direct causal connection between what happens in one mind and what happens in another. Only through the medium of the public physical world can the mind of one person make a difference to the mind of another. The mind is its own place and in his inner life each of us lives the life of a ghostly Robinson Crusoe. People can see, hear and jolt one another's bodies, but they are irremediably blind and deaf to the workings of one another's minds and inoperative upon them. . . .

THE ABSURDITY OF THE OFFICIAL DOCTRINE

Such in outline is the official theory. I shall often speak of it, with deliberate abusiveness, as "the dogma of the Ghost in the Machine." I hope to prove that it is entirely false, and false not in detail but in principle. It is not merely an assemblage of particular mistakes. It is one big mistake and a mistake of a special kind. It is, namely, a category mistake. It represents the facts of mental life as if they belonged to one logical type or category (or range of types or categories), when they actually belong to another. The dogma is therefore a philosopher's myth. . . .

I must first indicate what is meant by the phrase "category mistake." This I do in a series of illustrations.

A foreigner visiting Oxford or Cambridge for the first time is shown a number of colleges, libraries, playing fields, museums, scientific departments and administrative offices. He then asks, "But where is the University? I have seen where the members of the Colleges live, where the Registrar works, where the scientists experiment and the rest. But I have not yet seen the University in which reside and work the members of your University." It has then to be explained to him that the University is not another collateral institution, some ulterior counterpart to the colleges, laboratories and offices which he has seen. The University is just the way in which all that he has already seen is organized. When they are seen and when their coordination is understood, the University has been seen. His mistake lay in his innocent assumption that it was correct to speak of Christ Church, the Bodleian Library, the Ashmolean Museum *and* the University, to speak, that is, as if "the University" stood for an extra member of the class of which these other units are members. He was mistakenly allocating the University to the same category as that to which the other institutions belong.

The same mistake would be made by a child witnessing the march-past of a division, who, having had pointed out to him such and such battalions, batteries, squadrons, etc., asked when the division was going to appear. He would be supposing that a division was a counterpart to the units already seen, partly similar to them and partly unlike them. He would be shown his mistake by being told that in watching the battalions, batteries, and squadrons marching past he had been watching the division marching past. The march-past was not a parade of battalions, batteries, squadrons *and* a division; it was a parade of the battalions, batteries and squadrons *of* a division.

One more illustration. A foreigner watching his first game of cricket learns what are the functions of the bowlers, the batsmen, the fielders, the umpires and the scorers. He then says, "But there is no one left on the field to contribute the famous element of team spirit. I see who does the bowling, the batting and the wicket-keeping; but I do not see whose role it is to exercise *esprit de corps*." Once more, it would have to be explained that he was looking for the wrong type of thing. Team spirit is not another cricketing-operation supplementary to all of the other special tasks. It is, roughly, the keenness with which each of the special tasks is performed, and performing a task keenly is not performing two tasks. Certainly exhibiting team spirit is not the same thing as bowling or catching, but nor is it a third thing such that we can say that the bowler first bowls *and* then exhibits team spirit or that a fielder is at a given moment *either* catching *or* displaying *esprit de corps*.

These illustrations of category mistakes have a common feature which must be noticed. The mistakes were made by people who did not know how to wield the concepts *University, division* and *team spirit*. Their puzzles arose from inability to use certain items in the English vocabulary.

The theoretically interesting category mistakes are those made by people who are perfectly competent to apply concepts, at least in the situations with which they are familiar, but are still liable in their abstract thinking to allocate those concepts to logical types to which they do not belong. An instance of a mistake of this sort would be the following story. A student of politics has learned the main differences between the British, the French and the American Constitutions, and has learned also the differences and connections between the Cabinet, Parliament, the various Ministries, the Judicature and the Church of England. But he still becomes embarrassed when asked questions about the connections between the Church of England, the Home Office and the British Constitution. For while the Church and the Home Office are institutions, the British Constitution is not another institution in the same sense of that noun. So inter-institutional relations which can be asserted or denied to hold between the Church and the Home Office cannot be asserted or denied to hold between either of them and the British Constitution. "The British Constitution" is not a term of the same logical type as "the Home Office" and "the Church of England." In a partially similar way, John Doe may be a relative, a friend, an enemy or a stranger to Richard Roe; but he cannot be any of these things to the Average Taxpayer. He knows how to talk sense in certain sorts of discussions about the Average Taxpayer, but he is baffled to say why he could not come across him in the street as he can come across Richard Roe.

It is pertinent to our main subject to notice that, so long as the student of politics continues to think of the British Constitution as a counterpart to the other institutions, he will tend to describe it as a mysteriously occult institution; and so long as John Doe continues to think of the Average Taxpayer as a fellow citizen, he will tend to think of him as an elusive insubstantial man, a ghost who is everywhere yet nowhere.

My destructive purpose is to show that a family of radical category mistakes is the source of the double-life theory. The representation of a person as a ghost mysteriously ensconced in a machine derives from this argument.

STUDY QUESTIONS

1. What does Ryle mean by "the dogma of the Ghost in the Machine"?
2. What does Ryle mean by a "category mistake"?
3. According to Ryle, how does the dogma of the Ghost in the Machine involve a category mistake?
4. Present your own example of a category mistake.

Body and Soul

RICHARD TAYLOR

Dualism is the view that a person is a combination of a mind and a body. Materialism is the view that a person is just a body. If the materialist is correct, then how can a person think and feel? Can a mere body do that?

These issues are explored in the next article, by Richard Taylor (1919–2003), who was Professor of Philosophy at the University of Rochester.

....

All forms of dualism arise from the alleged disparity between persons and physical objects. People, it is rightly noted, are capable of thinking, believing, feeling, wishing, and so on, but bodies, it is claimed, are capable of none of these things, and the conclusion is drawn that people are not bodies. Yet it cannot be denied that they *have* bodies; hence, it is decided that a person is a nonphysical entity, somehow more or less intimately related to a body. But here it is rarely noted that whatever difficulties there may be in applying personal and psychological predicates and descriptions to bodies, precisely the same difficulties are involved in applying such predicates and descriptions to *anything whatever,* including spirits or souls. If, for example, a philosopher reasons that a body cannot think and thereby affirms that, since a person thinks, a person is a soul or spirit or mind rather than a body, we are entitled to ask how a spirit can think. For surely if a spirit or soul can think, we can affirm that a body can do so; and if we are asked *how* a body can think, our reply can be that it thinks in precisely the manner in which the dualist supposes a soul thinks. The difficulty of imagining how a body thinks is not in the least lessened by asserting that something else, which is not a body, thinks. And so it is with every other personal predicate or description. Whenever faced with the dualist's challenge to explain how a body can have desires, wishes, how it can deliberate, choose, repent, how it can be intelligent or stupid, virtuous or wicked, and so on, our reply can always be: The body can do these things, and be these things, in whatever manner one imagines the soul can do these things and be these things. For to repeat, the difficulty here is in seeing how *anything at all* can deliberate, choose, repent, think, be virtuous or wicked, and so on, and *that* difficulty is not removed but simply glossed over by the invention of some new thing, henceforth to be called the "mind" or "soul."

It becomes quite obvious what is the source of dualistic metaphysics when the dualist or soul philosopher is pressed for some description of the mind or soul. The mind or soul, it turns out in such descriptions, is just whatever it is that thinks, reasons, deliberates, chooses, feels, and so on. But the fact with which we began was that *human beings* think, reason, deliberate, choose, feel, and so on. And we do in fact have some fairly clear notion of what we mean by a human being, for we think of an individual person as existing in space and time, having a certain height and weight—as a being, in short, having many things in common with other objects in space and time, and particularly with those that are living, i.e., with other animals. But the dualist, noting that a human being is significantly different from other beings, insofar as he, unlike most of them, is capable of thinking, deliberating, choosing, and so on, suddenly asserts that it is not a person, as previously conceived, that does these things at all, but something else, namely, a mind or soul, or something that does not exist in space and time nor have any height and weight, nor have, in fact, any material properties at all. And then when we seek some understanding of what this mind or soul is, we find it simply described as a thing that thinks, deliberates, feels, and so on. But surely the proper inference should have been that people are like all other physical objects in some respects— e.g., in having size, mass, and location in space and time; that they are like some physical objects but unlike others in certain further respects—e.g., in being living, sentient, and so on; and like no other physical objects at all in still other respects—e.g., in being rational, deliberative, and so on. And of course none of this suggests that people are not physical objects, but rather that they are precisely physical objects, like other bodies in some ways, unlike many other bodies in other ways, and unlike any other bodies in still other respects.

The dualist or soul philosopher reasons that since people think, feel, desire, choose, and so on, and since such things cannot be asserted of bodies, then people are not bodies. Reasoning in this fashion, we are forced to the conclusion that people are not bodies—though it is a stubborn fact that they nevertheless *have* bodies. So the great problem then is to connect people, now conceived as souls or minds, to their bodies. But philosophically, it is just exactly as good to reason that, since people think, feel, desire, choose, etc., and since people are bodies—i.e., are living animal organisms having the essential material attributes of weight, size, and so on—then *some* bodies think, feel, desire, choose, etc. This argument is just as good as the dualist's argument and does not lead us into a morass of problems concerning the connection between soul and body. . . .

This point can perhaps be borne home to the imagination by the following sort of consideration: Suppose one feels, as probably everyone more or less does, that a *person* cannot be a mere *body,* and that no increase in the physical, biological, and physiological complexity of any body can bridge the gulf between being a body, albeit a complicated and living one, and being a person. Consider, then, a highly complex and living animal organism, physically and biologically identical in every respect to a living man, but lacking that one thing that is, we are supposing, still needed in order to convert this body into a person. Now just what can this extra essential ingredient be? What do we need to *add* to convert a mere body into a person?

Let us suppose it is a *soul.* If we add a soul to this living, complicated animal organism, let us suppose, then *lo!* it will cease to be a mere body and become a person. No one knows, however, exactly what a soul is or what properties it must possess in order to confer personality upon something. All we can say is that it is what distinguishes a person from a mere body, which of course tells us nothing here. So let us give it some definite properties. It does not matter what properties we give it, as we shall shortly see, so to make it simple and easy to grasp, let us suppose that this soul is a small round ball, about the size of a marble, transparent and indestructible. Now clearly, by implanting *that* anywhere in the living organism we get no closer to converting it from a mere body to a person. We manage only to add one further, trivial complication. But why so? Why are we now no closer to having a person than before? Is it just because the "soul" we added is itself a mere body? If that is the difficulty, then let us remove its corporeality. Let us suppose that the soul we add to this living animal organism is not a small round *physical* ball but a non-physical one. This will permit us to retain its transparency. If, being nonphysical, it can no longer be described as a ball, then we can drop that part of the description too. Let the thing we add be, in short, anything one likes. Let it be a small hard ball, a small soft ball, an immaterial ball, or something that is neither material nor a ball. The point is that no matter *what* it is that is added, it goes not the least way toward converting what was a mere body into a person. If a small hard ball does not bridge the gap, then we get no closer to bridging it by simply removing its properties of hardness, smallness, and sphericity—by making it, in short, something that is merely *non*physical. What we need to do is state just what positive properties this extra thing must possess, in order to elevate an animal body to the status of a person, and no positive properties suggest themselves at all. We cannot give it psychological properties—by saying, for example, that this soul thinks, desires, deliberates, wills, believes, repents, and so on; for if the thing we are adding has *those* properties, then it is *already* a person in its own right, and there is no question of *adding* it to something in order to *get* a person. We could as easily have given *those* properties to the animal organism with which we began as to give them to something else and then superfluously amalgamate the two things. Plainly, there are no positive properties of any "soul" that will do the trick. The best we can do is to say that the extra something required—the soul, or the mind, or whatever we choose to call this additional thing—is that which, when added, makes up the difference between being a mere animal body and being a person. This is about as good a way as one could find for indicating that he has no idea what he is talking about.

STUDY QUESTIONS

1. According to Taylor, how do all forms of dualism arise?
2. Can a physical object think?
3. Because a person can think, does it follow that a person is more than a physical object?
4. What does Taylor mean by a "soul"?

The Mind–Body Problem

PAUL M. CHURCHLAND

Paul M. Churchland is Professor Emeritus of Philosophy at the University of California, San Diego. He explores different forms of dualism, concluding that none is persuasive.

From Paul M. Churchland, *Matter and Consciousness,* third edition, MIT Press, 2013. Reprinted by permission of the publisher.

The dualistic approach to mind encompasses several quite different theories, but they are all agreed that the essential nature of conscious intelligence resides in something *nonphysical*, in something forever beyond the scope of sciences like physics, neurophysiology, and computer science. Dualism is not the most widely held view in the current philosophical and scientific community, but it is the most common theory of mind in the public at large, it is deeply entrenched in most of the world's popular religions, and it has been the dominant theory of mind for most of Western history. It is thus an appropriate place to begin our discussion.

SUBSTANCE DUALISM

The distinguishing claim of this view is that each mind is a distinct nonphysical thing, an individual "package" of nonphysical substance, a thing whose identity is independent of any physical body to which it may be temporarily "attached." Mental states and activities derive their special character, on this view, from their being states and activities of this unique, nonphysical substance.

This leaves us wanting to ask for more in the way of a *positive* characterization of the proposed mind-stuff. It is a frequent complaint with the substance dualist's approach that his characterization of it is so far almost entirely negative. This need not be a fatal flaw, however, since we no doubt have much to learn about the underlying nature of mind, and perhaps the deficit here can eventually be made good. On this score, the philosopher René Descartes (1596–1650) has done as much as anyone to provide a positive account of the nature of the proposed mind-stuff, and his views are worthy of examination.

Descartes theorized that reality divides into two basic kinds of substance. The first is ordinary matter, and the essential feature of this kind of substance is that it is extended in space: any instance of it has length, breadth, and height and occupies a determinate position in space. Descartes did not attempt to play down the importance of this type of matter. On the contrary, he was one of the most imaginative physicists of his time, and he was an enthusiastic advocate of what was then called "the mechanical philosophy." But there was one isolated corner of reality he thought could not be accounted for in terms of the mechanics of matter: the conscious reason of Man. This was his motive for proposing a second and radically different kind of substance, a substance that has no spatial extension or spatial position whatever, a substance whose essential feature is the activity of *thinking*. This view is known as *Cartesian dualism*.

As Descartes saw it, the real *you* is not your material body, but rather a nonspatial thinking substance, an individual unit of mind-stuff quite distinct from your material body. This nonphysical mind is in systematic causal interaction with your body. The physical state of your body's sense organs, for example, causes visual/auditory/tactile experiences in your mind. And the desires and decisions of your nonphysical mind cause your body to behave in purposeful ways. Its causal connections to your mind are what make your body yours, and not someone else's.

The main reasons offered in support of this view were straightforward enough. First, Descartes thought that he could determine, by direct introspection alone, that he was essentially a thinking substance and nothing else. And second, he could not imagine how a purely physical system could ever use *language* in a relevant way, or engage in mathematical *reasoning,* as any normal human can. Whether these are good reasons, we shall discuss presently. Let us first notice a difficulty that even Descartes regarded as a problem.

If "mind-stuff" is so utterly different from "matter-stuff" in its nature—different to the point that it has no mass whatever, no shape whatever, and no position anywhere in space—then how is it possible for my mind to have any causal influence on my body at all? As Descartes himself was aware (he was one of the first to formulate the law of the conservation of momentum), ordinary matter in space behaves according to rigid laws, and one cannot get bodily movement (= momentum) from nothing. How is this utterly insubstantial "thinking substance" to have any influence on ponderous matter? How can two such different things be in any sort of causal contact? Descartes proposed a very subtle material substance—"animal spirits"—to convey the mind's influence to the body in general. But this does not provide us with a solution, since it leaves us with the same problem with which we started: how something ponderous and spatial (even "animal spirits") can interact with something entirely nonspatial.

In any case, the basic principle of division used by Descartes is no longer as plausible as it was in his day. It is now neither useful nor accurate to characterize ordinary matter as that-which-has-extension-in-space. Electrons, for example, are bits of matter, but our best current theories describe the electron as a point-particle with no extension whatever (it even lacks a determinate spatial position). And according to Einstein's theory of gravity, an entire star can achieve this same status, if it undergoes a complete gravitational collapse. If there truly is a division between mind and body, it appears that Descartes did not put his finger on the dividing line.

Such difficulties with Cartesian dualism provide a motive for considering a less radical form of substance dualism, and that is what we find in a view I shall call *popular dualism.* This is the theory that a person is literally a "ghost in a machine," where the machine is the human body, and the ghost is a spiritual substance, quite unlike physical matter in its internal constitution, but fully possessed of spatial properties even so. In particular, minds are commonly held to be *inside* the bodies they control; inside the head, on most views, in intimate contact with the brain.

This view need not have the difficulties of Descartes'. The mind is right there in contact with the brain, and their interaction can perhaps be understood in terms of their exchanging energy of a form that our science has not yet recognized or understood. Ordinary matter, you may recall, is just a form or manifestation of energy. (You may think of a grain of sand as a great deal of energy condensed or frozen into a small package, according to Einstein's relation, $E = mc^2$.) Perhaps mind-stuff is a well-behaved form or manifestation of energy also, but a different form of it. It is thus *possible* that a dualism of this alternative sort be consistent with familiar laws concerning the conservation of momentum and energy. This is fortunate for dualism, since those particular laws are very well established indeed.

This view will appeal to many for the further reason that it at least holds out the possibility (though it certainly does not guarantee) that the mind might survive the death of the body. It does not guarantee the mind's survival because it remains possible that the peculiar form of energy here supposed to constitute a mind can be produced and sustained only in conjunction with the highly intricate form of matter we call the brain, and must disintegrate when the brain disintegrates. So the prospects for surviving death are quite unclear even on the assumption that popular dualism is true. But even if survival were a clear consequence of the theory, there is a pitfall to be avoided here. Its promise of survival might be a reason for *wishing* dualism to be true, but it does not constitute a reason for *believing* that it *is* true. For that, we would need independent empirical evidence that minds do indeed survive the permanent death of the body. Regrettably, and despite the exploitative blatherings of the supermarket tabloids (TOP DOCS PROVE LIFE AFTER DEATH!!!), we possess no such evidence.

As we shall see later in this section, when we turn to evaluation, positive evidence for the existence of this novel, nonmaterial, thinking *substance* is in general on the slim side. This has moved many dualists to articulate still less extreme forms of dualism, in hopes of narrowing further the gap between theory and available evidence.

PROPERTY DUALISM

The basic idea of the theories under this heading is that while there is no *substance* to be dealt with here beyond the physical brain, the brain has a special set of *properties* possessed by no other kind of physical object. It is these special properties that are nonphysical: hence the term *property dualism*. The properties in question are the ones you would expect: the property of having a pain, of having a sensation of red, of thinking that *P*, of desiring that *Q*, and so forth. These are the properties that are characteristic of conscious intelligence. They are held to be nonphysical in the sense that they cannot ever be reduced to or explained solely in terms of the concepts of the familiar physical sciences. They will require a wholly new and autonomous science—the "science of mental phenomena"—if they are ever to be adequately understood.

From here, important differences among the positions emerge. Let us begin with what is perhaps the oldest version of property dualism: *epiphenomenalism*. This term is rather a mouthful, but its meaning is simple. The Greek prefix "epi-" means "above," and the position at issue holds that mental phenomena are not a part of the physical phenomena in the brain that ultimately determine our actions and behavior, but rather ride "above the fray." Mental phenomena are thus *epiphenomena*. They are held to just appear or emerge when the growing brain passes a certain level of complexity.

But there is more. The epiphenomenalist holds that while mental phenomena are caused to occur by the various activities of the brain, *they do not have any causal effects in turn.* They are entirely impotent with respect to causal effects on the physical world. They are *mere* epiphenomena. (To fix our ideas, a vague metaphor may be helpful here. Think of our conscious mental states as little sparkles of shimmering light that occur on the wrinkled surface of the brain, sparkles which are caused to occur by physical activity in the brain, but which have no causal effects on the brain in return.) This means that the universal conviction that one's actions are determined by one's desires, decisions, and volitions is false! One's actions are exhaustively determined by physical events in the brain, which events *also* cause the epiphenomena we call desires, decisions, and volitions. There is therefore a constant conjunction between volitions and actions. But according to the epiphenomenalist, it is mere illusion that the former cause the latter.

What could motivate such a strange view? In fact, it is not too difficult to understand why someone might take it seriously. Put yourself in the shoes of a neuroscientist who is concerned to trace the origins of behavior back up the motor nerves to the active cells in the motor cortex of the cerebrum, and to trace in turn their activity into inputs from other parts of the brain, and from the various sensory nerves. She finds a thoroughly physical system of awesome structure and delicacy, and much intricate activity, all of it unambiguously chemical or electrical in nature, and she finds no hint at all of any nonphysical inputs of the kind that substance dualism proposes. What is she to think? From the standpoint of her researches, human behavior is exhaustively a function of the activity of the physical brain. And this opinion is further supported by her confidence that the brain has the behavior-controlling features it does exactly because those features have been ruthlessly selected for during the brain's long evolutionary history. In sum, the seat of human behavior appears entirely physical in its constitution, in its origins, and in its internal activities.

On the other hand, our neuroscientist has the testimony of her own introspection to account for as well. She can hardly deny that she has experiences, beliefs, and desires, nor that they are connected in some way with her behavior. One bargain that can be struck here is to admit the *reality* of mental properties, as nonphysical properties, but demote them to the status of impotent epiphenomena that have nothing to do with the scientific explanation of human and animal behavior. This is the position the epiphenomenalist takes, and the reader can now perceive the rationale behind it. It is a bargain struck between the desire to respect a rigorously scientific approach to the explanation of behavior and the desire to respect the testimony of introspection.

The epiphenomenalist's "demotion" of mental properties—to causally impotent by-products of brain activity—has seemed too extreme for most property dualists, and a theory closer to the convictions of common sense has enjoyed somewhat greater popularity. This view, which we may call *interactionist property dualism,* differs from the previous view in only one essential respect: the interactionist asserts that mental properties do indeed have causal effects on the brain and, thereby, on behavior. The mental properties of the brain are an integrated part of the general causal fray, in systematic interaction with the brain's physical properties. One's actions, therefore, are held to be caused by one's desires and volitions after all.

As before, mental properties are here said to be *emergent* properties, properties that do not appear at all until ordinary physical matter has managed to organize itself, through the evolutionary process, into a system of sufficient complexity. Examples of properties that are emergent in this sense would be the property of being *solid*, the property of being *colored*, and the property of being *alive*. All of these require matter to be suitably organized before they can be displayed. With this much, any materialist will agree. But any property dualist makes the further claim that mental states and properties are *irreducible*, in the sense that they are not just organizational features of physical matter, as are the examples cited. They are said to be novel properties beyond prediction or explanation by physical science.

This last condition—the irreducibility of mental properties—is an important one, since this is what makes the position a dualist position. But it sits poorly with the joint claim that mental properties emerge from nothing more than the organizational achievements of physical matter. If that is how mental properties are produced, then one would expect a physical account of them to be possible. The simultaneous claim of evolutionary emergence *and* physical irreducibility is prima facie puzzling.

A property dualist is not absolutely bound to insist on both claims. He could let go the thesis of evolutionary emergence and also claim that mental properties are *fundamental* properties of reality, properties that have been here from the universe's inception, properties on a par with length, mass, electric charge, and other fundamental properties. There is even an historical precedent for a position of this kind. At the turn of this century it was still widely believed that electromagnetic phenomena (such as electric charge and magnetic attraction) were just an unusually subtle manifestation of purely *mechanical* phenomena. Some scientists thought that a reduction of electromagnetics to mechanics was more or less in the bag. They thought that radio waves, for example, would turn out to be just travelling oscillations in a very subtle but jellylike aether that fills space everywhere. But the aether turned out not to exist. So electromagnetic properties turned out to be fundamental properties in their own right, and we were forced to add electric charge to the existing list of fundamental properties (mass, length, and duration).

Perhaps mental properties enjoy a status like that of electromagnetic properties: irreducible, but not emergent. Such a view may be called *elemental-property dualism*, and it has the advantage of clarity over the previous view. Unfortunately, the parallel with electromagnetic phenomena has one very obvious failure. Unlike electromagnetic properties, which are displayed at all levels of reality from the subatomic level on up, mental properties are displayed only in large physical systems that have evolved a very complex internal organization. The case for the evolutionary emergence of mental properties through the organization of matter is extremely strong. They do not appear to be basic or elemental at all. This returns us, therefore, to the issue of their irreducibility. Why should we accept this most basic of the dualist's claims? Why be a dualist?

ARGUMENTS FOR DUALISM

Here we shall examine some of the main considerations commonly offered in support of dualism. Criticism will be postponed for a moment so that we may appreciate the collective force of these supporting considerations.

A major source of dualistic convictions is the religious belief many of us bring to these issues. Each of the major religions is in its way a theory about the cause or purpose of the universe, and Man's place within it, and many of them are committed to the notion of an immortal soul—that is, to some form of substance dualism. Supposing that one is consistent, to consider disbelieving dualism is to consider disbelieving one's religious heritage, and some of us find that difficult to do. Call this the *argument from religion.*

A more universal consideration is the *argument from introspection.* The fact is, when you center your attention on the contents of your consciousness, you do not clearly apprehend a neural network pulsing with electrochemical activity: you apprehend a flux of thoughts, sensations, desires, and emotions. It seems that mental states and properties, as revealed in introspection, could hardly be more different from physical states and properties if they tried. The verdict of introspection, therefore, seems strongly on the side of some form of dualism—on the side of property dualism, at a minimum.

A cluster of important considerations can be collected under the *argument from irreducibility.* Here one points to a variety of mental phenomena where it seems clear that no purely physical explanation could possibly account for what is going on. Descartes has already cited our ability to use language in a way that is relevant to our changing circumstances, and he was impressed also with our faculty of Reason, particularly as it is displayed in our capacity for mathematical reasoning. These abilities, he thought, must surely be beyond the capacity of any physical system. More recently, the introspectible qualities of our sensations (sensory "qualia"), and the meaningful content of our thoughts and beliefs, have also been cited as phenomena that will forever resist reduction to the physical. Consider, for example, seeing the color or smelling the fragrance of a rose. A physicist or chemist might know everything about the molecular structure of the rose, and of the human brain, argues the dualist, but that knowledge would not enable him to predict or anticipate the quality of these inexpressible experiences.

Finally, parapsychological phenomena are occasionally cited in favor of dualism. Telepathy (mind reading), precognition (seeing the future), telekinesis (thought control of material objects), and clairvoyance (knowledge of distant objects) are all awkward to explain within the normal confines of psychology and physics. If these phenomena are real, they might well be reflecting the super-physical nature that the dualist ascribes to the mind. Trivially they are *mental* phenomena, and if they are also forever beyond physical explanation, then at least some mental phenomena must be irreducibly nonphysical.

Collectively, these considerations may seem compelling. But there are serious criticisms of each, and we must examine them as well. Consider first the argument from religion. There is certainly nothing wrong in principle with appealing to a more general theory that bears on the case at issue, which is what the appeal to religion amounts to. But the appeal can only be as good as the scientific credentials of the religion(s) being appealed to, and here the appeals tend to fall down rather badly. In general, attempts to decide scientific questions by appeal to religious orthodoxy have a very sorry history. That the stars are other suns, that the earth is not the center of the universe, that diseases are caused by microorganisms, that the earth is billions of years old, that life is a physicochemical phenomenon; all of these crucial insights were strongly and sometimes viciously resisted, because the dominant religion of the time happened to think otherwise. Giordano Bruno was burned at the stake for urging the first view; Galileo was forced by threat of torture in the Vatican's basement to recant the second view; the firm belief that disease was a punishment visited by the Devil allowed public health practices that brought chronic plagues to most of the cities of Europe; and the age of the earth and the evolution of life were forced to fight an uphill battle against religious prejudice even in an age of supposed enlightenment.

History aside, the almost universal opinion that one's own religious convictions are the reasoned outcome of a dispassionate evaluation of all of the major alternatives is almost demonstrably false for humanity in general. If that really were the genesis of most people's convictions, then one would expect the major faiths to be distributed more or less randomly or evenly over the globe. But in fact they show a very strong tendency to cluster: Christianity is centered in Europe and the Americas, Islam in Africa and the Middle East, Hinduism in India, and Buddhism in the Orient. Which illustrates what we all suspected anyway: that *social forces* are the primary determinants of religious belief for people in general. To decide scientific questions by appeal to religious orthodoxy would therefore be to put social forces in place of empirical evidence. For all of these reasons, professional scientists and philosophers concerned with the nature of mind generally do their best to keep religious appeals out of the discussion entirely.

The argument from introspection is a much more interesting argument, since it tries to appeal to the direct experience of everyman. But the argument is deeply suspect, in that it assumes that our faculty of inner observation or introspection reveals things as they really are in their innermost nature. This assumption is suspect because we already know that our other forms of observation—sight, hearing, touch, and so on—do no such thing. The red surface of an apple does not *look* like a matrix of molecules reflecting photons at certain critical wavelengths, but that is what it is. The sound of a flute does not *sound* like a sinusoidal compression wave train in the atmosphere, but that is what it is. The warmth of the summer air does not *feel* like the mean kinetic energy of millions of tiny molecules, but that is what it is. If one's pains and hopes and beliefs do not *introspectively* seem like electrochemical states in a neural network, that may be only because our faculty of introspection, like our other senses, is not sufficiently penetrating to reveal such hidden details. Which is just what one would expect anyway. The argument from introspection is therefore entirely without force, unless we can somehow argue that the faculty of introspection is quite different from all other forms of observation.

The argument from irreducibility presents a more serious challenge, but here also its force is less than first impression suggests. Consider first our capacity for mathematical reasoning which so impressed Descartes. The last ten years have made available, to anyone with fifty dollars to spend, electronic calculators whose capacity for mathematical reasoning—the calculational part, at least—far surpasses that of any normal human. The fact is, in the centuries since Descartes' writings, philosophers, logicians, mathematicians, and computer scientists have managed to isolate the general principles of mathematical reasoning, and electronics engineers have created machines that compute in accord with those principles. The result is a hand-held object that would have astonished Descartes. This outcome is impressive not just because machines have proved capable of some of the capacities boasted by human reason, but because some of those achievements invade areas of human reason that past dualistic philosophers have held up as forever closed to mere physical devices.

Although debate on the matter remains open, Descartes' argument from language use is equally dubious. The notion of a *computer language* is by now a commonplace: consider BASIC, PASCAL, FORTRAN, APL, LISP, and so on. Granted, these artificial "languages" are much simpler in structure and content than human natural language, but the differences may be differences only of degree, and not of kind. As well, the theoretical work of Noam Chomsky and the generative grammar approach to linguistics have done a great deal to explain the human capacity for language use in terms that invite simulation by computers. I do not mean to suggest that truly conversational computers are just around the corner. We have a great deal yet to learn, and fundamental problems yet to solve (mostly having to do with our capacity for inductive or theoretical reasoning). But recent progress here does nothing to support the claim that language use must be forever impossible for a purely physical system. On the contrary, such a claim now appears rather arbitrary and dogmatic.

The next issue is also a live problem: How can we possibly hope to explain or to predict the intrinsic qualities of our sensations, or the meaningful content of our beliefs and desires, in purely physical terms? This is a major challenge to the materialist. But as we shall see in later sections, active research programs are already under way on both problems, and positive suggestions are being explored. It is in fact not impossible to imagine how such explanations might go, though the materialist cannot yet pretend to have solved either problem. Until he does, the dualist will retain a bargaining chip here, but that is about all. What the dualists need in order to establish their case is the conclusion that a physical reduction is outright impossible, and that is a conclusion they have failed to establish. Rhetorical questions, like the one that opens this paragraph, do not constitute arguments. And it is equally difficult, note, to imagine how the relevant phenomena could be explained or predicted solely in terms of the substance dualist's nonphysical mind-stuff. The explanatory problem here is a major challenge to everybody, not just to the materialist. On this issue then, we have a rough standoff.

The final argument in support of dualism urged the existence of parapsycho-logical phenomena such as telepathy and telekinesis, the point being that such mental phenomena are (a) real and (b) beyond purely physical explanation. This argument is really another instance of the argument from irreducibility discussed above, and as before, it is not entirely clear that such phenomena, even if real, must forever escape a purely physical explanation. The materialist can already suggest a possible mechanism for telepathy, for example. On his view, thinking is an electrical activity within the brain. But according to electromagnetic theory, such changing motions of electric charges must produce electromagnetic waves radiating at the speed of light in all directions, waves that will contain information about the electrical activity that produced them. Such waves can subsequently have effects on the electrical activity of other brains, that is, on their thinking. Call this the "radio transmitter/receiver" theory of telepathy.

I do not for a moment suggest that this theory is true; the electromagnetic waves emitted by the brain are fantastically weak (billions of times weaker than the ever present background electromagnetic flux produced by commercial radio stations), and they are almost certain to be hopelessly jumbled together as well. This is one reason why, in the absence of systematic, compelling, and repeatable evidence for the existence of telepathy, one must doubt its possibility. But it is significant that the materialist has the theoretical resources to suggest a detailed possible explanation of telepathy, if it were real, which is more than any dualist has so far done. It is not at all clear, then, that the materialist *must* be at an explanatory disadvantage in these matters. Quite the reverse.

Put the preceding aside, if you wish, for the main difficulty with the argument from parapsychological phenomena is much, much simpler. Despite the endless pronouncements and anecdotes in the popular press, and despite a steady trickle of serious research on such things, there is no significant or trustworthy evidence that such phenomena even exist. The wide gap between popular conviction on this matter, and the actual evidence, is something that itself calls for research. For there is not a single parapsychological effect that can be repeatedly or reliably produced in any laboratory suitably equipped to perform and control the experiment. Not one. Honest researchers have been repeatedly hoodwinked by "psychic" charlatans with skills derived from the magician's trade, and the history of the subject is largely a history of gullibility, selection of evidence, poor experimental controls, and out-right fraud by the occasional researcher as well. If someone really does discover a repeatable parapsychological effect, then we shall have to reevaluate the situation, but as things stand, there is nothing here to support a dualist theory of mind.

Upon critical examination, the arguments in support of dualism lose much of their force. But we are not yet done: there are arguments against dualism, and these also require examination.

ARGUMENTS AGAINST DUALISM

The first argument against dualism urged by the materialists appeals to the greater *simplicity* of their view. It is a principle of rational methodology that, if all else is equal, the simpler of two competing hypotheses should be preferred. This principle is sometimes called "Ockham's Razor"—after William of Ockham, the medieval philosopher who first enunciated it—and it can also be expressed as follows: "Do not multiply entities beyond what is strictly necessary to explain the phenomena." The materialist postulates only one kind of substance (physical matter) and one class of properties (physical properties), whereas the dualist postulates two kinds of matter and/or two classes of properties. And to no explanatory advantage, charges the materialist.

This is not yet a decisive point against dualism, since neither dualism nor materialism can yet explain all of the phenomena to be explained. But the objection does have some force, especially since there is no doubt at all that physical matter exists, while spiritual matter remains a tenuous hypothesis.

If this latter hypothesis brought us some definite explanatory advantage obtainable in no other way, then we would happily violate the demand for simplicity, and we would be right to do so. But it does not, claims the materialist. In fact, the advantage is just the other way around, he argues, and this brings us to the second objection to dualism: the relative *explanatory impotence* of dualism as compared to materialism.

Consider, very briefly, the explanatory resources already available to the neurosciences. We know that the brain exists and what it is made of. We know much of its microstructure: how the neurons are organized into systems and how distinct systems are connected to one another, to the motor nerves going out to the muscles, and to the sensory nerves coming in from the sense organs. We know much of their microchemistry: how the nerve cells fire tiny electrochemical pulses along their various fibers, and how they make other cells fire also, or cease firing. We know some of how such activity processes sensory information, selecting salient or subtle bits to be sent on to higher systems. And we know some of how such activity initiates and coordinates bodily behavior. Thanks mainly to neurology (the branch of medicine concerned with brain pathology), we know a great deal about the correlations between damage to various parts of the human brain, and various behavioral and cognitive deficits from which the victims suffer. There are a great many isolated deficits—some gross, some subtle—that are familiar to neurologists (inability to speak, or to read, or to understand speech, or to recognize faces, or to add/subtract, or to move a certain limb, or to put information into long-term memory, and so on), and their appearance is closely tied to the occurrence of damage to very specific parts of the brain.

Nor are we limited to cataloguing traumas. The growth and development of the brain's microstructure is also something that neuroscience has explored, and such development appears to be the basis of various kinds of learning by the organism. Learning, that is, involves lasting chemical and physical changes in the brain. In sum, the neuroscientist can tell us a great deal about the brain, about its constitution and the physical laws that govern it; he can already explain much of our behavior in terms of the physical, chemical, and electrical properties of the brain; and he has the theoretical resources available to explain a good deal more as our explorations continue.

Compare now what the neuroscientist can tell us about the brain, and what he can do with that knowledge, with what the dualist can tell us about spiritual substance, and what he can do with those assumptions. Can the dualist tell us anything about the internal constitution of mind-stuff? Of the nonmaterial elements that make it up? Of the laws that govern their behavior? Of the mind's structural connections with the body? Of the manner of its operations? Can he explain human capacities and pathologies in terms of its structures and its defects? The fact is, the dualist can do none of these things, because no detailed theory of mind-stuff has ever been formulated. Compared to the rich resources and explanatory successes of current materialism, dualism is less a theory of mind than it is an empty space waiting for a genuine theory of mind to be put in it.

Thus argues the materialist. But again, this is not a completely decisive point against dualism. The dualist can admit that the brain plays a major role in the administration of both perception and behavior—on his view the brain is the *mediator* between the mind and the body—but he may attempt to argue that the materialist's current successes and future explanatory prospects concern only the mediative functions of the brain, not the *central* capacities of the nonphysical mind, capacities such as reason, emotion, and consciousness itself. On these latter topics, he may argue, both dualism *and* materialism currently draw a blank.

But this reply is not a very good one. So far as the capacity for reasoning is concerned, machines already exist that execute in minutes sophisticated deductive and mathematical calculations that would take a human a lifetime to execute. And so far as the other two mental capacities are concerned, studies of such things as depression, motivation, attention, and sleep have revealed many interesting and puzzling facts about the neurochemical and neurodynamical basis of both emotion and consciousness. The *central* capacities, no less than the peripheral, have been addressed with profit by various materialist research programs.

In any case, the (substance) dualist's attempt to draw a sharp distinction between the unique "mental" capacities proper to the nonmaterial mind, and the merely mediative capacities of the brain, prompts an argument that comes close to being an outright refutation of (substance) dualism. If there really is a distinct entity in which reasoning, emotion, and consciousness take place, and if that entity is dependent on the brain for nothing more than sensory experiences as input and volitional executions as output, *then one would expect reason, emotion, and consciousness to be relatively invulnerable to direct control or pathology by manipulation or damage to the brain.* But in fact the exact opposite is true. Alcohol, narcotics, or senile degeneration of nerve tissue will impair, cripple, or even destroy one's capacity for rational thought. Psychiatry knows of hundreds of emotion-controlling chemicals (lithium, chlorpromazine, amphetamine, cocaine, and so on) that do their work when vectored into the brain. And the vulnerability of consciousness to the anesthetics, to caffeine, and to something as simple as a sharp blow to the head shows its very close dependence on neural activity in the brain. All of this makes perfect sense if reason, emotion, and consciousness are activities of the brain itself. But it makes very little sense if they are activities of something else entirely.

We may call this the argument from the *neural dependence* of all known mental phenomena. Property dualism, note, is not threatened by this argument, since, like materialism, property dualism reckons the brain as the seat of all mental activity. We shall conclude this section, however, with an argument that cuts against both varieties of dualism: the argument from *evolutionary history*.

What is the origin of a complex and sophisticated species such as ours? What, for that matter, is the origin of the dolphin, the mouse, or the housefly? Thanks to the fossil record, comparative anatomy, and the biochemistry of proteins and nucleic acids, there is no longer any significant doubt on this matter. Each existing species is a surviving type from a number of variations on an earlier type of organism; each earlier type is in turn a surviving type from a number of variations on a still earlier type of organism; and so on down the branches of the evolutionary tree until, some three billion years ago, we find a trunk of just one or a handful of very simple organisms. These organisms, like their more complex offspring, are just self-repairing, self-replicating, energy-driven molecular structures. (That evolutionary trunk has its own roots in an earlier era of purely chemical evolution, in which the molecular elements of life were themselves pieced together.) The mechanism of development that has structured this tree has two main elements: (1) the occasional blind variation in types of reproducing creature and (2) the selective survival of some of these types due to the relative reproductive advantage enjoyed by individuals of those types. Over periods of geological time, such a process can produce an enormous variety of organisms, some of them very complex indeed.

For purposes of our discussion, the important point about the standard evolutionary story is that the human species and all of its features are the wholly physical outcome of a purely physical process. Like all but the simplest of organisms, we have a nervous system. And for the same reason: a nervous system permits the discriminative guidance of behavior. But a nervous system is just an active matrix of cells, and a cell is just an active matrix of molecules. We are notable only in that our nervous system is more complex and powerful than those of our fellow creatures. Our inner nature differs from that of simpler creatures in degree, but not in kind.

If this is the correct account of our origins, then there seems neither need, nor room, to fit any nonphysical substances or properties into our theoretical account of ourselves. We are creatures of matter. And we should learn to live with that fact.

Arguments like these have moved most (but not all) of the professional community to embrace some form of materialism. This has not produced much unanimity, however, since the differences between the several materialist positions are even wider than the differences that divide dualism.

STUDY QUESTIONS

1. Explain the difference between substance dualism and property dualism.
2. Present two arguments in favor of dualism.
3. Present two arguments against dualism.
4. According to Churchland, what is the connection between evolution and dualism?

What Is It Like to Be a Bat?

THOMAS NAGEL

If materialism is correct and a person is identical with a body, can we explain
the phenomenon we all experience of being conscious? How can my body be
conscious? Is my consciousness like yours? Is ours like that of animals? This last
question is explored by Thomas Nagel, Professor of Philosophy at New York
University, who wonders what it would be like to be a bat and goes on to explain
how the question bears directly on the mind–body problem.

Conscious experience is a widespread phenomenon. It occurs at many levels of
animal life, though we cannot be sure of its presence in the simpler organisms, and
it is very difficult to say in general what provides evidence of it. (Some extremists have been prepared to deny it even of mammals other than man.) No doubt
it occurs in countless forms totally unimaginable to us, on other planets in other
solar systems throughout the universe. But no matter how the form may vary, the
fact that an organism has conscious experiences *at all* means, basically, that there
is something it is like to *be* that organism. . . .

We may call this the subjective character of experience. . . . It is useless to base
the defense of materialism on any analysis of mental phenomena that fails to deal
explicitly with their subjective character. . . . [T]o make evident the importance of
subjective features, it will help to explore the matter in relation to an example. . . .

I assume we all believe that bats have experience. After all, they are mammals, and there is no more doubt that they have experience than that mice or
pigeons or whales have experience. I have chosen bats instead of wasps or floun-
ders because if one travels too far down the phylogenetic tree, people gradually
shed their faith that there is experience there at all. Bats, although more closely
related to us than those other species, nevertheless present a range of activity
and a sensory apparatus so different from ours that the problem I want to pose is
exceptionally vivid (though it certainly could be raised with other species). Even
without the benefit of philosophical reflection, anyone who has spent some time
in an enclosed space with an excited bat knows what it is to encounter a fundamentally *alien* form of life.

I have said that the essence of the belief that bats have experience is that
there is something that it is like to be a bat. Now we know that most bats (the

From Thomas Nagel, "What Is It Like to Be a Bat?" in *The Philosophical Review*, Volume
LXXXIII, no. 4, pp. 435–450. Copyright © 1974 by Duke University Press. Reprinted by
permission of the publisher. All rights reserved.

microchiroptera, to be precise) perceive the external world primarily by sonar, or echolocation, detecting the reflections, from objects within range, of their own rapid, subtly modulated, high-frequency shrieks. Their brains are designed to correlate the outgoing impulses with the subsequent echoes, and the information thus acquired enables bats to make precise discrimination of distance, size, shape, motion, and texture comparable to those we make by vision. But bat sonar, though clearly a form of perception, is not similar in its operation to any sense that we possess, and there is no reason to suppose that it is subjectively like anything we can experience or imagine. This appears to create difficulties for the notion of what it is like to be a bat. We must consider whether any method will permit us to extrapolate to the inner life of the bat from our own case[1] and, if not, what alternative methods there may be for understanding the notion.

Our own experience provides the basic material for our imagination, whose range is therefore limited. It will not help to try to imagine that one has webbing on one's arms, which enables one to fly around at dusk and dawn catching insects in one's mouth; that one has very poor vision, and perceives the surrounding world by a system of reflected high-frequency sound signals; and that one spends the day hanging upside down by one's feet in an attic. Insofar as I can imagine this (which is not very far), it tells me only what it would be like for *me* to behave as a bat behaves. But that is not the question. I want to know what it is like for a *bat* to be a bat. Yet if I try to imagine this, I am restricted to the resources of my own mind, and those resources are inadequate to the task. I cannot perform it either by imagining additions to my present experience, or by imagining segments gradually subtracted from it, or by imagining some combination of additions, subtractions, and modifications.

To the extent that I could look and behave like a wasp or a bat without changing my fundamental structure, my experiences would not be anything like the experiences of those animals. On the other hand, it is doubtful that any meaning can be attached to the supposition that I should possess the internal neurophysiological constitution of a bat. Even if I could by gradual degrees be transformed into a bat, nothing in my present constitution enables me to imagine what the experiences of such a future stage of myself thus metamorphosed would be like. The best evidence would come from the experiences of bats, if we only knew what they were like.

So if extrapolation from our own case is involved in the idea of what it is like to be a bat, the extrapolation must be incompletable. We cannot form more than a schematic conception of what it *is* like. For example, we may ascribe general *types* of experience on the basis of the animal's structure and behavior. Thus we describe bat sonar as a form of three-dimensional forward perception; we believe that bats feel some versions of pain, fear, hunger, and lust and that they have other, more familiar types of perception besides sonar. But we believe that these experiences also have in each case a specific subjective character, which it is beyond our ability to conceive. And if there is conscious life elsewhere in the universe, it is likely that some of it will not be describable even in the most general experiential terms available to us.[2] (The problem is not confined to exotic cases, however, for it exists between one person and another. The subjective character of the experience of a person deaf and blind from birth is not accessible to me, for example, nor presumably is mine to him. This does not prevent us each from believing that the other's experience has such a subjective character.)

If anyone is inclined to deny that we can believe in the existence of facts like this whose exact nature we cannot possibly conceive, he should reflect that in contemplating the bats we are in much the same position that intelligent bats or Martians[3] would occupy if they tried to form a conception of what it was like to be us. The structure of their own minds might make it impossible for them to succeed, but we know they would be wrong to conclude that there is not anything precise that it is like to be us: that only certain general types of mental state could be ascribed to us (perhaps perception and appetite would be concepts common to us both; perhaps not). We know they would be wrong to draw such a skeptical conclusion because we know what it is like to be us. And we know that while it includes an enormous amount of variation and complexity, and while we do not possess the vocabulary to describe it adequately, its subjective character is highly specific, and in some respects describable in terms that can be understood only by creatures like us. The fact that we cannot expect ever to accommodate in our language a detailed description of Martian or bat phenomenology should not lead us to dismiss as meaningless the claim that bats and Martians have experiences fully comparable in richness of detail to our own. It would be fine if someone were to develop concepts and a theory that enabled us to think about those things, but such an understanding may be permanently denied to us by the limits of our nature. . . .

My realism about the subjective domain in all its forms implies a belief in the existence of facts beyond the reach of human concepts. Certainly it is possible for a human being to believe that there are facts which humans never *will* possess the requisite concepts to represent or comprehend. Indeed, it would be foolish to doubt this, given the finiteness of humanity's expectations. . . . But one might also believe that there are facts which *could* not ever be represented or comprehended by human beings, even if the species lasted for ever—simply because our structure does not permit us to operate with concepts of the requisite type. . . . Reflection on what it is like to be a bat seems to lead us, therefore, to the conclusion that there are facts that do not consist in the truth of propositions expressible in a human language. . . .

This bears directly on the mind–body problem. For if the facts of experience—facts about what it is like *for* the experiencing organism—are accessible only from one point of view, then it is a mystery how the true character of experiences could be revealed in the physical operation of that organism. The latter is a domain of objective facts par excellence—the kind that can be observed and understood from many points of view and by individuals with differing perceptual systems. There are no comparable imaginative obstacles to the acquisition of knowledge about bat neurophysiology by human scientists, and intelligent bats or Martians might learn more about the human brain than we ever will. . . .

In the case of experience, on the other hand, the connexion with a particular point of view seems much closer. It is difficult to understand what could be meant by the *objective* character of an experience, apart from the particular point of view from which its subject apprehends it. After all, what would be left of what it was like to be a bat if one removed the viewpoint of the bat?

NOTES

1. By "our own case," I do not mean just "my own case," but rather the mentalistic ideas that we apply unproblematically to ourselves and other human beings.
2. Therefore the analogical form of the English expression "what it is *like*" is misleading. It does not mean "what (in our experience) it *resembles*," but rather "how it is for the subject himself."
3. Any intelligent extraterrestrial beings totally different from us.

STUDY QUESTIONS

1. What does Nagel mean by "the subjective character of experience"?
2. Do you agree that bats have experiences?
3. Does Nagel believe in the existence of facts beyond the reach of human concept?
4. According to Nagel, how does reflection on what it is like to be a bat relate to the mind–body problem?

The Qualia Problem

FRANK JACKSON

Frank Jackson is Professor of Philosophy at Australian National University. He offers two examples to suggest that the world contains not only physical objects but also qualia, the felt qualities of experience. These present a challenge to materialism, sometimes referred to as physicalism.

People vary considerably in their ability to discriminate colors. Suppose that in an experiment to catalog this variation Fred is discovered. Fred has better color vision

From Frank Jackson, "Epiphenomenal Qualities," *Philosophical Quarterly*, 32 (1982). Reprinted by permission of Blackwell Publishing.

than anyone else on record; he makes every discrimination that anyone has ever made, and moreover he makes one that we cannot even begin to make. Show him a batch of ripe tomatoes and he sorts them into two roughly equal groups and does so with complete consistency. That is, if you blindfold him, shuffle the tomatoes up, and then remove the blindfold and ask him to sort them out again, he sorts them into exactly the same two groups.

We ask Fred how he does it. He explains that all ripe tomatoes do not look the same color to him, and in fact that this is true of a great many objects that we classify together as red. He sees two colors where we see one, and he has in consequence developed for his own use two words "red$_1$" and "red$_2$" to mark the difference. Perhaps he tells us that he has often tried to teach the difference between red$_1$ and red$_2$ to his friends but has gotten nowhere and has concluded that the rest of the world is red$_1$–red$_2$ color-blind—or perhaps he has had partial success with his children; it doesn't matter. In any case he explains to us that it would be quite wrong to think that because "red" appears in both "red$_1$" and "red$_2$," the two colors are shades of the one color. He only uses the common term "red" to fit more easily into our restricted usage. To him red$_1$ and red$_2$ are as different from each other and all the other colors as yellow is from blue. And his discriminatory behavior bears this out: He sorts red$_1$ from red$_2$ tomatoes with the greatest of ease in a wide variety of viewing circumstances. Moreover, an investigation of the physiological basis of Fred's exceptional ability reveals that Fred's optical system is able to separate out two groups of wavelengths in the red spectrum as sharply as we are able to sort out yellow from blue.

I think that we should admit that Fred can see, really see, at least one more color than we can; red$_1$ is a different color from red$_2$. We are to Fred as a totally red–green color-blind person is to us. H. G. Wells' story "The Country of the Blind" is about a sighted person in a totally blind community. This person never manages to convince them that he can see, that he has an extra sense. They ridicule this sense as quite inconceivable, and they treat his capacity to avoid falling into ditches, to win fights, and so on as precisely that capacity and nothing more. We would be making their mistake if we refused to allow that Fred can see one more color than we can.

What kind of experience does Fred have when he sees red$_1$ and red$_2$? What is the new color or colors like? We would dearly like to know but do not; and it seems that no amount of physical information about Fred's brain and optical system tells us. We find out perhaps that Fred's cones respond differentially to certain light waves in the red section of the spectrum that make no difference to ours (or perhaps he has an extra cone) and that this leads in Fred to a wider range of those brain states responsible for visual discriminatory behavior. But none of this tells us what we really want to know about his color experience. There is something about it we don't know. But we know, we may suppose, everything about Fred's body, his behavior and dispositions to behavior and about his internal physiology, and everything about his history and relation to others that can be given in physical accounts of persons. We have all the physical information. Therefore, knowing all this is *not* knowing everything about Fred. It follows that Physicalism leaves something out.

To reinforce this conclusion, imagine that as a result of our investigations into the internal workings of Fred we find out how to make everyone's physiology like Fred's in the relevant respects; or perhaps Fred donates his body to science and on his death we are able to transplant his optical system into someone else—again the fine detail doesn't matter. The important point is that such a happening would create enormous interest. People would say "At last we will know what it is like to see the extra color, at last we will know how Fred has differed from us in the way he has struggled to tell us about for so long." Then it cannot be that we knew all along all about Fred. But *ex hypothesi* we did know all along everything about Fred that features in the physicalist scheme; hence the physicalist scheme leaves something out.

Put it this way. *After* the operation, we will know *more* about Fred and especially about his color experiences. But beforehand we had all the physical information we could desire about his body and brain, and indeed everything that has ever featured in physicalist accounts of mind and consciousness. Hence there is more to know than all that. Hence Physicalism is incomplete.

Fred and the new color(s) are of course essentially rhetorical devices. The same point can be made with normal people and familiar colors. Mary is a brilliant scientist who is, for whatever reason, forced to investigate the world from a black-and-white room *via* a black-and-white television monitor. She specializes in the neurophysiology of vision and acquires, let us suppose, all the physical information there is to obtain about what goes on when we see ripe tomatoes, or the sky, and use terms like "red," "blue," and so on. She discovers, for example, just which wavelength combinations from the sky stimulate the retina, and exactly how this produces *via* the central nervous system the contraction of the vocal chords and expulsion of air from the lungs that results in the uttering of the sentence "The sky is blue."

What will happen when Mary is released from her black-and-white room or is given a color television monitor? Will she *learn* anything or not? It just seems obvious that she will learn something about the world and our visual experience of it. But then it is inescapable that her previous knowledge was incomplete. But she had *all* the physical information. *Ergo* there is more to have than that, and Physicalism is false.

Clearly the same style of Knowledge argument could be deployed for taste, hearing, the bodily sensations, and generally speaking for the various mental states that are said to have (as it is variously put) raw feels, phenomenal features, or qualia. The conclusion in each case is that the qualia are left out of the physicalist story. And the polemical strength of the Knowledge argument is that it is so hard to deny the central claim that one can have all the physical information without having all the information there is to have.

STUDY QUESTIONS

1. What are qualia?
2. Why do qualia present a problem for materialists?
3. Will Mary learn anything when she experiences colors?
4. If Mary learns something when she experiences colors, is materialism false?

Knowing What It's Like

DAVID LEWIS

A materialist believes that reality consists only of physical objects and their properties. Can materialism, however, account for phenomenal qualities, that is, what it is like to have a certain kind of experience? In the previous articles Nagel and Jackson raised this challenge to materialism. In our next selection David Lewis (1941–2001), who was Professor of Philosophy at Princeton University, provides an answer to anyone who would appeal to qualia to defend some version of a dualism of mind and body.

....

The most formidable challenge to any sort of *materialism* . . . comes from the friend of *phenomenal qualia*. He says we leave out the phenomenal aspect of mental life: we forget that pain is a feeling, that there is something it is like to hold one's hand in a flame, that we are aware of something when we suffer pain, that we can recognize that something when it comes again. . . .

Suppose he makes his case as follows.[1]

> You have not tasted Vegemite (a celebrated yeast based condiment). So you do not know what it is like to taste Vegemite. And you never will, unless you taste Vegemite. (Or unless the same experience, or counterfeit traces of it, are somehow produced in you by artificial means.) No amount of the information whereof materialists and functionalists speak will help you at all. But if you taste Vegemite, *then* you will know what it is like. So you will have gained a sort of information that the materialists and functionalists overlook entirely. Call this *phenomenal information*. By *qualia* I mean the special subject matter of this phenomenal information. . . .

From *Philosophical Papers* vol. 1, Oxford University Press, where it appears as a postscript to "Mad Pain and Martian Pain." Copyright © 1983 by David Lewis. Reprinted by permission of Oxford University Press.

Our proper answer, I think, is that knowing what it's like is not the possession of information at all. It isn't the elimination of any hitherto open possibilities. Rather, knowing what it's like is the possession of abilities: abilities to recognize, abilities to imagine, abilities to predict one's behavior by means of imaginative experiments. (Someone who knows what it's like to taste Vegemite can easily and reliably predict whether he would eat a second helping of Vegemite ice cream.) Lessons cannot impart these abilities—who would have thought they could? There is a state of knowing what it's like sure enough. And Vegemite has a special power to produce that state. But phenomenal information and its special subject matter do not exist.[2]

Imagine a smart data bank. It can be told things, it can store the information it is given, it can reason with it, it can answer questions on the basis of its stored information. Now imagine a pattern-recognizing device that works as follows. When exposed to a pattern it makes a sort of template, which it then applies to patterns presented to it in the future. Now imagine one device with both faculties, rather like a clock radio. There is no reason to think that any such device must have a third faculty: a faculty of making templates for patterns it has never been exposed to, using its stored information about these patterns. If it has a full description about a pattern but no template for it, it lacks an ability but it doesn't lack information. (Rather, it lacks information in usable form.) When it is shown the pattern it makes a template and gains abilities, but it gains no information. We might be rather like that.

NOTES

1. This is the "knowledge argument" of Frank Jackson, "Epiphenomenal Qualia," *Philosophical Quarterly* 32 (1982): 127–36. It appears also, in less purified form, in Thomas Nagel, "What Is It Like to Be a Bat?" *Philosophical Review* 83 (1974): 435–50; and in Paul Meehl, "The Compleat Autocerebroscopist," in Paul Feyerabend and Grover Maxwell, eds., *Mind, Matter, and Method: Essays in Philosophy and Science in Honor of Herbert Feigl* (Minneapolis: University of Minnesota Press, 1966).

2. This defense against the knowledge argument is presented in detail in Laurence Nemirow, *Functionalism and the Subjective Quality of Experience* (Ph.D. dissertation, Stanford University, 1979), chapter 2; and more briefly in his review of Thomas Nagel's *Mortal Questions, Philosophical Review* 89 (1980): 473–77.

STUDY QUESTIONS

1. What does Lewis mean by "the friend of phenomenal qualia"?
2. Explain the point of the case of Vegemite.
3. How does Lewis reply to that case?
4. Is knowing what it's like to eat chocolate ice cream the possession of information?

Computing Machinery
and Intelligence

ALAN TURING

In a previous article Thomas Nagel explored the consciousness of a bat. But
do only living things think? What about a computer? Does it have conscious
thoughts?

Alan Turing (1912–1954) was an English mathematician, scientist, and philosopher. He proposes what has come to be known as the "Turing test," in which
a human interrogator asks questions and tries to determine whether the answers
are being given by a computer or a human being. Turing believes that a computer
could be so programmed that its answers would be indistinguishable from those
of a human being. In that case the computer would appropriately be described as
intelligent.

I propose to consider the question, "Can machines think?" This should begin with
definitions of the meaning of the terms "machine" and "think." The definitions
might be framed so as to reflect so far as possible the normal use of the words, but
this attitude is dangerous. If the meaning of the words "machine" and "think" are
to be found by examining how they are commonly used, it is difficult to escape
the conclusion that the meaning and the answer to the question, "Can machines
think?" is to be sought in a statistical survey such as a Gallup poll. But this is
absurd. Instead of attempting such a definition, I shall replace the question by
another, which is closely related to it and is expressed in relatively unambiguous
words.

The new form of the problem can be described in terms of a game which we
call the "imitation game." It is played with three people, a man (A), a woman (B),
and an interrogator (C) who may be of either sex. The interrogator stays in a room
apart from the other two. The object of the game for the interrogator is to determine which of the other two is the man and which is the woman. He knows them
by labels X and Y, and at the end of the game he says either "X is A and Y is B" or
"X is B and Y is A." The interrogator is allowed to put questions to A and B thus:

C: Will X please tell me the length of his or her hair?

From Alan Turing, "Computing Machinery and Intelligence," *Mind*, LIX (1950). Reprinted
by permission of Oxford University Press.

Now suppose X is actually A, then A must answer. It is A's object in the game to try to cause C to make the wrong identification. His answer might therefore be

"My hair is shingled, and the longest strands are about nine inches long."

In order that tones of voice may not help the interrogator, the answers should be written, or better still, typewritten. The ideal arrangement is to have a tele-printer communicating between the two rooms. Alternatively the question and answers can be repeated by an intermediary. The object of the game for the third player (B) is to help the interrogator. The best strategy for her is probably to give truthful answers. She can add such things as "I am the woman, don't listen to him!" to her answers, but it will avail nothing as the man can make similar remarks.

We now ask the question, "What will happen when a machine takes the part of A in this game?" Will the interrogator decide wrongly as often when the game is played like this as he does when the game is played between a man and a woman? These questions replace our original, "Can machines think?" . . .

It will simplify matters for the reader if I explain first my own beliefs in the matter. . . . I believe that in about fifty years' time it will be possible to program computers . . . to make them play the imitation game so well that an average inter-rogator will not have more than 70 percent chance of making the right identifica-tion after five minutes of questioning. . . .

I now proceed to consider opinions opposed to my own. . . .

THE ARGUMENT FROM CONSCIOUSNESS

This argument is very well expressed in Professor Jefferson's Lister Oration for 1949, from which I quote. "Not until a machine can write a sonnet or compose a concerto because of thoughts and emotions felt, and not by the chance fall of symbols, could we agree that machine equals brain—that is, not only write it but know that it had written it. No mechanism could feel (and not merely artificially signal, an easy contrivance) pleasure at its successes, grief when its valves fuse, be warmed by flattery, be made miserable by its mistakes, be charmed by sex, be angry or depressed when it cannot get what it wants."

This argument appears to be a denial of the validity of our test. According to the most extreme form of this view the only way by which one could be sure that a machine thinks is to *be* the machine and to feel oneself thinking. One could then describe these feelings to the world, but of course no one would be justified in tak-ing any notice. Likewise according to this view the only way to know that a *man* thinks is to be that particular man. It is in fact the solipsist point of view. It may be the most logical view to hold but it makes communication of ideas difficult. A is liable to believe "A thinks but B does not" while B believes "B thinks but A does not." Instead of arguing continually over this point it is usual to have the polite convention that everyone thinks.

I am sure that Professor Jefferson does not wish to adopt the extreme and solipsist point of view. Probably he would be quite willing to accept the imitation game as a test. The game (with the player B omitted) is frequently used in practice under the name of *viva voce* to discover whether someone really understands something or has "learned it parrot fashion." Let us listen to a part of such a *viva voce:*

INTERROGATOR: In the first line of your sonnet which reads "Shall I compare thee to a summer's day," would not "a spring day" do as well or better?

WITNESS: It wouldn't scan.

INTERROGATOR: How about "a winter's day." That would scan all right.

WITNESS: Yes, but nobody wants to be compared to a winter's day.

INTERROGATOR: Would you say Mr. Pickwick reminded you of Christmas?

WITNESS: In a way.

INTERROGATOR: Yet Christmas is a winter's day, and I do not think Mr. Pickwick would mind the comparison.

WITNESS: I don't think you're serious. By a winter's day one means a typical winter's day, rather than a special one like Christmas.

And so on. What would Professor Jefferson say if the sonnet-writing machine was able to answer like this in the *viva voce*? I do not know whether he would regard the machine as "merely artificially signaling" these answers, but if the answers were as satisfactory and sustained as in the above passage, I do not think he would describe it as "an easy contrivance." This phrase is, I think, intended to cover such devices as the inclusion in the machine of a record of someone reading a sonnet, with appropriate switching to turn it on from time to time.

In short then, I think that most of those who support the argument from consciousness could be persuaded to abandon it rather than be forced into the solipsist position. They will then probably be willing to accept our test.

I do not wish to give the impression that I think there is no mystery about consciousness. There is, for instance, something of a paradox connected with any attempt to localize it. But I do not think these mysteries necessarily need to be solved before we can answer the question with which we are concerned in this paper.

ARGUMENTS FROM VARIOUS DISABILITIES

These arguments take the form, "I grant you that you can make machines do all the things you have mentioned but you will never be able to make one to do X." Numerous features X are suggested in this connection. I offer a selection:

Be kind, resourceful, beautiful, friendly . . . , have initiative, have a sense of humor, tell right from wrong, make mistakes . . . , fall in love, enjoy strawberries and cream, make someone fall in love with it, learn from experience . . . , use words properly, be the subject of its own thought . . . , have as much diversity of behavior as a man, do something really new. . . .

No support is usually offered for these statements. I believe they are mostly founded on the principle of scientific induction. A man has seen thousands of machines in his lifetime. From what he sees of them he draws a number of general conclusions. They are ugly, each is designed for a very limited purpose, when required for a minutely different purpose they are useless, the variety of behavior of any one of them is very small, etc., etc. Naturally he concludes that these are necessary properties of machines in general. Many of these limitations are associated with the very small storage capacity of most machines. . . . A few years ago, when very little had been heard of digital computers, it was possible to elicit much incredulity concerning them, if one mentioned their properties without describing their construction. That was presumably due to a similar application of the principle of scientific induction. These applications of the principle are of course largely unconscious. When a burned child fears the fire and shows that he fears it by avoiding it, I should say that he was applying scientific induction. (I could of course also describe his behavior in many other ways.) The works and customs of mankind do not seem to be very suitable material to which to apply scientific induction. A very large part of space–time must be investigated if reliable results are to be obtained. Otherwise we may (as most English children do) decide that everybody speaks English and that it is silly to learn French.

There are, however, special remarks to be made about many of the disabilities that have been mentioned. The inability to enjoy strawberries and cream may have struck the reader as frivolous. Possibly a machine might be made to enjoy this delicious dish, but any attempt to make one do so would be idiotic. . . .

The claim that "machines cannot make mistakes" seems a curious one. One is tempted to retort, "Are they any the worse for that?" But let us adopt a more sympathetic attitude and try to see what is really meant. I think this criticism can be explained in terms of the imitation game. It is claimed that the interrogator could distinguish the machine from the man simply by setting them a number of problems in arithmetic. The machine would be unmasked because of its deadly accuracy. The reply to this is simple. The machine (programmed for playing the game) would not attempt to give the *right* answers to the arithmetic problems. It would deliberately introduce mistakes in a manner calculated to confuse the interrogator. A mechanical fault would probably show itself through an unsuitable decision as to what sort of mistake to make in the arithmetic. Even this interpretation of the criticism is not sufficiently sympathetic. But we cannot afford the space to go into it much further. It seems to me that this criticism depends on a confusion between two kinds of mistakes. We may call them "errors of functioning" and "errors of conclusion." Errors of functioning are due to some mechanical or electrical fault which causes the machine to behave otherwise than it was designed to do. In philosophical discussions one likes to ignore the possibility of such errors; one is therefore discussing "abstract machines." These abstract machines are mathematical fictions rather than physical objects. By definition they are incapable of errors of functioning. In this sense we can truly say that "machines can never make mistakes." Errors of conclusion can only arise when some meaning is attached to the output signals from the machine. The machine might, for instance, type out mathematical equations, or sentences in English. When a false proposition is typed, we say that the machine has committed an error of conclusion. There is clearly no reason at all for saying that a machine cannot make this kind of mistake. It might do nothing but type out repeatedly "$0 = 1$." To take a less perverse example, it might have some method for drawing conclusions by scientific induction. We must expect such a method to lead occasionally to erroneous results.

The claim that a machine cannot be the subject of its own thought can of course only be answered if it can be shown that the machine has *some* thought with *some* subject matter. Nevertheless, "the subject matter of a machine's operations" does seem to mean something, at least to the people who deal with it. If, for instance, the machine was trying to find a solution of the equation $x^2 - 40x - 11 = 0$, one would be tempted to describe this equation as part of the machine's subject matter at that moment. In this sort of sense a machine undoubtedly can be its own subject matter. It may be used to help in making up its own programs, or to predict the effect of alterations in its own structure. By observing the results of its own behavior it can modify its own programs so as to achieve some purpose more effectively. These are possibilities of the near future, rather than Utopian dreams.

STUDY QUESTIONS

1. What does Turing mean by the "imitation game"?
2. Can a machine make a mistake?
3. Could a machine be programmed to appear to think and yet not be thinking?
4. Do you believe that the imitation game offers a decisive test of whether a machine can think?

Do Computers Think?

JOHN SEARLE

A reply to the sort of argument Turing presented is offered by John Searle, Professor of Philosophy at the University of California, Berkeley.

He asks us to consider a man with no knowledge of Chinese who is placed in a room containing a basket of Chinese symbols and a rule book telling him which Chinese symbols to match with others solely on the basis of their shape. Using the rule book, he is able to answer in Chinese questions posed in Chinese. His successful manipulation of the Chinese symbols, however, does not give him an

From John Searle, "Is the Brain's Mind a Computer Program?" *Scientific American,* 1990. Reprinted by permission of the journal.

understanding of Chinese. So too, according to Searle, a computer's following its program does not give it thought.

....

Can a machine think? Can a machine have conscious thoughts in exactly the same sense that you and I have? If by "machine" one means a physical system capable of performing certain functions (and what else can one mean?), then humans are machines of a special biological kind, and humans can think, and so of course machines can think. And, for all we know, it might be possible to produce a thinking machine out of different materials altogether—say, out of silicon chips or vacuum tubes. Maybe it will turn out to be impossible, but we certainly do not know that yet.

In recent decades, however, the question of whether a machine can think has been given a different interpretation entirely. The question that has been posed in its place is, Could a machine think just by virtue of implementing a computer program? Is the program by itself constitutive of thinking? This is a completely different question because it is not about the physical, causal properties of actual or possible physical systems but rather about the abstract, computational properties of formal computer programs that can be implemented in any sort of substance at all, provided only that the substance is able to carry the program.

A fair number of researchers in artificial intelligence (AI) believe the answer to the second question is yes; that is, they believe that by designing the right programs with the right inputs and outputs, they are literally creating minds. They believe furthermore that they have a scientific test for determining success or failure: the Turing test devised by Alan M. Turing, the founding father of artificial intelligence. The Turing test, as currently understood, is simply this: if a computer can perform in such a way that an expert cannot distinguish its performance from that of a human who has a certain cognitive ability—say, the ability to do addition or to understand Chinese—then the computer also has that ability. So the goal is to design programs that will simulate human cognition in such a way as to pass the Turing test. What is more, such a program would not merely be a model of the mind; it would literally be a mind, in the same sense that a human mind is a mind.

By no means does every worker in artificial intelligence accept so extreme a view. A more cautious approach is to think of computer models as being useful in studying the mind in the same way that they are useful in studying the weather, economics or molecular biology. To distinguish these two approaches, I call the first strong AI and the second weak AI. It is important to see just how bold an approach strong AI is. Strong AI claims that thinking is merely the manipulation of formal symbols, and that is exactly what the computer does: manipulate formal symbols. This view is often summarized by saying, "The mind is to the brain as the program is to the hardware."

Strong AI is unusual among theories of the mind in at least two respects: it can be stated clearly, and it admits of a simple and decisive refutation. The refutation is one that any person can try for himself or herself. Here is how it goes. Consider a language you don't understand. In my case, I do not understand Chinese. To me, Chinese writing looks like so many meaningless squiggles. Now suppose I am placed in a room containing baskets full of Chinese symbols. Suppose also that I am given a rule book in English for matching Chinese symbols with other Chinese symbols. The rules identify the symbols entirely by their shapes and do not require that I understand any of them. The rules might say such things as, "Take a squiggle–squiggle sign from basket number one and put it next to a squoggle–squoggle sign from basket number two."

Imagine that people outside the room who understand Chinese hand in small bunches of symbols and that in response I manipulate the symbols according to the rule book and hand back more small bunches of symbols. Now, the rule book is the "computer program." The people who wrote it are "programmers," and I am the "computer." The baskets full of symbols are the "data base," the small bunches that are handed in to me are "questions" and the bunches I then hand out are "answers."

Now suppose that the rule book is written in such a way that my "answers" to the "questions" are indistinguishable from those of a native Chinese speaker. For example, the people outside might hand me some symbols that unknown to me mean, "What's your favorite color?" and I might after going through the rules give back symbols that, also unknown to me, mean, "My favorite is blue, but I also like green a lot." I satisfy the Turing test for understanding Chinese. All the same, I am totally ignorant of Chinese. And there is no way I could come to understand Chinese in the system as described, since there is no way that I can learn the meanings of any of the symbols. Like a computer, I manipulate symbols, but I attach no meaning to the symbols.

The point of the thought experiment is this: if I do not understand Chinese solely on the basis of running a computer program for understanding Chinese, then neither does any other digital computer solely on that basis. Digital computers merely manipulate formal symbols according to rules in the program.

What goes for Chinese goes for other forms of cognition as well. Just manipulating the symbols is not by itself enough to guarantee cognition, perception, understanding, thinking and so forth. And since computers, qua computers, are symbol-manipulating devices, merely running the computer program is not enough to guarantee cognition.

This simple argument is decisive against the claims of strong AI.

STUDY QUESTIONS

1. Does Searle believe a machine can think?
2. Explain the experiment that uses Chinese symbols.
3. What does Searle believe that the experiment proves?
4. What do you believe that the experiment proves?

The Body Problem

BARBARA MONTERO

Barbara Montero is Professor of Philosophy at the College of Staten Island and the Graduate Center of the City University of New York. She points out that the question of whether the mind is physical presumes an understanding of what counts as physical, a point on which agreement is lacking.

Is the mind physical? Are mental properties, such as the property of *being in pain* or *thinking about the higher orders of infinity,* actually physical properties? Many philosophers think that they are. For no matter how strange and remarkable consciousness and cognition may be, many hold that they are, nevertheless, entirely physical. While some take this view as a starting point in their discussions about the mind, others, well aware that there are dissenters among the ranks, argue for it strenuously. One wonders, however, just what is being assumed, argued for, or denied. In other words, one wonders: Just what does it mean to be physical? This is the question I call, "the body problem."

As I see it, there is little use in arguing about whether the mind is physical, or whether mental properties are physical properties unless we have at least some understanding of what it means to be physical. In other words, in order to solve the mind–body problem, we must solve the body problem. It strikes me as odd that while bookstores and journals are overflowing with debates about whether consciousness is physical, hardly anyone is concerned with "What counts as physical?" Moreover, it would not be much of an exaggeration to say today, as John Earman did more than twenty years ago, that "attempts to answer this question that have appeared in the philosophical literature are for the most part notable only for their glaring inadequacies."[1] If we want to discuss whether the mind is physical, we should say something about what it means to be physical.

Some may argue that such clarification is unnecessary. They may point out that while we cannot provide necessary and sufficient conditions for *tablehood,* we nonetheless understand the concept, because we can readily identify things that are clearly tables and things that are clearly not. They claim the same is true of our notion of the physical. But the situations are not analogous. While we can identify central cases of being physical—what could be clearer examples of physical than rocks and

From Steven M. Cahn and Maureen Eckert, eds., *Philosophical Horizons*, second edition, Wadsworth, 2012. Reprinted by permission of the publisher.

trees (except, perhaps, quarks and leptons)?—an extra wrinkle is that rocks and trees (as well as quarks and leptons) are clear cases only assuming that idealism is false. In any case, something needs to be said about how to determine what we can place in the category along with rocks and trees. In certain ways, beliefs and desires *are* like rocks and trees, while quarks and leptons are not. For example, talk of beliefs and desires plays a role in our ordinary folk understanding of the world, while talk of quarks and leptons does not. Beliefs and desires also are part of the same macro-level causal network as rocks and trees, while quarks and leptons are not. But few physicalists think that from our central examples of physical objects we should infer that quarks and leptons are nonphysical.

Perhaps these problems could be overlooked if we had clear intuitions regarding the nonphysical. But do we? The stock example of a nonphysical entity is some kind of ghost. For example, Jaegwon Kim defines "ontological physicalism" as the view that "there are no nonphysical residues (e.g. Cartesian souls, entelechies, and the like)."[2] And Jeffrey Poland states that the physicalist's bottom line is really: "There are no ghosts!"[3] But why is a ghost nonphysical? Is it that they can pass through walls without disturbing them? Neutrinos, I am told, can pass right through the earth without disturbing it, yet neutrinos are classified as physical. Is it that they have no mass? Photons have no mass yet are considered physical. Perhaps it is that they supposedly do not take up space. But if taking up no space shows that something is nonphysical, point particles (if they exist) would have to be classified as nonphysical. Yet physicalists, I take it, would not accept this view. So to say that the physical means "no spooky stuff" does not help matters.

Perhaps physicalism at least excludes the possibility of a ghost in a machine, that is, the view that there is some type of mental substance completely different in kind from physical substance. But what does this view amount to, since most physicalists are happy to admit that there is more than one kind of elementary particle? Perhaps the idea is that whether only one basic particle exists, say, strings, or it turns out that in addition to strings there are also Ferris wheels, physicalism holds that everything nonbasic is composed of the same kind, or kinds of basic particles. But this view cannot be right. For example, some evidence indicates that what physicists call "dark matter" is composed entirely of axions, hypothetical new elementary particles.[4] Yet dark matter is no threat to physicalism. So the simple notion of *stuff of a different kind* does not provide us with a notion of nonphysical. But what, then, does?

Philosophers commonly answer this question by deferring to the physicists. The physical is said to be whatever the physicist, or more precisely, the particle physicist, tells us exists (what we might now think of as quarks and leptons, as well as the exchange particles, gluons, gravitons, etc.). And the nonphysical is whatever remains, if there is anything. On this view, physicalists—that is, those who hold that everything is physical—claim that physics provides us with an exhaustive and exclusive line to all reality. Here is a straightforward answer to the body problem, but one that is too simple, since most philosophers believe that things like rocks, tables, and chairs are just as physical as quarks, leptons, and gluons.

Granted, whether to say that the physical is only what the physicists take as fundamental is partially a terminological issue. But while the question whether to reserve the name "physical" for just the fundamental constituents of reality or to use it more broadly *is* terminological, the question of how many layers of reality to countenance is not. Because most physicalists allow for not only the smallest stuff, but also for atoms, molecules, rocks and galaxies, the leave-it-to-the-physicists approach is usually amended to the view that the physical world is the world of the fundamental particles, forces, laws and such *as well as* whatever depends on this physical stuff. As such, we can allow for the possibility that rocks may be physical.

My concern, however, is not with the dependence relation *per se* but with what everything is being related to: the lower level dependence base or what is often referred to as "the microphysical." One thinks of microphysical phenomena as described by the most recent microphysics. But if the physical is defined in terms of current microphysics, and a new particle is discovered next week, the particle will not be physical—a consequence most philosophers want to avoid. But if not current microphysics, what else could the microphysical be?

Carl Hempel posed a dilemma for those attempting to define the physical in reference to microphysics.[5] On the one hand, we cannot define the physical in terms of current microphysics since today's microphysics is probably neither entirely true (some of our theories may look as wrong-headed to future generations as phlogiston theory looks to us now) nor complete (more remains to be explained). On the other hand, if we take microphysics to be some future unspecified theory, the claim that the mind is physical is vague, since we currently have no idea of that theory. Faced with this dilemma, what is a physicalist to do?

Some try to take the middle road, explaining the "microphysical" by referring to "something like current microphysics—but just improved."[6] But in what respect is this future microphysics like current microphysics? And in what respect will it be improved? Since these questions are usually not addressed (save, of course, for the implication that it is similar enough to be intelligible yet different enough to be true), it seems that Hempel's dilemma recurs for these compromise views. For the theory in question will be false if it is significantly similar to current physics, and if not, we are left with no clear notion of the physical.

Taking the first horn of Hempel's dilemma, that is, defining the physical in terms of current microphysics, does not provide us with a comfortable solution to the body problem. For it is rather awkward to hold a theory that one knows is false.[7] But does taking the second horn fare any better? David Armstrong thinks so. He explicitly tells us that when he says "physical properties" he is not talking about the properties specified by current physics, but rather "whatever set of properties the physicist in the end will appeal to."[8] Similarly, Frank Jackson holds that the physical facts encompass "everything in a completed physics, chemistry, and neurophysiology, and all there is to know about the causal and relational facts consequent upon all this."[9] As Barry Loewer puts it, "what many have on their minds when they speak of fundamental physical properties is that they are the properties expressed by simple predicates of the true comprehensive fundamental physical theory."[10] So for Armstrong and others the physical is to be defined over a completed physics, a physics in the end. But what is this final physics? The answer, as Hempel has pointed out, is unknown.

Basing one's notion of the physical on an unfathomable theory seems to be a serious enough problem to discourage defining the physical over a final theory. But most philosophers ignore this problem and charge ahead to the more juicy questions, such as whether knowledge of all the physical facts (whatever they may be) enables us to know what it is like to see colors. So consider that another consequence of using the notion of a completed physics to explain the physical is that, at least under one interpretation, it trivially excludes the possibility that the mind is not physical. For on one understanding of it, a completed physics amounts to a physics that explains *everything*. So if mentality is a feature of the world, a completed physics, on this definition, will explain it too. While there is nothing wrong with trivial truth *per se,* this is not the solution to the mind-body problem most philosophers would accept. For neither physicalists nor their foes think that we already know by definition that the mind is physical.

Chomsky has identified a related problem for those who define the physical in terms of a final physics. His point is that since we cannot predict the course of physics, we cannot be sure that a final physics will not include mental properties, qua mental, as fundamental properties.[11] Yet if final physics takes the mental realm to be fundamental, the difference dissolves between physicalists who claim that mental properties will be accounted for in final physics and dualists who claim that mental properties are fundamental.

A solution to the body problem is not forthcoming. Perhaps we should focus on questions other than the question "Is the mind physical?" So let me conclude with a suggestion. Physicalism is, at least partly, motivated by the belief that the mental is ultimately nonmental, that is, that mental properties are not fundamental properties, whereas dualism holds, precisely, that they are. So a crucial question is whether the mental is ultimately nonmental. Of course, the notion of the nonmental is also open-ended. And, for this reason, it may be just as difficult to see what sort of considerations are relevant in determining what counts as nonmental as it is to see what sort of considerations are relevant in determining what counts as physical. However, we do have a grasp of one side of the divide—that is, the mental. So, rather than worrying about whether the mind is physical, we should be concerned with whether it is nonmental. And this question has little to do with what current physics, future physics, or a final physics says about the world.

NOTES

1. John Earman, "What is Physicalism?" *Journal of Philosophy* 72 (1975), p. 566.
2. Jaegwon Kim, "Supervenience, Emergence, Realization in Philosophy of Mind," in M. Carrier and P. Machamer (eds.), *Mindscapes: Philosophy, Science, and the Mind,* Pittsburgh, University of Pittsburgh Press, 1997.

3. Jeffery Poland, *Physicalism: The Philosophical Foundations,* Oxford: Oxford University Press, 1994, p. 15. He emphasizes this point again later: "ghosts, gods, and the paranormal are genuine threats to physicalism" (p. 228). That is, according to Poland, if ghosts were to exist, physicalism would be false.

4. See Leslie Rosenberg, "The Search for Dark Matter Axions," *Particle World* 4 (1995), pp. 3–10.

5. See Carl Hempel, "Comments on Goodman's Ways of Worldmaking," *Synthese* 45 (1980), pp. 193–9. Also see Hempel, "Reduction: Ontological and Linguistic Facets," in S. Morgenbesser, P. Suppes and M. Whit (eds.), *Philosophy, Science and Method: Essays in Honor of Ernest Nagel,* New York: St. Martin's Press, 1969. I am using different terminology from Hempel, and my emphasis is on the question of whether the mind is physical rather than the question of physicalism in general, but the point is essentially the same.

6. See for example, David Lewis, "New Work for a Theory of Universals," *Australasian Journal of Philosophy* 61 (1983), pp. 343–77 and Robert Kirk, *Raw Feeling: A Philosophical Account of the Essence of Consciousness,* New York: Oxford University Press, 1994.

7. For further discussion of this point see Barbara Montero, "The Body Problem," *Nous* 33 (1999), pp. 183–200.

8. David Armstrong, "The Causal Theory of Mind," in D. Rosenthal (ed.), *The Nature of Mind,* New York: Oxford University Press, 1991, p. 186. Of course, not all properties the physicist appeals to are relevant: when a physicist is explaining a proposed budget in a grant application or explaining to her supervisor why she was late to work, she may be appealing to very different properties than when she is applying her mathematical skills in computing a wave function. But perhaps this distinction is intuitive enough.

9. Frank Jackson, "What Mary Didn't Know," in D. Rosenthal (ed.), *The Nature of Mind,* New York: Oxford University Press, 1991, p. 291.

10. Barry Loewer, "Humean Supervenience," *Philosophical Topics* 24 (1996), p. 103.

11. See Noam Chomsky, "Language and Nature," *Mind* 104 (1995), pp. 1–61 and *Language and Thought,* Rhode Island: Moyer Bell, 1993.

STUDY QUESTIONS

1. According to Montero, what is the "body problem"?
2. How does the body problem differ from the mind–body problem?
3. Does Montero agree that a ghost is nonphysical?
4. According to Montero, do we have a clearer grasp of the mental than the physical?

Meditations on First Philosophy

RENÉ DESCARTES

We return now to Descartes' *Meditations* at the point at which he had wondered whether we can be sure of any truth. He believes we can. The principle he proposes as certain is best known as formulated in another of his works as "I think; therefore, I am," in Latin, "Cogito, ergo sum." According to Descartes, the Cogito, as it is called by philosophers, is undeniable, for, in the act of attempting to deny one is thinking, one thinks and so renders the denial false.

Using the Cogito as the premise of his philosophical system, Descartes argues that because he is certain he is thinking but not certain of the existence of anything other than his own mind, he is to be identified with his mind. He claims further that by relying on the judgments of his mind rather than the evidence of his senses, he can attain knowledge.

....

SECOND MEDITATION

The Nature of the Human Mind, and How It Is Better Known Than the Body

So serious are the doubts into which I have been thrown as a result of yesterday's meditation that I can neither put them out of my mind nor see any way of resolving them. It feels as if I have fallen unexpectedly into a deep whirlpool which tumbles me around so that I can neither stand on the bottom nor swim up to the top. Nevertheless I will make an effort and once more attempt the same path which I started on yesterday. Anything which admits of the slightest doubt I will set aside just as if I had found it to be wholly false; and I will proceed in this way until I recognize something certain, or, if nothing else, until I at least recognize for certain that there is no certainty. Archimedes used to demand just one firm and immovable point in order to shift the entire earth; so I too can hope for great things if I manage to find just one thing, however slight, that is certain and unshakeable.

I will suppose then, that everything I see is spurious. I will believe that my memory tells me lies, and that none of the things that it reports ever happened. I have no senses. Body, shape, extension, movement, and place are chimeras. So what remains true? Perhaps just the one fact that nothing is certain.

Yet apart from everything I have just listed, how do I know that there is not something else which does not allow even the slightest occasion for doubt? Is there not a God, or whatever I may call him, who puts into me the thoughts I am now having? But why do I think this, since I myself may perhaps be the author of these thoughts? In that case am not I, at least, something? But I have just said that I have no senses and no body. This is the sticking point: what follows from this? Am I not so bound up with a body and with senses that I cannot exist without them? But I have convinced myself that there is absolutely nothing in the world, no sky, no earth, no minds, no bodies. Does it now follow that I too do not exist? No: if I convinced myself of something, then I certainly existed. But there is a deceiver of supreme power and cunning who is deliberately and constantly deceiving me. In that case I too undoubtedly exist, if he is deceiving me; and let him deceive me as much as he can, he will never bring it about that I am nothing so long as I think that I am something. So after considering everything very thoroughly, I must finally conclude that this proposition, *I am, I exist,* is necessarily true whenever it is put forward by me or conceived in my mind.

But I do not yet have a sufficient understanding of what this "I" is, that now necessarily exists. So I must be on my guard against carelessly taking something else to be this "I," and so making a mistake in the very item of knowledge that I maintain is the most certain and evident of all. I will therefore go back and meditate on what I originally believed myself to be, before I embarked on this present train of thought. I will then subtract anything capable of being weakened, even minimally, by the arguments now introduced, so that what is left at the end may be exactly and only what is certain and unshakeable.

What then did I formerly think I was? A man. But what is a man? Shall I say "a rational animal"? No; for then I should have to inquire what an animal is, what rationality is, and in this way one question would lead me down the slope to other harder ones, and I do not now have the time to waste on subtleties of this kind. Instead I propose to concentrate on what came into my thoughts spontaneously and quite naturally whenever I used to consider what I was. Well, the first thought to come to mind was that I had a face, hands, arms, and the whole mechanical structure of limbs which can be seen in a corpse, and which I called the body. The next thought was that I was nourished, that I moved about, and that I engaged in sense-perception and thinking; and these actions I attributed to the soul. But as to the nature of this soul, either I did not think about this or else I imagined it to be something tenuous, like a wind or fire or ether, which permeated my more solid parts. As to the body, however, I had no doubts about it, but thought I knew its nature distinctly. If I had tried to describe the mental conception I had of it, I would have expressed it as follows: by a body I understand whatever has a determinable shape and a definable location and can occupy a space in such a way as to exclude any other body; it can be perceived by touch, sight, hearing, taste, or smell, and can be moved in various ways, not by itself but by whatever else comes into contact with it. For, according to my judgement, the power of self-movement, like the power of sensation or of thought, was quite foreign to the nature of a body; indeed, it was a source of wonder to me that certain bodies were found to contain faculties of this kind.

But what shall I now say that I am, when I am supposing that there is some supremely powerful and, if it is permissible to say so, malicious deceiver, who is deliberately trying to trick me in every way he can? Can I now assert that I possess even the most insignificant of all the attributes which I have just said belong to the nature of a body? I scrutinize them, think about them, go over them again, but nothing suggests itself; it is tiresome and pointless to go through the list once more. But what about the attributes I assigned to the soul? Nutrition or movement? Since now I do not have a body, these are mere fabrications. Sense-perception? This surely does not occur without a body, and besides, when asleep I have appeared to perceive through the senses many things which I afterwards realized I did not perceive through the senses at all. Thinking? At last I have discovered it—thought; this alone is inseparable from me. I am, I exist—that is certain. But for how long? For as long as I am thinking. For it could be that were I totally to cease from thinking, I should totally cease to exist. At present I am not admitting anything except what is necessarily true. I am, then, in the strict sense only a thing that thinks; that is, I am a mind, or intelligence, or intellect, or reason—words whose meaning I have been ignorant of until now. But for all that I am a thing which is real and which truly exists. But what kind of a thing? As I have just said—a thinking thing.

What else am I? I will use my imagination. I am not that structure of limbs which is called a human body. I am not even some thin vapour which permeates the limbs—a wind, fire, air, breath, or whatever I depict in my imagination; for these are things which I have supposed to be nothing. Let this supposition stand; for all that I am still something. And yet may it not perhaps be the case that these very things which I am supposing to be nothing, because they are unknown to me, are in reality identical with the "I" of which I am aware? I do not know, and for the moment I shall not argue the point, since I can make judgements only about things which are known to me. I know that I exist; the question is, what is this "I" that I know? If the "I" is understood strictly as we have been taking it, then it is quite certain that knowledge of it does not depend on things of whose existence I am as yet unaware; so it cannot depend on any of the things which I invent in my imagination. And this very word "invent" shows me my mistake. It would indeed be a case of fictitious invention if I used my imagination to establish that I was something or other; for imagining is simply contemplating the shape or image of a corporeal thing. Yet now I know for certain both that I exist and at the same time that all such images and, in general, everything relating to the nature of body, could be mere dreams (and chimeras). Once this point has been grasped, to say "I will use my imagination to get to know more distinctly what I am" would seem to be as silly as saying "I am now awake, and see some truth; but since my vision is not yet clear enough, I will deliberately fall asleep so that my dreams may provide a truer and clearer representation." I thus realize that none of the things that the imagination enables me to grasp is at all relevant to this knowledge of myself which I possess, and that the mind must therefore be most carefully diverted from such things if it is to perceive its own nature as distinctly as possible.

But what then am I? A thing that thinks. What is that? A thing that doubts, understands, affirms, denies, is willing, is unwilling, and also imagines and has sensory perceptions.

This is a considerable list, if everything on it belongs to me. But does it? Is it not one and the same "I" who is now doubting almost everything, who nonetheless understands some things, who affirms that this one thing is true, denies everything else, desires to know more, is unwilling to be deceived, imagines many things even involuntarily, and is aware of many things which apparently come from the senses? Are not all these things just as true as the fact that I exist, even if I am asleep all the time, and even if he who created me is doing all he can to deceive me? Which of all these activities is distinct from my thinking? Which of them can be said to be separate from myself? The fact that it is I who am doubting and understanding and willing is so evident that I see no way of making it any clearer. But it is also the case that the "I" who imagines is the same "I." For even if, as I have supposed, none of the objects of imagination are real, the power of imagination is something which really exists and is part of my thinking. Lastly, it is also the same "I" who has sensory perceptions, or is aware of bodily things as it were through the senses. For example, I am now seeing light, hearing a noise, feeling heat. But I am asleep, so all this is false. Yet I certainly *seem* to see, to hear, and to be warmed. This cannot be false; what is called "having a sensory perception" is strictly just this, and in this restricted sense of the term it is simply thinking.

From all this I am beginning to have a rather better understanding of what I am. But it still appears—and I cannot stop thinking this—that the corporeal things of which images are formed in my thought, and which the senses investigate, are known with much more distinctness than this puzzling "I" which cannot be pictured in the imagination. And yet it is surely surprising that I should have a more distinct grasp of things which I realize are doubtful, unknown, and foreign to me, than I have of that which is true and known—my own self. But I see what it is: my mind enjoys wandering off and will not yet submit to being restrained within the bounds of truth. Very well then; just this once let us give it a completely free rein, so that after a while, when it is time to tighten the reins, it may more readily submit to being curbed.

Let us consider the things which people commonly think they understand most distinctly of all; that is, the bodies which we touch and see. I do not mean bodies in general—for general perceptions are apt to be somewhat more confused—but one particular body. Let us take, for example, this piece of wax. It has just been taken from the honeycomb; it has not yet quite lost the taste of the honey; it retains some of the scent of the flowers from which it was gathered; its colour, shape, and size are plain to see; it is hard, cold and can be handled without difficulty; if you rap it with your knuckle, it makes a sound. In short, it has everything which appears necessary to enable a body to be known as distinctly as possible. But even as I speak, I put the wax by the fire and look: the residual taste is eliminated, the smell goes away, the colour changes, the shape is lost, the size increases; it becomes liquid and hot; you can hardly touch it, and if you strike it, it no longer makes a sound. But does the same wax remain? It must be admitted that it does; no one denies it, no one thinks otherwise. So what was it in the wax that I understood with such distinctness? Evidently none of the features which I arrived at by means of the senses; for whatever came under taste, smell, sight, touch, or hearing has now altered—yet the wax remains.

Perhaps the answer lies in the thought which now comes to my mind; namely, the wax was not after all the sweetness of the honey, or the fragrance of the flowers, or the whiteness, or the shape, or the sound, but was rather a body which presented itself to me in these various forms a little while ago, but which now exhibits different ones. But what exactly is it that I am now imagining? Let us concentrate, take away everything which does not belong to the wax, and see what is left: merely something extended, flexible, and changeable. But what is meant here by "flexible" and "changeable"? Is it what I picture in my imagination: that this piece of wax is capable of changing from a round shape to a square shape, or from a square shape to a triangular shape? Not at all; for I can grasp that the wax is capable of countless changes of this kind, yet I am unable to run through this immeasurable number of changes in my imagination, from which it follows that it is not the faculty of imagination that gives me my grasp of the wax as flexible and changeable. And what is meant by "extended"? Is the extension of the wax also unknown? For it increases if the wax melts, increases again if it boils, and is greater still if the heat is increased. I would not be making a correct judgement about the nature of wax unless I believed it capable of being extended in many more different ways than I will ever encompass in my imagination. I must therefore admit that the nature of this piece of wax is in no way revealed by my imagination, but is perceived by the mind alone. (I am speaking of this particular piece of wax; the point is even clearer with regard to wax in general.) But what is this wax which is perceived by the mind alone? It is of course the same wax which I see, which I touch, which I picture in my imagination, in short the same wax which I thought it to be from the start. And yet, and here is the point, the perception I have of it is a case not of vision or touch or imagination—nor has it ever been, despite previous appearances—but of purely mental scrutiny; and this can be imperfect and confused, as it was before, or clear and distinct as it is now, depending on how carefully I concentrate on what the wax consists in.

But as I reach this conclusion I am amazed at how (weak and) prone to error my mind is. For although I am thinking about these matters within myself, silently and without speaking, nonetheless the actual words bring me up short, and I am almost tricked by ordinary ways of talking. We say that we see the wax itself, if it is there before us, not that we judge it to be there from its colour or shape; and this might lead me to conclude without more ado that knowledge of the wax comes from what the eye sees, and not from the scrutiny of the mind alone. But then if I look out of the window and see men crossing the square, as I just happen to have done, I normally say that I see the men themselves, just as I say that I see the wax. Yet do I see any more than hats and coats which could conceal automatons? I *judge* that they are men. And so something which I thought I was seeing with my eyes is in fact grasped solely by the faculty of judgement which is in my mind.

However, one who wants to achieve knowledge above the ordinary level should feel ashamed at having taken ordinary ways of talking as a basis for doubt. So let us proceed, and consider on which occasion my perception of the nature of the wax was more perfect and evident. Was it when I first looked at it, and believed I knew it by my external senses, or at least by what they call the "common" sense—that is, the power of imagination? Or is my knowledge more perfect now, after a more careful investigation of the nature of the wax and of the means by which it is known? Any doubt on this issue would clearly be foolish; for what distinctness was there in my earlier perception? Was there anything in it which an animal could not possess? But when I distinguish the wax from its outward forms—take the clothes off, as it were, and consider it naked—then although my judgement may still contain errors, at least my perception now requires a human mind.

But what am I to say about this mind, or about myself? (So far, remember, I am not admitting that there is anything else in me except a mind.) What, I ask, is this "I" which seems to perceive the wax so distinctly? Surely my awareness of my own self is not merely much truer and more certain than my awareness of the wax, but also much more distinct and evident. For if I judge that the wax exists from the fact that I see it, clearly this same fact entails much more evidently that I myself also exist. It is possible that what I see is not really the wax; it is possible that I do not even have eyes with which to see anything. But when I see, or think I see (I am not here distinguishing the two), it is simply not possible that I who am now thinking am not something. By the same token, if I judge that the wax exists from the fact that I touch it, the same result follows, namely, that I exist. If I judge that it exists from the fact that I imagine it, or for any other reason, exactly the same thing follows. And the result that I have grasped in the case of the wax may be applied to everything else located outside me. Moreover, if my perception of the wax seemed more distinct after it was established not just by sight or touch but by many other considerations, it must be admitted that I now know myself even more distinctly. This is because every consideration whatsoever which contributes to my perception of the wax, or of any other body, cannot but establish even more effectively the nature of my own mind. But besides this, there is so much else in the mind itself which can serve to make my knowledge of it more distinct, that it scarcely seems worth going through the contributions made by considering bodily things.

I see that without any effort I have now finally got back to where I wanted. I now know that even bodies are not strictly perceived by the senses or the faculty of imagination but by the intellect alone, and that this perception derives not from their being touched or seen but from their being understood; and in view of this I know plainly that I can achieve an easier and more evident perception of my own mind than of anything else. But since the habit of holding on to old opinions cannot be set aside so quickly, I should like to stop here and meditate for some time on this new knowledge I have gained, so as to fix it more deeply in my memory.

STUDY QUESTIONS

1. According to Descartes, which proposition is necessarily true?
2. By what argument does Descartes reach the conclusion that he is a mind?
3. What implications does Descartes draw from the example of the piece of wax?
4. Do you agree with Descartes that you can achieve an easier understanding of your own mind than of anything else?

PART 5

Free Will

Free Will

Thomas Nagel

We turn next to one of the most-discussed philosophical questions: Do human beings ever act freely? It might seem obvious that they do. Consider an ordinary human action—for instance, raising your hand at a meeting to attract the speaker's attention. If you are attending a lecture and the time comes for questions from the audience, you believe it is within your power to raise your hand and within your power not to raise it. The choice is yours.

Equally obvious, however, is that whenever an event occurs, a causal explanation can account for the occurrence of the event. If you feel a pain in your arm, then something is causing that pain. If nothing were causing it, you wouldn't be in pain. This same line of reasoning applies whether the event to be explained is a loud noise, a change in the weather, or an individual's action. If the event were uncaused, it wouldn't have occurred.

But if all actions are part of a causal chain extending back beyond your birth, how is it possible that any of your actions is free?

Our first reading is by Thomas Nagel, whose work we read previously. He explains the problem and concludes by suggesting that perhaps the feeling of free will is an illusion.

....

Suppose you're going through a cafeteria line and when you come to the desserts, you hesitate between a peach and a big wedge of chocolate cake with creamy icing. The cake looks good, but you know it's fattening. Still, you take it and eat it with pleasure. The next day you look in the mirror or get on the scale and think, "I wish I hadn't eaten that chocolate cake. I could have had a peach instead."

"I could have had a peach instead." What does that mean, and is it true?

Peaches were available when you went through the cafeteria line: you had the *opportunity* to take a peach instead. But that isn't all you mean. You mean you could have *taken* the peach instead of the cake. You could have *done* something different from what you actually did. Before you made up your mind, it was open whether you would take fruit or cake, and it was only your choice that decided which it would be.

Is that it? When you say, "I could have had a peach instead," do you mean that it depended only on your choice? You chose chocolate cake, so that's what you had, but *if* you had chosen the peach, you would have had that.

This still doesn't seem to be enough. You don't mean only that *if* you had chosen the peach, you would have had it. When you say, "I could have had a peach instead," you also mean that you *could have chosen* it—no "ifs" about it. But what does that mean?

It can't be explained by pointing out other occasions when you *have* chosen fruit. And it can't be explained by saying that if you had thought about it harder, or if a friend had been with you who eats like a bird, you *would* have chosen it. What you are saying is that you could have chosen a peach instead of chocolate cake *just then, as things actually were.* You think you could have chosen a peach even if everything else had been exactly the same as it was up to the point when you in fact chose chocolate cake. The only difference would have been that instead of thinking, "Oh well," and reaching for the cake, you would have thought, "Better not," and reached for the peach.

This is an idea of "can" or "could have" which we apply only to people (and maybe some animals). When we say, "The car could have climbed to the top of the hill," we mean the car had enough power to reach the top of the hill *if* someone drove it there. We don't mean that on an occasion when it was parked at the bottom of the hill, the car could have just taken off and climbed to the top, instead of continuing to sit there. Something else would have had to happen differently first, like a person getting in and starting the motor. But when it comes to people, we seem to think that they can do various things they don't actually do, *just like that,* without anything else happening differently first. What does this mean?

Part of what it means may be this: Nothing up to the point at which you choose determines irrevocably what your choice will be. It remains an *open possibility* that you will choose a peach until the moment when you actually choose chocolate cake. It isn't determined in advance.

Some things that happen *are* determined in advance. For instance, it seems to be determined in advance that the sun will rise tomorrow at a certain hour. It is not an open possibility that tomorrow the sun won't rise and night will just continue. That is not possible because it could happen only if the earth stopped rotating, or the sun stopped existing, and there is nothing going on in our galaxy which might make either of those things happen. The earth will continue rotating unless it is stopped, and tomorrow morning its rotation will bring us back around to face inward in the solar system, toward the sun, instead of outward, away from it. If there is no possibility that the earth will stop or that the sun won't be there, there is no possibility that the sun won't rise tomorrow.

When you say you could have had a peach instead of chocolate cake, part of what you mean may be that it wasn't determined in advance what you would do, as it *is* determined in advance that the sun will rise tomorrow. There were no processes or forces at work before you made your choice that made it inevitable that you would choose chocolate cake.

That may not be all you mean, but it seems to be at least part of what you mean. For if it was really determined in advance that you would choose cake, how could it also be true that you could have chosen fruit? It would be true that nothing would have prevented you from having a peach if you had chosen it instead of cake. But these *ifs* are not the same as saying you could have chosen a peach, period. You couldn't have chosen it unless the possibility remained open until you closed it off by choosing cake.

Some people have thought that it is never possible for us to do anything different from what we actually do, in this absolute sense. They acknowledge that what we do depends on our choices, decisions, and wants and that we make different choices in different circumstances: we're not like the earth rotating on its axis with monotonous regularity. But the claim is that, in each case, the circumstances that exist before we act determine our actions and make them inevitable. The sum total of a person's experiences, desires and knowledge, his hereditary constitution, the social circumstances and the nature of the choice facing him, together with other factors that we may not know about, all combine to make a particular action in the circumstances inevitable.

This view is called determinism. The idea is not that we can know all the laws of the universe and use them to *predict* what will happen. First of all, we can't know all the complex circumstances that affect a human choice. Secondly, even when we do learn something about the circumstances and try to make a prediction, that is itself a *change* in the circumstances, which may change the predicted result. But predictability isn't the point. The hypothesis is that there *are* laws of nature, like those that govern the movement of the planets, which govern everything that happens in the world, and that in accordance with those laws, the circumstances before an action determine that it will happen and will rule out any other possibility.

If that is true, then even while you were making up your mind about dessert, it was already determined by the many factors working on you and in you that you would choose cake. You *couldn't* have chosen the peach, even though you thought you could: the process of decision is just the working out of the determined result inside your mind.

If determinism is true for everything that happens, it was already determined before you were born that you would choose cake. Your choice was determined by the situation immediately before, and *that* situation was determined by the situation before *it*, and so on as far back as you want to go.

Even if determinism isn't true for everything that happens—even if some things just happen without being determined by causes that were there in advance—it would still be very significant if everything *we did* were determined before we did it. However free you might feel when choosing between fruit and cake, or between two candidates in an election, you would really be able to make only one choice in those circumstances—though if the circumstances or your desires had been different, you would have chosen differently.

If you believed that about yourself and other people, it would probably change the way you felt about things. For instance, could you blame yourself for giving in to temptation and having the cake? Would it make sense to say, "I really should have had a peach instead," if you *couldn't* have chosen a peach instead? It certainly wouldn't make sense to say it if there *was* no fruit. So how can it make sense if there *was* fruit, but you couldn't have chosen it because it was determined in advance that you would choose cake?

This seems to have serious consequences. Besides not being able sensibly to blame yourself for having had cake, you probably wouldn't be able sensibly to blame anyone at all for doing something bad, or praise them for doing something good. If it was determined in advance that they would do it, it was inevitable: they couldn't have done anything else, given the circumstances as they were. So how can we hold them responsible?

You may be very mad at someone who comes to a party at your house and steals all your Glenn Gould records, but suppose you believed that his action was determined in advance by his nature and the situation. Suppose you believed that everything he did, including the earlier actions that had contributed to the formation of his character, was determined in advance by earlier circumstances. Could you still hold him responsible for such low-grade behavior? Or would it be more reasonable to regard him as a kind of natural disaster—as if your records had been eaten by termites?

People disagree about this. Some think that if determinism is true, no one can reasonably be praised or blamed for anything, any more than the rain can be praised or blamed for falling. Others think that it still makes sense to praise good actions and condemn bad ones, even if they were inevitable. After all, the fact that someone was determined in advance to behave badly doesn't mean that he *didn't* behave badly. If he steals your records, that shows inconsiderateness and dishonesty, whether it was determined or not. Furthermore, if we don't blame him, or perhaps even punish him, he'll probably do it again.

On the other hand, if we think that what he did was determined in advance, this seems more like punishing a dog for chewing on the rug. It doesn't mean we hold him responsible for what he did: we're just trying to influence his behavior in the future. I myself don't think it makes sense to blame someone for doing what it was impossible for him not to do. (Though of course determinism implies that it was determined in advance that I would think this.)

These are the problems we must face if determinism is true. But perhaps it isn't true. Many scientists now believe that it isn't true for the basic particles of matter—that in a given situation, there's more than one thing that an electron may do. Perhaps if determinism isn't true for human actions, either, this leaves room for free will and responsibility. What if human actions, or at least some of them, are not determined in advance? What if, up to the moment when you choose, it's an open possibility that you will choose either chocolate cake or a peach? Then, so far as what has happened before is concerned, you *could* choose either one. Even if you actually choose cake, you could have chosen a peach.

But is even this enough for free will? Is this all you mean when you say, "I could have chosen fruit instead?"—that the choice wasn't determined in advance? No, you believe something more. You believe that *you* determined what you would do, by *doing* it. It wasn't determined in advance, but it didn't *just happen*, either. *You did it*, and you could have done the opposite. But what does that mean?

This is a funny question: we all know what it means to *do* something. But the problem is, if the act wasn't determined in advance, by your desires, beliefs, and personality, among other things, it seems to be something that just happened, without any explanation. And in that case, how was it *your doing*?

One possible reply would be that there is no answer to that question. Free action is just a basic feature of the world, and it can't be analyzed. There's a difference between something just happening without a cause and an action just being *done* without a cause. It's a difference we all understand, even if we can't explain it.

Some people would leave it at that. But others find it suspicious that we must appeal to this unexplained idea to explain the sense in which you could have chosen fruit instead of cake. Up to now it has seemed that determinism is the big threat to responsibility. But now it seems that even if our choices are not determined in advance, it is still hard to understand in what way we *can* do what we don't do. Either of two choices may be possible in advance, but unless I determine which of them occurs, it is no more my responsibility than if it was determined by causes beyond my control. And how can *I* determine it if *nothing* determines it?

This raises the alarming possibility that we're not responsible for our actions whether determinism is true *or* whether it's false. If determinism is true, antecedent circumstances are responsible. If determinism is false, nothing is responsible. That would really be a dead end.

There is another possible view, completely opposite to most of what we've been saying. Some people think responsibility for our actions *requires* that our actions be determined, rather than requiring that they not be. The claim is that for an action to be something you have done, it has to be produced by certain kinds of causes in you. For instance, when you chose the chocolate cake, that was something you did, rather than something that just happened, because you wanted chocolate cake more than you wanted a peach. Because your appetite for cake was stronger at the time than your desire to avoid gaining weight, it resulted in your choosing the cake. In other cases of action, the psychological explanation will be more complex, but there will always be one—otherwise the action wouldn't be yours. This explanation seems to mean that what you did was determined in advance after all. If it wasn't determined by anything, it was just an unexplained event, something that happened out of the blue rather than something that you did.

According to this position, causal determination by itself does not threaten freedom—only a certain *kind* of cause does that. If you grabbed the cake because someone else pushed you into it, then it wouldn't be a free choice. But free action doesn't require that there be no determining cause at all: it means that the cause has to be of a familiar psychological type.

I myself can't accept this solution. If I thought that everything I did was determined by my circumstances and my psychological condition, I would feel trapped. And if I thought the same about everybody else, I would feel that they were like a lot of puppets. It wouldn't make sense to hold them responsible for their actions any more than you hold a dog or a cat or even an elevator responsible.

On the other hand, I'm not sure I understand how responsibility for our choices makes sense if they are *not* determined. It's not clear what it means to say *I* determine the choice, if nothing about me determines it. So perhaps the feeling that you could have chosen a peach instead of a piece of cake is a philosophical illusion, and couldn't be right whatever was the case.

STUDY QUESTIONS

1. What is determinism?
2. If you chose one apple rather than another seemingly as good, was your choice determined?
3. Would you, like Nagel, believe yourself trapped if everything you did was determined by your circumstances and psychological conditions?
4. Why does Nagel doubt that we are responsible for our choices if they are not determined?

Free Will and Determinism

W. T. STACE

In the previous essay Nagel defended the view that free will and determinism are incompatible, that one or the other is false. Many philosophers, however, believe the two theses are compatible and that both are true.

These philosophers are sympathetic to the sort of argument presented in our next selection by W. T. Stace (1886–1967), an Englishman who became Professor of Philosophy at Princeton University. He maintains that once we define "free will" properly, any apparent incompatibility with determinism disappears.

[T]hose learned professors of philosophy or psychology who deny the existence of free will do so only in their professional moments and in their studies and lecture rooms. For when it comes to doing anything practical, even of the most trivial kind, they invariably behave as if they and others were free. They inquire from you at dinner whether you will choose this dish or that dish. They will ask a child why he told a lie, and will punish him for not having chosen the way of truthfulness. All of which

Specified excerpts from *Religion and the Modern Mind* by W. T. Stace. Copyright © 1952 by W. T. Stace. Copyright renewed. Reprinted by permission of HarperCollins Publishers, Inc.

is inconsistent with a disbelief in free will. This should cause us to suspect that the problem is not a real one; and this, I believe, is the case. The dispute is merely verbal, and is due to nothing but a confusion about the meanings of words. . . .

Throughout the modern period, until quite recently, it was assumed, both by the philosophers who denied free will and by those who defended it, that *determinism is inconsistent with free will*. If a man's actions were wholly determined by chains of causes stretching back into the remote past, so that they could be predicted beforehand by a mind which knew all the causes, it was assumed that they could not in that case be free. This implies that a certain definition of actions done from free will was assumed, namely that they are actions *not* wholly determined by causes or predictable beforehand. Let us shorten this by saying that free will was defined as meaning indeterminism. This is the incorrect definition which has led to the denial of free will. As soon as we see what the true definition is, we shall find that the question whether the world is deterministic, as Newtonian science implied, or in a measure indeterministic, as current physics teaches, is wholly irrelevant to the problem. . . .

At a recent murder trial in Trenton, some of the accused had signed confessions, but afterwards asserted that they had done so under police duress. The following exchange might have occurred:

JUDGE: Did you sign this confession of your own free will?
PRISONER: No. I signed it because the police beat me up.

Now suppose that a philosopher had been a member of the jury. We could imagine this conversation taking place in the jury room.

FOREMAN OF THE JURY: The prisoner says he signed the confession because he was beaten, and not of his own free will.
PHILOSOPHER: This is quite irrelevant to the case. There is no such thing as free will.
FOREMAN: Do you mean to say that it makes no difference whether he signed because his conscience made him want to tell the truth or because he was beaten?
PHILOSOPHER: None at all. Whether he was caused to sign by a beating or by some desire of his own—the desire to tell the truth, for example—in either case his signing was causally determined, and therefore in neither case did he act of his own free will. Since there is no such thing as free will, the question whether he signed of his own free will ought not to be discussed by us.

The foreman and the rest of the jury would rightly conclude that the philosopher must be making some mistake. What sort of a mistake could it be? There is only one possible answer. The philosopher must be using the phrase "free will" in some peculiar way of his own which is not the way in which men usually use it. . . .

What, then, is the difference between acts which are freely done and those which are not? . . . The free acts are all caused by desires, or motives, or by some sort of internal psychological states of the agent's mind. The unfree acts, on the other hand, are all caused by physical forces or physical conditions, outside the agent. . . . We may therefore frame the following rough definitions. *Acts freely done are those whose immediate causes are psychological states in the agent. Acts not freely done are those whose immediate causes are states of affairs external to the agent.*

It is plain that if we define free will in this way, then free will certainly exists, and the philosopher's denial of its existence is seen to be what it is—nonsense. For it is obvious that all those actions of men which we should ordinarily attribute to the exercise of their free will, or of which we should say that they freely chose to do them, are in fact actions which have been caused by their own desires, wishes, thoughts, emotions, impulses, or other psychological states.

In applying our definition we shall find that it usually works well, but that there are some puzzling cases which it does not seem exactly to fit. These puzzles can always be solved by paying careful attention to the ways in which words are used, and remembering that they are not always used consistently. I have space for only one example. Suppose that a thug threatens to shoot you unless you give him your wallet, and suppose that you do so. Do you, in giving him your wallet, do so of your own free will or not? If we apply our definition, we find that you acted freely, since the immediate cause of the action was not an actual outside force but the fear of death, which is a psychological cause. Most people, however, would say that you did not act of your own free will but under compulsion. Does this show that our definition is wrong? I do not think so. . . . In the case under discussion, though no actual force was used, the gun at your forehead so nearly approximated to actual force that we tend to say the case was one of compulsion. It is a borderline case.

Here is what may seem like another kind of puzzle. According to our view, an action may be free though it could have been predicted beforehand with certainty. But suppose you told a lie, and it was certain beforehand that you would tell it. How could one then say, "You could have told the truth"? The answer is that it is perfectly true that you could have told the truth *if* you had wanted to. In fact you would have done so, for in that case the causes producing your action, namely your desires, would have been different and would therefore have produced different effects. It is a delusion that predictability and free will are incompatible. This agrees with common sense. For if, knowing your character, I predict that you will act honorably, no one would say when you do act honorably, that this shows you did not do so of your own free will.

STUDY QUESTIONS

1. If you deny the existence of free will, is your position undermined by the observation that you act as if people had free will?
2. How does Stace argue in behalf of the compatibility of free will and determinism?
3. What does Stace believe is the difference between acts that are freely done and those that are not?
4. If someone can predict with certainty what you will do, might your action nevertheless be free?

Freedom or Determinism?

STEVEN M. CAHN

In the next essay I offer an overview of the problem of free will and argue against Stace's view that freedom is compatible with determinism. The discussion begins with an account of one of the twentieth century's most famous criminal trials. How did it involve a philosophical issue? Let us see.

In 1924 the American people were horrified by a senseless crime of extraordinary brutality. The defendants were eighteen-year-old Nathan Leopold and seventeen-year-old Richard Loeb, the sons of Chicago millionaires, and brilliant students who had led seemingly idyllic lives. Leopold was the youngest graduate in the history of the University of Chicago, and Loeb the youngest graduate in the history of the University of Michigan. Suddenly they were accused of the kidnapping and vicious murder of fourteen-year-old Bobby Franks, a cousin of Loeb's. Before the trial even began, Leopold and Loeb both confessed, and from across the country came an outcry for their execution.

The lawyer who agreed to defend them was Clarence Darrow, the outstanding defense attorney of his time. Because Leopold and Loeb had already admitted their crime, Darrow's only chance was to explain their behavior in such a way that his clients could escape the death penalty. He was forced to argue that Leopold and Loeb were not morally responsible for what they had done, that they were not to be blamed for their actions. But how could he possibly maintain that position?

Darrow's defense was a landmark in the history of criminal law. He argued that the actions of his clients were a direct and necessary result of hereditary and environmental forces beyond their control.[1] Leopold suffered from a glandular disease that left him depressed and moody. Originally shy with girls, he had been sent to an all-girls school as a cure but had sustained deep psychic scars from which he never recovered. In addition, his parents instilled in him the belief that his wealth absolved him of any responsibility toward others. Pathologically inferior because of his diminutive size, and pathologically superior because of his wealth, he became an acute schizophrenic.

Loeb suffered from a nervous disorder that caused fainting spells. During his unhappy childhood, he had often thought of committing suicide. He was under the control of a domineering governess and was forced to lie and cheat to deceive her.

His wealth led him to believe that he was superior to all those around him, and he developed a fascination for crime, an activity in which he could demonstrate his superiority. By the time he reached college he was severely psychotic.

In his final plea, Darrow recounted these facts. His central theme was that Leopold and Loeb were in the grip of powers beyond their control, that they themselves were victims.

> I do not know what it was that made these boys do this mad act, but I do know there is a reason for it. I know they did not beget themselves. I know that any one of an infinite number of causes reaching back to the beginning might be working out in these boys' minds, whom you are asked to hang in malice and in hatred and in injustice, because someone in the past has sinned against them. . . . What had this boy to do with it? He was not his own father; he was not his own mother; he was not his own grandparents. All of this was handed to him. He did not surround himself with governesses and wealth. He did not make himself. And yet he is to be compelled to pay.[2]

Darrow's plea was successful, for Leopold and Loeb escaped execution and were sentenced to life imprisonment. Although they had committed crimes and were legally responsible for their actions, the judge believed they were not morally responsible, for they had not acted freely.

If the line of argument that Darrow utilized in the Leopold–Loeb case is sound, then not only were Leopold and Loeb not to blame for what they had done, but no person is ever to blame for any actions. As Darrow himself put it, "We are all helpless."[3] But is Darrow's argument sound? Does the conclusion follow from the premises, and are the premises true?

We can formalize his argument as follows:

Premise 1:   No action is free if it must occur.
Premise 2:   In the case of every event that occurs, antecedent
                conditions, known or unknown, ensure the event's
                occurrence.
Conclusion: Therefore, no action is free.

Premise (1) assumes that an action is free only if it is within the agent's power to perform it and within the agent's power not to perform it. In other words, whether a free action will occur is up to the agent. If circumstances require the agent to perform a certain action or require the agent not to perform that action, then the action is not free.

Premise (2) is the thesis known as *determinism*. Put graphically, it is the claim that if at any time a being knew the position of every particle in the universe and all the forces acting on each particle, then that being could predict with certainty every future event. Determinism does not presume such a being exists; the being is only imagined in order to illustrate what the world would be like if determinism were true.

Darrow's conclusion, which is supposed to follow from premises (1) and (2), is that no person has free will. Note that to have free will does not imply being free with regard to all actions, for only the mythical Superman is free to leap tall buildings at a single bound. But so long as at least some of an agent's actions are free, the agent is said to have free will. What Darrow's argument purports to prove is that not a single human action that has ever been performed has been performed freely.

Does the conclusion of Darrow's argument follow from the premises? If premise (2) is true, then every event that occurs must occur, for its occurrence is ensured by antecedent conditions. Because every action is an event, it follows from premise (2) that every action that occurs must occur. But according to premise (1), no action is free if it must occur. Thus, if premises (1) and (2) are true, it follows that no action is free—the conclusion of Darrow's argument.

Even granting that Darrow's reasoning is unassailable, we need not accept the conclusion of his argument unless we grant the truth of his premises. Should we do so?

Hard determinism is the view that both premises of Darrow's argument are correct. In other words, a hard determinist believes that determinism is true and that, as a consequence, no person has free will.[4] Determinists note that whenever an event occurs, we all assume that a causal explanation can account for the occurrence of the event. Suppose, for example, you feel a pain in your arm and are prompted to visit a physician. After examining you, the doctor announces that the pain has no cause, either physical or psychological. In other words, you are supposed to be suffering from an uncaused pain. On hearing this diagnosis, you would surely switch doctors. After all, no one may be able to discover the cause of your pain, but surely something is causing it. If nothing were causing it, you wouldn't be in pain. This same line of reasoning applies whether the event to be explained is a loud noise, a change in the weather, or an individual's action. If the event were uncaused, it wouldn't have occurred.

We may agree, however, that the principle of determinism holds in the vast majority of cases, yet doubt its applicability in the realm of human action. While causal explanations may be found for rocks falling and birds flying, people are far more complex than rocks or birds.

The determinist responds to this objection by asking us to consider any specific action: for instance, your decision to read this book. You may suppose your decision was uncaused, but did you not wish to acquire information about philosophy? The determinist argues that your desire for such information, together with your belief that the information is found in this book, caused you to read. Just as physical forces cause rocks and birds to do things, so human actions are caused by desires and beliefs.

If you doubt this claim, the determinist can call attention to our success in predicting people's behavior. For example, a store owner who reduces prices can depend on increasing visits by shoppers; an athlete who wins a major championship can rely on greater attention from the press. Furthermore, when we read novels or see plays, we expect to understand why the characters act as they do, and an author who fails to provide such explanations is charged with poor writing. The similarity of people's reactions to the human condition also accounts for the popularity of the incisive psychological insights of a writer such as La Rochefoucauld, the French aphorist. We read one of his maxims, for instance, "When our integrity declines, our taste does also,"[5] and we nod our heads with approval, but are we not agreeing to a plausible generalization about the workings of the human psyche?

Granted, people's behavior cannot be predicted with certainty, but the hard determinist reminds us that each individual is influenced by a unique combination of hereditary and environmental factors. Just as each rock is slightly different from every other rock, and each bird is somewhat different from every other bird, so human beings differ from each other. Yet just as rocks and birds are part of an unbroken chain of causes and effects, so human beings, too, are part of that chain. Just as a rock falls because it breaks off from a cliff, so people act because of their desires and beliefs. And just as a rock has no control over the wind that causes it to break off, so people have no control over the desires and beliefs that cause them to act. In short, we are said to have no more control over our desires and beliefs than Leopold and Loeb had over theirs. If you can control your desire for food and your friend cannot, the explanation is that your will is of a sort that can control your desire and your friend's will is of a sort that cannot. That your will is of one sort and your friend's will of another is not within the control of either of you. As one hard determinist has written, "If we can overcome the effects of early environment, the ability to do so is itself a product of the early environment. We did not give ourselves this ability; and if we lack it we cannot be blamed for not having it."[6]

At this point in the argument, an antideterminist is apt to call attention to recent developments in physics that have been interpreted by some thinkers as a refutation of determinism. They claim that work in quantum mechanics demonstrates that certain subatomic events are uncaused and inherently unpredictable. Yet some physicists and philosophers of science argue that determinism has not been refuted, because the experimental results can be understood in causal terms.[7] The outcome of this dispute, however, seems irrelevant to the issue of human freedom, because the events we are discussing are not subatomic, and indeterminism on that level is compatible with the universal causation of events on the much larger level of human action.

Here, then, is a summary of hard determinism: According to this view, determinism is true and no person has free will. Every event that occurs is caused to occur, for otherwise why would it occur? Your present actions are events caused by your previous desires and beliefs, which themselves are accounted for by hereditary and environmental factors. These are part of a causal chain extending back far before your birth, and each link of the chain determines the succeeding link. Because you obviously have no control over events that occurred before your birth, and because these earlier events determined the later ones, it follows that you have no control over your present actions. In short, you do not have free will.

The hard determinist's argument may appear plausible, yet few of us are inclined to accept its shocking conclusion. We opt, therefore, to deny one of its two premises. *Soft determinism* is the view that the conclusion is false because premise 1 is false. In other words, a soft determinist believes both that determinism is true and that human beings have free will. The implication of the position is that an action may be free even if it is part of a causal chain extending back to events outside the agent's control. While this view may at first appear implausible, it has been defended throughout the centuries by many eminent philosophers, including David Hume and John Stuart Mill.

An approach employed explicitly or implicitly by many soft determinists has come to be known as "the paradigm-case argument." Consider it first in another setting, where its use is a classic of philosophical argumentation.

In studying physics, we learn that ordinary objects like tables and chairs are composed of sparsely scattered, minute particles. This fact may lead us to suppose that such objects are not solid. As Sir Arthur Eddington, the noted physicist, put it, a "plank has no solidity of substance. To step on it is like stepping on a swarm of flies."[8]

Eddington's view that a plank is not solid was forcefully attacked by the British philosopher L. Susan Stebbing. She pointed out that the word "solid" derives its meaning from examples such as planks.

> For "solid" just is the word we use to describe a certain respect in which a plank of wood resembles a block of marble, a piece of paper, and a cricket ball, and in which each of these differs from a sponge, from the interior of a soap-bubble, and from the holes in a net. . . . The point is that the common usage of language enables us to attribute a meaning to the phrase "a solid plank"; but there is no common usage of language that provides a meaning for the word "solid" that would make sense to say that the plank on which I stand is not solid.[9]

In other words, a plank is a paradigm case of solidity. Anyone who claims that a plank is not solid does not know how the word "solid" is used in the English language. Note that Stebbing is not criticizing Eddington's scientific views but only the manner in which he interpreted them.

The paradigm-case argument is useful to soft determinists, for in the face of the hard determinist's claim that no human action is free, soft determinists respond by pointing to a paradigm case of a free action, for instance, a person walking down the street. They stipulate that the individual is not under the influence of drugs, is not attached to ropes, is not sleepwalking, and so on; in other words, they refer to a normal, everyday instance of a person walking down the street. Soft determinists claim that the behavior described is a paradigm case of a free action, clearly distinguishable from instances in which a person is, in fact, under the influence of drugs, attached to ropes, or sleepwalking. These latter cases are not examples of free actions, or are at best problematic examples, while the case the soft determinists cite is clear and seemingly indisputable. Indeed, according to soft determinists, anyone who claims the act of walking down the street is not free does not know how the word "free" is used in English. Thus people certainly have free will, for we can cite obvious cases in which they act freely.

How do soft determinists define a "free action"? According to them, actions are free if the persons who perform them wish to do so and could, if they wished, not perform them. If your arm is forcibly raised, you did not act freely, for you did not wish to raise your arm. If you were locked in a room, you would also not be free, even if you wished to be there, for if you wished to leave, you couldn't.

Soft determinists emphasize that once we define "freedom" correctly, any apparent incompatibility between freedom and determinism disappears. Consider some particular action I perform that is free in the sense explicated by soft determinists. Even if the action is one link in a causal chain extending far back beyond my birth, nevertheless I am free with regard to that action, for I wish to perform it, and if I did not wish to, I would not do so. This description of the situation is consistent with supposing that my wish is a result of hereditary and environmental factors over which I have no control. The presence of such factors is, according to the soft determinists, irrelevant to the question of whether my action is free. I may be walking down a particular street because of my desire to buy a coat and my belief that I am heading toward a clothing store, and this desire and belief may themselves be caused by any number of other factors. But because I desire to walk down the street and could walk down some other street if I so desired, it follows that I am freely walking down the street. By this line of reasoning soft determinists affirm both free will and determinism, finding no incompatibility between them.

Soft determinism is an inviting doctrine, for it allows us to maintain a belief in free will without having to relinquish the belief that every event has a cause. Soft determinism, however, is open to objections that have led some philosophers to abandon the position.

The fundamental problem for soft determinists is that their definition of "freedom" does not seem in accordance with the ordinary way in which we use the term. Note that soft determinists and hard determinists offer two different definitions of "freedom." According to the hard determinist, an action is free if it is within my power to perform it and also within my power not to perform it. According to the soft determinist, an action is free if it is such that if I wish to perform it I can, and if I wish not to perform it I also can. To highlight the difference between these definitions, consider the case of a man who has been hypnotized and rolls up the leg of his pants as if to cross a stream. Is his action free? According to the hard determinist, the man's action is not free, for it is not within his power to refrain from rolling up the leg of his pants. According to the soft determinist's definition of "freedom," the action would be considered free, for the agent desires to perform it, and if he didn't desire to, he wouldn't. But a man under hypnosis is not free. Therefore, the soft determinist's definition of "freedom" seems unsatisfactory.

Perhaps this objection to soft determinism is unfair, because the desires of the hypnotized man are not his own but are controlled by the hypnotist. The force of the objection to soft determinism, however, is that the soft determinist overlooks whether a person's wishes or desires are themselves within that individual's control. The hard determinist emphasizes that my action is free only if it is up to me whether to perform it. But in order for an action to be up to me, I need to have control over my own wishes or desires. If I do not, my desires might be controlled by a hypnotist, a brainwasher, my family, hereditary factors, and so on, and thus I would not be free. Soft determinists do not appear to take such possibilities seriously, because, according to them, I would be free even if my desires were not within my control, so long as I was acting according to my desires and could act differently if my desires were different. But could my desires have been different? That is the crucial question. If my desires could not have been different, then I could not have acted in any way other than I did, which is the description of a person who is not free.

By failing to consider the ways in which a person's desires can be controlled by external forces beyond the individual's control, soft determinists offer a definition of "freedom" that I find not in accord with our normal use of the term. They may, of course, define terms as they wish, but we are interested in the concept of freedom relevant to questions of moral responsibility. Any concept of freedom implying that hypnotized or brainwashed individuals are morally responsible for their actions is not the concept in question.

What of the soft determinist's claim that a person's walking down the street is a paradigm case of a free action? Although I agree that the paradigm-case argument can sometimes be used effectively, the soft determinist's appeal to it does not seem convincing. To see why, imagine that we traveled to a land in which the inhabitants believed that every woman born on February 29 was a witch, and that every witch had the power to cause droughts. If we refused to believe that any woman was a witch, the philosophically sophisticated inhabitants might try to convince us by appealing to the paradigm-case argument, claiming that anyone born on February 29 is a paradigm case of a witch.

What would we say in response? How does this appeal to a paradigm case differ from Susan Stebbing's appeal to a plank as a paradigm case of solidity? No one doubts that a plank can hold significant weight and is, in that sense, solid. But until women born on February 29 demonstrate supernatural powers and are in that sense witches, the linguistic claim alone has no force.

Are soft determinists appealing to an indisputable instance when they claim that a person's walking down the street is a paradigm case of a free action? Not at all, for as we saw in the trial of Leopold and Loeb, such apparently free actions may not turn out to be judged as free. By appealing to a disputable example as a paradigm case, soft determinists assume what they are supposed to be proving. They are supposed to demonstrate that actions such as walking down the street are examples of free actions. Merely asserting that such actions are free is to overlook the hard determinist's argument that such actions are not free. No questionable instance can be used as a paradigm case, and walking down the street is, as Darrow demonstrated, a questionable example of a free action. Thus soft determinism appears to have a serious weakness.

Remember that the hard determinist argues that because premises 1 and 2 of Darrow's argument are true, so is the conclusion. Soft determinists argue that premise 1 is false. If they are mistaken, then the only way to avoid hard determinism is to reject premise 2. That position is known as *libertarianism*.

The libertarian agrees with the hard determinist that if an action must occur, it is not free. For the libertarian as well as for the hard determinist, I am free with regard to a particular action only if it is within my power to perform the action and within my power not to perform it. But do persons ever act freely? The hard determinist believes that people are never free, because in the case of every action, antecedent conditions, known or unknown, ensure the action's occurrence. Libertarians refuse to accept this conclusion, but find it impossible to reject premise 1 of Darrow's argument. Therefore their only recourse is to reject premise 2. As Sherlock Holmes noted, "When you have eliminated the impossible, whatever remains, however improbable, must be the truth."[10] The libertarian thus denies that every event has a cause.

But why is the libertarian so convinced that people sometimes act freely? Consider an ordinary human action—for instance, raising your hand at a meeting to attract the speaker's attention. If you are attending a lecture and the time comes for questions from the audience, you believe it is within your power to raise your hand and also within your power not to raise it. The choice is yours. Nothing forces you to ask a question, and nothing prevents you from asking one. What could be more obvious? If this description of the situation is accurate, then hard determinism is incorrect, for you are free with regard to the act of raising your hand.

The heart of the libertarian's position is that innumerable examples of this sort are conclusive evidence for free will. Indeed, we normally accept them as such. We assume on most occasions that we are free with regard to our actions, and, moreover, we assume that other persons are free with regard to theirs. If a friend agrees to meet us at six o'clock for dinner and arrives an hour late claiming to have lost track of time, we blame her for her tardiness, because we assume she had it within her power to act otherwise. All she had to do was glance at her watch, and assuming no special circumstances were involved, it was within her power to do so. She was simply negligent and deserves to be blamed, for she could have acted conscientiously. But to believe she could have acted in a way other than she did is to believe she was free.

How do hard determinists respond to such examples? They argue that such situations need to be examined in greater detail. In the case of our friend who arrives an hour late for dinner, we assume she is to blame for her actions, but the hard determinist points out that some motive impelled her to be late. Perhaps she was more interested in finishing her work at the office than in arriving on time for dinner. But why was she more interested in finishing her work than in arriving on time? Perhaps her parents had instilled in her the importance of work but not promptness. Hard determinists stress that whatever the explanation for her lateness, the motive causing it was stronger than the motive impelling her to arrive on time. She acted as she did because her strongest motive prevailed. Which motive was the strongest, however, was not within her control, and thus she was not free.

The hard determinist's reply may seem persuasive. How can I deny that I am invariably caused to act by my strongest motive? Analysis reveals, however, that the thesis is tautological, immune from refutation, and so devoid of empirical content. No matter what example of a human action is presented, a defender of the thesis could argue that the person's action resulted from the strongest motive. If I take a swim, taking a swim must have been my strongest motive. If I decide to forgo the swim and read a book instead, then reading a book must have been my strongest motive. How do we know that my motive to read a book was stronger than my motive to take a swim? Because I read a book and did not take a swim. If this line of argument appears powerful, the illusion will last only so long as we do not ask how we are to identify a person's strongest motive. The only possible answer appears to be that the strongest motive is the motive that prevails, the motive that causes the person to act. If the strongest motive is the motive causing the person to act, what force is there in the claim that the motive causing a person to act is causing the person to act? No insight into the complexities of human action is obtained by trumpeting such an empty redundancy.

Thus the hard determinist does not so easily succeed in overturning the examples of free actions offered by the libertarian. However, both hard and soft determinists have another argument to offer against the libertarian's position. If the libertarian is correct that free actions are uncaused, why do they occur? Are they inexplicable occurrences? If so, to act freely would be to act in a random, chaotic, unintelligible fashion. Yet holding people morally blameworthy for inexplicable actions is unreasonable. If you are driving a car and, to your surprise, find yourself turning the wheel to the right, we can hardly blame you if an accident occurs, for what happened was beyond your control.

So determinists argue that libertarians are caught in a dilemma. If we are caused to do whatever we do, libertarians assert we are not morally responsible for our actions. Yet if our actions are uncaused and inexplicable, libertarians again must deny our moral responsibility. How then can libertarians claim we ever act responsibly?

To understand the libertarian response, consider the simple act of a man picking up a telephone. Suppose we want to understand what he is doing and are told he is calling his stockbroker. The man has decided to buy some stock and wishes his broker to place the appropriate order. With this explanation, we now know why this man has picked up the telephone. Although we may be interested in learning more about the man or his choice of stocks, we have a complete explanation of his action, which turns out not to be random, chaotic, or unintelligible. We may not know what, if anything, is causing the man to act, but we do know the reason for the man's action. The libertarian thus replies to the determinist's dilemma by arguing that an action can be uncaused yet understandable, explicable in terms of the agent's intentions or purposes.

Now contrast the libertarian's description of a particular action with a determinist's. Let the action be your moving your arm to adjust your television set. A determinist claims you were caused to move your arm by your desire to adjust the set and your belief that you could make this adjustment by turning the dials. A libertarian claims you moved your arm in order to adjust the set.

Note that the libertarian explains human actions fundamentally differently from the way in which we explain the movements of rocks or rivers. If we speak of a rock's purpose in falling off a cliff or a river's purpose in flowing south, we do so only metaphorically, for we believe that rocks and rivers have no purposes of their own but are caused to do what they do. Strictly speaking, a rock does not fall in order to hit the ground, and a river does not flow in order to reach the south. But libertarians are speaking not metaphorically but literally when they say that people act in order to achieve their purposes. After all, not even the most complex machine can act as a person does. A machine can break down and fail to operate, but only a human being can protest and stop work on purpose.

Is the libertarian's view correct? I doubt anyone is justified in answering that question with certainty, but if the libertarian is right, human beings are often morally responsible for their actions. They deserve praise when acting admirably and blame when acting reprehensibly. Darrow may have been correct in arguing that Leopold and Loeb were not free agents, but if the libertarian is right, the burden of proof lay with Darrow, for he had to demonstrate that these boys were in that respect unlike the rest of us.

What if the libertarian is not correct? What if all human actions are caused by antecedent conditions, known or unknown, that ensure their occurrence? Moral responsibility would vanish; but even so, people could be held legally responsible for their actions. Just as we need to be safeguarded against mad dogs, so we need protection from dangerous people. Thus even if no person were morally responsible, we would still have a legal system, courts, criminals, and prisons. Remember that Darrow's eloquence did not free his clients; indeed, he did not ask that they be freed. Although he did not blame them for their actions, he did not want those actions repeated. To Darrow, Leopold and Loeb were sick men who needed the same care as sick persons with a contagious disease. After all, in a world without freedom, events need not be viewed as agreeable; they should, however, be understood as necessary.

NOTES

1. The following information is found in Irving Stone, *Clarence Darrow for the Defense* (Garden City, NY: Doubleday, Doran, 1941), pp. 384–91.
2. *Attorney for the Damned,* ed. Arthur Weinberg (New York: Simon and Schuster, 1957), pp. 37, 65.
3. Ibid., p. 37.
4. The expressions "hard determinism" and "soft determinism" were coined by William James in his essay "The Dilemma of Determinism," reprinted in *Essays on Faith and Morals* (Cleveland: World, 1962).
5. *The Maxims of La Rochefoucauld,* trans. Louis Kronenberger (New York: Random House, 1959), #379.
6. John Hospers, "What Means This Freedom," *Determinism and Freedom in the Age of Modern Science,* ed. Sidney Hook (New York: Collier, 1961), p. 138.

7. For a detailed discussion of the philosophical implications of quantum mechanics, see Ernest Nagel, *The Structure of Science* (New York: Harcourt Brace Jovanovich, 1961), ch. 10.
8. A. S. Eddington, *The Nature of the Physical World* (New York: Macmillan, 1928), p. 342.
9. L. Susan Stebbing, *Philosophy and the Physicists* (New York: Dover, 1958), pp. 51–52.
10. Sir Arthur Conan Doyle, "The Sign of Four," in *The Complete Sherlock Holmes* (Garden City, NY: Doubleday, n.d.), p. 111.

STUDY QUESTIONS

1. Is a hard determinist more committed to determinism than a soft determinist?
2. What reply does Cahn offer to the sort of argument presented by Stace in the preceding selection?
3. Are reasons a type of cause?
4. Can a machine make a mistake on purpose?

The Principle of Alternative Possibilities

HARRY FRANKFURT

Our previous selections on free will have taken for granted that if people cannot act otherwise than as they do, then they do not act freely. But is this assumption correct? Harry Frankfurt, who is Professor Emeritus of Philosophy at Princeton University, argues that the assumption is mistaken, and he offers an intriguing example to defend his position.

....

A dominant role in nearly all recent inquiries into the free-will problem has been played by a principle which I shall call "the principle of alternate possibilities." This principle states that a person is morally responsible for what he has done only if he could have done otherwise. . . . Practically no one . . . seems inclined to deny or even to question that the principle of alternate possibilities . . . is true. . . .

But the principle of alternate possibilities is false. A person may well be morally responsible for what he has done even though he could not have done

---

From Harry Frankfurt, "Alternative Possibilities and Moral Responsibility," *The Journal of Philosophy*, LXVI, 23 (1969). Reprinted by permission of the journal and the author.

otherwise. The principle's plausibility is an illusion, which can be made to vanish by bringing the relevant moral phenomena into sharper focus. . . .

Suppose someone—Black, let us say—wants Jones to perform a certain action. Black is prepared to go to considerable lengths to get his way, but he prefers to avoid showing his hand unnecessarily. So he waits until Jones is about to make up his mind what to do, and he does nothing unless it is clear to him (Black is an excellent judge of such things) that Jones is going to decide to do something *other* than what he wants him to do. If it does become clear that Jones is going to decide to do something else, Black takes effective steps to ensure that Jones decides to do, and that he does do, what he wants him to do. Whatever Jones's initial preferences and inclinations, then, Black will have his way.

What steps will Black take, if he believes he must take steps, in order to ensure that Jones decides and acts as he wishes? Anyone with a theory concerning what "could have done otherwise" means may answer this question for himself by describing whatever measures he would regard as sufficient to guarantee that, in the relevant sense, Jones cannot do otherwise. Let Black pronounce a terrible threat, and in this way both force Jones to perform the desired action and prevent him from performing a forbidden one. Let Black give Jones a potion, or put him under hypnosis, and in some such way as these generate in Jones an irresistible inner compulsion to perform the act Black wants performed and to avoid others. Or let Black manipulate the minute processes of Jones's brain and nervous system in some more direct way, so that causal forces running in and out of his synapses and along the poor man's nerves determine that he chooses to act and that he does act in the one way and not in any other. Given any conditions under which it will be maintained that Jones cannot do otherwise, in other words, let Black bring it about that those conditions prevail. The structure of the example is flexible enough, I think, to find a way around any charge of irrelevance by accommodating the doctrine on which the charge is based.

Now suppose that Black never has to show his hand because Jones, for reasons of his own, decides to perform and does perform the very action Black wants him to perform. In that case, it seems clear, Jones will bear precisely the same moral responsibility for what he does as he would have borne if Black had not been ready to take steps to ensure that he do it. It would be quite unreasonable to excuse Jones for his action, or to withhold the praise to which it would normally entitle him, on the basis of the fact that he could not have done otherwise. This fact played no role at all in leading him to act as he did. He would have acted the same even if it had not been a fact. Indeed, everything happened just as it would have happened without Black's presence in the situation and without his readiness to intrude into it.

In this example there are sufficient conditions for Jones's performing the action in question. What action he performs is not up to him. Of course it is in a way up to him whether he acts on his own or as a result of Black's intervention. That depends upon what action he himself is inclined to perform. But whether he finally acts on his own or as a result of Black's intervention, he performs the same action. He has no alternative but to do what Black wants him to do. If he does it on his own, however, his moral responsibility for doing it is not affected by the fact that Black was lurking in the background with sinister intent, since this intent never comes into play. . . .

This, then, is why the principle of alternate possibilities is mistaken. It asserts that a person bears no moral responsibility—that is, he is to be excused—for having performed an action if there were circumstances that made it impossible for him to avoid performing it. But there may be circumstances that make it impossible for a person to avoid performing some action without those circumstances in any way bringing it about that he performs that action. It would surely be no good for the person to refer to circumstances of this sort in an effort to absolve himself of moral responsibility for performing the action in question. For those circumstances, by hypothesis, actually had nothing to do with his having done what he did. He would have done precisely the same thing, and he would have been led or made in precisely the same way to do it, even if they had not prevailed. . . .

STUDY QUESTIONS

1. What is "the principle of alternate possibilities"?
2. Explain in your own words the case of Black and Jones.
3. Does this case disprove the principle of alternate possibilities?
4. Is Frankfurt's view consistent with soft determinism?

The Capacities of Agents

NEIL LEVY

Neil Levy holds research positions at both the University of Melbourne and the University of Oxford. In his reply to the previous selection by Frankfurt, Levy identifies the case of Black and Jones as a clever variation on an example offered by John Locke and argues that our capacities may be strengthened or weakened by the circumstances in which others place us. Thus Levy finds that in the case Frankfurt offers, Jones's freedom is undermined by Black's role. Here is a typical

Neil Levy, "Counterfactual Intervention and Agents' Capacities." Reprinted from *The Journal of Philosophy*, vol. CV, no. 5 (2008), by permission of the journal and the author.

philosophical dispute that may appear unconnected to real-life problems and yet turns out to lie at the heart of the issue of free will, which, as we have seen in the Leopold–Loeb case, can even have life-or-death consequences.

······································

It is widely held that Frankfurt-style cases (FSCs) decisively alter the landscape of debates over free will. Prior to their emergence, the debate between compatibilists and incompatibilists seemed irretrievably bogged down in the morass created by differing intuitions and different analyses of the central terms upon which the debate turned. For each of the central concepts—*abilities, alternative possibilities, capacities*—there were compatibilist and incompatibilist analyses available, and there seemed to be no decisive nonquestion-begging reasons to prefer one kind to the other. . . . FSCs changed all that, by showing (to the satisfaction of most) that alternative possibilities, and therefore agents' abilities to actualize such possibilities, are not necessary for moral responsibility. . . . Though agents lack alternative possibilities in FSCs, the features that explain why they lack such alternatives play no role in the explanation of what they do. Given that fact, agents in FSCs act "on their own" and are therefore apparently responsible for what they do.

In this paper I shall argue that this conclusion is unwarranted. FSCs can show that agents are responsible for their actions, despite lacking alternative possibilities, only if we are justified in believing not only that the agents they feature act "on their own," but also that their actions are an expression of *their* normal capacities for evaluating and responding to reasons. And we are justified in thinking that agents in FSCs act in a way that expresses their normal capacities only if we are justified in distinguishing between the intrinsic, responsibility-ensuring capacities of the agent and the features of her context. I shall show that there is no principled, non-*ad hoc* manner of making this latter distinction. I shall do this fighting thought experiment with thought experiment: by introducing a new kind of case, Frankfurt-enabler cases (FECs), in which agents apparently *gain* a capacity due to the presence of a counterfactual intervener. In FECs, the intuition that agents gain a capacity due to the presence of a counterfactual intervener depends upon our regarding the agent as an ensemble: agent-plus-intervener. But there is no principled reason, I claim, why we should distinguish between the agent and her context in FSCs, but fail to make this distinction in FECs. We should treat the cases alike. I argue that we can never understand agents' capacities, and thus the sensitivity to reasons of the mechanisms upon which they act, except by considering the context in which they are embedded. Hence, we are not entitled to conclude that the capacities of agents in FSCs are unchanged by the presence of the counterfactual intervener. . . .

In an FSC, an agent performs a morally significant action—say, voting for a political candidate in an election—in what is apparently the normal way, and therefore seems morally responsible for her action. However, due to circumstances of which the agent is unaware, she lacks alternatives: she cannot do otherwise than choose to vote in the way she does. Consider the following, more or less typical, FSC:

> *Voting*: When she enters the voting booth, Connie has not yet made up her mind whether to vote Democratic or Republican. Unbeknownst to her, an evil but gifted neuroscientist monitors her neural states using a computer chip he has implanted in her brain. The chip gives the neuroscientist the power to intervene in Connie's neural processes. Connie is psychologically constituted so that it is a necessary (though not sufficient) condition of her voting Democratic that she thinks deeply about a certain policy; were Connie to think deeply about this policy, the neuroscientist would intervene, causing her to choose to vote Republican. But Connie does not think deeply about the policy and proceeds to vote Republican on her own. The neuroscientist and his device play no role in bringing about Connie's vote.

Connie lacks any alternative to voting Republican; were she to think deeply about the policy that might motivate her to vote Democratic, the neuroscientist would intervene to bring it about that she votes Republican. But since she acts entirely on her own, she seems responsible for deciding to vote Republican and for voting Republican.

On the basis of cases like this, Frankfurt and his followers conclude that moral responsibility does not require alternative possibilities. . . .

As many people have pointed out, Frankfurt's original case can be understood as a clever variation on an example of John Locke's. In Locke's thought experiment, a man is carried into a room while he is asleep and the door is locked. When he awakes, he finds himself in the company of someone "he longs to see and speak with"; as a consequence he stays in the room willingly. Locke claims that we cannot doubt that the man stays in the room voluntarily, though "it is evident [. . .] he has not freedom to be gone."[1] In an FSC, the agent does not merely lose the ability to succeed in performing an action which he decides not to try performing, he loses the ability even to *try* to perform the action and yet he seems to decide, on his own, not to try, because he retains the relevant, responsibility-underlying capacities; in particular the capacities to respond and to react to reasons. In what follows, I aim to show that these capacities are lost. My strategy will be to . . . show that capacities can be *gained* through . . . intervention. Demonstrating this matters because . . . [if] it is true that agents can gain capacities merely by being in the presence of . . . interveners, then we are not entitled to conclude that they cannot lose them in the same way . . .

Consider this variation . . .

> . . . Jillian is walking along the beach when she notices a drowning. Jillian is a good swimmer, but she is pathologically afraid of deep water. She is so constituted that her phobia would prevent her from rescuing the child were she to attempt to; she would be overcome by feelings of panic. Nevertheless, she is capable of *trying* to rescue the child, and she knows that she is capable of trying. Indeed, though she knows that she has the phobia, she does not know just how powerful it is; she thinks (wrongly) that she could affect the rescue. Unbeknownst to Jillian,

a good-hearted neurosurgeon has implanted her with a chip with which he monitors Jillian's neural states, and through which he can intervene if he desires to. Should Jillian decide (on her own) to rescue the child, the neurosurgeon will intervene to dampen her fear; she will not panic and will succeed, despite her anxiety, in swimming out to the child and rescuing her.

... Jillian thinks she can save the child, and she seems to be right. ... The presence of the ... intervener has given her a capacity that she would otherwise have lacked. ...

Agents in FSCs are, supposedly, responsible for what they do because they do it on their own, in the sense that their decision or action is the product of mechanisms which belong to or which constitute them. They express their, or their mechanisms', unhindered capacities in decisions or actions. But we are entitled to conclude that these agents have their capacities intact only if we are entitled to bracket the counterfactual intervener. ... [W]e are not so entitled. In FECs agents *gain* capacities, due to the presence of a counterfactual intervener. We can only properly grasp the manner in which the relevant capacities are gained by, precisely, *not* bracketing the counterfactual intervener. The rationale for the claim that agents in FSCs do not lose the relevant, responsibility-ensuring capacities is therefore undermined. If we do not bracket the intervener in FSCs, in testing agents' capacities, then we are led to the conclusion that these capacities are *lost*. We are, therefore, not entitled to the intuition that agents in FSCs are morally responsible. ...

Human beings routinely gain capacities, including mental capacities, by learning to manipulate external symbols, or by interfacing with features of their environment, including other agents. FECs seem exotic, but they are merely an unusual variation on a ubiquitous phenomenon. But if we gain capacities due to the presence of interveners, even counterfactual interveners, then why can we not lose capacities in the same way? If agents like Jillian can gain in receptivity or reactivity to reasons, then why cannot agents like Connie, in the original voting case, lose such receptivity or reactivity? If they can, then FSCs fail to show that agents can be responsible even in the absence of alternative possibilities. At the very least, I think, proponents of FSCs are not entitled to appeal to the intuition that agents in these cases act in the normal way. They owe us an argument to that effect. For the time being, FSCs should not be seen as having broken the dialectical stalemate that characterized the free will debate before they burst onto the scene.

NOTE

1. Locke, *An Essay Concerning Human Understanding*, II.XXL.10.

STUDY QUESTIONS

1. What strategy does Levy adopt in replying to Frankfurt?
2. Explain in your own words the case of Jillian.
3. Can an agent gain powers in changed circumstances?
4. Can an agent lose powers in changed circumstances?

An Enquiry Concerning Human Understanding

DAVID HUME

We return to Hume's *An Enquiry Concerning Human Understanding* to read his defense of the compatibility of free will and determinism.

Hume first develops his view that all events are separate; none is necessarily connected to another. When we say that one event caused another event, we mean not that the first necessitated the second but only that events of the first sort are invariably followed by events of the second sort.

As to free will, Hume finds no incompatibility between determinism, the thesis that every event has a cause, and liberty, the claim that persons sometimes have the power to act or not act in accord with what they will. Whether Hume's solution to the problem is acceptable has long been a matter of dispute.

....

OF THE IDEA OF NECESSARY CONNECTION

... There are no ideas, which occur in metaphysics more obscure and uncertain, than those of *power, force, energy* or *necessary connection*, of which it is every moment necessary for us to treat in all our disquisitions. We shall, therefore, endeavor, in this section, to fix, if possible, the precise meaning of these terms and thereby remove some part of that obscurity, which is so much complained of in this species of philosophy.

It seems a proposition, which will not admit of much dispute, that all our ideas are nothing but copies of our impressions, or, in other words, that it is impossible for us to *think* of anything, which we have not antecedently *felt*, by either our external or internal senses. I have endeavored to explain and prove this proposition and have expressed my hopes that, by a proper application of it, men may reach a greater clearness and precision in philosophical reasonings than what they have hitherto been able to attain. Complex ideas may, perhaps, be well known by definition, which is nothing but an enumeration of those parts or simple ideas that compose them. But when we have pushed up definitions to the most simple ideas and find still some ambiguity and obscurity, what resource are we then possessed of?

From *An Enquiry Concerning Human Understanding* by David Hume (1748).

By what invention can we throw light upon these ideas, and render them altogether precise and determinate to our intellectual view! Produce the impressions or original sentiments, from which the ideas are copied. These impressions are all strong and sensible. They admit not of ambiguity. They are not only placed in a full light themselves, but may throw light on their correspondent ideas, which lie in obscurity. And by this means, we may, perhaps, attain a new microscope or species of optics, by which, in the moral sciences, the most minute and most simple ideas may be so enlarged as to fall readily under our apprehension, and be equally known with the grossest and most sensible ideas, which can be the object of our inquiry.

To be fully acquainted, therefore, with the idea of power or necessary connection, let us examine its impression; and in order to find the impression with greater certainty, let us search for it in all the sources, from which it may possibly be derived.

When we look about us towards external objects and consider the operation of causes, we are never able, in a single instance, to discover any power or necessary connection, nor any quality which binds the effect to the cause and renders the one an infallible consequence of the other. We only find that the one does actually, in fact, follow the other. The impulse of one billiard ball is attended with motion in the second. This is the whole that appears to the *outward* senses. The mind feels no sentiment or *inward* impression from this succession of objects: consequently there is not, in any single, particular instance of cause and effect, anything which can suggest the idea of power or necessary connection.

From the first appearance of an object, we never can conjecture what effect will result from it. But were the power or energy of any cause discoverable by the mind, we could foresee the effect, even without experience; and might, at first, pronounce with certainty concerning it, by mere dint of thought and reasoning.

In reality, there is no part of matter that does ever, by its sensible qualities, discover any power or energy, or give us ground to imagine that it could produce anything, or be followed by any other object, which we could denominate its effect. Solidity, extension, motion; these qualities are all complete in themselves and never point out any other event which may result from them. The scenes of the universe are continually shifting, and one object follows another in an uninterrupted succession; but the power of force, which actuates the whole machine, is entirely concealed from us, and never discovers itself in any of the sensible qualities of body. We know, that, in fact, heat is a constant attendant of flame; but what is the connection between them, we have no room so much as to conjecture or imagine. It is impossible, therefore, that the idea of power can be derived from the contemplation of bodies, in single instances of their operation, because no bodies ever discover any power, which can be the original of this idea. . . .

Part II
But to hasten to a conclusion of this argument, which is already drawn out to too great a length: we have sought in vain for an idea of power or necessary connection

in all the sources from which we could suppose it to be derived. It appears that, in single instances of the operation of bodies, we never can, by our utmost scrutiny, discover anything but one event following another, without being able to comprehend any force or power by which the cause operates, or any connection between it and its supposed effect. The same difficulty occurs in contemplating the operations of mind on body—where we observe the motion of the latter to follow upon the volition of the former, but are not able to observe or conceive the tie which binds together the motion and volition, or the energy by which the mind produces this effect. The authority of the will over its own faculties and ideas is not a whit more comprehensible: so that, upon the whole, there appears not, throughout all nature, any one instance of connection which is conceivable by us. All events seem entirely loose and separate. One event follows another; but we never can observe any tie between them. They seem *conjoined*, but never *connected*. And as we can have no idea of anything which never appeared to our outward sense or inward sentiment, the necessary conclusion *seems* to be that we have no idea of connection or power at all, and that these words are absolutely without any meaning, when employed either in philosophical reasonings or common life.

But there still remains one method of avoiding this conclusion, and one source which we have not yet examined. When any natural object or event is presented, it is impossible for us, by any sagacity or penetration, to discover, or even conjecture, without experience, what event will result from it, or to carry our foresight beyond that object which is immediately present to the memory and senses. Even after one instance or experiment where we have observed a particular event to follow upon another, we are not entitled to form a general rule, or foretell what will happen in like cases; it being justly esteemed an unpardonable temerity to judge of the whole course of nature from one single experiment, however accurate or certain. But when one particular species of event has always, in all instances, been conjoined with another, we make no longer any scruple of foretelling one upon the appearance of the other, and of employing that reasoning which can alone assure us of any matter of fact or existence. We then call the one object, *cause*; the other, *effect*. We suppose that there is some connection between them; some power in the one, by which it infallibly produces the other and operates with the greatest certainty and strongest necessity.

It appears, then, that this idea of a necessary connection among events arises from a number of similar instances which occur of the constant conjunction of these events; nor can that idea ever be suggested by any one of these instances, surveyed in all possible lights and positions. But there is nothing in a number of instances, different from every single instance, which is supposed to be exactly similar; except only, that after a repetition of similar instances, the mind is carried by habit, upon the appearance of one event, to expect its usual attendant and to believe that it will exist. This connection, therefore, which we *feel* in the mind, this customary transition of the imagination from one object to its usual attendant, is the sentiment or impression from which we form the idea of power or necessary connection. Nothing further is in the case. Contemplate the subject on all sides;

you will never find any other origin of that idea. This is the sole difference between one instance, from which we can never receive the idea of connection, and a number of similar instances, by which it is suggested. The first time a man saw the communication of motion by impulse, as by the shock of two billiard balls, he could not pronounce that the one event was *connected*, but only that it was *conjoined* with the other. After he has observed several instances of this nature, he then pronounces them to be *connected*. What alteration has happened to give rise to this new idea of *connection*? Nothing but that he now *feels* these events to be *connected* in his imagination and can readily foretell the existence of one from the appearance of the other. When we say, therefore, that one object is connected with another, we mean only that they have acquired a connection in our thought, and give rise to this inference, by which they become proofs of each other's existence: a conclusion which is somewhat extraordinary, but which seems founded on sufficient evidence. Nor will its evidence be weakened by any general diffidence of the understanding, or sceptical suspicion concerning every conclusion which is new and extraordinary. No conclusions can be more agreeable to scepticism than such as make discoveries concerning the weakness and narrow limits of human reason and capacity.

And what stronger instance can be produced of the surprising ignorance and weakness of the understanding than the present? For surely, if there be any relation among objects which it imports to us to know perfectly, it is that of cause and effect. On this are founded all our reasonings concerning matter of fact or existence. By means of it alone we attain any assurance concerning objects which are removed from the present testimony of our memory and senses. The only immediate utility of all sciences is to teach us how to control and regulate future events by their causes. Our thoughts and inquiries are, therefore, every moment, employed about this relation: yet so imperfect are the ideas which we form concerning it, that it is impossible to give any just definition of cause, except what is drawn from something extraneous and foreign to it. Similar objects are always conjoined with similar. Of this we have experience. Suitably to this experience, therefore, we may define a cause to be *an object, followed by another, and where all the objects similar to the first are followed by objects similar to the second.* Or in other words *where, if the first object had not been, the second never had existed.* The appearance of a cause always conveys the mind, by a customary transition, to the idea of the effect. Of this also we have experience. We may, therefore, suitably to this experience, form another definition of cause and call it *an object followed by another, and whose appearance always conveys the thought to that other.* But though both these definitions are drawn from circumstances foreign to the cause, we cannot remedy this inconvenience or attain any more perfect definition, which may point out that circumstances are the cause, which gives it a connection with its effect. We have no idea of this connection, nor even any distinct notion of what it is we desire to know, when we endeavor at a conception of it. We say, for instance, that the vibration of this string is the cause of this particular sound. But what do we mean by that affirmation? We either mean *that this vibration is followed by this sound and that all similar vibrations have been followed by similar sounds,* or, *that this vibration is followed by this sound and that upon the appearance of one the mind anticipates the senses and forms immediately an idea of the other.* We may consider the relation of cause and effect in either of these two lights; but beyond these, we have no idea of it.

To recapitulate, therefore, the reasonings of this section: every idea is copied from some preceding impression or sentiment; and where we cannot find any impression, we may be certain that there is no idea. In all single instances of the operation of bodies or minds, there is nothing that produces any impression, nor consequently can suggest any idea of power or necessary connection. But when many uniform instances appear, and the same object is always followed by the same event, we then begin to entertain the notion of cause and connection. We then feel a new sentiment or impression, to wit, a customary connection in the thought or imagination between one object and its usual attendant; and this sentiment is the original of that idea which we seek for. For as this idea arises from a number of similar instances, and not from any single instance, it must arise from that circumstance, in which the number of instances differ from every individual instance. But this customary connection or transition of the imagination is the only circumstance in which they differ. In every other particular they are alike. The first instance which we saw of motion communicated by the shock of two billiard balls (to return to this obvious illustration) is exactly similar to any instance that may, at present, occur to us; except only, that we could not, at first, *infer* one event from the other; which we are enabled to do at present, after so long a course of uniform experience. I know not whether the reader will readily apprehend this reasoning. I am afraid that, should I multiply words about it, or throw it into a greater variety of lights, it would only become more obscure and intricate. In all abstract reasonings there is one point of view which, if we can happily hit, we shall go farther towards illustrating the subject than by all the eloquence in the world. This point of view we should endeavor to reach, and reserve the flowers of rhetoric for subjects which are more adapted to them.

OF LIBERTY AND NECESSITY

It might reasonably be expected in questions which have been canvassed and disputed with great eagerness, since the first origin of science and philosophy, that is, the meaning of all the terms, at least, should have been agreed upon among the disputants; and our inquiries, in the course of two thousand years, should have been able to pass from words to the true and real subject of the controversy. For how easy may it seem to give exact definitions of the terms employed in reasoning, and make these definitions, not the mere sound of words, the object of future scrutiny and examination? But if we consider the matter more narrowly, we shall be apt to draw a quite opposite conclusion. From this circumstance alone, that a controversy has been long kept on foot, and remains still undecided, we may presume that there is some ambiguity in the expression and that the disputants affix different ideas to the terms employed in the controversy. For as the faculties of the mind are supposed to be naturally alike in every individual; otherwise nothing could be more fruitless than to reason or dispute together; it would be impossible, if men affix the same ideas to their terms, that they could so long form different opinions of the same subject; especially when they communicate their views, and each party turn themselves on all sides, in search of arguments which may give them the victory over their antagonists. It is true, if men attempt the discussion of questions which lie entirely beyond the reach of human capacity, such as those concerning the origin of worlds, or the economy of the intellectual system or region of spirits, they may long beat the air in their fruitless contests, and never arrive at any determinate conclusion. But if the question regards any subject of common life and experience, nothing, one would think, could preserve the dispute so long undecided but some ambiguous expressions, which keep the antagonists still at a distance and hinder them from grappling with each other.

This has been the case in the long disputed question concerning liberty and necessity; and to so remarkable a degree that, if I be not much mistaken, we shall find that all mankind, both learned and ignorant, have always been of the same opinion with regard to this subject, and that a few intelligible definitions would immediately have put an end to the whole controversy. I own that this dispute has been so much canvassed on all hands and has led philosophers into such a labyrinth of obscure sophistry that it is no wonder, if a sensible reader indulge his ease so far as to turn a deaf ear to the proposal of such a question, from which he can expect neither instruction nor entertainment. But the state of the argument here proposed may, perhaps, serve to renew his attention; as it has more novelty, promises at least some decision of the controversy, and will not much disturb his ease by any intricate or obscure reasoning.

I hope, therefore, to make it appear that all men have ever agreed in the doctrine both of necessity and of liberty, according to any reasonable sense, which can be put on these terms; and that the whole controversy has hitherto turned merely upon words. We shall begin with examining the doctrine of necessity.

It is universally allowed that matter, in all its operations, is actuated by a necessary force and that every natural effect is so precisely determined by the energy of its cause that no other effect, in such particular circumstances, could possibly have resulted from it. The degree and direction of every motion is, by the laws of nature, prescribed with such exactness that a living creature may as soon arise from the shock of two bodies as motion in any other degree or direction than what is actually produced by it. Would we, therefore, form a just and precise idea of *necessity*, we must consider whence that idea arises when we apply it to the operation of bodies.

It seems evident that, if all the scenes of nature were continually shifted in such a manner that no two events bore any resemblance to each other, but every object was entirely new, without any similitude to whatever had been seen before, we should never, in that case, have attained the least idea of necessity, or of a connection among these objects. We might say, upon such a supposition, that one object or event has followed another; not that one was produced by the other. The relation of cause and effect must be utterly unknown to mankind. Inference and reasoning concerning the operations of nature would, from that moment, be at an end; and the memory and senses remain the only canals, by which the knowledge of any real existence could possibly have access to the mind. Our idea, therefore, of necessity and causation arises entirely from the uniformity observable in the operations of nature, where similar objects are constantly conjoined together, and the mind is determined by custom to infer the one from the appearance of the other. These two circumstances form the whole of that necessity, which we ascribe to matter. Beyond the constant *conjunction* of similar objects, and the consequent *inference* from one to the other, we have no notion of any necessity or connection. . . .

I have frequently considered what could possibly be the reason why all mankind, though they have ever, without hesitation, acknowledged the doctrine of necessity in their whole practice and reasoning, have yet discovered such a reluctance to acknowledge it in words and have rather shown a propensity, in all ages, to profess the contrary opinion. The matter, I think, may be accounted for after the following manner. If we examine the operations of body, and the production of effects from their causes, we shall find that all our faculties can never carry us farther in our knowledge of this relation than barely to observe that particular objects are *constantly conjoined* together and that the mind is carried, by a *customary transition*, from the appearance of one to the belief of the other. But though this conclusion concerning human ignorance be the result of the strictest scrutiny of this subject, men still entertain a strong propensity to believe that they penetrate farther into the powers of nature and perceive something like a necessary connection between the cause and the effect. When again they turn their reflections towards the operations of their own minds and *feel* no such connection of the motive and the action, they are thence apt to suppose that there is a difference between the effects which result from material force and those which arise from thought and intelligence. But being once convinced that we know nothing farther of causation of any kind than merely the *constant conjunction* of objects, and the consequent *inference* of the mind from one to another, and finding that these two circumstances are universally allowed to have place in voluntary actions, we may be more easily led to own the same necessity common to all causes. And though this reasoning may contradict the systems of many philosophers, in ascribing necessity to the determinations of the will, we shall find, upon reflection, that they dissent from it in words only, not in their real sentiment. Necessity, according to the sense in which it is here taken, has never yet been rejected, nor can ever, I think, be rejected by any philosopher. It may only, perhaps, be pretended that the mind can perceive, in the operations of matter, some farther connection between the cause and effect; and connection that has not place in voluntary actions of intelligent beings. Now whether it be so or not can only appear upon examination; and it is incumbent on these philosophers to make good their assertion, by defining or describing that necessity and pointing it out to us in the operations of material causes.

It would seem, indeed, that men begin at the wrong end of this question concerning liberty and necessity, when they enter upon it by examining the faculties of the soul, the influence of the understanding, and the operations of the will. Let them first discuss a more simple question, namely, the operations of body and of brute unintelligent matter; and try whether they can there form any idea of causation and necessity, except that of a constant conjunction of objects, and subsequent inference of the mind from one to another. If these circumstances form, in reality, the whole of that necessity, which we conceive in matter, and if these circumstances be also universally acknowledged to take place in the operations of the mind, the dispute is at an end; at least, must be owned to be thenceforth merely verbal. But as long as we will rashly suppose that we have some farther idea of necessity and causation in the operations of external objects; at the same time, that we can find nothing farther in the voluntary actions of the mind; there is no possibility of bringing the question to any determinate issue, while we proceed upon so erroneous a supposition. The only method of undeceiving us is to mount up higher; to examine the narrow extent of science when applied to material causes; and to convince ourselves that all we know of them is the constant conjunction and inference above mentioned. We may, perhaps, find that it is with difficulty we are induced to fix such narrow limits to human understanding: but we can afterwards find no difficulty when we come to apply this doctrine to the actions of the will. For as it is evident that these have a regular conjunction with motives and circumstances and characters, and as we always draw inferences from one to the other, we must be obliged to acknowledge in words that necessity, which we have already avowed, in every deliberation of our lives and in every step of our conduct and behavior.

But to proceed in this reconciling project with regard to the question of liberty and necessity; the most contentious question of metaphysics, the most contentious science; it will not require many words to prove that all mankind have ever agreed in the doctrine of liberty as well as in that of necessity, and that the whole dispute, in this respect also, has been hitherto merely verbal. For what is meant by liberty, when applied to voluntary actions? We cannot surely mean that actions have so little connection with motives, inclinations, and circumstances, that one does not follow with a certain degree of uniformity from the other, and that one affords no inference by which we can conclude the existence of the other. For these are plain and acknowledged matters of fact. By liberty, then, we can only mean *a power of acting or not acting, according to the determinations of the will*; that is, if we choose to remain at rest, we may; if we choose to move, we also may. Now this hypothetical liberty is universally allowed to belong to everyone who is not a prisoner and in chains. Here, then, is no subject of dispute.

Whatever definition we may give of liberty, we should be careful to observe two requisite circumstances; *first*, that it be consistent with plain matter of fact; *secondly*, that it be consistent with itself. If we observe these circumstances and render our definition intelligible, I am persuaded that all mankind will be found of one opinion with regard to it.

It is universally allowed that nothing exists without a cause of its existence and that chance, when strictly examined, is a mere negative word and means not any real power which has anywhere a being in nature. But it is pretended that some causes are necessary, some not necessary. Here then is the advantage of definitions. Let anyone *define* a cause, without comprehending, as a part of the definition, a *necessary connection* with its effect; and let him show distinctly the origin of the idea, expressed by the definition; and I shall readily give up the whole controversy. But if the foregoing explication of the matter be received, this must be absolutely impracticable. Had not objects a regular conjunction with each other, we should never have entertained any notion of cause and effect; and this regular conjunction produces that inference of the understanding, which is the only connection that we can have any comprehension of. Whoever attempts a definition of cause, exclusive of these circumstances, will be obliged either to employ unintelligible terms or such as we are synonymous to the term which he endeavors to define. And if the definition above mentioned be admitted; liberty, when opposed to necessity, not to constraint, is the same thing with chance, which is universally allowed to have no existence.

STUDY QUESTIONS

1. What does Hume mean by "necessary connection"?
2. What does Hume mean by one event causing another?
3. How does Hume's notion of causality affect his views on the compatibility of liberty and necessity?
4. According to Hume, does anything exist by chance?

The Dilemma of Determinism

WILLIAM JAMES

William James (1842–1910) was Professor of Philosophy and of Psychology at Harvard University. A critical figure in the development of American thought, he explores philosophical issues in a refreshing, accessible style, as in the case of this essay, originally delivered as an address to the Harvard University Divinity

Reprinted from William James, *The Will to Believe and Other Essays in Popular Philosophy* (1898).

students. James does not believe free will can be proved or disproved but explains why he assumes it to be true and acts as if it were true.

....

A common opinion prevails that the juice has ages ago been pressed out of the free-will controversy, and that no new champion can do more than warm up stale arguments which everyone has heard. This is a radical mistake. I know of no subject less worn out, or in which inventive genius has a better chance of breaking open new ground—not, perhaps, of forcing a conclusion or of coercing assent, but of deepening our sense of what the issue between the two parties really is, and of what the ideas of fate and of free will imply. . . . [M]y ambition limits itself to just one little point. If I can make two of the necessarily implied corollaries of determinism clearer to you than they have been made before, I shall have made it possible for you to decide before or against that doctrine with a better understanding of what you are about. And if you prefer not to decide at all, but to remain doubters, you will at least see more plainly what the subject of your hesitation is. I thus declaim openly on the threshold all pretension to prove to you that the freedom of the will is true. The most I hope is to induce some of you to follow my own example in assuming it true, and acting as if it were true. If it be true, it seems to me that this is involved in the strict logic of the case. Its truth ought not to be forced willy-nilly down our indifferent throats. It ought to be freely espoused by men who can equally well turn their backs upon it. In other words, our first act of freedom, if we are free, ought in all inward propriety to be to affirm that we are free. This should exclude, it seems to me, from the free-will side of the question all hope of a coercive demonstration—a demonstration which I, for one, am perfectly contented to go without.

With thus much understood at the outset, we can advance. But, not without one more point understood as well. The arguments I am about to urge all proceed on two suppositions: first, when we make theories about the world and discuss them with one another, we do so in order to attain a conception of things which shall give us subjective satisfaction; and, second, if there be two conceptions, and the one seems to us, on the whole, more rational than the other, we are entitled to suppose that the more rational one is truer of the two. I hope that you are all willing to make these suppositions with me; for I am afraid that if there be any of you here who are not, they will find little edification in the rest of what I have to say. I cannot stop to argue the point; but I myself believe that all the magnificent achievements of mathematical and physical science—our doctrines of evolution, of uniformity of law, and the rest—proceed from our indomitable desire to cast the world into a more rational shape in our minds than the shape into which it is thrown there by the crude order of our experience. The world has shown itself, to a great extent, plastic to this demand of ours for rationality. How much farther it will show itself plastic, no one can say. Our only means of finding out is to try; and I, for one, feel as free to try conceptions of moral as of mechanical or of logical rationality.

If a certain formula for expressing the nature of the world violates my moral demand, I shall feel free to throw it overboard, or at least to doubt it, as if it disappointed my demand for uniformity of sequence, for example; the one demand being, so far as I can see, quite as subjective and emotional as the other is. The principle of causality, for example—what is it but a postulate, an empty name covering simply a demand that the sequence of events shall some day manifest a deeper kind of belonging of one thing with another than the mere juxtaposition which now phenomenally appears? It is as much an altar to an unknown god as the one that Saint Paul found at Athens. All our scientific and philosophic ideals are altars to unknown gods. Uniformity is as much so as is free will. If this be admitted, we can debate on even terms. But if any one pretends that while freedom and variety are, in the first instance, subjective demands, necessity and uniformity are something altogether different, I do not see how we can debate at all.

To begin, then, I must suppose you are acquainted with all the usual arguments on the subject. I cannot stop to take up the old proofs from causation, from statistics, from the certainty with which we can foretell one another's conduct, from the fixity of character, and all the rest. But there are two *words* which usually encumber these classical arguments, and which we must immediately dispose of if we are to make any progress. One is the eulogistic word *freedom,* and the other is the opprobrious word *chance.* The word "chance" I wish to keep, but I wish to get rid of the word "freedom." Its eulogistic associations have so far overshadowed all the rest of its meaning that both parties claim the sole right to use it, and determinists today insist that they alone are freedom's champions. Old-fashioned determinism was what we may call *hard* determinism. It did not shrink from such words as fatality, bondage of the will, necessitation, and the like. Nowadays, we have a *soft* determinism which abhors harsh words and, repudiating fatality, necessity, and even predetermination, says that its real name is freedom; for freedom is only necessity understood, and bondage to the highest is identical with true freedom. Even a writer as little used to making capital out of soft words as Mr. Hodgson hesitates not to call himself a "free-will determinist."

Now, all this is a quagmire of evasion under which the real issue of fact has been entirely smothered. Freedom in all these senses presents simply no problem at all. No matter what the soft determinist means by it—whether he means the acting without external constraint, whether he means the acting rightly, or whether he means the acquiescing in the law of the whole—who cannot answer him that sometimes we are free and sometimes we are not? But there *is* a problem, an issue of fact and not of words, an issue of the most momentous importance, which is often decided without discussion in one sentence—nay, in one clause of a sentence—by those very writers who spin out whole chapters in their efforts to show what "true" freedom is; and that is the question of determinism, about which we are to talk tonight.

Fortunately, no ambiguities hang about this word or about its opposite, indeterminism. Both designate an outward way in which things may happen, and their cold and mathematical sound has no sentimental associations that can bribe our partiality either way in advance. Now, evidence of an external kind to decide between determinism and indeterminism is, as I intimated a while back, strictly impossible to find. Let us look at the difference between them and see for ourselves. What does determinism profess?

It professes that those parts of the universe already laid down absolutely appoint and decree what the other parts shall be. The future has no ambiguous possibilities hidden in its womb: the part we call the present is compatible with only one totality. Any other future complement than the one fixed from eternity is impossible. The whole is in each and every part, and welds it with the rest into an absolute unity, an iron block, in which there can be no equivocation or shadow of turning.

> With earth's first clay they did the last man knead,
> And there of the last harvest sowed the seed.
> And the first morning of creation wrote
> What the last dawn of reckoning shall read.

Indeterminism, on the contrary, says that the parts have a certain amount of loose play on one another, so that the laying down of one of them does not necessarily determine what the others shall be. It admits that possibilities may be in excess of actualities and that things not yet revealed to our knowledge may really in themselves be ambiguous. Of two alternative futures which we conceive, both may now be really possible; and the one becomes impossible only at the very moment when the other excludes it by becoming real itself. Indeterminism thus denies the world to be one unbending unit of fact. It says there is a certain ultimate pluralism in it; and, so saying, it corroborates our ordinary unsophisticated view of things. To that view, actualities seem to float in a wider sea of possibilities from out of which they are chosen; and, somewhere, indeterminism says, such possibilities exist and form a part of truth.

Determinism, on the contrary, says they exist *nowhere* and that necessity on the one hand and impossibility on the other are the sole categories of the real. Possibilities that fail to get realized are, for determinism, pure illusions: they never were possibilities at all. There is nothing inchoate, it says, about this universe of ours, all that was or is or shall be actual in it having been from eternity virtually there. The cloud of alternatives our minds escort this mass of actuality withal is a cloud of sheer deceptions, to which "impossibilities" is the only name which rightfully belongs.

The issue, it will be seen, is a perfectly sharp one, which no eulogistic terminology can smear over or wipe out. The truth *must* lie with one side or the other, and its lying with one side makes the other false.

The question relates solely to the existence of possibilities, in the strict sense of the term, as things that may, but need not, be. Both sides admit that a volition, for instance, has occurred. The indeterminists say another volition might have occurred in its place: the determinists swear that nothing could possibly have occurred in its place. Now, can science be called in to tell us which of these two point-blank contradicters of each other is right? Science professes to draw no conclusions but such as are based on matters of fact, things that have actually happened; but how can any amount of assurance that something actually happened give us the least grain of information as to whether another thing might or might not have happened in its place? Only facts can be proved by other facts. With things that are possibilities and not facts, facts have no concern. If we have no other evidence than the evidence of existing facts, the possibility-question must remain a mystery never to be cleared up.

And the truth is that facts practically have hardly anything to do with making us either determinists or indeterminists. Sure enough, we make a flourish of quoting facts this way or that; and if we are determinists, we talk about the infallibility with which we can predict one another's conduct; while if we are indeterminists, we lay great stress on the fact that it is just because we cannot foretell one another's conduct, either in war or statecraft or in any of the great and small intrigues and businesses of men, that life is so intensely anxious and hazardous a game. But who does not see the wretched insufficiency of this so-called objective testimony on both sides? What fills up the gaps in our minds is something not objective, not external. What divides us into *possibility* men and *anti-possibility* men is different faiths or postulates—postulates of rationality. To this man the world seems more rational with possibilities in it—to that man more rational with possibilities excluded; and talk as we will about having to yield to evidence, what makes us monists or pluralists, determinists or indeterminists, is at bottom always some sentiment like this.

The stronghold of the deterministic sentiment is the antipathy to the idea of chance. As soon as we begin to talk indeterminism to our friends, we find a number of them shaking their heads. This notion of alternative possibility, they say, this admission that any one of several things may come to pass, is, after all, only a round-about name for chance; and chance is something the notion of which no sane mind can for an instant tolerate in the world. What is it, they ask, but barefaced crazy unreason, the negation of intelligibility and law? And if the slightest particle of it exists anywhere, what is to prevent the whole fabric from falling together, the stars from going out, and chaos from recommencing her topsy-turvy reign?

Remarks of this sort about chance will put an end to discussion as quickly as anything one can find. I have already told you that "chance" was a word I wished to keep and use. Let us then examine exactly what it means, and see whether it ought to be such a terrible bugbear to us. I fancy that squeezing the thistle boldly will rob it of its sting.

The sting of the word "chance" seems to lie in the assumption that it means something positive, and that if anything happens by chance, it must needs be something of an intrinsically irrational and preposterous sort. Now, chance means nothing of the kind. It is a purely negative and relative term, giving us no information about that of which it is predicated, except that it happens to be disconnected with something else—not controlled, secured, or necessitated by other things in advance of its own actual presence. As this point is the most subtle one of the whole lecture, and at the same time the point on which all the rest hinges, I beg you to pay particular attention to it. What I say is that it tells us nothing about what a thing may be in itself to call it "chance." It may be a bad thing, it may be a good thing. It may be lucidity, transparency, fitness incarnate, matching the whole system of other things, when it has once befallen, in an unimaginably perfect way. All you mean by calling it "chance" is that this is not guaranteed, that it may also fall out otherwise. For the system of other things has no positive hold on the chance-thing. Its origin is in a certain fashion negative: it escapes and says, "Hands off!" coming, when it comes, as a free gift, or not at all.

This negativeness, however, and this opacity of the chance-thing when thus considered *ab extra*, or from the point of view of previous things or distant things, do not preclude its having any amount of positiveness and luminosity from within, and at its own place and moment. All that its chance-character asserts about it is that there is something in it really of its own, something that is not the unconditional property of the whole. If the whole wants this property, the whole must wait till it can get it, if it be a matter of chance. That the universe may actually be a sort of joint-stock society of this sort, in which the sharers have both limited liabilities and limited powers, is of course a simple and conceivable notion.

Nevertheless, many persons talk as if the minutest dose of disconnectedness of one part with another, the smallest modicum of independence, the faintest tremor of ambiguity about the future, for example, would ruin everything and turn this goodly universe into a sort of insane sand-heap or nulliverse—no universe at all. Since future human volitions are, as a matter of fact, the only ambiguous things we are tempted to believe in, let us stop for a moment to make ourselves sure whether their independent and accidental character need be fraught with such direful consequences to the universe as these.

What is meant by saying that my choice of which way to walk home after the lecture is ambiguous and matter of chance as far as the present moment is concerned? It means that both Divinity Avenue and Oxford Street are called; but that only one, and that one *either* one shall be chosen. Now, I ask you seriously to suppose that this ambiguity of my choice is real; and then to make the impossible hypothesis that the choice is made twice over, and each time falls on a different street. In other words, imagine that I first walk through Divinity Avenue, and then imagine that the powers governing the universe annihilate ten minutes of time with all that it contained, and set me back at the door of this hall just as I was before the choice was made. Imagine then that, everything else being the same, I now make a different choice and traverse Oxford Street. You, as passive spectators, look on and see the two alternative universes—one of them with me walking through Divinity Avenue in it, the other with the same me walking through Oxford Street. Now, if you are determinists, you believe one of these universes to have been from eternity impossible: you believe it to have been impossible because of the intrinsic irrationality or accidentality somewhere involved in it. But looking outwardly at these universes, can you say which is the impossible and accidental one, and which the rational and necessary one? I doubt if the most iron-clad determinist among you could have the slightest glimmer of light at this point. In other words, either universe *after the fact* and once there would, to our means of observation and understanding, appear just as rational as the other. There would be absolutely no criterion by which we might judge one necessary and the other matter of chance. Suppose now we relieve the gods of their hypothetical task and assume my choice, once made, to be made forever. I go through Divinity Avenue for good and all. If, as good determinists, you now begin to affirm, what all good determinists punc- tually do affirm, that in the nature of things I couldn't have gone through Oxford Street—had I done so it would have been chance, irrationality, insanity, a horrid gap in nature—I simply call your attention to this, that your affirmation is what the Germans call a *Machtspruch*, a mere conception fulminated as a dogma and based on no insight into details. Before my choice, either street seemed as natural to you as to me. Had I happened to take Oxford Street, Divinity Avenue would have figured in your philosophy as the gap in nature; and you would have so pro- claimed it with the best deterministic conscience in the world.

But what a hollow outcry, then, is this against a chance which, if it were pres- ent to us, we could by no character whatever distinguish from a rational neces- sity! I have taken the most trivial of examples, but no possible example could lead to any different result. For what are the alternatives which, in point of fact, offer themselves to human volition? What are those futures that now seem matters of chance? Are they not one and all like the Divinity Avenue and Oxford Street of our example? Are they not all of them *kinds* of things already here and based in the existing frame of nature? Is any one ever tempted to produce an *absolute* accident, something utterly irrelevant to the rest of the world? Do not all the motives that assail us, all the futures that offer themselves to our choice, spring equally from the soil of the past; and would not either one of them, whether realized through chance or through necessity, the moment it was realized, seem to us to fit that past, and in the completest and most continuous manner to interdigitate with the phenomena already there?[1]

The more one thinks of the matter, the more one wonders that so empty and gratuitous a hubbub as this outcry against chance should have found so great an echo in the hearts of men. It is a word which tells us absolutely nothing about what chances, or about the *modus operandi* of the chancing; and the use of it as a war-cry shows only a temper of intellectual absolutism, a demand that the world shall be a solid block, subject to one control—which temper, which demand, the world may not be bound to gratify at all. In every outwardly verifiable and practi- cal respect, a world in which the alternatives that now actually distract *your* choice were decided by pure chance would be by *me* absolutely undistinguished from the world in which I now live. I am, therefore, entirely willing to call it, so far as your choices go, a world of chance for me. To *yourselves*, it is true, those very acts of choice, which to me are so blind, opaque, and external, are the opposites of this, for you are within them and effect them. To you they appear as decisions; and decisions, for him who makes them, are altogether peculiar psychic facts.

Self-luminous and self-justifying at the living moment in which they occur, they appeal to no outside moment to put its stamp upon them or make them continuous with the rest of nature. Themselves it is rather who seem to make nature continuous; and in their strange and intense function of granting consent to one possibility and withholding it from another, to transform an equivocal and double future into an inalterable and simple past.

But with the psychology of the matter, we have no concern this evening. The quarrel which determinism has with chance fortunately has nothing to do with this or that psychological detail. It is a quarrel altogether metaphysical. Determinism denies the ambiguity of future volitions, because it affirms that nothing future can be ambiguous. But we have said enough to meet the issue. Indeterminate future volitions *do* mean chance. Let us not fear to shout it from the house-tops if need be; for we now know that the idea of chance is, at bottom, exactly the same thing as the idea of gift—the one simply being a disparaging, and the other a eulogistic, name for anything on which we have no effective *claim*. And whether the world be the better or the worse for having either chances or gifts in it will depend altogether on *what* these uncertain and unclaimable things turn out to be.

And this at last brings us within sight of our subject. We have seen what determinism means: we have seen that indeterminism is rightly described as meaning chance; and we have seen that chance, the very name of which we are urged to shrink from as from a metaphysical pestilence, means only the negative fact that no part of the world, however big, can claim to control absolutely the destinies of the whole. But although, in discussing the word "chance," I may at moments have seemed to be arguing for its real existence, I have not meant to do so yet. We have not yet ascertained whether this is a world of chance or no; at most, we have agreed that it seems so. And I now repeat what I said at the outset, that, from any strict theoretical point of view, the question is insoluble. To deepen our theoretic sense of the *difference* between a world with chances in it and a deterministic world is the most I can hope to do; and this I may now at last begin upon, after all our tedious clearing of the way.

I wish first of all to show you just what the notion that this is a deterministic world implies. The implications I call your attention to are all bound up with the fact that it is a world in which we constantly have to make what I shall, with your permission, call judgments of regret. Hardly an hour passes in which we do not wish that something might be otherwise; and happy indeed are those of us whose hearts have never echoed the wish of Omar Khayyam—

> That we might clasp, ere closed, the book of fate,
>   And make the writer on a fairer leaf
> Inscribe our names, or quite obliterate.
>
> Ah! Love, could you and I with fate conspire
> To mend this sorry scheme of things entire,
>   Would we not shatter it to bits, and then
> Remould it nearer to the heart's desire?

Now, it is undeniable that most of these regrets are foolish, and quite on a par in point of philosophic value with the criticisms on the universe of that friend of our infancy, the hero of the fable, "The Atheist and the Acorn"—

Fool! had that bough a pumpkin bore,
Thy whimsies would have worked no more, etc.

Even from the point of view of our own ends, we should probably make a botch of remodelling the universe. How much more then from the point of view of ends we cannot see! Wise men therefore regret as little as they can. But still some regrets are pretty obstinate and hard to stifle—regrets for acts of wanton cruelty or treachery, for example, whether performed by others or by ourselves. Hardly any one can remain *entirely* optimistic after reading the confession of the murderer at Brockton the other day: how, to get rid of the wife whose continued existence bored him, he inveigled her into a deserted spot, shot her four times, and then, as she lay on the ground and said to him, "You didn't do it on purpose, did you, dear?" replied, "No, I didn't do it on purpose," as he raised a rock and smashed her skull. Such an occurrence, with the mild sentence and self-satisfaction of the prisoner, is a field for a crop of regrets, which one need not take up in detail. We feel that, although a perfect mechanical fit to the rest of the universe, it is a bad moral fit, and that something else would really have been better in its place.

But for the deterministic philosophy the murder, the sentence, and the pris-oner's optimism were all necessary from eternity; and nothing else for a moment had a ghost of a chance of being put in their place. To admit such a chance, the determinists tell us, would be to make a suicide of reason; so we must steel our hearts against the thought. And here our plot thickens, for we see the first of those difficult implications of determinism and monism which it is my purpose to make you feel. If this Brockton murder was called for by the rest of the universe, if it had come at its preappointed hour, and if nothing else would have been consistent with the sense of the whole, what are we to think of the universe? Are we stubbornly to stick to our judgment of regret, and say, though it *couldn't* be, yet it *would* have been a better universe with something different from this Brockton murder in it? That, of course, seems the natural and spontaneous thing for us to do; and yet it is nothing short of deliberately espousing a kind of *pessimism*. The judgment of regret calls the murder bad. Calling a thing bad means, if it means anything at all, that the thing ought not be, that something else ought to be in its stead. Determinism, in denying that anything else can be in its stead, virtually defines the universe as a place in which what ought to be is impossible—in other words, as an organism whose constitution is afflicted with an incurable taint and irremediable flaw. The pessimism of a Schopenhauer says no more than this—that the murder is a symptom; and that it is a vicious symptom because it belongs to a vicious whole, which can express its nature no otherwise than by bringing forth just such a symptom as that at this particular spot. Regret for the murder must transform itself, if we are determinists and wise, into a larger regret. It is absurd to regret the murder alone. Other things being what they are, *it* could not be different. What we should regret is that whole frame of things of which the murder is one member. I see no escape whatever from this pessimistic conclusion if, being determinists, our judgment of regret is to be allowed to stand at all.

The only deterministic escape from pessimism is everywhere to abandon the judgment of regret. That this can be done, history shows to be not impossible. The devil, *quoad existentiam*, may be good. That is, although he be a *principle* of evil, yet the universe, with such a principle in it, may practically be a better universe than it could have been without. On every hand, in a small way, we find that a certain amount of evil is a condition by which a higher form of good is brought. There is nothing to prevent anybody from generalizing this view, and trusting that if we could but see things in the largest of all ways, even such matters as this Brockton murder would appear to be paid for by the uses which follow in their train. An optimism *quand même*, a systematic and infatuated optimism like that ridiculed by Voltaire in his *Candide*, is one of the possible ideal ways in which a man may train himself to look upon life. Bereft of dogmatic hardness and lit up with the expression of a tender and pathetic hope, such an optimism has been the grace of some of the most religious characters that ever lived.

> Throb thine with Nature's throbbing breast,
> And all is clear from east to west.

Even cruelty and treachery may be among the absolutely blessed fruits of time, and to quarrel with any of their details may be blasphemy. The only real blasphemy, in short, may be that pessimistic temper of the soul which lets it give way to such things as regrets, remorse, and grief.

Thus, our deterministic pessimism may become a deterministic optimism at the price of extinguishing our judgments of regret.

But does not this immediately bring us into a curious logical predicament? Our determinism leads us to call our judgments of regret wrong, because they are pessimistic in implying that what is impossible yet ought to be. But how then about the judgments of regret themselves? If they are wrong, other judgments, judgments of approval presumably, ought to be in their place. But as they are necessitated, nothing else *can* be in their place; and the universe is just what it was before—namely, a place in which what ought to be appears impossible. We have got one foot out of the pessimistic bog, but the other one sinks all the deeper. We have rescued our actions from the bonds of evil, but our judgments are now held fast. When murders and treacheries cease to be sins, regrets are theoretic absurdities and errors. The theoretic and the active life thus play a kind of see-saw with each other on the ground of evil. The rise of either sends the other down. Murder and treachery cannot be good without regret being bad: regret cannot be good without treachery and murder being bad. Both, however, are supposed to have been foredoomed; so something must be fatally unreasonable, absurd, and wrong in the world. It must be a place of which either sin or error forms a necessary part. From this dilemma there seems at first sight no escape. Are we then so soon to fall back into the pessimism from which we thought we had emerged? And is there no possible way by which we may, with good intellectual consciences, call the cruelties and the treacheries, the reluctances and the regrets, *all* good together?

Certainly there is such a way, and you are probably most of you ready to formulate it yourselves. But, before doing so, remark how inevitably the question of determinism and indeterminism slides us into the question of optimism and pessimism, or, as our fathers called it, "The question of evil." The theological form of all these disputes is simplest and the deepest, the form from which there is the least escape—not because, as some have sarcastically said, remorse and regret are clung to with a morbid fondness by the theologians as spiritual luxuries, but because they are existing facts in the world, and as such must be taken into account in the deterministic interpretation of all that is fated to be. If they are fated to be error, does not the bat's wing of irrationality cast its shadow over the world? . . .

[T]he only consistent way of representing a pluralism and a world whose parts may affect one another through their conduct being either good or bad is the indeterministic way. What interest, zest, or excitement can there be in achieving the right way, unless we are enabled to feel that the wrong way is also a possible and a natural way—nay, more, a menacing and an imminent way? And what sense can there be in condemning ourselves for taking the wrong way, unless we need have done nothing of the sort, unless the right way was open to us as well? I cannot understand the willingness to act, no matter how we feel, without the belief that acts are really good and bad. I cannot understand the belief that an act is bad, without regret at its happening. I cannot understand regret without the admission of real, genuine possibilities in the world. Only then is it other than a mockery to feel, after we have failed to do our best, that an irreparable opportunity is gone from the universe, the loss of which it must forever after mourn.

If you insist that this is all superstition, that possibility is in the eye of science and reason impossibility, and that if I act badly 'tis that the universe was foredoomed to suffer this defect, you fall right back into the dilemma, the labyrinth, of pessimism and subjectivism, from out of whose toils we have just wound our way.

Now, we are of course free to fall back, if we please. For my own part, though, whatever difficulties may beset the philosophy of objective right and wrong, and the indeterminism it seems to imply, determinism, with its alternative pessimism or romanticism, contains difficulties that are greater still. But you will remember that I expressly repudiated awhile ago the pretension to offer any arguments which could be coercive in a so-called scientific fashion in this matter. And I consequently find myself, at the end of this long talk, obliged to state my conclusions in an altogether personal way. This personal method of appeal seems to be among the very conditions of the problem; and the most any one can do is to confess as candidly as he can the grounds for the faith that is in him, and leave his example to work on others as it may.

Let me, then, without circumlocution say just this. The world is enigmatical enough in all conscience, whatever theory we may take up toward it. The indeterminism I defend, the free-will theory of popular sense based on the judgment of regret, represents that world as vulnerable, and liable to be injured by certain of its parts if they act wrong. And it represents their acting wrong as a matter of possibility or accident, neither inevitable nor yet to be infallibly warded off. In all this, it is a theory devoid either of transparency or of stability. It gives us a pluralistic, restless universe, in which no single point of view can ever take in the whole scene; and to a mind possessed of the love of unity at any cost, it will, no doubt, remain forever inacceptable. A friend with such a mind once told me that the thought of my universe made him sick, like the sight of the horrible motion of a mass of maggots in their carrion bed.

But while I freely admit that the pluralism and the restlessness are repugnant and irrational in a certain way, I find that every alternative to them is irrational in a deeper way. The indeterminism with its maggots, if you please to speak so about it, offends only the native absolutism of my intellect—an absolutism which, after all, perhaps, deserves to be snubbed and kept in check. But the determinism with its necessary carrion, to continue the figure of speech, and with no possible maggots to eat the latter up, violates my sense of moral reality through and through. When, for example, I imagine such carrion as the Brockton murder, I cannot conceive it as an act by which the universe, as a whole, logically and necessarily expresses its nature without shrinking from complicity with such a whole. And I deliberately refuse to keep on terms of loyalty with the universe by saying blankly that the murder, since it does flow from the nature of the whole, is not carrion. There are *some* instinctive reactions which I, for one, will not tamper with. The only remaining alternative, the attitude of gnostical romanticism, wrenches my personal instincts in quite as violent a way. It falsifies the simple objectivity of their deliverance. It makes the goose-flesh the murder excites in me a sufficient reason for the perpetration of the crime. It transforms life from a tragic reality into an insincere melodramatic exhibition, as foul or as tawdry as any one's diseased curiosity pleases to carry it out. And with its consecration of the *roman naturaliste* state of mind, and its enthronement of the baser crew of Parisian *littérateurs* among the eternally indispensable organs by which the infinite spirit of things attains to that subjective illumination which is the task of its life, it leaves me in presence of a sort of subjective carrion considerably more noisome than the objective carrion I called it in to take away.

No! better a thousand times than such systematic corruption of our moral sanity, the plainest pessimism, so that it be straightforward; but better far than that, the world of chance. Make as great an uproar about chance as you please, I know that chance means pluralism and nothing more. If some of the members of the pluralism are bad, the philosophy of pluralism, whatever broad views it may deny me, permits me, at least, to turn to the other members with a clean breast of affection and an unsophisticated moral sense. And if I still wish to think of the world as a totality, it lets me feel that a world with a chance in it of being altogether good, even if the chance never comes to pass, is better than a world with no such chance at all. That "chance" whose very notion I am exhorted and conjured to banish from my view of the future as the suicide of reason concerning it, that "chance" is—what? Just this—the chance that in moral respects the future may be other and better than the past has been. This is the only chance we have any motive for supposing to exist. Shame, rather, on its repudiation and its denial! For its presence is the vital air which lets the world live, the salt which keeps it sweet.

NOTE

1. A favorite argument against free will is that if it be true, a man's murderer may as probably be his best friend as his worst enemy, a mother be as likely to strangle as to suckle her first-born, and all of us be as ready to jump from fourth-story windows as to go out of front doors, etc. Users of this argument should probably be excluded from debate till they learn what the real question is. "Free-will" does not say that everything that is physically conceivable is also morally possible. It merely says that of alternatives that really *tempt* our will more than one is really possible. Of course, the alternatives that do thus tempt our will are vastly fewer than the physical possibilities we can coldly fancy. Persons really tempted often do murder their best friends, mothers do strangle their first-borns, people do jump out of fourth stories, etc.

STUDY QUESTIONS

1. Explain the significance for James of his choice whether to walk home on Oxford Street or Divinity Avenue.
2. According to James, why does determinism imply that the world must be a place of which either sin or error forms a necessary part?
3. According to James, why is the issue of freedom and determinism insoluble?
4. If an issue is insoluble, are we still being reasonable if we take a position on it?

PART 6

Identity

A Case of Identity

BRIAN SMART

Another metaphysical question concerns personal identity. What makes you the person you are? When you undergo physical or psychological changes, which element remains the same throughout, thus identifying you as the same individual before and after the changes?

Rather than beginning with the identifies of persons, however, let us start simply with the identities of objects. Imagine that you leave your car in a parking lot and return some hours later to discover that your vehicle has been hit by a huge truck and smashed to smithereens. A towing service arrives and takes the remaining pieces of your car to a repair garage, where you are assured that your car will be completely fixed. When you come to the garage two weeks later you are shown a car in perfect condition and told that it's your old car, now repaired. But is this car the same one you had left in the parking lot, or is it a new car? And how would you know? Suppose the original automobile was a gift that you valued highly. Do you still have that gift? Or has it been lost and replaced?

The following selection is by Brian Smart, who was Professor of Philosophy at the University of Keele. His example concerns a ship rather than a car, and he shows how a metaphysical issue about identity can lie at the heart of a legal dispute about ownership. See whether you believe the judges in the case ruled correctly.

....

A ship, X, is composed of a thousand old, but perfectly seaworthy, planks. It is brought into dock A where at hour 1 one of X's planks is removed to dock B and is replaced by a new plank. At hour 2 the same process is repeated so that by hour 1000 we have a ship Y in dock A composed of a thousand new planks and (since X's old planks have been reassembled as a ship) a ship Z in dock B composed of a thousand old planks. The problem is: with which ship—Y or Z—, if either, is X identical?

Let us give this problem a fictitious, but practical, setting.

Two shipowners, Morion and Bombos, are involved in a legal dispute. Morion had ordered a new ship from the Proteus brothers, shipbuilders and shiprepairers. Bombos had sent his ship, X, along to the same firm for a complete renewal of all its parts. (It should be explained that such a renewal would involve only half the labour costs of building a new ship from scratch.) Now the scheming Proteus brothers had persuaded Morion that what he wanted was a ship with well-seasoned timber and told him that his "new" ship was under construction in dock B. They saw their way to an enormous profit. For, while they would require a thousand

From Brian Smart, "How to Reidentify the Ship of Theseus," *Analysis*, 32:5, 1972. Reprinted by permission of the author.

new planks for renovating the ship that belonged to the shrewder and potentially more troublesome Bombos, they would clearly not need a second batch of new planks for building Morion's ship: they would use Bombos's old ones.

However the brothers' plans misfired all too literally. Just after Morion and Bombos had paid their bills, but before they had taken possession of Y and Z, there was a fire in dock B and Z was reduced to ashes. Under the law of Oudamou, where all these events occurred, the brothers were responsible for Z until Morion had taken possession. Unfortunately, they had not had Z insured. The insurance would have had to be for a "new" ship but under Oudamou law the newness of a ship was decided by the newness of its component parts.

Seeing their vast profits about to disappear the Proteus brothers, in heavy disguise, left Oudamou abandoning Y in dock A.

Morion was quickly persuaded by his lawyer to claim ownership of Y as he had paid for a new ship and Y was new under Oudamou law. Bombos's lawyer naturally put in a claim on his client's behalf for possession of Y on the ground that Y was identical with X.

When the case was heard . . . Bombos's lawyer argued . . . as follows. Over a period of time, objects like the human body can undergo a change of identity in all their parts. All that is required is that the overall *form* of the object is retained and that it occupies a continuous space-time path. The ship in dock A satisfies this condition, and so X, his client's ship, is identical with Y. X is not identical with Z precisely because the form of Z cannot be linked to the form of X by a continuous space–time path.

Morion's lawyer attacked this argument. . . . He urged that the spatio-temporal continuity of form was neither a necessary nor a sufficient condition of identity. It was not a necessary condition since a watch could be dismantled and the same parts reassembled to form the same watch. X had in fact been gradually dismantled in dock A and reassembled in dock B. The necessary and sufficient condition to be met was the identity of the parts of X with the parts of Z. This condition had been met by Z. Hence it was Bombos's ship that had been destroyed and his client's ship which remained. . . .

The judges agreed that objects could be dismantled and reassembled elsewhere, still retaining their identity. . . . They contended that the requirement was that the object's *parts* had been reassembled. . . . They claimed that Z did not contain X's parts at all. If the case had been one in which only the original planks were involved, there would be no difficulty over identifying Z's parts with X's parts. But the case was not as simple as that.

Their reasoning was this. When a plank had been removed from X and replaced by a new plank, it was the new plank that was now a part of X. The old plank *had been* a part of X but was no longer. Rather it was a part of Z which gradually came into being from hour 1 onwards. When completed, Z was not composed of any of X's parts but rather of what had been X's parts. "Being a part of X" was merely a temporary role in the career of the old planks which were now parts of Z. Using this line of argument, it was clear that X had simply changed the identity of its parts and that now its parts were identical with the parts of Y. Hence X was identical with Y. X was not identical with Z for they had no parts in common.

Thus they found in favour of Bombos.

STUDY QUESTIONS

1. Explain in your own words the case of Morion versus Bombos.
2. What are the strongest arguments Morion can offer?
3. What are the strongest arguments Bombos can offer?
4. Is any decision in the case arbitrary?

The Problem of Personal Identity

JOHN PERRY

So much for the identity of objects. Now what about the identity of persons? The issue is explained here by John Perry, Professor Emeritus of Philosophy at Stanford University.

....

Imagine the following. Elected to the Senate from your home state, you have become a key member of the Committee on Health, Education, and Welfare. This committee meets tomorrow to vote on a bill to fund a feasibility study of a new method for manufacturing shoes, which is alleged to produce a high-quality, inexpensive shoe that never wears out. Your support of the bill is essential; it has faced the bitter and unflagging opposition of the American Cobblers Association (ACA), led by their high-pressure lobbyist Peter Pressher, and a number of committee members intend to vote against it.

The morning of the committee vote you wake up, open your eyes, and glance at the clock on the shelf beyond the bed. Something seems strange. The bump in the covers you take to be your feet seems strangely distant. As you get out of bed you hit your head on a shelf that used to be a good three or four inches above it. You notice you are wearing a leather apron, which you are certain you didn't wear to bed. Puzzled, you go to the mirror. Staring out you see not your familiar clean-shaven face and squatty body, but the strapping frame and bearded countenance of Peter Pressher.

From John Perry, ed., *Personal Identity*, Berkeley, University of California Press, 1975. Reprinted by permission of the publisher.

You don't know what to think. Are you dreaming? Is this some kind of a trick? But you perform various tests to eliminate these possibilities. No doubt can remain: the body you have looks just like the body Peter Pressher normally has; it seems to be that very body.

Hearing laughter, you turn toward your living room. There on the sofa sits a person who looks exactly like you. That is exactly like you used to look, down to the inevitable magenta hollyhock (your state's flower) in the lapel. Before you can speak, he says,

"Surprised, Senator? I've made sacrifices for the Cobblers before. Getting this squatty body must take the prize. But I'll vote to kill that bill this afternoon, and it will be worth it . . ."

He speaks with your own deep and resonant voice, but the syntax and the fanatic overtones are unmistakably those of . . .

"Peter Pressher! . . ."

"Right, Senator, it's me. But as far as the rest of the world will ever know, it's really you. We snuck into your apartment last night and my brother Bimo, the brain surgeon, carefully removed your brain and put it in my body—or should I say your body. And vice versa. It's a new operation he's pioneering; he calls it a 'body transplant.'"

"You'll never get away with it . . ."

"Forget it. You have two choices. You can go around telling people that you're you, in which case I will sue you and my family, thinking they are your family, will sign papers to have you put away. Or you can start acting like me—become Peter Pressher—we think you'd make a good lobbyist. Almost as good a lobbyist as I'll make a senator!"

An incredible story? Let's hope so. Impossible? In one sense, yes. Physicians cannot now perform body transplants with human beings. But in another sense the case is perfectly possible. The day when such operations can be performed may not be so far away. Such an operation is possible in the sense of being conceivable. The story was not self-contradictory or incoherent. As a piece of science fiction, it's pretty mild stuff. . . .

Why are such cases puzzling, and why is the puzzlement of philosophical interest? Because they seem to disprove the view that a person is just a live human body. If we can have the same person on two different occasions when we don't have the same live human body, then it seems that a person cannot be identified with his body, and personal identity cannot be identified with bodily identity. This is puzzling simply because the assumption that the two go together plays a large role in our daily lives. We make it when we identify others on the basis of appearance, or observed movements, or fingerprints. What is the justification for this assumption? The abandonment of the simple theory that personal identity is just bodily identity carries with it the need to formulate an alternative account of personal identity.

But perhaps we are moving too fast. Are we so sure that the puzzle cases prove what they are alleged to? Perhaps the events imagined have been wrongly described, and the right description would go something like this:

You are a senator from your home state. One morning you wake up on the sofa, seeming to remember being Peter Pressher, a lobbyist for the ACA. A man emerges from a bedroom, who seems to remember being you. But subsequent tests—fingerprints, testimony of close friends, comparison of medical records, etc.—establish, to your delight and his dismay, that you are a duly elected senator with delusions (which you keep quiet about) of having been a lobbyist, while he is a lobbyist with delusions of having been a senator. His situation is rather ironic. He willingly participated in a scheme where his brain (and so various of his psychological characteristics) were exchanged for your brain (and so various of your psychological characteristics). He seems to have thought that would somehow constitute a "body transfer," and he would wind up in the Senate. (He was taught this by a philosophy professor in college, whom he is suing.) What actually happened, of course, is that two people underwent radical changes in character and personality, and acquired delusive memories, as a result of brain surgery.

How shall we decide between these two descriptions? In a sense, they do not disagree about what happened—which sounds emanated from which bodies, and so forth. So neither can be proven incorrect by reference to the occurrence of these events. But in another sense they are blatantly contradictory, and one must be wrong.

STUDY QUESTIONS

1. In Perry's story, are you Peter Pressher?
2. How do you decide the matter?
3. Could you be mistaken about who you are?
4. Is any decision in the matter arbitrary?

The Unimportance of Identity

DEREK PARFIT

Derek Parfit (1942–2017) was Emeritus Fellow at All Souls College of the University of Oxford. Using a variety of unusual yet provocative thought experiments, he argues against the importance of personal identity.

From Henry Harris, ed., *Identity*, Clarendon Press, 1995. Reprinted by permission of the publisher.

Personal identity is widely thought to have great rational and moral significance. Thus it is the fact of identity which is thought to give us our reason for concern about our own future. And several moral principles, such as those of desert or distributive justice, presuppose claims about identity. The separateness of persons, or the non-identity of different people, has been called "the basic fact for morals."

I can comment here on only one of these questions: what matters in our survival. I mean by that, not what makes our survival good, but what makes our survival matter, whether it will be good or bad. What is it, in our survival, that gives us a reason for special anticipatory or prudential concern? . . .

Most of us believe that we should care about our future because it will be *our* future. I believe that what matters is not identity but certain other relations. To help us to decide between these views, we should consider cases where identity and those relations do not coincide.

Which these cases are depends on which criterion of identity we accept. I shall start with the simplest form of the Physical Criterion, according to which a person continues to exist if and only if that person's body continues to exist. That must be the view of those who believe that persons just are bodies. And it is the view of several of the people who identify persons with human beings. Let's call this the *Bodily Criterion*.

Suppose that, because of damage to my spine, I have become partly paralysed. I have a brother, who is dying of a brain disease. With the aid of new techniques, when my brother's brain ceases to function, my head could be grafted onto the rest of my brother's body. Since we are identical twins, my brain would then control a body that is just like mine, except that it would not be paralysed.

Should I accept this operation? Of those who assume that identity is what matters, three groups would answer No. Some accept the Bodily Criterion. These people believe that, if this operation were performed, I would die. The person with my head tomorrow would be my brother, who would mistakenly think that he was me. Other people are uncertain what would happen. They believe that it would be risky to accept this operation, since the resulting person might not be me. Others give a different reason why I should reject this operation: that it would be indeterminate whether that person would be me. On all these views, it matters who that person would be.

On my view, that question is unimportant. If this operation were performed, the person with my head tomorrow would not only believe that he was me, seem to remember living my life, and be in every other way psychologically like me. These facts would also have their normal cause, the continued existence of my brain. And this person's body would be just like mine. For all these reasons, his life would be just like the life that I would have lived, if my paralysis had been cured. I believe that, given these facts, I should accept this operation. It is irrelevant whether this person would be me.

That may seem all important. After all, if he would not be me, I shall have ceased to exist. But, if that person would not be me, this fact would just consist in another fact. It would just consist in the fact that my body will have been replaced below the neck. When considered on its own, is that second fact important? Can it matter in itself that the blood that will keep my brain alive will circulate, not through my own heart and lungs, but through my brother's heart and lungs? Can it matter in itself that my brain will control, not the rest of my body, but the rest of another body that is exactly similar? . . .

According to my argument, we should now conclude that neither of these facts could matter greatly. Since it would not be in itself important that my head would be grafted onto this body, and that would be all there was to the fact that the resulting person would not be me, it would not be in itself important that this person would not be me. Perhaps it would not be irrational to regret these facts a little. But, I believe, they would be heavily outweighed by the fact that, unlike me, the resulting person would not be paralysed. . . .

On my view, what matters is what is going to happen. If I knew that my head could be grafted onto the rest of a body that is just like mine, and that the resulting person would be just like me, I need not ask whether the resulting person could be correctly called me. That is not a further difference in what is going to happen. . . .

It may now be objected: "By choosing this example, you are cheating. Of course you should accept this operation. But that is because the resulting person *would* be you. We should reject the Bodily Criterion. So this case cannot show that identity is not what matters."

Since there are people who accept this criterion, I am not cheating. It is worth trying to show these people that identity is not what matters. But I accept part of this objection. I agree that we should reject the Bodily Criterion. . . .

I am now assuming that we accept the Brain-Based Psychological Criterion. We believe that, if there will be one future person who will have enough of my brain to be psychologically continuous with me, that person would be me. On this view, there is another way to argue that identity is not what matters.

We can first note that, just as I could survive with less than my whole body, I could survive with less than my whole brain. People have survived, and with little psychological change, even when, through a stroke or injury, they have lost the use of half their brain.

Let us next suppose that the two halves of my brain could each fully support ordinary psychological functioning. That may in fact be true of certain people. If it is not, we can suppose that, through some technological advance, it has been made true of me. Since our aim is to test our beliefs about what matters, there is no harm in making such assumptions.

We can now compare two more possible operations. In the first, after half my brain is destroyed, the other half would be successfully transplanted into the empty skull of a body that is just like mine. Given our assumptions, we should conclude that, here too, I would survive. Since I would survive if my brain were transplanted, and I would survive with only half my brain, it would be unreasonable to deny that I would survive if that remaining half were transplanted. So, in this *Single Case*, the resulting person would be me.

Consider next the *Double Case*, or *My Division*. Both halves of my brain would be successfully transplanted, into different bodies that are just like mine. Two people would wake up, each of whom has half my brain, and is, both physically and psychologically, just like me.

Since these would be two different people, it cannot be true that each of them is me. That would be a contradiction. If each of them was me, each would be one and the same person: me. So they could not be two different people.

Could it be true that only one of them is me? That is not a contradiction. But, since I have the same relation to each of these people, there is nothing that could make me one of them rather than the other. It cannot be true, of either of these people, that he is the one who could be correctly called me.

How should I regard these two operations? Would they preserve what matters in survival? In the Single Case, the one resulting person would be me. The relation between me now and that future person is just an instance of the relation between me now and myself tomorrow. So that relation would contain what matters. In the Double Case, my relation to that person would be just the same. So this relation must still contain what matters. Nothing is missing. But that person cannot here be claimed to be me. So identity cannot be what matters.

We may object that, if that person isn't me, something *is* missing. *I'm* missing. That may seem to make all the difference. How can everything still be there if *I'm* not there?

Everything is still there. The fact that I'm not there is not a real absence. The relation between me now and that future person is in itself the same. As in the Single Case, he has half my brain, and he is just like me. The difference is only that, in this Double Case, I also have the same relation to the other resulting person. Why am I not there? The explanation is only this. When this relation holds between me now and a single person in the future, we can be called one and the same person. When this relation holds between me now and *two* future people, I cannot be called one and the same as each of these people. But that is not a difference in the nature or the content of this relation. In the Single Case, where half my brain will be successfully transplanted, my prospect is survival. That prospect contains what matters. In the Double Case, where both halves will be successfully transplanted, nothing would be lost.

It can be hard to believe that identity is not what matters. But that is easier to accept when we see why, in this example, it is true. It may help to consider this analogy. Imagine a community of persons who are like us, but with two exceptions. First, because of facts about their reproductive system, each couple has only two children, who are always twins. Second, because of special features of their psychology, it is of great importance for the development of each child that it should not, through the death of its sibling, become an only child. Such children suffer psychological damage. It is thus believed, in this community, that it matters greatly that each child should have a twin.

Now suppose that, because of some biological change, some of the children in this community start to be born as triplets. Should their parents think this a disaster, because these children don't have twins? Clearly not. These children don't have twins only because they each have *two* siblings. Since each child has two siblings, the trio must be called, not twins, but triplets. But none of them will suffer damage as an only child. These people should revise their view. What matters isn't having a twin: it is having at least one sibling.

In the same way, we should revise our view about identity over time. What matters isn't that there will be someone alive who will be me. It is rather that there will be at least one living person who will be psychologically continuous with me as I am now, and/or who has enough of my brain. When there will be only one such person, he can be described as me. When there will be two such people, we cannot claim that each will be me. But that is as trivial as the fact that, if I had two identical siblings, they could not be called my twins.

If, as I have argued, personal identity is not what matters, we must ask what does matter. There are several possible answers. And, depending on our answer, there are several further implications. Thus there are several moral questions which I have no time even to mention. I shall end with another remark about our concern for our own future.

That concern is of several kinds. We may want to survive partly so that our hopes and ambitions will be achieved. We may also care about our future in the kind of way in which we care about the well-being of certain other people, such as our relatives or friends. But most of us have, in addition, a distinctive kind of egoistic concern. If I know that my child will be in pain, I may care about his pain more than I would about my own future pain. But I cannot fearfully anticipate my child's pain. And if I knew that my Replica would take up my life where I leave off, I would not look forward to that life.

This kind of concern may, I believe, be weakened, and be seen to have no ground, if we come to accept [my] view. In our thoughts about our own identity, we are prone to illusions. That is why the so-called "problem cases" seem to raise problems: why we find it hard to believe that, when we know the other facts, it is an empty or a merely verbal question whether we shall still exist. Even after we accept [my] view, we may continue, at some level, to think and feel as if that view were not true. Our own continued existence may still seem an independent fact, of a peculiarly deep and simple kind. And that belief may underlie our anticipatory concern about our own future. . . .

Even the use of the word "I" can lead us astray. Consider the fact that, in a few years, I shall be dead. This fact can seem depressing. But the reality is only this. After a certain time, none of the thoughts and experiences that occur will be directly causally related to this brain, or be connected in certain ways to these present experiences. That is all this fact involves. And, in that redescription, my death seems to disappear.

STUDY QUESTIONS

1. How do you analyze the Single Case?
2. How do you analyze the Double Case?
3. Do you agree with Parfit that identity is unimportant?
4. Do you believe that the strangeness of the cases Parfit discusses weakens his conclusion?

An Essay Concerning Human Understanding

JOHN LOCKE

John Locke, whose work we read previously, differentiates between the concepts of same body and same person. Bodily identity is determined for a man or woman the same way it is determined for a ship or a swan. The criterion for personal identity, however, is continuity of consciousness, that is, memory. If you remember scoring the winning goal in a crucial game a decade ago, then you are the person who scored that goal.

Locke's position has the advantage of reconciling his materialism with the possibility of immortality, because a person's identity would not depend on bodily survival. An apparent disadvantage of Locke's position, however, is the fallibility of memory. For instance, you might be the person who scored that winning goal, yet you might not remember doing so.

9. ... [T]o find wherein personal identity consists, we must consider what *person* stands for;—which, I think, is a thinking intelligent being that has reason and reflection and can consider itself as itself, the same thinking thing, in different times and places; which it does only by that consciousness which is inseparable from thinking, and, as it seems to me, essential to it: it being impossible for any one to perceive without *perceiving* that he does perceive. When we see, hear, smell, taste, feel, meditate, or will anything, we know that we do so. Thus it is always as to our present sensations and perceptions: and by this every one is to himself that which he calls self:—it not being considered, in this case, whether the same self be continued in the same or divers substances. For, since consciousness always accompanies thinking, and it is that which makes every one to be what he calls self, and thereby distinguishes himself from all other thinking things, in this alone consists personal identity, i.e., the sameness of a rational being: and as far as this consciousness can be extended backwards to any past action or thought, so far reaches the identity of that person; it is the same self now it was then; and it is by the same self with this present one that now reflects on it, that that action was done.

From *An Essay Concerning Human Understanding* by John Locke (1690), Book II, Chapter 27.

10. But it is further inquired, whether it be the same identical substance. This few would think they had reason to doubt of, if these perceptions, with their consciousness, always remained present in the mind, whereby the same thinking thing would be always consciously present, and, as would be thought, evidently the same to itself. But that which seems to make the difficulty is this, that this consciousness being interrupted always by forgetfulness, there being no moment of our lives wherein we have the whole train of all our past actions before our eyes in one view, but even the best memories losing the sight of one part whilst they are viewing another; and we sometimes, and that the greatest part of our lives, not reflecting on our past selves, being intent on our present thoughts, and in sound sleep having no thoughts at all, or at least none with that consciousness which remarks our waking thoughts,—I say, in all these cases, our consciousness being interrupted, and we losing the sight of our past selves, doubts are raised whether we are the same thinking thing, i.e., the same *substance* or no. Which, however reasonable or unreasonable, concerns not *personal* identity at all. The question being what makes the same person; and not whether it be the same identical substance, which always thinks in the same person, which, in the case, matters not at all: different substances, by the same consciousness (where they do partake in it) being united into one person, as well as different bodies by the same life are united into one animal, whose identity is preserved in that change of substances by the unity of one continued life. For, it being the same consciousness that makes a man be himself to himself, personal identity depends on that only, whether it be annexed solely to one individual substance, or can be continued in a succession of several substances. For as far as any intelligent being *can* repeat the idea of any past action with the same consciousness it had of it at first, and with the same consciousness it has of any present action; so far it is the same personal self. For it is by the consciousness it has of its present thoughts and actions, that it is *self to itself* now, and so will be the same self, as far as the same consciousness can extend to actions past or to come; and would be by distance of time, or change of substance, no more two persons, than a man be two men by wearing other clothes today than he did yesterday, with a long or a short sleep between: the same consciousness uniting those distant actions in the same person, whatever substances contributed to their production.

11. That this is so, we have some kind of evidence in our very bodies, all whose particles, whilst vitally united to this same thinking conscious self, so that *we feel* when they are touched, and are affected by, and conscious of good or harm that happens to them, are a part of ourselves, i.e., of our thinking conscious self. Thus, the limbs of his body are to every one a part of himself; he sympathizes and is concerned for them. Cut off a hand, and thereby separate it from that consciousness he had of its heat, cold, and other affections, and it is then no longer a part of that which is himself, any more than the remotest part of matter. Thus, we see the *substance* whereof personal self consisted at one time may be varied at another, without the change of personal identity; there being no question about the same person, though the limbs which but now were a part of it, be cut off. . . .

15. And thus may we be able, without any difficulty, to conceive the same person at the resurrection, though in a body not exactly in make or parts the same

which he had here,—the same consciousness going along with the soul that inhabits it. But yet the soul alone, in the change of bodies, would scarce to any one but to him that makes the soul the man, be enough to make the same man. For should the soul of a prince, carrying with it the consciousness of the prince's past life, enter and inform the body of a cobbler, as soon as deserted by his own soul, every one sees he would be the same *person* with the prince, accountable only for the prince's actions: but who would say it was the same *man*? The body too goes to the making the man, and would, I guess, to everybody determine the man in this case, wherein the soul, with all its princely thoughts about it, would not make another man: but he would be the same cobbler to every one besides himself. I know that, in the ordinary way of speaking, the same person, and the same man, stand for one and the same thing. And indeed every one will always have a liberty to speak as he pleases, and to apply what articulate sounds to what ideas he thinks fit, and change them as often as he pleases. But yet, when we will inquire what makes the same *spirit, man,* or *person,* we must fix the ideas of spirit, man, or person in our minds; and having resolved with ourselves what we mean by them, it will not be hard to determine in either of them, or the like, when it is the same, and when not.

16. But though the immaterial substance or soul does not alone, wherever it be, and in whatsoever state, make the same *man;* yet it is plain, consciousness, as far as ever it can be extended—should it be to ages past—unites existences and actions very remote in time into the same *person,* as well as it does the existences and actions of the immediately preceding moment: so that whatever has the consciousness of present and past actions, is the same person to whom they both belong. Had I the same consciousness that I saw the ark and Noah's flood, as that I saw an overflowing of the Thames last winter, or as that I write now, I could no more doubt that I who write this now, that saw the Thames overflowed last winter, and that viewed the flood at the general deluge, was the same *self,*—place that self in what *substance* you please—than that I who write this am the same *myself* now whilst I write (whether I consist of all the same substance, material or immaterial, or no) that I was yesterday. For as to this point of being the same self, it matters not whether this present self be made up of the same or other substances—I being as much concerned, and as justly accountable for any action that was done a thousand years since, appropriated to me now by this self-consciousness, as I am for what I did the last moment. . . .

20. But yet possibly it will still be objected,—Suppose I wholly lose the memory of some parts of my life, beyond a possibility of retrieving them, so that perhaps I shall never be conscious of them again; yet am I not the same person that did those actions, had those thoughts that I once was conscious of, though I have now forgot them? To which I answer, that we must here take notice what the word *I* is applied to; which, in this case, is the *man* only. And the same man being presumed to be the same person, I is easily here supposed to stand also for the same person. But if it be possible for the same man to have distinct incommunicable consciousness at different times, it is past doubt the same man would at different times make different persons; which, we see, is the sense of mankind in the solemnest declaration of their opinions, human laws not punishing the mad man for

the sober man's actions, nor the sober man for what the mad man did,—thereby making them two persons: which is somewhat explained by our way of speaking in English when we say such an one is "not himself," or is "beside himself"; in which phrases it is insinuated, as if those who now, or at least first used them, thought that self was changed; the selfsame person was no longer in that man.

STUDY QUESTIONS

1. According to Locke, what is a person?
2. According to Locke, could a person remain the same but with an entirely changed body?
3. How does Locke respond to the observation that a person can lose memories?
4. What does Locke's view of personal identity imply about the possibility of immortality?

A Treatise of Human Nature

DAVID HUME

David Hume, whose work we read previously, denies the view that we are conscious of a simple self, identical from one time to another. Instead, Hume maintains that we are but a collection of perceptions succeeding each other with great rapidity. A person's identity is no more invariable than that of a plant or vegetable. In short, the concept of a human soul is a fiction.

OF PERSONAL IDENTITY

There are some philosophers who imagine we are every moment intimately conscious of what we call our self, that we feel its existence and its continuance in existence, and are certain beyond the evidence of a demonstration both of its perfect identity and simplicity. . . .

Unluckily all these positive assertions are contrary to that very experience which is pleaded for them, nor have we any idea of *self* after the manner it is here explained. For from what impression could this idea be derived? This question it is impossible to answer without a manifest contradiction and absurdity, and yet it is a question which must necessarily be answered, if we would have the idea of

From *A Treatise of Human Nature* by David Hume (1738).

self pass for clear and intelligible. It must be some one impression that gives rise to every real idea. But self or person is not any one impression, but that to which our several impressions and ideas are supposed to have a reference. If any impression gives rise to the idea of self, that impression must continue invariably the same through the whole course of our lives, since self is supposed to exist after that manner. But there is no impression constant and invariable. Pain and pleasure, grief and joy, passions and sensations succeed each other and never all exist at the same time. It cannot, therefore, be from any of these impressions or from any other that the idea of self is derived, and, consequently, there is no such idea.

But further, what must become of all our particular perceptions upon this hypothesis? All these are different, and distinguishable, and separable from each other, and may be separately considered, and may exist separately, and have no need of anything to support their existence. After what manner therefore do they belong to self and how are they connected with it? For my part, when I enter most intimately into what I call *myself*, I always stumble on some particular perception or other, of heat or cold, light or shade, love or hatred, pain or pleasure. I never can catch *myself* at any time without a perception and never can observe anything but the perception. When my perceptions are removed for any time, as by sound sleep, so long am I insensible of myself and may truly be said not to exist. And were all my perceptions removed by death and could I neither think, nor feel, nor see, nor love, nor hate after the dissolution of my body. I should be entirely annihilated, nor do I conceive what is further requisite to make me a perfect nonentity. If anyone, upon serious and unprejudiced reflection, thinks he has a different notion of *himself*, I must confess I can reason no longer with him. All I can allow him is that he may be in the right as well as I and that we are essentially different in this particular. He may, perhaps, perceive something simple and continued which he calls *himself*, though I am certain there is no such principle in me.

But setting aside some metaphysicians of this kind, I may venture to affirm of the rest of mankind that they are nothing but a bundle or collection of different perceptions which succeed each other with an inconceivable rapidity and are in a perpetual flux and movement. Our eyes cannot turn in their sockets without varying our perceptions. Our thought is still more variable than our sight and all our other senses and faculties contribute to this change; nor is there any single power of the soul which remains unalterably the same perhaps for one moment. The mind is a kind of theater where several perceptions successively make their appearance, pass, repass, glide away, and mingle in an infinite variety of postures and situations. There is properly no *simplicity* in it at one time nor *identity* in different, whatever natural propensity we may have to imagine that simplicity and identity. The comparison of the theater must not mislead us. They are the successive perceptions only that constitute the mind, nor have we the most distant notion of the place where these scenes are represented or of the materials of which it is composed.

What, then, gives us so great a propensity to ascribe an identity to these successive perceptions and to suppose ourselves possessed of an invariable and uninterrupted existence through the whole course of our lives? . . .

We have a distinct idea of an object that remains invariable and uninterrupted through a supposed variation of time and this idea we call that of *identity* or *sameness*. We have also a distinct idea of several different objects existing in succession and connected together by a close relation, and this, to an accurate view, affords as perfect a notion of *diversity* as if there was no manner of relation among the objects. But though these two ideas of identity and a succession of related objects be in themselves perfectly distinct and even contrary, yet it is certain that, in our common way of thinking, they are generally confounded with each other. That action of the imagination by which we consider the uninterrupted and invariable object and that by which we reflect on the succession of related objects are almost the same to the feeling, nor is there much more effort of thought required in the latter case than in the former. The relation facilitates the transition of the mind from one object to another and renders its passage as smooth as if it contemplated one continued object. This resemblance is the cause of the confusion and mistake and makes us substitute the notion of identity instead of that of related objects. However at one instant we may consider the related succession as variable or interrupted, we are sure the next to ascribe to it a perfect identity and regard it as invariable and uninterrupted. Our propensity to this mistake is so great from the resemblance above mentioned that we fall into it before we are aware, and though we incessantly correct ourselves by reflection and return to a more accurate method of thinking, yet we cannot long sustain our philosophy or take off this bias from the imagination. Our last resource is to yield to it and boldly assert that these different related objects are in effect the same, however interrupted and variable. In order to justify to ourselves this absurdity, we often feign some new and unintelligible principle that connects the objects together and prevents their interruption or variation. Thus we feign the continued existence of the perceptions of our senses to remove the interruption and run into the notion of a *soul*, and *self*, and *substance* to disguise the variation. But, we may further observe that where we do not give rise to such a fiction, our propensity to confound identity with relation is so great that we are apt to imagine something unknown and mysterious, connecting the parts, besides their relation, and this I take to be the case with regard to the identity we ascribe to plants and vegetables. And even when this does not take place, we still feel a propensity to confound these ideas, though we are not able fully to satisfy ourselves in that particular nor find anything invariable and uninterrupted to justify our notion of identity.

Thus the controversy concerning identity is not merely a dispute of words. For when we attribute identity, in an improper sense, to variable or interrupted objects, our mistake is not confined to the expression, but is commonly attended with a fiction, either of something invariable and uninterrupted, or of something mysterious and inexplicable, or at least with a propensity to such fictions. What will suffice to prove this hypothesis to the satisfaction of every fair inquirer is to show from daily experience and observation that the objects which are variable or interrupted, and yet are supposed to continue the same, are such only as consist of a succession of parts, connected together by resemblance, contiguity, or causation. . . .

A ship of which a considerable part has been changed by frequent repairs is still considered as the same, nor does the difference of the materials hinder us from ascribing an identity to it. The common end, in which the parts conspire, is the same under all their variations and affords an easy transition of the imagination from one situation of the body to another. . . .

[T]hough everyone must allow that in a very few years both vegetables and animals endure a *total* change, yet we still attribute identity to them, while their form, size, and substance are entirely altered. An oak that grows from a small plant to a large tree is still the same oak, though there is not one particle of matter or figure of its parts the same. An infant becomes a man and is sometimes fat, sometimes lean without any change in his identity. . . .

[A] man who hears a noise that is frequently interrupted and renewed says it is still the same noise, though it is evident the sounds have only a specific identity or resemblance and there is nothing numerically the same but the cause which produced them. In like manner it may be said without breach of the propriety of language that such a church, which was formerly of brick, fell to ruin and that the parish rebuilt the same church of freestone and according to modern architecture. Here neither the form nor materials are the same, nor is there anything common to the two objects but their relation to the inhabitants of the parish. Yet this alone is sufficient to make us denominate them the same. But we must observe that in these cases the first object is in a manner annihilated before the second comes into existence, by which means we are never presented in any one point of time with the idea of difference and multiplicity and, for that reason, are less scrupulous in calling them the same. . . .

The identity which we ascribe to the mind of man is only a fictitious one and of a like kind with that which we ascribe to vegetables and animal bodies. It cannot, therefore, have a different origin, but must proceed from a like operation of the imagination upon like objects.

But lest this argument should not convince the reader, though in my opinion perfectly decisive, let him weigh the following reasoning, which is still closer and more immediate. It is evident that the identity which we attribute to the human mind, however perfect we may imagine it to be, is not able to run the several different perceptions into one and make them lose their characters of distinction and difference which are essential to them. It is still true that every distinct perception which enters into the composition of the mind is a distinct existence, and is different, and distinguishable, and separable from every other perception, either contemporary or successive. But as, notwithstanding this distinction and separability, we suppose the whole train of perceptions to be united by identity, a question naturally arises concerning this relation of identity, whether it is something that really binds our several perceptions together or only associates their ideas in the imagination, that is, in other words, whether, in pronouncing concerning the identity of a person, we observe some real bond among his perceptions or only feel one among the ideas we form of them. This question we might easily decide if we would recollect what has been already proved at large, namely, that the understanding never observes any real connection among objects and that even the union of cause and effect, when strictly examined, resolves itself into a customary association of ideas. For from this it evidently follows that identity is nothing really belonging to these different perceptions and uniting them together but rather is merely a quality which we attribute to them because of the union of their ideas in the imagination when we reflect upon them. . . .

The only question, therefore, which remains is by what relations this uninterrupted progress of our thought is produced when we consider the successive existence of a mind or thinking person. And here it is evident we must confine ourselves to resemblance and causation. . . .

As memory alone acquaints us with the continuance and extent of this succession of perceptions, it is to be considered upon that account chiefly as the source of personal identity. Had we no memory, we never should have any notion of causation nor consequently of that chain of causes and effects which constitute our self or person. But having once acquired this notion of causation from the memory, we can extend the same chain of causes and consequently the identity of our persons beyond our memory and can comprehend times, circumstances, and actions which we have entirely forgotten, but suppose in general to have existed. For how few of our past actions are there of which we have any memory? Who can tell me, for instance, what were his thoughts and actions on the 1st of January 1715, the 11th of March 1719, and the 3rd of August 1733? Or will he affirm, because he has entirely forgotten the incidents of these days, that the present self is not the same person with the self of that time, and by that means overturn all the most established notions of personal identity? In this view, therefore, memory does not so much *produce* as *discover* personal identity by showing us the relation of cause and effect among our different perceptions. It will be incumbent on those who affirm that memory produces entirely our personal identity to give a reason why we can thus extend our identity beyond our memory.

The whole of this doctrine leads us to a conclusion which is of great importance in the present affair, namely that all the nice and subtle questions concerning personal identity can never possibly be decided and are to be regarded rather as grammatical than as philosophical difficulties. Identity depends on the relations of ideas, and these relations produce identity by means of that easy transition they occasion. But as the relations and the easiness of the transition may diminish by insensible degrees, we have no just standard by which we can decide any dispute concerning the time when they acquire or lose a title to the name of identity. All the disputes concerning the identity of connected objects are merely verbal, except so far as the relation of parts gives rise to some fiction or imaginary principle of union as we have already observed.

STUDY QUESTIONS

1. According to Hume, what is the self?
2. According to Hume, why are we confused about the nature of the self?
3. Why does Hume conclude that questions concerning personal identity raise grammatical rather than philosophical difficulties?
4. What does Hume's view of personal identity imply about the possibility of immortality?

Essays on the Intellectual Powers of Man

THOMAS REID

Thomas Reid (1710–1796) was the founder of what became known as the Scottish "common sense" school of philosophy. He was Professor of Moral Philosophy at the University of Glasgow.

Reid was a critic of the empiricism of Locke and Hume. Reid affirms that persons are permanent, indivisible, immaterial substances, and he appeals to memory as the basis for our knowledge of our personal identity. Unlike Locke, however, whose views he criticizes, Reid emphasizes that memory provides the evidence of my personal identity but doesn't make me the person I am.

....

OF IDENTITY

The conviction which every man has of his Identity, as far back as his memory reaches, needs no aid of philosophy to strengthen it; and no philosophy can weaken it, without first producing some degree of insanity.

The philosopher, however, may very properly consider this conviction as a phaenomenon of human nature worthy of his attention. If he can discover its cause, an addition is made to his stock of knowledge. If not, it must be held as a part of our original constitution, or an effect of that constitution produced in a manner unknown to us. . . .

That we may form as distinct a notion as we are able of this phenomenon of the human mind, it is proper to consider what is meant by identity in general, what by our own personal identity, and how we are led into that invincible belief and conviction which every man has of his own personal identity, as far as his memory reaches.

Identity in general, I take to be a relation between a thing which is known to exist at one time, and a thing which is known to have existed at another time. If you ask whether they are one and the same, or two different things, every man of common sense understands the meaning of your question perfectly. Whence we may infer with certainty that every man of common sense has a clear and distinct notion of identity.

If you ask a definition of identity, I confess I can give none; it is too simple a notion to admit of logical definition. I can say it is a relation; but I cannot find words to express the specific difference between this and other relations, though I am in no danger of confounding it with any other. I can say that diversity is

From *Essays on the Intellectual Powers of Man* by Thomas Reid (1785), Essay III.

a contrary relation and that similitude and dissimilitude are another couple of contrary relations, which every man easily distinguishes in his conception from identity and diversity.

I see evidently that identity supposes an uninterrupted continuance of existence. That which hath ceased to exist cannot be the same with that which afterwards begins to exist; for this would be to suppose a being to exist after it ceased to exist, and to have had existence before it was produced, which are manifest contradictions. Continued uninterrupted existence is therefore necessarily implied in identity.

Hence we may infer that identity cannot, in its proper sense, be applied to our pains, our pleasures, our thoughts, or any operation of our minds. The pain felt this day is not the same individual pain which I felt yesterday, though they may be similar in kind and degree and have the same cause. The same may be said of every feeling and of every operation of mind: they are all successive in their nature, like time itself, no two moments of which can be the same moment.

It is otherwise with the parts of absolute space. They always are, and were, and will be the same. So far, I think, we proceed upon clear ground in fixing the notion of identity in general.

It is, perhaps, more difficult to ascertain with precision the meaning of Personality; but it is not necessary in the present subject: it is sufficient for our purpose to observe, that all mankind place their personality in something that cannot be divided, or consist of parts. A part of a person is a manifest absurdity.

When a man loses his estate, his health, his strength, he is still the same person and has lost nothing of his personality. If he has a leg or an arm cut off, he is the same person he was before. The amputated member is no part of his person, otherwise it would have a right to a part of his estate and be liable for a part of his engagements; it would be entitled to a share of his merit and demerit—which is manifestly absurd. A person is something indivisible. . . .

My personal identity, therefore, implies the continued existence of that indivisible thing which I call myself. Whatever this self may be, it is something which thinks, and deliberates, and resolves, and acts, and suffers. I am not thought, I am not action. I am not feeling; I am something that thinks, and acts, and suffers. My thoughts, and actions, and feelings, change every moment—they have no continued, but a successive existence: but that *self* or *I*, to which they belong, is permanent and has the same relation to all the succeeding thoughts, actions, and feelings, which I call mine.

Such are the notions that I have of my personal identity. But perhaps it may be said, this may all be fancy without reality. How do you know?—what evidence have you, that there is such a permanent self which has a claim to all the thoughts, actions, and feelings, which you call yours?

To this I answer, that the proper evidence I have of all this is remembrance. I remember that, twenty years ago, I conversed with such a person; I remember several things that passed in that conversation; my memory testifies not only that this was done, but that it was done by me who now remember it. If it was done by me, I must have existed at that time and continued to exist from that time to the present:

if the identical person whom I call myself had not a part in that conversation, my memory is fallacious—it gives a distinct and positive testimony of what is not true. Every man in his senses believes what he distinctly remembers, and everything he remembers convinces him that he existed at the time remembered.

Although memory gives the most irresistible evidence of my being the identical person that did such a thing, at such a time, I may have other good evidence of things which befell me and which I do not remember: I know who bare me and suckled me, but I do not remember these events.

It may here be observed (though the observation would have been unnecessary, if some great philosophers had not contradicted it) that it is not my remembering any action of mine that *makes* me to be the person who did it. This remembrance makes me to *know* assuredly that I did it; *but I might have done it, though I did not remember it*. That relation to me, which is expressed by saying that *I did it*, would be the same, though I had not the least remembrance of it. To say that my remembering that I did such a thing, or, as some choose to express it, my being conscious that I did it, makes me to have done it, appears to me as great an absurdity as it would be to say that my belief that the world was created made it to be created.

When we pass judgment on the identity of other persons than ourselves, we proceed upon other grounds, and determine from a variety of circumstances, which sometimes produce the firmest assurance, and sometimes leave room for doubt. The identity of persons has often furnished matter of serious litigation before tribunals of justice. But no man of a sound mind ever doubted of his own identity, as far as he distinctly remembered.

The identity of a person is a perfect identity: wherever it is real, it admits of no degrees; and it is impossible that a person should be in part the same and in part different; because a person is a *monad* and is not divisible into parts. The evidence of identity in other persons than ourselves does indeed admit of all degrees, from what we account certainty, to the least degree of probability. But still it is true that the same person is perfectly the same and cannot be so in part, or in some degree only.

For this cause, I have first considered personal identity as that which is perfect in its kind, and the natural measure of that which is imperfect.

We probably at first derive our notion of identity from that natural conviction which every man has from the dawn of reason of *his own* identity and continued existence. The operations of our minds are all successive and have no continued existence. But the thinking being has a continued existence, and we have an invincible belief that it remains the same when all its thoughts and operations change.

Our judgments of the identity of objects of sense seem to be formed much upon the same grounds as our judgments of the identity of *other persons* than ourselves. Wherever we observe great *similarity*, we are apt to presume identity if no reason appears to the contrary. Two objects ever so like, when they are perceived at the same time, cannot be the same; but if they are presented to our senses at different times, we are apt to think them the same merely from their similarity.

Whether this be a natural prejudice or from whatever cause it proceeds, it certainly appears in children from infancy; and when we grow up, it is confirmed in most instances by experience: for we rarely find two individuals of the same species that are not distinguishable by obvious differences. A man challenges a thief whom he finds in possession of his horse or his watch, only on similarity. When the watchmaker swears that he sold this watch to such a person, his testimony is grounded on similarity. The testimony of witnesses to the identity of a person is commonly grounded on no other evidence.

Thus it appears that the evidence we have of our own identity, as far back as we remember, is totally of a different kind from the evidence we have of the identity of other persons, or of objects of sense. The first is grounded on *memory* and gives undoubted certainty. The last is grounded on *similarity* and on other circumstances, which in many cases are not so decisive as to leave no room for doubt.

It may likewise be observed that the identity of *objects of sense* is never perfect. All bodies, as they consist of innumerable parts that may be disjoined from them by a great variety of causes, are subject to continual changes of their substance, increasing, diminishing, changing insensibly. When such alterations are gradual, because language could not afford a different name for every different state of such a changeable being, it retains the same name and is considered as the same thing. Thus we say of an old regiment that it did such a thing a century ago, though there now is not a man alive who then belonged to it. We say a tree is the same in the seed-bed and in the forest. A ship of war, which has successively changed her anchors, her tackle, her sails, her masts, her planks, and her timbers, while she keeps the same name, is the same.

The identity, therefore, which we ascribe to bodies, whether natural or artificial, is not perfect identity; it is rather something which, for the conveniency of speech, we call identity. It admits of a great change of the subject, providing the change be *gradual*; sometimes, even of a total change. And the changes which in common language are made consistent with identity differ from those that are thought to destroy it, not in *kind* but in *number* and *degree*. It has no fixed nature when applied to bodies; and questions about the identity of a body are very often questions about words. But identity, when applied to persons, has no ambiguity, and admits not of degrees, or of more and less. It is the foundation of all rights and obligations and of all accountableness; and the notion of it is fixed and precise.

. . . OF MR. LOCKE'S ACCOUNT OF OUR PERSONAL IDENTITY

. . . Mr. Locke tells us . . . "that personal identity—that is, the sameness of a rational being—consists in consciousness alone, and, as far as this consciousness can be extended backwards to any past action or thought, so far reaches the identity of that person. So that, whatever hath the consciousness of present and past actions, is the same person to whom they belong."

This doctrine hath some strange consequences, which the author was aware of, such as, that, if the same consciousness can be transferred from one intelligent being to another, which he thinks we cannot shew to be impossible, then two or twenty intelligent beings may be the same person. And if the intelligent being may lose the consciousness of the actions done by him, which surely is possible, then he is not the person that did those actions; so that one intelligent being may be two or twenty different persons, if he shall so often lose the consciousness of his former actions.

There is another consequence of this doctrine, which follows no less necessarily, though Mr. Locke probably did not see it. It is that a man may be, and at the same time not be, the person that did a particular action.

Suppose a brave officer to have been flogged when a boy at school, for robbing an orchard, to have taken a standard from the enemy in his first campaign, and to have been made a general in advanced life: Suppose also, which must be admitted to be possible, that, when he took the standard, he was conscious of his having been flogged at school, and that when made a general he was conscious of his taking the standard, but had absolutely lost the consciousness of his flogging.

These things being supposed, it follows, from Mr. Locke's doctrine, that he who was flogged at school is the same person who took the standard, and that he who took the standard is the same person who was made a general. Whence it follows, if there be any truth in logic, that the general is the same person with him who was flogged at school. But the general's consciousness does not reach so far back as his flogging—therefore, according to Mr. Locke's doctrine, he is not the person who was flogged. Therefore, the general is, and at the same time is not, the same person with him who was flogged at school.

STUDY QUESTIONS

1. How does Reid respond to the request for a definition of identity?
2. What evidence does Reid offer for the existence of a permanent self?
3. How does the evidence we have for our own identity differ from the evidence we have for the identity of other persons?
4. According to Reid, why does Locke's theory of personal identity lead to a contradiction?

PART 7

God

Does God Exist?

ERNEST NAGEL

One metaphysical issue that interests us all is whether God exists. A theist believes God does exist. An atheist believes God does not exist. An agnostic believes the available evidence is insufficient to decide the matter. Which of these positions is the most reasonable?

The first step in answering this question is to determine what is meant by the term "God." Let us adopt a view common to many religious believers that "God" refers to an all-good, all-powerful, eternal Creator of the world. The question then is whether a being of that description exists.

The next essay considers various arguments for and against the existence of God. The author is Ernest Nagel (1901–1985), who was Professor of Philosophy at Columbia University.

....

1

I want now to discuss three classical arguments for the existence of God, arguments which have constituted at least a partial basis for theistic commitments. As long as theism is defended simply as a dogma, asserted as a matter of direct revelation or as the deliverance of authority, belief in the dogma is impregnable to rational argument. In fact, however, reasons are frequently advanced in support of the theistic creed, and these reasons have been the subject of acute philosophical critiques.

One of the oldest intellectual defenses of theism is the cosmological argument, also known as the argument from a first cause. Briefly put, the argument runs as follows. Every event must have a cause. Hence an event A must have as cause some event B, which in turn must have a cause C, and so on. But if there is no end to this backward progression of causes, the progression will be infinite; and in the opinion of those who use this argument, an infinite series of actual events is unintelligible and absurd. Hence there must be a first cause, and this first cause is God, the initiator of all change in the universe.

The argument is an ancient one, and . . . it has impressed many generations of exceptionally keen minds. The argument is nonetheless a weak reed on which to rest the theistic thesis. Let us waive any question concerning the validity of the principle that every event has a cause, for though the question is important,

From *Basic Beliefs,* ed. J. E. Fairchild. Copyright © 1959 by Sheridan House, Inc. Reprinted by permission of the publisher.

its discussion would lead us far afield. However, if the principle is assumed, it is surely incongruous to postulate a first cause as a way of escaping from the coils of an infinite series. For if everything must have a cause, why does not God require one for His own existence? The standard answer is that He does not need any, because He is self-caused. But if God can be self-caused, why cannot the world itself be self-caused? Why do we require a God transcending the world to bring the world into existence and to initiate changes in it? On the other hand, the supposed inconceivability and absurdity of an infinite series of regressive causes will be admitted by no one who has competent familiarity with the modern mathematical analysis of infinity. The cosmological argument does not stand up under scrutiny.

The second "proof" of God's existence is usually called the ontological argument. It too has a long history going back to early Christian days, though it acquired great prominence only in medieval times. The argument can be stated in several ways, one of which is the following. Since God is conceived to be omnipotent, he is a perfect being. A perfect being is defined as one whose essence or nature lacks no attributes (or properties) whatsoever, one whose nature is complete in every respect. But it is evident that we have an idea of a perfect being, for we have just defined the idea; and since this is so, the argument continues, God who is the perfect being must exist. Why must he? Because his existence follows from his defined nature. For if God lacked the attribute of existence, he would be lacking at least one attribute and would therefore not be perfect. To sum up, since we have an idea of God as a perfect being, God must exist.

There are several ways of approaching this argument, but I shall consider only one. The argument was exploded by the eighteenth-century philosopher Immanuel Kant. The substance of Kant's criticism is that it is just a confusion to say that existence is an attribute, and that though the *word* "existence" may occur as the grammatical predicate in a sentence, no attribute is being predicated of a thing when we say that the thing exists or has existence. Thus, to use Kant's example, when we think of $100 we are thinking of the nature of this sum of money; but the nature of $100 remains the same whether we have $100 in our pockets or not. Accordingly, we are confounding grammar with logic if we suppose that some characteristic is being attributed to the nature of $100 when we say that a hundred dollar bill exists in someone's pocket.

To make the point clearer, consider another example. When we say that a lion has a tawny color, we are predicating a certain attribute of the animal, and similarly when we say that the lion is fierce or is hungry. But when we say the lion exists, all that we are saying is that something is (or has the nature of) a lion; we are not specifying an attribute which belongs to the nature of anything that is a lion. In short, the word "existence" does not signify any attribute, and in consequence no attribute that belongs to the nature of anything. Accordingly, it does not follow from the assumption that we have an idea of a perfect being that such a being exists. For the idea of a perfect being does not involve the attribute of existence as a constituent of that idea, since there is no such attribute. The ontological argument thus has a serious leak, and it can hold no water.

2

The two arguments discussed thus far are purely dialectical, and attempt to establish God's existence without any appeal to empirical data. The next argument, called the argument from design, is different in character, for it is based on what purports to be empirical evidence. I wish to examine two forms of this argument.

One variant of it calls attention to the remarkable way in which different things and processes in the world are integrated with each other, and concludes that this mutual "fitness" of things can be explained only by the assumption of a divine architect who planned the world and everything in it. For example, living organisms can maintain themselves in a variety of environments, and do so in virtue of their delicate mechanisms which adapt the organisms to all sorts of environmental changes. There is thus an intricate pattern of means and ends throughout the animate world. But the existence of this pattern is unintelligible, so the argument runs, except on the hypothesis that the pattern has been deliberately instituted by a Supreme Designer. If we find a watch in some deserted spot, we do not think it came into existence by chance, and we do not hesitate to conclude that an intelligent creature designed and made it. But the world and all its contents exhibit mechanisms and mutual adjustments that are far more complicated and subtle than are those of a watch. Must we not therefore conclude that these things too have a Creator?

The conclusion of this argument is based on an inference from analogy: the watch and the world are alike in possessing a congruence of parts and an adjustment of means to ends; the watch has a watch-maker; hence the world has a worldmaker. But is the analogy a good one? Let us once more waive some important issues, in particular the issue whether the universe is the unified system such as the watch admittedly is. And let us concentrate on the question, What is the ground for our assurance that watches do not come into existence except through the operations of intelligent manufacturers? The answer is plain. We have never run across a watch which has not been deliberately made by someone. But the situation is nothing like this in the case of the innumerable animate and inanimate systems with which we are familiar. Even in the case of living organisms, though they are generated by their parent organisms, the parents do not "make" their progeny in the same sense in which watch-makers make watches. And once this point is clear, the inference from the existence of living organisms to the existence of a supreme designer no longer appears credible.

Moreover, the argument loses all its force if the facts which the hypothesis of a divine designer is supposed to explain can be understood on the basis of a better supported assumption. And indeed, such an alternative explanation is one of the achievements of Darwinian biology. For Darwin showed that one can account for the variety of biological species, as well as for their adaptations to their environments, without invoking a divine creator and acts of special creation. The Darwinian theory explains the diversity of biological species in terms of chance variations in the structure of organisms, and of a mechanism of selection which retains those variant forms that possess some advantages for survival. The evidence for these assumptions is considerable; and developments subsequent to Darwin have only strengthened the case for a thoroughly naturalistic explanation of the facts of biological adaptation. In any event, this version of the argument from design has nothing to recommend it.

A second form of this argument has been recently revived in the speculations of some modern physicists. No one who is familiar with the facts can fail to be impressed by the success with which the use of mathematical methods has enabled us to obtain intellectual mastery of many parts of nature. But some thinkers have therefore concluded that since the book of nature is ostensibly written in mathematical language, nature must be the creation of a divine mathematician. However, the argument is most dubious. For it rests, among other things, on the assumption that mathematical tools can be successfully used only if the events of nature exhibit some *special* kind of order, and on the further assumption that if the structure of things were different from what they are, mathematical language would be inadequate for describing such structure. But it can be shown that no matter what the world were like—even if it impressed us as being utterly chaotic—it would still possess some order and would in principle be amenable to a mathematical description. In point of fact, it makes no sense to say that there is absolutely *no* pattern in any conceivable subject matter. To be sure, there are differences in complexities of structure, and if the patterns of events were sufficiently complex, we might not be able to unravel them. But however that may be, the success of mathematical physics in giving us some understanding of the world around us does not yield the conclusion that only a mathematician could have devised the patterns of order we have discovered in nature.

3

The inconclusiveness of the three classical arguments for the existence of God was already made evident by Kant, in a manner substantially not different from the above discussion. There are, however, other types of arguments for theism that have been influential in the history of thought, two of which I wish to consider, even if only briefly.

Indeed, though Kant destroyed the classical intellectual foundations for theism, he himself invented a fresh argument for it. Kant's attempted proof is not intended to be a purely theoretical demonstration and is based on the supposed facts of our moral nature. It has exerted an enormous influence on subsequent theological speculation. In barest outline, the argument is as follows. According to Kant, we are subject not only to physical laws like the rest of nature, but also to moral ones. These moral laws are categorical imperatives, which we must

heed not because of their utilitarian consequences, but simply because as autonomous moral agents it is our duty to accept them as binding. However, Kant was
keenly aware that though virtue may be its reward, the virtuous man (that is,
the man who acts out of a sense of duty and in conformity with the moral law)
does not always receive his just desserts in this world; nor did he shut his eyes
to the fact that evil men frequently enjoy the best things this world has to
offer. In short, virtue does not always reap happiness. Nevertheless, the highest human good is the realization of happiness commensurate with one's virtue;
and Kant believed that it is a practical postulate of the moral life to promote
this good. But what can guarantee that the highest good is realizable? Such a
guarantee can be found only in God, who must therefore exist if the highest
good is not to be a fatuous ideal. The existence of an omnipotent, omniscient,
and omnibenevolent God is thus postulated as a necessary condition for the
possibility of a moral life.

Despite the prestige this argument has acquired, it is difficult to grant it
any force. It is easy enough to postulate God's existence. But as Bertrand Russell
observed in another connection, postulation has all the advantages of theft over
honest toil. No postulation carries with it any assurance that what is postulated is
actually the case. And though we may postulate God's existence as a means to guar-
anteeing the possibility of realizing happiness together with virtue, the postulation
establishes neither the actual realizability of this ideal nor the fact of his existence.
Moreover, the argument is not made more cogent when we recognize that it is
based squarely on the highly dubious conception that considerations of utility and
human happiness must not enter into the determination of what is morally obligatory. Having built his moral theory on a radical separation of means from ends,
Kant was driven to the desperate postulation of God's existence in order to relate
them again. The argument is thus at best a *tour de force,* contrived to remedy a
fatal flaw in Kant's initial moral assumptions. It carries no conviction to anyone
who does not commit Kant's initial blunder.

One further type of argument, pervasive in much Protestant theological literature, deserves brief mention. Arguments of this type take their point of departure from the psychology of religious and mystical experience. Those who have
undergone such experiences often report that during the experience they feel
themselves to be in the presence of the divine and holy, that they lose their sense
of self-identity and become merged with some fundamental reality, or that they
enjoy a feeling of total dependence upon some ultimate power. The overwhelming sense of transcending one's finitude which characterizes such vivid periods of
life, and of coalescing with some ultimate source of all existence, is then taken to
be compelling evidence for the existence of a supreme being. In a variant form of
this argument, other theologians have identified God as the object which satisfies
the commonly experienced need for integrating one's scattered and conflicting
impulses into a coherent unity, or as the subject which is of ultimate concern to us.
In short, a proof of God's existence is found in the occurrence of certain distinctive
experiences.

It would be flying in the face of well-attested facts were one to deny that such experiences frequently occur. But do these facts constitute evidence for the conclusion based on them? Does the fact, for example, that an individual experiences a profound sense of direct contact with an alleged transcendent ground of all reality constitute competent evidence for the claim that there is such a ground and that it is the immediate cause of the experience? If well-established canons for evaluating evidence are accepted, the answer is surely negative. No one will dispute that many men do have vivid experiences in which such things as ghosts or pink elephants appear before them; but only the hopelessly credulous will without further ado count such experiences as establishing the existence of ghosts and pink elephants. To establish the existence of such things, evidence is required that is obtained under controlled conditions and that can be confirmed by independent inquirers. Again, though a man's report that he is suffering pain may be taken at face value, one cannot take at face value the claim, were he to make it, that it is the food he ate which is the cause (or a contributory cause) of his felt pain—not even if the man were to report a vivid feeling of abdominal disturbance. And similarly, an overwhelming feeling of being in the presence of the Divine is evidence enough for admitting the genuineness of such feeling; it is no evidence for the claim that a supreme being with a substantial existence independent of the experience is the cause of the experience.

4

Thus far the discussion has been concerned with noting inadequacies in various arguments widely used to support theism. However, much atheistic criticism is also directed toward exposing incoherencies in the very thesis of theism. I want therefore to consider this aspect of the atheistic critique, though I will restrict myself to the central difficulty in the theistic position which arises from the simultaneous attribution of omnipotence, omniscience, and omnibenevolence to the Deity. The difficulty is that of reconciling these attributes with the occurrence of evil in the world. Accordingly, the question to which I now turn is whether, despite the existence of evil, it is possible to construct a theodicy which will justify the ways of an infinitely powerful and just God to man.

Two main types of solutions have been proposed for this problem. One way that is frequently used is to maintain that what is commonly called evil is only an illusion, or at worst only the "privation" or absence of good. Accordingly, evil is not "really real," it is only the "negative" side of God's beneficence, it is only the product of our limited intelligence which fails to plumb the true character of God's creative bounty. A sufficient comment on this proposed solution is that facts are not altered or abolished by rebaptizing them. Evil may indeed be only an appearance and not genuine. But this does not eliminate from the realm of appearance the tragedies, the sufferings, and the iniquities which men so frequently endure. And it raises once more, though on another level, the problem of reconciling the fact that there is evil in the realm of appearance with God's alleged omnibenevolence. In any event, it is small comfort to anyone suffering a cruel misfortune for which he is in no way responsible, to be told that what he is undergoing is only the absence of good. It is a gratuitous insult to mankind, a symptom of insensitivity and indifference to human suffering, to be assured that all the miseries and agonies men experience are only illusory.

Another gambit often played in attempting to justify the ways of God to man is to argue that the things called evil are evil only because they are viewed in isolation; they are not evil when viewed in proper perspective and in relation to the rest of creation. Thus, if one attends to but a single instrument in an orchestra, the sounds issuing from it may indeed be harsh and discordant. But if one is placed at a proper distance from the whole orchestra, the sounds of that single instrument will mingle with the sounds issuing from the other players to produce a marvellous bit of symphonic music. Analogously, experiences we call painful undoubtedly occur and are real enough. But the pain is judged to be an evil only because it is experienced in a limited perspective—the pain is there for the sake of a more inclusive good, whose reality eludes us because our intelligences are too weak to apprehend things in their entirety.

It is an appropriate retort to this argument that of course we judge things to be evil in a human perspective, but that since we are not God this is the only proper perspective in which to judge them. It may indeed be the case that what is evil for us is not evil for some other part of creation. However, we are not this other part of creation, and it is irrelevant to argue that were we something other than what we are, our evaluations of what is good and bad would be different. Moreover, the worthlessness of the argument becomes even more evident if we remind ourselves that it is unsupported speculation to suppose that whatever is evil in a finite perspective is good from the purported perspective of the totality of things. For the argument can be turned around: what we judge to be a good is a good only because it is viewed in isolation; when it is viewed in proper perspective and in relation to the entire scheme of things, it is an evil. This is in fact a standard form of the argument for a universal pessimism. Is it any worse than the similar argument for a universal optimism? The very raising of this question is a *reductio ad absurdum* of the proposed solution to the ancient problem of evil.

I do not believe it is possible to reconcile the alleged omnipotence and omnibenevolence of God with the unvarnished facts of human existence. In point of fact, many theologians have concurred in this conclusion; for in order to escape from the difficulty which the traditional attributes of God present, they have assumed that God is not all powerful, and that there are limits as to what He can do in his efforts to establish a righteous order in the universe. But whether such a modified theology is better off is doubtful; and in any event, the question still remains whether the facts of human life support the claim that an omnibenevolent Deity, though limited in power, is revealed in the ordering of human history. It is pertinent to note in this connection that though there have been many historians who have made the effort, no historian has yet succeeded in showing to the satisfaction of his professional colleagues that the hypothesis of a Divine Providence is capable of explaining anything which cannot be explained just as well without this hypothesis.

STUDY QUESTIONS

1. What connection does Nagel find between Darwinian biology and the design argument?
2. What is Nagel's assessment of the evidence for God's existence drawn from mystical experience?
3. How does Nagel respond to the claim that evil is only an illusion?
4. If the existence of God is compatible with the worst evils imaginable, what comfort is provided by believing in God?

Why God Allows Evil

RICHARD SWINBURNE

Richard Swinburne, who taught at the University of Oxford, is a leading proponent of theism and other tenets of Christianity. In our next selection he offers a theodicy, a defense of God's goodness and omnipotence in the face of the existence of evil.

The world . . . contains much evil. An omnipotent God could have prevented this evil, and surely a perfectly good and omnipotent God would have done so. So why is there this evil? Is not its existence strong evidence against the existence of God? It would be unless we can construct what is known as a theodicy, an explanation of why God would allow such evil to occur. I believe that that can be done, and I shall outline a theodicy. . . . I emphasize that . . . in writing that God would do this or that, I am not taking for granted the existence of God, but merely claiming that, if there is a God, it is to be expected that he would do certain things, including allowing the occurrence of certain evils; and so, I am claiming, their occurrence is not evidence against his existence.

It is inevitable that any attempt by myself or anyone else to construct a theodicy will sound callous, indeed totally insensitive to human suffering. Many theists, as well as atheists, have felt that any attempt to construct a theodicy evinces an immoral approach to suffering. I can only ask the reader to believe that I am not totally insensitive to human suffering, and that I do mind about the agony of poisoning, child abuse, bereavement, solitary imprisonment, and marital infidelity as much as anyone else. True, I would not in most cases recommend that a pastor give this chapter to victims of sudden distress at their worst moment to read for consolation.

From *Is There a God?* by Richard Swinburne. Copyright ©1996 by the author. Reprinted by permission of Oxford University Press.

But this is not because its arguments are unsound; it is simply that most people in deep distress need comfort, not argument. Yet there is a problem about why God allows evil, and, if the theist does not have (in a cool moment) a satisfactory answer to it, then his belief in God is less than rational, and there is no reason why the atheist should share it. To appreciate the argument of this chapter, each of us needs to stand back a bit from the particular situation of his or her own life and that of close relatives and friends (which can so easily seem the only important thing in the world), and ask very generally what good things would a generous and everlasting God give to human beings in the course of a short earthly life. Of course thrills of pleasure and periods of contentment are good things, and—other things being equal—God would certainly seek to provide plenty of those. But a generous God will seek to give deeper good things than these. He will seek to give us great responsibility for ourselves, each other, and the world, and thus a share in his own creative activity of determining what sort of world it is to be. And he will seek to make our lives valuable, of great use to ourselves and each other. The problem is that God cannot give us these goods in full measure without allowing much evil on the way. . . .

[T]here are plenty of evils, positive bad states, which God could if he chose remove. I divide these into moral evils and natural evils. I understand by "natural evil" all evil which is not deliberately produced by human beings and which is not allowed by human beings to occur as a result of their negligence. Natural evil includes both physical suffering and mental suffering, of animals as well as humans; all the trial of suffering which disease, natural disasters, and accidents unpredictable by humans bring in their train. "Moral evil" I understand as including all evil caused deliberately by humans doing what they ought not to do (or allowed to occur by humans negligently failing to do what they ought to do) *and* also the evil constituted by such deliberate actions or negligent failure. It includes the sensory pain of the blow inflicted by the bad parent on his child, the mental pain of the parent depriving the child of love, the starvation allowed to occur in Africa because of negligence by members of foreign governments who could have prevented it, and also the evil of the parent or politician deliberately bringing about the pain or not trying to prevent the starvation.

MORAL EVIL

The central core of any theodicy must, I believe, be the "free-will defence," which deals—to start with—with moral evil, but can be extended to deal with much natural evil as well. The free-will defence claims that it is a great good that humans have a certain sort of free will which I shall call free and responsible choice, but that, if they do, then necessarily there will be the natural possibility of moral evil. (By the "natural possibility" I mean that it will not be determined in advance whether or not the evil will occur.) A God who gives humans such free will necessarily brings about the possibility and puts outside his own control whether or not that evil occurs. It is not logically possible—that is, it would be self-contradictory to suppose—that God could give us such free will and yet ensure that we always use it in the right way.

Free and responsible choice is not just free will in the narrow sense of being able to choose between alternative actions, without our choice being causally necessitated by some prior cause. . . . [H]umans could have that kind of free will merely in virtue of being able to choose freely between two equally good and unimportant alternatives. Free and responsible choice is rather free will (of the kind discussed) to make significant choices between good and evil, which make a big difference to the agent, to others, and to the world.

Given that we have free will, we certainly have free and responsible choice. Let us remind ourselves of the difference that humans can make to themselves, others, and the world. Humans have opportunities to give themselves and others pleasurable sensations and to pursue worthwhile activities—to play tennis or the piano, to acquire knowledge of history and science and philosophy, and to help others to do so, and thereby to build deep personal relations founded upon such sensations and activities. And humans are so made that they can form their characters. Aristotle famously remarked: "we become just by doing just acts, prudent by doing prudent acts, brave by doing brave acts." That is, by doing a just act when it is difficult—when it goes against our natural inclinations (which is what I understand by desires)—we make it easier to do a just act next time. We can gradually change our desires, so that—for example—doing just acts becomes natural. Thereby we can free ourselves from the power of the less good desires to which we are subject. And, by choosing to acquire knowledge and to use it to build machines of various sorts, humans can extend the range of the differences they can make to the world—they can build universities to last for centuries, or save energy for the next generation; and by cooperative effort over many decades they can eliminate poverty. The possibilities for free and responsible choice are enormous.

It is good that the free choices of humans should include *genuine* responsibility for other humans, and that involves the opportunity to benefit *or* harm them. God has the power to benefit or to harm humans. If other agents are to be given a share in his creative work, it is good that they have that power too (although perhaps to a lesser degree). A world in which agents can benefit each other but not do each other harm is one where they have only very limited responsibility for each other. If my responsibility for you is limited to whether or not to give you a camcorder, but I cannot cause you pain, stunt your growth, or limit your education, then I do not have a great deal of responsibility for you. A God who gave agents only such limited responsibilities for their fellows would not have given much. God would have reserved for himself the all-important choice of the kind of world it was to be, while simply allowing humans the minor choice of filling in the details. He would be like a father asking his elder son to look after the younger son, and adding that he would be watching the elder son's every move and would intervene the moment the elder son did a thing wrong. The elder son might justly retort that, while he would be happy to share his father's work, he could really do so only if he were left to make his own judgements as to what to do within a significant range of the options available to the father. A good God, like a good father, will delegate responsibility. In order to allow creatures a share in creation, he will allow them the choice of hurting and maiming, of frustrating the divine plan. Our world is one where creatures have just such deep responsibility for each other. I cannot only benefit my children, but harm them. One way in which I can harm them is that I can inflict physical pain on them. But there are much more damaging things which I can do to them. Above all I can stop them growing into creatures with significant knowledge, power, and freedom; I can determine whether they come to have the kind of free and responsible choice which I have. The possibility of humans bringing about significant evil is a logical consequence of their having this free and responsible choice. Not even God could give us this choice without the possibility of resulting evil.

Now . . . an action would not be intentional unless it was done for a reason—that is, seen as in some way a good thing (either in itself or because of its consequences). And, if reasons alone influence actions, that regarded by the subject as most important will determine what is done; an agent under the influence of reason alone will inevitably do the action which he regards as overall the best. If an agent does not do the action which he regards as overall the best, he must have allowed factors other than reason to exert an influence on him. In other words, he must have allowed desires for what he regards as good only in a certain respect, but not overall, to influence his conduct. So, in order to have a choice between good and evil, agents need already a certain depravity, in the sense of a system of desires for what they correctly believe to be evil. I need to *want* to overeat, get more than my fair share of money or power, indulge my sexual appetites even by deceiving my spouse or partner, and see you hurt, if I am to have choice between good and evil. This depravity is itself an evil which is a necessary condition of a greater good. It makes possible a choice made seriously and deliberately, because it is made in the face of a genuine alternative. I stress that, according to the free-will defence, it is the natural possibility of moral evil which is the necessary condition of the great good, not the actual evil itself. Whether that occurs is (through God's choice) outside God's control and up to us.

Note further and crucially that, if I suffer in consequence of your freely chosen bad action, that is not by any means pure loss for me. In a certain respect it is a good for *me*. My suffering would be pure loss for me if the only good thing in life was sensory pleasure, and the only bad thing sensory pain; and it is because the modern world tends to think in those terms that the problem of evil seems so acute. If these were the only good and bad things, the occurrence of suffering would indeed be a conclusive objection to the existence of God. But we have already noted the great good of freely choosing and influencing our future, that of our fellows, and that of the world. And now note another great good—the good of our life serving a purpose, of being of use to ourselves and others. Recall the words of Christ, "it is more blessed to give than to receive" (as quoted by St. Paul (Acts 20: 35)). We tend to think, when the beggar appears on our doorstep and we feel obliged to give and do give, that that was lucky for him but not for us who happened to be at home. That is not what Christ's words say. They say that *we* are the lucky ones, not just because we have a lot, out of which we can give a little, but because we are privileged to contribute to the beggar's happiness—and that privilege is worth a lot more than money. And, just as it is a great good freely to choose to do good, so it is also a good to be used by someone else for a worthy purpose (so long, that is, that he or she has the right, the authority, to use us in this way). Being allowed to suffer to make possible a great good is a privilege, even if the privilege is forced upon you. Those who are allowed to die for their country and thereby save their country from foreign oppression are privileged. Cultures less obsessed than our own by the evil of purely physical pain have always recognized that. And they have recognized that it is still a blessing, even if the one who died had been conscripted to fight.

And even twentieth-century man can begin to see that—sometimes—when he seeks to help prisoners, not by giving them more comfortable quarters, but by letting them help the handicapped; or when he pities rather than envies the "poor little rich girl" who has everything and does nothing for anyone else. And one phenomenon prevalent in end-of-century Britain draws this especially to our attention—the evil of unemployment. Because of our system of Social Security, the unemployed on the whole have enough money to live without too much discomfort; certainly they are a lot better off than are many employed in Africa or Asia or Victorian Britain. What is evil about unemployment is not so much any resulting poverty but the uselessness of the unemployed. They often report feeling unvalued by society, of no use, "on the scrap heap." They rightly think it would be a good for them to contribute; but they cannot. Many of them would welcome a system where they were obliged to do useful work in preference to one where society has no use for them.

It follows from that fact that being of use is a benefit for him who is of use, and that those who suffer at the hands of others, and thereby make possible the good of those others who have free and responsible choice, are themselves benefited in this respect. I am fortunate if the natural possibility of my suffering if you choose to hurt me is the vehicle which makes your choice really matter. My vulnerability, my openness to suffering (which necessarily involves my actually suffering if you make the wrong choice), means that you are not just like a pilot in a simulator, where it does not matter if mistakes are made. That our choices matter tremendously, that we can make great differences to things for good or ill, is one of the greatest gifts a creator can give us. And if my suffering is the means by which he can give you that choice, I too am in this respect fortunate. Though of course suffering is in itself a bad thing, my good fortune is that the suffering is not random, pointless suffering. It is suffering which is a consequence of my vulnerability which makes me of such use.

Someone may object that the only good thing is not *being* of use (dying for one's country or being vulnerable to suffering at your hands), but *believing* that one is of use—believing that one is dying for one's country and that this is of use; the "feel-good" experience. But that cannot be correct. Having comforting beliefs is only a good thing if they are true beliefs. It is not a good thing to believe that things are going well when they are not, or that your life is of use when it is not. Getting pleasure out of a comforting falsehood is a cheat. But if I get pleasure out of a true belief, it must be that I regard the state of things which I believe to hold to be a good thing. If I get pleasure out of the true belief that my daughter is doing well at school, it must be that I regard it as a good thing that my daughter does well at school (whether or not I believe that she is doing well). If I did not think the latter, I would not get any pleasure out of believing that she is doing well. Likewise, the belief that I am vulnerable to suffering at your hands, and that that is a good thing, can only be a good thing if being vulnerable to suffering at your hands is itself a good thing (independently of whether I believe it or not). Certainly, when my life is of use and that is a good for me, it is even better if I believe it and get comfort therefrom; but it can only be even better if it is already a good for me whether I believe it or not.

But though suffering may in these ways serve good purposes, does God have the right to allow me to suffer for your benefit, without asking my permission? For surely, an objector will say, no one has the right to allow one person A to suffer for the benefit of another one B without A's consent. We judge that doctors who use patients as involuntary objects of experimentation in medical experiments which they hope will produce results which can be used to benefit others are doing something wrong. After all, if my arguments about the utility of suffering are sound, ought we not all to be causing suffering to others in order that those others may have the opportunity to react in the right way?

There are, however, crucial differences between God and the doctors. The first is that God as the author of our being has certain rights, a certain authority over us, which we do not have over our fellow humans. He is the cause of our existence at each moment of our existence and sustains the laws of nature which give us everything we are and have. To allow someone to suffer for his own good or that of others, one has to stand in some kind of parental relationship towards him. I do not have the right to let some stranger suffer for the sake of some good, when I could easily prevent this, but I do have *some* right of this kind in respect of my own children. I may let the younger son suffer *somewhat* for his own good or that of his brother. I have this right because in small part I am responsible for the younger son's existence, his beginning and continuance. If I have begotten him, nourished, and educated him, I have some limited rights over him in return; to a *very limited* extent I can use him for some worthy purpose. If this is correct, then a God who is so much more the author of our being than are our parents has so much more right in this respect. Doctors do have over us even the rights of parents.

But secondly and all-importantly, the doctors *could* have asked the patients for permission; and the patients, being free agents of some power and knowledge, could have made an informed choice of whether or not to allow themselves to be used. By contrast, God's choice is not about how to use already existing agents, but about the sort of agents to make and the sort of world into which to put them. In God's situation there are no agents to be asked. I am arguing that it is good that one agent A should have deep responsibility for another B (who in turn could have deep responsibility for another C). It is not logically possible for God to have asked B if he wanted things thus, for, if A is to be responsible for B's growth in freedom, knowledge, and power, there will not be a B with enough freedom and knowledge to make any choice, before God has to choose whether or not to give A responsibility for him. One cannot ask a baby into which sort of world he or she wishes to be born. The creator has to make the choice independently of his creatures.

He will seek on balance to benefit them—all of them. And, in giving them the gift of life—whatever suffering goes with it—that is a substantial benefit. But when one suffers at the hands of another, often perhaps it is not enough of a benefit to outweigh the suffering. Here is the point to recall that it is an additional benefit to the sufferer that his suffering is the means whereby the one who hurt him had the opportunity to make a significant choice between good and evil which otherwise he would not have had.

Although for these reasons, as I have been urging, God has the right to allow humans to cause each other to suffer, there must be a limit to the amount of suffering which he has the right to allow a human being to suffer for the sake of a great good. A parent may allow an elder child to have the power to do some harm to a younger child for the sake of the responsibility given to the elder child; but there are limits. And there are limits even to the moral right of God, our creator and sustainer, to use free sentient beings as pawns in a greater game. Yet, if these limits were too narrow, God would be unable to give humans much real responsibility; he would be able to allow them only to play a toy game. Still, limits there must be to God's rights to allow humans to hurt each other; and limits there are in the world to the extent to which they can hurt each other, provided above all by the short finite life enjoyed by humans and other creatures—one human can hurt another for no more than eighty years or so. And there are a number of other safety-devices in-built into our physiology and psychology, limiting the amount of pain we can suffer. But the primary safety limit is that provided by the shortness of our finite life. Unending, unchosen suffering would indeed to my mind provide a very strong argument against the existence of God. But that is not the human situation.

So then God, without asking humans, has to choose for them between the kinds of world in which they can live—basically either a world in which there is very little opportunity for humans to benefit or harm each other, or a world in which there is considerable opportunity. How shall he choose? There are clearly reasons for both choices. But it seems to me (just, on balance) that his choosing to create the world in which we have considerable opportunity to benefit or harm each other is to bring about a good at least as great as the evil which he thereby allows to occur. *Of course* the suffering he allows is a bad thing; and, other things being equal, to be avoided. But having the natural possibility of causing suffering makes possible a greater good. God, in creating humans who (of logical necessity) cannot choose for themselves the kind of world into which they are to come, plausibly exhibits his goodness in making for them the heroic choice that they come into a risky world where they may have to suffer for the good of others.

NATURAL EVIL

Natural evil is not to be accounted for along the same lines as moral evil. Its main role rather, I suggest, is to make it possible for humans to have the kind of choice which the free-will defence extols, and to make available to humans specially worthwhile kinds of choice.

There are two ways in which natural evil operates to give humans those choices. First, the operation of natural laws producing evils gives humans knowledge (if they choose to seek it) of how to bring about such evils themselves. Observing you catch some disease by the operation of natural processes gives me the power either to use those processes to give that disease to other people, or through negligence to allow others to catch it, or to take measures to prevent others from catching the disease. Study of the mechanisms of nature producing various evils (and goods) opens up for humans a wide range of choice. This is the way in which in fact we learn how to bring about (good and) evil. But could not God give us the requisite knowledge (of how to bring about good or evil) which we need in order to have free and responsible choice by a less costly means? Could he not just whisper in our ears from time to time what are the different consequences of different actions of ours? Yes. But anyone who believed that an action of his would have some effect because he believed that God had told him so would see all his actions as done under the all-watchful eye of God. He would not merely believe strongly that there was a God, but would know it with real certainty. That knowledge would greatly inhibit his freedom of choice and would make it very difficult for him to choose to do evil. This is because we all have a natural inclination to wish to be thought well of by everyone, and above all by an all-good God; that we have such an inclination is a very good feature of humans, without which we would be less than human. Also, if we were directly informed of the consequences of our actions, we would be deprived of the choice whether to seek to discover what the consequences were through experiment and hard cooperative work. Knowledge would be available on tap. Natural processes alone give humans knowledge of the effects of their actions without inhibiting their freedom, and if evil is to be a possibility for them they must know how to allow it to occur.

The other way in which natural evil operates to give humans their freedom is that it makes possible certain kinds of action towards it between which agents can choose. It increases the range of significant choice. A particular natural evil, such as physical pain, gives to the sufferer a choice—whether to endure it with patience or to bemoan his lot. His friend can choose whether to show compassion towards the sufferer or to be callous. The pain makes possible these choices, which would not otherwise exist. There is no guarantee that our actions in response to the pain will be good ones, but the pain gives us the opportunity to perform good actions. The good or bad actions which we perform in the face of natural evil themselves provide opportunities for further choice—of good or evil stances towards the former actions. If I am patient with my suffering, you can choose whether to encourage or laugh at my patience; if I bemoan my lot, you can teach me by word and example what a good thing patience is. If you are sympathetic, I have then the opportunity to show gratitude for the sympathy or to be so self-involved that I ignore it. If you are callous, I can choose whether to ignore this or to resent it for life. And so on. I do not think that there can be much doubt that natural evil, such as physical pain, makes available these sorts of choice. The actions which natural evil makes possible are ones which allow us to perform at our best and interact with our fellows at the deepest level.

It may, however, be suggested that adequate opportunity for these great good actions would be provided by the occurrence of moral evil without any need for suffering to be caused by natural processes. You can show courage when threatened by a gunman, as well as when threatened by cancer; and show sympathy to those likely to be killed by gunmen as well as to those likely to die of cancer. But just imagine all the suffering of mind and body caused by disease, earthquake, and accident unpreventable by humans removed at a stroke from our society. No sickness, no bereavement in consequence of the untimely death of the young. Many of us would then have such an easy life that we simply would not have much opportunity to show courage or, indeed, manifest much in the way of great goodness at all. We need those insidious processes of decay and dissolution which money and strength cannot ward off for long to give us the opportunities, so easy otherwise to avoid, to become heroes.

God has the right to allow natural evils to occur (for the same reason as he has the right to allow moral evils to occur)—up to a limit. It would, of course, be crazy for God to multiply evils more and more in order to give endless opportunity for heroism, but to have *some* significant opportunity for real heroism and consequent character formation is a benefit for the person to whom it is given. Natural evils give to us the knowledge to make a range of choices between good and evil and also give us the opportunity to perform actions of especially valuable kinds.

There is, however, no reason to suppose that animals have free will. So what about their suffering? Animals had been suffering for a long time before humans appeared on this planet—just how long depends on which animals are conscious beings. The first thing to take into account here is that, while the higher animals, at any rate the vertebrates, suffer, it is most unlikely that they suffer nearly as much as humans do. Given that suffering depends directly on brain events (in turn caused by events in other parts of the body), then, since the lower animals do not suffer at all and humans suffer a lot, animals of intermediate complexity (it is reasonable to suppose) suffer only a moderate amount. So, while one does need a theodicy to account for why God allows animals to suffer, one does not need as powerful a theodicy as one does in respect of humans. One only needs reasons adequate to account for God allowing an amount of suffering much less than that of humans. That said, there is, I believe, available for animals parts of the theodicy which I have outlined above for humans.

The good of animals, like that of humans, does not consist solely in thrills of pleasure. For animals, too, there are more worthwhile things, and in particular intentional actions, and among them serious significant intentional actions. The life of animals involves many serious significant intentional actions. Animals look for a mate, despite being tired and failing to find one. They take great trouble to build nests and feed their young, to decoy predators, and to explore. But all this inevitably involves pain (going on despite being tired) and danger. An animal cannot intentionally avoid forest fires, or take trouble to rescue its offspring from forest fires, unless there exists a serious danger of getting caught in a forest fire. The action of rescuing despite danger simply cannot be done unless the danger exists—and the danger will not exist unless there is a significant natural probability of being caught in the fire. Animals do not choose freely to do such actions, but the actions are nevertheless worthwhile. It is great that animals feed their young, not just themselves; that animals explore when they know it to be dangerous; that animals save each other from predators, and so on. These are the things that give the lives of animals their value. But they do often involve some suffering to some creature.

To return to the central case of humans—the reader will agree with me to the extent to which he or she values responsibility, free choice, and being of use very much more than thrills of pleasure or absence of pain. There is no other way to get the evils of this world into the right perspective, except to reflect at length on innumerable very detailed thought experiments (in addition to actual experiences of life) in which we postulate very different sorts of worlds from our own, and then ask ourselves whether the perfect goodness of God would require him to create one of these (or no world at all) rather than our own. But I conclude with a very small thought experiment, which may help to begin this process. Suppose that you exist in another world before your birth in this one, and are given a choice as to the sort of life you are to have in this one. You are told that you are to have only a short life, maybe of only a few minutes, although it will be an adult life in the sense that you will have the richness of sensation and belief characteristic of adults. You have a choice as to the sort of life you will have. You can have either a few minutes of very considerable pleasure, of the kind produced by some drug such as heroin, which you will experience by yourself and which will have no effects at all in the world (for example, no one else will know about it); or you can have a few minutes of considerable pain, such as the pain of childbirth, which will have (unknown to you at the time of pain) considerable good effects on others over a few years. You are told that, if you do not make the second choice, those others will never exist—and so you are under no moral obligation to make the second choice. But you seek to make the choice which will make *your* own life the best life for *you* to have led. How will you choose? The choice is, I hope, obvious. You should choose the second alternative.

For someone who remains unconvinced by my claims about the relative strengths of the good and evils involved—holding that, great though the goods are, they do not justify the evils which they involve—there is a fall-back position. My arguments may have convinced you of the greatness of the goods involved sufficiently for you to allow that a perfectly good God would be justified in bringing about the evils for the sake of the good which they make possible, if and only if God also provided compensation in the form of happiness after death to the victims whose sufferings make possible the goods. . . . While believing that God does provide at any rate for many humans such life after death, I have expounded a theodicy without relying on this assumption. But I can understand someone thinking that the assumption is needed, especially when we are considering the worst evils. (This compensatory afterlife need not necessarily be the everlasting life of Heaven.)

It remains the case, however, that evil is evil, and there is a substantial price to pay for the goods of our world which it makes possible. God would not be less than perfectly good if he created instead a world without pain and suffering, and so without the particular goods which those evils make possible. Christian, Islamic, and much Jewish tradition claims that God has created worlds of both kinds—our world, and the Heaven of the blessed. The latter is a marvellous world with a vast range of possible deep goods, but it lacks a few goods which our world contains, including the good of being able to reject the good. A generous God might well choose to give some of us the choice of rejecting the good in a world like ours before giving to those who embrace it a wonderful world in which the former possibility no longer exists.

STUDY QUESTIONS

1. Explain Swinburne's distinction between moral evil and natural evil.
2. Do you find his explanation of one of these two types of evil more persuasive than his explanation of the other?
3. Do his explanations depend on how much evil is found in the world?
4. If evil makes our world better, why would evil not make heaven better?

Pascal's Wager

SIMON BLACKBURN

Blaise Pascal (1623–1662) was a French mathematician, physicist, and philosopher who developed a justification for believing in the existence of God even in the absence of a sound proof for God's existence. According to Pascal's celebrated "wager" argument, if we believe and God exists, then we attain heavenly bliss; if we believe and God doesn't exist, little is lost. On the other hand, if we don't believe and God does exist, then we are doomed to the torments of damnation; if we don't believe and God doesn't exist, little is gained. So belief is the safest strategy.

Simon Blackburn, who taught at the University of Cambridge, doesn't find Pascal's argument persuasive. Do you?

None of the metaphysical arguments . . . do much to confirm the hypothesis that the universe is the creation of a traditional God. . . . Faced with these blanks, religious faith may try to find other arguments.

An interesting and ingenious one is due to the French mathematician and theologian, Blaise Pascal, and is known as Pascal's wager. Unlike the arguments we have been considering, it is not presented as an argument for the *truth* of religious belief, but for the *utility* of believing in some version of a monotheistic, Judaic, Christian, or Islamic, God.

The argument is this. First, Pascal confesses to metaphysical ignorance:

> Let us now speak according to natural lights.
>
> If there is a God, he is infinitely incomprehensible, since, having neither parts, nor limits, He has no affinity to us. We are therefore incapable of knowing either what He is, or if He is . . . Who then will blame the Christians for not being able to give a reason for their belief, since they profess a religion for which they cannot give a reason?

It is not too clear why this excuse is offered for the Christians, as opposed to those of other faiths, as well as believers in fairies, ghosts, the living Elvis, and L. Ron Hubbard. Still, suppose the choice is between religious belief and a life of religious doubt or denial:

> You must wager. It is not optional. Which will you choose then? . . . Let us weigh the gain and the loss in wagering that God is. Let us estimate these two chances. If you gain, you gain all; if you lose, you lose nothing. Wager, then, without hesitation that He is.

With great clarity Pascal realizes that this is rather an odd reason for choosing a belief. But he also says, perceptively, that

> your inability to believe is the result of your passions, since reason brings you to this, and yet you cannot believe . . . Learn of those who have been bound like you, and who now stake all their possessions . . . Follow the way by which they began; by acting as if they believe, taking the holy water, having masses said, etc. Even this will naturally make you believe, and deaden your acuteness.

After you have "stupefied" yourself, you have become a believer. And then you will reap the rewards of belief: infinite rewards, if the kind of God you believe in exists. And if it does not? Well, you have lost very little, in comparison with infinity: only what Pascal calls the "poisonous pleasures" of things like playing golf on Sundays instead of going to mass.

The standard way to present this argument is in terms of a two-by-two box of the options:

	God exists	God does not
I believe in him	+infinity!	0
I do not believe in him	–infinity!	0

The zeros on the right correspond to the thought that not much goes better or worse in this life, whether or not we believe. This life is of vanishingly little account compared to what is promised to believers. The plus-infinity figure corresponds to infinite bliss. The minus-infinity figure in the bottom left corresponds to the traditional jealous God, who sends to Hell those who do not believe in him, and of course encourages his followers to give them a hard time here, as well. But the minus-infinity figure can be soft-pedalled. Even if we put 0 in the bottom left-hand box, the wager looks good. It would be good even if God does not punish disbelief, because there is still that terrific payoff of "+infinity" cranking up the choice. . . . [T]he option of belief . . . can win and cannot lose. So—go for it!

Unfortunately the lethal problem with this argument is simple, once it is pointed out.

Pascal starts from a position of metaphysical ignorance. We just know nothing about the realm beyond experience. But the set-up of the wager presumes that we *do* know something. We are supposed to know the rewards and penalties attached to belief in a Christian God. This is a God who will be pleasured and reward us for our attendance at mass, and will either be indifferent or, in the minus-infinity option, seriously discombobulated by our nonattendance. But this is a case of false options. For consider that if we are really ignorant metaphysically, then it is at least as likely that the options pan out like this:

> There is indeed a very powerful, very benevolent deity. He (or she or they or it) has determined as follows. The good human beings are those who follow the natural light of reason, which is given to them to control their beliefs. These good humans follow the arguments, and hence avoid religious convictions. These ones with the strength of mind not to believe in such things go to Heaven. The rest go to Hell.

This is not such a familiar deity as the traditional jealous God, who cares above all that people believe in him. (Why is God so jealous? Alas, might his jealousy be a projection of human sectarian ambitions and emotions? Either you are with us or against us! The French sceptic Voltaire said that God created mankind in his image, and mankind returned the compliment.) But the problem for Pascal is that if we really know nothing, then we do not know whether the scenario just described is any less likely than the Christian one he presented. In fact, for my money, a God that punishes belief is just as likely, and a lot more reasonable, than one that punishes disbelief.

And of course, we could add the Humean point that whilst for Pascal it was a simple two-way question of mass versus disbelief, in the wider world it is also a question of the Koran versus mass, or L. Ron Hubbard versus the Swami Maharishi, or the Aquarian Concepts Community Divine New Order Government versus the First Internet Church of All. The wager has to be silent about those choices.

STUDY QUESTIONS

1. What is Pascal's wager?
2. According to Blackburn, what is the lethal problem with Pascal's wager?
3. Do you believe Pascal's wager overlooked some relevant options?
4. Why would an all-powerful, all-good God be more concerned with your theological beliefs rather than your commitment to cure illness, relieve poverty, or help others in need?

Pascal's Wager: An Assessment

Linda Zagzebski

In the next selection Linda Zagzebski, whose work we read previously, considers
three objections to Pascal's wager. She finds that they point to problems with the
wager but may not require that Pascal's line of reasoning be abandoned.

....

Pascal's wager has a number of well-known objections, some of them coming from
theists and some from nontheists. Let us consider three of them.

1. *The many gods objection.* Pascal assumes the wager is over belief in the
Christian God. It is a God who promises eternal life for belief in him. But this
means that the wager is between the existence of a God of a certain kind and no
God. That is not a forced wager because there are other possibilities. To put the
point another way, there are many wagers: Christian God or no Christian God,
Muslim God or no Muslim God, Hindu God or no Hindu God, etc. And this is a
problem because for some of these you could make the same kind of wager, yet you
really can only bet on one, assuming that betting on one commits you to betting
against the others. But which one should you bet on?

One answer to this objection is that Pascal is thinking of live options, something you could really believe. Presumably he thinks that the God of only one religion would be a possibility for you. Pascal's era was not one in which there were
churches, temples, mosques, and synagogues within easy driving distance of the
average person making the wager. So it means that Pascal's wager is not intended
for everybody. It is for people who: (1) think both Christianity and atheism are
intellectually unproven but also unrefuted, so from a rational viewpoint both are
live options; (2) have a roughly Christian view of God as a being who rewards his
worshipers with heaven; and (3) are in the emotional position of struggle, trying
to choose. Presumably that would apply to many people, and many other people
would be in the analogous position of betting on the God of a different religion.
Clearly, though, the situation is much more complex for a person for whom more
than one religion that promises an infinite payoff is a live option.

2. *The wager presupposes a low view of God and religious faith.* A second
objection is that God does not want believers who believe on the basis of a wager
motivated by self-interest. This is not what religious faith is all about. This
objection is often expressed by religious people who find the wager repugnant.

From Linda Zagzebski, *Philosophy of Religion: An Historical Introduction*. Blackwell Publishing,
2007. Reprinted by permission of the publisher.

The reply to this objection is that Pascal is formulating an appeal to a certain kind of person, one who is perched precariously between belief and unbelief. Given that he thought of the wager as the precursor to real faith, not faith itself, the person who makes the wager would sincerely try to believe in God. She would not remain indefinitely in the state of the gambler who is motivated only by potential gain. There is no guarantee that she will eventually acquire real faith, but she won't unless she tries, just as the entrepreneur has no guarantee of success in business, but he knows for sure that he won't succeed if he doesn't make the attempt. If the theistic bettor succeeds, her original motive will eventually be replaced by the attitude of religious faith. . . .

3. *We can't believe by making a choice.* There are many things you can't just decide to believe. Suppose somebody tries to bribe you into believing there will be an earthquake in Antarctica on April 19, 2020. Could you do it? You can't just believe because it is in your interest to do so. No matter how much money you are offered, it is probably impossible to make yourself believe certain things if the evidence does not support it. If the choice is not forced, your reason tells you to withhold judgment. And it is hard to see how you could muster the motive to believe, given that earthquakes in Antarctica probably do not connect to anything you already care about at all.

But there are several disanalogies between the Antarctica example and Pascal's wager. As we have seen, Pascal does not think you can start believing in an instant. Second, Pascal thinks the choice is forced, and it is about something you already care about. If you take the time to cultivate the belief by acting as if you believe, you may eventually end up really believing. Here is an analogy given by James Cargile[1] defending Pascal's view that you could get yourself to believe in God given (a) the right motivation, (b) no firm belief to begin with, and (c) a bit of time. Suppose a billionaire jazz lover declares that in two years he will toss a coin. If it comes up heads, he will give a million dollars to every devoted jazz fan. If it comes up tails, he won't do anything. Every Sunday for the next two years a one-hour jazz concert is scheduled. If you attend these concerts religiously, listen to jazz at every other opportunity, and avoid listening to any other kind of music, it is quite likely that you will become a lover of jazz. Of course, it's not likely to work if you hated jazz from the beginning, but if you start out neutral, there is a good chance it will work. In any case, Pascal is addressing someone who is neutral about the existence of God.

But here is another analogy that is more problematic. It highlights both the issue of whether you can make yourself feel something and whether it is morally reprehensible to do so even if you can. Suppose a wealthy man falls in love with a poor woman and wants to marry her, but she feels nothing for him, neither positive nor negative. If she can get herself to love him, she will get a lot of money. One problem is that she has to try to love the man, and while the chances that she will succeed vary with the case, there is rarely a very high probability that it will. But that is not an unsurmountable problem, since even a low probability of success may be enough to make the effort to love him worthwhile. The real problem is that the motive is suspect. No one objects when a woman tries to love a man in order to have a happy relationship with someone she does not want to hurt, but the situation is problematic when she is motivated by the prospect of a reward external to the relationship itself. Nonetheless, human motives are complex, and we often consider it acceptable, even commendable, when people consider the external rewards of a marriage to some extent. Parents routinely advise their children to pick a mate with a good income, and nobody considers that deplorable. But it would be a foolhardy parent who would advise her child to choose a mate with the best income and *then* try to love the person. Is Pascal's wager analogous to the foolhardy parent? If so, can it be altered to avoid the problematic features of the marriage analogy?

NOTE

1. James Cargile, "Pascal's Wager," in Steven M. Cahn and David Shatz, eds., *Contemporary Philosophy of Religion*. Oxford University Press, 1982, pp. 229–236.

STUDY QUESTIONS

1. What is the "many gods" objection to Pascal's wager?
2. What is Zagzebski's response to the many gods objection?
3. Can you decide to believe something?
4. Might acting as religious adherents act lead you to believe what religious adherents believe?

The Problem of Hell

MARILYN McCORD ADAMS

Marilyn McCord Adams is a Visiting Professor of Philosophy at Rutgers University. She is also an ordained priest of the Episcopal Church. She argues that a God who condemned people to hell would be cruel and thus not perfectly good.

So-called atheologians have advanced as an argument against the existence of God the alleged logical incompossibility of the statements

From Eleonore Stump, ed., *Reasoned Faith: Essays in Philosophical Theology in Honor of Norman Kretzmann*, Cornell University Press, 1993. Reprinted by permission of the publisher.

(I) God exists, and is essentially omnipotent, omniscient, and perfectly good

and

(II) Evil exists.

. . .

My own view is that hell poses the principal problem of evil for Christians. Its challenge is so deep and decisive that to spill bottles of ink defending the logical compossibility of (I) with this-worldly evils while holding a closeted belief that

(III) Some created persons will be consigned to hell forever

is at best incongruous and at worst disingenuous. . . .

. . . [A] realistic picture of human agency should recognize the following: (a) We human beings start life ignorant, weak, and helpless, psychologically so lacking in a self-concept as to be incapable of choice. (b) We learn to "construct" a picture of the world, ourselves, and other people only with difficulty over a long period of time and under the extensive influence of other non-ideal choosers. (c) Human development is the interactive product of human nature and its environment, and from early on we humans are confronted with problems that we cannot adequately grasp or cope with, and in response to which we mount (without fully conscious calculation) inefficient adaptational strategies. (d) Yet, the human psyche forms habits in such a way that these reactive patterns, based as they are on a child's inaccurate view of the world and its strategic options, become entrenched in the individual's personality. (e) Typically, the habits are unconsciously "acted out" for years, causing much suffering to self and others before (if ever) they are recognized and undone through a difficult and painful process of therapy and/or spiritual formation. (f) Having thus begun *immature*, we arrive at adulthood in a state of *impaired freedom*, as our childhood adaptational strategies continue to distort our perceptions and behavior. (g) We adults with impaired freedom are responsible for our choices, actions, and even the character molded by our unconscious adaptational strategies, in the sense that we are the *agent causes* of them. (h) Our assessments of moral responsibility, praise, and blame cannot afford to take this impairment into account, because we are not as humans capable of organizing and regulating ourselves in that fine-tuned a way. And so, except for the most severe cases of impairment, we continue to hold ourselves *responsible to one another*.

Taking these estimates of human nature to heart, I draw two conclusions: first, that such impaired adult human agency is no more competent to be entrusted with its (individual or collective) eternal destiny than two-year-old agency is to be allowed choices that could result in its death or serious physical impairment; and second, that the fact that the choices of such impaired agents come between the divine creator of the environment and their infernal outcome no more reduces divine responsibility for the damnation than two-year-old agency reduces the responsibility of the adult caretaker. Suppose, for example, that a parent introduces a two-year-old child into a room filled with gas that is safe to breathe but will explode if ignited. Assume further that the room contains a stove with brightly colored knobs, which if turned will light the burners and ignite the gas. If the parent warns the child not to turn the knobs and leaves, whereupon the child turns the knobs and blows itself up, surely the child is at most marginally to blame, even if it knew enough to obey the parent, while the parent is both primarily responsible and highly culpable. Or suppose a terrorist announces his intention to kill one hundred citizens if anyone in a certain village wears a red shirt on Tuesday. The village takes the threat seriously, and everyone is informed. If some adult citizen slips up and wears his favorite red shirt on Tuesday, he will be responsible and culpable, but the terrorist who set up the situation will be much more culpable.

Once again, my further conclusion is not that God would (like the parent and the terrorist) be culpable if He were to insert humans into a situation in which their eternal destiny depended on their exercise of impaired agency, for I deny that God has any obligations to creatures. . . . Rather, God (like the parent or the terrorist) would bear primary responsibility for any tragic outcomes, and God would be cruel to create human beings in a world with combinations of obstacles and opportunities such as are found in the actual world and govern us under a scheme according to which whether or not we go to the traditional hell depends on how we exercise our impaired adult agency in this life—cruel, by virtue of imposing horrendous consequences on our all-too-likely failures.

STUDY QUESTIONS

1. According to Adams, what is the "problem of hell"?
2. Do you agree with Adams's picture of human nature?
3. Do you accept Adams's view of human agency?
4. Could any finite wrongdoing deserve infinite punishment?

Faith and Reason

MICHAEL SCRIVEN

Michael Scriven, a philosopher at Claremont Graduate University, argues that reason and faith are not on a par, because reason has passed tests of effectiveness that faith has not. Furthermore, while every religious believer relies on reason to assess the claims of ordinary experience, those who are not religious believers

From *Primary Philosophy* by Michael Scriven. Reprinted by permission of The McGraw-Hill Companies.

have no need to rely on religious faith in any aspect of their lives. If the criteria for religious truth are not connected with the criteria for everyday truth, faith, unlike reason, does not provide a reliable guide for our lives.

....

We must now contend with the suggestion that reason is irrelevant to the commitment to theism because this territory is the domain of another faculty: the faculty of faith. It is sometimes even hinted that it is morally wrong and certainly foolish to suggest we should be reasoning about God. For this is the domain of faith or of the "venture of faith," of the "knowledge that passeth understanding," of religious experience and mystic insight.

Now the normal meaning of *faith* is simply "confidence"; we say that we have great faith in someone or in some claim or product, meaning that we believe and act as if they were very reliable. Of such faith we can properly say that it is well founded or not, depending on the evidence for whatever it is in which we have faith. So there is no incompatibility between this kind of faith and reason; the two are from different families and can make a very good marriage. Indeed if they do not join forces, then the resulting ill-based or inadequate confidence will probably lead to disaster. So faith, in this sense, means only a high degree of belief and may be reasonable or unreasonable.

But the term is sometimes used to mean an *alternative to reason* instead of something that should be founded on reason. Unfortunately, the mere use of the term in this way does not demonstrate that faith is a possible route to truth. It is like using the term "winning" as a synonym for "playing" instead of one possible outcome of playing. This is quaint, but it could hardly be called a satisfactory way of proving that we are winning; any time we "win" by changing the meaning of winning, the victory is merely illusory. And so it proves in this case. To use "faith" *as if* it were an alternative way to the truth cannot by-pass the crucial question whether such results really have any likelihood of being true. A rose by any other name will smell the same, and the inescapable facts about "faith" in the new sense are that it is still *applied to* a belief and is still supposed to imply *confidence in* that belief: the belief in the existence and goodness of God. So we can still ask the same old question about that belief: Is the confidence justified or misplaced? To say we "take it on faith" does not get it off parole.

Suppose someone replies that theism is a kind of belief that does not need justification by evidence. This means either that no one cares whether it is correct or not or that there is some other way of checking that it is correct besides looking at the evidence for it, i.e., giving reasons for believing it. But the first alternative is false since very many people care whether there is a God or not; and the second alternative is false because any method of showing that belief is likely to be true is, by definition, a justification of that belief, i.e., an appeal to reason. You certainly cannot show that a belief in God is likely to be true just by having confidence in it and by saying this is a case of knowledge "based on" faith, any more than you can win a game just by playing it and by calling that winning.

It is psychologically possible to have faith in something without any basis in fact, and once in a while you will turn out to be lucky and to have backed the right belief. This does not show you "really knew all along"; it only shows you cannot be unlucky all the time. . . . But, in general, beliefs without foundations lead to an early grave or to an accumulation of superstitions, which are usually troublesome and always false beliefs. It is hardly possible to defend this approach just by *saying* that you have decided that in this area confidence is its own justification.

Of course, you might try to *prove* that a feeling of great confidence about certain types of propositions is a reliable indication of their truth. If you succeeded, you would indeed have shown that the belief was justified; you would have done *this* by justifying it. To do this, you would have to show what the real facts were and show that when someone had the kind of faith we are now talking about, it usually turned out that the facts were as he believed, just as we might justify the claims of a telepath. The catch in all this is simply that you have got to show what the real facts are in some way *other* than by appealing to faith, since that would simply be assuming what you are trying to prove. And if you can show what the facts are in this other way, you do not need faith in any new sense at all; you are already perfectly entitled to confidence in any belief that you have shown to be well supported.

How are you going to show what the real facts are? You show this by any method of investigation that has itself been tested, the testing being done by still another tested method, etc., through a series of tested connections that eventually terminates in our ordinary everyday reasoning and testing procedures of logic and observation.

Is it not prejudiced to require that the validation of beliefs always involve ultimate reference to our ordinary logic and everyday-plus-scientific knowledge? May not faith (religious experience, mystic insight) give us access to some new domain of truth? It is certainly possible that it does this. But, of course, it is also possible that it lies. One can hardly accept the reports of those with faith or, indeed, the apparent revelations of one's own religious experiences on the ground that they *might* be right. So *might* be a fervent materialist who saw his interpretation as a revelation. Possibility is not veracity. Is it not of the very greatest importance that we should try to find out whether we really can justify the use of the term "truth or knowledge" in describing the content of faith? If it is, then we must find something in that content that is known to be true in some other way, because to get off the ground we must first push off against the ground—we cannot lift ourselves by our shoelaces. If the new realm of knowledge is to be a realm of knowledge and not mythology, then it must tell us something which relates it to the kind of case that gives meaning to the term "truth." If you want to use the old word for the new events, you must show that it is applicable.

Could not the validating experience, which religious experience must have if it is to be called true, be the experience of others who also have or have had religious experiences? The religious community could, surely, provide a basis of agreement analogous to that which ultimately underlies scientific truth. Unfortunately, agreement is not the only requirement for avoiding error, for all may be in error.

The difficulty for the religious community is to show that its agreement is not simply agreement about a shared mistake. If agreement were the only criterion of truth, there could never be a shared mistake; but clearly either the atheist group or the theist group shares a mistake. To decide which is wrong must involve appeal to something other than mere agreement. And, of course, it is clear that particular religious beliefs are mistaken, since religious groups do not all agree and they cannot all be right.

Might not some or all scientific beliefs be wrong, too? This is conceivable, but there are crucial differences between the two kinds of belief. In the first place, any commonly agreed religious beliefs concern only one or a few entities and their properties and histories. What for convenience we are here calling "scientific belief" is actually the sum total of all conventionally founded human knowledge, much of it not part of any science, and it embraces billions upon billions of facts, each of them perpetually or frequently subject to checking by independent means, each connected with a million others. The success of *this* system of knowledge shows up every day in everything that we do: we eat, and the food is not poison; we read, and the pages do not turn to dust; we slip, and gravity does not fail to pull us down. We are not just relying on the existence of agreement about the interpretation of a certain experience among a small part of the population. We are relying directly on our extremely reliable, nearly universal, and independently tested senses, and each of us is constantly obtaining independent confirmation for claims based on these, many of these confirmations being obtained for many claims, independently of each other. It is the wildest flight of fancy to suppose that there is a body of common religious beliefs which can be set out to exhibit this degree of repeated checking by religious experiences. In fact, there is not only gross disagreement on even the most fundamental claims in the creeds of different churches, each of which is supported by appeal to religious experience or faith, but where there is agreement by many people, it is all too easily open to the criticism that it arises from the common cultural exposure of the child or the adult convert and hence is not independent in the required way.

This claim that the agreement between judges is spurious in a particular case because it only reflects previous common indoctrination of those in agreement is a serious one. It must always be met by direct disproof whenever agreement is appealed to in science, and it is. The claim that the food is not poison cannot be explained away as a myth of some subculture, for anyone, even if told nothing about the eaters in advance, will judge that the people who ate it are still well. The whole methodology of testing is committed to the doctrine that any judges who could have learned what they are expected to say about the matter they are judging are completely valueless. Now anyone exposed to religious teaching, whether a believer or not, has long known the standard for such experiences, the usual symbols, the appropriate circumstances, and so on. These suggestions are usually very deeply implanted, so that they cannot be avoided by good intentions, and consequently members of our culture are rendered entirely incapable *of* being independent observers. Whenever observers are not free from previous contamination in this manner, the only way to support their claims is to examine independently testable *consequences* of the novel claims, such as predictions about the future. In the absence of these, the religious-experience gambit, whether involving literal or analogical claims, is wholly abortive.

A still more fundamental point counts against the idea that agreement among the religious can help support the idea of faith as an alternative path to truth. It is that every sane theist also believes in the claims of ordinary experience, while the reverse is not the case. Hence, the burden of proof is on the theist to show that the *further step* he wishes to take will not take him beyond the realm of truth. The two positions, of science and religion, are not symmetrical; the adherent of one of them suggests that we extend the range of allowable beliefs and yet is unable to produce the same degree of acceptance or "proving out" in the ordinary field of human activities that he insists on before believing in a new instrument or source of information. The atheist obviously cannot be shown his error in the way someone who thinks that there are no electrons can be shown his, *unless some of the arguments for the existence of God are sound. . . .* If some of them work, the position of religious knowledge is secure; if they do not, nothing else will make it secure.

In sum, the idea of separating religious from scientific knowledge and making each an independent realm with its own basis in experience of quite different kinds is a counsel of despair and not a product of true sophistication, for one cannot break the connection between everyday experience and religious claims, for purposes of defending the latter, without eliminating the consequences of religion for everyday life. There is no way out of this inexorable contract: if you want to support your beliefs, you must produce some experience which can be shown to be a reliable indicator of truth, and that can be done only by showing a connection between the experience and what we know to be true in a previously established way.

So, if the criteria of religious truth are not connected with the criteria of everyday truth, then they are not criteria of truth at all and the beliefs they "establish" have no essential bearing on our lives, constitute no explanation of what we see around us, and provide no guidance for our course through time.

STUDY QUESTIONS

1. Can knowledge be based on faith?
2. Can you believe strongly and be wrong?
3. According to Scriven, why are faith and reason not symmetrical?
4. Is your life invariably improved by holding justified beliefs rather than unjustified ones?

God and Morality

STEVEN M. CAHN

Would the existence of God have implications for morality? Some believe so, but in the next selection I argue against that claim.

According to many religions, although not all, the world was created by God, an all-powerful, all-knowing, all-good being. Although God's existence has been doubted, let us for the moment assume its truth. What implications of this supposition would be relevant to our lives?

Some people would feel more secure in the knowledge that the world had been planned by an all-good being. Others would feel insecure, realizing the extent to which their existence depended on a decision of this being. In any case, most people, out of either fear or respect, would wish to act in accord with God's will.

Belief in God by itself, however, provides no hint whatsoever which actions God wishes us to perform, or what we ought to do to please or obey God. We may affirm that God is all-good, yet have no way of knowing the highest moral standards. All we may presume is that, whatever these standards, God always acts in accordance with them. We might expect God to have implanted the correct moral standards in our minds, but this supposition is doubtful in view of the conflicts among people's intuitions. Furthermore, even if consensus prevailed, it might be only a means by which God tests us to see whether we have the courage to dissent from popular opinion.

Some would argue that if God exists, then murder is immoral, because it destroys what God with infinite wisdom created. This argument, however, fails on several grounds. First, God also created germs, viruses, and disease-carrying rats. Because God created these things, ought they not be eliminated? Second, if God arranged for us to live, God also arranged for us to die. By killing, are we thereby assisting the work of God? Third, God provided us with the mental and physical potential to commit murder. Does God wish us to fulfill this potential?

Thus God's existence alone does not imply any particular moral precepts. We may hope our actions are in accord with God's standards, but no test is available to check whether what we do is best in God's eyes. Some seemingly good people suffer great ills, whereas some seemingly evil people achieve happiness. Perhaps in a future life these outcomes will be reversed, but we have no way of ascertaining who, if anyone, is ultimately punished and who ultimately rewarded.

Over the course of history, those who believed in God's existence typically were eager to learn God's will and tended to rely on those individuals who claimed to possess such insight. Diviners, seers, and priests were given positions of great influence. Competition among them was severe, however, for no one could be sure which oracle to believe.

In any case prophets died, and their supposedly revelatory powers disappeared with them. For practical purposes what was needed was a permanent record of God's will. This requirement was met by the writing of holy books in which God's will was revealed to all.

But even though many such books were supposed to embody the will of God, they conflicted with one another. Which was to be accepted? Belief in the existence of God by itself yields no answer.

Let us suppose, however, that an individual becomes persuaded that a reliable guide to God's will is contained in the Ten Commandments. This person, therefore, believes that to murder, steal, or commit adultery is wrong.

But why is it wrong? Is it wrong because God says so, or does God say so because it *is* wrong?

This crucial issue was raised more than two thousand years ago in Plato's remarkable dialogue, the *Euthyphro*. Plato's teacher, Socrates, who in most of Plato's works is given the leading role, asks the overconfident Euthyphro whether actions are right because God says they are right, or whether God says actions are right because they are right.

In other words, Socrates is inquiring whether actions are right because of God's fiat or whether God is subject to moral standards. If actions are right because of God's command, then anything God commands would be right. Had God commanded adultery, stealing, and murder, then adultery, stealing, and murder would be right—surely an unsettling and to many an unacceptable conclusion.

Granted, some may be willing to adopt this discomforting view, but then they face another difficulty. If the good is whatever God commands, to say that God's commands are good amounts to saying that God's commands are God's commands, a mere tautology or repetition of words. In that case, the possibility of meaningfully praising the goodness of God would be lost.

The lesson here is that might does not make right, even if the might is the infinite might of God. To act morally is not to act out of fear of punishment; it is not to act as one is commanded to act. Rather, it is to act as one ought to act, and how one ought to act is not dependent on anyone's power, even if the power be divine.

Thus actions are not right because God commands them; on the contrary, God commands them because they are right. What is right is independent of what God commands, for to be right, what God commands must conform to an independent standard.

We could act intentionally in accord with this standard without believing in the existence of God; therefore morality does not rest on that belief. Consequently those who do not believe in God can be highly moral (as well as immoral) people, and those who do believe in the existence of God can be highly immoral (as well as moral) people. This conclusion should come as no surprise to anyone who has contrasted the benevolent life of the inspiring teacher, the Buddha, an atheist, with the malevolent life of the monk Torquemada, who devised and enforced the boundless cruelties of the Spanish Inquisition.

In short, believing in the existence of God does not by itself imply any specific moral principles, and knowing God's will does not provide any justification for morality. Thus regardless of our religious commitments, the moral dimension of our lives remains to be explored.

STUDY QUESTIONS

1. If God exists, is murder immoral?
2. Is murder wrong because God prohibits it, or does God prohibit murder because it is wrong?
3. Can atheists be moral persons?
4. Can theists be immoral persons?

HISTORICAL SOURCES

The Ontological Argument

ANSELM AND GAUNILO

Throughout the history of philosophy, various arguments have been offered to prove God's existence. Only one, however, the ontological argument, is *a priori*, making no appeal to empirical evidence and relying solely on an analysis of the concept of God.

Its classic formulation was provided by Saint Anselm (1033–1109), who was born in a village that is now part of Italy, was educated in a Benedictine monastery, and became Archbishop of Canterbury. He understands God to be the Being greater than which none can be conceived. Anselm reasons that if God did not exist, then a greater being could be conceived, namely, a being that exists. In that case, the Being greater than which none can be conceived would not be the Being greater than which none can be conceived, which is a contradiction. So the Being greater than which none can be conceived must exist, that is, God must exist. Indeed, Anselm goes on to claim that God cannot even be thought not to exist, because a being that *cannot* be thought not to exist is greater than one that *can* be thought not to exist.

From Brian Davies and G. R. Evans, eds., *Anselm of Canterbury: The Major Works*. Reprinted by permission of Oxford University Press. The words enclosed in brackets have been interpolated by the translator, M. J. Charlesworth, to make the meaning clearer.

The first known response to Anselm's argument was offered by his contemporary Gaunilo, a monk of Marmoutier, France, about whom little is known. Gaunilo maintains that Anselm's line of reasoning could be used to prove the existence of an island greater than which none can be conceived, an absurd conclusion. In reply, Anselm maintains that the argument did not apply to an island because, unlike God, an island has a beginning and end and so can be thought not to exist.

The ontological argument has continued to intrigue thinkers throughout the centuries. While its intricacy may not win many converts to theism, the argument retains the power to fascinate philosophers.

PROSLOGION

2

Well then, Lord, You who give understanding to faith, grant me that I may understand, as much as You see fit, that You exist as we believe You to exist, and that You are what we believe You to be. Now we believe that You are something than which nothing greater can be thought. Or can it be that a thing of such a nature does not exist, since "the Fool has said in his heart, there is no God" [Ps. 13:1; 52:1]? But surely, when this same Fool hears what I am speaking about, namely, "something-than-which-nothing-greater-can-be-thought," he understands what he hears, and what he understands is in his mind, even if he does not understand that it actually exists. For it is one thing for an object to exist in the mind, and another thing to understand that an object actually exists. Thus, when a painter plans beforehand what he is going to execute, he has [the picture] in his mind, but he does not yet think that it actually exists because he has not yet executed it. However, when he has actually painted it, then he both has it in his mind and understands that it exists because he has now made it. Even the Fool, then, is forced to agree that something-than-which-nothing-greater-can-be-thought exists in the mind, since he understands this when he hears it, and whatever is understood is in the mind. And surely that-than-which-a-greater-cannot-be-thought cannot exist in the mind alone. For if it exists solely in the mind, it can be thought to exist in reality also, which is greater. If then that-than-which-a-greater-cannot-be-thought exists in the mind alone, this same that-than-which-a-greater-*cannot*-be-thought is that-than-which-a-greater-*can*-be-thought. But this is obviously impossible. Therefore there is absolutely no doubt that something-than-which-a-greater-cannot-be-thought exists both in the mind and in reality.

3

And certainly this being so truly exists that it cannot be even thought not to exist. For something can be thought to exist that cannot be thought not to exist, and this is greater than that which can be thought not to exist. Hence, if that-than-which-a-greater-cannot-be-thought can be thought not to exist, then that-than-which-a-greater-cannot-be-thought is not the same as that-than-which-a-greater-cannot-be-thought, which is absurd. Something-than-which-a-greater-cannot-be-thought exists so truly then, that it cannot be even thought not to exist.

And You, Lord our God, are this being. You exist so truly, Lord my God, that You cannot even be thought not to exist. And this is as it should be, for if some intelligence could think of something better than You, the creature would be above its Creator and would judge its Creator—and that is completely absurd. In fact, everything else there is, except You alone can be thought of as not existing. You alone, then, of all things most truly exist and therefore of all things possess existence to the highest degree; for anything else does not exist as truly, and so possesses existence to a lesser degree. Why then did "the Fool say in his heart, there is no God" [Ps. 13:1; 52:1] when it is so evident to any rational mind that You of all things exist to the highest degree? Why indeed, unless because he was stupid and a fool?

4

How indeed has he "said in his heart" what he could not think; or how could he not think what he "said in his heart," since to "say in one's heart" and to "think" are the same? But if he really (indeed, since he really) both thought because he "said in his heart" and did not "say in his heart" because he could not think, there is not only one sense in which something is "said in one's heart" or thought. For in one sense a thing is thought when the word signifying it is thought; in another sense when the very object which the thing is is understood. In the first sense, then, God can be thought not to exist, but not at all in the second sense. No one, indeed, understanding what God is can think that God does not exist, even though he may say these words in his heart either without any [objective] signification or with some peculiar signification. For God is that-than-which-nothing-greater-can-be-thought. Whoever really understands this understands clearly that this same being so exists that not even in thought can it not exist. Thus whoever understands that God exists in such a way cannot think of Him as not existing.

I give thanks, good Lord, I give thanks to You, since what I believed before through Your free gift I now so understand through Your illumination, that if I did not want to *believe* that You existed, I should nevertheless be unable not to *understand* it.

ON BEHALF OF THE FOOL

Gaunilo

1

To one doubting whether there is, or denying that there is, something of such a nature than which nothing greater can be thought, it is said here that its existence is proved, first because the very one who denies or doubts it already has it in his mind, since when he hears it spoken of he understands what is said; and further, because what he understands is necessarily such that it exists not only in the mind but also in reality. And this is proved by the fact that it is greater to exist both in the mind and in reality than in the mind alone. For if this same being exists in the mind alone, anything that existed also in reality would be greater than this being, and thus that which is greater than everything would be less than some thing and would not be greater than everything, which is obviously contradictory. Therefore, it is necessarily the case that that which is greater than everything, being already proved to exist in the mind, should exist not only in the mind but also in reality, since otherwise it would not be greater than everything.

2

But he [the Fool] can perhaps reply that this thing is said already to exist in the mind only in the sense that I understand what is said. For could I not say that all kinds of unreal things, not existing in themselves in any way at all, are equally in the mind since if anyone speaks about them I understand whatever he says? . . .

6

For example: they say that there is in the ocean somewhere an island which, because of the difficulty (or rather the impossibility) of finding that which does not exist, some have called the "Lost Island." And the story goes that it is blessed with all manner of priceless riches and delights in abundance, much more even than the Happy Isles, and, having no owner or inhabitant, it is superior everywhere in abundance of riches to all those other lands that men inhabit. Now, if anyone tell me that it is like this, I shall easily understand what is said, since nothing is difficult about it. But if he should then go on to say, as though it were a logical consequence of this: You cannot any more doubt that this island that is more excellent than all other lands truly exists somewhere in reality than you can doubt that it is in your mind; and since it is more excellent to exist not only in the mind alone but also in reality, therefore it must needs be that it exists. For if it did not exist, any other land existing in reality would be more excellent than it, and so this island, already conceived by you to be more excellent than others, will not be more excellent. If, I say, someone wishes thus to persuade me that this island really exists beyond all doubt, I should either think that he was joking or I should find it hard to decide which of us I ought to judge the bigger fool—I, if I agreed with him, or he, if he thought that he had proved the existence of this island with any certainty, unless he had first convinced me that its very excellence exists in my mind precisely as a thing existing truly and indubitably and not just as something unreal or doubtfully real.

REPLY TO GAUNILO

You claim, however, that this is as though someone asserted that it cannot be doubted that a certain island in the ocean (which is more fertile than all other lands and which, because of the difficulty or even the impossibility of discovering what does not exist, is called the "Lost Island") truly exists in reality since anyone easily understands it when it is described in words. Now, I truly promise that if anyone should discover for me something existing either in reality or in the mind alone—except "that-than-which-a-greater-cannot-be-thought"—to which the logic of my argument would apply, then I shall find that Lost Island and give it, never more to be lost, to that person. It has already been clearly seen, however, that "that-than-which-a-greater-cannot-be-thought" cannot be thought not to exist, because it exists as a matter of such certain truth. Otherwise it would not exist at all. In short, if anyone says that he thinks that this being does not exist, I reply that, when he thinks of this, either he thinks of something than which a greater cannot be thought, or he does not think of it. If he does not think of it, then he does not think that what he does not think of does not exist. If, however, he does think of it, then indeed he thinks of something which cannot be even thought not to exist. For if it could be thought not to exist, it could be thought to have a beginning and an end—but this cannot be. Thus, he who thinks of it thinks of something that cannot be thought not to exist; indeed, he who thinks of this does not think of it as not existing, otherwise he would think what cannot be thought. Therefore "that-than-which-a-greater-cannot-be-thought" cannot be thought not to exist.

STUDY QUESTIONS

1. Why is the ontological argument considered an *a priori* argument?
2. What are the premises Anselm uses to prove the existence of God?
3. What is Gaunilo's criticism of Anselm's argument?
4. Do you find Gaunilo's criticism persuasive?

Summa Theologiae

THOMAS AQUINAS

Thomas Aquinas (1225–1274), born near Naples, was the most influential philosopher of the medieval period. He joined the Dominican order and taught at the University of Paris. In his vast writings, composed in Latin, he seeks to demonstrate that Christian belief is consistent with reason.

Aquinas's greatest work was the *Summa Theologiae,* and its most famous passage, reprinted here, is the five ways to prove the existence of God. While Aquinas believes that not all the tenets of Christian doctrine can be demonstrated without reliance on Divine revelation, he maintains that the existence of God is provable without any appeal to faith.

In the fourth way Aquinas cites "*Metaph.* ii." The reference is to the second book of the *Metaphysics* of Aristotle, and serves as a reminder of Aquinas's regard for that highly influential Greek thinker.

....

The existence of God can be proved in five ways.

The first and more manifest way is the argument from motion. It is certain, and evident to our senses, that in the world some things are in motion. Now whatever is moved is moved by another, for nothing can be moved except it is in potentiality to that towards which it is moved; whereas a thing moves inasmuch as it is in act. For motion is nothing else than the reduction of something from potentiality to actuality. But nothing can be reduced from potentiality to actuality, except by something in a state of actuality. Thus that which is actually hot, as fire, makes wood, which is potentially hot, to be actually hot, and thereby moves and changes it. Now it is not possible that the same thing should be at once in actuality and potentiality in the same respect, but only in different respects. For what is actually hot cannot simultaneously be potentially hot; but it is simultaneously potentially cold. It is therefore impossible that in the same respect and in the same way a thing should be both mover and moved, i.e., that it should move itself. Therefore, whatever is moved must be moved by another. If that by which it is moved be itself moved, then this also must need to be moved by another, and that by another again. But this cannot go on to infinity, because then there would be no first mover and, consequently, no other mover, seeing that subsequent movers move only inasmuch as they are moved by the first mover; as the staff moves only because it is moved by the hand. Therefore it is necessary to arrive at a first mover, moved by no other; and this everyone understands to be God.

The second way is from the nature of efficient cause. In the world of sensible things we find there is an order of efficient causes. There is no case known (neither is it, indeed, possible) in which a thing is found to be the efficient cause of itself; for so it would be prior to itself, which is impossible. Now in efficient causes it is not possible to go on to infinity, because in all efficient causes following in order, the first is the cause of the intermediate cause, and the intermediate is the cause of the ultimate cause, whether the intermediate cause be several, or one only. Now to take away the cause is to take away the effect. Therefore, if there be no first cause among efficient causes, there will be no ultimate, nor any intermediate, cause. But if in efficient causes it is possible to go on to infinity, there will be no first efficient cause, neither will there be an ultimate effect, nor any intermediate efficient causes; all of which is plainly false. Therefore it is necessary to admit a first efficient cause, to which everyone gives the name of God.

The third way is taken from possibility and necessity, and runs thus. We find in nature things that are possible to be and not to be, since they are found to be generated, and to be corrupted, and consequently, it is possible for them to be and not to be. But it is impossible for these always to exist, for that which can not-be at some time is not. Therefore, if everything can not-be, then at one time there was nothing in existence. Now if this were true, even now there would be nothing in existence, because that which does not exist begins to exist only through something already existing. Therefore, if at one time nothing was in existence, it would have been impossible for anything to have begun to exist; and thus even now nothing would be in existence—which is absurd. Therefore, not all beings are merely possible, but there must exist something the existence of which is necessary. But every necessary thing either has its necessity caused by another or does not. Now it is impossible to go on to infinity in necessary things which have their necessity caused by another, as has been already proved in regard to efficient causes. Therefore we cannot but admit the existence of some being having of itself its own necessity, and not receiving it from another, but rather causing in others their necessity. This all men speak of as God.

The fourth way is taken from the gradation to be found in things. Among beings there are some more and some less good, true, noble, and the like. But *more* and *less* are predicated of different things according as they resemble in their different ways something which is the maximum, as a thing is said to be hotter according as it more nearly resembles that which is hottest; so that there is something which is truest, something best, something noblest, and, consequently, something which is most being, for those things that are greatest in truth are greatest in being, as it is written in *Metaph*. ii. Now the maximum in any genus is the cause of all in that genus, as fire, which is the maximum of heat, is the cause of all hot things, as is said in the same book. Therefore there must also be something which is to all beings the cause of their being, goodness, and every other perfection: and this we call God.

The fifth way is taken from the governance of the world. We see that things which lack knowledge, such as natural bodies, act for an end, and this is evident from their acting always, or nearly always, in the same way, so as to obtain the best result. Hence it is plain that they achieve their end, not fortuitously but designedly. Now whatever lacks knowledge cannot move towards an end, unless it be directed by some being endowed with knowledge and intelligence; as the arrow is directed by the archer. Therefore some intelligent being exists by whom all natural things are directed to their end; and this being we call God.

STUDY QUESTIONS

1. Do Aquinas's five ways all reach the same conclusion?
2. If whatever is moved must be moved by another, how is an unmoved mover possible?
3. Do the terms "more" and "less" always presuppose a maximum?
4. Does a river flowing toward the sea act for an end?

Dialogues Concerning Natural Religion

DAVID HUME

David Hume's extraordinarily powerful *Dialogues Concerning Natural Religion* is one of the most important books in the philosophy of religion. During his lifetime, his friends, fearful of public disapproval, had dissuaded him from publishing the manuscript, but he took great pains to ensure that the work would not be lost, and it appeared in print three years after his death, although without any publisher's name attached.

"Natural religion" was the term used by eighteenth-century writers to refer to theological tenets that are provable by reason without appeal to revelation. The three participants in the *Dialogues* are distinguished by their views concerning the scope and limits of reason. Cleanthes claims that he can present arguments that demonstrate the truth of traditional Christian theology. Demea is committed to that theology but does not believe empirical evidence can provide any defense for his faith. Philo doubts that reason yields conclusive results in any field of inquiry and is especially critical of theological dogmatism.

By subtle interplay among these three characters, Hume seeks to show the surprising affinity between Philo and Demea, as well as the equally surprising lack of affinity between Demea and Cleanthes.

In the sections of the book reprinted here, the argument to design is subjected to trenchant criticism. In addition, Hume develops in detail what is probably the strongest argument against the existence of God, namely, the problem of evil: How can evil exist in a world created by an all-good, all-powerful God?

PART II

... Not to lose any time in circumlocutions, said Cleanthes, ... I shall briefly explain how I conceive this matter. Look round the world, contemplate the whole and every part of it: you will find it to be nothing but one great machine, subdivided into an infinite number of lesser machines, which again admit of subdivisions to a degree beyond what human senses and faculties can trace and explain. All these various machines, and even their most minute parts, are adjusted to each other with an accuracy which ravishes into admiration all men who have ever contemplated them. The curious adapting of means to ends, throughout all nature, resembles exactly, though it much exceeds, the productions of human

From *Dialogues Concerning Natural Religion* (1779) by David Hume.

contrivance—of human design, thought, wisdom, and intelligence. Since therefore the effects resemble each other, we are led to infer, by all the rules of analogy, that the causes also resemble, and that the Author of nature is somewhat similar to the mind of man, though possessed of much larger faculties, proportioned to the grandeur of the work which he has executed. By this argument a posteriori, and by this argument alone, do we prove at once the existence of a Deity and his similarity to human mind and intelligence.

I shall be so free, Cleanthes, said Demea, as to tell you that from the beginning I could not approve of your conclusion concerning the similarity of the Deity to men, still less can I approve of the mediums by which you endeavour to establish it. What! No demonstration of the Being of God! No abstract arguments! No proofs a priori! Are these which have hitherto been so much insisted on by philosophers all fallacy, all sophism? Can we reach no farther in this subject than experience and probability? I will not say that this is betraying the cause of a Deity; but surely, by this affected candour, you give advantages to atheists which they never could obtain by the mere dint of argument and reasoning.

What I chiefly scruple in this subject, said Philo, is not so much that all religious arguments are by Cleanthes reduced to experience, as that they appear not to be even the most certain and irrefragable of that inferior kind. That a stone will fall, that fire will burn, that the earth has solidity, we have observed a thousand and a thousand times; and when any new instance of this nature is presented, we draw without hesitation the accustomed inference. The exact similarity of the cases gives us a perfect assurance of a similar event, and a stronger evidence is never desired nor sought after. But wherever you depart, in the least, from the similarity of the cases, you diminish proportionably the evidence, and may at last bring it to a very weak *analogy*, which is confessedly liable to error and uncertainty. After having experienced the circulation of the blood in human creatures, we make no doubt that it takes place in Titius and Maevius,[1] but from its circulation in frogs and fishes it is only a presumption, though a strong one, from analogy that it takes place in men and other animals. The analogical reasoning is much weaker when we infer the circulation of the sap in vegetables from our experience that the blood circulates in animals; and those who hastily followed that imperfect analogy are found, by more accurate experiments, to have been mistaken.

If we see a house, Cleanthes, we conclude, with the greatest certainty, that it had an architect or builder because this is precisely that species of effect which we have experienced to proceed from that species of cause. But surely you will not affirm that the universe bears such a resemblance to a house that we can with the same certainty infer a similar cause, or that the analogy is here entire and perfect. The dissimilitude is so striking that the utmost you can here pretend to is a guess, conjecture, a presumption concerning a similar cause; and how that pretension will be received in the world, I leave you to consider.

It would surely be very ill received, replied Cleanthes; and I should be deservedly blamed and detested did I allow that the proofs of Deity amounted to no more than a guess or conjecture. But is the whole adjustment of means to ends in a house and in the universe so slight a resemblance? the economy of final causes? the order, proportion, and arrangement of every part? Steps of a stair are plainly contrived that human legs may use them in mounting; and this inference is certain and infallible. Human legs are also contrived for walking and mounting; and this inference, I allow, is not altogether so certain because of the dissimilarity which you remark; but does it, therefore, deserve the name only of presumption or conjecture?

Good God! cried Demea, interrupting him, where are we? Zealous defenders of religion allow that the proofs of a Deity fall short of perfect evidence! And you, Philo, on whose assistance I depended in proving the adorable mysteriousness of the Divine Nature, do you assent to all these extravagant opinions of Cleanthes? For what other name can I give them? or, why spare my censure when such principles are advanced, supported by such an authority, before so young a man as Pamphilus?

You seem not to apprehend, replied Philo, that I argue with Cleanthes in his own way, and, by showing him the dangerous consequences of his tenets, hope at last to reduce him to our opinion. But what sticks most with you, observe, is the representation which Cleanthes has made of the argument a posteriori; and, finding that the argument is likely to escape your hold and vanish into air, you think it so disguised that you can scarcely believe it to be set in its true light. Now, however much I may dissent, in other respects, from the dangerous principle of Cleanthes, I must allow that he has fairly represented that argument, and I shall endeavour so to state the matter to you that you will entertain no further scruples with regard to it.

Were a man to abstract from everything which he knows or has seen, he would be altogether incapable, merely from his own ideas, to determine what kind of scene the universe must be, or to give the preference to one state or situation of things above another. For as nothing which he clearly conceives could be esteemed impossible or implying a contradiction, every chimera of his fancy would be upon an equal footing; nor could he assign any just reason why he adheres to one idea or system, and rejects the others which are equally possible.

Again, after he opens his eyes and contemplates the world as it really is, it would be impossible for him at first to assign the cause of any one event, much less of the whole of things, or of the universe. He might set his fancy a rambling, and she might bring him in an infinite variety of reports and representations. These would all be possible, but, being all equally possible, he would never of himself give a satisfactory account for his preferring one of them to the rest. Experience alone can point out to him the true cause of any phenomenon.

Now, according to this method of reasoning, Demea, it follows (and is, indeed, tacitly allowed by Cleanthes himself) that order, arrangement, or the adjustment of final causes, is not of itself any proof of design, but only so far as it has been experienced to proceed from that principle. For aught we can know a priori, matter may contain the source or spring of order originally within itself, as well as mind does; and there is no more difficulty in conceiving that the several elements, from an internal unknown cause, may fall into the most exquisite arrangement, than to conceive that their ideas, in the great universal mind, from a like internal unknown cause, fall into that arrangement. The equal possibility of both these suppositions is allowed. But, by experience, we find (according to Cleanthes) that there is a difference between them. Throw several pieces of steel together, without shape or form, they will never arrange themselves so as to compose a watch. Stone and mortar and wood, without an architect, never erect a house. But the ideas in a human mind, we see, by an unknown, inexplicable economy, arrange themselves so as to form the plan of a watch or house. Experience, therefore, proves that there is an original principle of order in mind, not in matter. From similar effects we infer similar causes. The adjustment of means to ends is alike in the universe, as in a machine of human contrivance. The causes, therefore, must be resembling.

I was from the beginning scandalized, I must own, with this resemblance which is asserted between the Deity and human creatures, and must conceive it to imply such a degradation of the Supreme Being as no sound theist could endure. With your assistance, therefore, Demea, I shall endeavour to defend what you justly call the adorable mysteriousness of the Divine Nature, and shall refute this reasoning of Cleanthes, provided he allows that I have made a fair representation of it.

When Cleanthes had assented, Philo, after a short pause, proceeded in the following manner.

That all inferences, Cleanthes, concerning fact are founded on experience, and that all experimental reasonings are founded on the supposition that similar causes prove similar effects, and similar effects similar causes, I shall not at present much dispute with you. But observe, I entreat you, with what extreme caution all just reasoners proceed in the transferring of experiments to similar cases. Unless the cases be exactly similar, they repose no perfect confidence in applying their past observation to any particular phenomenon. Every alteration of circumstances occasions a doubt concerning the event; and it requires new experiments to prove certainly that the new circumstances are of no moment or importance. A change in bulk, situation, arrangement, age, disposition of the air, or surrounding bodies— any of these particulars may be attended with the most unexpected consequences. And unless the objects be quite familiar to us, it is the highest temerity to expect with assurance, after any of these changes, an event similar to that which before fell under our observation. The slow and deliberate steps of philosophers here, if anywhere, are distinguished from the precipitate march of the vulgar, who, hurried on by the smallest similitude, are incapable of all discernment or consideration.

But can you think, Cleanthes, that your usual phlegm and philosophy have been preserved in so wide a step as you have taken when you compared to the universe houses, ships, furniture, machines, and, from their similarity in some circumstances, inferred a similarity in their causes? Thought, design, intelligence, such as we discover in men and other animals, is no more than one of the springs and principles of the universe, as well as heat or cold, attraction or repulsion, and a hundred others which fall under daily observation. It is an active cause by which some particular parts of nature, we find, produce alterations on other parts. But can a conclusion, with any propriety, be transferred from parts to the whole? Does not the great disproportion bar all comparison and inference? From observing the growth of a hair, can we learn anything concerning the generation of a man? Would the manner of a leaf's blowing, even though perfectly known, afford us any instruction concerning the vegetation of a tree?

But allowing that we were to take the *operations* of one part of nature upon another for the foundation of our judgment concerning the *origin* of the whole (which never can be admitted), yet why select so minute, so weak, so bounded a principle as the reason and design of animals is found to be upon this planet? What peculiar privilege has this little agitation of the brain which we call *thought*, that we must thus make it the model of the whole universe? Our partiality in our own favour does indeed present it on all occasions, but sound philosophy ought carefully to guard against so natural an illusion.

So far from admitting, continued Philo, that the operations of a part can afford us any just conclusion concerning the origin of the whole, I will not allow any one part to form a rule for another part if the latter be very remote from the former. Is there any reasonable ground to conclude that the inhabitants of other planets possess thought, intelligence, reason, or anything similar to these faculties in men? When nature has so extremely diversified her manner of operation in this small globe, can we imagine that she incessantly copies herself throughout so immense a universe? And if thought, as we may well suppose, be confined merely to this narrow corner and has even there so limited a sphere of action, with what propriety can we assign it for the original cause of all things? The narrow views of a peasant who makes his domestic economy the rule for the government of kingdoms is in comparison a pardonable sophism.

But were we ever so much assured that a thought and reason resembling the human were to be found throughout the whole universe, and were its activity elsewhere vastly greater and more commanding than it appears in this globe, yet I cannot see why the operations of a world constituted, arranged, adjusted can with any propriety be extended to a world which is in its embryo state, and is advancing towards that constitution and arrangement. By observation we know somewhat of the economy, action, and nourishment of a finished animal, but we must transfer with great caution that observation to the growth of a fetus in the womb, and still more to the formation of an animalcule in the loins of its male parent. Nature, we find, even from our limited experience, possesses an infinite number of springs and principles which incessantly discover themselves on every change of her position and situation. And what new and unknown principles would actuate her in so new and unknown a situation as that of the formation of a universe, we cannot, without the utmost temerity, pretend to determine.

A very small part of this great system, during a very short time, is very imperfectly discovered to us; and do we thence pronounce decisively concerning the origin of the whole?

Admirable conclusion! Stone, wood, brick, iron, brass, have not, at this time, in this minute globe of earth, an order or arrangement without human art and contrivance; therefore, the universe could not originally attain its order and arrangement without something similar to human art. But is a part of nature a rule for another part very wide of the former? Is it a rule for the whole? Is a very small part a rule for the universe? Is nature in one situation a certain rule for nature in another situation vastly different from the former?

And can you blame me, Cleanthes, if I here imitate the prudent reserve of Simonides,[2] who, according to the noted story, being asked by Hiero,[3] *What God was?* desired a day to think of it, and then two days more; and after that manner continually prolonged the term, without ever bringing in his definition or description? Could you even blame me if I had answered, at first, *that I did not know*, and was sensible that this subject lay vastly beyond the reach of my faculties? You might cry out sceptic and raillier, as much as you pleased; but, having found in so many other subjects much more familiar the imperfections and even contradictions of human reason, I never should expect any success from its feeble conjectures in a subject so sublime and so remote from the sphere of our observation. When two *species* of objects have always been observed to be conjoined together, I can *infer*, by custom, the existence of one wherever I *see* the existence of the other; and this I call an argument from experience. But how this argument can have place where the objects, as in the present case, are single, individual, without parallel or specific resemblance may be difficult to explain. And will any man tell me with a serious countenance that an orderly universe must arise from some thought and art like the human because we have experience of it? To ascertain this reasoning, it was requisite that we had experience of the origin of worlds; and it is not sufficient, surely, that we have seen ships and cities arise from human art and contrivance. . . .

PART V

But to show you still more inconveniences, continued Philo, in your anthropomorphism, please to take a new survey of your principles. *Like effects prove like causes.* This is the experimental argument, and this, you say too, is the sole theological argument. Now it is certain that the liker the effects are which are seen and the liker the causes which are inferred, the stronger is the argument. Every departure on either side diminishes the probability and renders the experiment less conclusive. You cannot doubt of the principle; neither ought you to reject its consequences.

All the new discoveries in astronomy which prove the immense grandeur and magnificence of the works of nature are so many additional arguments for a Deity, according to the true system of theism; but, according to your hypothesis of experimental theism, they become so many objections, by removing the effect still farther from all resemblance to the effects of human art and contrivance. . . .

If this argument, I say, had any force in former ages, how much greater must it have at present when the bounds of Nature are so infinitely enlarged and such a magnificent scene is opened to us? It is still more unreasonable to form our idea of so unlimited a cause from our experience of the narrow productions of human design and invention.

The discoveries by microscopes, as they open a new universe in miniature, are still objections, according to you, arguments, according to me. The further we push our researches of this kind, we are still led to infer the universal cause of all to be vastly different from mankind, or from any object of human experience and observation.

And what say you to the discoveries in anatomy, chemistry, botany? . . . These surely are no objections, replied Cleanthes; they only discover new instances of art and contrivance, it is still the image of mind reflected on us from innumerable objects. Add a mind *like the human*, said Philo. I know of no other, replied Cleanthes. And the liker, the better, insisted Philo. To be sure, said Cleanthes.

Now, Cleanthes, said Philo, with an air of alacrity and triumph, mark the consequences. *First*, by this method of reasoning you renounce all claim to infinity in any of the attributes of the Deity. For, as the cause ought only to be proportioned to the effect, and the effect, so far as it falls under our cognizance, is not infinite, what pretensions have we, upon your suppositions, to ascribe that attribute to the Divine Being? You will still insist that, by removing him so much from all similarity to human creatures, we give in to the most arbitrary hypothesis, and at the same time weaken all proofs of his existence.

Secondly, you have no reason, on your theory, for ascribing perfection to the Deity, even in his finite capacity, or for supposing him free from every error, mistake, or incoherence, in his undertakings. There are many inexplicable difficulties in the works of nature which, if we allow a perfect author to be proved a priori, are easily solved, and become only seeming difficulties from the narrow capacity of man, who cannot trace infinite relations. But according to your method of reasoning, these difficulties become all real, and, perhaps, will be insisted on as new instances of likeness to human art and contrivance. At least, you must acknowledge that it is impossible for us to tell, from our limited views, whether this system contains any great faults or deserves any considerable praise if compared to other possible and even real systems. Could a peasant, if the *Aeneid* were read to him, pronounce that poem to be absolutely faultless, or even assign to it its proper rank among the productions of human wit, he who had never seen any other production?

But were this world ever so perfect a production, it must still remain uncertain whether all the excellences of the work can justly be ascribed to the workman. If we survey a ship, what an exalted idea must we form of the ingenuity of the carpenter who framed so complicated, useful, and beautiful a machine? And what surprise must we feel when we find him a stupid mechanic who imitated others, and copied an art which, through a long succession of ages, after multiplied trials, mistakes, corrections, deliberations, and controversies, had been gradually improving? Many worlds might have been botched and bungled, throughout an eternity, ere this system was struck out; much labour lost, many fruitless trials made, and a slow but continued improvement carried on during infinite ages in the art of world-making. In such subjects, who can determine where the truth, nay, who can conjecture where the probability lies, amidst a great number of hypotheses which may be proposed, and a still greater which may be imagined?

And what shadow of an argument, continued Philo, can you produce from your hypothesis to prove the unity of the Deity? A great number of men join in building a house or ship, in rearing a city, in framing a commonwealth; why may not several deities combine in contriving and framing a world? This is only so much greater similarity to human affairs. By sharing the work among several, we may so much further limit the attributes of each, and get rid of that extensive power and knowledge which must be supposed in one deity, and which, according to you, can only serve to weaken the proof of his existence. And if such foolish, such vicious creatures as man can yet often unite in framing and executing one plan, how much more those deities or demons, whom we may suppose several degrees more perfect!

To multiply causes without necessity is indeed contrary to true philosophy, but this principle applies not to the present case. Were one deity antecedently proved by your theory who was possessed of every attribute requisite to the production of the universe, it would be needless, I own (though not absurd) to suppose any other deity existent. But while it is still a question whether all these attributes are united in one subject or dispersed among several independent beings, by what phenomena in nature can we pretend to decide the controversy? Where we see a body raised in a scale, we are sure that there is in the opposite scale, however concealed from sight, some counterpoising weight equal to it; but it is still allowed to doubt whether that weight be an aggregate of several distinct bodies or one uniform united mass. And if the weight requisite very much exceeds anything which we have ever seen conjoined in any single body, the former supposition becomes still more probable and natural. An intelligent being of such vast power and capacity as is necessary to produce the universe, or, to speak in the language of ancient philosophy, so prodigious an animal exceeds all analogy and even comprehension.

But further, Cleanthes: Men are mortal, and renew their species by generation; and this is common to all living creatures. The two great sexes of male and female, says Milton, animate the world. Why must this circumstance, so universal, so essential, be excluded from those numerous and limited deities? Behold, then, the theogeny of ancient times brought back upon us.

And why not become a perfect anthropomorphite? Why not assert the deity or deities to be corporeal, and to have eyes, a nose, mouth, ears, etc.? Epicurus maintained that no man had ever seen reason but in a human figure; therefore, the gods must have a human figure. And this argument, which is deservedly so much ridiculed by Cicero, becomes, according to you, solid and philosophical.

In a word, Cleanthes, a man who follows your hypothesis, is able, perhaps, to assert or conjecture that the universe sometime arose from something like design; but beyond that position he cannot ascertain one single circumstance, and is left afterwards to fix every point of his theology by the utmost license of fancy and hypothesis. This world, for aught he knows, is very faulty and imperfect, compared to a superior standard, and was only the first rude essay of some infant deity who afterwards abandoned it, ashamed of his lame performance; it is the work only of some dependent, inferior deity, and is the object of derision to his superiors; it is the production of old age and dotage in some superannuated deity, and ever since his death has run on at adventures, from the first impulse and active force which it received from him. You justly give signs of horror, Demea, at these strange suppositions; but these, and a thousand more of the same kind, are Cleanthes' suppositions, not mine. From the moment the attributes of the Deity are supposed finite, all these have place. And I cannot, for my part, think that so wild and unsettled a system of theology is, in any respect, preferable to none at all.

These suppositions I absolutely disown, cried Cleanthes: they strike me, however, with no horror, especially when proposed in that rambling way in which they drop from you. On the contrary, they give me pleasure when I see that, by the utmost indulgence of your imagination, you never get rid of the hypothesis of design in the universe, but are obliged at every turn to have recourse to it. To this concession I adhere steadily; and this I regard as a sufficient foundation for religion.

PART VI

It must be a slight fabric, indeed, said Demea, which can be erected on so tottering a foundation. While we are uncertain whether there is one deity or many, whether the deity or deities, to whom we owe our existence, be perfect or imperfect, subordinate or supreme, dead or alive, what trust or confidence can we repose in them? What devotion or worship address to them? What veneration or obedience pay them? To all the purposes of life the theory of religion becomes altogether useless; and even with regard to speculative consequences its uncertainty, according to you, must render it totally precarious and unsatisfactory.

To render it still more unsatisfactory, said Philo, there occurs to me another hypothesis which must acquire an air of probability from the method of reasoning so much insisted on by Cleanthes. That like effects arise from like causes—this principle he supposes the foundation of all religion. But there is another principle of the same kind, no less certain and derived from the same source of experience, that, where several known circumstances are observed to be similar, the unknown will also be found similar. Thus, if we see the limbs of a human body, we conclude that it is also attended with a human head, though hid from us. Thus, if we see, through a chink in a wall, a small part of the sun, we conclude that were the wall removed we should see the whole body. In short, this method of reasoning is so obvious and familiar that no scruple can ever be made with regard to its solidity.

Now, if we survey the universe, so far as it falls under our knowledge, it bears a great resemblance to an animal or organized body, and seems actuated with a like principle of life and motion. A continual circulation of matter in it produces no disorder; a continual waste in every part is incessantly repaired; the closest sympathy is perceived throughout the entire system; and each part or member, in performing its proper offices, operates both to its own preservation and to that of the whole. The world, therefore, I infer, is an animal; and the Deity is the *soul* of the world, actuating it, and actuated by it. . . .

This theory, I own, replied Cleanthes, has never before occurred to me, though a pretty natural one; and I cannot readily, upon so short an examination and reflection, deliver any opinion with regard to it. You are very scrupulous, indeed, said Philo; were I to examine any system of yours, I should not have acted with half that caution and reserve, in starting objections and difficulties to it. However, if anything occur to you, you will oblige us by proposing it.

Why then, replied Cleanthes, it seems to me that, though the world does, in many circumstances, resemble an animal body, yet is the analogy also defective in many circumstances the most material: no organs of sense, no seat of thought or reason; no one precise origin of motion and action. In short, it seems to bear a stronger resemblance to a vegetable than to an animal, and your inference would be so far inconclusive in favor of the soul of the world. . . .

PART VII

But here, continued Philo, in examining the ancient system of the soul of the world there strikes me, all of a sudden, a new idea which, if just, must go near to subvert all your reasoning, and destroy even your first inferences on which you repose such confidence. If the universe bears a greater likeness to animal bodies and to vegetables than to the works of human art, it is more probable that its cause resembles the cause of the former than that of the latter, and its origin ought rather to be ascribed to generation or vegetation than to reason or design. Your conclusion, even according to your own principles, is therefore lame and defective.

Pray open up this argument a little further, said Demea, for I do not rightly apprehend it in that concise manner in which you have expressed it.

Our friend Cleanthes, replied Philo, as you have heard, asserts that since no question of fact can be proved otherwise than by experience, the existence of a Deity admits not of proof from any other medium. The world, says he, resembles the works of human contrivance; therefore its cause must also resemble that of the other. Here we may remark that the operation of one very small part of nature, to wit, man, upon another very small part, to wit, that inanimate matter lying within his reach, is the rule by which Cleanthes judges of the origin of the whole; and he measures objects, so widely disproportioned, by the same individual standard. But to waive all objections drawn from this topic, I affirm that there are other parts of the universe (besides the machines of human invention) which bear still a greater resemblance to the fabric of the world, and which, therefore, afford a better conjecture concerning the universal origin of this system. These parts are animals and vegetables. The world plainly resembles more an animal or a vegetable than it does a watch or a knitting loom. Its cause, therefore, it is more probable, resembles the cause of the former. The cause of the former is generation or vegetation. The cause, therefore, of the world we may infer to be something similar or analogous to generation or vegetation.

But how is it conceivable, said Demea, that the world can arise from anything similar to vegetation or generation?

Very easily, replied Philo. In like manner as a tree sheds its seed into the neighboring fields and produces other trees; so the great vegetable, the world, or this planetary system, produces within itself certain seeds which, being scattered into the surrounding chaos, vegetate into new worlds. A comet, for instance, is the seed of a world; and after it has been fully ripened, by passing from sun to sun, and star to star, it is at last tossed into the unformed elements which everywhere surround this universe, and immediately sprouts up into a new system.

Or if, for the sake of variety (for I see no other advantage) we should suppose this world to be an animal; a comet is the egg of this animal; and in like manner as an ostrich lays its egg in the sand, which, without any further care, hatches the egg and produces a new animal, so . . . I understand you, says Demea: But what wild, arbitrary suppositions are these? What *data* have you for such extraordinary conclusions? And is the slight, imaginary resemblance of the world to a vegetable or an animal sufficient to establish the same inference with regard to both? Objects which are in general so widely different; ought they to be a standard for each other?

Right, cries Philo: This is the topic on which I have all along insisted. I have still asserted that we have no *data* to establish any system of cosmogony. Our experience, so imperfect in itself and so limited both in extent and duration, can afford us no probable conjecture concerning the whole of things. But if we must need fix on some hypothesis, by what rule, pray, ought we to determine our choice? Is there any other rule than the great similarity of the objects compared? And does not a plant or an animal, which springs from vegetation or generation, bear a stronger resemblance to the world than does any artificial machine, which arises from reason and design?

But what is this vegetation and generation of which you talk? said Demea. Can you explain their operations and anatomize that fine internal structure on which they depend?

As much, at least, replied Philo, as Cleanthes can explain the operations of reason, or anatomize that internal structure on which *it* depends. But without any such elaborate disquisitions, when I see an animal, I infer that it sprang from generation; and that with as great certainty as you conclude a house to have been reared by design. These words *generation, reason* mark only certain powers and energies in nature whose effects are known, but whose essence is incomprehensible; and one of these principles, more than the other, has no privilege for being made a standard to the whole of nature.

In reality, Demea, it may reasonably be expected that the larger the views are which we take of things, the better will they conduct us in our conclusions concerning such extraordinary and such magnificent subjects. In this little corner of the world alone, there are four principles, *reason, instinct, generation, vegetation*, which are similar to each other, and are the causes of similar effects. What a number of other principles may we naturally suppose in the immense extent and variety of the universe could we travel from planet to planet, and from system to system, in order to examine each part of this mighty fabric? Any one of these four principles above mentioned (and a hundred others which lie open to our conjecture) may afford us a theory by which to judge of the origin of the world; and it is a palpable and egregious partiality to confine our view entirely to that principle by which our own minds operate. Were this principle more intelligible on that account, such a partiality might be somewhat excusable; but reason, in its internal fabric and structure, is really as little known to us as instinct or vegetation; and, perhaps, even that vague, undeterminate word *nature* to which the vulgar refer everything is not at the bottom more inexplicable. The effects of these principles are all known to us from experience; but the principles themselves and their manner of operation are totally unknown; nor is it less intelligible or less conformable to experience to say that the world arose by vegetation, from a seed shed by another world, than to say that it arose from a divine reason or contrivance, according to the sense in which Cleanthes understands it.

But methinks, said Demea, if the world had a vegetative quality and could sow the seeds of new worlds into the infinite chaos, this power would be still an additional argument for design in its author. For whence could arise so wonderful a faculty but from design? Or how can order spring from anything which perceives not that order which it bestows?

You need only look around you, replied Philo, to satisfy yourself with regard to this question. A tree bestows order and organization on that tree which springs from it, without knowing the order; an animal in the same manner on its offspring; a bird on its nest; and instances of this kind are even more frequent in the world than those of order which arise from reason and contrivance. To say that all this order in animals and vegetables proceeds ultimately from design is begging the question; nor can that great point be ascertained otherwise than by proving, a priori, both that order is, from its nature, inseparably attached to thought and that it can never of itself or from original unknown principles belong to matter. . . .

PART X

It is my opinion, I own, replied Demea, that each man feels, in a manner, the truth of religion within his own breast, and, from a consciousness of his imbecility and misery rather than from any reasoning, is led to seek protection from that Being on whom he and all nature is dependent. So anxious or so tedious are even the best scenes of life that futurity is still the object of all our hopes and fears. We incessantly look forward and endeavour, by prayers, adoration, and sacrifice, to appease those unknown powers whom we find, by experience, so able to afflict and oppress us. Wretched creatures that we are! What resource for us amidst the innumerable ills of life did not religion suggest some methods of atonement, and appease those terrors with which we are incessantly agitated and tormented?

I am indeed persuaded, said Philo, that the best and indeed the only method of bringing everyone to a due sense of religion is by just representations of the misery and wickedness of men. And for that purpose a talent of eloquence and strong imagery is more requisite than that of reasoning and argument. For is it necessary to prove what everyone feels within himself? It is only necessary to make us feel it, if possible, more intimately and sensibly.

The people, indeed, replied Demea, are sufficiently convinced of this great and melancholy truth. The miseries of life, the unhappiness of man, the general corruptions of our nature, the unsatisfactory enjoyment of pleasures, riches, honours—these phrases have become almost proverbial in all languages. And who can doubt what all men declare from their own immediate feeling and experience?

In this point, said Philo, the learned are perfectly agreed with the vulgar; and in all letters, *sacred* and *profane*, the topic of human misery has been insisted on with the most pathetic eloquence that sorrow and melancholy could inspire. The poets, who speak from sentiment, without a system, and whose testimony has therefore the more authority, abound in images of this nature. From Homer down to Dr. Young[4] the whole inspired tribe have ever been sensible that no other representation of things would suit the feeling and observation of each individual.

As to authorities, replied Demea, you need not seek them. Look round this library of Cleanthes. I shall venture to affirm that, except authors of particular sciences, such as chemistry or botany, who have no occasion to treat of human life, there is scarce one of those innumerable writers from whom the sense of human misery has not, in some passage or other, extorted a complaint and confession of it. At least, the chance is entirely on that side; and no one author has ever, so far as I can recollect, been so extravagant as to deny it.

There you must excuse me, said Philo: Leibniz[5] has denied it and is perhaps the first who ventured upon so bold and paradoxical an opinion; at least, the first who made it essential to his philosophical system.

And by being the first, replied Demea, might he not have been sensible of his error? For is this a subject in which philosophers can propose to make discoveries especially in so late an age? And can any man hope by a simple denial (for the subject scarcely admits of reasoning) to bear down the united testimony of mankind, founded on sense and consciousness?

And why should man, added he, pretend to an exemption from the lot of all other animals? The whole earth, believe me, Philo, is cursed and polluted. A perpetual war is kindled amongst all living creatures. Necessity, hunger, want stimulate the strong and courageous; fear, anxiety, terror agitate the weak and infirm. The first entrance into life gives anguish to the new-born infant and to its wretched parent; weakness, impotence, distress attend each stage of that life, and it is, at last finished in agony and horror.

Observe, too, says Philo, the curious artifices of nature in order to embitter the life of every living being. The stronger prey upon the weaker and keep them in perpetual terror and anxiety. The weaker, too, in their turn, often prey upon the stronger, and vex and molest them without relaxation. Consider that innumerable race of insects, which either are bred on the body of each animal or, flying about, infix their stings in him. These insects have others still less than themselves which torment them. And thus on each hand, before and behind, above and below, every animal is surrounded with enemies which incessantly seek his misery and destruction.

Man alone, said Demea, seems to be, in part, an exception to this rule. For by combination in society he can easily master lions, tigers, and bears, whose greater strength and agility naturally enable them to prey upon him.

On the contrary, it is here chiefly, cried Philo, that the uniform and equal maxims of nature are most apparent. Man, it is true, can, by combination, surmount all his *real* enemies and become master of the whole animal creation; but does he not immediately raise up to himself *imaginary* enemies, the demons of his fancy, who haunt him with superstitious terrors and blast every enjoyment of life? His pleasure, as he imagines, becomes in their eyes a crime; his food and repose give them umbrage and offence; his very sleep and dreams furnish new materials to anxious fear; and even death, his refuge from every other ill, presents only the dread of endless and innumerable woes. Nor does the wolf molest more the timid flock than superstition does the anxious breast of wretched mortals.

Besides, consider, Demea: This very society by which we surmount those wild beasts, our natural enemies, what new enemies does it not raise to us? What woe and misery does it not occasion? Man is the greatest enemy of man. Oppression, injustice, contempt, contumely, violence, sedition, war, calumny, treachery, fraud—by these they mutually torment each other, and they would soon dissolve that society which they had formed were it not for the dread of still greater ills which must attend their separation.

But though these external insults, said Demea, from animals, from men, from all the elements, which assault us from a frightful catalogue of woes, they are nothing in comparison of those which arise within ourselves, from the distempered condition of our mind and body. How many lie under the lingering torment of diseases? . . .

The disorders of the mind, continued Demea, though more secret, are not perhaps less dismal and vexatious. Remorse, shame, anguish, rage, disappointment, anxiety, fear, dejection, despair—who has ever passed through life without cruel inroads from these tormentors? How many have scarcely ever felt any better sensations? Labour and poverty, so abhorred by everyone, are the certain lot of the far greater number; and those few privileged persons who enjoy ease and opulence never reach contentment or true felicity. All the goods of life united would not make a very happy man, but all the ills united would make a wretch indeed, and any one of them almost (and who can be free from every one?), nay, often the absence of one good (and who can possess all?) is sufficient to render life ineligible.

Were a stranger to drop on a sudden into this world, I would show him, as a specimen of its ills, an hospital full of diseases, a prison crowded with malefactors and debtors, a field of battle strewed with carcases, a fleet floundering in the ocean, a nation languishing under tyranny, famine, or pestilence. To turn the gay side of life to him and give him a notion of its pleasures—whither should I conduct him?

To a ball, to an opera, to court? He might justly think that I was only showing him a diversity of distress and sorrow.

There is no evading such striking instances, said Philo, but by apologies which still further aggravate the charge. Why have all men, I ask, in all ages, complained incessantly of the miseries of life? . . . They have no just reason, says one: these complaints proceed only from their discontented, repining, anxious disposition. . . . And can there possibly, I reply, be a more certain foundation of misery than such a wretched temper?

But if they were really as unhappy as they pretend, says my antagonist, why do they remain in life? . . .

Not satisfied with life, afraid of death—

This is the secret chain, say I, that holds us. We are terrified, not bribed to the continuance of our existence.

It is only a false delicacy, he may insist, which a few refined spirits indulge, and which has spread these complaints among the whole race of mankind. . . . And what is this delicacy, I ask, which you blame? Is it anything but a greater sensibility to all the pleasures and pains of life? And if the man of a delicate, refined temper, by being so much more alive than the rest of the world, is only so much more unhappy, what judgment must we form in general of human life?

Let men remain at rest, says our adversary, and they will be easy. They are willing artificers of their own misery. . . . No! reply I: an anxious languor follows their repose: disappointment, vexation, trouble, their activity and ambition.

I can observe something like what you mention in some others, replied Cleanthes, but I confess I feel little or nothing of it in myself, and hope that it is not so common as you represent it.

If you feel not human misery yourself, cried Demea, I congratulate you on so happy a singularity. Others, seemingly the most prosperous, have not been ashamed to vent their complaints in the most melancholy strains. Let us attend to the great, the fortunate emperor, Charles V,[6] when tired with human grandeur, he resigned all his extensive dominions into the hands of his son. In the last harangue which he made on that memorable occasion, he publicly avowed *that the greatest prosperities which he had ever enjoyed had been mixed with so many adversities that he might truly say he had never enjoyed any satisfaction or contentment.* But did the retired life in which he sought for shelter afford him any greater happiness? If we may credit his son's account, his repentance commenced the very day of his resignation.

Cicero's[7] fortune, from small beginnings, rose to the greatest luster and renown; yet what pathetic complaints of the ills of life do his familiar letters, as well as philosophical discourses, contain? And suitably to his own experience, he introduces Cato,[8] the great, the fortunate Cato protesting in his old age that had he a new life in his offer he would reject the present.

Ask yourself, ask any of your acquaintance, whether they would live over again the last ten or twenty years of their life. No! but the next twenty, they say, will be better. . . .

Thus, at last, they find (such is the greatness of human misery, it reconciles even contradictions) that they complain at once of the shortness of life and of its vanity and sorrow.

And is it possible, Cleanthes, said Philo, that after all these reflections, and infinitely more which might be suggested, you can still perservere in your anthropomorphism and assert the moral attributes of the Deity, his justice, benevolence, mercy, and rectitude to be of the same nature with these virtues in human creatures? His power, we allow, is infinite; whatever he wills is executed; but neither man nor any other animal is happy; therefore, he does not will their happiness. His wisdom is infinite; he is never mistaken in choosing the means to any end; but the course of nature tends not to human or animal felicity; therefore, it is not established for that purpose. Through the whole compass of human knowledge there are no inferences more certain and infallible than these. In what respect, then, do his benevolence and mercy resemble the benevolence and mercy of men?

Epicurus' old questions are yet unanswered.

Is he willing to prevent evil, but not able? then is he impotent. Is he able, but not willing? then is he malevolent. Is he both able and willing? whence then is evil?

You ascribe, Cleanthes (and I believe justly), a purpose and intention to nature. But what, I beseech you, is the object of that curious artifice and machinery which she has displayed in all animals—the preservation alone of individuals, and propagation of the species? It seems enough for her purpose, if such a rank be barely upheld in the universe, without any care or concern for the happiness of the members that compose it. No resource for this purpose: no machinery in order merely to give pleasure or ease; no fund of pure joy and contentment; no indulgence without some want or necessity accompanying it. At least, the few phenomena of this nature are over-balanced by opposite phenomena of still greater importance.

Our sense of music, harmony, and indeed beauty of all kinds gives satisfaction, without being absolutely necessary to the preservation and propagation of the species. But what racking pains, on the other hand, arise from gouts, gravels, megrims, toothaches, rheumatisms, where the injury to the animal machinery is either small or incurable? Mirth, laughter, play, frolic seem gratuitous satisfactions which have no further tendency; spleen, melancholy, discontent, superstition are pains of the same nature. How then does the Divine benevolence display itself, in the sense of you anthropomorphites? None but we mystics, as you were pleased to call us, can account for this strange mixture of phenomena, by deriving it from attributes infinitely perfect but incomprehensible.

And have you, at last, said Cleanthes smiling, betrayed your intentions, Philo? Your long agreement with Demea did indeed a little surprise me, but I find you were all the while erecting a concealed battery against me. And I must confess that you have now fallen upon a subject worthy of your noble spirit of opposition and controversy. If you can make out the present point, and prove mankind to be unhappy or corrupted, there is an end at once of all religion. For to what purpose establish the natural attributes of the Deity, while the moral are still doubtful and uncertain?

You take umbrage very easily, replied Demea, at opinions the most innocent and the most generally received, even amongst the religious and devout themselves; and nothing can be more surprising than to find a topic like this—concerning the wickedness and misery of man—charged with no less than atheism and profaneness. Have not all pious divines and preachers who have indulged their rhetoric on so fertile a subject, have they not easily, I say, given a solution of any difficulties which may attend it? This world is but a point in comparison of the universe, this life but a moment in comparison of eternity. The present evil phenomena, therefore, are rectified in other regions, and in some future period of existence. And the eyes of men, being then opened to larger views of things, see the whole connection of general laws, and trace, with adoration, the benevolence and rectitude of the Deity through all the mazes and intricacies of his providence.

No! replied Cleanthes, no! These arbitrary suppositions can never be admitted, contrary to matter of fact, visible and uncontroverted. Whence can any cause be known but from its known effects? Whence can any hypothesis be proved but from the apparent phenomena? To establish one hypothesis upon another is building entirely in the air; and the utmost we ever attain by these conjectures and fictions is to ascertain the bare possibility of our opinion, but never can we, upon such terms, establish its reality.

The only method of supporting Divine benevolence—and it is what I willingly embrace—is to deny absolutely the misery and wickedness of man. Your representations are exaggerated; your melancholy views mostly fictitious; your inferences contrary to fact and experience. Health is more common than sickness; pleasure than pain; happiness than misery. And for one vexation which we meet with, we attain, upon computation, a hundred enjoyments.

Admitting your position, replied Philo, which yet is extremely doubtful, you must at the same time allow that, if pain be less frequent than pleasure, it is infinitely more violent and durable. One hour of it is often able to outweigh a day, a week, a month of our common insipid enjoyments; and how many days, weeks, and months are passed by several in the most acute torments? Pleasure, scarcely in one instance, is ever able to reach ecstasy and rapture; and in no one instance can it continue for any time at its highest pitch and altitude. The spirits evaporate, the nerves relax, the fabric is disordered, and the enjoyment quickly degenerates into fatigue and uneasiness. But pain often, good God, how often! rises to torture and agony; and the longer it continues, it becomes still more genuine agony and torture. Patience is exhausted, courage languishes, melancholy seizes us, and nothing terminates our misery but the removal of its cause or another event which is the sole cure of all evil, but which, from our natural folly, we regard with still greater horror and consternation.

But not to insist upon these topics, continued Philo, though most obvious, certain, and important, I must use the freedom to admonish you, Cleanthes, that you have put the controversy upon a most dangerous issue, and are unawares introducing a total scepticism into the most essential articles of natural and revealed theology. What! no method of fixing a just foundation for religion unless we allow the happiness of human life, and maintain a continued existence even in this world, with all our present pains, infirmities, vexations, and follies, to be eligible and desirable! But this is contrary to everyone's feeling and experience; it is contrary to an authority so established as nothing can subvert. No decisive proofs can ever be produced against this authority; nor is it possible for you to compute, estimate, and compare all the pains and all the pleasures in the lives of all men and of all animals; and thus, by your resting the whole system of religion on a point which, from its very nature, must for ever be uncertain, you tacitly confess that that system is equally uncertain.

But allowing you what never will be believed, at least, what you never possibly can prove, that animal or, at least, human happiness in this life exceeds its misery, you have yet done nothing; for this is not, by any means, what we expect from infinite power, infinite wisdom, and infinite goodness. Why is there any misery at all in the world? Not by chance, surely. From some cause then. Is it from the intention of the Deity? But he is perfectly benevolent. Is it contrary to his intention? But he is almighty. Nothing can shake the solidity of this reasoning, so short, so clear, so decisive, except we assert that these subjects exceed all human capacity and that our common measures of truth and falsehood are not applicable to them—a topic which I have all along insisted on, but which you have, from the beginning, rejected with scorn and indignation.

But I will be contented to retire still from this entrenchment, for I deny that you can ever force me in it. I will allow that pain or misery in man is *compatible* with infinite power and goodness in the Deity, even in your sense of these attributes: what are you advanced by all these concessions? A mere possible compatibility is not sufficient. You must *prove* these pure, unmixed, and uncontrollable attributes from the present mixed and confused phenomena, and from these alone. A hopeful undertaking! Were the phenomena ever so pure and unmixed, yet, being finite, they would be insufficient for that purpose. How much more, where they are also so jarring and discordant!

Here, Cleanthes, I find myself at ease in my argument. Here I triumph. Formerly, when we argued concerning the natural attributes of intelligence and design, I needed all my sceptical and metaphysical subtlety to elude your grasp. In many views of the universe and of its parts, particularly the latter, the beauty and fitness of final causes strike us with such irresistible force that all objections appear (what I believe they really are) mere cavils and sophisms; nor can we then imagine how it was ever possible for us to repose any weight on them. But there is no view of human life or of the condition of mankind from which, without the greatest violence, we can infer the moral attributes or learn that infinite benevolence, conjoined with infinite power and infinite wisdom, which we must discover by the eyes of faith alone. It is your turn now to tug the labouring oar, and to support your philosophical subtleties against the dictates of plain reason and experience.

NOTES

1. [Conventional names of ordinary persons, such as Smith and Jones.—S.M.C.]
2. [Simonides of Ceos (c. 548–468 B.C.) was a Greek poet.]

3. [The reference is to Hiero I, a fifth-century B.C. ruler of Syracuse, noted as a patron of literature.]
4. [The reference is to Edward Young (1683–1765), an English poet.]
5. [The reference is to the renowned German philosopher Gottfried Wilhelm Leibniz (1646–1716).]
6. [Charles V (1500–1588) was king of Spain for forty years.]
7. [Marcus Tullius Cicero (106–43 B.C.), the statesman and philosopher, was considered the greatest Roman orator.]
8. [The reference is to Marcus Porcius Cato the Elder (234–149 B.C.), a Roman statesman.]

STUDY QUESTIONS

1. In what ways is the world similar to a machine, and in what ways dissimilar?
2. Does the nature of the world give evidence suggesting more strongly one creator or many creators?
3. If you would not be willing to live over again the last ten years of your life, does that reluctance amount to evidence against theism?
4. At what point in the argument does Philo declare, "Here I triumph"?

The Wager

BLAISE PASCAL

> Here, translated from the original French, is the passage in which Blaise Pascal presents his much-discussed wager, examined in previous selections by Simon Blackburn and Linda Zagzebski.

If there is a God, he is infinitely beyond our comprehension, since, having neither parts nor limits, he bears no relation to ourselves. We are therefore incapable of knowing either what he is, or if he is. That being so, who will dare to undertake a resolution of this question? It cannot be us, who bear no relationship to him.

Who will then blame the Christians for being unable to provide a rational basis for their belief, they who profess a religion for which they cannot provide a rational basis? They declare that it is a folly (1 Cor. 1: 18) in laying it before the world: and then you complain that they do not prove it! If they did prove it, they

---

From Blaise Pascal, *Pensées*, trans. Honor Levi. Reprinted by permission of Oxford University Press.

would not be keeping their word. It is by the lack of proof that they do not lack sense. "Yes, but although that excuses those who offer their religion as it is, and that takes away the blame from them of producing it without a rational basis, it does not excuse those who accept it."

Let us therefore examine this point, and say: God is, or is not. But towards which side will we lean? Reason cannot decide anything. There is an infinite chaos separating us. At the far end of this infinite distance a game is being played and the coin will come down heads or tails. How will you wager? Reason cannot make you choose one way or the other, reason cannot make you defend either of the two choices.

So do not accuse those who have made a choice of being wrong, for you know nothing about it! "No, but I will blame them not for having made this choice, but for having made any choice. For, though the one who chooses heads and the other one are equally wrong, they are both wrong. The right thing is not to wager at all."

Yes, but you have to wager. It is not up to you, you are already committed. Which then will you choose? Let us see. Since you have to choose, let us see which interests you the least. You have two things to lose: the truth and the good, and two things to stake: your reason and will, your knowledge and beatitude; and your nature has two things to avoid: error and wretchedness. Your reason is not hurt more by choosing one rather than the other, since you do have to make the choice. That is one point disposed of. But your beatitude? Let us weigh up the gain and the loss by calling heads that God exists. Let us assess the two cases: if you win, you win everything; if you lose, you lose nothing. Wager that he exists then, without hesitating! "This is wonderful. Yes, I must wager. But perhaps I am betting too much." Let us see. Since there is an equal chance of gain and loss, if you won only two lives instead of one, you could still put on a bet. But if there were three lives to win, you would have to play (since you must necessarily play), and you would be unwise, once forced to play, not to chance your life to win three in a game where there is an equal chance of losing and winning. But there is an eternity of life and happiness. And that being so, even though there were an infinite number of chances of which only one were in your favour, you would still be right to wager one in order to win two, and you would be acting wrongly, since you are obliged to play, by refusing to stake one life against three in a game where out of an infinite number of chances there is one in your favour, if there were an infinitely happy infinity of life to be won. But here there is an infinitely happy infinity of life to be won, one chance of winning against a finite number of chances of losing, and what you are staking is finite. That removes all choice: wherever there is infinity and where there is no infinity of chances of losing against one of winning, there is no scope for wavering, you have to chance everything. And thus, as you are forced to gamble, you have to have discarded reason if you cling on to your life, rather than risk it for the infinite prize which is just as likely to happen as the loss of nothingness.

For it is no good saying that it is uncertain if you will win, that it is certain you are taking a risk, and that the infinite distance between the *certainty* of what you are risking and the *uncertainty* of whether you win makes the finite good of what you are certainly risking equal to the uncertainty of the infinite. It does not work like that. Every gambler takes a certain risk for an uncertain gain; nevertheless he certainly risks the finite uncertainty in order to win a finite gain, without sinning against reason. There is no infinite distance between this certainty of what is being risked and the uncertainty of what might be gained: that is untrue. There is, indeed, an infinite distance between the certainty of winning and the certainty of losing. But the uncertainty of winning is proportional to the certainty of the risk, according to the chances of winning or losing. And hence, if there are as many chances on one side as on the other, the odds are even, and then the certainty of what you risk is equal to the uncertainty of winning. It is very far from being infinitely distant from it. So our argument is infinitely strong, when the finite is at stake in a game where there are equal chances of winning and losing, and the infinite is to be won.

That is conclusive, and, if human beings are capable of understanding any truth at all, this is the one.

"I confess it, I admit it, but even so . . . Is there no way of seeing underneath the cards?" "Yes, Scripture and the rest, etc." "Yes, but my hands are tied and I cannot speak a word. I am being forced to wager and I am not free, they will not let me go. And I am made in such a way that I cannot believe. So what do you want me to do?" "That is true. But at least realize that your inability to believe, since reason urges you to do so and yet you cannot, arises from your passions. So concentrate not on convincing yourself by increasing the number of proofs of God but on diminishing your passions. You want to find faith and you do not know the way? You want to cure yourself of unbelief and you ask for the remedies? Learn from those who have been bound like you, and who now wager all they have. They are people who know the road you want to follow and have been cured of the affliction of which you want to be cured. Follow the way by which they began: by behaving just as if they believed, taking holy water, having masses said, etc. That will make you believe quite naturally, and according to your animal reactions." "But that is what I am afraid of." "Why? What do you have to lose?"

STUDY QUESTIONS

1. If God is, as Pascal declares, "infinitely beyond our comprehension," does this admission undermine his subsequent argument?
2. Is believing in God for the reasons Pascal offers a legitimate basis for religious commitment?
3. If you follow Pascal's advice and engage in Christian rituals, are you more likely to accept Christian beliefs?
4. Might God reward thoughtful unbelievers for having the strength of their convictions?

Natural Theology

WILLIAM PALEY

William Paley (1743–1805) was an English theologian and moral philosopher. He gives a classic presentation of another argument for the existence of God, the so-called teleological argument or argument to design. This argument proceeds from the premise of the world's magnificent order to the conclusion that the world must be the work of a Supreme Mind responsible for this order.

CHAPTER I: THE STATE OF THE ARGUMENT

In crossing a heath, suppose I pitched my foot against a stone and were asked how the stone came to be there. I might possibly answer that for anything I knew to the contrary it had lain there forever; nor would it, perhaps, be very easy to show the absurdity of this answer. But suppose I had found a watch upon the ground, and it should be inquired how the watch happened to be in that place. I should hardly think of the answer which I had before given, that for anything I knew the watch might have always been there. Yet why should not this answer serve for the watch as well as for the stone? Why is it not as admissible in the second case as in the first? For this reason, and for no other, namely, that when we come to inspect the watch, we perceive—what we could not discover in the stone—that its several parts are framed and put together for a purpose, e.g., that they are so formed and adjusted as to produce motion, and that motion so regulated as to point out the hour of the day; that if the different parts had been differently shaped from what they are, of a different size from what they are, or placed after any other manner or in any other order than that in which they are placed, either no motion at all would have been carried on in the machine, or none which would have answered the use that is now served by it. To reckon up a few of the plainest of these parts and of their offices, all tending to one result; we see a cylindrical box containing a coiled elastic spring, which, by its endeavor to relax itself, turns round the box. We next observe a flexible chain—artificially wrought for the sake of flexure—communicating the action of the spring from the box to the fusee. We then find a series of wheels, the teeth of which catch in and apply to each other, conducting the motion from the fusee to the balance and from the balance to the pointer, and at the same time, by the size and shape

From William Paley, *Natural Theology* (1802).

of those wheels, so regulating that motion as to terminate in causing an index, by an equable and measured progression, to pass over a given space in a given time. We take notice that the wheels are made of brass, in order to keep them from rust; the springs of steel, no other metal being so elastic; that over the face of the watch there is placed a glass, a material employed in no other part of the work, but in the room of which, if there had been any other than a transparent substance, the hour could not be seen without opening the case. This mechanism being observed—it requires indeed an examination of the instrument, and perhaps some previous knowledge of the subject, to perceive and understand it; but being once, as we have said, observed and understood—the inference we think is inevitable, that the watch must have had a maker—that there must have existed, at some time and at some place or other, an artificer or artificers who formed it for the purpose which we find it actually to answer, who comprehended its construction and designed its use.

I. Nor would it, I apprehend, weaken the conclusion, that we had never seen a watch made—that we had never known an artist capable of making one—that we were altogether incapable of executing such a piece of workmanship ourselves, or of understanding in what manner it was performed; all this being no more than what is true of some exquisite remains of ancient art, of some lost arts, and, to the generality of mankind, of the more curious productions of modern manufacture. Does one man in a million know how oval frames are turned? Ignorance of this kind exalts our opinion of the unseen and unknown artist's skill, if he is unseen and unknown, but raises no doubt in our minds of the existence and agency of such an artist, at some former time and in some place or other. Nor can I perceive that it varies at all the inference, whether the question arises concerning a human agent or concerning an agent of a different species, or an agent possessing in some respects a different nature.

II. Neither, secondly, would it invalidate our conclusion, that the watch sometimes went wrong or that it seldom went exactly right. The purpose of the machinery, the design, and the designer might be evident, and in the case supposed, would be evident, in whatever way we accounted for the irregularity of the movement, or whether we could account for it or not. It is not necessary that a machine be perfect in order to show with what design it was made: still less necessary, where the only question is whether it were made with any design at all.

III. Nor, thirdly, would it bring any uncertainty into the argument, if there were a few parts of the watch, concerning which we could not discover or had not yet discovered in what manner they conduced to the general effect; or even some parts, concerning which we could not ascertain whether they conduced to that effect in any manner whatever. For, as to the first branch of the case, if by the loss, or disorder, or decay of the parts in question, the movement of the watch were found in fact to be stopped, or disturbed, or retarded, no doubt would remain in our minds as to the utility or intention of these parts, although we should be unable to investigate the manner according to which, or the connection by which, the ultimate effect depended upon their action or assistance; and the more complex is the machine, the more likely is this obscurity to arise. Then, as to the second thing supposed, namely, that there were parts which might be spared without prejudice to the movement of the watch, and that we had proved this by experiment, these superfluous parts, even if we were completely assured that they were such, would not vacate the reasoning which we had instituted concerning other parts. The indication of contrivance remained, with respect to them, nearly as it was before.

IV. Nor, fourthly, would any man in his senses think the existence of the watch with its various machinery accounted for, by being told that it was one out of possible combinations of material forms; that whatever he had found in the place where he found the watch must have contained some internal configuration or other; and that this configuration might be the structure now exhibited, namely, of the works of a watch, as well as a different structure.

V. Nor, fifthly, would it yield his inquiry more satisfaction, to be answered that there existed in things a principle of order, which had disposed the parts of the watch into their present form and situation. He never knew a watch made by the principle of order; nor can he even form to himself an idea of what is meant by a principle of order distinct from the intelligence of the watchmaker.

VI. Sixthly, he would be surprised to hear that the mechanism of the watch was no proof of contrivance, only a motive to induce the mind to think so:

VII. And not less surprised to be informed that the watch in his hand was nothing more than the result of the laws of *metallic* nature. It is a perversion of language to assign any law as the efficient, operative cause of any thing. A law presupposes an agent, for it is only the mode according to which an agent proceeds; it implies a power, for it is the order according to which that power acts. Without this agent, without this power, which are both distinct from itself, the *law* does nothing, is nothing. The expression, "the law of metallic nature," may sound strange and harsh to a philosophic ear; but it seems quite as justifiable as some others which are more familiar to him, such as "the law of vegetable nature," "the law of animal nature," or, indeed, "the law of nature" in general, when assigned as the cause of phenomena, in exclusion of agency and power, or when it is substituted into the place of these.

VIII. Neither, lastly, would our observer be driven out of his conclusion or from his confidence in its truth by being told that he knew nothing at all about the matter. He knows enough for his argument; he knows the utility of the end; he knows the subserviency and adaptation of the means to the end. These points being known, his ignorance of other points, his doubts concerning other points affect not the certainty of his reasoning. The consciousness of knowing little need not beget a distrust of that which he does know. . . .

CHAPTER III: APPLICATION OF THE ARGUMENT

. . . Every indication of contrivance, every manifestation of design, which existed in the watch, exists in the works of nature; with the difference, on the side of nature, of being greater and more, and that in a degree which exceeds all computation. I mean that the contrivances of nature surpass the contrivances of art in the complexity, subtility, and curiosity of the mechanism; and still more, if possible, do they go beyond them in number and variety; yet, in a multitude of cases, are not less evidently mechanical, not less evidently contrivances, not less evidently accommodated to their end, or suited to their office, than are the most perfect productions of human ingenuity. . . .

I know no better method of introducing so large a subject than that of comparing a single thing with a single thing; an eye, for example, with a telescope. As far as the examination of the instrument goes, there is precisely the same proof that the eye was made for vision, as there is that the telescope was made for assisting it. They are made upon the same principles, both being adjusted to the laws by which the transmission and reflection of rays of light are regulated. I speak not of the origin of the laws themselves; but such laws being fixed, the construction, in both cases, is adapted to them. For instance, these laws require, in order to produce the same effect, that the rays of light, in passing from water into the eye, should be refracted by a more convex surface than when it passes out of air into the eye. Accordingly we find, that the eye of a fish, in that part of it called the crystalline lens, is much rounder than the eye of terrestrial animals. What plainer manifestation of design can there be than this difference? What could a mathematical instrument-maker have done more, to show his knowledge of his principle, his application of that knowledge, his suiting of his means to his end; I will not say to display the compass or excellence of his skill and art, for in these all comparison is indecorous, but to testify counsel, choice, consideration, purpose?

STUDY QUESTIONS

1. In what circumstances might it appear that a stone was designed?
2. Does it seem that dinosaurs were designed?
3. How would you know if something was designed, but badly?
4. Do the evils of the world suggest that it was designed?

The Will to Believe

WILLIAM JAMES

William James, whose work we read previously, contends that when you face an important choice between two appealing options and cannot wait for further evidence, you are justified in believing and acting as your passion decides. According to James, we should not allow the fear of holding a false belief to prevent us from losing the benefits of believing what may be true.

James asserts that the essence of religion is contained in two fundamental claims: (1) the best things are the more eternal things, and (2) we are better off if we believe (1). Note that in a footnote he says that "if the action required or inspired by the religious hypothesis is in no way different from that dictated by the naturalistic hypothesis, then religious faith is a pure superfluity, better pruned away, and controversy about its legitimacy is a piece of idle trifling, unworthy of serious minds." An intriguing question is whether believing in (1) and (2), which James considers the core of the religious attitude, requires different action than rejecting (1) and (2).

In the recently published *Life* by Leslie Stephen[1] of his brother, Fitz-James,[2] there is an account of a school to which the latter went when he was a boy. The teacher, a certain Mr. Guest, used to converse with his pupils in this wise, "Gurney, what is the difference between justification and sanctification?—Stephen, prove the omnipotence of God!" etc. In the midst of our Harvard freethinking and indifference we are prone to imagine that here at your good old orthodox College conversation continues to be somewhat upon this order; and to show you that we at Harvard have not lost all interest in these vital subjects, I have brought with me tonight something like a sermon on justification by faith to read to you,—I mean an essay in justification *of* faith, a defence of our right to adopt a believing attitude in religious matters, in spite of the fact that our merely logical intellect may not have been coerced. "The Will to Believe," accordingly, is the title of my paper. . . .

I have long defended to my own students the lawfulness of voluntarily adopted faith; but as soon as they have become well imbued with the logical spirit, they have as a rule refused to admit my contention to be lawful philosophically, even though in point of fact they were personally all the time chock full of some faith or other themselves. I am all the while, however, so profoundly convinced that my own position is correct, that your invitation has seemed to me a good occasion to make my statements more clear. Perhaps your minds will be more open than those

---

An address delivered before the Philosophical Clubs of Yale and Brown Universities. Published in 1896.

with which I have hitherto had to deal. I will be as little technical as I can, though I must begin by setting up some technical distinctions that will help us in the end.

I

Let us give the name of hypothesis to anything that may be proposed to our belief; and just as the electricians speak of *live* and *dead* wires, let us speak of any hypothesis as either live or dead. A live hypothesis is one which appeals as a real possibility to him to whom it is proposed. If I ask you to believe in the Mahdi,[3] the notion makes no electric connection with your nature—it refuses to scintillate with any credibility at all. As an hypothesis it is completely dead. To an Arab, however (even if he be not one of the Mahdi's followers), the hypothesis is among the mind's possibilities: It is alive. This shows that deadness and liveness in an hypothesis are not intrinsic properties, but relations to the individual thinker. They are measured by his willingness to act. The maximum of liveness in an hypothesis means willingness to act irrevocably. Practically, that means belief; but there is some believing tendency wherever there is willingness to act at all.

Next, let us call the decision between two hypotheses an *option*. Options may be of several kinds. They may be first, *living* or *dead*; secondly, *forced* or *avoidable*; thirdly, *momentous* or *trivial*; and for our purposes we may call an option a *genuine* option when it is of the forced, living, and momentous kind.

1. A living option is one in which both hypotheses are live ones. If I say to you: "Be a theosophist or be a Mohammedan," it is probably a dead option, because for you neither hypothesis is likely to be alive. But if I say: "Be an agnostic or be a Christian," it is otherwise; trained as you are, each hypothesis makes some appeal, however small, to your belief.

2. Next, if I say to you: "Choose between going out with your umbrella or without it," I do not offer you a genuine option, for it is not forced. You can easily avoid it by not going out at all. Similarly, if I say, "Either love me or hate me," "Either call my theory true or call it false," your option is avoidable. You may remain indifferent to me, neither loving nor hating, and you may decline to offer any judgment as to my theory. But if I say, "Either accept this truth or go without it," I put on you a forced option, for there is no standing place outside of the alternative. Every dilemma based on a complete logical disjunction, with no possibility of not choosing, is an option of this forced kind.

3. Finally, if I were Dr. Nansen[4] and proposed to you to join my North Pole expedition, your option would be momentous; for this would probably be your only similar opportunity, and your choice now would either exclude you from the North Pole sort of immortality altogether or put at least the chance of it into your hands. He who refuses to embrace a unique opportunity loses the prize as surely as if he tried and failed. *Per contra,*[5] the option is trivial when the opportunity is not unique, when the stake is insignificant, or when the decision is reversible if it later proves unwise. Such trivial options abound in the scientific life. A chemist finds an hypothesis live enough to spend a year in its verification: he believes in it to that

extent. But if his experiments prove inconclusive either way, he is quit for his loss of time, no vital harm being done.

It will facilitate our discussion if we keep all these distinctions well in mind.

II

The next matter to consider is the actual psychology of human opinion. When we look at certain facts, it seems as if our passional and volitional nature lay at the root of all our convictions. When we look at others, it seems as if they could do nothing when the intellect had once said its say. Let us take the latter facts up first.

Does it not seem preposterous on the very face of it to talk of our opinions being modifiable at will? Can our will either help or hinder our intellect in its perceptions of truth? Can we, by just willing it, believe that Abraham Lincoln's existence is a myth and that the portraits of him in *McClure's Magazine* are all of some one else? Can we, by any effort of our will, or by any strength of wish that it were true, believe ourselves well and about when we are roaring with rheumatism in bed, or feel certain that the sum of the two one-dollar bills in our pocket must be a hundred dollars? We can *say* any of these things, but we are absolutely impotent to believe them; and of just such things is the whole fabric of the truths that we do believe in made up—matters of fact, immediate or remote, as Hume said, and relations between ideas, which are either there or not there for us if we see them so, and which if not there cannot be put there by any action of our own.

In Pascal's *Thoughts* there is a celebrated passage known in literature as Pascal's wager. In it he tries to force us into Christianity by reasoning as if our concern with truth resembled our concern with the stakes in a game of chance. Translated freely his words are these: You must either believe or not believe that God is—which will you do? Your human reason cannot say. A game is going on between you and the nature of things which at the day of judgment will bring out either heads or tails. Weigh what your gains and your losses would be if you should stake all you have on heads, or God's existence; if you win in such case, you gain eternal beatitude; if you lose, you lose nothing at all. If there were an infinity of chances, and only one for God in this wager, still you ought to stake your all on God; for though you surely risk a finite loss by this procedure, any finite loss is reasonable, even a certain one is reasonable, if there is but the possibility of infinite gain. Go, then, and take holy water, and have masses said; belief will come and stupefy your scruples. . . . Why should you not? At bottom, what have you to lose?

You probably feel that when religious faith expresses itself thus, in the language of the gaming table, it is put to its last trumps. Surely Pascal's own personal belief in masses and holy water had far other springs; and this celebrated page of his is but an argument for others, a last desperate snatch at a weapon against the hardness of the unbelieving heart. We feel that a faith in masses and holy water adopted wilfully after such a mechanical calculation would lack the inner soul of faith's reality; and if we were ourselves in the place of the Deity, we should probably take particular pleasure in cutting off believers of this pattern from their infinite reward. It is evident that unless there be some preexisting tendency to believe in masses and holy water, the option offered to the will by Pascal is not a living option. Certainly no Turk ever took to masses and holy water on its account; and even to us Protestants these means of salvation seem such foregone impossibilities that Pascal's logic, invoked for them specifically, leaves us unmoved. As well might the Mahdi write to us, saying, "I am the Expected One whom God has created in his effulgence. You shall be infinitely happy if you confess me; otherwise you shall be cut off from the light of the sun. Weigh, then, your infinite gain if I am genuine against your finite sacrifice if I am not!" His logic would be that of Pascal; but he would vainly use it on us, for the hypothesis he offers us is dead. No tendency to act on it exists in us to any degree.

The talk of believing by our volition seems, then, from one point of view, simply silly. From another point of view it is worse than silly, it is vile. When one turns to the magnificent edifice of the physical sciences, and sees how it was reared; what thousands of disinterested moral lives of men lie buried in its mere foundations; what patience and postponement, what choking down of preference, what submission to the icy laws of outer fact are wrought into its very stones and mortar; how absolutely impersonal it stands in its vast augustness—then how besotted and contemptible seems every little sentimentalist who comes blowing his voluntary smokewreaths, and pretending to decide things from out of his private dream! Can we wonder if those bred in the rugged and manly school of science should feel like spewing such subjectivism out of their mouths? The whole system of loyalties which grow up in the schools of science go dead against its toleration; so that it is only natural that those who have caught the scientific fever should pass over to the opposite extreme, and write sometimes as if the incorruptibly truthful intellect ought positively to prefer bitterness and unacceptableness to the heart in its cup.

> It fortifies my soul to know
> That though I perish, Truth is so

sings Clough,[6] while Huxley[7] exclaims: "My only consolation lies in the reflection that, however bad our posterity may become, so far as they hold by the plain rule of not pretending to believe what they have no reason to believe, because it may be to their advantage so to pretend [the word 'pretend' is surely here redundant], they will not have reached the lowest depth of immorality." And that delicious *enfant terrible*[8] Clifford writes: "Belief is desecrated when given to unproved and unquestioned statements for the solace and private pleasure of the believer. . . . Whoso would deserve well of his fellows in this matter will guard the purity of his belief with a very fanaticism of jealous care, lest at any time it should rest on an unworthy object, and catch a stain which can never be wiped away. . . . If [a] belief has been accepted on insufficient evidence [even though the belief be true, as Clifford on the same page explains] the pleasure is a stolen one. . . . It is sinful because it is stolen in defiance of our duty to mankind. That duty is to guard ourselves from such beliefs as from a pestilence which may shortly master our own body and then spread to the rest of the town. . . . It is wrong always, everywhere, and for every one, to believe anything upon insufficient evidence."

III

All this strikes one as healthy, even when expressed, as by Clifford, with somewhat too much of robustious pathos in the voice. Free will and simple wishing do seem, in the matter of our credences, to be only fifth wheels to the coach. Yet if any one should thereupon assume that intellectual insight is what remains after wish and will and sentimental preference have taken wing, or that pure reason is what then settles our opinions, he would fly quite as directly in the teeth of the facts.

It is only our already dead hypotheses that our willing nature is unable to bring to life again. But what has made them dead for us is for the most part a previous action of our willing nature of an antagonistic kind. When I say "willing nature," I do not mean only such deliberate volitions as may have set up habits of belief that we cannot now escape from—I mean all such factors of belief as fear and hope, prejudice and passion, imitation and partisanship, the circumpressure of our caste and set. As a matter of fact we find ourselves believing, we hardly know how or why. Mr. Balfour[9] gives the name of "authority" to all those influences, born of the intellectual climate, that make hypotheses possible or impossible for us, alive or dead. Here in this room, we all of us believe in molecules and the conservation of energy, in democracy and necessary progress, in Protestant Christianity and the duty of fighting for "the doctrine of the immortal Monroe,"[10] all for no reasons worthy of the name. We see into these matters with no more inner clearness, and probably with much less, than any disbeliever in them might possess. His unconventionality would probably have some grounds to show for its conclusions; but for us, not insight, but the *prestige* of the opinions, is what makes the spark shoot from them and light up our sleeping magazines of faith. Our reason is quite satisfied, in nine hundred and ninety-nine cases out of every thousand of us, if it can find a few arguments that will do to recite in case our credulity is criticized by some one else. Our faith is faith in some one else's faith, and in the greatest matters this is the most the case. . . .

Evidently, then, our non-intellectual nature does influence our convictions. There are passional tendencies and volitions which run before and others which come after belief, and it is only the latter that are too late for the fair; and they are not too late when the previous passional work has been already in their own direction. Pascal's argument, instead of being powerless, then seems a regular clincher, and is the last stroke needed to make our faith in masses and holy water complete. The state of things is evidently far from simple; and pure insight and logic, whatever they might do ideally, are not the only things that really do produce our creeds.

IV

Our next duty, having recognized this mixed-up state of affairs, is to ask whether it be simply reprehensible and pathological, or whether, on the contrary, we must treat it as a normal element in making up our minds. The thesis I defend is, briefly stated, this: Our passional nature not only lawfully may, but must, decide an option between propositions, whenever it is a genuine option that cannot by its nature be decided on intellectual grounds; for to say, under such circumstances, "Do not decide, but leave the question open," is itself a passional decision—just like deciding yes or no—and is attended with the same risk of losing the truth. . . .

VII

One more point, small but important, and our preliminaries are done. There are two ways of looking at our duty in the matter of opinion—ways entirely different, and yet ways about whose difference the theory of knowledge seems hitherto to have shown very little concern. *We must know the truth;* and *we must avoid error—* these are our first and great commandments as would-be knowers; but they are not two ways of stating an identical commandment, they are two separable laws. Although it may indeed happen that when we believe the truth A, we escape as an incidental consequence from believing the falsehood B, it hardly ever happens that by merely disbelieving B we necessarily believe A. We may in escaping B fall into believing other falsehoods, C or D, just as bad as B; or we may escape B by not believing anything at all, not even A.

Believe truth! Shun error!—these, we see, are two materially different laws; and by choosing between them we may end by coloring differently our whole intellectual life. We may regard the chase for truth as paramount, and the avoidance of error as secondary; or we may, on the other hand, treat the avoidance of error as more imperative, and let truth take its chance. Clifford, in the instructive passage which I have quoted, exhorts us to the latter course. Believe nothing, he tells us, keep your mind in suspense forever, rather than by closing it on insufficient evidence incur the awful risk of believing lies. You, on the other hand, may think that the risk of being in error is a very small matter when compared with the blessings of real knowledge, and be ready to be duped many times in your investigation rather than postpone indefinitely the chance of guessing true. I myself find it impossible to go with Clifford. We must remember that these feelings of our duty about either truth or error are in any case only expressions of our passional life. Biologically considered, our minds are as ready to grind out falsehood as veracity, and he who says, "Better go without belief forever than believe a lie!" merely shows his own preponderant private horror of becoming a dupe. He may be critical of many of his desires and fears, but this fear he slavishly obeys. He cannot imagine any one questioning its binding force. For my own part, I have also a horror of being duped; but I can believe that worse things than being duped may happen to a man in this world; so Clifford's exhortation has to my ears a thoroughly fantastic sound. It is like a general informing his soldiers that it is better to keep out of battle forever than to risk a single wound. Not so are victories either over enemies or over nature gained. Our errors are surely not such awfully solemn things. In a world where we are so certain to incur them in spite of all our caution, a certain lightness of heart seems healthier than this excessive nervousness on their behalf. At any rate, it seems the fittest thing for the empiricist philosopher.

VIII

And now, after all this introduction, let us go straight at our question. I have said, and now repeat it, that not only as a matter of fact do we find our passional nature influencing us in our opinions, but that there are some options between opinions in which this influence must be regarded both as an inevitable and as a lawful determinant of our choice.

I fear here that some of you my hearers will begin to scent danger, and lend an inhospitable ear. Two first steps of passion you have indeed had to admit as necessary—we must think so as to avoid dupery, and we must think so as to gain truth; but the surest path to those ideal consummations, you will probably consider, is from now onwards to take no further passional step.

Well, of course, I agree as far as the facts will allow. Wherever the option between losing truth and gaining it is not momentous, we can throw the chance of *gaining truth* away, and at any rate save ourselves from any chance of *believing falsehood*, by not making up our minds at all till objective evidence has come. In scientific questions, this is almost always the case; and even in human affairs in general, the need of acting is seldom so urgent that a false belief to act on is better than no belief at all. Law courts, indeed, have to decide on the best evidence attainable for the moment, because a judge's duty is to make law as well as to ascertain it, and (as a learned judge once said to me) few cases are worth spending much time over; the great thing is to have them decided on *any* acceptable principle, and gotten out of the way. But in our dealings with objective nature we obviously are recorders, not makers, of the truth; and decisions for the mere sake of deciding promptly and getting on to the next business would be wholly out of place. Throughout the breadth of physical nature facts are what they are quite independently of us, and seldom is there any such hurry about them that the risks of being duped by believing a premature theory need be faced. The questions here are always trivial options, the hypotheses are hardly living (at any rate not living for us spectators), the choice between believing truth or falsehood is seldom forced. The attitude of sceptical balance is therefore the absolutely wise one if we would escape mistakes. What difference, indeed, does it make to most of us whether we have or have not a theory of the Röntgen[11] rays, whether we believe or not in mind-stuff, or have a conviction about the causality of conscious states? It makes no difference. Such options are not forced on us. On every account it is better not to make them, but still keep weighing reasons *pro et contra*[12] with an indifferent hand.

I speak, of course, here of the purely judging mind. For purposes of discovery, such indifference is to be less highly recommended, and science would be far less advanced than she is if the passionate desires of individuals to get their own faiths confirmed had been kept out of the game. See for example the sagacity which Spencer[13] and Weismann[14] now display. On the other hand, if you want an absolute duffer in an investigation, you must, after all, take the man who has no interest whatever in its results: he is the warranted incapable, the positive fool. The most useful investigator, because the most sensitive observer, is always he whose eager interest in one side of the question is balanced by an equally keen nervousness lest he become deceived. Science has organized this nervousness into a regular *technique*, her so-called method of verification; and she has fallen so deeply in love with the method that one may even say she has ceased to care for truth by itself at all. It is only truth as technically verified that interests her. The truth of truths might come in merely affirmative form, and she would decline to touch it. Such truth as that, she might repeat with Clifford, would be stolen in defiance of her duty to mankind. Human passions, however, are stronger than technical rules. "*Le coeur a ses raisons*" as Pascal says, "*que la raison ne connait pas*"[15]; and however indifferent to all but the bare rules of the game the umpire, the abstract intellect, may be, the concrete players who furnish him the materials to judge of are usually, each one of them, in love with some pet "live hypothesis" of his own. Let us agree, however, that wherever there is no forced option, the dispassionately judicial intellect with no pet hypothesis, saving us, as it does, from dupery at any rate, ought to be our ideal.

The question next arises: Are there not somewhere forced options in our speculative questions, and can we (as men who may be interested at least as much in positively gaining truth as in merely escaping dupery) always wait with impunity till the coercive evidence shall have arrived? It seems *a priori* improbable that the truth should be so nicely adjusted to our needs and powers as that. In the great boarding-house of nature, the cakes and the butter and the syrup seldom come out so even and leave the plates so clean. Indeed, we should view them with scientific suspicion if they did.

IX

Moral questions immediately present themselves as questions whose solution cannot wait for sensible proof. A moral question is a question not of what sensibly exists, but of what is good, or would be good if it did exist. Science can tell us what exists; but to compare the *worths*, both of what exists and of what does not exist, we must consult not science, but what Pascal calls our heart. . . .

Turn now from these wide questions of good to a certain class of questions of fact, questions concerning personal relations, states of mind between one man and another. *Do you like me or not?*—for example. Whether you do or not depends, in countless instances, on whether I meet you halfway, am willing to assume that you must like me, and show you trust and expectation. The previous faith on my part in your liking's existence is in such cases what makes your liking come. But if I stand aloof, and refuse to budge an inch until I have objective evidence, until you shall have done something apt, as the absolutists say, *ad extorquendum assensum meum*,[16] ten to one your liking never comes. How many women's hearts are vanquished by the mere sanguine insistence of some man that they *must* love him! He will not consent to the hypothesis that they cannot. The desire for a certain kind of truth here brings about that special truth's existence; and so it is in innumerable cases of other sorts. . . . *And where faith in a fact can help create the fact*, that would be an insane logic which should say that faith running ahead of scientific evidence is the "lowest kind of immorality" into which a thinking being can fall. Yet such is the logic by which our scientific absolutists pretend to regulate our lives!

X

In truths dependent on our personal action, then, faith based on desire is certainly a lawful and possibly an indispensable thing.

But now, it will be said, these are all childish human cases and have nothing to do with great cosmical matters, like the question of religious faith. Let us then pass on to that. Religions differ so much in their accidents that in discussing the religious question we must make it very generic and broad. What then do we now mean by the religious hypothesis? Science says things are; morality says some things are better than other things; and religion says essentially two things.

First, she says that the best things are the more eternal things, the overlapping things, the things in the universe that throw the last stone, so to speak, and say the final word. "Perfection is eternal"—this phrase of Charles Secrétan[17] seems a good way of putting this first affirmation of religion, an affirmation which obviously cannot yet be verified scientifically at all.

The second affirmation of religion is that we are better off even now if we believe her first affirmation to be true.

Now, let us consider what the logical elements of this situation are *in case the religious hypothesis in both its branches be really true.* (Of course, we must admit that possibility at the outset. If we are to discuss the question at all, it must involve a living option. If for any of you religion be a hypothesis that cannot, by any living possibility, be true, then you need go no farther. I speak to the "saving remnant" alone.) So proceeding, we see, first, that religion offers itself as a *momentous* option. We are supposed to gain, even now, by our belief, and to lose by our nonbelief, a certain vital good. Secondly, religion is a *forced* option, so far as that good goes. We cannot escape the issue by remaining sceptical and waiting for more light, because, although we do avoid error in that way *if religion be untrue*, we lose the good, *if it be true*, just as certainly as if we positively chose to disbelieve. It is as if a man should hesitate indefinitely to ask a certain woman to marry him because he was not perfectly sure that she would prove an angel after he brought her home.

Would he not cut himself off from that particular angel-possibility as decisively as if he went and married someone else? Scepticism, then, is not avoidance of option; it is option of a certain particular kind of risk. *Better risk loss of truth than chance of error*—that is your faith-vetoer's exact position. He is actively playing his stake as much as the believer is; he is backing the field against the religious hypothesis, just as the believer is backing the religious hypothesis against the field. To preach scepticism to us as a duty until "sufficient evidence" for religion is found is tantamount therefore to telling us, when in presence of the religious hypothesis, that to yield to our fear of its being error is wiser and better than to yield to our hope that it may be true. It is not intellect against all passion, then; it is only intellect with one passion laying down its law. And by what, forsooth, is the supreme wisdom of this passion warranted? Dupery for dupery, what proof is there that dupery through hope is so much worse than dupery through fear? I, for one, can see no proof; and I simply refuse obedience to the scientist's command to imitate his kind of option, in a case where my own stake is important enough to give me the right to choose my own form of risk. If religion is true and the evidence for it is still insufficient, I do not wish, by putting your extinguisher upon my nature (which feels to me as if it had after all some business in this matter), to forfeit my sole chance in life of getting upon the winning side—that chance depending, of course, on my willingness to run the risk of acting as if my passional need of taking the world religiously might be prophetic and right.

All this is on the supposition that it really may be prophetic and right, and that, even to us who are discussing the matter, religion is a live hypothesis which may be true. Now, to most of us religion comes in a still further way that makes a veto on our active faith even more illogical. The more perfect and more eternal aspect of the universe is represented in our religions as having personal form. The universe is no longer a mere *It* to us, but a *Thou*, if we are religious; and any relation that may be possible from person to person might be possible here. For instance, although in one sense we are passive portions of the universe, in another we show a curious autonomy, as if we were small active centers on our own account. We feel, too, as if the appeal of religion to us were made to our own active goodwill, as if evidence might be forever withheld from us unless we met the hypothesis halfway to take a trivial illustration: just as a man who in a company of gentlemen made no advances, asked a warrant for every concession, and believed no one's word without proof, would cut himself off by such churlishness from all the social rewards that a more trusting spirit would earn—so here, one who should shut himself up in snarling logicality and try to make the gods extort his recognition willy-nilly, or not get it at all, might cut himself off forever from his only opportunity of making the gods' acquaintance. This feeling, forced on us we know not whence that by obstinately believing that there are gods (although not to do so would be so easy both for our logic and our life) we are doing the universe the deepest service we can, seems part of the living essence of the religious hypothesis. If the hypothesis *were* true in all its parts, including this one, then pure intellectualism, with its veto on our making willing advances, would be an absurdity; and some participation of our sympathetic nature would be logically required. I therefore, for one, cannot see my way to accepting the agnostic rules for truthseeking, or wilfully agree to keep my willing nature out of the game. I cannot do so for this plain reason, that *a rule of thinking which would absolutely prevent me from acknowledging certain kinds of truth if those kinds of truth were really there, would be an irrational rule.* That for me is the long and short of the formal logic of the situation, no matter what the kinds of truth might materially be.

I confess I do not see how this logic can be escaped. But sad experience makes me fear that some of you may still shrink from radically saying with me, *in abstracto,* that we have the right to believe at our own risk any hypothesis that is live enough to tempt our will. I suspect, however, that if this is so, it is because you have got away from the abstract logical point of view altogether, and are thinking (perhaps without realizing it) of some particular religious hypothesis which for you is dead. The freedom to "believe what we will" you apply to the case of some patent superstition; and the faith you think of is the faith defined by the schoolboy when he said, "is when you believe something that you know ain't true." I can only repeat that this is misapprehension. *In concreto,*[18] the freedom to believe can only cover living options which the intellect of the individual cannot by itself resolve; and living options never seem absurdities to him who has them to consider. When I look at the religious question as it really puts itself to concrete men, and when I think of all the possibilities which both practically and theoretically it involves, then this command that we shall put a stopper on our heart, instincts, and cour-age, and *wait*—acting of course meanwhile more or less as if religion were *not* true[19]—till doomsday, or till such time as our intellect and senses working together may have raked in evidence enough—this command, I say, seems to me the queer-est idol ever manufactured in the philosophic cave. Were we scholastic absolut-ists, there might be more excuse. If we had an infallible intellect with its objective certitudes, we might feel ourselves disloyal to such a perfect organ of knowledge in not trusting to it exclusively, in not waiting for its releasing word. But if we are empiricists, if we believe that no bell in us tolls to let us know for certain when truth is in our grasp, then it seems a piece of idle fantasticality to preach so sol-emnly our duty of waiting for the bell. Indeed we *may* wait if we will—I hope you do not think that I am denying that—but if we do so, we do so at our peril as much as if we believed. In either case we *act,* taking our life in our hands. No one of us ought to issue vetoes to the other, nor should we bandy words of abuse. We ought, on the contrary, delicately and profoundly to respect one another's mental free-dom: then only shall we bring about the intellectual republic; then only shall we have that spirit of inner tolerance without which all our outer tolerance is soulless, and which is empiricism's glory; then only shall we live and let live, in speculative as well as in practical things.

I began by a reference to Fitz-James Stephen; let me end by a quotation from him. "What do you think of yourself? What do you think of the world? . . . These are questions with which all must deal as it seems good to them. They are rid-dles of the Sphinx, and in some way or other we must deal with them. . . . In all important transactions of life we have to take a leap in the dark. . . . If we decide to leave the riddles unanswered, that is a choice; if we waver in our answer, that, too, is a choice: but whatever choice we make, we make it at our peril. If a man chooses to turn his back altogether on God and the future, no one can prevent him; no one can show beyond reasonable doubt that he is mistaken. If a man thinks otherwise and acts as he thinks, I do not see that any one can prove that *he* is mistaken. Each must act as he thinks best; and if he is wrong, so much the worse for him. We stand on a mountain pass in the midst of whirling snow and blinding mist, through which we get glimpses now and then of paths which may be deceptive. If we stand still, we shall be frozen to death. If we take the wrong road, we shall be dashed to pieces. We do not certainly know whether there is any right one. What must we do? 'Be strong and of a good courage.' Act for the best, hope for the best, and take what comes. . . . If death ends all, we cannot meet death better."[20]

NOTES

1. [The reference is to the English critic and philosopher Sir Leslie Stephen (1832–1904) and his 1895 book, *The Life of Sir James Fitzjames Stephen*—S.M.C.]
2. [The reference is to the English jurist and journalist Sir James Fitzjames Stephen (1829–1894).]
3. [The redeemer, according to Islam, who will come to bring justice on earth and establish universal Islam.]
4. [The reference is to the Norwegian explorer Fridtjof Nansen (1861–1930).]
5. [In contrast.]
6. [The reference is to the British poet Arthur Hugh Clough (1819–1861).]
7. [The reference is to the English biologist Thomas Henry Huxley (1825–1895), who was a leading exponent of the evolutionary theory of Charles Darwin.]
8. [One who is strikingly unorthodox.]
9. [The reference is to the British prime minister and philosopher Arthur James Balfour (1848–1930).]
10. [The reference is to James Monroe (1758–1831), fifth president of the United States, whose doctrine prohibited European colonization or intervention in the American continents.]
11. [The reference is to the German physicist Wilhelm Conrad Röntgen, discover of the X-ray, for which he received in 1901 the first Nobel Prize in Physics.]
12. [For and against.]
13. [The reference is to the English philosopher Herbert Spencer (1820–1903), a leading exponent of the theory of evolution.]
14. [The reference is to the German biologist August Weismann (1834–1914).]
15. [The heart has its reasons, which reason does not know.]
16. [For compelling my assent.]
17. [The reference is to the Swiss philosopher Charles Secrétan (1815–1895).]
18. [In practice.]
19. Since belief is measured by action, he who forbids us to believe religion to be true, necessarily also forbids us to act as we should if we did believe it to be true. The whole defence of religious faith hangs upon action. If the action required or inspired by the

religious hypothesis is in no way different from that dictated by the naturalistic hypothesis, then religious faith is a pure superfluity, better pruned away, and controversy about its legitimacy is a piece of idle trifling, unworthy of serious minds. I myself believe, of course, that the religious hypothesis gives to the world an expression which specifically determines our reactions, and makes them in a large part unlike what they might be on a purely naturalistic scheme of belief.

20. *Liberty, Equality, Fraternity,* p. 353, 2d edition, London, 1874.

STUDY QUESTIONS

1. In what ways is James's reasoning different from Pascal's wager?
2. According to James, what two things does religion say?
3. Does it makes any difference to James which religion you practice?
4. Do religious believers act differently than others?

PART 8

Moral Theory

How Not to Answer
Moral Questions

TOM REGAN

We turn now to that major field of philosophy known as "ethics," a term derived
from the Greek word *ethos,* meaning "character." The subject, which may also
be referred to as "moral philosophy," focuses on the nature of a moral judgment,
the principles that ought to guide a good life, and the resolution of such thorny
practical issues as abortion or euthanasia.

Faced with an ethical issue, some people challenge the supposition that the
problem can be resolved through reasoned discussion. They claim that moral
judgments are merely expressions of personal preference, matters of individual
opinion, reflections of majority will, or commands of a supposed higher authority, such as God. In any of these cases, reasoning about ethics is useless. All we
can do is express our feelings, reiterate our beliefs, consult polls, or perhaps seek
divine guidance. In the following selection Tom Regan, Professor Emeritus of
Philosophy at North Carolina State University, argues that none of these ways of
dealing with moral questions is appropriate.

MORAL JUDGEMENTS AND PERSONAL PREFERENCES

Some people like New Age music; others do not. Some people think bourbon is
just great; others detest its taste. Some people will go to a lot of trouble to spend
an afternoon in the hot sun at the beach; others can think of nothing worse. In all
these cases, disagreement in preference exists. Someone likes something; someone
else does not. Are moral disagreements, disagreements over whether something is
morally right or wrong, good or bad, just or unjust, the same as disagreements in
preference?

It does not appear so. For one thing, when a person (say, Jack) says he likes
something, he is not denying what another person (Jill) says if she says she does
not like it. Suppose Jack says, "I (Jack) like the Grateful Dead," and Jill says, "I (Jill)
do not like the Grateful Dead." Then clearly Jill does not deny what Jack says. To
deny what Jack says, Jill would have to say, "You (Jack) do not like the Grateful
Dead," which is not what she says. So, in general, when two people express different personal preferences, the one does not deny what the other affirms. It is

perfectly possible for two opposing expressions of personal preference to be true at the same time.

When two people express conflicting judgements about the morality of something, however, the disagreement is importantly different. Suppose Jack says, "All wars are unjust," while Jill says, "Some wars are just." Then Jill *is* denying what Jack affirms; she is *denying* that wars are unjust, so that if what she said were true, what Jack said would have to be false. Some philosophers have denied this. They have maintained that moral judgements should be understood as expressions of personal preferences. Though this view deserves to be mentioned with respect, it is doubtful that it is correct. When people say that something is morally right or wrong, it is always appropriate to ask them to give reasons to justify their judgement, reasons for accepting their judgement as *correct*. In the case of personal preferences, however, such requests are inappropriate. If Jack says he likes to go to the beach, it hardly seems apt to press him to give reasons to *justify* what he says. If he says abortion is always wrong, however, it is highly relevant to test Jack's judgement by examining the reasons he gives for thinking what he does. In this case we want to know whether Jack's judgement is correct, not merely what Jack likes or dislikes.

This difference between expressions of differing personal preference and conflicting moral judgements points to one way not to answer moral questions. Given that moral judgements are not just expressions of personal preference, it follows that moral right and wrong cannot be determined just by finding out about someone's personal preferences. This is true even in the case of our own preferences. Our personal preferences are certainly important, but we do not answer moral questions just by saying that we like some things and dislike others.

WHY THINKING IT SO DOES NOT MAKE IT SO

The same is true about what someone thinks. Quite aside from her personal preferences, Bonnie, if she is sincere, does think that we who are well off ought to make sacrifices to help feed the many starving people in the world if she says that we ought to do so. Nevertheless, if her judgement is a *moral* judgement, what she means cannot be "I (Bonnie) think we who are well off ought to make sacrifices to help feed the many starving people in the world." If it were, then she would not be affirming something that Clyde denies, when *he* says, "We who are well off ought not to make such sacrifices." Each would merely be stating that each thinks something, and it is certainly possible for it *both* to be true that Bonnie thinks that we ought to make sacrifices for those who are starving *and*, at the same time, that Clyde thinks we ought not. So if Clyde is denying what Bonnie affirms, he cannot merely be stating that *he* thinks that we ought not to make sacrifices for these people. Clearly, Clyde believes that *what* he says is *correct*; and whether it *is* correct is independent of his thinking that it is. Thus, the fact that Clyde happens to think what he does is just as irrelevant to establishing whether we ought or ought not to make sacrifices to help those who are starving as Jack's feelings about war. And the same is true concerning what *we* happen to think. Our thinking something right or wrong does not make it so.

THE IRRELEVANCE OF STATISTICS

Someone might think that though what one person thinks or feels about moral issues does not settle matters, what all or most people think or feel does. A single individual is only one voice; what most or all people think or feel is a great deal more. There is strength in numbers. Thus, the correct method for answering questions about right and wrong is to find out what most or all people think or feel. Opinion polls should be conducted, statistics compiled. That will reveal the truth.

This approach to moral questions is deficient. All that opinion polls can reveal is what all or most people think or feel about various controversial questions— for example, "Should convicted murderers be executed?" Twenty years ago most Americans believed that capital punishment should be abolished; today most Americans believe it should be retained. This is an important, interesting change in public opinion. . . . Clearly, however, merely establishing that most Americans today favor the death penalty or, to take another example, that most favor the legalization of euthanasia, is not to establish that the majority opinion is correct. In times past, virtually everyone believed that the world is flat, yet this consensus did not settle the correct description of its shape. There is no compelling reason to assume that the answers to moral questions differ in this respect. Questions of moral right and wrong, in short, cannot be answered just by taking a vote and seeing what the majority favors.

THE APPEAL TO A MORAL AUTHORITY

Suppose it is conceded that we cannot answer moral questions just by finding out what Jack or Jill or Bonnie and Clyde happen to think or feel, or by finding out what all or most people happen to think or feel. After all, single individuals like Jack or Jill, or most or all people like them, might think or feel one way when they should think or feel differently. We ordinary mortals, after all, are fallible. But now suppose there is someone who *never is mistaken* when it comes to moral questions: If this person judges that something is morally right, it *is* morally right; if it is judged wrong, it is wrong. No mistakes are made. Let us call such a person a moral authority. Might appealing to the judgements of a moral authority be the correct method for answering moral questions?

Most people who think there is a moral authority think this authority is not an ordinary mortal but a god. This causes problems immediately. Whether there is a god (or gods) is a very controversial question, and to rest questions of right and wrong on what an alleged god says (or the gods say) is already to base morality on an intellectually unsettled foundation. The difficulties go deeper than this, however, since even if there is a god who is a moral authority, very serious questions arise concerning whether people always understand what this authority says.

The difficulties that exist when Jews and Christians consult the Bible are illustrative. Problems of interpretation abound. Some who think that we were created to be vegetarians think they find evidence in the Bible that God thinks so too; others think they find evidence that God does not. Some who think that God allows us to exploit nature without regard to its values cite what they think are supporting chapters and verses; others cite other chapters and verses they think show that God does not allow this, or they cite the same passages and argue that they should be interpreted differently. The gravity of these and kindred problems of interpretation should not be underestimated. Even if there is a moral authority, and even if the God Jews and Christians worship should happen to be this authority, that would not make it easy to find out what is right and wrong. The problem of finding out what God thinks on these matters would still remain and would be especially acute in areas where the Bible offers very little, if any, direct guidance—on the ethics of the use of life-sustaining technology for the irreversibly comatose, for example.

Problems of interpretation aside, it is clear that the correct method for answering moral questions cannot consist merely in discovering what some alleged moral authority says. Even if there is a moral authority, those who are not moral authorities can have no good reason for thinking that there is one unless the judgements of this supposed authority can be checked for their truth or reasonableness, and it is not possible to do this unless what is true or reasonable regarding right and wrong can be known independently of what this supposed authority says. An example from another quarter might make this point clearer. A plumber proves his "authority as a plumber" not merely by what he says but by the quality of his work, which can be verified independently of what he says in any particular case. *After* we have come to know, on independent grounds, that a particular plumber's judgement is reliable, *then* we have reason to rely on his judgement in the future. The same is true of the authority of one's judgement in, say, science, economics, the law, and morality: One's "credentials" can be established in the case of moral judgements only if there are independent ways of testing the truth or reasonableness of moral judgements. Thus, because there must be some independent way of knowing what judgements are true or reasonable in order to test for the authority of another's moral judgements, to appeal to this or that "moral authority" cannot itself be the method that we seek for answering moral questions.

STUDY QUESTIONS

1. Are moral judgments merely personal preferences?
2. Can moral disagreements ever be resolved by statistics?
3. Can moral questions be decided by appealing to a moral authority?
4. If you firmly believe an action is moral, might you be wrong?

Moral Isolationism

MARY MIDGLEY

Some would claim that the search for universal answers to moral questions is futile because morality differs from one culture to another. This view, sometimes referred to as "cultural relativism," maintains that while we can seek understanding of a particular culture's moral system, we have no basis for judging it. Morality is just a matter of custom, as suggested by the origin of the term "morality," which comes from the Latin word *moralis*, relating to "custom."

In the next selection Mary Midgley, who was Senior Lecturer in Philosophy at Newcastle University in England, argues that moral reasoning requires the possibility of judging the practices of other cultures.

All of us are, more or less, in trouble today about trying to understand cultures strange to us. We hear constantly of alien customs. We see changes in our lifetime which would have astonished our parents. I want to discuss here one very short way of dealing with this difficulty, a drastic way which many people now theoretically favour. It consists in simply denying that we can ever understand any culture except our own well enough to make judgements about it. Those who recommend this hold that the world is sharply divided into separate societies, sealed units, each with its own system of thought. They feel that the respect and tolerance due from one system to another forbids us ever to take up a critical position to any other culture. Moral judgement, they suggest, is a kind of coinage valid only in its country of origin.

I shall call this position "moral isolationism." I shall suggest that it is certainly not forced upon us, and indeed that it makes no sense at all. People usually take it up because they think it is a respectful attitude to other cultures. In fact, however, it is not respectful. Nobody can respect what is entirely unintelligible to them. To respect someone, we have to know enough about him to make a *favourable* judgement, however general and tentative. And we do understand people in other cultures to this extent. Otherwise a great mass of our most valuable thinking would be paralysed.

To show this, I shall take a remote example, because we shall probably find it easier to think calmly about it than we should with a contemporary one, such as female circumcision in Africa or the Chinese Cultural Revolution. The principles

---

From Mary Midgley, *Heart and Mind: The Varieties of Moral Experience*, Routledge, 2003. Reprinted by permission of Taylor & Francis.

involved will still be the same. My example is this. There is, it seems, a verb in classical Japanese which means "to try out one's new sword on a chance wayfarer." (The word is *tsujigiri,* literally "crossroads-cut.") A samurai sword had to be tried out because, if it was to work properly, it had to slice through someone at a single blow, from the shoulder to the opposite flank. Otherwise, the warrior bungled his stroke. This could injure his honour, offend his ancestors, and even let down his emperor. So tests were needed, and wayfarers had to be expended. Any wayfarer would do—provided, of course, that he was not another Samurai. Scientists will recognize a familiar problem about the rights of experimental subjects.

Now when we hear of a custom like this, we may well reflect that we simply do not understand it; and therefore are not qualified to criticize it at all, because we are not members of that culture. But we are not members of any other culture either, except our own. So we extend the principle to cover all extraneous cultures, and we seem therefore to be moral isolationists. But this is, as we shall see, an impossible position. Let us ask what it would involve.

We must ask first: Does the isolating barrier work both ways? Are people in other cultures equally unable to criticize *us?* This question struck me sharply when I read a remark in *The Guardian* by an anthropologist about a South American Indian who had been taken into a Brazilian town for an operation, which saved his life. When he came back to his village, he made several highly critical remarks about the white Brazilians' way of life. They may very well have been justified. But the interesting point was that the anthropologist called these remarks "a damning indictment of Western civilization." Now the Indian had been in that town about two weeks. Was he in a position to deliver a damning indictment? Would we ourselves be qualified to deliver such an indictment on the Samurai, provided we could spend two weeks in ancient Japan? What do we really think about this?

My own impression is that we believe that outsiders can, in principle, deliver perfectly good indictments—only, it usually takes more than two weeks to make them damning. Understanding has degrees. It is not a slapdash yes-or-no matter. Intelligent outsiders can progress in it, and in some ways will be at an advantage over the locals. But if this is so, it must clearly apply to ourselves as much as anybody else.

Our next question is this: Does the isolating barrier between cultures block praise as well as blame? If I want to say that the Samurai culture has many virtues, or to praise the South American Indians, am I prevented from doing *that* by my outside status? Now, we certainly do need to praise other societies in this way. But it is hardly possible that we could praise them effectively if we could not, in principle, criticize them. Our praise would be worthless if it rested on no definite grounds, if it did not flow from some understanding. Certainly we may need to praise things which we do not *fully* understand. We say "there's something very good here, but I can't quite make out what it is yet." This happens when we want to learn from strangers. And we can learn from strangers. But to do this we have to distinguish between those strangers who are worth learning from and those who are not. Can we then judge which is which?

This brings us to our third question: What is involved in judging? Now plainly there is no question here of sitting on a bench in a red robe and sentencing people. Judging simply means forming an opinion, and expressing it if it is called for. Is there anything wrong about this? Naturally, we ought to avoid forming—and expressing—*crude* opinions, like that of a simple-minded missionary, who might dismiss the whole Samurai culture as entirely bad, because non-Christian. But this is a different objection. The trouble with crude opinions is that they are crude, whoever forms them, not that they are formed by the wrong people. Anthropologists, after all, are outsiders quite as much as missionaries. Moral isolationism forbids us to form *any* opinions on these matters. Its ground for doing so is that we don't understand them. But there is much that we don't understand in our own culture too. This brings us to our last question: If we can't judge other cultures, can we really judge our own? Our efforts to do so will be much damaged if we are really deprived of our opinions about other societies, because these provide the range of comparison, the spectrum of alternatives against which we set what we want to understand. We would have to stop using the mirror which anthropology so helpfully holds up to us.

In short, moral isolationism would lay down a general ban on moral reasoning. Essentially, this is the programme of immoralism, and it carries a distressing logical difficulty. Immoralists like Nietzsche are actually just a rather specialized sect of moralists. They can no more afford to put moralizing out of business than smugglers can afford to abolish customs regulations. The power of moral judgement is, in fact, not a luxury, not a perverse indulgence of the self-righteous. It is a necessity. When we judge something to be bad or good, better or worse than something else, we are taking it as an example to aim at or avoid. Without opinions of this sort, we would have no framework of comparison for our own policy, no chance of profiting by other people's insights or mistakes. In this vacuum, we could form no judgements on our own actions.

Now it would be odd if *Homo sapiens* had really got himself into a position as bad as this—a position where his main evolutionary asset, his brain, was so little use to him. None of us is going to accept this skeptical diagnosis. We cannot do so, because our involvement in moral isolationism does not flow from apathy, but from a rather acute concern about human hypocrisy and other forms of wickedness. But we polarize that concern around a few selected moral truths. We are rightly angry with those who despise, oppress or steamroll other cultures. We think that doing these things is actually *wrong*. But this is itself a moral judgement. We could not condemn oppression and insolence if we thought that all our condemnation were just a trivial local quirk of our own culture. We could still less do it if we tried to stop judging altogether.

Real moral skepticism, in fact, could lead only to inaction, to our losing all interest in moral questions, most of all in those which concern other societies.

When we discuss these things, it becomes instantly clear how far we are from doing this. Suppose, for instance, that I criticize the bisecting Samurai, that I say his behaviour is brutal. What will usually happen next is that someone will protest, will say that I have no right to make criticisms like that of another culture. But it is most unlikely that he will use this move to end the discussion of the subject. Instead, he will justify the Samurai. He will try to fill in the background, to make me understand the custom, by explaining the exalted ideals of discipline and devotion which produced it. He will probably talk of the lower value which the ancient Japanese placed on individual life generally. He may well suggest that this is a healthier attitude than our own obsession with security. He may add, too, that the wayfarers did not seriously mind being bisected, that in principle they accepted the whole arrangement.

Now an objector who talks like this is implying that it *is* possible to understand alien customs. That is just what he is trying to make me do. And he implies, too, that if I do succeed in understanding them, I shall do something better than giving up judging them. He expects me to change my present judgement to a truer one—namely, one that is favourable. And the standards I must use to do this cannot just be Samurai standards. They have to be ones current in my own culture. Ideals like discipline and devotion will not move anybody unless he himself accepts them. As it happens, neither discipline nor devotion is very popular in the West at present. Anyone who appeals to them may well have to do some more arguing to make *them* acceptable, before he can use them to explain the Samurai. But if he does succeed here, he will have persuaded us, not just that there was something to be said for them in ancient Japan, but that there would be here as well.

Isolating barriers simply cannot arise here. If we accept something as a serious moral truth about one culture, we can't refuse to apply it—in however different an outward form—to other cultures as well, wherever circumstances admit it. If we refuse to do this, we just are not taking the other culture seriously. This becomes clear if we look at the last argument used by my objector—that of justification by consent of the victim. It is suggested that sudden bisection is quite in order, *provided* that it takes place between consenting adults. I cannot now discuss how conclusive this justification is. What I am pointing out is simply that it can only work if we believe that *consent* can make such a transaction respectable—and this is a thoroughly modern and Western idea. It would probably never occur to a Samurai; if it did, it would surprise him very much. It is *our* standard. In applying it, too, we are likely to make another typically Western demand. We shall ask for good factual evidence that the wayfarers actually do have this rather surprising taste—that they are really willing to be bisected. In applying Western standards in this way, we are not being confused or irrelevant. We are asking the questions which arise *from where we stand,* questions which we can see the sense of. We do this because asking questions which you can't see the sense of is humbug. Certainly we can extend our questioning by imaginative effort. We can come to understand other societies better. By doing so, we may make their questions our own, or we may see that they are really forms of the questions which we are asking already. This is not impossible. It is just very hard work. The obstacles which often prevent it are simply those of ordinary ignorance, laziness and prejudice.

If there were really an isolating barrier, of course, our own culture could never have been formed. It is no sealed box, but a fertile jungle of different influences— Greek, Jewish, Roman, Norse, Celtic and so forth, into which further influences are still pouring—American, Indian, Japanese, Jamaican, you name it. The moral isolationist's picture of separate unmixable cultures is quite unreal. People who talk about British history usually stress the value of this fertilizing mix, no doubt rightly. But this is not just an odd fact about Britain. Except for the very smallest and most remote, all cultures are formed out of many streams. All have the problem of digesting and assimilating things which, at the start, they do not understand. All have the choice of learning something from this challenge, or, alternatively, of refusing to learn, and fighting it mindlessly instead.

This universal predicament has been obscured by the fact that anthropologists used to concentrate largely on very small and remote cultures, which did not seem to have this problem. These tiny societies, which had often forgotten their own history, made neat, self-contained subjects for study. No doubt it was valuable to emphasize their remoteness, their extreme strangeness, their independence of our cultural tradition. This emphasis was, I think, the root of moral isolationism. But, as the tribal studies themselves showed, even there the anthropologists were able to interpret what they saw and make judgements—often favourable—about the tribesmen. And the tribesmen, too, were quite equal to making judgements about the anthropologists—and about the tourists and Coca-Cola salesmen who followed them. Both sets of judgements, no doubt, were somewhat hasty, both have been refined in the light of further experience. A similar transaction between us and the Samurai might take even longer. But that is no reason at all for deeming it impossible. Morally as well as physically, there is only one world, and we all have to live in it.

STUDY QUESTIONS

1. What does Midgley mean by "moral isolationism"?
2. Are those who oppose judging other cultures equally opposed to other cultures judging ours?
3. Do those who live in a culture necessarily understand it better than those who don't live in that culture?
4. If criticisms of other cultures are always inappropriate, can praise of other cultures ever be appropriate?

Kant's Ethics

ONORA O'NEILL

Can we find a moral rule that offers us a defensible standard for making ethical judgments? One influential answer is provided by Immanuel Kant, who offers various formulations of what he terms the "categorical imperative"—categorical because it does not depend on anyone's particular desires, and an imperative because it is a command of reason.

In the next selection Onora O'Neill, who was Principal of Newnham College, University of Cambridge, explains one of Kant's versions of the categorical imperative, the requirement that each person be treated as an end and never merely as a means.

Kant's moral theory has acquired the reputation of being forbiddingly difficult to understand and, once understood, excessively demanding in its requirements. I don't believe that this reputation has been wholly earned, and I am going to try to undermine it. . . .

The main method by which I propose to avoid some of the difficulties of Kant's moral theory is by explaining only one part of the theory. This does not seem to me to be an irresponsible approach in this case. One of the things that makes Kant's moral theory hard to understand is that he gives a number of different versions of the principle that he calls the Supreme Principle of Morality, and these different versions don't look at all like one another. . . .

Kant calls his Supreme Principle the *Categorical Imperative;* its various versions also have sonorous names. . . . The one on which I shall concentrate is known as the *Formula of the End in Itself.* . . .

THE FORMULA OF THE END IN ITSELF

Kant states the Formula of the End in Itself as follows:

> Act in such a way that you always treat humanity, whether in your own person or in the person of any other, never simply as a means but always at the same time as an end.

To understand this we need to know what it is to treat a person as a means or as an end. According to Kant, each of our acts reflects one or more *maxims.* The maxim of the act is the principle on which one sees oneself as acting. A maxim expresses a person's policy, or if he or she has no settled policy, the principle underlying the particular intention or decision on which he or she acts. Thus, a person who decides, "This year I'll give 10 percent of my income to famine relief," has as a maxim the principle of tithing his or her income for famine relief. In practice, the difference between intentions and maxims is of little importance, for given any intention, we can formulate the corresponding maxim by deleting references to particular times, places, and persons. In what follows I shall take the terms "maxim" and "intention" as equivalent.

Whenever we act intentionally, we have at least one maxim and can, if we reflect, state what it is. (There is of course room for self-deception here—"I'm only keeping the wolf from the door," we may claim as we wolf down enough to keep ourselves overweight, or, more to the point, enough to feed someone else who hasn't enough food.)

When we want to work out whether an act we propose to do is right or wrong, according to Kant, we should look at our maxims and not at how much misery or happiness the act is likely to produce, and whether it does better at increasing happiness than other available acts. We just have to check that the act we have in mind will not use anyone as a mere means, and, if possible, that it will treat other persons as ends in themselves.

USING PERSONS AS MERE MEANS

To use someone as a *mere means* is to involve them in a scheme of action *to which they could not in principle consent*. Kant does not say that there is anything wrong about using someone as a means. Evidently we have to do so in any cooperative scheme of action. If I cash a check I use the teller as a means, without whom I could not lay my hands on the cash; the teller in turn uses me as a means to earn his or her living. But in this case, each party consents to her or his part in the transaction. Kant would say that though they use one another as means, they do not use one another as *mere* means. Each person assumes that the other has maxims of his or her own and is not just a thing or a prop to be manipulated.

But there are other situations where one person uses another in a way to which the other could not in principle consent. For example, one person may make a promise to another with every intention of breaking it. If the promise is accepted, then the person to whom it was given must be ignorant of what the promisor's intention (maxim) really is. If one knew that the promisor did not intend to do what he or she was promising, one would, after all, not accept or rely on the promise. It would be as though there had been no promise made. Successful false promising depends on deceiving the person to whom the promise is made about what one's real maxim is. And since the person who is deceived doesn't know that real maxim, he or she can't in principle consent to his or her part in the proposed scheme of action. The person who is deceived is, as it were, a prop or a tool—a mere means—in the false promisor's scheme. A person who promises falsely treats the acceptor of the promise as a prop or a thing and not as a person. In Kant's view, it is this that makes false promising wrong.

One standard way of using others as mere means is by deceiving them. By getting someone involved in a business scheme or a criminal activity on false pretenses, or by giving a misleading account of what one is about, or by making a false promise or a fraudulent contract, one involves another in something to which he or she in principle cannot consent, since the scheme requires that he or she doesn't know what is going on. Another standard way of using others as mere means is by coercing them. If a rich or powerful person threatens a debtor with bankruptcy unless he or she joins in some scheme, then the creditor's intention is to coerce; and the debtor, if coerced, cannot consent to his or her part in the creditor's scheme. To make the example more specific: If a moneylender in an Indian village threatens not to renew a vital loan unless he is given the debtor's land, then he uses the debtor as a mere means. He coerces the debtor, who cannot truly consent to this "offer he can't refuse." (Of course the outward form of such transactions may look like ordinary commercial dealings, but we know very well that some offers and demands couched in that form are coercive.)

In Kant's view, acts that are done on maxims that require deception or coercion of others, and so cannot have the consent of those others (for consent precludes both deception and coercion), are wrong. When we act on such maxims, we treat others as mere means, as things rather than as ends in themselves. If we act on such maxims, our acts are not only wrong but unjust: such acts wrong the particular others who are deceived or coerced.

STUDY QUESTIONS

1. According to Kant, is using someone as a means always wrong?
2. What does Kant mean by the maxim of an action?
3. Why is it wrong to deceive others?
4. Can you imagine circumstances in which breaking a promise would not be wrong?

Assessing Utilitarianism

LOUIS P. POJMAN

Whereas Kant's ethical system concentrates exclusively on the reasons for an action and does not take account of its results, an opposing ethical system developed by John Stuart Mill, the leading English philosopher of the nineteenth century, focuses only on consequences. He defends utilitarianism, the view that the supreme principle of morality is to act so as to produce as much happiness as possible, each person counting equally. By "happiness" Mill means pleasure and the absence of pain.

Utilitarianism is in many ways an appealing doctrine, but it has been attacked on various grounds. In the next selection Louis P. Pojman (1935–2005), who was Professor of Philosophy at the United States Military Academy, explains why utilitarianism has been thought mistaken and offers possible responses to criticisms of it.

....

There are two classical types of utilitarianism: act utilitarianism and rule utilitarianism. In applying the principle of utility, act utilitarians . . . say that ideally we ought to apply the principle to all of the alternatives open to us at any given moment. We may define act utilitarianism in this way:

> **act utilitarianism:** An act is right if and only if it results in as much good as any available alternative.

Of course, we cannot do the necessary calculations to determine which act is the correct one in each case, for often we must act spontaneously and quickly. So rules of thumb (for example, "In general don't lie," and "Generally keep your promises") are of practical importance. However, the right act is still that alternative that results in the most utility.

The obvious criticism of act utility is that it seems to fly in the face of fundamental intuitions about minimally correct behavior. Consider Richard Brandt's criticism of act utilitarianism:

> It implies that if you have employed a boy to mow your lawn and he has finished the job and asks for his pay, you should pay him what you promised only if you cannot find a better use for your money. It implies that when you bring home your monthly paycheck you should use it to support your family and yourself only if it cannot be used more effectively to supply the needs of others. It implies that if your father is ill and he has no prospect of good in his life, and maintaining him is a drain on the energy and enjoyments of others, then, if you can end his life without provoking any public scandal or setting a bad example, it is your positive duty to take matters into your own hands and bring his life to a close.[1]

Rule utilitarians like Brandt attempt to offer a more credible version of the theory. They state that an act is right if it conforms to a valid rule within a system of rules that, if followed, will result in the best possible state of affairs (or the least bad state of affairs, if it is a question of all the alternatives being bad). We may define rule utilitarianism this way:

> **rule utilitarianism:** An act is right if and only if it is required by a rule that is itself a member of a set of rules whose acceptance would lead to greater utility for society than any available alternative.

From Louis P. Pojman, *How Should We Live? An Introduction to Ethics.* Copyright © 2005. Reprinted by permission of Wadsworth, a part of Cengage Learning, Inc. Reproduced by permission, www.cengage.com/permissions. Some paragraphs have been reordered for the sake of continuity.

Human beings are rule-following creatures. We learn by adhering to the rules of a given subject, whether it is speaking a language, driving a car, dancing, writing an essay, rock climbing, or cooking. We want to have a set of action-guiding rules to live by. The act-utilitarian rule, to do the act that maximizes utility, is too general for most purposes. Often we don't have time to deliberate whether lying will produce more utility than truth telling, so we need a more specific rule prescribing truthfulness, which passes the test of rational scrutiny. Rule utilitarianism asserts that the best chance of maximizing utility is by following the *set of rules* most likely to give us our desired results. . . .

An often-debated question in ethics is whether rule utilitarianism is a consistent version of utilitarianism. . . . [F]or example, we could imagine a situation in which breaking the general rule "Never lie" in order to spare someone's feelings would create more utility . . . than keeping the rule would. It would seem that we could always improve on any version of rule utilitarianism by breaking the set of rules whenever we judge that by so doing we could produce even more utility than by following the set. . . .

Whatever the answers . . . utilitarianism does have two very positive features. It also has several problems. The first attraction or strength is that it is a single principle, an absolute system with a potential answer for every situation. Do what will promote the most utility! It's good to have a simple, action-guiding principle that is applicable to every occasion—even if it may be difficult to apply (life's not simple). Its second strength is that utilitarianism seems to get to the substance of morality. It is not merely a formal system (that is, a system that sets forth broad guidelines for choosing principles but offers no principles; such a guideline would be "Do whatever you can universalize") but rather has a material core: Promote human (and possibly animal) flourishing and ameliorate suffering. The first virtue gives us a clear decision procedure in arriving at our answer about what to do. The second virtue appeals to our sense that morality is made for humans (and other animals?) and that morality is not so much about rules as about helping people and alleviating the suffering in the world. . . .

Opponents raise several . . . objections against utilitarianism. We discuss five of them: (1) the no-rest objection, (2) the absurd-implications objection, (3) the integrity objection, (4) the justice objection, and (5) the publicity objection. . . .

Problem 1: The No-Rest Objection: According to utilitarianism, one should always do that act that promises to promote the most utility. However, there is usually an infinite set of possible acts to choose from, and even if I can be excused from considering all of them, I can be fairly sure that there is often a preferable act that I could be doing. For example, when I am about to go to the movies with a friend, I should ask myself if helping the homeless in my community wouldn't promote more utility. When I am about to go to sleep, I should ask myself whether I could at that moment be doing something to help save the ozone layer. And why not simply give all my assets (beyond what is absolutely necessary to keep me alive) to the poor in order to promote utility? Following utilitarianism, I should get little or no rest, and, certainly, I have no right to enjoy life when, by sacrificing, I can make others happier. Similar to this point is Peter Singer's contention that middle-class people have a duty to contribute to poor people (especially in undeveloped countries) more than one-third of their income and all of us have a duty to contribute every penny above $30,000 that we possess until we are only marginally better off than the worst-off people on Earth. But, the objection goes, this makes morality too demanding, creates a disincentive to work, and fails to account for differential obligation. So utilitarianism must be a false doctrine.

Response: The utilitarian responds . . . by insisting that a rule prescribing rest and entertainment is actually the kind of rule that would have a place in a utility-maximizing set of rules. The agent should aim at maximizing his or her own happiness as well as other people's happiness. For the same reason, it is best not to worry much about the needs of those not in our primary circle. Although we should be concerned about the needs of future and distant (especially poor) people, it actually would promote disutility for the average person to become preoccupied with these concerns. Peter Singer represents a radical act–utilitarian position, which fails to give adequate attention to the rules that promote human flourishing, such as the right to own property, educate one's children, and improve one's quality of life, all of which probably costs more than $30,000 per year in many parts of North America. But, the utilitarian would remind us, we can surely do a lot more for suffering humanity than we now are doing—especially if we join together and act cooperatively. And we can simplify our lives, cutting back on conspicuous consumption, while improving our overall quality.

Problem 2: The Absurd-Implications Objection: W. D. Ross has argued that utilitarianism is to be rejected because it is counterintuitive. If we accept it, we would have to accept an absurd implication. Consider two acts, A and B, that will both result in 100 hedons (units of pleasure of utility). The only difference is that A involves telling a lie and B involves telling the truth. The utilitarian must maintain that the two acts are of equal value. But this seems implausible; truth seems to be an intrinsically good thing. . . .

Response: . . . [U]tilitarians can agree that there is something counterintuitive in the calculus of equating an act of lying with one of honesty; but, they argue, we must be ready to change our culture-induced moral biases. What is so important about truth telling or so bad about lying? If it turned out that lying really promoted human welfare, we'd have to accept it. But that's not likely. Our happiness is tied up with a need for reliable information (truth) on how to achieve our ends. So truthfulness will be a member of rule utility's set. But when lying will clearly promote utility without undermining the general adherence to the rule, we simply ought to lie. Don't we already accept lying to a gangster or telling white lies to spare people's feelings? . . .

Problem 3: The Integrity Objection: Bernard Williams argues that utilitarianism violates personal integrity by commanding that we violate our most central and deeply held principles. He illustrates this with the following example:

> Jim finds himself in the central square of a small South American town. Tied up against the wall [is] a row of twenty Indians, most terrified, a few defiant, in front of them several armed men in uniform. A heavy man in a sweat-stained khaki shirt turns out to be the captain in charge and, after a good deal of questioning of Jim which establishes that he got there by accident while on a botanical expedition, explains that the Indians are a random group of inhabitants who, after recent acts of protest against the government, are just about to be killed to remind other possible protesters of the advantages of not protesting. However, since Jim is an honored visitor from another land, the captain is happy to offer him a guest's privilege of killing one of the Indians himself. If Jim accepts, then as a special mark of the occasion, the other Indians will be let off. Of course, if Jim refuses, then there is no special occasion, and Pedro here will do what he was about to do when Jim arrived, and kill them all. Jim, with some desperate recollection of schoolboy fiction, wonders whether if he got hold of a gun, he could hold the captain, Pedro and the rest of the soldiers to threat, but it is quite clear from the set-up that nothing of that kind is going to work: any attempt of that sort of thing will mean that all the Indians will be killed, and himself. The men against the wall, the other villagers, understand the situation, and are obviously begging him to accept. What should he do?[2]

Williams asks rhetorically,

> How can a man, as a utilitarian agent, come to regard as one satisfaction among others, and a dispensable one, a project or attitude round which he has built his life, just because someone else's projects have so structured the causal scene that *that* is how the utilitarian sum comes out?

Williams's conclusion is that utilitarianism leads to personal alienation and so is deeply flawed.

Response: ... [T]he utilitarian can argue that (1) some alienation may be necessary for the moral life but (2) the utilitarian (even the act utilitarian) can take this into account in devising strategies of action. That is, integrity is not an absolute that must be adhered to at all costs. Even when it is required that we sacrifice our lives or limit our freedom for others, we may have to limit or sacrifice something of what Williams calls our integrity. We may have to do the "lesser of evils" in many cases. If the utilitarian doctrine of negative responsibility is correct, we need to realize that we are responsible for the evil that we knowingly allow, as well as for the evil we commit.

But ... a utilitarian may realize that there are important social benefits in having people who are squeamish about committing acts of violence, even those that preliminary utility calculations seem to prescribe. It may be that becoming certain kinds of people (endorsed by utilitarianism) may rule out being able to commit certain kinds of horrors—like Jim's killing of an innocent Indian. That is, utilitarianism recognizes the utility of good character and conscience, which may militate against certain apparently utility-maximizing acts.

Problem 4: The Justice Objection: Suppose a rape and murder [are] committed in a racially volatile community. As the sheriff of the town, you have spent a lifetime working for racial harmony. Now, just when your goal is being realized, this incident occurs. The crime is thought to be racially motivated, and a riot is about to break out that will very likely result in the death of several people and create long-lasting racial antagonism. You see that you could frame a derelict for the crime so that a trial will find him guilty and he will be executed. There is every reason to believe that a speedy trial and execution will head off the riot and save community harmony. Only you (and the real criminal, who will keep quiet about it) will know that an innocent man has been tried and executed. What is the morally right thing to do? The utilitarian seems committed to framing the derelict, but many would find this appalling.

Or consider [that you] are a utilitarian physician who has five patients under your care. One needs a heart transplant, two need one lung each, one needs a liver, and the last one needs a kidney. Now into your office comes a healthy bachelor needing an immunization. You judge that he would make a perfect sacrifice for your five patients. Via a utility calculus, you determine that, without doubt, you could do the most good by injecting the healthy man with a fatal drug and then using his organs to save your five patients.

This cavalier view of justice offends us. The very fact that utilitarians even countenance such actions—that they would misuse the legal system or the medical system to carry out their schemes—seems frightening. . . .

Response: . . . The utilitarian counters that justice is not an absolute—mercy and benevolence and the good of the whole society sometimes should override it; but, the sophisticated utilitarian insists, it makes good utilitarian sense to have a principle of justice that we generally adhere to. It may not be clear what the sheriff should do in the racially torn community. . . . If we could be certain that it would not set a precedent of sacrificing innocent people, it may be right to sacrifice one person for the good of the whole. Wouldn't we all agree, the utilitarian continues, that it would be right to sacrifice one innocent person to prevent a great evil?

Virtually all standard moral systems have a rule against torturing innocent people. But suppose a maniac . . . has a lethal gas that will spread throughout the globe and wipe out all life within a few weeks. His psychiatrist knows the lunatic well and assures us that there is one way to stop him—torture his 10-year-old daughter and televise it. Suppose, for the sake of the argument, there is no way to simulate the torture. Would you not consider torturing the child in this situation?

Is it not right to sacrifice one innocent person to stop a war or to save the human race from destruction? We seem to proceed on this assumption in wartime, in every bombing raid. . . . We seem to be following this rule in our decision to drive automobiles and trucks even though we are fairly certain the practice will result in the death of thousands of innocent people each year.

On the other hand, the sophisticated utilitarian may argue that, in the case of the sheriff framing the innocent derelict, justice should not be overridden by current utility concerns, for human rights themselves are outcomes of utility consideration and should not lightly be violated. That is, because we tend subconsciously to favor our own interests and biases, we institute the principle of rights to protect ourselves and others from capricious and biased acts that would in the long run have great disutility. So we must not undermine institutional rights too easily—we should not kill the bachelor in order to provide a heart, two lungs, a liver, and one kidney to the five other patients—at least not at the present time, given people's expectations of what will happen to them when they enter hospitals. But neither should we worship rights! They are to be taken seriously but not given ultimate authority. The utilitarian cannot foreclose the possibility of sacrificing innocent people for the greater good of humanity. If slavery could be humane and yield great overall utility, utilitarians would accept it. . . .

Problem 5: The Publicity Objection: It is usually thought that all must know moral principles so that all may freely obey the principles. But utilitarians usually hesitate to recommend that everyone act as a utilitarian, especially an act utilitarian, for it takes a great deal of deliberation to work out the likely consequences of alternative courses of action. . . . So utilitarianism seems to contradict our notion of publicity.

Response: . . . [U]tilitarians have two responses. First, they can counter that the objection only works against act utilitarianism. Rule utilitarianism can allow for greater publicity, for it is not the individual act that is important but the set of rules that is likely to bring about the most good. But then the act utilitarian may respond that this objection only shows a bias toward publicity (or even democracy). It may well be that publicity is only a rule of thumb to be overridden whenever there is good reason to believe that we can obtain more utility by not publicizing act-utilitarian ideas. Since we need to coordinate our actions with other people, moral rules must be publicly announced, typically through legal statutes. I may profit from cutting across the grass in order to save a few minutes in getting to class, but I also value a beautiful green lawn. We need public rules to ensure the healthy state of the lawn. So we agree on a rule to prohibit walking on the grass—even when it may have a utility function. There are many activities that individually may bring about individual utility advancement or even communal good, which if done regularly, would be disastrous, such as cutting down trees in order to build houses or to make newspaper or paper for books like this one, valuable as it is. We thus regulate the lumber industry so that every tree cut down is replaced with a new one and large forests are kept inviolate. So moral rules must be publicly advertised, often made into laws and enforced.

There is one further criticism of rule utilitarianism, which should be mentioned. Sometimes students accuse this version as being relativistic, since it seems to endorse different rules in different societies. Society A may uphold polygamy, whereas our society defends monogamy. A desert society upholds the rule "Don't waste water," but in a community where water is plentiful no such rule exists.

However, this is not really conventional relativism, since the rule is not made valid by the community's choosing it but by the actual situation. In the first case, the situation is an imbalance in the ratio of women to men; in the second case, the situation is environmental factors, concerning the availability of water. . . .

The worry is that utilitarianism becomes so plastic as to be guilty of becoming a justification for our intuitions. Asked why we support justice . . . it seems too easy to respond, "Well, this principle will likely contribute to the greater utility in the long run." The utilitarian may sometimes become self-serving in such rationalizations. Nevertheless, there may be truth in such a defense.

NOTES

1. Richard Brandt, "Towards a Credible Form of Utilitarianism," in *Morality and the Language of Conduct*, ed. H. Castaneda and G. Naknikian (Detroit: Wayne State University Press, 1963), pp. 109–110.
2. Bernard Williams, "A Critique of Utilitarianism," in *Utilitarianism: For and Against*, ed. J. C. C. Smart and Bernard Williams (Cambridge, UK: Cambridge University Press, 1973), p. 98ff.

STUDY QUESTIONS

1. Explain the difference between act utilitarianism and rule utilitarianism.
2. What is the justice objection to utilitarianism?
3. What is the integrity objection to utilitarianism?
4. Does utilitarianism imply that under certain circumstances a physician might be morally justified in killing one patient to save the lives of five others?

Virtue Ethics

Julia Driver

Julia Driver is Professor of Philosophy at Washington University in St. Louis. In the next selection she explains the difference between an ethical theory, like Aristotle's, that focuses on the development of a person's character, and an ethical theory, like that of Kant or Mill, that concentrates on the formulation of rules for right action.

Sometimes, in deciding on what we ought to do, we first consider how we ought to be. For example, if faced with a situation that involves social injustice, we might pick someone whom we admired and wanted to be like—Gandhi, let's say, or Mother Teresa—and then ask "What would Gandhi do?" This doesn't give us a rigid formula or decision procedure to employ. Instead, it asks us to consider a virtuous person, to consider his or her virtues, and then ask what behavior people with these good traits and dispositions exemplify. Some writers have thought that a picture like this better reflects how people should go about making their moral decisions. They should do so on the basis of concrete virtue judgments instead of abstract principles, such as "Maximize the good" or "Never treat another person merely as a means," and so forth.

. . . [V]irtue ethics has actually been around in one form or another for thousands of years. Current virtue ethicists, in fact, tend to take their inspiration from Aristotle, who was a student of Plato, and certainly one of the greatest philosophers in the history of philosophy. Aristotle wrote the *Nicomachean Ethics,* which—as an aid to his son—spelled out the steps to a good life. Of course, "good" is a bit ambiguous—Is that morally good, or prudentially good, or intellectually good, or all of the above? Well, for Aristotle, the good human life had all these ingredients. A good human being was virtuous in the sense that he embodied all the excellences of human character. So, Aristotle is often held up as a paradigmatic virtue ethicist. Again, . . . virtue ethics maintains that character, human excellence, *virtues,* are the basic modes of evaluation in the theory, as opposed to act evaluations such as "right" and "wrong." . . . [A]ct evaluation is to be understood in terms of character evaluation. Virtue is the primary mode of evaluation, and all other modes are understood and defined *in terms of* virtue. . . . Most of the theoretical weight is therefore borne by the account of virtue provided in the theory. . . .

Aristotle famously believed in the claim that virtue is a mean state, that it lies between two opposed vices. This is referred to as the doctrine of the mean. The basic idea is that virtue will tend to lie between two extremes, each of which is a vice. So, bravery lies between cowardice and foolhardiness; temperance lies between gluttony and abstinence; and so forth. Some virtues can be hard to model on this view. Take honesty. Of course, failure to tell the truths—telling a lie—would be one extreme, but is there a vice of telling too much truth? Maybe . . . though I suspect there might be some disagreement over this. Part of the mean state concerned our emotions, however, and not just our actions. The virtuous person not only does the right thing, but he does the right thing in the right way—in the right sort of emotional or psychological state. Our emotions can be excessive or deficient as well. The person who runs into the battle to fight, but who is excessively fearful, is not fully virtuous. The truly well-functioning person is able to control and regulate his feelings and emotions, as well as act rightly.

Aristotle's picture, then, of the virtuous person is the person who functions harmoniously—his desires and emotions do not conflict with what he knows to be right. They go together. This leads him to view a person who acts rightly, but who feels badly about it, as not being virtuous. This person is merely "continent"—this person can control his actions, but needs to work on bringing his emotions in line with what reason tells him is the right and appropriate thing to do. So the excellent human being is not conflicted; he does not suffer inner turmoil and the struggle between reason and passion. . . .

Many challenges have been posed to virtue ethics. . . . One *general* criticism of the whole approach is that it fails to conform to what we know about how best to explain human behavior . . .

For example, John Doris proposes that the globalism of traditional virtue ethics be rejected.[1] There is no one "honesty" trait, for example. Instead, we may have 50 or more "honesties"; that is, narrowly circumscribed traits or dispositions to tell the truth. So, Joe might not have honesty 1, which is the disposition to tell the truth about how well he does on exams, but he might have honesty 34, the disposition to tell the truth about how tall he is. So, Doris thinks that . . . the experimental evidence supports the view that are no robust traits; that is, traits to tell the truth over all or even most contexts or situations. And this is a problem for a virtue ethics that understands virtue as a "stable" or "reliable" character trait.

Another challenge has been that virtue ethics doesn't provide a guide to action. "Be nice, dear"—Well, what is nice, and what are the circumstances under which I should be nice? That's what we really want to know. This shows that it is these other reasons that actually justify our behavior. This has been raised as a very standard problem for the theory, but virtue ethicists have spent a good deal of time trying to show how their theories could be applied. . . .

This challenge can be expanded by noting that virtue ethics has trouble telling us the right thing to do in conflict situations, where two virtues may conflict, and thus the corresponding rules—such as "Be honest" or "Be kind"—may conflict. But some virtue ethicists think that this is simply the way morality is—it is messy, and for any situation there may be more than one right answer. Insisting that morality is neat and tidy is simply to impose a misleading clarity on moral decision-making.

. . . Virtue ethics remains an interesting alternative approach to moral evaluation and moral guidance.

NOTE

1. John Doris, *Lack of Character: Personality and Moral Behavior* (Cambridge, UK: Cambridge University Press, 2002), p. 31.

STUDY QUESTIONS

1. When you make a moral judgment, which question should you ask yourself: "What should I do?" or "What sort of person should I be?"
2. Should moral decisions always be based on rules?
3. Can findings in psychology be relevant to assessing moral theories?
4. Might a moral question have more than one right answer?

The Ethics of Care

VIRGINIA HELD

Virginia Held is Professor Emerita of Philosophy at Hunter College and The
Graduate Center of The City University of New York. In the following selection
she develops what she terms "the ethics of care," which some philosophers have
viewed as one form of virtue ethics. She emphasizes, however, that while the two
are in some ways similar, virtue ethics focuses on the character of individuals,
whereas the ethics of care is concerned especially with fostering connectedness
among people.

I

The ethics of care is only a few decades old. Some theorists do not like the term
"care" to designate this approach to moral issues and have tried substituting "the
ethic of love," or "relational ethics," but the discourse keeps returning to "care"
as the so far more satisfactory of the terms considered, though dissatisfactions
with it remain. The concept of care has the advantage of not losing sight of the
work involved in caring for people and of not lending itself to the interpretation
of morality as ideal but impractical to which advocates of the ethics of care often
object. Care is both value and practice. . . .

I think one can discern among various versions of the ethics of care a number
of major features.

First, the central focus of the ethics of care is on the compelling moral salience
of attending to and meeting the needs of the particular others for whom we take
responsibility. Caring for one's child, for instance, may well and defensibly be
at the forefront of a person's moral concerns. The ethics of care recognizes that
human beings are dependent for many years of their lives, that the moral claim
of those dependent on us for the care they need is pressing, and that there are
highly important moral aspects in developing the relations of caring that enable
human beings to live and progress. All persons need care for at least their early
years. Prospects for human progress and flourishing hinge fundamentally on the
care that those needing it receive, and the ethics of care stresses the moral force
of the responsibility to respond to the needs of the dependent. Many persons will
become ill and dependent for some periods of their later lives, including in frail
old age, and some who are permanently disabled will need care the whole of their

lives. Moralities built on the image of the independent, autonomous, rational individual largely overlook the reality of human dependence and the morality for which it calls. The ethics of care attends to this central concern of human life and delineates the moral values involved. . . .

Second, in the epistemological process of trying to understand what morality would recommend and what it would be morally best for us to do and to be, the ethics of care values emotion rather than rejects it. Not all emotion is valued, of course, but in contrast with the dominant rationalist approaches, such emotions as sympathy, empathy, sensitivity, and responsiveness are seen as the kind of moral emotions that need to be cultivated not only to help in the implementation of the dictates of reason but to better ascertain what morality recommends. Even anger may be a component of the moral indignation that should be felt when people are treated unjustly or inhumanely, and it may contribute to (rather than interfere with) an appropriate interpretation of the moral wrong. This is not to say that raw emotion can be a guide to morality; feelings need to be reflected on and educated. But from the care perspective, moral inquiries that rely entirely on reason and rationalistic deductions or calculations are seen as deficient.

The emotions that are typically considered and rejected in rationalistic moral theories are the egoistic feelings that undermine universal moral norms, the favoritism that interferes with impartiality, and the aggressive and vengeful impulses for which morality is to provide restraints. The ethics of care, in contrast, typically appreciates the emotions and relational capabilities that enable morally concerned persons in actual interpersonal contexts to understand what would be best. Since even the helpful emotions can often become misguided or worse—as when excessive empathy with others leads to a wrongful degree of self-denial or when benevolent concern crosses over into controlling domination—we need an *ethics* of care, not just care itself. The various aspects and expressions of care and caring relations need to be subjected to moral scrutiny and *evaluated*, not just observed and described.

Third, the ethics of care rejects the view of the dominant moral theories that the more abstract the reasoning about a moral problem the better because the more likely to avoid bias and arbitrariness, the more nearly to achieve impartiality. The ethics of care respects rather than removes itself from the claims of particular others with whom we share actual relationships. It calls into question the universalistic and abstract rules of the dominant theories. When the latter consider such actual relations as between a parent and child, if they say anything about them at all, they may see them as permitted and cultivating them a preference that a person may have. Or they may recognize a universal obligation for all parents to care for their children. But they do not permit actual relations ever to take priority over the requirements of impartiality. . . .

The ethics of care may seek to limit the applicability of universal rules to certain domains where they are more appropriate, like the domain of law, and resist their extension to other domains. Such rules may simply be inappropriate in, for instance, the contexts of family and friendship, yet relations in these domains should certainly be *evaluated,* not merely described, hence morality should not be limited to abstract rules. We should be able to give moral guidance concerning actual relations that are trusting, considerate, and caring and concerning those that are not.

Dominant moral theories tend to interpret moral problems as if they were conflicts between egoistic individual interests on the one hand, and universal moral principles on the other. The extremes of "selfish individual" and "humanity" are recognized, but what lies between these is often overlooked. The ethics of care, in contrast, focuses especially on the area between these extremes. Those who conscientiously care for others are not seeking primarily to further their own *individual* interests; their interests are intertwined with the persons they care for. Neither are they acting for the sake of *all others* or *humanity in general*; they seek instead to preserve or promote an actual human relation between themselves and *particular others*. Persons in caring relations are acting for self-and-other together. Their characteristic stance is neither egoistic nor altruistic; these are the options in a conflictual situation, but the well-being of a caring relation involves the cooperative well-being of those in the relation and the well-being of the relation itself. . . .

II

What *is* care? What do we mean by the term "care"? Can we define it in anything like a precise way? There is not yet anything close to agreement among those writing on care on what exactly we should take the meaning of this term to be, but there have been many suggestions, tacit and occasionally explicit.

For over two decades, the concept of care as it figures in the ethics of care has been assumed, explored, elaborated, and employed in the development of theory. But definitions have often been imprecise, or trying to arrive at them has simply been postponed (as in my own case), in the growing discourse. Perhaps this is entirely appropriate for new explorations, but the time may have come to seek greater clarity. Some of those writing on care have attempted to be precise, with mixed results, whereas others have proceeded with the tacit understanding that of course to a considerable extent we know what we are talking about when we speak of taking care of a child or providing care for the ill. But care has many forms, and as the ethics of care evolves, so should our understanding of what care is.

The last words I spoke to my older brother after a brief visit and with special feeling were: "take care." He had not been taking good care of himself, and I hoped he would do better; not many days later he died, of problems quite possibly unrelated to those to which I had been referring. "Take care" was not an expression he and I grew up with. I acquired it over the years in my life in New York City. It may be illuminating to begin thinking about the meaning of "care" with an examination of this expression.

We often say "take care" as routinely as "goodbye" or some abbreviation and with as little emotion. But even then it does convey some sense of connectedness.

More often, when said with some feeling, it means something like "take care of yourself because I care about you." Sometimes we say it, especially to children or to someone embarking on a trip or an endeavor, meaning "I care what happens to you, so please don't do anything dangerous or foolish." Or, if we know the danger is inevitable and inescapable, it may be more like a wish that the elements will let the person take care so the worst can be evaded. And sometimes we mean it as a plea: Be careful not to harm yourself or others because our connection will make us feel with and for you. We may be harmed ourselves or partly responsible, or if you do something you will regret we will share that regret.

One way or another, this expression (like many others) illustrates human relatedness and the daily reaffirmations of connection. It is the relatedness of human beings, built and rebuilt, that the ethics of care is being developed to try to understand, evaluate, and guide. The expression has more to do with the feelings and awareness of the persons expressing and the persons receiving such expressions than with the actual tasks and work of "taking care" of a person who is dependent on us, or in need of care, but such attitudes and shared awareness seem at least one important component of care.

A seemingly easy distinction to make is between care as the activity of taking care of someone and the mere "caring about" of how we feel about certain issues. Actually "caring for" a small child or a person who is ill is quite different from merely "caring for" something (or not) in the sense of liking it or not, as in "I don't care for that kind of music." But these distinctions may not be as clear as they appear, since when we take care of a child, for instance, we usually also care about him or her, and although we could take care of a child we do not like, the caring will usually be better care if we care for the child in both senses. If we really do care about world hunger, we will probably be doing something about it, such as at least giving money to alleviate it or to change the conditions that bring it about, and thus establishing some connection between ourselves and the hungry we say we care about. And if we really do care about global climate change and the harm it will bring to future generations, we imagine a connection between ourselves and those future people who will judge our irresponsibility, and we change our consumption practices or political activities to decrease the likely harm. . . .

My own view, then, is that care is both a practice and a value. As a practice, it shows us how to respond to needs and why we should. It builds trust and mutual concern and connectedness between persons. It is not a series of individual actions, but a practice that develops, along with its appropriate attitudes. It has attributes and standards that can be described, but more important that can be recommended and that should be continually improved as adequate care comes closer to being good care. Practices of care should express the caring relations that bring persons together, and they should do so in ways that are progressively more morally satisfactory. Caring practices should gradually transform children and others into human beings who are increasingly morally admirable. . . .

In addition to being a practice, care is also a value. Caring persons and caring attitudes should be valued, and we can organize many evaluations of how persons are interrelated around a constellation of moral considerations associated with care or its absence. For instance, we can ask of a relation whether it is trusting and mutually considerate or hostile and vindictive. We can ask if persons are attentive and responsive to each other's needs or indifferent and self-absorbed. Care is not the same as benevolence, in my view, since it is more the characterization of a social relation than the description of an individual disposition, and social relations are not reducible to individual states. Caring relations ought to be cultivated, between persons in their personal lives and between the members of caring societies. Such relations are often reciprocal over time if not at given times. The values of caring are especially exemplified in caring relations, rather than in persons as individuals.

STUDY QUESTIONS

1. According to Held, what is "the ethics of care"?
2. What does Held mean by her claim that care is both a practice and a value?
3. Is the ethics of care a form of virtue ethics?
4. Does analyzing a moral problem from the perspective of the ethics of care sometimes yield a different result than that obtained by using either a Kantian or a utilitarian standard?

Egoism and Moral Skepticism

JAMES RACHELS

Morality involves taking into account interests apart from our own. Do we ever do so? According to psychological egoism, we don't, because all human behavior is motivated only by self-interest. According to ethical egoism, even if we could act in the interest of others, we ought not do so but should be concerned only with ourselves. In the next selection James Rachels (1941–2003), who was Professor of Philosophy at the University of Alabama at Birmingham, considers both psychological and ethical egoism, concluding that neither is acceptable.

1. Our ordinary thinking about morality is full of assumptions that we almost never question. We assume, for example, that we have an obligation to consider the welfare of other people when we decide what actions to perform or what rules

to obey; we think that we must refrain from acting in ways harmful to others, and that we must respect their rights and interests as well as our own. We also assume that people are in fact capable of being motivated by such considerations, that is, that people are not wholly selfish and that they do sometimes act in the interests of others.

Both of these assumptions have come under attack by moral skeptics, as long ago as by Glaucon in Book II of Plato's *Republic*. Glaucon recalls the legend of Gyges, a shepherd who was said to have found a magic ring in a fissure opened by an earthquake. The ring would make its wearer invisible and thus would enable him to go anywhere and do anything undetected. Gyges used the power of the ring to gain entry to the Royal Palace, where he seduced the Queen, murdered the King, and subsequently seized the throne. Now Glaucon asks us to imagine that there are two such rings, one given to a man of virtue and one given to a rogue. The rogue, of course, will use his ring unscrupulously and do anything necessary to increase his own wealth and power. He will recognize no moral constraints on his conduct, and, since the cloak of invisibility will protect him from discovery, he can do anything he pleases without fear of reprisal. So, there will be no end to the mischief he will do. But how will the so-called virtuous man behave? Glaucon suggests that he will behave no better than the rogue: "No one, it is commonly believed, would have such iron strength of mind as to stand fast in doing right or keep his hands off other men's goods, when he could go to the market-place and fearlessly help himself to anything he wanted, enter houses and sleep with any woman he chose, set prisoners free and kill men at his pleasure, and in a word go about among men with the powers of a god. He would behave no better than the other; both would take the same course."[1] Moreover, why shouldn't he? Once he is freed from the fear of reprisal, why shouldn't a man simply do what he pleases, or what he thinks is best for himself? What reason is there for him to continue being "moral" when it is clearly not to his own advantage to do so?

These skeptical views suggested by Glaucon have come to be known as *psychological egoism* and *ethical egoism,* respectively. Psychological egoism is the view that all men are selfish in everything that they do, that is, that the only motive from which anyone ever acts is self-interest. On this view, even when men are acting in ways apparently calculated to benefit others, they are actually motivated by the belief that acting in this way is to their own advantage, and if they did not believe this, they would not be doing that action. Ethical egoism is, by contrast, a normative view about how men *ought* to act. It is the view that, regardless of how men do in fact behave, they have no obligation to do anything except what is in their own interests. According to ethical egoists, a person is always justified in doing whatever is in his own interests, regardless of the effect on others.

Clearly, if either of these views is correct, then "the moral institution of life" (to use Butler's well-turned phrase) is very different than what we normally think. The majority of mankind is grossly deceived about what is, or ought to be, the case, where morals are concerned.

2. Psychological egoism seems to fly in the face of the facts. We are tempted to say, "Of course people act unselfishly all the time. For example, Smith gives up a trip to the country, which he would have enjoyed very much, in order to stay behind and help a friend with his studies, which is a miserable way to pass the time. This is a perfectly clear case of unselfish behavior, and if the psychological egoist thinks that such cases do not occur, then he is just mistaken." Given such obvious instances of "unselfish behavior," what reply can the egoist make? There are two general arguments by which he might try to show that all actions, including those such as the one just outlined, are in fact motivated by self-interest. Let us examine these in turn:

a. The first argument goes as follows: If we describe one person's action as selfish, and another person's action as unselfish, we are overlooking the crucial fact that in both cases, assuming that the action is done voluntarily, *the agent is merely doing what he most wants to do.* If Smith stays behind to help his friend, that only shows that he wanted to help his friend more than he wanted to go to the country. And why should he be praised for his "unselfishness" when he is only doing what he most wants to do? So, since Smith is only doing what he wants to do, he cannot be said to be acting unselfishly.

This argument is so bad that it would not deserve to be taken seriously except for the fact that so many otherwise intelligent people have been taken in by it. First, the argument rests on the premise that people never voluntarily do anything except what they want to do. But this is patently false; there are at least two classes of actions that are exceptions to this generalization. One is the set of actions which we may not want to do, but which we do anyway as a means to an end which we want to achieve, for example, going to the dentist in order to stop a toothache, or going to work every day in order to be able to draw our pay at the end of the month. These cases may be regarded as consistent with the spirit of the egoist argument, however, since the ends mentioned are wanted by the agent. But the other set of actions are those which we do, not because we want to, nor even because there is an end which we want to achieve, but because we feel ourselves *under an obligation* to do them. For example, someone may do something because he has promised to do it, and thus feels obligated, even though he does not want to do it. It is sometimes suggested that in such cases we do the action because, after all, we want to keep our promises; so, even here, we are doing what we want. However, this dodge will not work: if I have promised to do something, and if I do not want to do it, then it is simply false to say that I want to keep my promise. In such cases we feel a conflict precisely because we do *not* want to do what we feel obligated to do. It is reasonable to think that Smith's action falls roughly into this second category: he might stay behind, not because he wants to, but because he feels that this friend needs help.

But suppose we were to concede, for the sake of the argument, that all voluntary action is motivated by the agent's wants, or at least that Smith is so motivated. Even if this were granted, it would not follow that Smith is acting selfishly or from self-interest. For if Smith wants to do something that will help his friend, even when it means forgoing his own enjoyments, that is precisely what makes him *un*selfish. What else could unselfishness be, if not wanting to help others? Another way to put the same point is to say that it is the *object* of a want that determines whether it is selfish or not. The mere fact that I am acting on *my* wants does not mean that I am acting selfishly; that depends on *what it is* that I want. If I want only my own good, and care nothing for others, then I am selfish; but if I also want other people to be well-off and happy, and if I act on *that* desire, then my action is not selfish. So much for this argument.

b. The second argument for psychological egoism is this: Since so-called unselfish actions always produce a sense of self-satisfaction in the agent,[2] and since this sense of satisfaction is a pleasant state of consciousness, it follows that the point of the action is really to achieve a pleasant state of consciousness, rather than to bring about any good for others. Therefore, the action is "unselfish" only at a superficial level of analysis. Smith will feel much better with himself for having stayed to help his friend—if he had gone to the country, he would have felt terrible about it—and that is the real point of the action. According to a well-known story, this argument was once expressed by Abraham Lincoln:

> Mr. Lincoln once remarked to a fellow passenger on an old-time mud-coach that all men were prompted by selfishness in doing good. His fellow-passenger was antagonizing this position when they were passing over a corduroy bridge that spanned a slough. As they crossed this bridge they espied an old razor-backed sow on the bank making a terrible noise because her pigs had got into the slough and were in danger of drowning. As the old coach began to climb the hill, Mr. Lincoln called out, "Driver, can't you stop just a moment?" Then Mr. Lincoln jumped out, ran back, and lifted the little pigs out of the mud and water and placed them on the bank. When he returned, his companion remarked: "Now, Abe, where does selfishness come in on this little episode?" "Why, bless your soul, Ed, that was the very essence of selfishness. I should have had no peace of mind all day had I gone on and left that suffering old sow worrying over those pigs. I did it to get peace of mind, don't you see?"[3]

This argument suffers from defects similar to the previous one. Why should we think that merely because someone derives satisfaction from helping others this makes him selfish? Isn't the unselfish man precisely the one who *does* derive satisfaction from helping others, while the selfish man does not? If Lincoln "got peace of mind" from rescuing the piglets, does this show him to be selfish, or, on the contrary, doesn't it show him to be compassionate and good-hearted? (If a man were truly selfish, why should it bother his conscience that *others* suffer—much less pigs?) Similarly, it is nothing more than shabby sophistry to say, because Smith takes satisfaction in helping his friend, that he is behaving selfishly. If we say this rapidly, while thinking about something else, perhaps it will sound all right; but if we speak slowly, and pay attention to what we are saying, it sounds plain silly.

Moreover, suppose we ask *why* Smith derives satisfaction from helping his friend. The answer will be, it is because Smith cares for him and wants him to succeed. If Smith did not have these concerns, then he would take no pleasure in assisting him; and these concerns, as we have already seen, are the marks of unselfishness, not selfishness. To put the point more generally: if we have a positive attitude toward the attainment of some goal, then we may derive satisfaction from attaining that goal. But the *object* of our attitude is *the attainment of that goal*; and we must want to attain the goal *before* we can find any satisfaction in it. We do not, in other words, desire some sort of "pleasurable consciousness" and then try to figure out how to achieve it; rather, we desire all sorts of different things— money, a new fishing boat, to be a better chess player, to get a promotion in our work, etc.—and because we desire these things, we derive satisfaction from attaining them. And so, if someone desires the welfare and happiness of another person, he will derive satisfaction from that; but this does not mean that this satisfaction is the object of his desire, or that he is in any way selfish on account of it.

It is a measure of the weakness of psychological egoism that these insupportable arguments are the ones most often advanced in its favor. Why, then, should anyone ever have thought it a true view? Perhaps because of a desire for theoretical simplicity: In thinking about human conduct, it would be nice if there were some simple formula that would unite the diverse phenomena of human behavior under a single explanatory principle, just as simple formulae in physics bring together a great many apparently different phenomena. And since it is obvious that self-regard is an overwhelmingly important factor in motivation, it is only natural to wonder whether all motivation might not be explained in these terms. But the answer is clearly No; while a great many human actions are motivated entirely or in part by self-interest, only by a deliberate distortion of the facts can we say that all conduct is so motivated. This will be clear, I think, if we correct three confusions which are commonplace. The exposure of these confusions will remove the last traces of plausibility from the psychological egoist thesis.

The first is the confusion of selfishness with self-interest. The two are clearly not the same. If I see a physician when I am feeling poorly, I am acting in my own interest but no one would think of calling me "selfish" on account of it. Similarly, brushing my teeth, working hard at my job, and obeying the law are all in my self-interest but none of these are examples of selfish conduct. This is because selfish behavior is behavior that ignores the interests of others, in circumstances in which their interests ought not to be ignored. This concept has a definite evaluative flavor; to call someone "selfish" is not just to describe his action but to condemn it. Thus, you would not call me selfish for eating a normal meal in normal circumstances (although it may surely be in my self-interest); but you would call me selfish for hoarding food while others about are starving.

The second confusion is the assumption that every action is done *either* from self-interest or from other-regarding motives. Thus, the egoist concludes that if there is no such thing as genuine altruism then all actions must be done from self-interest. But this is certainly a false dichotomy. The man who continues to smoke cigarettes, even after learning about the connection between smoking and cancer, is surely not acting from self-interest, not even by his own standards—self-interest would dictate that he quit smoking at once—and he is not acting altruistically either. He *is,* no doubt, smoking for the pleasure of it, but all that this shows is that undisciplined pleasure-seeking and acting from self-interest are very different. This is what led Butler to remark that "the thing to be lamented is, not that men have so great regard to their own good or interest in the present world, for they have not enough."[4]

The last two paragraphs show *(a)* that it is false that all actions are selfish and *(b)* that it is false that all actions are done out of self-interest. And it should be noted that these two points can be made, and were, without any appeal to putative examples of altruism.

The third confusion is the common but false assumption that a concern for one's own welfare is incompatible with any genuine concern for the welfare of others. Thus, since it is obvious that everyone (or very nearly everyone) does desire his own well-being, it might be thought that no one can really be concerned with others. But again, this is false. There is no inconsistency in desiring that everyone, including oneself *and* others, be well-off and happy. To be sure, it may happen on occasion that our own interests conflict with the interests of others, and in these cases we will have to make hard choices. But even in these cases we might sometimes opt for the interests of others, especially when the others involved are our family or friends. But more importantly, not all cases are like this: sometimes we are able to promote the welfare of others when our own interests are not involved at all. In these cases not even the strongest self-regard need prevent us from acting considerately toward others.

Once these confusions are cleared away, it seems to me obvious enough that there is no reason whatever to accept psychological egoism. On the contrary, if we simply observe people's behavior with an open mind, we may find that a great deal of it is motivated by self-regard, but by no means all of it; and that there is no reason to deny that "the moral institution of life" can include a place for the virtue of beneficence.[5]

3. The ethical egoist would say at this point, "Of course it is possible for people to act altruistically, and perhaps many people do act that way—but there is no reason why they *should* do so. A person is under no obligation to do anything except what is in his own interests."[6] This is really quite a radical doctrine. Suppose I have an urge to set fire to some public building (say, a department store) just for the fascination of watching the spectacular blaze: according to this view, the fact that several people might be burned to death provides no reason whatever why I should not do it. After all, this only concerns *their* welfare, not my own, and according to the ethical egoist the only person I need think of is myself.

Some might deny that ethical egoism has any such monstrous consequences. They would point out that it is really to my own advantage not to set the fire—for, if I do that I may be caught and put into prison (unlike Gyges, I have no magic ring for protection). Moreover, even if I could avoid being caught it is still to my advantage to respect the rights and interests of others, for it is to my advantage to live in a society in which people's rights and interests are respected. Only in such a society can I live a happy and secure life; so, in acting kindly toward others, I would merely be doing my part to create and maintain the sort of society which it is to my advantage to have.[7] Therefore, it is said, the egoist would not be such a bad man; he would be as kindly and considerate as anyone else, because he would see that it is to his own advantage to be kindly and considerate.

This is a seductive line of thought, but it seems to me mistaken. Certainly it is to everyone's advantage (including the egoist's) to preserve stable society where people's interests are generally protected. But there is no reason for the egoist to think that merely because *he* will not honor the rules of the social game, decent society will collapse. For the vast majority of people are not egoists, and there is no reason to think that they will be converted by his example—especially if he is discreet and does not unduly flaunt his style of life. What this line of reasoning shows is not that the egoist himself must act benevolently, but that he must encourage *others* to do so. He must take care to conceal from public view his own self-centered method of decision making, and urge others to act on precepts very different from those on which he is willing to act.

The rational egoist, then, cannot advocate that egoism be universally adopted by everyone. For he wants a world in which his own interests are maximized; and if other people adopted the egoistic policy of pursuing their own interests to the exclusion of his interests, as he pursues his interests to the exclusion of theirs, then such a world would be impossible. So he himself will be an egoist, but he will want others to be altruists.

This brings us to what is perhaps the most popular "refutation" of ethical egoism current among philosophical writers—the argument that ethical egoism is at bottom inconsistent because it cannot be universalized.[8] The argument goes like this:

To say that any action or policy of action is *right* (or that it *ought* to be adopted) entails that it is right for *anyone* in the same sort of circumstances. I cannot, for example, say that it is right for me to lie to you, and yet object when you lie to me (provided, of course, that the circumstances are the same). I cannot hold that it is all right for me to drink your beer and then complain when you drink mine. This is just the requirement that we be consistent in our evaluations; it is a requirement of logic. Now it is said that ethical egoism cannot meet this requirement because, as we have already seen, the egoist would not want others to act in the same way that he acts. Moreover, suppose he *did* advocate the universal adoption of egoistic policies: he would be saying to Peter, "You ought to pursue your own interests even if it means destroying Paul"; and he would be saying to Paul, "You ought to pursue your own interests even if it means destroying Peter." The attitudes expressed in these two recommendations seem clearly inconsistent—he is urging the advancement of Peter's interests at one moment, and countenancing their defeat at the next. Therefore, the argument goes, there is no way to maintain the doctrine of ethical egoism as a consistent view about how we ought to act. We will fall into inconsistency whenever we try.

What are we to make of this argument? Are we to conclude that ethical egoism has been refuted? Such a conclusion, I think, would be unwarranted; for I think that we can show, contrary to this argument, how ethical egoism can be maintained consistently. We need only to interpret the egoist's position in a sympathetic way: we should say that he has in mind a certain kind of world which he would prefer over all others; it would be a world in which his own interests were maximized, regardless of the effects on the other people. The egoist's primary policy of action, then, would be to act in such a way as to bring about, as nearly as possible, this sort of world. Regardless of however morally reprehensible we might find it, there is nothing *inconsistent* in someone's adopting this as his ideal and acting in a way calculated to bring it about. And if someone did adopt this as his ideal, then he would not advocate universal egoism; as we have already seen, he would want other people to be altruists. So, if he advocates any principles of conduct for the general public, they will be altruistic principles. This could not be inconsistent; on the contrary, it would be perfectly consistent with his goal of creating a world in which his own interests are maximized. To be sure, he would have to be deceitful; in order to secure the good will of others, and a favorable hearing for his exhortations to altruism, he would have to pretend that he was himself prepared to accept altruistic principles. But again, that would be all right; from the egoist's point of view, this would merely be a matter of adopting the necessary means to the achievement of his goal—and while we might not approve of this, there is nothing inconsistent about it. Again, it might be said, "He advocates one thing, but does another. Surely *that's* inconsistent." But it is not; for what he advocates and what he does are both calculated as means to an end (the *same* end, we might note); and as such, he is doing what is rationally required in each case. Therefore, contrary to the previous argument, there is nothing inconsistent in the ethical egoist's view. He cannot be refuted by the claim that he contradicts himself.

Is there, then, no way to refute the ethical egoist? If by "refute" we mean show that he has made some *logical* error, the answer is that there is not. However, there is something more that can be said. The egoist challenge to our ordinary moral convictions amounts to a demand for an explanation of why we should adopt certain policies of action, namely, policies in which the good of others is given importance. We can give an answer to this demand, albeit an indirect one. The reason one ought not to do actions that would hurt other people is other people would be hurt. The reason one ought to do actions that would benefit other people is other people would be benefited. This may at first seem like a piece of philosophical sleight-of-hand, but it is not. The point is that the welfare of human beings is something that most of us value *for its own sake,* and not merely for the sake of something else. Therefore, when *further* reasons are demanded for valuing the welfare of human beings, we cannot point to anything further to satisfy this demand. It is not that we have no reason for pursuing these policies, but that our reason *is* that these policies are for the good of human beings.

So if we are asked, "Why shouldn't I set fire to this department store?" one answer would be, "Because if you do, people may be burned to death." This is a complete, sufficient reason which does not require qualification or supplementation of any sort. If someone seriously wants to know why this action shouldn't be done, that's the reason. If we are pressed further and asked the skeptical question, "But why shouldn't I do actions that will harm others?" we may not know what to say—but this is because the questioner has included in his question the very answer we would like to give: "Why shouldn't you do actions that will harm others? Because, doing those actions would harm others."

The egoist, no doubt, will not be happy with this. He will protest that *we* may accept this as a reason, but *he* does not. And here the argument stops: there are limits to what can be accomplished by argument, and if the egoist really doesn't care about other people—if he honestly doesn't care whether they are helped or hurt by his actions—then we have reached those limits. If we want to persuade him to act decently toward his fellow humans, we will have to make our appeal to such other attitudes as he does possess, by threats, bribes, or other cajolery. That is all that we can do.

Though some may find this situation distressing (we would like to be able to show that the egoist is just *wrong),* it holds no embarrassment for common morality. What we have come up against is simply a fundamental requirement of rational action, namely, that the existence of reasons for action always depends on the prior existence of certain attitudes in the agent. For example, the fact that a certain course of action would make the agent a lot of money is a reason for doing it only if the agent wants to make money; the fact that practicing at chess makes one a better player is a reason for practicing only if one wants to be a better player; and so on. Similarly, the fact that a certain action would help the agent is a reason for doing the action only if the agent cares about his own welfare, and the fact that an action would help others is a reason for doing it only if the agent cares about others. In this respect, ethical egoism and what we might call ethical altruism are in exactly the same fix: both require that the agent *care* about himself, or about other people, before they can get started.

So a nonegoist will accept "It would harm another person" as a reason not to do an action simply because he cares about what happens to that other person. When the egoist says that he does *not* accept that as a reason, he is saying something quite extraordinary. He is saying that he has no affection for friends or family, that he never feels pity or compassion, that he is the sort of person who can look on scenes of human misery with complete indifference, so long as he is not the one suffering. Genuine egoists, people who really don't care at all about anyone other than themselves, are rare. It is important to keep this in mind when thinking about ethical egoism; it is easy to forget just how fundamental to human psychological makeup the feeling of sympathy is. Indeed, a man without any sympathy at all would scarcely be recognizable as a man; and that is what makes ethical egoism such a disturbing doctrine in the first place.

4. There are, of course, many different ways in which the skeptic might challenge the assumptions underlying our moral practice. In this essay I have discussed only two of them, the two put forward by Glaucon in the passage that I cited from Plato's *Republic*. It is important that the assumptions underlying our moral practice should not be confused with particular judgments made within that practice. To defend one is not to defend the other. We may assume—quite properly, if my analysis has been correct—that the virtue of beneficence does, and indeed should, occupy an important place in "the moral institution of life"; and yet we may make constant and miserable errors when it comes to judging when and in what ways this virtue is to be exercised. Even worse, we may often be able to make accurate moral judgments, and know what we ought to do, but not do it. For these ills, philosophy alone is not the cure.

NOTES

1. *The Republic of Plato*, translated by F. M. Cornford (Oxford, 1941), p. 45.
2. Or, as it is sometimes said, "It gives him a clear conscience," or "He couldn't sleep at night if he had done otherwise," or "He would have been ashamed of himself for not doing it," and so on.
3. Frank C. Sharp, *Ethics* (New York, 1928), pp. 74–75. Quoted from the Springfield (IL) *Monitor* in the *Outlook*, vol. 56, p. 1059.
4. *The Works of Joseph Butler*, edited by W. E. Gladstone (Oxford, 1896), vol. II, p. 26. It should be noted that most of the points I am making against psychological egoism were first made by Joseph Butler. Butler made all the important points; all that is left for us is to remember them.
5. The capacity for altruistic behavior is not unique to human beings. Some interesting experiments with rhesus monkeys have shown that these animals will refrain from operating a device for securing food if this causes other animals to suffer pain. See Jules H. Masserman, Stanley Wechkin, and William Terris, "'Altruistic' Behavior in Rhesus Monkeys," *American Journal of Psychiatry*, vol. 121 (1964), pp. 584–85.
6. I take this to be the view of Ayn Rand, insofar as I understand her confused doctrine.
7. Cf. Thomas Hobbes, *Leviathan* (London, 1651), chap. 17.
8. See, for example, Brian Medlin, "Ultimate Principles and Ethical Egoism," *Australasian Journal of Philosophy*, vol. 35 (1957), pp. 111–18; and D. H. Monro, *Empiricism and Ethics* (Cambridge, 1967), chap. 16.

STUDY QUESTIONS

1. Explain the distinction between psychological egoism and ethical egoism.
2. In the story about Abraham Lincoln, was his action motivated by selfishness?
3. Is a concern for one's own welfare incompatible with a concern for the welfare of others?
4. Is it self-defeating for an ethical egoist to urge everyone to act egoistically?

Happiness and Morality

CHRISTINE VITRANO

Does your acting morally guarantee your happiness? Does your acting immorally guarantee your unhappiness? Christine Vitrano, Associate Professor of Philosophy at Brooklyn College of The City University of New York, answers both questions in the negative. Thus she offers a challenge to those who would defend morality by presuming that your making an ethical choice always works out to your satisfaction.

....

Although happiness and morality are conceptually independent, an empirical correlation exists between a person's moral character and happiness. Because most of us desire to develop and sustain relationships with others who will be more likely to react positively to us if we are kind and trustworthy, being moral enhances our potential for happiness. Alternatively, a person's nastiness and treachery will win few friends.

I am not denying the possibility of the happy tyrant, the happy hermit, or the happy immoralist; however, most of us rely on the good will of others in order to be happy. Psychologists studying happiness have found a positive correlation between people's social contacts (including family and friends) and the level of satisfaction with their lives. As the psychologist Michael Argyle notes, "In many studies [social relationships] come out as the greatest single source of happiness."[1] Because having a social network is for most people an important source of happiness, almost all of us have an interest in being viewed favorably by others. Acting immorally might result in short-term gains but in the longer run will besmirch our reputations.

While no controversy surrounds the recognition of an empirical connection between a person's moral character and happiness, a crucial issue often overlooked is whether the benefit to us derives from our being moral or merely appearing to be moral. The virtuous person is bound by moral obligations and so is unable to capitalize on opportunities to increase happiness through immoral actions. The person who merely appears to be virtuous will enjoy exactly the same advantages in reputation gained by someone who actually is virtuous, but will be able to exploit situations in which immorality enhances happiness. Thus what is crucial for maximal happiness is not being moral but appearing to be moral.

To develop this point more fully, consider these four cases: (1) a moral person who appears to be moral; (2) an immoral person who appears to be moral; (3) a moral person who appears to be immoral; (4) an immoral person who appears to be immoral.

Case (4) is worst for the subject. The blatant immoralist may be able to achieve some short-term gains but once recognized as immoral will be unlikely to be happy, because immoral actions will lead at least to social disapproval, if not a jail term.

Case (3), a moral person who appears to be immoral, is almost as bad for promoting happiness. Although the subject can take pride in knowing that she is acting morally, she will nevertheless suffer all the negative consequences associated with the blatant immoralist. Consider the example of an attorney who, believing that justice requires all those accused of crimes to have competent counsel, agrees to defend a terrorist accused of a murderous bombing. The attorney has no sympathy whatever for the deadly attack but does her best in the interest of her client. The public fails to appreciate her position and views her as a terrorist-sympathizer. Threats are made against her and her family, and she is eventually forced to give up her practice and move to another locale. She has acted morally and may receive some personal satisfaction from having taken a courageous stand, but because the public views her actions as immoral, she has impaired her happiness, just as she would have had she acted immorally.

Case (1), a moral person who appears to be moral, offers a commonly accepted model for achieving happiness but still has drawbacks. In those circumstances in which happiness depends on acting immorally, the moral person will be forced to sacrifice happiness for the sake of morality. Do such circumstances actually arise? Only those in the grip of an unrealistic philosophical theory would deny the possibility.

Consider the example of Anne, who is invited to go to a concert that takes place at the same time her sister is moving into a new apartment. Anne had promised to help her sister move, but the band is Anne's favorite, and this appearance is their last engagement before they break up. Anne does not want to miss this once-in-a-lifetime opportunity, but her sister would be greatly upset if Anne broke her promise. What should she do?

As a virtuous person she has no choice but to honor her commitment, thus missing an opportunity that would bring her happiness. If, however, she were not virtuous, she might fabricate a compelling excuse and achieve greater happiness. Some might suppose that Anne's lie would in some way bring her unhappiness, but that assumption, while perhaps comforting, is unwarranted. We could tell a story about how Anne's breaking her promise worked out badly for her and her sister, but we could equally easily tell a story about how the lie worked out well for both of them.

Sometimes the path of morality leads to misery. For example, someone may stop his car to help a stranger fix a flat tire, only to be hit by an oncoming truck. The whistle blower may as a result of telling the truth be fired, while the politician who refuses to vote against conscience may thereby forfeit a realistic chance for reelection. In all such cases the individual's happiness is lost as a result of adhering to moral standards.

In case (2), however, an immoral person who appears to be moral, the subject possesses all the advantages of a reputation for being moral while avoiding the disadvantages of always acting as morality dictates. Such an individual retains the option of acting immorally, whenever greater happiness would result. Admittedly, the person does take a significant risk, because exposure might bring ruin, but by striving to develop a reputation for being moral, and acting immorally only when the payoff is huge and the chances of being caught are small, the crafty immoralist may find more happiness than anyone else.

Once we recognize the independence of happiness and morality, we open the door to the dreaded question: Why be moral? If we acknowledge that the desire for happiness can come into conflict with acting morally, and that to pursue one's own happiness is rational, we are forced to acknowledge that sometimes acting immorally could be rational.

Faced with this conclusion, many philosophers have been tempted to deny that morality and happiness can conflict, a position that flies in the face of ordinary language or common experience. Another strategy to defuse the problem is to focus on cases of extreme depravity and then make the obvious point that such behavior is less preferable than adherence to conventional morality. The more realistic choice that confronts each person, however, is not whether to choose unmitigated evils but whether to do wrong when such action offers a plausible path to happiness. In the end, as we face critical decisions in what may be highly tempting circumstances, we shall define ourselves by our actions.

NOTE

1. Michael Argyle, "Subjective Well-Being," in *In Pursuit of the Quality of Life*, ed. Avner Offer (New York: Oxford University Press, 1996), p. 26.

STUDY QUESTIONS

1. Can an immoral person be happy?
2. Can a happy person be immoral?
3. According to Vitrano, under what circumstances can appearing to be moral lead to greater happiness than being moral?
4. Do you agree with Vitrano that one can appear to be moral without actually being moral?

Existentialism

JEAN-PAUL SARTRE

Jean-Paul Sartre (1905–1980) was a leading French philosopher, who was also a major playwright, novelist, and literary critic. He was offered but declined the 1964 Nobel Prize for Literature. He defends existentialism, according to which human agents, through their own thoughts and activities, freely shape themselves but, having no prior concepts on which to rely, are condemned to forlornness.

Let us consider some object that is manufactured, for example, a book or a paper-cutter: here is an object which has been made by an artisan whose inspiration came from a concept. He referred to the concept of what a paper-cutter is and likewise to a known method of production, which is part of the concept, something which is, by and large, a routine. Thus, the paper-cutter is at once an object produced in a certain way and, on the other hand, one having a specific use; and one cannot postulate a man who produces a paper-cutter but does not know what it is used for. Therefore, let us say that, for the paper-cutter, essence—that is, the ensemble of both the production routines and the properties which enable it to be both produced and defined—precedes existence. . . .

When we conceive God as the Creator, He is generally thought of as a superior sort of artisan. . . . He knows exactly what He is creating. Thus, the concept of man in the mind of God is comparable to the concept of paper-cutter in the mind of the manufacturer, and, following certain techniques and a conception, God produces man, just as the artisan, following a definition and a technique, makes a paper-cutter. Thus, the individual man is the realization of a certain concept in the divine intelligence. . . .

Atheistic existentialism, which I represent, . . . states that if God does not exist, there is at least one being in whom existence precedes essence, a being who exists before he can be defined by any concept, and that this being is man. . . . What is meant here by saying that existence precedes essence? It means that, first of all, man exists, turns up, appears on the scene, and only afterwards defines himself. If man, as the existentialist conceives him, is indefinable, it is because at first he is nothing. Only afterward will he be something, and he himself will have made what he will be. Thus, there is no human nature, since there is no God to conceive it. Not only is man what he conceives himself to be, but he is also only what he wills himself to be after this thrust toward existence.

From *Existentialism and Human Emotions* by Jean-Paul Sartre, translated by Bernard Frechtman, A Philosophical Library Book, Citadel, 2001. Reprinted by permission of Kensington Publishing Corp.

Man is nothing else but what he makes of himself. Such is the first principle of existentialism. . . .

The existentialist . . . thinks it very distressing that God does not exist, because all possibility of finding values in a heaven of ideas disappears along with Him; there can no longer be an a priori Good, since there is no infinite and perfect conscious-ness to think it. Nowhere is it written that the Good exists, that we must be honest, that we must not lie, because the fact is we are on a plane where there are only men. Dostoevsky said, "If God didn't exist, everything would be possible." That is the very starting point of existentialism. Indeed, everything is permissible if God does not exist, and as a result man is forlorn, because neither within him nor without does he find anything to cling to. He can't start making excuses for himself.

If existence really does precede essence, there is no explaining things away by reference to a fixed and given human nature. In other words, there is no determin-ism, man is free, man is freedom. On the other hand, if God does not exist, we find no values or commands to turn to which legitimize our conduct. So, in the bright realm of values, we have no excuse behind us, nor justification before us. We are alone, with no excuses.

That is the idea I shall try to convey when I say that man is condemned to be free. Condemned, because he did not create himself, yet, in other respects is free; because, once thrown into the world, he is responsible for everything he does. . . . But then we are forlorn.

To give you an example which will enable you to understand forlornness better, I shall cite the case of one of my students who came to see me under the following cir-cumstances: his father was on bad terms with his mother, and, moreover, was inclined to be a collaborationist; his older brother had been killed in the German offensive of 1940, and the young man, with somewhat immature but generous feelings, wanted to avenge him. His mother lived alone with him, very much upset by the half-treason of her husband and the death of her older son; the boy was her only consolation.

The boy was faced with the choice of leaving for England and joining the Free French Forces—that is, leaving his mother behind—or remaining with his mother and helping her to carry on. He was fully aware that the woman lived only for him and that his going-off—and perhaps his death—would plunge her into despair. He was also aware that every act that he did for his mother's sake was a sure thing, in the sense that it was helping her to carry on, whereas every effort he made toward going off and fighting was an uncertain move which might run aground and prove com-pletely useless; for example, on his way to England he might, while passing through Spain, be detained indefinitely in a Spanish camp; he might reach England or Algiers and be stuck in an office at a desk job. As a result, he was faced with two very differ-ent kinds of action: one, concrete, immediate, but concerning only one individual; the other concerned an incomparably vaster group, a national collectivity, but for that very reason was dubious, and might be interrupted en route. And, at the same time, he was wavering between two kinds of ethics. On the one hand, an ethics of sympathy, of personal devotion; on the other hand, a broader ethics, but one whose efficacy was more dubious. He had to choose between the two.

Who could help him choose? Christian doctrine? No. Christian doctrine says, "Be charitable, love your neighbor, take the more rugged path, etc., etc." But which is the more rugged path? Whom should he love as a brother? The fighting man or his mother? Which does the greater good, the vague act of fighting in a group, or the concrete one of helping a particular human being to go on living? Who can decide a priori? Nobody. No book of ethics can tell him. The Kantian ethics says, "Never treat any person as a means, but as an end." Very well, if I stay with my mother, I'll treat her as an end and not as a means; but by virtue of this very fact, I'm running the risk of treating the people around me who are fighting, as means; and, conversely, if I go to join those who are fighting, I'll be treating them as an end, and, by doing that, I run the risk of treating my mother as a means.

If values are vague, and if they are always too broad for the concrete and specific case that we are considering, the only thing left for us is to trust our instincts. That's what this young man tried to do; and when I saw him, he said, "In the end, feeling is what counts. I ought to choose whichever pushes me in one direction. If I feel that I love my mother enough to sacrifice everything else for her—my desire for vengeance, for action, for adventure—then I'll stay with her. If, on the contrary, I feel that my love for my mother isn't enough, I'll leave."

But how is the value of a feeling determined? What gives his feeling for his mother value? Precisely the fact that he remained with her. I may say that I like so-and-so well enough to sacrifice a certain amount of money for him, but I may say so only if I've done it. I may say "I love my mother well enough to remain with her" if I have remained with her. The only way to determine the value of this affection is, precisely, to perform an act which confirms and defines it. But, since I require this affection to justify my act, I find myself caught in a vicious circle.

On the other hand, Gide has well said that a mock feeling and a true feeling are almost indistinguishable; to decide that I love my mother and will remain with her, or to remain with her by putting on an act, amount somewhat to the same thing. In other words, the feeling is formed by the acts one performs; so, I cannot refer to it in order to act upon it. Which means that I can neither seek within myself the true condition which will impel me to act, nor apply to a system of ethics for concepts which will permit me to act. You will say, "At least, he did go to a teacher for advice." But if you seek advice from a priest, for example, you have chosen this priest; you already knew, more or less, just about what advice he was going to give you. In other words, choosing your adviser is involving yourself. The proof of this is that if you are a Christian, you will say, "Consult a priest." But some priests are collaborating, some are just marking time, some are resisting. Which to choose? If the young man chooses a priest who is resisting or collaborating, he has already decided on the kind of advice he's going to get. Therefore, in coming to see me he knew the answer I was going to give him, and I had only one answer to give: "You're free, choose, that is, invent." No general ethics can show you what is to be done; there are no omens in the world. The Catholics will reply, "But there are." Granted—but, in any case, I myself choose the meaning they have.

When I was a prisoner, I knew a rather remarkable young man who was a Jesuit. He had entered the Jesuit order in the following way: he had had a number of very bad breaks; in childhood, his father died, leaving him in poverty, and he was a scholarship student at a religious institution where he was constantly made to feel that he was being kept out of charity; then, he failed to get any of the honors and distinctions that children like; later on, at about eighteen, he bungled a love affair; finally at twenty-two, he failed in military training, a childish enough matter, but it was the last straw.

This young fellow might well have felt that he had botched everything. It was a sign of something, but of what? He might have taken refuge in bitterness or despair. But he very wisely looked upon all this as a sign that he was not made for secular triumphs, and that only the triumphs of religion, holiness, and faith were open to him. He saw the hand of God in all this, and so he entered the order. Who can help seeing that he alone decided what the sign meant?

Some other interpretation might have been drawn from this series of setbacks; for example, that he might have done better to turn carpenter or revolutionist. Therefore, he is fully responsible for the interpretation. Forlornness implies that we ourselves choose our being.

STUDY QUESTIONS

1. What does Sartre mean by his claim that existence precedes essence?
2. According to Sartre, why are human beings forlorn?
3. Do you agree with Sartre that our feelings are formed by the acts we perform?
4. Do you agree with Sartre's analysis of the case of the boy faced with the choice of joining the Free French Forces or staying with his mother?

Nicomachean Ethics

ARISTOTLE

Aristotle (384–322 B.C.E.) was born in Macedonia, located between the Balkans and the Greek peninsula. At the age of eighteen he entered Plato's Academy, where he remained for two decades until Plato's death. He then taught outside Athens, including service as tutor to the young prince who later became known as Alexander the Great. Subsequently, Aristotle returned to Athens and founded his own school, the Lyceum. A dozen years later, when an outbreak of anti-Macedonian feeling swept Athens, Aristotle left the city, "lest," he reportedly said, "the Athenians should sin twice against philosophy," referring, of course, to the case of Socrates.

The *Nicomachean Ethics,* named after Aristotle's son Nicomachus, is widely regarded as one of the great books of moral philosophy. Aristotle grounds morality in human nature, viewing the good as the fulfillment of the human potential to live well. To live well is to live in accordance with virtue. But how does one acquire virtue? Aristotle's answer depends on his distinction between moral and intellectual virtue. Moral virtue, which we might call "goodness of character," is formed by habit. One becomes good by doing good. Repeated acts of justice and self-control result in a just, self-controlled person who not only performs just, self-controlled actions but does so from a fixed character. Intellectual virtue, on the other hand, which we might refer to as "wisdom," requires sophisticated intelligence and is acquired by teaching.

Virtuous activities are those that avoid the two extremes of excess and deficiency. For example, if you fear too much, you become cowardly; if you fear too little, you become rash. The mean is courage. To achieve the mean, you need to make a special effort to avoid that extreme to which you happen to be prone. Thus if you tend to be foolhardy, aim at timidity, and you will achieve the right measure of boldness.

The translation from the Greek is by David Ross (1877–1971), updated by J. L. Ackrill (1921–2007) and J. O. Urmson (1915–2008), all of the University of Oxford.

Every art and every inquiry, and similarly every action and pursuit, is thought to aim at some good; and for this reason the good has rightly been declared to be that at which all things aim. . . .

From *The Nicomachean Ethics,* translated by David Ross, revised by J. L. Ackrill and J. O. Urmson. Reprinted by permission of Oxford University Press.

If, then, there is some end of the things we do, which we desire for its own sake (everything else being desired for the sake of this), . . . clearly this must be . . . the chief good. . . .

Now such a thing happiness, above all else, is held to be; for this we choose always for itself and never for the sake of something else. . . .

Presumably, however, to say that happiness is the chief good seems a platitude, and a clearer account of what it is is still desired. This might perhaps be given, if we could first ascertain the function of man. For just as for a flute-player, a sculptor, or any artist, and, in general, for all things that have a function or activity, the good and the "well" is thought to reside in the function, so would it seem to be for man, if he has a function. Have the carpenter, then, and the tanner certain functions or activities, and has man none? Is he born without a function? Or as eye, hand, foot, and in general each of the parts evidently has a function, may one lay it down that man similarly has a function apart from all these? What then can this be? Life seems to belong even to plants, but we are seeking what is peculiar to man. Let us exclude, therefore, the life of nutrition and growth. Next there would be a life of perception, but *it* also seems to be shared even by the horse, the ox, and every animal. There remains, then, an active life of the element that has a rational principle. . . . Now if the function of man is an activity of soul which follows or implies a rational principle, and if . . . any action is well performed when it is performed in accordance with the appropriate excellence . . . human good turns out to be activity of soul exhibiting excellence. . . .

But we must add "in a complete life." For one swallow does not make a summer, nor does one day; and so too one day, or a short time, does not make a man blessed and happy. . . .

Virtue, then, being of two kinds, intellectual and moral, intellectual virtue in the main owes both its birth and its growth to teaching (for which reason it requires experience and time), while moral virtue comes about as a result of habit. . . . From this it is also plain that none of the moral virtues arises in us by nature; for nothing that exists by nature can form a habit contrary to its nature. For instance the stone which by nature moves downwards cannot be habituated to move upwards, not even if one tries to train it by throwing it up ten thousand times; nor can fire be habituated to move downwards, nor can anything else that by nature behaves in one way be trained to behave in another. Neither by nature, then, nor contrary to nature do the virtues arise in us; rather we are adapted by nature to receive them, and are made perfect by habit.

Again, of all the things that come to us by nature we first acquire the potentiality and later exhibit the activity (this is plain in the case of the senses; for it was not by often seeing or often hearing that we got these senses, but on the contrary we had them before we used them, and did not come to have them by using them); but the virtues we get by first exercising them, as also happens in the case of the arts as well. For the things we have to learn before we can do them, we learn by doing them, e.g., men become builders by building and lyre-players by playing the lyre; so too we become just by doing just acts, temperate by doing temperate acts, brave by doing brave acts. . . .

It makes no small difference, then, whether we form habits of one kind or of another from our very youth; it makes a very great difference, or rather *all* the difference.

Since, then, the present inquiry does not aim at theoretical knowledge like the others (for we are inquiring not in order to know what virtue is, but in order to become good, since otherwise our inquiry would have been of no use), we must examine the nature of actions, namely how we ought to do them; for these determine also the nature of the states of character that are produced, as we have said. . . .

First, then, let us consider this, that it is the nature of such things to be destroyed by defect and excess, as we see in the case of strength and of health (for to gain light on things imperceptible we must use the evidence of sensible things); exercise either excessive or defective destroys the strength, and similarly drink or food which is above or below a certain amount destroys the health, while that which is proportionate both produces and increases and preserves it. So too is it, then, in the case of temperance and courage and the other virtues. For the man who flies from and fears everything and does not stand his ground against anything becomes a coward, and the man who fears nothing at all but goes to meet every danger becomes rash; and similarly the man who indulges in every pleasure and abstains from none becomes self-indulgent, while the man who shuns every pleasure, as boors do, becomes in a way insensible; temperance and courage, then, are destroyed by excess and defect, and preserved by the mean.

But not only are the sources and causes of their origination and growth the same as those of their destruction, but also the sphere of their actualization will be the same; for this is also true of the things which are more evident to sense, e.g., of strength; it is produced by taking much food and undergoing much exertion, and it is the strong man that will be most able to do these things. So too is it with the virtues; by abstaining from pleasures we become temperate, and it is when we have become so that we are most able to abstain from them; and similarly too in the case of courage; for by being habituated to despise things that are fearful and to stand our ground against them we become brave, and it is when we have become so that we shall be most able to stand our ground against them. . . .

The question might be asked, what we mean by saying that we must become just by doing just acts, and temperate by doing temperate acts; for if men do just and temperate acts, they are already just and temperate, exactly as, if they do what is in accordance with the laws of grammar and of music, they are grammarians and musicians.

Or is this not true even of the arts? It is possible to do something that is in accordance with the laws of grammar, either by chance or under the guidance of another. A man will be a grammarian, then, only when he has both said something grammatical and said it grammatically; and this means doing it in accordance with the grammatical knowledge in himself.

Again, the case of the arts and that of the virtues are not similar; for the products of the arts have their goodness in themselves, so that it is enough that they should have a certain character, but if the acts that are in accordance with the virtues have themselves a certain character it does not follow that they are done justly or temperately. The agent also must be in a certain condition when he does them; in the first place he must have knowledge, secondly he must choose the acts, and choose them for their own sakes, and thirdly his action must proceed from a firm and unchangeable character. These are not reckoned in as conditions of the possession of the arts, except the bare knowledge; but as a condition of the possession of the virtues knowledge has little or no weight, while the other conditions count not for a little but for everything, i.e., the very conditions which result from often doing just and temperate acts.

Actions, then, are called just and temperate when they are such as the just or the temperate man would do; but it is not the man who does these that is just and temperate, but the man who also does them *as* just and temperate men do them. It is well said, then, that it is by doing just acts that the just man is produced, and by doing temperate acts the temperate man; without doing these no one would have even a prospect of becoming good.

But most people do not do these, but take refuge in theory and think they are being philosophers and will become good in this way, behaving somewhat like patients who listen attentively to their doctors, but do none of the things they are ordered to do. As the latter will not be made well in body by such a course of treatment, the former will not be made well in soul by such a course of philosophy. . . .

[E]very virtue or excellence both brings into good condition the thing of which it is the excellence and makes the work of that thing be done well; e.g., the excellence of the eye makes both the eye and its work good; for it is by the excellence of the eye that we see well. Similarly the excellence of the horse makes a horse both good in itself and good at running and at carrying its rider and at awaiting the attack of the enemy. Therefore, if this is true in every case, the virtue of man also will be the state of character which makes a man good and which makes him do his own work well.

How this is to happen we have stated already, but it will be made plain also by the following consideration of the specific nature of virtue. In everything that is continuous and divisible it is possible to take more, less, or an equal amount, and that either in terms of the thing itself or relatively to us; and the equal is an intermediate between excess and defect. By the intermediate in the object I mean that which is equidistant from each of the extremes, which is one and the same for all men; by the intermediate relatively to us that which is neither too much nor too little—and this is not one, nor the same for all. For instance, if ten is many and two is few, six is the intermediate, taken in terms of the object; for it exceeds and is exceeded by an equal amount; this is intermediate according to arithmetical proportion. But the intermediate relatively to us is not to be taken so; if ten pounds are too much for a particular person to eat and two too little, it does not follow that the trainer will order six pounds; for this also is perhaps too much for the person who is to take it, or too little—too little for Milo, too much for the beginner in athletic exercises. The same is true of running and wrestling. Thus a master of any art avoids excess and defect, but seeks the intermediate and chooses this—the intermediate not in the object but relatively to us.

If it is thus, then, that every art does its work well—by looking to the intermediate and judging its works by this standard (so that we often say of good works of art that it is not possible either to take away or to add anything, implying that excess and defect destroy the goodness of works of art, while the mean preserves it; and good artists, as we say, look to this in their work), and if, further, virtue is more exact and better than any art, as nature also is, then virtue must have the quality of aiming at the intermediate. I mean moral virtue; for it is this that is concerned with passions and actions, and in these there is excess, defect, and the intermediate. For instance, both fear and confidence and appetite and anger and pity and in general pleasure and pain may be felt both too much and too little, and in both cases not well; but to feel them at the right times, with reference to the right objects, towards the right people, with the right motive, and in the right way, is what is both intermediate and best, and this is characteristic of virtue. Similarly with regard to actions also there is excess, defect, and the intermediate. Now virtue is concerned with passions and actions, in which excess is a form of failure, and so is defect, while the intermediate is praised and is a form of success; and being praised and being successful are both characteristics of virtue. Therefore virtue is a kind of mean, since, as we have seen, it aims at what is intermediate. . . .

But not every action nor every passion admits of a mean; for some have names that already imply badness, e.g., spite, shamelessness, envy, and in the case of actions adultery, theft, murder; for all of these and suchlike things imply by their names that they are themselves bad, and not the excesses or deficiencies of them. It is not possible, then, ever to be right with regard to them; one must always be wrong. Nor does goodness or badness with regard to such things depend on committing adultery with the right woman, at the right time, and in the right way, but simply to do any of them is to go wrong. . . .

That moral virtue is a mean, then, and in what sense it is so, and that it is a mean between two vices, the one involving excess, the other deficiency, and that it is such because its character is to aim at what is intermediate in passions and in actions, has been sufficiently stated. Hence also it is no easy task to be good. For in everything it is no easy task to find the middle, e.g., to find the middle of a circle is not for everyone but for him who knows; so, too, anyone can get angry—that is easy—or give or spend money; but to do this to the right person, to the right extent, at the right time, with the right motive, and in the right way, *that* is not for everyone, nor is it easy; wherefore goodness is both rare and laudable and noble. . . .

But we must consider the things towards which we ourselves also are easily carried away; for some of us tend to one thing, some to another; and this will be recognizable from the pleasure and the pain we feel. We must drag ourselves away to the contrary extreme; for we shall get into the intermediate state by drawing well away from error. . . .

So much, then, is plain, that the intermediate state is in all things to be praised, but that we must incline sometimes towards the excess, sometimes towards the deficiency; for so shall we most easily hit the mean and what is right.

STUDY QUESTIONS

1. According to Aristotle, what is the function of a human being?
2. How does moral virtue differ from intellectual virtue?
3. How is moral virtue acquired?
4. What is Aristotle's doctrine of the mean?

Groundwork of the Metaphysics of Morals

IMMANUEL KANT

Immanuel Kant, whose work we read previously, is a central figure in the history of ethics. The selection that follows comes from a short work of his which, although intended only as a preliminary presentation of the main themes of his moral philosophy, has become the most widely read of all his ethical writings. By the "metaphysics of morals" Kant means the philosophical study of moral principles, as opposed to the anthropological survey of moral practices.

....

Everything in nature works in accordance with laws. Only a rational being has the power to act in accordance with the idea of laws—that is, in accordance with principles—and thus has a will. . . .

The idea of an objective principle, in so far as it constrains a will, is called a commandment (of reason), and the formulation of this commandment is called an Imperative. . . .

All imperatives command either hypothetically or categorically. Hypothetical imperatives declare a possible action to be practically necessary as a means to the attainment of something else that one wants (or that one may want). A categorical imperative would be one that represented an action as itself objectively necessary, without regard to any further end. . . .

If the action would be good only as a means to something else, the imperative is hypothetical; if the action is thought of as good in itself and therefore as necessary for a will which of itself conforms to reason as its principle, then the imperative is categorical. . . .

If I think of a *hypothetical* imperative as such, I do not know beforehand what it will contain—not until I am given its condition. But if I think of a *categorical imperative*, I know right away what it contains. For since this imperative contains, besides the law, only the necessity that the maxim[1] conform to this law, while the law, as we have seen, contains no condition limiting it, there is nothing left over to which the maxim of action should conform except the universality of a law as such; and it is only this conformity that the imperative asserts to be necessary.

There is therefore only one categorical imperative and it is this: "Act only on that maxim by which you can at the same time will that it should become a universal law." . . .

We shall now enumerate some duties. . . .

1. A man feels sick of life as the result of a mounting series of misfortunes that has reduced him to hopelessness, but he still possesses enough of his reason to ask himself whether it would not be contrary to his duty to himself to take his own life. Now he tests whether the maxim of his action could really become a universal law of nature. His maxim, however, is: "I make it my principle out of self-love to shorten my life if its continuance threatens more evil than it promises advantage." The only further question is whether this principle of self-love can become a universal law of nature. But one sees at once that a nature whose law was that the very same feeling meant to promote life should actually destroy life would contradict itself, and hence would not endure as nature. The maxim therefore could not possibly be a general law of nature and thus it wholly contradicts the supreme principle of all duty.

2. Another finds himself driven by need to borrow money. He knows very well that he will not be able to pay it back, but he sees too that nobody will lend him anything unless he firmly promises to pay it back within a fixed time. He wants to make such a promise, but he still has enough conscience to ask himself, "Isn't it impermissible and contrary to duty to get out of one's difficulties this way?" Suppose, however, that he did decide to do it. The maxim of his action would run thus: "When I believe myself short of money, I will borrow money and promise to pay it back, even though I know that this will never be done." Now this principle of self-love or personal advantage is perhaps quite compatible with my own entire future welfare; only there remains the question "Is it right?" I therefore transform the unfair demand of self-love into a universal law and frame my question thus: "How would things stand if my maxim became a universal law?" I then see immediately that this maxim can never qualify as a self-consistent universal law of nature, but must necessarily contradict itself. For the universality of a law

that permits anyone who believes himself to be in need to make any promise he pleases with the intention of not keeping it would make promising, and the very purpose one has in promising, itself impossible. For no one would believe he was being promised anything, but would laugh at any such utterance as hollow pretence.

3. A third finds in himself a talent that, with a certain amount of cultivation, could make him a useful man for all sorts of purposes. But he sees himself in comfortable circumstances, and he prefers to give himself up to pleasure rather than to bother about increasing and improving his fortunate natural aptitudes. Yet he asks himself further "Does my maxim of neglecting my natural gifts, besides agreeing with my taste for amusement, agree also with what is called duty?" He then sees that a nature could indeed endure under such a universal law, even if (like the South Sea Islanders) every man should let his talents rust and should be bent on devoting his life solely to idleness, amusement, procreation—in a word, to enjoyment. Only he cannot possibly *will* that this should become a universal law of nature or should be implanted in us as such a law by a natural instinct. For as a rational being he necessarily wills that all his powers should be developed, since they are after all useful to him and given to him for all sorts of possible purposes.

4. A fourth man, who is himself flourishing but sees others who have to struggle with great hardships (and whom he could easily help) thinks to himself: "What do I care? Let every one be as happy as Heaven intends or as he can make himself; I won't deprive him of anything; I won't even envy him; but I don't feel like contributing anything to his well-being or to helping him in his distress!" Now admittedly if such an attitude were a universal law of nature, the human race could survive perfectly well and doubtless even better than when everybody chatters about sympathy and good will, and even makes an effort, now and then, to practise them, but, when one can get away with it, swindles, traffics in human rights, or violates them in other ways. But although it is possible that a universal law of nature in accord with this maxim could exist, it is impossible to *will* that such a principle should hold everywhere as a law of nature. For a will that intended this would be in conflict with itself, since many situations might arise in which the man needs love and sympathy from others, and in which, by such a law of nature generated by his own will, he would rob himself of all hope of the help he wants.

These are some of the many actual duties—or at least of what we take to be actual—whose derivation from the single principle cited above is perspicuous. We must be able to will that a maxim of our action should become a universal law—this is the authoritative model for moral judging of action generally. Some actions are so constituted that we cannot even *conceive* without contradiction that their maxim be a universal law of nature, let alone that we could *will* that it *ought* to become one. In the case of other actions, we do not find this inner impossibility, but it is still impossible to *will* that their maxim should be raised to the universality of a law of nature, because such a will would contradict itself. . . .

If we now look at ourselves whenever we transgress a duty, we find that we in fact do not intend that our maxim should become a universal law. For this is impossible for us. What we really intend is rather that its opposite should remain a law generally; we only take the liberty of making an *exception* to it, for ourselves or (of course just this once) to satisfy our inclination. Consequently if we weighed it all up from one and the same perspective—that of reason—we should find a contradiction in our own will, the contradiction that a certain principle should be objectively necessary as a universal law and yet subjectively should not hold universally but should admit of exceptions. . . .

Suppose, however, there were something *whose existence in itself* had an absolute worth, something that, as an end *in itself,* could be a ground of definite laws. Then in it and in it alone, would the ground of a possible categorical imperative, that is, of a practical law, reside.

Now, I say, a human being, and in general every rational being, *does exist* as an end in himself, *not merely as a means* to be used by this or that will as it pleases. In all his actions, whether they are directed to himself or to other rational beings, a human being must always be viewed *at the same time as an end.* . . .

Beings whose existence depends not on our will but on nature still have only a relative value as means and are therefore called *things,* if they lack reason. Rational beings, on the other hand, are called *persons* because, their nature already marks them out as ends in themselves—that is, as something which ought not to be used *merely* as a means—and consequently imposes restrictions on all choice making (and is an object of respect). Persons, therefore, are not merely subjective ends whose existence as an effect of our actions has a value *for us.* They are *objective ends*—that is, things whose existence is in itself an end, and indeed an end such that no other end can be substituted for it, no end to which they should serve *merely* as a means. For if this were not so, there would be nothing at all having *absolute value* anywhere. But if all value were conditional, and thus contingent, then no supreme principle could be found for reason at all.

If then there is to be a supreme practical principle and a categorical imperative for the human will, it must be such that it forms an objective principle of the will from the idea of something which is necessarily an end for everyone because *it is an end in itself,* a principle that can therefore serve as a universal practical law. The ground of this principle is: *Rational nature exists as an end in itself.* This is the way in which a human being necessarily conceives his own existence, and it is therefore a *subjective* principle of human actions. But it is also the way in which every other rational being conceives his existence, on the same rational ground which holds also for me; hence it is at the same time an *objective* principle from which, since it is a supreme practical ground, it must be possible to derive all laws of the will. The practical imperative will therefore be the following: *Act in such a way that you treat humanity, whether in your own person or in any other person, always at the same time as an end, never merely as a means.* We will now see whether this can be carried out in practice.

Let us keep to our previous examples.

First, . . . the man who contemplates suicide will ask himself whether his action could be compatible with the Idea of humanity as *an end in itself.* If he damages himself in order to escape from a painful situation, he is making use of a person *merely as a means* to maintain a tolerable state of affairs till the end of his life. But a human being is not a thing—not something to be used *merely* as a means: he must always in all his actions be regarded as an end in himself. Hence I cannot dispose of a human being in my own person, by maiming, corrupting, or killing him. (I must here forego a more precise definition of this principle that would forestall any misunderstanding—for example, as to having limbs amputated to save myself or exposing my life to danger in order to preserve it, and so on—this discussion belongs to ethics proper.)

Secondly, . . . the man who has in mind making a false promise to others will see at once that he is intending to make use of another person *merely as a means* to an end which that person does not share. For the person whom I seek to use for my own purposes by such a promise cannot possibly agree with my way of treating him, and so cannot himself share the end of the action. This incompatibility with the principle of duty to others can be seen more distinctly when we bring in examples of attacks on the freedom and property of others. For then it is manifest that a violator of the rights of human beings intends to use the person of others merely as a means without taking into consideration that, as rational beings, they must always at the same time be valued as ends—that is, treated only as beings who must themselves be able to share in the end of the very same action.

Thirdly, . . . it is not enough that an action not conflict with humanity in our own person as an end in itself: it must also *harmonize with this end.* Now there are in humanity capacities for greater perfection that form part of nature's purpose for humanity in our own person. To neglect these can perhaps be compatible with the *survival* of humanity as an end in itself, but not with the *promotion* of that end.

Fourthly, . . . the natural end that all human beings seek is their own perfect happiness. Now the human race might indeed exist if everybody contributed nothing to the happiness of others but at the same time refrained from deliberately impairing it. This harmonizing with humanity *as an end in itself* would, however, be merely negative and not positive, unless everyone also endeavours, as far as he can, to further the ends of others. For the ends of any person who is an end in himself must, if this idea is to have its full effect in me, be also, as far as possible, *my* ends.

NOTE

1. [A maxim is the principle according to which the subject acts.—S. M. C.]

STUDY QUESTIONS

1. According to Kant, is using someone as a means always wrong?
2. What does Kant mean by the maxim of an action?
3. Why is it wrong to deceive others?
4. Can you imagine circumstances in which breaking a promise would not be wrong?

Utilitarianism

JOHN STUART MILL

John Stuart Mill (1806–1873), born in London, received an intense early education from his father, James Mill, a philosophical and political writer. While pursuing a career in the East India Company, John Stuart Mill published widely in philosophy, political theory, and economics. A strong influence on his life and thought was Harriet Taylor, whom he met in 1831 and married two decades later following the death of her husband. She herself died seven years afterward. Subsequently, Mill served as a member of Parliament, then retired and spent much of his time in Avignon, France, where his wife was buried.

The best known of his ethical writings is *Utilitarianism,* originally published in three installments in *Fraser's Magazine* of 1861. More than 150 years later, the book remains enormously influential. As a concise, yet comprehensive, presentation of its subject, the work has never been equaled.

CHAPTER II

WHAT UTILITARIANISM IS

. . . The creed which accepts as the foundation of morals "utility" or the "greatest happiness principle" holds that actions are right in proportion as they tend to promote happiness; wrong as they tend to produce the reverse of happiness. By happiness is intended pleasure and the absence of pain; by unhappiness, pain and the privation of pleasure. To give a clear view of the moral standard set up by the theory, much more requires to be said; in particular, what things it includes in the ideas of pain and pleasure, and to what extent this is left an open question. But these supplementary explanations do not affect the theory of life on which this theory of morality is

From *Utilitarianism* by John Stuart Mill (1863).

grounded—namely, that pleasure and freedom from pain are the only things desirable as ends; and that all desirable things (which are as numerous in the utilitarian as in any other scheme) are desirable either for pleasure inherent in themselves or as means to the promotion of pleasure and the prevention of pain. . . .

It is quite compatible with the principle of utility to recognize the fact that some kinds of pleasure are more desirable and more valuable than others. It would be absurd that, while in estimating all other things quality is considered as well as quantity, the estimation of pleasure should be supposed to depend on quantity alone.

If I am asked what I mean by difference of quality in pleasures, or what makes one pleasure more valuable than another, merely as a pleasure, except its being greater in amount, there is but one possible answer. Of two pleasures, if there be one to which all or almost all who have experience of both give a decided preference, irrespective of any feeling of moral obligation to prefer it, that is the more desirable pleasure. If one of the two is, by those who are competently acquainted with both, placed so far above the other that they prefer it, even though knowing it to be attended with a greater amount of discontent, and would not resign it for any quantity of the other pleasure which their nature is capable of, we are justified in ascribing to the preferred enjoyment a superiority in quality so far outweighing quantity as to render it, in comparison, of small account.

Now it is an unquestionable fact that those who are equally acquainted with and equally capable of appreciating and enjoying both do give a most marked preference to the manner of existence which employs their higher faculties. Few human creatures would consent to be changed into any of the lower animals for a promise of the fullest allowance of a beast's pleasures; no intelligent human being would consent to be a fool, no instructed person would be an ignoramus, no person of feeling and conscience would be selfish and base, even though they should be persuaded that the fool, the dunce, or the rascal is better satisfied with his lot than they are with theirs. They would not resign what they possess more than he for the most complete satisfaction of all the desires which they have in common with him. If they ever fancy they would, it is only in cases of unhappiness so extreme that to escape from it they would exchange their lot for almost any other, however undesirable in their own eyes. A being of higher faculties requires more to make him happy, is capable probably of more acute suffering, and certainly accessible to it at more points, than one of an inferior type; but in spite of these liabilities, he can never really wish to sink into what he feels to be a lower grade of existence. . . .

It is better to be a human being dissatisfied than a pig satisfied; better to be Socrates dissatisfied than a fool satisfied. And if the fool, or the pig, are of a different opinion, it is because they only know their own side of the question. The other party to the comparison knows both sides. . . .

From this verdict of the only competent judges, I apprehend there can be no appeal. On a question which is the best worth having of two pleasures, or which of two modes of existence is the most grateful to the feelings, apart from its moral attributes and from its consequences, the judgment of those who are qualified by knowledge of both, or, if they differ, that of the majority among them, must be admitted as final. And there needs be the less hesitation to accept this judgment respecting the quality of pleasures, since there is no other tribunal to be referred to even on the question of quantity. What means are there of determining which is the acutest of two pains, or the intensest of two pleasurable sensations, except the general suffrage of those who are familiar with both?. . .

I have dwelt on this point as being a necessary part of a perfectly just conception of utility or happiness considered as the directive rule of human conduct. But it is by no means an indispensable condition to the acceptance of the utilitarian standard; for that standard is not the agent's own greatest happiness, but the greatest amount of happiness altogether; and if it may possibly be doubted whether a noble character is always the happier for its nobleness, there can be no doubt that it makes other people happier, and that the world in general is immensely a gainer by it. Utilitarianism, therefore, could only attain its end by the general cultivation of nobleness of character, even if each individual were only benefited by the nobleness of others, and his own, so far as happiness is concerned, were a sheer deduction from the benefit. But the bare enunciation of such an absurdity as this last renders refutation superfluous.

According to the greatest happiness principle, as above explained, the ultimate end, with reference to and for the sake of which all other things are desirable—whether we are considering our own good or that of other people—is an existence exempt as far as possible from pain, and as rich as possible in enjoyments, both in point of quantity and quality; the test of quality and the rule for measuring it against quantity being the preference felt by those who, in their opportunities of experience, to which must be added their habits of self-consciousness and self-observation, are best furnished with the means of comparison. This, being according to the utilitarian opinion the end of human action, is necessarily also the standard of morality, which may accordingly be defined "the rules and precepts for human conduct," by the observance of which an existence such as has been described might be, to the greatest extent possible, secured to all mankind; and not to them only, but, so far as the nature of things admits, to the whole sentient creation. . . .

I must again repeat what the assailants of utilitarianism seldom have the justice to acknowledge, that the happiness which forms the utilitarian standard of what is right in conduct is not the agent's own happiness but that of all concerned. As between his own happiness and that of others, utilitarianism requires him to be as strictly impartial as a disinterested and benevolent spectator. In the golden rule of Jesus of Nazareth, we read the complete spirit of the ethics of utility. "To do as you would be done by," and "to love your neighbor as yourself," constitute the ideal perfection of utilitarian morality. As the means of making the nearest approach to this ideal, utility would enjoin, first, that laws and social arrangements should place the happiness or (as, speaking practically, it may be called) the interest of every individual as nearly as possible in harmony with the interest of the whole; and, secondly, that education and opinion, which have so vast a power over human character, should so use that power as to establish in the mind of every individual an indissoluble association between his own happiness and the good of the whole, especially between his own happiness and the practice of such modes of conduct, negative and positive, as regard for the universal happiness prescribes; so that not only he may be unable to conceive the possibility of happiness to himself, consistently with conduct opposed to the general good, but also that a direct impulse to promote the general good may be in every individual one of the habitual motives of action, and the sentiments connected therewith may fill a large and prominent place in every human being's sentient existence. If the impugners of the utilitarian morality represented it to their own minds in this its true character, I know not what recommendation possessed by any other morality they could possibly affirm to be wanting to it; what more beautiful or more exalted developments of human nature any other ethical system can be supposed to foster, or what springs of action, not accessible to the utilitarian, such systems rely on for giving effect to their mandates.

The objectors to utilitarianism cannot always be charged with representing it in a discreditable light. On the contrary, those among them who entertain anything like a just idea of its disinterested character sometimes find fault with its standard as being too high for humanity. They say it is exacting too much to require that people shall always act from the inducement of promoting the general interests of society. But this is to mistake the very meaning of a standard of morals and confound the rule of action with the motive of it. It is the business of ethics to tell us what are our duties, or by what test we may know them; but no system of ethics requires that the sole motive of all we do shall be a feeling of duty; on the contrary, ninety-nine hundredths of all our actions are done from other motives, and rightly so done if the rule of duty does not condemn them. It is the more unjust to utilitarianism that this particular misapprehension should be made a ground of objection to it, inasmuch as utilitarian moralists have gone beyond almost all others in affirming that the motive has nothing to do with the morality of the action, though much with the worth of the agent. He who saves a fellow creature from drowning does what is morally right, whether his motive be duty or the hope of being paid for his trouble; he who betrays the friend that trusts him is guilty of a crime, even if his object be to serve another friend to whom he is under greater obligations. But to speak only of actions done from the motive of duty, and in direct obedience to principle: it is a misapprehension of the utilitarian mode of thought to conceive it as implying that people should fix their minds upon so wide a generality as the world, or society at large. The great majority of good actions are intended not for the benefit of the world, but for that of individuals, of which the good of the world is made up; and the thoughts of the most virtuous man need not on these occasions travel beyond the particular persons concerned, except so far as is necessary to assure himself that in benefiting them he is not violating the rights, that is, the legitimate and authorized expectations, of anyone else. The multiplication of happiness is, according to the utilitarian ethics, the object of virtue: the occasions on which any person (except one in a thousand) has it in his power to do this on an extended scale—in other words, to be a public benefactor—are but exceptional; and on these occasions alone is he called on to consider public utility; in every other case, private utility, the interest or happiness of some few persons, is all he has to attend to. Those alone the influence of whose actions extends to society in general need concern themselves habitually about so large an object. In the case of abstinences indeed—of things which people forbear to do from moral considerations, though the consequences in the particular case might be beneficial—it would be unworthy of an intelligent agent not to be consciously aware that the action is of a class which, if practiced generally, would be generally injurious, and that this is the ground of the obligation to abstain from it. The amount of regard for the public interest implied in this recognition is no greater than is demanded by every system of morals, for they all enjoin to abstain from whatever is manifestly pernicious to society. . . .

Again, utility is often summarily stigmatized as an immoral doctrine by giving it the name of "expediency" and taking advantage of the popular use of that term to contrast it with principle. But the expedient, in the sense in which it is opposed to the right, generally means that which is expedient for the particular interest of the agent himself; as when a minister sacrifices the interests of his country to keep himself in place. When it means anything better than this, it means that which is expedient for some immediate object, some temporary purpose, but which violates a rule whose observance is expedient in a much higher degree. The expedient, in this sense, instead of being the same thing with the useful, is a branch of the hurtful. Thus it would often be expedient, for the purpose of getting over some momentary embarrassment, or attaining some object immediately useful to ourselves or others, to tell a lie. But inasmuch as the cultivation in ourselves of a sensitive feeling on the subject of veracity is one of the most useful, and the enfeeblement of that feeling one of the most hurtful, things to which our conduct can be instrumental; and inasmuch as any, even unintentional, deviation from truth does that much toward weakening the trustworthiness of human assertion, which is not only the principal support of all present social well-being, but the insufficiency of which does more than any one thing that can be named to keep back civilization, virtue, everything on which human happiness on the largest scale depends—we feel that the violation, for a present advantage, of a rule of such transcendent expediency is not expedient, and that he who, for the sake of convenience to himself or to some other individual, does what depends on him to deprive mankind of the good, and inflict upon them the evil, involved in the greater or less reliance which they can place in each other's word, acts the part of one of their worst enemies. Yet that even this rule, sacred as it is, admits of possible exceptions is acknowledged by all moralists; the chief of which is when the withholding of some fact (as of information from a malefactor, or of bad news from a person dangerously ill) would save an individual (especially an individual other than oneself) from great and unmerited evil, and when the withholding can only be effected by denial. But in order that the exception may not extend itself beyond the need, and may have the least possible effect in weakening reliance on veracity, it ought to be recognized and, if possible, its limits defined; and, if the principle of utility is good for anything, it must be good for weighing these conflicting utilities against one another and marking out the region within which one or the other preponderates.

CHAPTER IV

OF WHAT SORT OF PROOF THE PRINCIPLE
OF UTILITY IS SUSCEPTIBLE

. . . Questions about ends are, in other words, questions about what things are desirable. The utilitarian doctrine is that happiness is desirable, and the only thing desirable, as an end; all other things being only desirable as means to that end. What ought to be required of this doctrine, what conditions is it requisite that the doctrine should fulfill—to make good its claim to be believed?

The only proof capable of being given that an object is visible is that people actually see it. The only proof that a sound is audible is that people hear it; and so of the other sources of our experience. In like manner, I apprehend, the sole evidence it is possible to produce that anything is desirable is that people do actually desire it. If the end which the utilitarian doctrine proposes to itself were not, in theory and in practice, acknowledged to be an end, nothing could ever convince any person that it was so. No reason can be given why the general happiness is desirable, except that each person, so far as he believes it to be attainable, desires his own happiness. This, however, being a fact, we have not only all the proof which the case admits of, but all which it is possible to require, that happiness is a good, that each person's happiness is a good to that person, and the general happiness, therefore, a good to the aggregate of all persons. Happiness has made out its title as *one* of the ends of conduct and, consequently, one of the criteria of morality.

But it has not, by this alone, proved itself to be the sole criterion. To do that, it would seem, by the same rule, necessary to show, not only that people desire happiness, but that they never desire anything else. Now it is palpable that they do desire things which, in common language, are decidedly distinguished from happiness. They desire, for example, virtue and the absence of vice no less really than pleasure and the absence of pain. The desire of virtue is not as universal, but it is as authentic a fact as the desire of happiness. And hence the opponents of the utilitarian standard deem that they have a right to infer that there are other ends of human action besides happiness, and that happiness is not the standard of approbation and disapprobation.

But does the utilitarian doctrine deny that people desire virtue, or maintain that virtue is not a thing to be desired? The very reverse. It maintains not only that virtue is to be desired, but that it is to be desired disinterestedly, for itself. Whatever may be the opinion of utilitarian moralists as to the original conditions by which virtue is made virtue, however they may believe (as they do) that actions and dispositions are only virtuous because they promote another end than virtue, yet this being granted, and it having been decided, from considerations of this description, what *is* virtuous, they not only place virtue at the very head of the things which are good as means to the ultimate end, but they also recognize as a psychological fact the possibility of its being, to the individual, a good in itself, without looking to any end beyond it; and hold that the mind is not in a right state, not in a state conformable to utility, not in the state most conducive to the general happiness, unless it does love virtue in this manner—as a thing desirable in itself, even although, in the individual instance, it should not produce those other desirable consequences which it tends to produce, and on account of which it is held to be virtue. This opinion is not, in the smallest degree, a departure from the happiness principle. The ingredients of happiness are very various, and each of them is desirable in itself, and not merely when considered as swelling an aggregate. The principle of utility does not mean that any given pleasure, as music, for instance, or any given exemption from pain, as for example health, is to be looked upon as means to a collective something termed happiness, and to be desired on that account. They are desired and desirable in and for themselves; besides being means, they are a part of the end. Virtue, according to the utilitarian doctrine is not naturally and originally part of the end, but it is capable of becoming so; and in those who live it disinterestedly it has become so, and is desired and cherished, not as a means to happiness, but as a part of their happiness.

To illustrate this further, we may remember that virtue is not the only thing originally a means, and which if it were not a means to anything else would be and remain indifferent, but which by association with what it is a means to comes to be desired for itself, and that too with the utmost intensity. What, for example, shall we say of the love of money? There is nothing originally more desirable about money than about any heap of glittering pebbles. Its worth is solely that of the things which it will buy; the desires for other things than itself, which it is a means of gratifying. Yet the love of money is not only one of the strongest moving forces of human life, but money is, in many cases, desired in and for itself; the desire to possess it is often stronger than the desire to use it, and goes on increasing when all the desires which point to ends beyond it, to be compassed by it, are falling off. It may, then, be said truly that money is desired not for the sake of an end, but as part of the end. From being a means to happiness, it has come to be itself a principal ingredient of the individual's conception of happiness. The same may be said of the majority of the great objects of human life: power, for example, or fame, except that to each of these there is a certain amount of immediate pleasure annexed, which has at least the semblance of being naturally inherent in them—a thing which cannot be said of money. Still, however, the strongest natural attraction, both of power and of fame, is the immense aid they give to the attainment of our other wishes; and it is the strong association thus generated between them and all our objects of desire which gives to the direct desire of them the intensity it often assumes, so as in some characters to surpass in strength all other desires. In these cases the means have become a part of the end, and a more important part of it than any of the things which they are means to. What was once desired as an instrument for the attainment of happiness has come to be desired for its own sake. In being desired for its own sake it is, however, desired as *part* of happiness. The person is made, or thinks he would be made, happy by its mere possession; and is made unhappy by failure to obtain it. The desire of it is not a different thing from the desire of happiness any more than the love of music or the desire of health. They are included in happiness. They are some of the elements of which the desire of happiness is made up. Happiness is not an abstract idea but a concrete whole; and these are some of its parts. And the utilitarian standard sanctions and approves their being so. Life would be a poor thing, very ill provided with sources of happiness, if there were not this provision of nature by which things originally indifferent, but conducive to, or otherwise associated with, the satisfaction of our primitive desires, become in themselves sources of pleasure more valuable than the primitive pleasures, both in permanency, in the space of human existence that they are capable of covering, and even in intensity.

Virtue, according to the utilitarian conception, is a good of this description. There was no original desire of it, or motive to it, save its conduciveness to pleasure, and especially to protection from pain. But through the association thus formed it may be felt a good in itself, and desired as such with as great intensity as any other good; and with this difference between it and the love of money, of power, or of fame—that all of these may, and often do, render the individual noxious to the other members of the society to which he belongs, whereas there is nothing which makes him so much a blessing to them as the cultivation of the disinterested love of virtue. And consequently, the utilitarian standard, while it tolerates and approves those other acquired desires, up to the point beyond which they would be more injurious to the general happiness than promotive of it, enjoins and requires the cultivation of the love of virtue up to the greatest strength possible, as being above all things important to the general happiness.

It results from the preceding considerations that there is in reality nothing desired except happiness. Whatever is desired otherwise than as a means to some end beyond itself, and ultimately to happiness, is desired as itself a part of happiness, and is not desired for itself until it has become so. Those who desire virtue for its own sake desire it either because the consciousness of it is a pleasure, or because the consciousness of being without it is a pain, or for both reasons united, as in truth the pleasure and pain seldom exist separately, but almost always together—the same person feeling pleasure in the degree of virtue attained, and pain in not having attained more. If one of these gave him no pleasure, and the other no pain, he would not love or desire virtue, or would desire it only for the other benefits which it might produce to himself or to persons whom he cared for.

We have now, then, an answer to the question, of what sort of proof the principle of utility is susceptible.

STUDY QUESTIONS

1. According to Mill, is the agent's own happiness the standard of right conduct?
2. Are some types of pleasure more worthwhile than others?
3. Why does Mill believe lying is wrong?
4. Does Mill believe the principle of utilitarianism can be proven?

PART 9

Moral Problems

A Defense of Abortion

JUDITH JARVIS THOMSON

Consider the following argument:

1. A fetus is an innocent human being.
2. Killing an innocent human being is always wrong.
3. Therefore killing a fetus is always wrong.

This argument is valid because the premises imply the conclusion. But is the argument sound? In other words, are both its premises true?

Premise 1 is open to question, for arguably the earliest embryo is not a human person. Yet some believe it is and may defend their view on religious grounds. In any case you might suppose that if premise 1 were granted, then the conclusion of the argument would be acceptable, because premise 2 may appear uncontroversial. Much philosophical discussion, however, has hypothesized that premise 1 is true and nevertheless denied the argument's conclusion by claiming that premise 2 is false.

On what grounds, if any, can premise 2 be rejected? That question lies at the heart of the following essay by Judith Jarvis Thomson, who is Professor Emerita of Philosophy at the Massachusetts Institute of Technology. She argues that even if the human fetus is a person, abortion remains morally permissible in a variety of cases in which the mother's life is not threatened.

Most opposition to abortion relies on the premise that the fetus is a human being, a person, from the moment of conception. The premise is argued for, but, as I think, not well. Take, for example, the most common argument. We are asked to notice that the development of a human being from conception through birth into childhood is continuous; then it is said that to draw a line, to choose a point in this development and say "before this point the thing is not a person, after this point it is a person" is to make an arbitrary choice, a choice for which in the nature of things no good reason can be given. It is concluded that the fetus is, or anyway that we had better say it is, a person from the moment of conception. But this conclusion does not follow. Similar things might be said about the development of an acorn into an oak tree, and it does not follow that acorns are oak trees, or that we had better say they are. Arguments of this form are sometimes called "slippery slope arguments"—the phrase is perhaps self-explanatory—and it is dismaying that opponents of abortion rely on them so heavily and uncritically.

From Judith Jarvis Thomson, "A Defense of Abortion," *Philosophy & Public Affairs* 1 (1971). Reprinted by permission of Blackwell Publishers.

I am inclined to agree, however, that the prospects for "drawing a line" in the development of the fetus look dim. I am inclined to think also that we shall probably have to agree that the fetus has already become a human person well before birth. Indeed, it comes as a surprise when one first learns how early in its life it begins to acquire human characteristics. By the tenth week, for example, it already has a face, arms and legs, fingers and toes; it has internal organs, and brain activity is detectable. On the other hand, I think that the premise is false, that the fetus is not a person from the moment of conception. A newly fertilized ovum, a newly implanted clump of cells, is no more a person than an acorn is an oak tree. But I shall not discuss any of this. For it seems to me to be of great interest to ask what happens if, for the sake of argument, we allow the premise. How, precisely, are we supposed to get from there to the conclusion that abortion is morally impermissible? Opponents of abortion commonly spend most of their time establishing that the fetus is a person, and hardly any time explaining the step from there to the impermissibility of abortion. Perhaps they think the step too simple and obvious to require much comment. Or perhaps instead they are simply being economical in argument. Many of those who defend abortion rely on the premise that the fetus is not a person, but only a bit of tissue that will become a person at birth; and why pay out more arguments than you have to? Whatever the explanation, I suggest that the step they take is neither easy nor obvious, that it calls for closer examination than it is commonly given, and that when we do give it this closer examination we shall feel inclined to reject it.

I propose, then, that we grant that the fetus is a person from the moment of conception. How does the argument go from here? Something like this, I take it. Every person has a right to life. So the fetus has a right to life. No doubt the mother has a right to decide what shall happen in and to her body; everyone would grant that. But surely a person's right to life is stronger and more stringent than the mother's right to decide what happens in and to her body, and so outweighs it. So the fetus may not be killed; an abortion may not be performed.

It sounds plausible. But now let me ask you to imagine this. You wake up in the morning and find yourself back to back in bed with an unconscious violinist. A famous unconscious violinist. He has been found to have a fatal kidney ailment, and the Society of Music Lovers has canvassed all the available medical records and found that you alone have the right blood type to help. They have therefore kidnapped you, and last night the violinist's circulatory system was plugged into yours, so that your kidneys can be used to extract poisons from his blood as well as your own. The director of the hospital now tells you, "Look, we're sorry the Society of Music Lovers did this to you—we would never have permitted it if we had known. But still, they did it, and the violinist now is plugged into you. To unplug you would be to kill him. But never mind, it's only for nine months. By then he will have recovered from his ailment, and can safely be unplugged from you." Is it morally incumbent on you to accede to this situation? No doubt it would be very nice of you if you did, a great kindness. But do you *have* to accede to it? What if it were not nine months, but nine years? Or longer still? What if the director of the hospital says, "Tough luck, I agree, but you've now got to stay in bed, with the violinist plugged into you, for the rest of your life. Because remember this. All persons have a right to life, and violinists are persons. Granted you have a right to decide what happens in and to your body, but a person's right to life outweighs your right to decide what happens in and to your body. So you cannot ever be unplugged from him." I imagine you would regard this as outrageous, which suggests that something really is wrong with that plausible-sounding argument I mentioned a moment ago.

In this case, of course, you were kidnapped; you didn't volunteer for the operation that plugged the violinist into your kidneys. Can those who oppose abortion on the ground I mentioned make an exception for a pregnancy due to rape? Certainly. They can say that persons have a right to life only if they didn't come into existence because of rape; or they can say that all persons have a right to life, but that some have less of a right to life than others, in particular, that those who came into existence because of rape have less. But these statements have a rather unpleasant sound. Surely the question of whether you have a right to life at all, or how much of it you have, shouldn't turn on the question of whether or not you are the product of a rape. And in fact the people who oppose abortion on the ground I mentioned do not make this distinction, and hence do not make an exception in case of rape.

Nor do they make an exception for a case in which the mother has to spend the nine months of her pregnancy in bed. They would agree that would be a great pity, and hard on the mother; but all the same, all persons have a right to life, the fetus is a person, and so on. I suspect, in fact, that they would not make an exception for a case in which, miraculously enough, the pregnancy went on for nine years, or even the rest of the mother's life.

Some won't even make an exception for a case in which continuation of the pregnancy is likely to shorten the mother's life; they regard abortion as impermissible even to save the mother's life. Such cases are nowadays very rare, and many opponents of abortion do not accept this extreme view. All the same, it is a good place to begin: a number of points of interest come out in respect to it.

1. Let us call the view that abortion is impermissible even to save the mother's life "the extreme view." I want to suggest first that it does not issue from the argument I mentioned earlier without the addition of some fairly powerful premises. Suppose a woman has become pregnant and now learns that she has a cardiac condition such that she will die if she carries the baby to term. What may be done for her? The fetus, being a person, has a right to life, but as the mother is a person too, so has she a right to life. Presumably they have an equal right to life. How is it supposed to come out that an abortion may not be performed? If mother and child have an equal right to life, shouldn't we perhaps flip a coin? Or should we add to the mother's right to life her right to decide what happens in and to her body, which everybody seems to be ready to grant—the sum of her rights now outweighing the fetus' right to life?

The most familiar argument here is the following. We are told that performing the abortion would be directly killing[1] the child, whereas doing nothing would not be killing the mother, but only letting her die. Moreover, in killing the child, one would be killing an innocent person, for the child has committed no crime and is not aiming at his mother's death. And then there are a variety of ways in which this might be continued. (1) But as directly killing an innocent person is always and absolutely impermissible, an abortion may not be performed. Or, (2) as directly killing an innocent person is murder, and murder is always and absolutely impermissible, an abortion may not be performed. Or, (3) as one's duty to refrain from directly killing an innocent person is more stringent than one's duty to keep a person from dying, an abortion may not be performed. Or, (4) if one's only options are directly killing an innocent person or letting a person die, one must prefer letting the person die, and thus an abortion may not be performed.[2]

Some people seem to have thought that these are not further premises which must be added if the conclusion is to be reached, but that they follow from the very fact that an innocent person has a right to life. But this seems to me to be a mistake, and perhaps the simplest way to show this is to bring out that while we must certainly grant that innocent persons have a right to life, the theses in (1) through (4) are all false. Take (2), for example. If directly killing an innocent person is murder, and thus is impermissible, then the mother's directly killing the innocent person inside her is murder and thus is impermissible. But it cannot seriously be thought to be murder if the mother performs an abortion on herself to save her life. It cannot seriously be said that she *must* refrain, that she *must* sit passively by and wait for her death. Let us look again at the case of you and the violinist. There you are, in bed with the violinist, and the director of the hospital says to you, "It's all most distressing, and I deeply sympathize, but you see this is putting an additional strain on your kidneys, and you'll be dead within the month. But you *have* to stay where you are all the same. Because unplugging you would be directly killing an innocent violinist, and that's murder, and that's impermissible." If anything in the world is true, it is that you do not commit murder, you do not do what is impermissible, if you reach around to your back and unplug yourself from that violinist to save your life.

The main focus of attention in writings on abortion has been on what a third party may or may not do in answer to a request from a woman for an abortion. This is in a way understandable. Things being as they are, there isn't much a woman can safely do to abort herself. So the question asked is what a third party may do and what the mother may do, if it is mentioned at all, is deduced, almost as an afterthought, from what it is concluded that third parties may do. But it seems to me that to treat the matter in this way is to refuse to grant to the mother that very status of person which is so firmly insisted on for the fetus. For we cannot simply read off what a person may do from what a third party may do. Suppose you find yourself trapped in a tiny house with a growing child. I mean a very tiny house and a rapidly growing child—you are already up against the wall of the house and in a few minutes you'll be crushed to death. The child on the other hand won't be crushed to death; if nothing is done to stop him from growing he'll be hurt, but in the end he'll simply burst open the house and walk out a free man. Now I could well understand it if a bystander were to say, "There's nothing we can do for you. We cannot choose between your life and his, we cannot be the ones to decide who is to live, we cannot intervene." But it cannot be concluded that you too can do nothing, that you cannot attack it to save your life. However innocent the child may be, you do not have to wait passively while it crushes you to death. Perhaps a pregnant woman is vaguely felt to have the status of house, to which we don't allow the right of self-defense. But if the woman houses the child, it should be remembered that she is a person who houses it.

I should perhaps stop to say explicitly that I am not claiming that people have a right to do anything whatever to save their lives. I think, rather, that there are drastic limits to the right of self-defense. If someone threatens you with death unless you torture someone else to death, I think you have not the right, even to save your life, to do so. But the case under consideration here is very different. In our case there are only two people involved, one whose life is threatened and one who threatens it. Both are innocent: the one who is threatened is not threatened because of any fault, the one who threatens does not threaten because of any fault. For this reason we may feel that we bystanders cannot intervene. But the person threatened can.

In sum, a woman surely can defend her life against the threat to it posed by the unborn child, even if doing so involves its death. And this shows not merely that the theses in (1) through (4) are false; it shows also that the extreme view of abortion is false, and so we need not canvass any other possible ways of arriving at it from the argument I mentioned at the outset.

2. The extreme view could of course be weakened to say that while abortion is permissible to save the mother's life, it may not be performed by a third party, but only by the mother herself. But this cannot be right either. For what we have to keep in mind is that the mother and the unborn child are not like two tenants in a small house which has, by an unfortunate mistake, been rented to both: the mother *owns* the house. The fact that she does adds to the offensiveness of deducing that the mother can do nothing from the supposition that third parties can do nothing. But it does more than this: it casts a bright light on the supposition that third parties can do nothing. Certainly it lets us see that a third party who says "I cannot choose between you" is fooling himself if he thinks this is impartiality. If Jones has found and fastened on a certain coat, which he needs to keep him from freezing, but which Smith also needs to keep him from freezing, then it is not impartiality that says "I cannot choose between you" when Smith owns the coat. Women have said again and again "This body is *my* body!" and they have reason to feel angry, reason to feel that it has been like shouting into the wind. Smith, after all, is hardly likely to bless us if we say to him, "Of course it's your coat, anybody would grant that it is. But no one may choose between you and Jones who is to have it."

We should really ask what it is that says "no one may choose" in the face of the fact that the body that houses the child is the mother's body. It may be simply a failure to appreciate this fact. But it may be something more interesting, namely, the sense that one has a right to refuse to lay hands on people, even where it would be just and fair to do so, even where justice seems to require that somebody do so. Thus justice might call for somebody to get Smith's coat back from Jones, and yet you have a right to refuse to be the one to lay hands on Jones, a right to refuse to do physical violence to him. This, I think, must be granted. But then what should be said is not "no one may choose," but only "*I* cannot choose," and indeed not even this, but "*I* will not *act*," leaving it open that somebody else can or should, and in particular that anyone in a position of authority, with the job of securing people's rights, both can and should. So this is no difficulty. I have not been arguing that any given third party must accede to the mother's request that he perform an abortion to save her life, but only that he may.

I suppose that in some views of human life the mother's body is only on loan to her, the loan not being one which gives her any prior claim to it. One who held this view might well think it impartiality to say "I cannot choose." But I shall simply ignore this possibility. My own view is that if a human being has any just, prior claim to anything at all, he has a just, prior claim to his own body. And perhaps this needn't be argued for here anyway, since, as I mentioned, the arguments against abortion we are looking at do grant that the woman has a right to decide what happens in and to her body.

But although they do grant it, I have tried to show that they do not take seriously what is done in granting it. I suggest the same thing will reappear even more clearly when we turn away from cases in which the mother's life is at stake, and attend, as I propose we now do, to the vastly more common cases in which a woman wants an abortion for some less weighty reason than preserving her own life.

3. Where the mother's life is not at stake, the argument I mentioned at the outset seems to have a much stronger pull. "Everyone has a right to life, so the unborn person has a right to life." And isn't the child's right to life weightier than anything other than the mother's own right to life, which she might put forward as ground for an abortion?

This argument treats the right to life as if it were unproblematic. It is not, and this seems to me to be precisely the source of the mistake.

For we should now, at long last, ask what it comes to, to have a right to life. In some views having a right to life includes having a right to be given at least the bare minimum one needs for continued life. But suppose that what in fact *is* the bare minimum a man needs for continued life is something he has no right at all to be given? If I am sick unto death, and the only thing that will save my life is the touch of Henry Fonda's cool hand on my fevered brow, then all the same, I have no right to be given the touch of Henry Fonda's cool hand on my fevered brow. It would be frightfully nice of him to fly in from the West Coast to provide it. It would be less nice, though no doubt well meant, if my friends flew out to the West Coast and carried Henry Fonda back with them. But I have no right at all against anybody that he should do this for me. Or again, to return to the story I told earlier, the fact that for continued life that violinist needs the continued use of your kidneys does not establish that he has a right to be given the continued use of your kidneys. He certainly has no right against you that *you* should give him continued use of your kidneys. For nobody has any right to use your kidneys unless you give him such a right; and nobody has the right against you that you shall give him this right—if you do allow him to go on using your kidneys, this is a kindness on your part, and not something he can claim from you as his due. Nor has he any right against anybody else that they should give him continued use of your kidneys. Certainly he had no right against the Society of Music Lovers that *they* should plug him into you in the first place. And if you now start to unplug yourself, having learned that you will otherwise have to spend nine years in bed with him, there is nobody in the world who must try to prevent you, in order to see to it that he is given something he has a right to be given.

Some people are rather stricter about the right to life. In their view, it does not include the right to be given anything, but amounts to, and only to, the right not to be killed by anybody. But here a related difficulty arises. If everybody is to refrain from killing that violinist, then everybody must refrain from doing a great many different sorts of things. Everybody must refrain from slitting his throat, everybody must refrain from shooting him—and everybody must refrain from unplugging you from him. But does he have a right against everybody that they shall refrain from unplugging you from him? To refrain from doing this is to allow him to continue to use your kidneys. It could be argued that he has a right against us that *we* should allow him to continue to use your kidneys. That is, while he had no right against us that we should give him the use of your kidneys, it might be argued that he anyway has a right against us that we shall not now intervene and deprive him of the use of your kidneys. I shall come back to third-party interventions later. But certainly the violinist has no right against you that *you* shall allow him to continue to use your kidneys. As I said, if you do allow him to continue to use them, it is a kindness on your part and not something you owe him.

The difficulty I point to here is not peculiar to the right to life. It reappears in connection with all the other natural rights; and it is something which an adequate account of rights must deal with. For present purposes it is enough just to draw attention to it. But I would stress that I am not arguing that people do not have a right to life—quite to the contrary, it seems to me that the primary control we must place on the acceptability of an account of rights is that it should turn out in that account to be a truth that all persons have a right to life. I am arguing only that having a right to life does not guarantee having either a right to be given the use of or a right to be allowed continued use of another person's body—even if one needs it for life itself. So the right to life will not serve the opponents of abortion in the very simple and clear way in which they seem to have thought it would.

4. There is another way to bring out the difficulty. In the most ordinary sort of case, to deprive someone of what he has a right to is to treat him unjustly. Suppose a boy and his small brother are jointly given a box of chocolates for Christmas. If the older boy takes the box and refuses to give his brother any of the chocolates, he is unjust to him, for the brother has been given a right to half of them.

But suppose that, having learned that otherwise it means nine years in bed with that violinist, you unplug yourself from him. You surely are not being unjust to him, for you gave him no right to use your kidneys, and no one else can have given him any such right. But we have to notice that in unplugging yourself, you are killing him; and violinists, like everybody else, have a right to life, and thus in the view we were considering just now, the right not to be killed. So here you do what he supposedly has a right you shall not do, but you do not act unjustly to him in doing it.

The emendation which may be made at this point is this: the right to life consists not in the right not to be killed, but rather in the right not to be killed unjustly. This runs a risk of circularity, but never mind: it would enable us to square the fact that the violinist has a right to life with the fact that you do not act unjustly toward him in unplugging yourself, thereby killing him. For if you do not kill him unjustly, you do not violate his right to life, and so it is no wonder you do him no injustice.

But if this emendation is accepted, the gap in the argument against abortion stares us plainly in the face: it is by no means enough to show that the fetus is a person, and to remind us that all persons have a right to life—we need to be shown also that killing the fetus violates its right to life, i.e., that abortion is unjust killing. And is it?

I suppose we may take it as a datum that in a case of pregnancy due to rape the mother has not given the unborn person a right to the use of her body for food and shelter. Indeed, in what pregnancy could it be supposed that the mother has given the unborn person such a right? It is not as if there were unborn persons drifting about the world, to whom a woman who wants a child says "I invite you in."

But it might be argued that there are other ways one can have acquired a right to the use of another person's body than by having been invited to use it by that person. Suppose a woman voluntarily indulges in intercourse, knowing of the chance it will issue in pregnancy, and then she does become pregnant; is she not in part responsible for the presence, in fact the very existence, of the unborn person inside her? No doubt she did not invite it in. But doesn't her partial responsibility for its being there itself give it a right to the use of her body? If so, then her aborting it would be more like the boy's taking away the chocolates, and less like your unplugging yourself from the violinist—doing so would be depriving it of what it does have a right to, and thus would be doing it an injustice.

And then, too, it might be asked whether or not she can kill it even to save her own life: If she voluntarily called it into existence, how can she now kill it, even in self-defense?

The first thing to be said about this is that it is something new. Opponents of abortion have been so concerned to make out the independence of the fetus, in order to establish that it has a right to life, just as its mother does, that they have tended to overlook the possible support they might gain from making out that the fetus is *dependent* on the mother, in order to establish that she has a special kind of responsibility for it, a responsibility that gives it rights against her which are not possessed by any independent person—such as an ailing violinist who is a stranger to her.

On the other hand, this argument would give the unborn person a right to its mother's body only if her pregnancy resulted from a voluntary act, undertaken in full knowledge of the chance a pregnancy might result from it. It would leave out entirely the unborn person whose existence is due to rape. Pending the availability of some further argument, then, we would be left with the conclusion that unborn persons whose existence is due to rape have no right to the use of their mothers' bodies, and thus that aborting them is not depriving them of anything they have a right to and hence is not unjust killing.

And we should also notice that it is not at all plain that this argument really does go even as far as it purports to. For there are cases and cases, and the details make a difference. If the room is stuffy, and I therefore open a window to air it, and a burglar climbs in, it would be absurd to say, "Ah, now he can stay, she's given him a right to the use of her house—for she is partially responsible for his presence there, having voluntarily done what enabled him to get in, in full knowledge that there are such things as burglars, and that burglars burgle." It would be still more absurd to say this if I had had bars installed outside my windows, precisely to prevent burglars from getting in, and a burglar got in only because of a defect in the bars. It remains equally absurd if we imagine it is not a burglar who climbs in, but an innocent person who blunders or falls in. Again, suppose it were like this: people-seeds drift about in the air like pollen, and if you open your windows, one may drift in and take root in your carpets or upholstery. You don't want children, so you fix up your windows with fine mesh screens, the very best you can buy. As can happen, however, and on very, very rare occasions does happen, one of the screens is defective; and a seed drifts in and takes root. Does the person-plant who now develops have a right to the use of your house? Surely not—despite the fact that you voluntarily opened your windows, you knowingly kept carpets and upholstered furniture, and you knew that screens were sometimes defective. Someone may argue that you are responsible for its rooting, that it does have a right to your house, because after all you *could* have lived out your life with bare floors and furniture, or with sealed windows and doors. But this won't do—for by the same token anyone can avoid a pregnancy due to rape by having a hysterectomy, or anyway by never leaving home without a (reliable!) army.

It seems to me that the argument we are looking at can establish at most that there are *some* cases in which the unborn person has a right to the use of its mother's body, and therefore *some* cases in which abortion is unjust killing. There is room for much discussion and argument as to precisely which, if any. But I think we should sidestep this issue and leave it open, for at any rate the argument certainly does not establish that all abortion is unjust killing.

5. There is room for yet another argument here, however. We surely must all grant that there may be cases in which it would be morally indecent to detach a person from your body at the cost of his life. Suppose you learn that what the

violinist needs is not nine years of your life, but only one hour: all you need do to save his life is to spend one hour in that bed with him. Suppose also that letting him use your kidneys for that one hour would not affect your health in the slightest. Admittedly you were kidnapped. Admittedly you did not give anyone permission to plug him into you. Nevertheless it seems to me plain you *ought* to allow him to use your kidneys for that hour—it would be indecent to refuse.

Again, suppose pregnancy lasted only an hour, and constituted no threat to life or health. And suppose that a woman becomes pregnant as a result of rape. Admittedly she did not voluntarily do anything to bring about the existence of a child. Admittedly she did nothing at all which would give the unborn person a right to the use of her body. All the same it might well be said, as in the newly emended violinist story, that she *ought* to allow it to remain for that hour—that it would be indecent of her to refuse.

Now some people are inclined to use the term "right" in such a way that it follows from the fact that you ought to allow a person to use your body for the hour he needs, that he has a right to use your body for the hour he needs, even though he has not been given that right by any person or act. They may say that it follows also that if you refuse, you act unjustly toward him. This use of the term is perhaps so common that it cannot be called wrong; nevertheless it seems to me to be an unfortunate loosening of what we would do better to keep a tight rein on. Suppose that box of chocolates I mentioned earlier had not been given to both boys jointly, but was given only to the older boy. There he sits, stolidly eating his way through the box, his small brother watching enviously. Here we are likely to say, "You ought not to be so mean. You ought to give your brother some of those chocolates." My own view is that it just does not follow from the truth of this that the brother has any right to any of the chocolates. If the boy refuses to give his brother any, he is greedy, stingy, callous—but not unjust. I suppose that the people I have in mind will say it does follow that the brother has a right to some of the chocolates, and thus that the boy does act unjustly if he refuses to give his brother any. But the effect of saying this is to obscure what we should keep distinct, namely, the difference between the boy's refusal in this case and the boy's refusal in the earlier case, in which the box was given to both boys jointly, and in which the small brother thus had what was from any point of view clear title to half.

A further objection to so using the term "right" that from the fact that A ought to do a thing for B, it follows that B has a right against A that A do it for him, is that it is going to make the question of whether or not a man has a right to a thing turn on how easy it is to provide him with it; and this seems not merely unfortunate, but morally unacceptable. Take the case of Henry Fonda again. I said earlier that I had no right to the touch of his cool hand on my fevered brow, even though I needed it to save my life. I said it would be frightfully nice of him to fly in from the West Coast to provide me with it, but that I had no right against him that he should do so. But suppose he isn't on the West Coast. Suppose he has only to walk across the room, place a hand briefly on my brow—and lo, my life is saved. Then surely he ought to do it, it would be indecent to refuse. Is it to be said, "Ah, well, it follows that in this case she has a right to the touch of his hand on her brow, and so it would be an injustice in him to refuse"? So that I have a right to it when it is easy for him to provide it, though no right when it's hard? It's rather a shocking idea that anyone's rights should fade away and disappear as it gets harder and harder to accord them to him.

So my own view is that even though you ought to let the violinist use your kidneys for the one hour he needs, we should not conclude that he has a right to do so—we should say that if you refuse, you are, like the boy who owns all the chocolates and will give none away, self-centered and callous, indecent in fact, but not unjust. And similarly, that even supposing a case in which a woman pregnant due to rape ought to allow the unborn person to use her body for the hour he needs, we should not conclude that he has a right to do so; we should conclude that she is self-centered, callous, indecent, but not unjust, if she refuses. The complaints are no less grave; they are just different. However, there is no need to insist on this point. If anyone does wish to deduce "he has a right" from "you ought," then all the same he must surely grant that there are cases in which it is not morally required of you that you allow that violinist to use your kidneys, and in which he does not have a right to use them, and in which you do not do him an injustice if you refuse. And so also for mother and unborn child. Except in such cases as the unborn person has a right to demand it—and we were leaving open the possibility that there may be such cases—nobody is morally *required* to make large sacrifices, of health, of all other interests and concerns, of all other duties and commitments, for nine years, or even for nine months, in order to keep another person alive.

6. We have in fact to distinguish between two kinds of Samaritan: the Good Samaritan and what we might call the Minimally Decent Samaritan. The story of the Good Samaritan, you will remember, goes like this:

> A certain man went down from Jerusalem to Jericho, and fell among thieves, which stripped him of his raiment, and wounded him, and departed, leaving him half dead.
>
> And by chance there came down a certain priest that way; and when he saw him, he passed by on the other side.
>
> And likewise a Levite, when he was at the place, came and looked on him, and passed by on the other side.
>
> But a certain Samaritan, as he journeyed, came where he was; and when he saw him he had compassion on him.
>
> And went to him, and bound up his wounds, pouring in oil and wine, and set him on his own beast, and brought him to an inn, and took care of him.
>
> And on the morrow, when he departed, he took out two pence, and gave them to the host, and said unto him, "Take care of him; and whatsoever thou spendest more, when I come again, I will repay thee."
>
> —(Luke 10:30–35)

The Good Samaritan went out of his way, at some cost to himself, to help one in need of it. We are not told what the options were, that is, whether or not the priest and the Levite could have helped by doing less than the Good Samaritan did, but assuming they could have, then the fact they did nothing at all shows they were not even Minimally Decent Samaritans, not because they were not Samaritans, but because they were not even minimally decent. . . .

After telling the story of the Good Samaritan, Jesus said, "Go, and do thou likewise." Perhaps he meant that we are morally required to act as the Good Samaritan did. Perhaps he was urging people to do more than is morally required of them. At all events it seems plain that . . . it is not morally required of anyone that he give long stretches of his life—nine years or nine months—to sustaining the life of a person who has no special right (we were leaving open the possibility of this) to demand it. . . .

We have . . . to look now at third-party interventions. I have been arguing that no person is morally required to make large sacrifices to sustain the life of another who has no right to demand them, and this even where the sacrifices do not include life itself; we are not morally required to be Good Samaritans or anyway Very Good Samaritans to one another. But what if a man cannot extricate himself from such a situation? What if he appeals to us to extricate him? It seems to me plain that there are cases in which we can, cases in which a Good Samaritan would extricate him. There you are, you were kidnapped, and nine years in bed with that violinist lie ahead of you. You have your own life to lead. You are sorry, but you simply cannot see giving up so much of your life to the sustaining of his. You cannot extricate yourself, and ask us to do so. I should have thought that—in light of his having no right to the use of your body—it was obvious that we do not have to accede to your being forced to give up so much. We can do what you ask. There is no injustice to the violinist in our doing so.

7. Following the lead of the opponents of abortion, I have throughout been speaking of the fetus merely as a person, and what I have been asking is whether or not the argument we began with, which proceeds only from the fetus' being a person, really does establish its conclusion. I have argued that it does not.

But of course there are arguments and arguments, and it may be said that I have simply fastened on the wrong one. It may be said that what is important is not merely the fact that the fetus is a person, but that it is a person for whom the woman has a special kind of responsibility issuing from the fact that she is its mother. And it might be argued that all my analogies are therefore irrelevant—for you do not have that special kind of responsibility for that violinist, Henry Fonda does not have that special kind of responsibility for me. . . .

I have in effect dealt (briefly) with this argument in section 4 above; but a (still briefer) recapitulation now may be in order. Surely we do not have any such "special responsibility" for a person unless we have assumed it, explicitly or implicitly. If a set of parents do not try to prevent pregnancy, do not obtain an abortion, and then at the time of birth of the child do not put it out for adoption, but rather take it home with them, then they have assumed responsibility for it, they have given it rights, and they cannot *now* withdraw support from it at the cost of its life because they now find it difficult to go on providing for it. But if they have taken all reasonable precautions against having a child, they do not simply by virtue of their biological relationship to the child who comes into existence have a special responsibility for it. They may wish to assume responsibility for it, or they may not wish to. And I am suggesting that if assuming responsibility for it would require large sacrifices, then they may refuse. A Good Samaritan would not refuse—or anyway, a Splendid Samaritan, if the sacrifices that had to be made were enormous. But then so would a Good Samaritan assume responsibility for that violinist; so would Henry Fonda, if he is a Good Samaritan, fly in from the West Coast and assume responsibility for me.

8. My argument will be found unsatisfactory on two counts by many of those who want to regard abortion as morally permissible. First, while I do argue that abortion is not impermissible, I do not argue that it is always permissible. There may well be cases in which carrying the child to term requires only Minimally Decent Samaritanism of the mother, and this is a standard we must not fall below. I am inclined to think it a merit of my account precisely that it does *not* give a general yes or a general no. It allows for and supports our sense that, for example, a sick and desperately frightened fourteen-year-old schoolgirl, pregnant due to rape, may *of course* choose abortion, and that any law which rules this out is an insane law. And it also allows for and supports our sense that in other cases resort to abortion is even positively indecent. It would be indecent in the woman to request an abortion, and indecent in a doctor to perform it, if she is in her seventh month, and wants the abortion just to avoid the nuisance of postponing a trip abroad. The very fact that the arguments I have been drawing attention to treat all cases of abortion, or even all cases of abortion in which the mother's life is not at stake, as morally on a par ought to have made them suspect at the outset.

Secondly, while I am arguing for the permissibility of abortion in some cases, I am not arguing for the right to secure the death of the unborn child. It is easy to confuse these two things in that up to a certain point in the life of the fetus it is not able to survive outside the mother's body; hence removing it from her body guarantees its death. But they are importantly different. I have argued that you are not morally required to spend nine months in bed, sustaining the life of that violinist; but to say this is by no means to say that if, when you unplug yourself, there is a miracle and he survives, you then have a right to turn round and slit his throat. You may detach yourself even if this costs him his life; you have no right to be guaranteed his death, by some other means, if unplugging yourself does not kill him. There are some people who will feel dissatisfied by this feature of my argument. A woman may be utterly devastated by the thought of a child, a bit of herself, put out for adoption and never seen or heard of again. She may therefore want not merely that the child be detached from her, but more, that it die. Some opponents of abortion are inclined to regard this as beneath contempt—thereby showing insensitivity to what is surely a powerful source of despair. All the same, I agree that the desire for the child's death is not one which anybody may gratify, should it turn out to be possible to detach the child alive.

At this place, however, it should be remembered that we have only been pretending throughout that the fetus is a human being from the moment of conception. A very early abortion is surely not the killing of a person, and so is not dealt with by anything I have said here.

NOTES

1. The term "direct" in the arguments I refer to is a technical one. Roughly, what is meant by "direct killing" is either killing as an end in itself, or killing as a means of some end, for example, the end of saving someone else's life.

2. The thesis in (4) is in an interesting way weaker than those in (1), (2), and (3): they rule out abortion even in cases in which both mother *and* child will die if the abortion is not performed. By contrast, one who held the view expressed in (4) could consistently say that one needn't prefer letting two persons die to killing one.

STUDY QUESTIONS

1. What are the main points Thomson seeks to make by the example of the unconscious violinist?

2. Does the morality of aborting a fetus depend on the conditions surrounding its conception?

3. If abortion is murder, who is the murderer and what is the appropriate punishment?

4. If the abortion controversy is described as a debate between those who believe in a right to life and those who affirm a woman's right to choose, on which side is Thomson?

On the Moral and Legal Status of Abortion

Mary Anne Warren

Mary Anne Warren (1942–2010) was Professor of Philosophy at San Francisco State University. She argues that because women are persons and fetuses are not, women's rights override whatever right to life a fetus may possess.

For our purposes, abortion may be defined as the act a woman performs in deliberately terminating her pregnancy before it comes to term, or in allowing another person to terminate it. Abortion usually entails the death of a fetus. Nevertheless,

I will argue that it is morally permissible and should be neither legally prohibited nor made needlessly difficult to obtain, e.g., by obstructive legal regulations.

Some philosophers have argued that the moral status of abortion cannot be resolved by rational means. If this is so, then liberty should prevail; for it is not a proper function of the law to enforce prohibitions upon personal behavior that cannot clearly be shown to be morally objectionable, and seriously so. But the advocates of prohibition believe that their position is objectively correct, and not merely a result of religious beliefs or personal prejudices. They argue that the humanity of the fetus is a matter of scientific fact and that abortion is therefore the moral equivalent of murder and must be prohibited in all or most cases. (Some would make an exception when the woman's life is in danger or when the pregnancy is due to rape or incest; others would prohibit abortion even in these cases.)

In response, advocates of a right to choose abortion point to the terrible consequences of prohibiting it, especially while contraception is still unreliable, and is financially beyond the reach of much of the world's population. Worldwide, hundreds of thousands of women die each year from illegal abortions, and many more suffer from complications that may leave them injured or infertile. Women who are poor, underage, disabled, or otherwise vulnerable, suffer most from the absence of safe and legal abortion. Advocates of choice also argue that to deny a woman access to abortion is to deprive her of the right to control her own body—a right so fundamental that without it other rights are often all but meaningless.

These arguments do not convince abortion opponents. The tragic consequences of prohibition leave them unmoved, because they regard the deliberate killing of fetuses as even more tragic. Nor do appeals to the right to control one's own body impress them, since they deny that this right includes the right to destroy a fetus. We cannot hope to persuade those who equate abortion with murder that they are mistaken, unless we can refute the standard anti-abortion argument: that because fetuses are human beings, they have a right to life equal to that of any other human being. Unfortunately, confusion has prevailed with respect to the two important questions which that argument raises: (1) Is a human fetus really a human being at all stages of prenatal development? and (2) If so, what (if anything) follows about the moral and legal status of abortion? . . .

My own inquiry will also have two stages. In Section I, I consider whether abortion can be shown to be morally permissible even on the assumption that a fetus is a human being with a strong right to life. I argue that this cannot be established, except in special cases. Consequently, we cannot avoid facing the question of whether or not a fetus has the same right to life as any human being.

In Section II, I propose an answer to this question, namely, that a fetus is not a member of the moral community—the set of beings with full and equal moral rights. The reason that a fetus is not a member of the moral community is that it is not yet a person, nor is it enough like a person in the morally relevant respects to be regarded the equal of those human beings who are persons. I argue that it is personhood, and not genetic humanity, which is the fundamental basis for membership in the moral community. A fetus, especially in the early stages of its development, satisfies none of the criteria of personhood. Consequently, it makes no sense to grant it moral rights strong enough to override the woman's moral rights to liberty, bodily integrity, and sometimes life itself. Unlike an infant who has already been born, a fetus cannot be granted full and equal moral rights without severely threatening the rights and well-being of women. Nor, as we will see, is a fetus's *potential* personhood a threat to the moral permissibility of abortion, since merely potential persons do not have a moral right to become actual—or none that is strong enough to override the fundamental moral rights of actual persons.

I

Judith Thomson argues that, even if a fetus has a right to life, abortion is often morally permissible. Her argument is based upon an imaginative analogy. She asks you to picture yourself waking up one day, in bed with a famous violinist, who is a stranger to you. Imagine that you have been kidnapped, and your bloodstream connected to that of the violinist, who has an ailment that will kill him unless he is permitted to share your kidneys for nine months. No one else can save him, since you alone have the right type of blood. Consequently, the Society of Music Lovers has arranged for you to be kidnapped and hooked up. If you unhook yourself, he will die. But if you remain in bed with him, then after nine months he will be cured and able to survive without further assistance from you.

Now, Thomson asks, what are your obligations in this situation? To be consistent, the anti-abortionist must say that you are obliged to stay in bed with the violinist: for violinists are human beings, and all human beings have a right to life. But this is outrageous; thus, there must be something very wrong with the same argument when it is applied to abortion. It would be extremely generous of you to agree to stay in bed with the violinist; but it is absurd to suggest that your refusal to do so would be the moral equivalent of murder. The violinist's right to life does not oblige you to do whatever is required to keep him alive; still less does it justify anyone else in forcing you to do so. A law which required you to stay in bed with the violinist would be an unjust law, since unwilling persons ought not to be required to be Extremely Good Samaritans, i.e., to make enormous personal sacrifices for the sake of other individuals toward whom they have no special prior obligation.

Thomson concludes that we can grant the anti-abortionist his claim that a fetus is a human being with a right to life, and still hold that a pregnant woman is morally entitled to refuse to be an Extremely Good Samaritan toward the fetus. For there is a great gap between the claim that a human being has a right to life, and the claim that other human beings are morally obligated to do whatever is necessary to keep him alive. One has no duty to keep another human being alive *at a great personal cost,* unless one has somehow contracted a special obligation toward that individual; and a woman who is pregnant may have done nothing that morally obliges her to make the burdensome personal sacrifices necessary to preserve the life of the fetus.

This argument is plausible, and in the case of pregnancy due to rape it is probably conclusive. Difficulties arise, however, when we attempt to specify the larger range of cases in which abortion can be justified on the basis of this argument. Thomson considers it a virtue of her argument that it does not imply that abortion is *always* morally permissible. It would, she says, be indecent for a woman in her seventh month of pregnancy to have an abortion in order to embark on a trip to Europe. On the other hand, the violinist analogy shows that, "a sick and desperately frightened fourteen-year-old schoolgirl, pregnant due to rape, may *of course* choose abortion, and that any law which rules this out is an insane law." So far, so good; but what are we to say about the woman who becomes pregnant not through rape but because she and her partner did not use available forms of contraception, or because their attempts at contraception failed? What about a woman who becomes pregnant intentionally, but then re-evaluates the wisdom of having a child? In such cases, the violinist analogy is considerably less useful to advocates of the right to choose abortion.

It is perhaps only when a woman's pregnancy is due to rape, or some other form of coercion, that the situation is sufficiently analogous to the violinist case for our moral intuitions to transfer convincingly from the one case to the other. One difference between a pregnancy caused by rape and most unwanted pregnancies is that only in the former case is it perfectly clear that the woman is in no way responsible for her predicament. In the other cases, she *might* have been able to avoid becoming pregnant, e.g., by taking birth control pills (more faithfully), or insisting upon the use of high-quality condoms, or even avoiding heterosexual intercourse altogether throughout her fertile years. In contrast, if you are suddenly kidnapped by strange music lovers and hooked up to a sick violinist, then you are in no way responsible for your situation, which you could not have foreseen or prevented. And responsibility does seem to matter here. If a person behaves in a way which she could have avoided, and which she knows might bring into existence a human being who will depend upon her for survival, then it is not entirely clear that if and when that happens she may rightly refuse to do what she must in order to keep that human being alive.

This argument shows that the violinist analogy provides a persuasive defense of a woman's right to choose abortion only in cases where she is in no way morally responsible for her own pregnancy. In all other cases, the assumption that a fetus has a strong right to life makes it necessary to look carefully at the particular circumstances in order to determine the extent of the woman's responsibility, and hence the extent of her obligation. This outcome is unsatisfactory to advocates of the right to choose abortion, because it suggests that the decision should not be left in the woman's own hands, but should be supervised by other persons, who will inquire into the most intimate aspects of her personal life in order to determine whether or not she is entitled to choose abortion.

A supporter of the violinist analogy might reply that it is absurd to suggest that forgetting her pill one day might be sufficient to morally oblige a woman to complete an unwanted pregnancy. And indeed it is absurd to suggest this. As we will see, a woman's moral right to choose abortion does not depend upon the extent to which she might be thought to be morally responsible for her own pregnancy. But once we allow the assumption that a fetus has a strong right to life, we cannot avoid taking this absurd suggestion seriously. On this assumption, it is a vexing question whether and when abortion is morally justifiable. The violinist analogy can at best show that aborting a pregnancy is a deeply tragic act, though one that is sometimes morally justified.

My conviction is that an abortion is not always this deeply tragic, because a fetus is not yet a person, and therefore does not yet have a strong moral right to life. Although the truth of this conviction may not be self-evident, it does, I believe, follow from some highly plausible claims about the appropriate grounds for ascribing moral rights. It is worth examining these grounds, since this has not been adequately done before.

II

The question we must answer in order to determine the moral status of abortion is, How are we to define the moral community, the set of beings with full and equal moral rights? What sort of entity has the inalienable moral rights to life, liberty, and the pursuit of happiness? . . .

On the Definition of "Human"
The term "human being" has two distinct, but not often distinguished, senses. This results in a slide of meaning, which serves to conceal the fallacy in the traditional argument that, since (1) it is wrong to kill innocent human beings, and (2) fetuses are innocent human beings, therefore (3) it is wrong to kill fetuses. For if "human being" is used in the same sense in both (1) and (2), then whichever of the two senses is meant, one of these premises is question-begging. And if it is used in different senses then the conclusion does not follow.

Thus, (1) is a generally accepted moral truth,[1] and one that does not beg the question about abortion, only if "human being" is used to mean something like "a full-fledged member of the moral community, who is also a member of the human species." I will call this the *moral* sense of "human being." It is not to be confused with what I will call the *genetic* sense, i.e., the sense in which any individual entity that belongs to the human species is a human being, regardless of whether or not it is rightly considered to be an equal member of the moral community. Premise (1) avoids begging the question only if the moral sense is intended, while premise (2) avoids it only if what is intended is the genetic sense. . . .

Defining the Moral Community
Is genetic humanity sufficient for moral humanity? There are good reasons for not defining the moral community in this way. I would suggest that the moral community consists, in the first instance, of all *persons,* rather than all genetically human entities.[2] It is persons who invent moral rights and who are (sometimes)

capable of respecting them. It does not follow from this that only persons can have moral rights. However, persons are wise not to ascribe to entities that clearly are not persons moral rights that cannot in practice be respected without severely undercutting the fundamental moral rights of those who clearly are.

What characteristics entitle an entity to be considered a person? This is not the place to attempt a complete analysis of the concept of personhood; but we do not need such an analysis to explain why a fetus is not a person. All we need is an approximate list of the most basic criteria of personhood. In searching for these criteria, it is useful to look beyond the set of people with whom we are acquainted, all of whom are human. Imagine, then, a space traveler who lands on a new planet and encounters organisms unlike any she has ever seen or heard of. If she wants to behave morally toward these organisms, she has somehow to determine whether they are people and thus have full moral rights, or whether they are things that she need not feel guilty about treating, for instance, as a source of food.

How should she go about making this determination? If she has some anthropological background, she might look for signs of religion, art, and the manufacturing of tools, weapons, or shelters, since these cultural traits have frequently been used to distinguish our human ancestors from prehuman beings, in what seems to be closer to the moral than the genetic sense of "human being." She would be right to take the presence of such traits as evidence that the extraterrestrials were persons. It would, however, be anthropocentric of her to take the absence of these traits as proof that they were not, since they could be people who have progressed beyond, or who have never needed, these particular cultural traits.

I suggest that among the characteristics which are central to the concept of personhood are the following:

1. *sentience*—the capacity to have conscious experiences, usually including the capacity to experience pain and pleasure;
2. *emotionality*—the capacity to feel happy, sad, angry, loving, etc.;
3. *reason*—the capacity to solve new and relatively complex problems;
4. *the capacity to communicate,* by whatever means, messages of an indefinite variety of types; that is, not just with an indefinite number of possible contents, but on indefinitely many possible topics;
5. *self-awareness*—having a concept of oneself as an individual and/or as a member of a social group; and finally
6. *moral agency*—the capacity to regulate one's own actions through moral principles or ideals.

It is difficult to produce precise definitions of these traits, let alone to specify universally valid behavioral indications that these traits are present. But let us assume that our explorer knows approximately what these six characteristics mean, and that she is able to observe whether or not the extraterrestrials possess these mental and behavioral capacities. How should she use her findings to decide whether or not they are persons?

An entity need not have *all* of these attributes to be a person. And perhaps none of them is absolutely necessary. For instance, the absence of emotion would not disqualify a being that was person-like in all other ways. Think, for instance, of two of the *Star Trek* characters, Mr. Spock (who is half human and half alien), and Data (who is an android). Both are depicted as lacking the capacity to feel emotion; yet both are sentient, reasoning, communicative, self-aware moral agents, and unquestionably persons. Some people are unemotional; some cannot communicate well; some lack self-awareness; and some are not moral agents. It should not surprise us that many people do not meet all of the criteria of personhood. Criteria for the applicability of complex concepts are often like this: none may be logically necessary, but the more criteria that are satisfied, the more confident we are that the concept is applicable. Conversely, the fewer criteria are satisfied, the less plausible it is to hold that the concept applies. And if none of the relevant criteria are met, then we may be confident that it does not.

Thus, to demonstrate that a fetus is not a person, all I need to claim is that an entity that has *none* of these six characteristics is not a person. Sentience is the most basic mental capacity, and the one that may have the best claim to being a necessary (though not sufficient) condition for personhood. Sentience can establish a claim to moral considerability, since sentient beings can be harmed in ways that matter to them; for instance, they can be caused to feel pain, or deprived of the continuation of a life that is pleasant to them. It is unlikely that an entirely insentient organism could develop the other mental behavioral capacities that are characteristic of persons. Consequently, it is odd to claim that an entity that is not sentient, and that has never been sentient, is nevertheless a person. Persons who have permanently and irreparably lost all capacity for sentience, but who remain biologically alive, arguably still have strong moral rights by virtue of what they have been in the past. But small fetuses, which have not yet begun to have experiences, are not persons yet and do not have the rights that persons do.

The presumption that all persons have full and equal basic moral rights may be part of the very concept of a person. If this is so, then the concept of a person is in part a moral one; once we have admitted that X is a person, we have implicitly committed ourselves to recognizing X's right to be treated as a member of the moral community. The claim that X is a *human being* may also be voiced as an appeal to treat X decently; but this is usually either because "human being" is used in the moral sense, or because of a confusion between genetic and moral humanity.

If (1)–(6) are the primary criteria of personhood, then genetic humanity is neither necessary nor sufficient for personhood. Some genetically human entities are not persons, and there may be persons who belong to other species. A man or woman whose consciousness has been permanently obliterated but who remains biologically alive is a human entity who may no longer be a person; and some unfortunate humans, who have never had any sensory or cognitive capacities at all, may not be people either. Similarly, an early fetus is a human entity which is not yet a person. It is not even minimally sentient, let alone capable of emotion, reason, sophisticated communication, self-awareness, or moral agency.[3] Thus, while it may be greatly valued as a future child, it does not yet have the claim to moral consideration that it may come to have later.

Moral agency matters to moral status, because it is moral agents who invent moral rights and who can be obliged to respect them. Human beings have become moral agents from social necessity. Most social animals exist well enough, with no evident notion of a moral right. But human beings need moral rights, because we are not only highly social, but also sufficiently clever and self-interested to be capable of undermining our societies through violence and duplicity. For human persons, moral rights are essential for peaceful and mutually beneficial social life. So long as some moral agents are denied basic rights, peaceful existence is difficult, since moral agents justly resent being treated as something less. If animals of some terrestrial species are found to be persons, or if alien persons come from other worlds, or if human beings someday invent machines whose mental and behavioral capacities make them persons, then we will be morally obliged to respect the moral rights of these nonhuman persons—at least to the extent that they are willing and able to respect ours in turn.

Although only those persons who are moral agents can participate directly in the shaping and enforcement of moral rights, they need not and usually do not ascribe moral rights only to themselves and other moral agents. Human beings are social creatures who naturally care for small children, and other members of the social community who are not currently capable of moral agency. Moreover, we are all vulnerable to the temporary or permanent loss of the mental capacities necessary for moral agency. Thus, we have self-interested as well as altruistic reasons for extending basic moral rights to infants and other sentient human beings who have already been born, but who currently lack some of these other mental capacities. These human beings, despite their current disabilities, are persons and members of the moral community.

But in extending moral rights to beings (human or otherwise) that have few or none of the morally significant characteristics of persons, we need to be careful not to burden human moral agents with obligations that they cannot possibly fulfill, except at unacceptably great cost to their own well-being and that of those they care about. Women often cannot complete unwanted pregnancies, except at intolerable mental, physical, and economic cost to themselves and their families. And heterosexual intercourse is too important a part of the social lives of most men and women to be reserved for times when pregnancy is an acceptable outcome.... If fetuses were persons, then they would have rights that must be respected, even at great social or personal cost. But given that early fetuses, at least, are unlike persons in the morally relevant respects, it is unreasonable to insist that they be accorded exactly the same moral and legal status.

Fetal Development and the Right to Life

Two questions arise regarding the application of these suggestions to the moral status of the fetus. First, if indeed fetuses are not yet persons, then might they nevertheless have strong moral rights based upon the degree to which they *resemble* persons? Secondly, to what extent, if any, does a fetus's potential to *become* a person imply that we ought to accord to it some of the same moral rights? Each of these questions requires comment.

It is reasonable to suggest that the more like a person something is—the more it appears to meet at least some of the criteria of personhood—the stronger is the case for according it a right to life, and perhaps the stronger its right to life is. That being the case, perhaps the fetus gradually gains a stronger right to life as it develops. We should take seriously the suggestion that, just as "the human individual develops biologically in a continuous fashion,

the rights of a human person . . . develop in the same way."[4]

A seven-month fetus can apparently feel pain and can respond to such stimuli as light and sound. Thus, it may have a rudimentary form of consciousness. Nevertheless, it is probably not as conscious, or as capable of emotion, as even a very young infant is; and it has as yet little or no capacity for reason, sophisticated intentional communication, or self-awareness. In these respects, even a late-term fetus is arguably less like a person than are many nonhuman animals. Many animals (e.g., large-brained mammals such as elephants, cetaceans, or apes) are not only sentient, but clearly possessed of a degree of reason, and perhaps even of self-awareness. Thus, on the basis of its resemblance to a person, even a late-term fetus can have no more right to life than do these animals.

Animals may, indeed, plausibly be held to have some moral rights, and perhaps rather strong ones. But it is impossible in practice to accord full and equal moral rights to all animals. When an animal poses a serious threat to the life or well-being of a person, we do not, as a rule, greatly blame the person for killing it; and there are good reasons for this species-based discrimination. Animals, however intelligent in their own domains, are generally not beings with whom we can reason; we cannot persuade mice not to invade our dwellings or consume our food. That is why their rights are necessarily weaker than those of a being who can understand and respect the rights of other beings.

But the probable sentience of late-term fetuses is not the only argument in favor of treating late abortion as a morally more serious matter than early abortion. Many—perhaps most—people are repulsed by the thought of needlessly aborting a late-term fetus. The late-term fetus has features which cause it to arouse in us almost the same powerful protective instinct as does a small infant.

This response needs to be taken seriously. If it were impossible to perform abortions early in pregnancy, then we might have to tolerate the mental and physical trauma that would be occasioned by the routine resort to late abortion. But where early abortion is safe, legal, and readily available to all women, it is not unreasonable to expect most women who wish to end a pregnancy to do so prior to the third trimester. Most women strongly prefer early to late abortion, because it is far less physically painful and emotionally traumatic. Other things being equal, it is better for all concerned that pregnancies that are not to be completed should be ended as early as possible. Few women would consider ending a pregnancy in the seventh month in order to take a trip to Europe. If, however, a woman's own life or health is at stake, or if the fetus has been found to be so severely abnormal as to be unlikely to survive or to have a life worth living, then late abortion may be the morally best choice. For even a late-term fetus is not a person yet, and its rights must yield to those of the woman whenever it is impossible for both to be respected.

Potential Personhood and the Right to Life

We have seen that a presentient fetus does not yet resemble a person in ways which support the claim that it has strong moral rights. But what about its *potential,* the fact that if nurtured and allowed to develop it may eventually become a person? Doesn't that potential give it at least some right to life? The fact that something is a potential person may be a reason for not destroying it; but we need not conclude from this that potential people have a strong right to life. It may be that the feeling that it is better not to destroy a potential person is largely due to the fact that potential people are felt to be an invaluable resource, not to be lightly squandered. If every speck of dust were a potential person, we would be less apt to suppose that all potential persons have a right to become actual.

We do not need to insist that a potential person has no right to life whatever. There may be something immoral, and not just imprudent, about wantonly destroying potential people, when doing so isn't necessary. But even if a potential person does have some right to life, that right could not outweigh the right of a woman to obtain an abortion; for the basic moral rights of an actual person outweigh the rights of a merely potential person, whenever the two conflict. Since this may not be immediately obvious in the case of a human fetus, let us look at another case.

Suppose that our space explorer falls into the hands of an extraterrestrial civilization, whose scientists decide to create a few thousand new human beings by killing her and using some of her cells to create clones. We may imagine that each of these newly created women will have all of the original woman's abilities, skills, knowledge, and so on, and will also have an individual self-concept; in short, that each of them will be a bona fide (though not genetically unique) person. Imagine, further, that our explorer knows all of this and knows that these people will be treated kindly and fairly. I maintain that in such a situation she would have the right to escape if she could, thus depriving all of the potential people of their potential lives. For her right to life outweighs all of theirs put together, even though they are not genetically human, and have a high probability of becoming people, if only she refrains from acting.

Indeed, I think that our space traveler would have a right to escape even if it were not her life which the aliens planned to take, but only a year of her freedom, or only a day. She would not be obliged to stay, even if she had been captured because of her own lack of caution—or even if she had done so deliberately, knowing the possible consequences. Regardless of why she was captured, she is not obliged to remain in captivity for *any* period of time in order to permit merely potential people to become actual people. By the same token, a woman's rights to liberty and the control of her own body outweigh whatever right a fetus may have merely by virtue of its potential personhood.

The Objection From Infanticide

One objection to my argument is that it appears to justify not only abortion, but also infanticide. A newborn infant is not much more personlike than a nine-month fetus, and thus it might appear that if late-term abortion is sometimes justified then infanticide must also sometimes be justified. Yet most people believe that infanticide is a form of murder, and virtually never justified.

This objection is less telling than it may seem. There are many reasons why infanticide is more difficult to justify than abortion, even though neither fetuses nor newborn infants are clearly persons. In this period of history, the deliberate killing of newborns is virtually never justified. This is in part because newborns are so close to being persons that to kill them requires a very strong moral justification— as does the killing of dolphins, chimpanzees, and other highly person-like creatures. It is certainly wrong to kill such beings for the sake of convenience, or financial profit, or "sport." Only the most vital human needs, such as the need to defend one's own life and physical integrity, can provide a plausible justification for killing such beings.

In the case of an infant, there is no such vital need, since in the contemporary world there are usually other people who are eager to provide a good home for an infant whose own parents are unable or unwilling to care for it. Many people wait years for the opportunity to adopt a child, and some are unable to do so, even though there is every reason to believe that they would be good parents. The needless destruction of a viable infant not only deprives a sentient human being of life, but also deprives other persons of a source of great satisfaction, perhaps severely impoverishing *their* lives.

Even if an infant is unadoptable (e.g., because of some severe physical disability), it is still wrong to kill it. For most of us value the lives of infants, and would greatly prefer to pay taxes to support foster care and state institutions for disabled children, rather than to allow them to be killed or abandoned. So long as most people feel this way, and so long as it is possible to provide care for infants who are unwanted, or who have special needs that their parents cannot meet without assistance, it is wrong to let any infant die who has a chance of living a reasonably good life.

If these arguments show that infanticide is wrong, at least in today's world, then why don't they also show that late-term abortion is always wrong? After all, third-trimester fetuses are almost as personlike as infants, and many people value them and would prefer that they be preserved. As a potential source of pleasure to some family, a fetus is just as valuable as an infant. But there is an important difference between these two cases: once the infant is born, its continued life cannot pose any serious threat to the woman's life or health, since she is free to put it up for adoption or to place it in foster care. While she might, in rare cases, prefer that the child die rather than being raised by others, such a preference would not establish a right on her part.

In contrast, a pregnant woman's right to protect her own life and health outweighs other people's desire that the fetus be preserved—just as, when a person's desire for life or health is threatened by an animal, and when the threat cannot be removed without killing the animal, that person's right to self-defense outweighs the desires of those who would prefer that the animal not be killed. Thus, while the moment of birth may mark no sharp discontinuity in the degree to which an infant resembles a person, it does mark the end of the mother's right to determine its fate. Indeed, if a late abortion can be safely performed without harming the fetus, the mother has in most cases no right to insist upon its death, for the same reason that she has no right to insist that a viable infant be killed or allowed to die.

It remains true that, on my view, neither abortion nor the killing of newborns is obviously a form of murder. Perhaps our legal system is correct in its classification of infanticide as murder, since no other legal category adequately expresses the force of our disapproval of this action. But some moral distinction remains, and it has important consequences. When a society cannot possibly care for all of the children who are born, without endangering the survival of adults and older children, allowing some infants to die may be the best of a bad set of options. Throughout history, most societies—from those that lived by gathering and hunting to the highly civilized Chinese, Japanese, Greeks, and Romans—have permitted infanticide under such unfortunate circumstances, regarding it as a necessary evil. It shows a lack of understanding to condemn these societies as morally benighted for this reason alone, since in the absence of safe and effective means of contraception and abortion, parents must sometimes have had no morally better options.

CONCLUSION

I have argued that fetuses are neither persons nor members of the moral community. Furthermore, neither a fetus's resemblance to a person, nor its potential for becoming a person, provides an adequate basis for the claim that it has a full and equal right to life. At the same time, there are medical as well as moral reasons for preferring early to late abortion when the pregnancy is unwanted.

Women, unlike fetuses, are undeniably persons and members of the human moral community. If unwanted or medically dangerous pregnancies never occurred, then it might be possible to respect women's basic moral rights, while at the same time extending the same basic rights to fetuses. But in the real world such pregnancies do occur—often despite the woman's best efforts to prevent them. Even if the perfect contraceptive were universally available, the continued occurrence of rape and incest would make access to abortion a vital human need. Because women are persons, and fetuses are not, women's rights to life, liberty, and physical integrity morally override whatever right to life it may be appropriate to ascribe to a fetus. Consequently, laws that deny women the right to obtain abortions, or that make safe early abortions difficult or impossible for some women to obtain, are an unjustified violation of basic moral and constitutional rights.

NOTES

1. The principle that it is always wrong to kill innocent human beings may be in need of other modifications, e.g., that it may be permissible to kill innocent human beings in order to save a larger number of equally innocent human beings; but we may ignore these complications here.
2. From here on, I will use "human" to mean "genetically human," since the moral sense of the term seems closely connected to, and perhaps derived from, the assumption that genetic humanity is both necessary and sufficient for membership in the moral community.
3. Fetal sentience is impossible prior to the development of neurological connections between the sense organs and the brain, and between the various parts of the brain involved in the processing of conscious experience. This stage of neurological development is currently thought to occur at some point in the late second or early third trimester.
4. Thomas L. Hayes, "A Biological View," *Commonweal* 85 (March 17, 1967): pp. 677–78; cited by Daniel Callahan in *Abortion: Law, Choice, and Morality* (London: Macmillan, 1970).

STUDY QUESTIONS

1. What characteristics entitle an entity to be considered a person?
2. Is infanticide more difficult to justify than abortion?
3. If a fetus is a human being, is abortion ever morally permissible?
4. If a fetus is not a human being, is abortion ever morally wrong?

Why Abortion Is Immoral

DON MARQUIS

Don Marquis, who is Professor Emeritus of Philosophy at the University of Kansas, disagrees with the position on abortion defended by Judith Jarvis Thomson. He argues that, with rare exceptions, abortion is immoral. Note that he does not base his reasoning on the claim that the fetus is a person but rather on the view that the fetus has a valuable future.

The view that abortion is, with rare exceptions, seriously immoral has received little support in the recent philosophical literature. No doubt most philosophers affiliated with secular institutions of higher education believe that the anti-abortion

From Don Marquis, "Why Abortion Is Immoral," *The Journal of Philosophy,* 86 (1989). Reprinted with the permission of the author and the journal.

position is either a symptom of irrational religious dogma or a conclusion generated by seriously confused philosophical argument. The purpose of this essay is to undermine this general belief. This essay sets out an argument that purports to show, as well as any argument in ethics can show, that abortion is, except possibly in rare cases, seriously immoral, that it is in the same moral category as killing an innocent adult human being. . . .

II

. . . [W]e can start from the following unproblematic assumption concerning our own case: it is wrong to kill *us*. Why is it wrong? Some answers can be easily eliminated. It might be said that what makes killing us wrong is that a killing brutalizes the one who kills. But the brutalization consists of being inured to the performance of an act that is hideously immoral; hence, the brutalization does not explain the immorality. It might be said that what makes killing us wrong is the great loss others would experience due to our absence. Although such hubris is understandable, such an explanation does not account for the wrongness of killing hermits, or those whose lives are relatively independent and whose friends find it easy to make new friends.

A more obvious answer is better. What primarily makes killing wrong is neither its effect on the murderer nor its effect on the victim's friends and relatives, but its effect on the victim. The loss of one's life is one of the greatest losses one can suffer. The loss of one's life deprives one of all the experiences, activities, projects, and enjoyments that would otherwise have constituted one's future. Therefore, killing someone is wrong, primarily because the killing inflicts (one of) the greatest possible losses on the victim. To describe this as the loss of life can be misleading, however. The change in my biological state does not by itself make killing me wrong. The effect of the loss of my biological life is the loss to me of all those activities, projects, experiences, and enjoyments which would otherwise have constituted my future personal life. These activities, projects, experiences, and enjoyments are either valuable for their own sakes or are means to something else that is valuable for its own sake. Some parts of my future are not valued by me now, but will come to be valued by me as I grow older and as my values and capacities change. When I am killed, I am deprived both of what I now value which would have been part of my future personal life, but also what I would come to value. Therefore, when I die, I am deprived of all of the value of my future. Inflicting this loss on me is ultimately what makes killing me wrong. This being the case, it would seem that what makes killing *any* adult human being prima facie seriously wrong is the loss of his or her future.

How should this rudimentary theory of the wrongness of killing be evaluated? It cannot be faulted for deriving an "ought" from an "is," for it does not. The analysis assumes that killing me (or you, reader) is prima facie seriously wrong. The point of the analysis is to establish which natural property ultimately explains the wrongness of the killing, given that it is wrong. A natural property will ultimately explain the wrongness of killing, only if (1) the explanation fits with our intuitions about the matter and (2) there is no other natural property that provides the basis for a better explanation of the wrongness of killing. This analysis rests on the intuition that what makes killing a particular human or animal wrong is what it does to that particular human or animal. What makes killing wrong is some natural effect or other of the killing. . . .

The claim that what makes killing wrong is the loss of the victim's future is directly supported by two considerations. In the first place, this theory explains why we regard killing as one of the worst of crimes. Killing is especially wrong, because it deprives the victim of more than perhaps any other crime. In the second place, people with AIDS or cancer who know they are dying believe, of course, that dying is a very bad thing for them. They believe that the loss of a future to them that they would otherwise have experienced is what makes their premature death a very bad thing for them. A better theory of the wrongness of killing would require a different natural property associated with killing which better fits with the attitudes of the dying. What could it be?

The view that what makes killing wrong is the loss to the victim of the value of the victim's future gains additional support when some of its implications are examined. In the first place, it is incompatible with the view that it is wrong to kill only beings who are biologically human. It is possible that there exists a different species from another planet whose members have a future like ours. Since having a future like that is what makes killing someone wrong, this theory entails that it would be wrong to kill members of such a species. Hence, this theory is opposed to the claim that only life that is biologically human has great moral worth, a claim which many anti-abortionists have seemed to adopt. This opposition . . . seems to be a merit of the theory.

In the second place, the claim that the loss of one's future is the wrong-making feature of one's being killed entails the possibility that the futures of some actual nonhuman mammals on our own planet are sufficiently like ours that it is seriously wrong to kill them also. Whether some animals do have the same right to life as human beings depends on adding to the account of the wrongness of killing some additional account of just what it is about my future or the futures of other adult human beings which makes it wrong to kill us. No such additional account will be offered in this essay. Undoubtedly, the provision of such an account would be a very difficult matter. Undoubtedly, any such account would be quite controversial. Hence, it surely should not reflect badly on this sketch of an elementary theory of the wrongness of killing that it is indeterminate with respect to some very difficult issues regarding animal rights.

In the third place, the claim that the loss of one's future is the wrong-making feature of one's being killed does not entail, as sanctity of human life theories do, that active euthanasia is wrong. Persons who are severely and incurably ill, who face a future of pain and despair, and who wish to die will not have suffered a loss if they are killed. It is, strictly speaking, the value of a human's future which makes killing wrong in this theory. This being so, killing does not necessarily wrong some persons who are sick and dying. Of course, there may be other reasons for a prohibition of active euthanasia, but that is another matter. Sanctity-of-human-life theories seem to hold that active euthanasia is seriously wrong even in an individual case where there seems to be good reason for it independently of public policy considerations. This consequence is most implausible, and it is a plus for the claim that the loss of a future of value is what makes killing wrong that it does not share this consequence.

In the fourth place, the account of the wrongness of killing defended in this essay does straightforwardly entail that it is prima facie seriously wrong to kill children and infants, for we do presume that they have futures of value. Since we do believe that it is wrong to kill defenseless babies, it is important that a theory of the wrongness of killing easily accounts for this. Personhood theories of the wrongness of killing, on the other hand, cannot straightforwardly account for the wrongness of killing infants and young children. Hence, such theories must add special ad hoc accounts of the wrongness of killing the young. The plausibility of such ad hoc theories seems to be a function of how desperately one wants such theories to work. The claim that the primary wrong-making feature of a killing is the loss to the victim of the value of its future accounts for the wrongness of killing young children and infants directly; it makes the wrongness of such acts as obvious as we actually think it is. This is a further merit of this theory. Accordingly, it seems that this value of a future-like-ours theory of the wrongness of killing shares strengths of both sanctity-of-life and personhood accounts while avoiding weaknesses of both. In addition, it meshes with a central intuition concerning what makes killing wrong.

The claim that the primary wrong-making feature of a killing is the loss to the victim of the value of its future has obvious consequences for the ethics of abortion. The future of a standard fetus includes a set of experiences, projects, activities, and such which are identical with the futures of adult human beings and are identical with the futures of young children. Since the reason that is sufficient to explain why it is wrong to kill human beings after the time of birth is a reason that also applies to fetuses, it follows that abortion is prima facie seriously morally wrong.

This argument does not rely on the invalid inference that, since it is wrong to kill persons, it is wrong to kill potential persons also. The category that is morally central to this analysis is the category of having a valuable future like ours; it is not the category of personhood. The argument to the conclusion that abortion is prima facie seriously morally wrong proceeded independently of the notion of person or potential person or any equivalent. Someone may wish to start with this analysis in terms of the value of a human future, conclude that abortion is, except perhaps in rare circumstances, seriously morally wrong, infer that fetuses have the right to life, and then call fetuses "persons" as a result of their having the right to life. Clearly, in this case, the category of person is being used to state the *conclusion* of the analysis rather than to generate the *argument* of the analysis. . . .

Of course, this value of a future-like-ours argument, if sound, shows only that abortion is prima facie wrong, not that it is wrong in any and all circumstances. Since the loss of the future to a standard fetus, if killed, is, however, at least as great a loss as the loss of the future to a standard adult human being who is killed, abortion, like ordinary killing, could be justified only by the most compelling reasons. The loss of one's life is almost the greatest misfortune that can happen to one. Presumably abortion could be justified in some circumstances, only if the loss consequent on failing to abort would be at least as great. Accordingly, morally permissible abortions will be rare indeed unless, perhaps, they occur so early in pregnancy that a fetus is not yet definitely an individual. Hence, this argument should be taken as showing that abortion is presumptively very seriously wrong, where the presumption is very strong—as strong as the presumption that killing another adult human being is wrong.

<h1 style="text-align:center">V</h1>

In this essay, it has been argued that the correct ethic of the wrongness of killing can be extended to fetal life and used to show that there is a strong presumption that any abortion is morally impermissible. If the ethic of killing adopted here entails, however, that contraception is also seriously immoral, then there would appear to be a difficulty with the analysis of this essay.

But this analysis does not entail that contraception is wrong. Of course, contraception prevents the actualization of a possible future of value. Hence, it follows from the claim that futures of value should be maximized that contraception is prima facie immoral. This obligation to maximize does not exist, however; furthermore, nothing in the ethics of killing in this paper entails that it does. The ethics of killing in this essay would entail that contraception is wrong only if something were denied a human future of value by contraception. Nothing at all is denied such a future by contraception, however.

Candidates for a subject of harm by contraception fall into four categories: (1) some sperm or other, (2) some ovum or other, (3) a sperm and an ovum separately, and (4) a sperm and an ovum together. Assigning the harm to some sperm is utterly arbitrary, for no reason can be given for making a sperm the subject of harm rather than an ovum. Assigning the harm to some ovum is utterly arbitrary, for no reason can be given for making an ovum the subject of harm rather than a sperm. One might attempt to avoid these problems by insisting that contraception deprives both the sperm and the ovum separately of a valuable future like ours. On this alternative, too many futures are lost. Contraception was supposed to be wrong, because it deprived us of one future of value, not two. One might attempt to avoid this problem by holding that contraception deprives the combination of sperm and ovum of a valuable future like ours. But here the definite article misleads. At the time of contraception, there are hundreds of millions of sperm, one (released) ovum and millions of possible combinations of all of these. There is no actual combination at all. Is the subject of the loss to be a merely possible combination? Which one? This alternative does not yield an actual subject of harm either. Accordingly, the immorality of contraception is not entailed by the loss of a future-like-ours argument simply because there is no nonarbitrarily identifiable subject of the loss in the case of contraception.

VI

The purpose of this essay has been to set out an argument for the serious presumptive wrongness of abortion subject to the assumption that the moral permissibility of abortion stands or falls on the moral status of the fetus. Since a fetus possesses a property, the possession of which in adult human beings is sufficient to make killing an adult human being wrong, abortion is wrong. This way of dealing with the problem of abortion seems superior to other approaches to the ethics of abortion, because it rests on an ethics of killing which is close to self-evident, because the crucial morally relevant property clearly applies to fetuses, and because the argument avoids the usual equivocations of "human life," "human being," or "person." . . . Its soundness is compatible with the moral permissibility of euthanasia and contraception. It deals with our intuitions concerning young children.

Finally, this analysis can be viewed as resolving a standard problem—indeed, *the* standard problem—concerning the ethics of abortion. Clearly, it is wrong to kill adult human beings. Clearly, it is not wrong to end the life of some arbitrarily chosen single human cell. Fetuses seem to be like arbitrarily chosen human cells in some respects and like adult humans in other respects. The problem of the ethics of abortion is the problem of determining the fetal property that settles this moral controversy. The thesis of this essay is that the problem of the ethics of abortion, so understood, is solvable.

STUDY QUESTIONS

1. Is the loss of one's future as devastating for a fetus as for a child?
2. Does Marquis's argument that abortion is immoral depend on religious considerations?
3. Does Marquis accept the argument that because killing persons is wrong, killing potential persons is also wrong?
4. According to Marquis, in what circumstances is abortion not wrong?

Virtue Theory and Abortion

ROSALIND HURSTHOUSE

Rosalind Hursthouse is Professor of Philosophy at the University of Auckland in
New Zealand. She demonstrates how virtue theory can be applied to the issue of
abortion. The term "deontological" that she uses refers to an ethical theory, such
as Kant's, based on fulfilling duties, as opposed to a consequentialist theory, such
as utilitarianism, that appeals to achieving good states of affairs.

The sort of ethical theory derived from Aristotle, variously described as virtue ethics, virtue-based ethics, or neo-Aristotelianism, is becoming better known and is
now quite widely recognized as at least a possible rival to deontological and utilitarian theories. . . . I aim to deepen that understanding . . . by illustrating what the
theory looks like when it is applied to a particular issue, in this case, abortion. . . .

As everyone knows, the morality of abortion is commonly discussed in relation to just two considerations: first, and predominantly, the status of the fetus and
whether or not it is the sort of thing that may or may not be innocuously or justifiably killed; and second, and less predominantly (when, that is, the discussion concerns
the *morality* of abortion rather than the question of permissible legislation in a just
society), women's rights. If one thinks within this familiar framework, one may well
be puzzled about what virtue theory, as such, could contribute. Some people assume
the discussion will be conducted solely in terms of what the virtuous agent would or
would not do. . . . Others assume that only justice, or at most justice and charity, will be
applied to the issue, generating a discussion very similar to Judith Jarvis Thomson's.[1]

Now if this is the way the virtue theorist's discussion of abortion is imagined to
be, no wonder people think little of it. It seems obvious in advance that in any such
discussion there must be either a great deal of extremely tendentious application
of the virtue terms *just, charitable*, and so on or a lot of rhetorical appeal to "this is
what only the virtuous agent knows." But these are caricatures; they fail to appreciate the way in which virtue theory quite transforms the discussion of abortion by
dismissing the two familiar dominating considerations as, in a way, fundamentally
irrelevant. In what way or ways, I hope to make both clear and plausible.

Let us first consider women's rights. Let me emphasize again that we are discussing the *morality* of abortion, not the rights and wrongs of laws prohibiting or
permitting it. If we suppose that women do have a moral right to do as they choose
with their own bodies, or, more particularly, to terminate their pregnancies, then
it may well follow that a *law* forbidding abortion would be unjust. Indeed, even

From *Philosophy & Public Affairs* 20 (1991), by permission of Blackwell Publishing.

if they have no such right, such a law might be, as things stand at the moment, unjust, or impractical, or inhumane: on this issue I have nothing to say in this article. But, putting all questions about the justice or injustice of laws to one side, and supposing only that women have such a moral right, *nothing* follows from this supposition about the morality of abortion, according to virtue theory, once it is noted (quite generally, not with particular reference to abortion) that in exercising a moral right I can do something cruel, or callous, or selfish, light-minded, self-righteous, stupid, inconsiderate, disloyal, dishonest—that is, act viciously.[2] Love and friendship do not survive their parties constantly insisting on their rights, nor do people live well when they think that getting what they have a right to is of preeminent importance; they harm others, and they harm themselves. So whether women have a moral right to terminate their pregnancies is irrelevant within virtue theory, for it is irrelevant to the question "In having an abortion in these circumstances, would the agent be acting virtuously or viciously or neither?"

What about the consideration of the status of the fetus—what can virtue theory say about that? One might say that this issue is not in the province of *any* moral theory; it is a metaphysical question, and an extremely difficult one at that. Must virtue theory then wait upon metaphysics to come up with the answer?

At first sight it might seem so. For virtue is said to involve knowledge, and part of this knowledge consists in having the *right* attitude to things. "Right" here does not just mean "morally right" or "proper" or "nice" in the modern sense; it means "accurate, true." One cannot have the right or correct attitude to something if the attitude is based on or involves false beliefs. And this suggests that if the status of the fetus is relevant to the rightness or wrongness of abortion, its status must be known, as a truth, to the fully wise and virtuous person.

But the sort of wisdom that the fully virtuous person has is not supposed to be recondite; it does not call for fancy philosophical sophistication, and it does not depend upon, let alone wait upon, the discoveries of academic philosophers.[3] And this entails the following, rather startling, conclusion: that the status of the fetus—that issue over which so much ink has been spilt—is, according to virtue theory, simply not relevant to the rightness or wrongness of abortion (within, that is, a secular morality).

Or rather, since that is clearly too radical a conclusion, it is in a sense relevant, but only in the sense that the familiar biological facts are relevant. By "the familiar biological facts" I mean the facts that most human societies are and have been familiar with—that, standardly (but not invariably), pregnancy occurs as the result of sexual intercourse, that it lasts about nine months, during which time the fetus grows and develops, that standardly it terminates in the birth of a living baby, and that this is how we all come to be.

It might be thought that this distinction—between the familiar biological facts and the status of the fetus—is a distinction without a difference. But this is not so. To attach relevance to the status of the fetus, in the sense in which virtue theory claims it is not relevant, is to be gripped by the conviction that we must go beyond the familiar biological facts, deriving some sort of conclusion from them, such as that the fetus has rights, or is not a person, or something similar. It is also to believe that this exhausts the relevance of the familiar biological facts, that all they are relevant to is the status of the fetus and whether or not it is the sort of thing that may or may not be killed.

These convictions, I suspect, are rooted in the desire to solve the problem of abortion by getting it to fall under some general rule such as "You ought not to kill anything with the right to life but may kill anything else." But they have resulted in what should surely strike any nonphilosopher as a most bizarre aspect of nearly all the current philosophical literature on abortion, namely, that, far from treating abortion as a unique moral problem, markedly unlike any other, nearly everything written on the status of the fetus and its bearing on the abortion issue would be consistent with the human reproductive facts' (to say nothing of family life) being totally different from what they are. Imagine that you are an alien extraterrestrial anthropologist who does not know that the human race is roughly 50 percent female and 50 percent male, or that our only (natural) form of reproduction involves heterosexual intercourse, viviparous birth, and the female's (and only the female's) being pregnant for nine months, or that females are capable of childbearing from late childhood to late middle age, or that childbearing is painful, dangerous, and emotionally charged—do you think you would pick up these facts from the hundreds of articles written on the status of the fetus? I am quite sure you would not. And that, I think, shows that the current philosophical literature on abortion has got badly out of touch with reality.

Now if we are using virtue theory, our first question is not "What do the familiar biological facts show—what can be derived from them about the status of the fetus?" but "How do these facts figure in the practical reasoning, actions and passions, thoughts and reactions, of the virtuous and the nonvirtuous? What is the mark of having the right attitude to these facts and what manifests having the wrong attitude to them?" This immediately makes essentially relevant not only all the facts about human reproduction I mentioned above, but a whole range of facts about our emotions in relation to them as well. I mean such facts as that human parents, both male and female, tend to care passionately about their offspring, and that family relationships are among the deepest and strongest in our lives—and, significantly, among the longest-lasting.

These facts make it obvious that pregnancy is not just one among many other physical conditions; and hence that anyone who genuinely believes that an abortion is comparable to a haircut or an appendectomy is mistaken.[4] The fact that the premature termination of a pregnancy is, in some sense, the cutting off of a new human life, and thereby, like the procreation of a new human life, connects with all our thoughts about human life and death, parenthood, and family relationships, must make it a serious matter. To disregard this fact about it, to think of abortion as nothing but the killing of something that does not matter, or as nothing but the exercise of some right or rights one has, or as the incidental means to some desirable state of affairs, is to do something callous and light-minded, the sort of thing that no virtuous and wise person would do. It is to have the wrong attitude not only to fetuses, but more generally to human life and death, parenthood, and family relationships.

Although I say that the facts make this obvious, I know that this is one of my tendentious points. In partial support of it I note that even the most dedicated proponents of the view that deliberate abortion is just like an appendectomy or haircut rarely hold the same view of spontaneous abortion, that is, miscarriage. It is not so tendentious of me to claim that to react to people's grief over miscarriage by saying, or even thinking, "What a fuss about nothing!" would be callous and light-minded, whereas to try to laugh someone out of grief over an appendectomy scar or a botched haircut would not be. It is hard to give this point due prominence within act-centered theories, for the inconsistency is an inconsistency in attitude about the seriousness of loss of life, not in beliefs about which acts are right or wrong. Moreover, an act-centered theorist may say, "Well, there is nothing wrong with *thinking* 'What a fuss about nothing!' as long as you do not say it and hurt the person who is grieving. And besides, we cannot be held responsible for our thoughts, only for the intentional actions they give rise to." But the character traits that virtue theory emphasizes are not simply dispositions to intentional actions, but a seamless disposition to certain actions and passions, thoughts and reactions.

To say that the cutting off of a human life is always a matter of some seriousness, at any stage, is not to deny the relevance of gradual fetal development. Notwithstanding the well-worn point that clear boundary lines cannot be drawn, our emotions and attitudes regarding the fetus do change as it develops, and again when it is born, and indeed further as the baby grows. Abortion for shallow reasons in the later stages is much more shocking than abortion for the same reasons in the early stages in a way that matches the fact that deep grief over miscarriage in the later stages is more appropriate than it is over miscarriage in the earlier stages (when, that is, the grief is solely about the loss of *this* child, not about, as might be the case, the loss of one's only hope of having a child or of having one's husband's child). Imagine (or recall) a woman who already has children; she had not intended to have more, but finds herself unexpectedly pregnant. Though contrary to her plans, the pregnancy, once established as a fact, is welcomed—and then she loses the embryo almost immediately. If this were bemoaned as a tragedy, it would, I think, be a misapplication of the concept of what is tragic. But it may still properly be mourned as a loss. The grief is expressed in such terms as "I shall always wonder how she or he would have turned out" or "When I look at the others, I shall think, 'How different their lives would have been if this other one had been part of them.'" It would, I take it, be callous and light-minded to say, or think, "Well, she has already *got* four children; what's the problem?"; it would be neither, nor arrogantly intrusive in the case of a close friend, to try to correct prolonged mourning by saying, "I know it's sad, but it's not a tragedy; rejoice in the ones you have." The application of *tragic* becomes more appropriate as the fetus grows, for the mere fact that one has lived with it for longer, conscious of its existence, makes a difference. To shrug off an early abortion is understandable just because it is very hard to be fully conscious of the fetus's existence in the early stages and hence hard to appreciate that an early abortion is the destruction of life. It is particularly hard for the young and inexperienced to appreciate this, because appreciation of it usually comes only with experience.

I do not mean "with the experience of having an abortion" (though that may be part of it) but, quite generally, "with the experience of life." Many women who have borne children contrast their later pregnancies with their first successful one, saying that in the later ones they were conscious of a new life growing in them from very early on. And, more generally, as one reaches the age at which the next generation is coming up close behind one, the counterfactuals "If I, or she, had had an abortion, Alice, or Bob, would not have been born" acquire a significant application, which casts a new light on the conditionals "If I or Alice have an abortion then some Caroline or Bill will not be born."

The fact that pregnancy is not just one among many physical conditions does not mean that one can never regard it in that light without manifesting a vice. When women are in very poor physical health, or worn out from childbearing, or forced to do very physically demanding jobs, then they cannot be described as self-indulgent, callous, irresponsible, or light-minded if they seek abortions mainly with a view to avoiding pregnancy as the physical condition that it is. To go through with a pregnancy when one is utterly exhausted, or when one's job consists of crawling along tunnels hauling coal, as many women in the nineteenth century were obliged to do, is perhaps heroic, but people who do not achieve heroism are not necessarily vicious. That they can view the pregnancy only as eight months of misery, followed by hours if not days of agony and exhaustion, and abortion only as the blessed escape from this prospect, is entirely understandable and does not manifest any lack of serious respect for human life or a shallow attitude to motherhood. What it does show is that something is terribly amiss in the conditions of their lives, which make it so hard to recognize pregnancy and childbearing as the good that they can be.

In relation to this last point I should draw attention to the way in which virtue theory has a sort of built-in indexicality. Philosophers arguing against anything remotely resembling a belief in the sanctity of life (which the above claims clearly embody) frequently appeal to the existence of other communities in which abortion and infanticide are practiced. We should not automatically assume that it is impossible that some other communities could be morally inferior to our own; maybe some are, or have been, precisely insofar as their members are, typically, callous or light-minded or unjust. But in communities in which life is a great deal tougher for everyone than it is in ours, having the right attitude to human life and death, parenthood, and family relationships might well manifest itself in ways that are unlike ours. When it is essential to survival that most members of the community fend for themselves at a very young age or work during most of their waking hours, selective abortion or infanticide might be practiced either as a form of genuine euthanasia or for the sake of the community and not, I think, be thought callous or light-minded. But this does not make everything all right; as before, it shows that there is something amiss with the conditions of their lives, which are making it impossible for them to live really well.

The foregoing discussion, insofar as it emphasizes the right attitude to human life and death, parallels to a certain extent those standard discussions of abortion that concentrate on it solely as an issue of killing. But it does not, as those discussions do, gloss over the fact, emphasized by those who discuss the morality of abortion in terms of women's rights, that abortion, wildly unlike any other form of killing, is the termination of a pregnancy, which is a condition of a woman's body and results in *her* having a child if it is not aborted. This fact is given due recognition not by appeal to women's rights but by emphasizing the relevance of the familiar biological and psychological facts and their connection with having the right attitude to parenthood and family relationships. But it may well be thought that failing to bring in women's rights still leaves some important aspects of the problem of abortion untouched.

Speaking in terms of women's rights, people sometimes say things like, "Well, it's her life you're talking about too, you know; she's got a right to her own life, her own happiness." And the discussion stops there. But in the context of virtue theory, given that we are particularly concerned with what constitutes a good human life, with what true happiness or *eudaimonia* is, this is no place to stop. We go on to ask, "And is this life of hers a good one? Is she living well?"

If we are to go on to talk about good human lives, in the context of abortion, we have to bring in our thoughts about the value of love and family life, and our proper emotional development through a natural life cycle. The familiar facts support the view that parenthood in general, and motherhood and childbearing in particular, are intrinsically worthwhile, are among the things that can be correctly thought to be partially constitutive of a flourishing human life.[5] If this is right, then a woman who opts for not being a mother (at all, or again, or now) by opting for abortion may thereby be manifesting a flawed grasp of what her life should be, and be about—a grasp that is childish, or grossly materialistic, or short-sighted, or shallow.

I said "*may* thereby"; this *need* not be so. Consider, for instance, a woman who has already had several children and fears that to have another will seriously affect her capacity to be a good mother to the ones she has—she does not show a lack of appreciation of the intrinsic value of being a parent by opting for abortion. Nor does a woman who has been a good mother and is approaching the age at which she may be looking forward to being a good grandmother. Nor does a woman who discovers that her pregnancy may well kill her, and opts for abortion and adoption. Nor, necessarily, does a woman who has decided to lead a life centered around some other worthwhile activity or activities with which motherhood would compete.

People who are childless by choice are sometimes described as "irresponsible," or "selfish," or "refusing to grow up," or "not knowing what life is about." But one can hold that having children is intrinsically worthwhile without endorsing this, for we are, after all, in the happy position of there being more worthwhile things to do than can be fitted into one lifetime. Parenthood, and motherhood in particular, even if granted to be intrinsically worthwhile, undoubtedly take up a lot of one's adult life, leaving no room for some other worthwhile pursuits. But some women who choose abortion rather than have their first child, and some men who encourage their partners to choose abortion, are not avoiding parenthood for the sake of other worthwhile pursuits, but for the worthless one of "having a good time," or for the pursuit of some false vision of the ideals of freedom or self-realization.

And some others who say "I am not ready for parenthood yet" are making some sort of mistake about the extent to which one can manipulate the circumstances of one's life so as to make it fulfill some dream that one has. Perhaps one's dream is to have two perfect children, a girl and a boy, within a perfect marriage, in financially secure circumstances, with an interesting job of one's own. But to care too much about that dream, to demand of life that it give it to one and act accordingly, may be both greedy and foolish, and is to run the risk of missing out on happiness entirely. Not only may fate make the dream impossible, or destroy it, but one's own attachment to it may make it impossible. Good marriages, and the most promising children, can be destroyed by just one adult's excessive demand for perfection.

Once again, this is not to deny that girls may quite properly say "I am not ready for motherhood yet," especially in our society, and, far from manifesting irresponsibility or light-mindedness, show an appropriate modesty or humility, or a fearfulness that does not amount to cowardice. However, even when the decision to have an abortion is the right decision—one that does not itself fall under a vice-related term and thereby one that the perfectly virtuous could recommend—it does not follow that there is no sense in which having the abortion is wrong, or guilt inappropriate. For, by virtue of the fact that a human life has been cut short, some evil has probably been brought about,[6] and that circumstances make the decision to bring about some evil the right decision will be a ground for guilt if getting into those circumstances in the first place itself manifested a flaw in character.

What "gets one into those circumstances" in the case of abortion is, except in the case of rape, one's sexual activity and one's choices, or the lack of them, about one's sexual partner and about contraception. The virtuous woman (which here of course does not mean simply "chaste woman" but "woman with the virtues") has such character traits as strength, independence, resoluteness, decisiveness, self-confidence, responsibility, serious-mindedness, and self-determination—and no one, I think, could deny that many women become pregnant in circumstances in which they cannot welcome or cannot face the thought of having *this* child precisely because they lack one or some of these character traits. So even in the cases where the decision to have an abortion is the right one, it can still be the reflection of a moral failing—not because the decision itself is weak or cowardly or irresolute or irresponsible or light-minded, but because lack of the requisite opposite of these failings landed one in the circumstances in the first place. Hence the common universalized claim that guilt and remorse are never appropriate emotions about an abortion is denied. They may be appropriate, and appropriately inculcated, even when the decision was the right one.

Another motivation for bringing women's rights into the discussion may be to attempt to correct the implication, carried by the killing-centered approach, that insofar as abortion is wrong, it is a wrong that only women do, or at least (given the preponderance of male doctors) that only women instigate. I do not myself believe that we can thus escape the fact that nature bears harder on women than it does on men,[7] but virtue theory can certainly correct many of the injustices that the emphasis on women's rights is rightly concerned about. With very little amendment, everything that has been said above applies to boys and men too. Although the abortion decision is, in a natural sense, the woman's decision, proper to her, boys and men are often party to it, for well or ill, and even when they are not, they are bound to have been party to the circumstances that brought it up. No less than girls and women, boys and men can, in their actions, manifest self-centeredness, callousness, and light-mindedness about life and parenthood in relation to abortion. They can be self-centered or courageous about the possibility of disability in their offspring; they need to reflect on their sexual activity and their choices, or the lack of them, about their sexual partner and contraception; they need to grow up and take responsibility for their own actions and life in relation to fatherhood. If it is true, as I maintain, that insofar as motherhood is intrinsically worthwhile, being a mother is an important purpose in women's lives, being a father (rather than a mere generator) is an important purpose in men's lives as well, and it is adolescent of men to turn a blind eye to this and pretend that they have many more important things to do.

Much more might be said, but I shall end the actual discussion of the problem of abortion here, and conclude by highlighting what I take to be its significant features. . . .

The discussion does not proceed simply by our trying to answer the question "Would a perfectly virtuous agent ever have an abortion and, if so, when?"; virtue theory is not limited to considering "Would Socrates have had an abortion if he were a raped, pregnant fifteen-year-old?" nor automatically stumped when we are considering circumstances into which no virtuous agent would have got herself. Instead, much of the discussion proceeds in the virtue- and vice-related terms whose application, in several cases, yields practical conclusions. . . . These terms are difficult to apply correctly, and anyone might challenge my application of any one of them. So, for example, I have claimed that some abortions, done for certain reasons, would be callous or light-minded; that others might indicate an appropriate modesty or humility; that others would reflect a greedy and foolish attitude to what one could expect out of life. Any of these examples may be disputed, but what is at issue is, should these difficult terms be there, or should the discussion be couched in terms that all clever adolescents can apply correctly? . . .

Proceeding as it does in the virtue- and vice-related terms, the discussion thereby, inevitably, also contains claims about what is worthwhile, serious and important, good and evil, in our lives. So, for example, I claimed that parenthood is intrinsically worthwhile, and that having a good time was a worthless end (in life, not on individual occasions); that losing a fetus is always a serious matter (albeit not a tragedy in itself in the first trimester) whereas acquiring an appendectomy scar is a trivial one; that (human) death is an evil. Once again, these are difficult matters, and anyone might challenge any one of my claims. But what is at issue is, as before, should those difficult claims be there or can one reach practical conclusions about real moral issues that are in no way determined by premises about such matters? . . .

The discussion also thereby, inevitably, contains claims about what life is like (e.g., my claim that love and friendship do not survive their parties' constantly insisting on their rights; or the claim that to demand perfection of life is to run the risk of missing out on happiness entirely). What is at issue is, should those disputable claims be there, or is our knowledge (or are our false opinions) about what life is like irrelevant to our understanding of real moral issues? . . .

Naturally, my own view is that all these concepts should be there in any discussion of real moral issues and that virtue theory, which uses all of them, is the right theory to apply to them. I do not pretend to have shown this. I realize that proponents of rival theories may say that, now that they have understood how virtue theory uses the range of concepts it draws on, they are more convinced than ever that such concepts should not figure in an adequate normative theory, because they are sectarian, or vague or too particular, or improperly anthropocentric. . . . Or, finding many of the details of the discussion appropriate, they may agree that many, perhaps even all, of the concepts should figure, but argue that virtue theory gives an inaccurate account of the way the concepts fit together (and indeed of the concepts themselves) and that another theory provides a better account; that would be interesting to see.

NOTES

1. Judith Jarvis Thomson, "A Defense of Abortion," *Philosophy & Public Affairs* 1, no. 1 (Fall 1971): 47–66. One could indeed regard this article as proto-virtue theory (no doubt to the surprise of the author) if the concepts of callousness and kindness were allowed more weight.

2. One possible qualification: if one ties the concept of justice very closely to rights, then if women do have a moral right to terminate their pregnancies it *may* follow that in doing so they do not act unjustly. (Cf. Thomson, "A Defense of Abortion.") But it is debatable whether even that much follows.

3. This is an assumption of virtue theory, and I do not attempt to defend it here. An adequate discussion of it would require a separate article, since, although most moral philosophers would be chary of claiming that intellectual sophistication is a necessary condition of moral wisdom or virtue, most of us, from Plato onward, tend to write as if this were so. Sorting out which claims about moral knowledge are committed to this kind of elitism and which can, albeit with difficulty, be reconciled with the idea that moral knowledge can be acquired by anyone who really wants it would be a major task.

4. Mary Anne Warren, in "On the Moral and Legal Status of Abortion," *Monist* 57 (1973), sec. 1, says of the opponents of restrictive laws governing abortion that "their conviction (for the most part) is that abortion is not a *morally* serious and extremely unfortunate, even though sometimes justified, act, comparable to killing in self-defense or to letting the violinist die, but rather is closer to being a *morally neutral* act, like cutting one's hair" (italics mine). I would like to think that no one *genuinely* believes this. But certainly in discussion, particularly when arguing against restrictive laws or the suggestion that remorse over abortion might be appropriate, I have found that some people *say* they believe it. . . . Those who allow that it is morally serious, and far from morally neutral, have to argue against restrictive laws, or the appropriateness of remorse, on a very different ground from that laid down by the premise "The fetus is just part of the woman's body (and she has a right to determine what happens to her body and should not feel guilt about anything she does to it)."

5. I take this as a premise here, but argue for it in some detail in my *Beginning Lives* (Oxford: Basil Blackwell, 1987). In this connection I also discuss adoption and the sense in which it may be regarded as "second best," and the difficult question of whether the good of parenthood may properly be sought, or indeed bought, by surrogacy.

6. I say "some evil has probably been brought about" on the ground that (human) life is (usually) a good and hence (human) death usually an evil. The exceptions would be (*a*) where death is actually a good or a benefit, because the baby that would come to be if the life were not cut short would be better off dead than alive, and (*b*) where death, though not a good, is not an evil either, because the life that would be led (e.g., in a state of permanent coma) would not be a good.

7. I discuss this point at greater length in *Beginning Lives*.

STUDY QUESTIONS

1. According to Hursthouse, do women's rights have anything to do with the morality of abortion?
2. According to Hursthouse, is the status of the fetus relevant to the rightness or wrongness of abortion?
3. What connections does Hursthouse draw between good human lives and a decision about abortion?
4. Can a correct moral decision result in some evil?

Active and Passive Euthanasia

JAMES RACHELS

The American Medical Association endorses the doctrine that at a patient's request a physician may withhold extraordinary means of prolonging life but may not take steps to terminate that life intentionally. Is this distinction viable? James Rachels, whose work we read previously, argues that it is not.

The distinction between active and passive euthanasia is thought to be crucial for medical ethics. The idea is that it is permissible, at least in some cases, to withhold treatment and allow a patient to die, but it is never permissible to take any direct action designed to kill the patient. This doctrine seems to be accepted by most doctors, and it is endorsed in a statement adopted by the House of Delegates of the American Medical Association on 4 December 1973:

> The intentional termination of the life of one human being by another—mercy killing—is contrary to that for which the medical profession stands and is contrary to the policy of the American Medical Association.
>
> The cessation of the employment of extraordinary means to prolong the life of the body when there is irrefutable evidence that biological death is imminent is the decision of the patient and/or his immediate family. The advice and judgement of the physician should be freely available to the patient and/or his immediate family.

However, a strong case can be made against this doctrine. In what follows I will set out some of the relevant arguments, and urge doctors to reconsider their views on this matter.

To begin with a familiar type of situation, a patient who is dying of incurable cancer of the throat is in terrible pain, which can no longer be satisfactorily alleviated. He is certain to die within a few days, even if present treatment is continued, but he does not want to go on living for those days since the pain is unbearable. So he asks the doctor for an end to it, and his family joins in the request.

Suppose the doctor agrees to withhold treatment, as the conventional doctrine says he may. The justification for his doing so is that the patient is in terrible agony, and since he is going to die anyway, it would be wrong to prolong his suffering needlessly. But now notice this. If one simply withholds treatment, it may take the patient longer to die, and so he may suffer more than he would if more direct action were taken and a lethal injection given. This fact provides strong reason for thinking that, once the initial decision not to prolong his agony has been made, active euthanasia is actually preferable to passive euthanasia, rather than the reverse. To say otherwise is to endorse the option that leads to more suffering rather than less, and is contrary to the humanitarian impulse that prompts the decision not to prolong his life in the first place.

Part of my point is that the process of being "allowed to die" can be relatively slow and painful, whereas being given a lethal injection is relatively quick and painless. Let me give a different sort of example. In the United States about one in 600 babies is born with Down's syndrome. Most of these babies are otherwise healthy—that is, with only the usual pediatric care, they will proceed to an otherwise normal infancy. Some, however, are born with congenital defects such as intestinal obstructions that require operations if they are to live. Sometimes, the parents and the doctor will decide not to operate, and let the infant die. Anthony Shaw describes what happens then:

> When surgery is denied [the doctor] must try to keep the infant from suffering while natural forces sap the baby's life away. As a surgeon whose natural inclination is to use the scalpel to fight off death, standing by and watching a salvageable baby die is the most emotionally exhausting experience I know. It is easy at a conference, in a theoretical discussion to decide that such infants should be allowed to die. It is altogether different to stand by in the nursery and watch as dehydration and infection wither a tiny being over hours and days. This is a

terrible ordeal for me and the hospital staff—much more so than for the parents who never set foot in the nursery.[1]

I can understand why some people are opposed to all euthanasia, and insist that such infants must be allowed to live. I think I can also understand why other people favour destroying these babies quickly and painlessly. But why should anyone favour letting "dehydration and infection wither a tiny being over hours and days"? The doctrine that says a baby may be allowed to dehydrate and wither, but may not be given an injection that would end its life without suffering, seems so patently cruel as to require no further refutation. The strong language is not intended to offend, but only to put the point in the clearest possible way.

My second argument is that the conventional doctrine leads to decisions concerning life and death made on irrelevant grounds.

Consider again the case of the infants with Down's syndrome who need operations for congenital defects unrelated to the syndrome to live. Sometimes, there is no operation, and the baby dies, but when there is no such defect, the baby lives on. Now, an operation such as that to remove an intestinal obstruction is not prohibitively difficult. The reason why such operations are not performed in these cases is, clearly, that the child has Down's syndrome and the parents and the doctor judge that because of that fact it is better for the child to die.

But notice that this situation is absurd, no matter what view one takes of the lives and potentials of such babies. If the life of such an infant is worth preserving, what does it matter if it needs a simple operation? Or, if one thinks it better that such a baby should not live on, what difference does it make that it happens to have an unobstructed intestinal tract? In either case, the matter of life and death is being decided on irrelevant grounds. It is the Down's syndrome, and not the intestines, that is the issue. The matter should be decided, if at all, on that basis, and not be allowed to depend on the essentially irrelevant question of whether the intestinal tract is blocked.

What makes this situation possible, of course, is the idea that when there is an intestinal blockage, one can "let the baby die," but when there is no such defect there is nothing that can be done, for one must not "kill" it. The fact that this idea leads to such results as deciding life or death on irrelevant grounds is another good reason why the doctrine would be rejected.

One reason why so many people think that there is an important moral difference between active and passive euthanasia is that they think killing someone is morally worse than letting someone die. But is it? Is killing, in itself, worse than letting die? To investigate this issue, two cases may be considered that are exactly alike except that one involves killing whereas the other involves letting someone die. Then, it can be asked whether this difference makes any difference to the moral assessments. It is important that the cases be exactly alike, except for this one difference, since otherwise one cannot be confident that it is this difference and not some other that accounts for any variation in the assessments of the two cases. So, let us consider this pair of cases:

In the first, Smith stands to gain a large inheritance if anything should happen to his six-year-old cousin. One evening while the child is taking his bath, Smith sneaks into the bathroom and drowns the child, and then arranges things so that it will look like an accident.

In the second, Jones also stands to gain if anything should happen to his six-year-old cousin. Like Smith, Jones sneaks in planning to drown the child in his bath. However, just as he enters the bathroom Jones sees the child slip and hit his head, and fall face down in the water. Jones is delighted; he stands by, ready to push the child's head back under if it is necessary, but it is not necessary. With only a little thrashing about, the child drowns all by himself, "accidentally," as Jones watches and does nothing.

Now Smith killed the child, whereas Jones "merely" let the child die. That is the only difference between them. Did either man behave better, from a moral point of view? If the difference between killing and letting die were in itself a morally important matter, one should say that Jones's behaviour was less reprehensible than Smith's. But does one really want to say that? I think not. In the first place, both men acted from the same motive, personal gain, and both had exactly the same end in view when they acted. It may be inferred from Smith's conduct that he is a bad man, although that judgement may be withdrawn or modified if certain further facts are learned about him—for example, that he is mentally deranged. But would not the very same thing be inferred about Jones from his conduct? And would not the same further considerations also be relevant to any modification of this judgement? Moreover, suppose Jones pleaded, in his own defence, "After all, I didn't do anything except just stand there and watch the child drown. I didn't kill him; I only let him die." Again, if letting die were in itself less bad than killing, this defence should have at least some weight. But it does not. Such a "defence" can only be regarded as a grotesque perversion of moral reasoning. Morally speaking, it is no defence at all.

Now, it may be pointed out, quite properly, that the cases of euthanasia with which doctors are concerned are not like this at all. They do not involve personal gain or the destruction of normal, healthy children. Doctors are concerned only with cases in which the patient's life is of no further use to him, or in which the patient's life has become or will soon become a terrible burden. However, the point is the same in these cases: the bare difference between killing and letting die does not, in itself, make a moral difference. If a doctor lets a patient die, for humane reasons, he is in the same moral position as if he had given the patient a lethal injection for humane reasons. If his decision was wrong—if, for example, the patient's illness was in fact curable—the decision would be equally regrettable no matter which method was used to carry it out. And if the doctor's decision was the right one, the method used is not in itself important.

The AMA policy statement isolates the crucial issue very well; the crucial issue is "the intentional termination of the life of one human being by another." But after identifying this issue, and forbidding "mercy killing," the statement goes on to deny that the cessation of treatment is the intentional termination of a life. This is where the mistake comes in, for what is the cessation of treatment, in these circumstances, if it is not "the intentional termination of the life of one human being by another"? Of course it is exactly that, and if it were not, there would be no point to it.

Many people will find this judgement hard to accept. One reason, I think, is that it is very easy to conflate the question of whether killing is, in itself, worse than letting die, with the very different question of whether most actual cases of killing are more reprehensible than most actual cases of letting die. Most actual cases of killing are clearly terrible (think, for example, of all the murders reported in the newspapers), and one hears of such cases every day. On the other hand, one hardly ever hears of a case of letting die, except for the actions of doctors who are motivated by humanitarian reasons. So one learns to think of killing in a much worse light than of letting die. But this does not mean that there is something about killing that makes it in itself worse than letting die, for it is not the bare difference between killing and letting die that makes the difference in these cases. Rather, the other factors—the murderer's motive of personal gain, for example, contrasted with the doctor's humanitarian motivation—account for different reactions to the different cases.

I have argued that killing is not in itself any worse than letting die; if my contention is right, it follows that active euthanasia is not any worse than passive euthanasia. What arguments can be given on the other side? The most common, I believe, is the following:

> The important difference between active and passive euthanasia is that, in passive euthanasia, the doctor does not do anything to bring about the patient's death. The doctor does nothing, and the patient dies of whatever ills already afflict him. In active euthanasia, however, the doctor does something to bring about the patient's death: he kills him. The doctor who gives the patient with cancer a lethal injection has himself caused his patient's death; whereas if he merely ceases treatment, the cancer is the cause of the death.

A number of points need to be made here. The first is that it is not exactly correct to say that in passive euthanasia the doctor does nothing, for he does do one thing that is very important: he lets the patient die. "Letting someone die" is certainly different, in some respects, from other types of action—mainly in that it is a kind of action that one may perform by way of not performing certain other actions. For example, one may let a patient die by way of not giving medication, just as one may insult someone by way of not shaking his hand. But for any purpose of moral assessment, it is a type of action nonetheless. The decision to let a patient die is subject to moral appraisal in the same way that a decision to kill him would be subject to moral appraisal: it may be assessed as wise or unwise, compassionate or sadistic, right or wrong. If a doctor deliberately let a patient die who was suffering from a routinely curable illness, the doctor would certainly be to blame for what he had done, just as he would be to blame if he had needlessly killed the patient. Charges against him would then be appropriate. If so, it would be no defence at all for him to insist that he didn't "do anything." He would have done something very serious indeed, for he let his patient die.

Fixing the cause of death may be very important from a legal point of view, for it may determine whether criminal charges are brought against the doctor. But I do not think that this notion can be used to show a moral difference between active and passive euthanasia. The reason why it is considered bad to be the cause of someone's death is that death is regarded as a great evil—and so it is. However, if it has been decided that euthanasia—even passive euthanasia—is desirable in a given case, it has also been decided that in this instance death is no greater an evil than the patient's continued existence. And if this is true, the usual reason for not wanting to be the cause of someone's death simply does not apply.

Finally, doctors may think that all of this is only of academic interest—the sort of thing that philosophers may worry about but that has no practical bearing on their own work. After all, doctors must be concerned about the legal consequences of what they do, and active euthanasia is clearly forbidden by the law. But even so, doctors should also be concerned with the fact that the law is forcing upon them a moral doctrine that may be indefensible, and has a considerable effect on their practices. Of course, most doctors are not now in the position of being coerced in this matter, for they do not regard themselves as merely going along with what the law requires. Rather, in statements such as the AMA policy statement that I have quoted, they are endorsing this doctrine as a central point of medical ethics. In that statement, active euthanasia is condemned not merely as illegal but as "contrary to that for which the medical profession stands," whereas passive euthanasia is approved. However, the preceding considerations suggest that there is really no moral difference between the two, considered in themselves (there may be important moral differences in some cases in their *consequences,* but, as I pointed out, these differences may make active euthanasia, and not passive euthanasia, the morally preferable option). So, whereas doctors may have to discriminate between active and passive euthanasia to satisfy the law, they should not do any more than that. In particular, they should not give the distinction any added authority and weight by writing it into official statements of medical ethics.

NOTE

1. Shaw, Anthony, "Doctor, Do We Have a Choice?" *The New York Times Magazine,* 30 Jan. 1972, p. 54.

STUDY QUESTIONS

1. According to Rachels, in passive euthanasia does the physician do anything?
2. Once a decision has been made for a terminally ill patient to die, is letting the person die better than killing the person?
3. Is someone who allows another person to drown morally guilty of killing the person?
4. According to Rachels, under what circumstances is active euthanasia morally preferable to passive euthanasia?

The Intentional Termination of Life

BONNIE STEINBOCK

Bonnie Steinbock, Professor Emerita of Philosophy at the University at Albany (State University of New York), wrote the following essay responding to the previous article by James Rachels. Who has the better of the argument? That question is for each reader to answer.

....

According to James Rachels, . . . a common mistake in medical ethics is the belief that there is a moral difference between active and passive euthanasia. This is a mistake [he argues] because the rationale underlying the distinction between active and passive euthanasia is the idea that there is a significant moral difference between intentionally killing and intentionally letting die. . . .

Whether . . . there is a significant moral difference . . . is not my concern here. For it is far from clear that this distinction is the basis of the doctrine of the American Medical Association which Rachels attacks. And if the killing/letting die distinction is not the basis of the AMA doctrine, then arguments showing that the distinction has no moral force do not, in themselves, reveal in the doctrine's adherents either "confused thinking" or "a moral point of view unrelated to the interests of individuals." Indeed, as we examine the AMA doctrine, I think it will become clear that it appeals to and makes use of a number of overlapping distinctions, which may have moral significance in particular cases, such as the distinction between intending and foreseeing, or between ordinary and extraordinary care. Let us then turn to the 1973 statement, from the House of Delegates of the American Medical Association, which Rachels cites:

> The intentional termination of the life of one human being by another—mercy killing—is contrary to that for which the medical profession stands and is contrary to the policy of the American Medical Association.
>
> The cessation of the employment of extraordinary means to prolong the life of the body when there is irrefutable evidence that biological death is imminent is the decision of the patient and/or his immediate family. The advice and judgment of the physician should be freely available to the patient and/or his immediate family.

Rachels attacks this statement because he believes that it contains a moral distinction between active and passive euthanasia. . . .

Bonnie Steinbock, "The Intentional Termination of Life," *Social Science & Medicine*, Vol. 6, No. 1, 1979, pp. 59–64. Reprinted by permission of the journal. The footnotes were edited.

[He takes] the AMA position to prohibit active euthanasia, while allowing, under certain conditions, passive euthanasia.

I intend to show that the AMA statement does not imply support of the active/passive euthanasia distinction. In forbidding the intentional termination of life, the statement rejects both active and passive euthanasia. It does allow for "the cessation of the employment of extraordinary means" to prolong life. The mistake Rachels . . . make[s] is in identifying the cessation of life-prolonging treatment with passive euthanasia, or intentionally letting die. If it were right to equate the two, then the AMA statement would be self-contradictory, for it would begin by condemning, and end by allowing, the intentional termination of life. But if the cessation of life-prolonging treatment is not always or necessarily passive euthanasia, then there is no confusion and no contradiction.

Why does Rachels think that the cessation of life-prolonging treatment is the intentional termination of life? He says:

> The AMA policy statement isolates the crucial issue very well: the crucial issue is "the intentional termination of the life of one human being by another." But after identifying this issue, and forbidding "mercy killing," the statement goes on to deny that the cessation of treatment is the intentional termination of a life. This is where the mistake comes in, for what is the cessation of treatment, in these circumstances, if it is not "the intentional termination of the life of one human being by another"? Of course it is exactly that, and if it were not, there would be no point to it.

However, there *can* be a point (to the cessation of life-prolonging treatment) other than an endeavor to bring about the patient's death, and so the blanket identification of cessation of treatment with the intentional termination of a life is inaccurate. There are at least two situations in which the termination of life-prolonging treatment cannot be identified with the intentional termination of the life of one human being by another.

The first situation concerns the patient's right to refuse treatment. . . . Rachels give[s] the example of a patient dying of an incurable disease, accompanied by unrelievable pain, who wants to end the treatment which cannot cure him but can only prolong his miserable existence. Why, they ask, may a doctor accede to the patient's request to stop treatment, but not provide a patient in a similar situation with a lethal dose? The answer lies in the patient's right to refuse treatment. In general, a competent adult has the right to refuse treatment, even where such treatment is necessary to prolong life. Indeed, the right to refuse treatment has been upheld even when the patient's reason for refusing treatment is generally agreed to be inadequate.[1] This right can be overridden (if, for example, the patient has dependent children) but, in general, no one may legally compel you to undergo treatment to which you have not consented. "Historically, surgical intrusion has always been considered a technical battery upon the person and one to be excused or justified by consent of the patient or justified by necessity created by the circumstances of the moment. . . . "[2]

At this point, an objection might be raised that if one has the right to refuse life-prolonging treatment, then consistency demands that one have the right to decide to end his or her life, and to obtain help in doing so. The idea is that the right to refuse treatment somehow implies a right to voluntary euthanasia, and we need to see why someone might think this. The right to refuse treatment has been considered by legal writers as an example of the right to privacy or, better, the right to bodily self-determination. You have the right to decide what happens to your own body, and the right to refuse treatment is an instance of that right. But if you have the right to determine what happens to your own body, then should you not have the right to choose to end your life, and even a right to get help in doing so?

However, it is important to see that the right to refuse treatment is not the same as, nor does it entail, a right to voluntary euthanasia, even if both can be derived from the right to bodily self-determination. The right to refuse treatment is not itself a "right to die"; that one may choose to exercise this right even at the risk of death, or even *in order to die*, is irrelevant. The purpose of the right to refuse medical treatment is not to give persons a right to decide whether to live or die, but to protect them from the unwanted interferences of others. Perhaps we ought to interpret the right to bodily self-determination more broadly, so as to include a right to die; but this would be a substantial extension of our present understanding of the right to bodily self-determination, and not a consequence of it. If we were to recognize a right to voluntary euthanasia, we would have to agree that people have the right not merely to be left alone but also the right to be killed. I leave to one side that substantive moral issue. My claim is simply that there can be a reason for terminating life-prolonging treatment other than "to bring about the patient's death."

The second case in which termination of treatment cannot be identified with intentional termination of life is where continued treatment has little chance of improving the patient's condition and brings greater discomfort than relief.

The question here is what treatment is appropriate to the particular case. A cancer specialist describes it in this way:

> My general rule is to administer therapy as long as a patient responds well and has the potential for a reasonably good quality of life. But when all feasible therapies have been administered and a patient shows signs of rapid deterioration, the continuation of therapy can cause more discomfort than the cancer. From that time I recommend surgery, radiotherapy, or chemotherapy only as a means of relieving pain. But if a patient's condition should once again stabilize after the withdrawal of active therapy and if it should appear that he could still gain some good time, I would immediately reinstitute active therapy. The decision to cease anticancer treatment is never irrevocable, and often the desire to live will push a patient to try for another remission, or even a few more days of life.[3]

The decision here to cease anticancer treatment cannot be construed as a decision that the patient die, or as the intentional termination of life. It is a decision to provide the most appropriate treatment for that patient at that time.

Rachels suggests that the point of the cessation of treatment is the intentional termination of life. But here the point of discontinuing treatment is not to bring about the patient's death but to avoid treatment that will cause more discomfort than the cancer and has little hope of benefiting the patient. Treatment that meets this description is often called "extraordinary."[4] The concept is flexible, and what might be considered "extraordinary" in one situation might be ordinary in another. The use of a respirator to sustain a patient through a severe bout with a respiratory disease would be considered ordinary; its use to sustain the life of a severely brain-damaged person in an irreversible coma would be considered extraordinary.

Contrasted with extraordinary treatment is ordinary treatment, the care a doctor would normally be expected to provide. Failure to provide ordinary care constitutes neglect, and can even be construed as the intentional infliction of harm, where there is a legal obligation to provide care. The importance of the ordinary/extraordinary care distinction lies partly in its connection to the doctor's intention. The withholding of extraordinary care should be seen as a decision not to inflict painful treatment on a patient without reasonable hope of success. The withholding of ordinary care, by contrast, must be seen as neglect. Thus, one doctor says, "We have to draw a distinction between ordinary and extraordinary means. We never withdraw what's needed to make a baby comfortable, we would never withdraw the care a parent would provide. We never kill a baby. . . . But we may decide certain heroic intervention is not worthwhile."[5]

We should keep in mind the ordinary/extraordinary care distinction when considering an example given by . . . Rachels to show the irrationality of the active/passive distinction with regard to infanticide. The example is this: a child is born with [Down] syndrome and also has an intestinal obstruction that requires corrective surgery. If the surgery is not performed, the infant will starve to death, since it cannot take food orally. This may take days or even weeks, as dehydration and infection set in. Commenting on this situation in his article in this book, Rachels says:

> I can understand why some people are opposed to all euthanasia, and insist that such infants must be allowed to live. I think I can also understand why other people favor destroying these babies quickly and painlessly. But why should anyone favor letting "dehydration and infection wither a tiny being over hours and days"? The doctrine that says that a baby may be allowed to dehydrate and wither, but may not be given an injection that would end its life without suffering, seems so patently cruel as to require no further refutation.

Such a doctrine perhaps does not need further refutation; but this is not the AMA doctrine. The AMA statement criticized by Rachels allows only for the cessation of extraordinary means to prolong life when death is imminent. Neither of these conditions is satisfied in this example. Death is not imminent in this situation, any more than it would be if a normal child had an attack of appendicitis. Neither the corrective surgery to remove the intestinal obstruction nor the intravenous feeding required to keep the infant alive until such surgery is performed can be regarded as extraordinary means, for neither is particularly expensive, nor does either place an overwhelming burden on the patient or others. (The continued existence of the child might be thought to place an overwhelming burden on its parents, but that has nothing to do with the characterization of the means to prolong its life as extraordinary. If it had, then *feeding* a severely defective child who required a great deal of care could be regarded as extraordinary.) The chances of success if the operation is undertaken are quite good, though there is always a risk in operating on infants. Though the [Down] syndrome will not be alleviated, the child will proceed to an otherwise normal infancy.

It cannot be argued that the treatment is withheld for the infant's sake, unless one is prepared to argue that all mentally retarded babies are better off dead. This is particularly implausible in the case of [Down] syndrome babies, who generally do not suffer and are capable of giving and receiving love, of learning and playing, to varying degrees.

In a film on this subject entitled "Who Should Survive?" a doctor defended a decision not to operate, saying that since the parents did not consent to the operation, the doctor's hands were tied. As we have seen, surgical intrusion requires consent, and in the case of infants, consent would normally come from the parents. But, as legal guardians, parents are required to provide medical care for their children, and failure to do so can constitute criminal neglect or even homicide. In general, courts have been understandably reluctant to recognize a parental right to terminate life-prolonging treatment.[6] Although prosecution is unlikely, physicians who comply with invalid instructions from the parents and permit the infant's death could be liable for aiding and abetting, failure to report child neglect, or even homicide. So it is not true that, in this situation, doctors are legally bound to do as the parents wish.

To sum up, I think that Rachels is right to regard the decision not to operate in the [Down] syndrome example as the intentional termination of life. But there is no reason to believe that either the law or the AMA would regard it otherwise. Certainly the decision to withhold treatment is not justified by the AMA statement. That such infants have been allowed to die cannot be denied; but this, I think, is the result of doctors misunderstanding the law and the AMA position.

Withholding treatment in this case is the intentional termination of life because the infant is deliberately allowed to die; that is the point of not operating. But there are other cases in which that is not the point. If the point is to avoid inflicting painful treatment on a patient with little or no reasonable hope of success, this is not the intentional termination of life. The permissibility of such withholding of treatment, then, would have no implications for the permissibility of euthanasia, active or passive.

The decision whether or not to operate, or to institute vigorous treatment, is particularly agonizing in the case of children born with spina bifida, an opening in the base of the spine usually accompanied by hydrocephalus and mental retardation. If left unoperated, these children usually die of meningitis or kidney failure within the first few years of life. Even if they survive, all affected children face a lifetime of illness, operations, and varying degrees of disability. The policy used to be to save as many as possible, but the trend now is toward selective treatment, based on the physician's estimate of the chances of success. If operating is not likely to improve significantly the child's condition, parents and doctors may agree not to operate. This is not the intentional termination of life, for again the purpose is not the termination of the child's life but the avoidance of painful and pointless treatment. Thus, the fact that withholding treatment is justified does not imply that killing the child would be equally justified.

Throughout the discussion, I have claimed that intentionally ceasing life-prolonging treatment is not the intentional termination of life unless the doctor has, as his or her purpose in stopping treatment, the patient's death.

It may be objected that I have incorrectly characterized the conditions for the intentional termination of life. Perhaps it is enough that the doctor intentionally ceases treatment, foreseeing that the patient will die.

In many cases, if one acts intentionally, foreseeing that a particular result will occur, one can be said to have brought about that result intentionally. Indeed, this is the general legal rule. Why, then, am I not willing to call the cessation of life-prolonging treatment, in compliance with the patient's right to refuse treatment, the intentional termination of life? It is not because such an *identification* is necessarily opprobrious; for we could go on to *discuss* whether such cessation of treatment is a *justifiable* intentional termination of life. Even in the law, some cases of homicide are justifiable; e.g., homicide in self-defense.

However, the cessation of life-prolonging treatment, in the cases which I have discussed, is not regarded in law as being justifiable homicide, because it is not homicide at all. Why is this? Is it because the doctor "doesn't do anything," and so cannot be guilty of homicide? Surely not, since, as I have indicated, the law sometimes treats an omission as the cause of death. A better explanation, I think, has to do with the fact that in the context of the patient's right to refuse treatment, a doctor is not at liberty to continue treatment. It seems a necessary ingredient of intentionally letting die that one could have done something to prevent the death. In this situation, of course the doctor can physically prevent the patient's death, but since we do not regard the doctor as *free* to continue treatment, we say that there is "nothing he can do." Therefore he does not intentionally let the patient die.

To discuss this suggestion fully, I would need to present a full-scale theory of intentional action. However, at least I have shown, through the discussion of the above examples, that such a theory will be very complex, and that one of the complexities concerns the agent's reason for acting. The reason why an agent acted (or failed to act) may affect the characterization of what he did intentionally. The mere fact that he did *something* intentionally, foreseeing a certain result, does not necessarily mean that he brought about that *result* intentionally.

In order to show that the cessation of life-prolonging treatment, in the cases I've discussed, is the intentional termination of life, one would either have to show that treatment was stopped in order to bring about the patient's death, or provide a theory of intentional action according to which the reason for ceasing treatment is irrelevant to its characterization as the intentional termination of life. I find this suggestion implausible, but am willing to consider arguments for it. Rachels has provided no such arguments: indeed, he apparently shares my view about the intentional termination of life. For when he claims that the cessation of life-prolonging treatment is the intentional termination of life, his reason for making the claim is that "if it were not, there would be no point to it." Rachels believes that the point of ceasing treatment, "in these cases," is to bring about the patient's death. If that were not the point, he suggests, why would the doctor cease treatment? I have shown, however, that there can be a point to ceasing treatment which is not the death of the patient. In showing this, I have refuted Rachels' reason for identifying the cessation of life-prolonging treatment with the intentional termination of life, and thus his argument against the AMA doctrine.

Here someone might say: Even if the withholding of treatment is not the intentional termination of life, does that make a difference, morally speaking? If life-prolonging treatment may be withheld, for the sake of the child, may not an easy death be provided, for the sake of the child, as well? The unoperated child with spina bifida may take months or even years to die. Distressed by the spectacle of children "lying around, waiting to die," one doctor has written, "It is time that society and medicine stopped perpetuating the fiction that withholding treatment is ethically different from terminating a life. It is time that society began to discuss mechanisms by which we can alleviate the pain and suffering for those individuals whom we cannot help."[7]

I do not deny that there may be cases in which death is in the best interests of the patient. In such cases, a quick and painless death may be the best thing. However, I do not think that, once active or vigorous treatment is stopped, a quick death is always preferable to a lingering one. We must be cautious about attributing to defective children *our* distress at seeing them linger. Waiting for them to die may be tough on parents, doctors, and nurses—it isn't necessarily tough on the child. The decision not to operate need not mean a decision to neglect, and it may be possible to make the remaining months of the child's life comfortable, pleasant, and filled with love. If this alternative is possible, surely it is more decent and humane than killing the child. In such a situation, withholding treatment, foreseeing the child's death, is not ethically equivalent to killing the child, and we cannot move from the permissibility of the former to that of the latter. I am worried that there will be a tendency to do precisely that if active euthanasia is regarded as morally equivalent to the withholding of life-prolonging treatment.

CONCLUSION

The AMA statement does not make the distinction Rachels . . . wish[es] to attack, that between active and passive euthanasia. Instead, the statement draws a distinction between the intentional termination of life, on the one hand, and the cessation of the employment of extraordinary means to prolong life, on the other. Nothing said by Rachels . . . shows that this distinction is confused. It may be that doctors have misinterpreted the AMA statement and that this has led, for example, to decisions to allow defective infants to starve slowly to death. I quite agree with Rachels . . . that the decisions to which they allude were cruel and made on irrelevant grounds. Certainly it is worth pointing out that allowing someone to die *can* be the intentional termination of life, and that it can be just as bad as, or worse than, killing someone. However, the withholding of life-prolonging treatment is not necessarily the intentional termination of life, so that if it is permissible to withhold life-prolonging treatment it does not follow that, other things being equal, it is permissible to kill. Furthermore, most of the time, other things are not equal. In many of the cases in which it would be right to cease treatment, I do not think that it would also be right to kill.

NOTES

1. For example, *In re Yetter*, 62 Pa. D & C. 2d 619 (C.P., Northampton County Ct. 1974).
2. David W. Meyers, "Legal Aspects of Voluntary Euthanasia," in *Dilemmas of Euthanasia*, ed. John Behnke and Sissela Bok (New York: Anchor Books, 1975), p. 56.
3. Ernest H. Rosenbaum, M.D., *Living With Cancer* (New York: Praeger, 1975), p. 27.
4. See Tristram Engelhardt, Jr., "Ethical Issues in Aiding the Death of Young Children," in *Beneficent Euthanasia*, ed. Marvin Kohl (Buffalo, N.Y.: Prometheus Books, 1975). . . .
5. B. D. Colen, *Karen Ann Quinlan: Living and Dying in the Age of Eternal Life* (Los Angeles: Nash, 1976), p. 115.
6. See Norman L. Cantor, "Law and the Termination of an Incompetent Patient's Life-Preserving Care," in *Dilemmas of Euthanasia*, pp. 69–105.
7. John Freeman, "Is There a Right to Die—Quickly?", *Journal of Pediatrics*, 80, no. 5 (1972), 904–905.

STUDY QUESTIONS

1. Is killing someone always worse than letting the person die?
2. Is the physician's intention crucial to assessing the morality of the means used to bring about death?
3. Are we ever justified in performing actions with unfortunate consequences in an effort to achieve other purposes?
4. What should a physician do if a paralyzed patient on life support asks to be euthanized?

Famine, Affluence, and Morality

PETER SINGER

What obligations do we have toward those around the globe who are suffering from a lack of food, shelter, or medical care? Does morality permit us to purchase luxuries for ourselves, our families, and our friends instead of providing needed resources to other people who are suffering in unfortunate circumstances? Peter Singer, who is Ira W. DeCamp Professor of Bioethics at the University Center for Human Values at Princeton University, argues that if we can prevent something bad without thereby sacrificing anything of comparable worth, we ought to do so.

As I write this, in November 1971, people are dying in East Bengal from lack of food, shelter, and medical care. The suffering and death that are occurring there now are not inevitable, not unavoidable in any fatalistic sense of the term. Constant poverty, a cyclone, and a civil war have turned at least nine million people into destitute refugees; nevertheless, it is not beyond the capacity of the richer nations to give enough assistance to reduce any further suffering to very small proportions. The decisions and actions of human beings can prevent this kind of suffering. Unfortunately, human beings have not made the necessary decisions. At the individual level, people have, with very few exceptions, not responded to the situation in any significant way. Generally speaking, people have not given large sums to relief funds; they have not written to their parliamentary representatives demanding increased government assistance; they have not demonstrated in the streets, held symbolic fasts, or done anything else directed toward providing the refugees with the means to satisfy their essential needs. At the government level, no government has given the sort of massive aid that would enable the refugees to survive for more than a few days. Britain, for instance, has given rather more than most countries. It has, to date, given £14,750,000. For comparative purposes, Britain's share of the nonrecoverable development costs of the Anglo-French Concorde project is already in excess of £275,000,000, and on present estimates will reach £400,000,000. The implication is that the British government values a supersonic transport more than thirty times as highly as it values the lives of the nine million refugees. Australia is another country which, on a per capita basis, is well up in the "aid to Bengal" table. Australia's aid, however, amounts to less than one-twelfth of the cost of Sydney's new opera house. The total amount given, from all sources, now stands at about £65,000,000.

The estimated cost of keeping the refugees alive for one year is £464,000,000. Most of the refugees have now been in the camps for more than six months. The World Bank has said that India needs a minimum of £300,000,000 in assistance from other countries before the end of the year. It seems obvious that assistance on this scale will not be forthcoming. India will be forced to choose between letting the refugees starve or diverting funds from her own development program, which will mean that more of her own people will starve in the future.[1]

These are the essential facts about the present situation in Bengal. So far as it concerns us here, there is nothing unique about this situation except its magnitude. The Bengal emergency is just the latest and most acute of a series of major emergencies in various parts of the world, arising both from natural and from man-made causes. There are also many parts of the world in which people die from malnutrition and lack of food independent of any special emergency. I take Bengal as my example only because it is the present concern, and because the size of the problem has ensured that it has been given adequate publicity. Neither individuals nor governments can claim to be unaware of what is happening there.

What are the moral implications of a situation like this? In what follows, I shall argue that the way people in relatively affluent countries react to a situation like that in Bengal cannot be justified; indeed, the whole way we look at moral issues—our moral conceptual scheme—needs to be altered, and with it, the way of life that has come to be taken for granted in our society.

In arguing for this conclusion I will not, of course, claim to be morally neutral. I shall, however, try to argue for the moral position that I take, so that anyone who accepts certain assumptions, to be made explicit, will, I hope, accept my conclusion.

I begin with the assumption that suffering and death from lack of food, shelter, and medical care are bad. I think most people will agree about this, although one may reach the same view by different routes. I shall not argue for this view. People can hold all sorts of eccentric positions, and perhaps from some of them it would not follow that death by starvation is in itself bad. It is difficult, perhaps impossible, to refute such positions, and so for brevity I will henceforth take this assumption as accepted. Those who disagree need read no further.

My next point is this: if it is in our power to prevent something bad from happening, without thereby sacrificing anything of comparable moral importance, we ought, morally, to do it. By "without sacrificing anything of comparable moral importance" I mean without causing anything else comparably bad to happen, or doing something that is wrong in itself, or failing to promote some moral good, comparable in significance to the bad thing that we can prevent. This principle seems almost as uncontroversial as the last one. It requires us only to prevent what is bad, and not to promote what is good, and it requires this of us only when we can do it without sacrificing anything that is, from the moral point of view, comparably important. I could even, as far as the application of my argument to the Bengal emergency is concerned, qualify the point so as to make it: if it is in our power to prevent something very bad from happening, without thereby sacrificing anything morally significant, we ought, morally, to do it. An application of this principle would be as follows: if I am walking past a shallow pond and see a child drowning in it, I ought to wade in and pull the child out. This will mean getting my clothes muddy, but this is insignificant, while the death of the child would presumably be a very bad thing.

The uncontroversial appearance of the principle just stated is deceptive. If it were acted upon, even in its qualified form, our lives, our society, and our world would be fundamentally changed. For the principle takes, firstly, no account of proximity or distance. It makes no moral difference whether the person I can help is a neighbor's child ten yards from me or a Bengali whose name I shall never know, ten thousand miles away. Secondly, the principle makes no distinction between cases in which I am the only person who could possibly do anything and cases in which I am just one among millions in the same position.

I do not think I need to say much in defense of the refusal to take proximity and distance into account. The fact that a person is physically near to us, so that we have personal contact with him, may make it more likely that we *shall* assist him, but this does not show that we *ought* to help him rather than another who happens to be further away. If we accept any principle of impartiality, universalizability, equality, or whatever, we cannot discriminate against someone merely because he is far away from us (or we are far away from him). Admittedly, it is possible that we are in a better position to judge what needs to be done to help a person near to us than one far away, and perhaps also to provide the assistance we judge to be necessary. If this were the case, it would be a reason for helping those near to us first. This may once have been a justification for being more concerned with the poor in one's own town than with famine victims in India. Unfortunately for those who like to keep their moral responsibilities limited, instant communication and swift transportation have changed the situation. From the moral point of view, the development of the world into a "global village" has made an important, though still unrecognized, difference to our moral situation. Expert observers and supervisors, sent out by famine relief organizations or permanently stationed in the famine-prone areas, can direct our aid to a refugee in Bengal almost as effectively as we could get it to someone in our own block. There would seem, therefore, to be no possible justification for discriminating on geographical grounds.

There may be a greater need to defend the second implication of my principle— that the fact that there are millions of other people in the same position, in respect to the Bengali refugees, as I am, does not make the situation significantly different from a situation in which I am the only person who can prevent something very bad from occurring. Again, of course, I admit that there is a psychological difference between the cases; one feels less guilty about doing nothing if one can point to others, similarly placed, who have also done nothing. Yet this can make no real difference to our moral obligations.[2] Should I consider that I am less obliged to pull the drowning child out of the pond if on looking around I see other people, no further away than I am, who have also noticed the child but are doing nothing? One has only to ask this question to see the absurdity of the view that numbers lessen obligation. It is a view that is an ideal excuse for inactivity; unfortunately most of the major evils—poverty, overpopulation, pollution—are problems in which everyone is almost equally involved.

The view that numbers do make a difference can be made plausible if stated in this way: if everyone in circumstances like mine gave £5 to the Bengal Relief Fund, there would be enough to provide food, shelter, and medical care for the refugees; there is no reason why I should give more than anyone else in the same circumstances as I am; therefore I have no obligation to give more than £5. Each premise in this argument is true, and the argument looks sound. It may convince us, unless we notice that it is based on a hypothetical premise, although the conclusion is not stated hypothetically. The argument would be sound if the conclusion were: if everyone in circumstances like mine were to give £5, I would have no obligation to give more than £5. If the conclusion were so stated, however, it would be obvious that the argument has no bearing on a situation in which it is not the case that everyone else gives £5. This, of course, is the actual situation. It is more or less certain that not everyone in circumstances like mine will give £5. So there will not be enough to provide the needed food, shelter, and medical care. Therefore by giving more than £5 I will prevent more suffering than I would if I gave just £5.

It might be thought that this argument has an absurd consequence. Since the situation appears to be that very few people are likely to give substantial amounts, it follows that I and everyone else in similar circumstances ought to give as much as possible, that is, at least up to the point at which by giving more one would begin to cause serious suffering for oneself and one's dependents—perhaps even beyond this point to the point of marginal utility, at which by giving more one would cause oneself and one's dependents as much suffering as one would prevent in Bengal. If everyone does this, however, there will be more than can be used for the benefit of the refugees, and some of the sacrifice will have been unnecessary. Thus, if everyone does what he ought to do, the result will not be as good as it would be if everyone did a little less than he ought to do, or if only some do all that they ought to do.

The paradox here arises only if we assume that the actions in question—sending money to the relief funds—are performed more or less simultaneously, and are also unexpected. For if it is to be expected that everyone is going to contribute something, then clearly each is not obliged to give as much as he would have been obliged to had others not been giving too. And if everyone is not acting more or less simultaneously, then those giving later will know how much more is needed, and will have no obligation to give more than is necessary to reach this amount. To say this is not to deny the principle that people in the same circumstances have the same obligations, but to point out that the fact that others have given, or may be expected to give, is a relevant circumstance: those giving after it has become known that many others are giving and those giving before are not in the same circumstances. So the seemingly absurd consequence of the principle I have put forward can occur only if people are in error about the actual circumstances—that is, if they think they are giving when others are not, but in fact they are giving when others are. The result of everyone doing what he really ought to do cannot be worse than the result of everyone doing less than he ought to do, although the result of everyone doing what he reasonably believes he ought to do could be.

If my argument so far has been sound, neither our distance from a preventable evil nor the number of other people who, in respect to that evil, are in the same situation as we are, lessens our obligation to mitigate or prevent that evil. I shall therefore take as established the principle I asserted earlier. As I have already said, I need to assert it only in its qualified form: if it is in our power to prevent something very bad from happening, without thereby sacrificing anything else morally significant, we ought, morally, to do it.

The outcome of this argument is that our traditional moral categories are upset. The traditional distinction between duty and charity cannot be drawn, or at least not in the place we normally draw it. Giving money to the Bengal Relief Fund is regarded as an act of charity in our society. The bodies which collect money are known as "charities." These organizations see themselves in this way—if you send them a check, you will be thanked for your "generosity." Because giving money is regarded as an act of charity, it is not thought that there is anything wrong with not giving. The charitable man may be praised, but the man who is not charitable is not condemned. People do not feel in any way ashamed or guilty about spending money on new clothes or a new car instead of giving it to famine relief. (Indeed, the alternative does not occur to them.) This way of looking at the matter cannot be justified. When we buy new clothes not to keep ourselves warm but to look "well-dressed" we are not providing for any important need. We would not be sacrificing anything significant if we were to continue to wear our old clothes, and give the money to famine relief. By doing so, we would be preventing another person from starving. It follows from what I have said earlier that we ought to give money away, rather than spend it on clothes which we do not need to keep us warm. To do so is not charitable, or generous. Nor is it the kind of act which philosophers and theologians have called "supererogatory"—an act which it would be good to do, but not wrong not to do. On the contrary, we ought to give the money away, and it is wrong not to do so.

I am not maintaining that there are no acts which are charitable, or that there are no acts which it would be good to do but not wrong not to do. It may be possible to redraw the distinction between duty and charity in some other place. All I am arguing here is that the present way of drawing the distinction, which makes it an act of charity for a man living at the level of affluence which most people in the "developed nations" enjoy to give money to save someone else from starvation, cannot be supported. It is beyond the scope of my argument to consider whether the distinction should be redrawn or abolished altogether. There would be many other possible ways of drawing the distinction—for instance, one might decide that it is good to make other people as happy as possible, but not wrong not to do so.

Despite the limited nature of the revision in our moral conceptual scheme which I am proposing, the revision would, given the extent of both affluence and famine in the world today, have radical implications. These implications may lead to further objections, distinct from those I have already considered. I shall discuss two of these.

One objection to the position I have taken might be simply that it is too drastic a revision of our moral scheme. People do not ordinarily judge in the way I have suggested they should. Most people reserve their moral condemnation for those who violate some moral norm, such as the norm against taking another person's property. They do not condemn those who indulge in luxury instead of giving to famine relief. But given that I did not set out to present a morally neutral description of the way people make moral judgments, the way people do in fact judge has nothing to do with the validity of my conclusion. My conclusion follows from the principle which I advanced earlier, and unless that principle is rejected, or the arguments shown to be unsound, I think the conclusion must stand, however strange it appears. . . .

The second objection to my attack on the present distinction between duty and charity is one which has from time to time been made against utilitarianism. It follows from some forms of utilitarian theory that we all ought, morally, to be working full time to increase the balance of happiness over misery. The position I have taken here would not lead to this conclusion in all circumstances, for if there were no bad occurrences that we could prevent without sacrificing something of comparable moral importance, my argument would have no application. Given the present conditions in many parts of the world, however, it does follow from my argument that we ought, morally, to be working full time to relieve great suffering of the sort that occurs as a result of famine or other disasters. Of course, mitigating circumstances can be adduced—for instance, that if we wear ourselves out through overwork, we shall be less effective than we would otherwise have been. Nevertheless, when all considerations of this sort have been taken into account, the conclusion remains: we ought to be preventing as much suffering as we can without sacrificing something else of comparable moral importance. This conclusion is one which we may be reluctant to face. I cannot see, though, why it should be regarded as a criticism of the position for which I have argued, rather than a criticism of our ordinary standards of behavior. Since most people are self-interested to some degree, very few of us are likely to do everything that we ought to do. It would, however, hardly be honest to take this as evidence that it is not the case that we ought to do it. . . .

A third point raised by the conclusion reached earlier relates to the question of just how much we all ought to be giving away. One possibility, which has already been mentioned, is that we ought to give until we reach the level of marginal utility—that is, the level at which, by giving more, I would cause as much suffering to myself or my dependents as I would relieve by my gift. This would mean, of course, that one would reduce oneself to very nearly the material circumstances of a Bengali refugee. It will be recalled that earlier I put forward both a strong and a moderate version of the principle of preventing bad occurrences. The strong version, which required us to prevent bad things from happening unless in doing so we would be sacrificing something of comparable moral significance, does seem to require reducing ourselves to the level of marginal utility. I should also say that the strong version seems to me to be the correct one. I proposed the more moderate version—that we should prevent bad occurrences unless, to do so, we had to sacrifice something morally significant—only in order to show that even on this surely undeniable principle a great change in our way of life is required. On the more moderate principle, it may not follow that we ought to reduce ourselves to the level of marginal utility, for one might hold that to reduce oneself and one's family to this level is to cause something significantly bad to happen. Whether this is so I shall not discuss, since, as I have said, I can see no good reason for holding the moderate version of the principle rather than the strong version. Even if we accepted the principle only in its moderate form, however, it should be clear that we would have to give away enough to ensure that the consumer society, dependent as it is on people spending on trivia rather than giving to famine relief, would slow down and perhaps disappear entirely. There are several reasons why this would be desirable in itself. The value and necessity of economic growth are now being questioned not only by conservationists, but by economists as well.[3] There is no doubt, too, that the consumer society has had a distorting effect on the goals and purposes of its members. Yet looking at the matter purely from the point of view of overseas aid, there must be a limit to the extent to which we should deliberately slow down our economy; for it might be the case that if we gave away, say, forty percent of our Gross National Product, we would slow down the economy so much that in absolute terms we would be giving less than if we gave twenty-five percent of the much larger GNP that we would have if we limited our contribution to this smaller percentage.

I mention this only as an indication of the sort of factor that one would have to take into account in working out an ideal. Since Western societies generally consider one percent of the GNP an acceptable level of overseas aid, the matter is entirely academic. Nor does it affect the question of how much an individual should give in a society in which very few are giving substantial amounts.

It is sometimes said, though less often now than it used to be, that philosophers have no special role to play in public affairs, since most public issues depend primarily on an assessment of facts. On questions of fact, it is said, philosophers as such have no special expertise, and so it has been possible to engage in philosophy without committing oneself to any position on major public issues. No doubt there are some issues of social policy and foreign policy about which it can truly be said that a really expert assessment of the facts is required before taking sides or acting, but the issue of famine is surely not one of these. The facts about the existence of suffering are beyond dispute. Nor, I think, is it disputed that we can do something about it, either through orthodox methods of famine relief or through population control or both. This is therefore an issue on which philosophers are competent to take a position. The issue is one which faces everyone who has more money than he needs to support himself and his dependents, or who is in a position to take some sort of political action. These categories must include practically every teacher and student of philosophy in the universities of the Western world. If philosophy is to deal with matters that are relevant to both teachers and students, this is an issue that philosophers should discuss.

Discussion, though, is not enough. What is the point of relating philosophy to public (and personal) affairs if we do not take our conclusions seriously? In this instance, taking our conclusion seriously means acting upon it. The philosopher will not find it any easier than anyone else to alter his attitudes and way of life to the extent that, if I am right, is involved in doing everything that we ought to be doing. At the very least, though, one can make a start. The philosopher who does so will have to sacrifice some of the benefits of the consumer society, but he can find compensation in the satisfaction of a way of life in which theory and practice, if not yet in harmony, are at least coming together.

NOTES

1. There was also a third possibility: that India would go to war to enable the refugees to return to their lands. Since I wrote this paper, India has taken this way out. The situation is no longer that described above, but this does not affect my argument, as the next paragraph indicates.

2. In view of the special sense philosophers often give to the term, I should say that I use "obligation" simply as the abstract noun derived from "ought," so that "I have an obligation to" means no more, and no less, than "I ought to." This usage is in accordance with the definition of "ought" given by the *Shorter Oxford English Dictionary*: "the general verb to express duty or obligation." I do not think any issue of substance hangs on the way the term is used; sentences in which I use "obligation" could all be rewritten, although somewhat clumsily, as sentences in which a clause containing "ought" replaces the term "obligation."

3. See, for instance, John Kenneth Galbraith, *The New Industrial State* (Boston, 1967); and E. J. Mishan, *The Costs of Economic Growth* (London, 1967).

STUDY QUESTIONS

1. If you can prevent something bad from happening at a comparatively small cost to yourself, are you obligated to do so?

2. Are you acting immorally by buying a luxury car while others are starving?

3. Are you acting immorally by paying college tuition for your own children while other children have no opportunity for any schooling?

4. Do we have a moral obligation to try to alleviate extreme poverty in our own country before attempting to do so in other countries?

A Reply to Singer

TRAVIS TIMMERMAN

Peter Singer argues that you are obligated to prevent something bad from happening if you can do so without thereby sacrificing anything of comparable moral importance. For example, you are morally obligated to save a child from drowning if you can do so without inconvenience. Travis Timmerman, assistant professor of philosophy at Seton Hall University, argues that the strength of your obligation depends on how many children need to be saved. If the number is large, then Singer's line of reasoning would obligate you to spend your entire life saving children. Are you not entitled at some point to pursue your own interests, even if they are not as morally weighty as saving the lives of children?

From Travis Timmerman, "Sometimes There Is Nothing Wrong with Letting a Child Drown," *Analysis* 75 (2015). Reprinted by permission of Oxford University Press. Footnotes omitted.

Peter Singer's "Famine, Affluence, and Morality" is undoubtedly one of the most influential and widely read pieces of contemporary philosophy. Yet, the majority of philosophers (including ethicists) reject Singer's conclusion that we are morally required to donate to aid agencies whenever we can do so without sacrificing anything nearly as important as the good that our donations could bring about. Many ignore Singer's argument simply because they believe morality would just be too demanding if it required people in affluent nations to donate significant sums of money to charity. Of course, merely rejecting Singer's conclusion because it seems absurd does not constitute a refutation of Singer's argument. More importantly, this standard demandingness objection is a particularly inappropriate dialectical move because Singer provides a valid argument for his (demanding) conclusion and, crucially, the argument only consists of ethical premisses that Singer takes his typical readers to already accept. Singer formulates his argument as follows.

1. Suffering and death from lack of food, shelter and medical care are bad.
2. If it is in your power to prevent something bad from happening, without sacrificing anything nearly as important, it is wrong not to do so.
3. By donating to aid agencies, you can prevent suffering and death from lack of food, shelter and medical care, without sacrificing anything nearly as important.
4. Therefore, if you do not donate to aid agencies, you are doing something wrong.

If it is not true that typical readers' existing ethical commitments entail that they accept premisses one and two, then they should be able to say which premiss(es) they reject and why. Those who believe that Singer's conclusion is too demanding will need to reject premiss two. This requires addressing Singer's infamous *Drowning Child* thought experiment, which elicits a common response that Singer believes demonstrates that his readers are already committed to the truth of premiss two. As such, Singer purports to demonstrate that the ethical commitments his typical readers already accept are demanding enough to require them to donate a substantial portion of their expendable income to aid organizations. . . .

Perhaps premiss two is true, but a proposition with such strong counterintuitive implications requires a strong defence, one that gives us reason to think that certain ordinary moral intuitions are radically misguided. Singer believes he has provided such a defence with *Drowning Child*. Aren't we morally obligated to sacrifice our new clothes to save the child *because* we are obligated to prevent something bad from happening whenever we can do so without sacrificing anything nearly as important? The short answer is 'No.' Here's why. Although Singer's description of *Drowning Child* is ahistorical, the implicit assumption is that *Drowning Child* is an anomalous event. People almost never find themselves in the situation Singer describes, so when they consider their obligations in *Drowning Child*, they implicitly assume that they have not frequently sacrificed their new clothes to save children in the past and will not need to do so frequently in the future.

Giving to aid organizations is, in this respect, unlike *Drowning Child*. Every individual in an affluent nation, so long as they have some expendable income, will always be in a position to save the lives of people living in extreme poverty by donating said income. It may be quite clear that one has a moral obligation to sacrifice $200 worth of new clothing a single time to prevent a child from drowning. It is much less clear that one is morally obligated to spend one's entire life making repeated $200 sacrifices to constantly prevent children from drowning. So, we may be obligated to save the child in *Drowning Child*, but still be disposed to believe that premiss two is false. I will expand on this asymmetry . . . by providing an altered version of Singer's thought experiment that more closely resembles the position those in affluent nations are in with respect to providing aid to those in extreme poverty. I suspect that most people's intuitions in such a case will show that they reject premiss two of Singer's argument.

People almost universally have the intuition that we are morally obligated to rescue the child in *Drowning Child*, but are not morally obligated to donate all their expendable income to aid agencies. Singer attempts to explain away this intuition as a mere psychological difference, a difference that results from our evolutionary history and socialization and not a moral difference. . . . However, there *is* a moral difference between the sacrifice required to save the child in *Drowning Child* (as it is imagined) and the sacrifice Singer believes people in affluent nations are required to make in order to donate the supposed obligatory amount to aid organizations.

This moral difference is easily overlooked because Singer's *Drowning Child* thought experiment is, in a crucial way, under-described. Once the necessary details are filled in, its inability to support premiss two will be made clear. My following *Drowning Children* case is not under-described and gives us reason to believe that there are times at which it is morally permissible to *not* prevent something bad from happening, even when one can do so at a comparably insignificant personal cost.

> **Drowning Children**: Unlucky Lisa gets a call from her 24-hr bank telling her that hackers have accessed her account and are taking $200 out of it every 5 min until Lisa shows up in person to put a hold on her account. Due to some legal loophole, the bank is not required to reimburse Lisa for any of the money she may lose nor will they. In fact, if her account is overdrawn, the bank will seize as much of her assets as is needed to pay the debt created by the hackers.
>
> Fortunately, for Lisa, the bank is just across the street from her work and she can get there in fewer than 5 min. She was even about to walk to the bank as part of her daily routine. On her way, Lisa notices a vast space of land covered with hundreds of newly formed shallow ponds, each of which contains a small child who will drown unless someone pulls them to safety. Lisa knows that for each child she rescues, an extra child will live who would have otherwise died. Now, it would take Lisa approximately 5 min to pull

each child to safety and, in what can only be the most horrifically surreal day of her life, Lisa has to decide how many children to rescue before entering the bank. Once she enters the bank, all the children who have not yet been rescued will drown.

Things only get worse for poor Lisa. For the remainder of her life, the hackers repeat their actions on a daily basis and, every day, the ponds adjacent to Lisa's bank are filled with drowning children.

The truth of premiss two would entail that Lisa is obligated to rescue children until almost all of her money and assets are gone. It might permit her to close her account before she is unable to rent a studio apartment and eat a healthy diet. However, it would require her to give up her house, her car, her books, her art and anything else not nearly as important as a child's life. That might not seem so counterintuitive if Lisa has to make this monumental sacrifice a single time. But, and here's the rub, premiss two would also prohibit Lisa from ever rebuilding her life. For every day Lisa earns money, she is forced to choose between saving children and letting the hackers steal from her. Lisa would only be permitted to go to the bank each day in time to maintain the things nearly as important as a child's life, which I take to be the basic necessities Lisa needs to lead a healthy life.

I propose that it's a viable option that morality permits Lisa to, *at least* on one day over the course of her entire life, stop the hackers in time to enjoy some good that is not nearly as important as a child's life. Maybe Lisa wants to experience theatre one last time before she spends the remainder of her days pulling children from shallow ponds and stopping hackers. Given the totality of the sacrifice Lisa is making, morality intuitively permits Lisa to indulge in theatre *at least* one time in, let's say, the remaining eighty years of her life. In fact, commonsense morality should permit Lisa to indulge in these comparably morally insignificant goods a non-trivial number of times, though a single instance is all that is required to demonstrate that premiss two is false and, consequently, Singer's argument is unsound. . . .

To sum up, the intuitive pull of premiss two is more apparent than real. . . . How much are we obligated to donate to aid organizations? I am not sure exactly, but it should be the same amount we would be obligated to sacrifice were we to find ourselves in Lisa's position.

STUDY QUESTIONS

1. If you buy a book instead of giving the money to help others in need, are you acting morally?
2. If you spend time studying philosophy instead of helping others in need, are you acting morally?
3. If you pay to send your child to college while other children are too poor to obtain food or clothing, are you acting morally?
4. When, if ever, are you entitled to pursue your own interests while you could, instead, be helping others in need of assistance?

The Case for Animal Rights

Tom Regan

Tom Regan, whose work we read previously, here develops the case for animal rights. He calls for the abolition of animal agriculture, commercial and sport hunting, and the use of animals in scientific research.

....

I regard myself as an advocate of animal rights—as a part of the animal rights movement. That movement, as I conceive it, is committed to a number of goals, including,

- the total abolition of the use of animals in science;
- the total dissolution of commercial animal agriculture;
- the total elimination of commercial and sport hunting and trapping.

There are, I know, people who profess to believe in animal rights but do not avow these goals. Factory farming, they say, is wrong—it violates animals' rights—but traditional animal agriculture is all right. Toxicity tests of cosmetics on animals violates their rights, but important medical research—cancer research, for example—does not. The clubbing of baby seals is abhorrent, but not the harvesting of adult seals. I used to think I understood this reasoning. Not anymore. You don't change unjust institutions by tidying them up.

What's wrong—fundamentally wrong—with the way animals are treated isn't the details that vary from case to case. It's the whole system. The forlornness of the veal calf is pathetic, heart wrenching; the pulsing pain of the chimp with electrodes planted deep in her brain is repulsive; the slow, tortuous death of the racoon caught in the leg-hold trap is agonizing. But what is wrong isn't the pain, isn't the suffering, isn't the deprivation. These compound what's wrong. Sometimes—often—they make it much, much worse. But they are not the fundamental wrong.

The fundamental wrong is the system that allows us to view animals as *our resources*, here for *us*—to be eaten, or surgically manipulated, or exploited for sport or money. Once we accept this view of animals—as our resources—the rest is as predictable as it is regrettable. Why worry about their loneliness, their pain, their death? Since animals exist for us, to benefit us in one way or another, what harms them really doesn't matter—or matters only if it starts to bother us, makes us feel a trifle uneasy when we eat our veal escalope, for example. So, yes, let us get veal calves out of solitary confinement, give them more space, a little straw, a few companions. But let us keep our veal escalope.

But a little straw, more space and a few companions won't eliminate—won't even touch—the basic wrong that attaches to our viewing and treating these animals as our resources. A veal calf killed to be eaten after living in close confinement is viewed and treated in this way: but so, too, is another who is raised (as they say) "more humanely." To right the wrong of our treatment of farm animals requires more than making rearing methods "more humane"; it requires the total dissolution of commercial animal agriculture. . . .

How to proceed? We begin by asking how the moral status of animals has been understood by thinkers who deny that animals have rights. Then we test the mettle of their ideas by seeing how well they stand up under the heat of fair criticism. If we start our thinking in this way, we soon find that some people believe that we have no duties directly to animals, that we owe nothing to them, that we can do nothing that wrongs them. Rather, we can do wrong acts that involve animals, and so we have duties regarding them, though none to them. Such views may be called indirect duty views. By way of illustration: suppose your neighbour kicks your dog. Then your neighbour has done something wrong. But not to your dog. The wrong that has been done is a wrong to you. After all, it is wrong to upset people, and your neighbour's kicking your dog upsets you. So you are the one who is wronged, not your dog. Or again: by kicking your dog your neighbour damages another person's property. And since it is wrong to damage another person's property, your neighbour has done something wrong—to you, of course, not to your dog. Your neighbour no more wrongs your dog than your car would be wronged if the windshield were smashed. Your neighbour's duties involving your dog are indirect duties to you. More generally, all of our duties regarding animals are indirect duties to one another—to humanity.

How could someone try to justify such a view? Someone might say that your dog doesn't feel anything and so isn't hurt by your neighbour's kick, doesn't care about pain since none is felt, is as unaware of anything as is your windshield. Someone might say this, but no rational person will, since, among other considerations, such a view will commit anyone who holds it to the position that no human being feels pain either—that human beings also don't care about what happens to them. A second possibility is that though both humans and your dog are hurt when kicked, it is only human pain that matters. But, again, no rational person can believe this. Pain is pain wherever it occurs. If your neighbour's causing you pain is wrong because of the pain that is caused, we cannot rationally ignore or dismiss the moral relevance of the pain that your dog feels. . . .

Indirect duty views, then, including the best among them, fail to command our rational assent. Whatever ethical theory we should accept rationally, therefore, it must at least recognize that we have some duties directly to animals, just as we have some duties directly to each other. The next two theories I'll sketch attempt to meet this requirement.

The first I call the cruelty–kindness view. Simply stated, this says that we have a direct duty to be kind to animals and a direct duty not to be cruel to them.

Despite the familiar, reassuring ring of these ideas, I do not believe that this view offers an adequate theory. To make this clearer, consider kindness. A kind person acts from a certain kind of motive—compassion or concern, for example. And that is a virtue. But there is no guarantee that a kind act is a right act. If I am a generous racist, for example, I will be inclined to act kindly towards members of my own race, favouring their interests above those of others. My kindness would be real and, so far as it goes, good. But I trust it is too obvious to require argument that my kind acts may not be above moral reproach—may, in fact, be positively wrong because rooted in injustice. So kindness, notwithstanding its status as a virtue to be encouraged, simply will not carry the weight of a theory of right action.

Cruelty fares no better. People or their acts are cruel if they display either a lack of sympathy for or, worse, the presence of enjoyment in another's suffering. Cruelty in all its guises is a bad thing, a tragic human failing. But just as a person's being motivated by kindness does not guarantee that he or she does what is right, so the absence of cruelty does not ensure that he or she avoids doing what is wrong. Many people who perform abortions, for example, are not cruel, sadistic people. But that fact alone does not settle the terribly difficult question of the morality of abortion. The case is no different when we examine the ethics of our treatment of animals. So, yes, let us be for kindness and against cruelty. But let us not suppose that being for the one and against the other answers questions about moral right and wrong.

Some people think that the theory we are looking for is utilitarianism. A utilitarian accepts two moral principles. The first is that of equality: everyone's interests count, and similar interests must be counted as having similar weight or importance. White or black, American or Iranian, human or animal—everyone's pain or frustration matters, and matters just as much as the equivalent pain or frustration of anyone else. The second principle a utilitarian accepts is that of utility: do the act that will bring about the best balance between satisfaction and frustration for everyone affected by the outcome.

As a utilitarian, then, here is how I am to approach the task of deciding what I morally ought to do: I must ask who will be affected if I choose to do one thing rather than another, how much each individual will be affected, and where the best results are most likely to lie—which option, in other words, is most likely to bring about the best results, the best balance between satisfaction and frustration. That option, whatever it may be, is the one I ought to choose. That is where my moral duty lies.

The great appeal of utilitarianism rests with its uncompromising *egalitarianism*: everyone's interests count and count as much as the like interests of everyone else. The kind of odious discrimination . . . based on race or sex, for example seems disallowed in principle by utilitarianism, as is speciesism, systematic discrimination based on species membership.

The equality we find in utilitarianism, however, is not the sort an advocate of animal or human rights should have in mind. Utilitarianism has no room for the equal moral rights of different individuals because it has no room for their equal inherent value or worth. What has value for the utilitarian is the satisfaction of an individual's interests, not the individual whose interests they are. A universe in which you satisfy your desire for water, food, and warmth is, other things being equal, better than a universe in which these desires are frustrated. And the same is true in the case of an animal with similar desires. But neither you nor the animal have any value in your own right. Only your feelings do.

Here is an analogy to help make the philosophical point clearer: a cup contains different liquids, sometimes sweet, sometimes bitter, sometimes a mix of the two. What has value are the liquids: the sweeter the better, the bitterer the worse. The cup, the container, has no value. It is what goes into it, not what they go into, that has value. For the utilitarian you and I are like the cup; we have no value as individuals and thus no equal value. What has value is what goes into us, what we serve as receptacles for; our feelings of satisfaction have positive value, our feelings of frustration negative value.

Serious problems arise for utilitarianism when we remind ourselves that it enjoins us to bring about the best consequences. What does this mean? It doesn't mean the best consequences for me alone, or for my family or friends, or any other person taken individually. No, what we must do is, roughly, as follows: we must add up . . . the separate satisfactions and frustrations of everyone likely to be affected by our choice, the satisfactions in one column, the frustrations in the other. We must total each column for each of the options before us. That is what it means to say the theory is aggregative. And then we must choose that option which is most likely to bring about the best balance of totalled satisfactions over totalled frustrations. Whatever act would lead to this outcome is the one we ought morally to perform—it is where our moral duty lies. And that act quite clearly might not be the same one that would bring about the best results for me personally, or for my family or friends, or for a lab animal. The best aggregated consequences for everyone concerned are not necessarily the best for each individual.

That utilitarianism is an aggregative theory—different individuals' satisfactions or frustrations are added, or summed, or totalled—is the key objection to this theory. My Aunt Bea is old, inactive, a cranky, sour person, though not physically ill. She prefers to go on living. She is also rather rich. I could make a fortune if I could get my hands on her money, money she intends to give me in any event, after she dies, but which she refuses to give me now. In order to avoid a huge tax bite, I plan to donate a handsome sum of my profits to a local children's hospital. Many, many children will benefit from my generosity, and much joy will be brought to their parents, relatives, and friends. If I don't get the money rather soon, all these ambitions will come to naught. The once-in-a-lifetime opportunity to make a real killing will be gone. Why, then, not kill my Aunt Bea? Oh, of course I *might* get caught. But I'm no fool and, besides, her doctor can be counted on to cooperate (he has an eye for the same investment and I happen to know a good deal about his shady past). The deed can be done . . . professionally, shall we say. There is *very* little chance of getting caught. And as for my conscience being guilt-ridden, I am a resourceful sort of fellow and will take more than sufficient comfort—as I lie on the beach at Acapulco—in contemplating the joy and health I have brought to so many others.

Suppose Aunt Bea is killed and the rest of the story comes out as told. Would I have done anything wrong? Anything immoral? One would have thought that I had. Not according to utilitarianism. Since what I have done has brought about the best balance between totalled satisfaction and frustration for all those affected by the outcome, my action is not wrong. Indeed, in killing Aunt Bea the physician and I did what duty required.

This same kind of argument can be repeated in all sorts of cases, illustrating, time after time, how the utilitarian's position leads to results that impartial people find morally callous. It *is* wrong to kill my Aunt Bea in the name of bringing about the best results for others. A good end does not justify an evil means. Any adequate moral theory will have to explain why this is so. Utilitarianism fails in this respect and so cannot be the theory we seek.

What to do? Where to begin anew? The place to begin, I think, is with the utilitarian's view of the value of the individual—or, rather, lack of value. In its place, suppose we consider that you and I, for example, do have value as individuals—what we'll call *inherent value.* To say we have such value is to say that we are something more than, something different from, mere receptacles. Moreover, to ensure that we do not pave the way for such injustices as slavery or sexual discrimination, we must believe that all who have inherent value have it equally, regardless of their sex, race, religion, birthplace, and so on. Similarly to be discarded as irrelevant are one's talents or skills, intelligence and wealth, personality or pathology, whether one is loved and admired or despised and loathed. The genius and the retarded child, the prince and the pauper, the brain surgeon and the fruit vendor, Mother Teresa and the most unscrupulous used-car salesman—all have inherent value, all possess it equally, and all have an equal right to be treated with respect, to be treated in ways that do not reduce them to the status of things, as if they existed as resources for others. My value as an individual is independent of my usefulness to you. Yours is not dependent on your usefulness to me. For either of us to treat the other in ways that fail to show respect for the other's independent value is to act immorally, to violate the individual's rights.

Some of the rational virtues of this view—what I call the rights view—should be evident. Unlike (crude) contractarianism, for example, the rights view *in principle* denies the moral tolerability of any and all forms of racial, sexual, or social discrimination; and unlike utilitarianism, this view *in principle* denies that we can justify good results by using evil means that violate an individual's rights—denies, for example, that it could be moral to kill my Aunt Bea to harvest beneficial consequences for others. That would be to sanction the disrespectful treatment of the individual in the name of the social good, something the rights view will not—categorically will not—ever allow.

The rights view, I believe, is rationally the most satisfactory moral theory. It surpasses all other theories in the degree to which it illuminates and explains the foundation of our duties to one another—the domain of human morality. On this score it has the best reasons, the best arguments, on its side. Of course, if it were possible to show that only human beings are included within its scope, then a person like myself, who believes in animal rights, would be obliged to look elsewhere.

But attempts to limit its scope to humans only can be shown to be rationally defective. Animals, it is true, lack many of the abilities humans possess. They can't read, do higher mathematics, build a bookcase, or make *baba ghanoush*. Neither can many human beings, however, and yet we don't (and shouldn't) say that they (these humans) therefore have less inherent value, less of a right to be treated with respect, than do others. It is the *similarities* between those human beings who most clearly, most noncontroversially have such value (the people reading this, for example), not our differences, that matter most. And the really crucial, the basic similarity is simply this: we are each of us the experiencing subject of a life, a conscious creature having an individual welfare that has importance to us whatever our usefulness to others. We want and prefer things, believe and feel things, recall and expect things. And all these dimensions of our life, including our pleasure and pain, our enjoyment and suffering, our satisfaction and frustration, our continued existence or our untimely death—all make a difference to the quality of our life as lived, as experienced, by us as individuals. As the same is true of those animals that concern us (the ones that are eaten and trapped, for example), they too must be viewed as the experiencing subjects of a life, with inherent value of their own.

Some there are who resist the idea that animals have inherent value. "Only humans have such value," they profess. How might this narrow view be defended? Shall we say that only humans have the requisite intelligence, or autonomy, or reason? But there are many, many humans who fail to meet these standards and yet are reasonably viewed as having value above and beyond their usefulness to others. Shall we claim that only humans belong to the right species, the species *Homo sapiens*? But this is blatant speciesism. Will it be said, then, that all—and only—humans have immortal souls? Then our opponents have their work cut out for them. I am myself not ill-disposed to the proposition that there are immortal souls. Personally, I profoundly hope I have one. But I would not want to rest my position on a controversial ethical issue on the even more controversial question about who or what has an immortal soul. That is to dig one's hole deeper, not to climb out. Rationally, it is better to resolve moral issues without making more controversial assumptions than are needed. The question of who has inherent value is such a question, one that is resolved more rationally without the introduction of the idea of immortal souls than by its use.

Well, perhaps some will say that animals have some inherent value, only less than we have. Once again, however, attempts to defend this view can be shown to lack rational justification. What could be the basis of our having more inherent value than animals? Their lack of reason, or autonomy, or intellect? Only if we are willing to make the same judgement in the case of humans who are similarly deficient. But it is not true that such humans—the retarded child, for example, or the mentally deranged—have less inherent value than you or I. Neither, then, can we rationally sustain the view that animals like them in being the experiencing subjects of a life have less inherent value. *All* who have inherent value have it *equally*, whether they be human animals or not.

Inherent value, then, belongs equally to those who are the experiencing subjects of a life. Whether it belongs to others—to rocks and rivers, trees and glaciers, for example—we do not know and may never know. But neither do we need to know, if we are to make the case for animal rights. We do not need to know, for example, how many people are eligible to vote in the next presidential election before we can know whether I am. Similarly, we do not need to know how many individuals have inherent value before we can know that some do. When it comes to the case for animal rights, then, what we need to know is whether the animals that, in our culture, are routinely eaten, hunted, and used in our laboratories, for example, are like us in being subjects of a life. And we do know this. We do know that many—literally, billions and billions—of these animals are the subjects of a life in the sense explained and so have inherent value if we do. And since, in order to arrive at the best theory of our duties to one another, we must recognize our equal inherent value as individuals, reason—not sentiment, not emotion—reason compels us to recognize the equal inherent value of these animals and, with this, their equal right to be treated with respect.

That, *very* roughly, is the shape and feel of the case for animal rights. . . . I must, in closing, limit myself to [two] final points.

The first is how the theory that underlies the case for animal rights shows that the animal rights movement is a part of, not antagonistic to, the human rights movement. The theory that rationally grounds the rights of animals also grounds the rights of humans. Thus those involved in the animal rights movement are partners in the struggle to secure respect for human rights—the rights of women, for example, or minorities, or workers. The animal rights movement is cut from the same moral cloth as these.

Second, having set out the broad outlines of the rights view, I can now say why its implications for farming and science, among other fields, are both clear and uncompromising. In the case of the use of animals in science, the rights view is categorically abolitionist. Lab animals are not our tasters; we are not their kings. Because these animals are treated routinely, systematically as if their value were reducible to their usefulness to others, they are routinely, systematically treated with a lack of respect, and thus their rights are routinely, systematically violated. This is just as true when they are used in trivial, duplicative, unnecessary, or unwise research as it is when they are used in studies that hold out real promise of human benefits. We can't justify harming or killing a human being (my Aunt Bea, for example) just for these sorts of reason. Neither can we do so even in the case of so lowly a creature as a laboratory rat. It is not just refinement or reduction that is called for, not just larger, cleaner cages, not just more generous use of anaesthetic or the elimination of multiple surgery, not just tidying up the system. It is complete replacement. The best we can do when it comes to using animals in science is—not to use them. That is where our duty lies, according to the rights view.

As for commercial animal agriculture, the rights view takes a similar abolitionist position. The fundamental moral wrong here is not that animals are kept in stressful close confinement or in isolation, or that their pain and suffering, their needs and preferences are ignored or discounted. All these *are* wrong, or course, but they are not the fundamental wrong. They are symptoms and effects of the deeper systematic wrong that allows these animals to be viewed and treated as lacking independent value, as resources for us—as, indeed, a renewable resource. Giving farm animals more space, more natural environments, more companions does not right the fundamental wrong, any more than giving lab animals more anaesthesia or bigger, cleaner cages would right the fundamental wrong in their case. Nothing less than the total dissolution of commercial animal agriculture will do this, just as, for similar reasons I won't develop at length here, morality requires nothing less than the total elimination of hunting and trapping for commercial and sporting ends. The rights view's implications, then, as I have said, are clear and uncompromising.

STUDY QUESTIONS

1. What are rights?
2. Do all human beings have rights?
3. If some nonhuman animals display mental skills beyond the capacity of human beings, might those nonhuman animals have rights?
4. If a lion was about to attack a zebra and a human being could save the life of the zebra, can you imagine circumstances in which such an intervention would be morally justified?

Speaking of Animal Rights

MARY ANNE WARREN

Mary Anne Warren, whose work we read previously, maintains that animals do have rights but not identical in strength to those of persons. She argues that practicality precludes our treating all animals as our moral equals.

....

Tom Regan has produced what is perhaps the definitive defense of the view that the basic moral rights of at least some non-human animals are in no way inferior to our own. In *The Case for Animal Rights,* he argues that all normal mammals over a year of age have the same basic moral rights.[1] Non-human mammals have

Mary Anne Warren, "Difficulties with the Strong Rights Position," from *Between the Species* 2, No. 4 (Fall 1987). Reprinted by permission.

essentially the same right not to be harmed or killed as we do. I shall call this "the strong animal rights position," although it is weaker than the claims made by some animal liberationists in that it ascribes rights to only some sentient animals.[2]

I will argue that Regan's case for the strong animal rights position is unpersuasive and that this position entails consequences which a reasonable person cannot accept. I do not deny that some non-human animals have moral rights; indeed, I would extend the scope of the rights claim to include all sentient animals, that is, all those capable of having experiences, including experiences of pleasure or satisfaction and pain, suffering, or frustration.[3] However, I do not think that the moral rights of most non-human animals are identical in strength to those of persons.[4] The rights of most non-human animals may be overridden in circumstances which would not justify overriding the rights of persons. There are, for instance, compelling realities which sometimes require that we kill animals for reasons which could not justify the killing of persons. I will call this view "the weak animal rights" position, even though it ascribes rights to a wider range of animals than does the strong animal rights position.

I will begin by summarizing Regan's case for the strong animal rights position and noting two problems with it. Next, I will explore some consequences of the strong animal rights position which I think are unacceptable. Finally, I will outline the case for the weak animal rights position.

REGAN'S CASE

Regan's argument moves through three stages. First, he argues that normal, mature mammals are not only sentient but have other mental capacities as well. These include the capacities for emotion, memory, belief, desire, the use of general concepts, intentional action, a sense of the future, and some degree of self-awareness. Creatures with such capacities are said to be subjects-of-a-life. They are not only alive in the biological sense but have a psychological identity over time and an existence which can go better or worse for them. Thus, they can be harmed or benefited. These are plausible claims, and well defended. . . . The second and third stages of the argument are more problematic.

In the second stage, Regan argues that subjects-of-a-life have inherent value. His concept of inherent value grows out of his opposition to utilitarianism. Utilitarian moral theory, he says, treats individuals as "mere receptacles" for morally significant value, in that harm to one individual may be justified by the production of a greater net benefit to other individuals. In opposition to this, he holds that subjects-of-a-life have a value independent of both the value they may place upon their lives or experiences and the value others may place upon them.

Inherent value, Regan argues, does not come in degrees. To hold that some individuals have more inherent value than others is to adopt a "perfectionist" theory, i.e., one which assigns different moral worth to individuals according to how well they are thought to exemplify some virtue(s), such as intelligence or moral autonomy. Perfectionist theories have been used, at least since the time of

Aristotle, to rationalize such injustices as slavery and male domination, as well as the unrestrained exploitation of animals. Regan argues that if we reject these injustices, then we must also reject perfectionism and conclude that all subjects-of-a-life have equal inherent value. Moral agents have no more inherent value than moral patients, i.e., subjects-of-a-life who are not morally responsible for their actions.

In the third phase of the argument, Regan uses the thesis of equal inherent value to derive strong moral rights for all subjects-of-a-life. This thesis underlies the Respect Principle, which forbids us to treat beings who have inherent value as mere receptacles, i.e., mere means to the production of the greatest overall good. This principle, in turn, underlies the Harm Principle, which says that we have a direct prima facie duty not to harm beings who have inherent value. Together, these principles give rise to moral rights. Rights are defined as valid claims, claims to certain goods and against certain beings, i.e., moral agents. Moral rights generate duties not only to refrain from inflicting harm upon beings with inherent value but also to come to their aid when they are threatened by other moral agents. Rights are not absolute but may be overridden in certain circumstances. Just what these circumstances are we will consider later. But first, let's look at some difficulties in the theory as thus far presented.

THE MYSTERY OF INHERENT VALUE

Inherent value is a key concept in Regan's theory. It is the bridge between the plausible claim that all normal, mature mammals—human or otherwise—are subjects-of-a-life and the more debatable claim that they all have basic moral rights of the same strength. But it is a highly obscure concept, and its obscurity makes it ill-suited to play this crucial role.

Inherent value is defined almost entirely in negative terms. It is not dependent upon the value which either the inherently valuable individual or anyone else may place upon that individual's life or experiences. It is not (necessarily) a function of sentience or any other mental capacity, because, Regan says, some entities which are not sentient (e.g., trees, rivers, or rocks) may, nevertheless, have inherent value. . . . It cannot attach to anything other than an individual; species, ecosystems, and the like cannot have inherent value.

These are some of the things which inherent value is not. But what is it? Unfortunately, we are not told. Inherent value appears as a mysterious non-natural property which we must take on faith. Regan says that it is a *postulate* that subjects-of-a-life have inherent value, a postulate justified by the fact that it avoids certain absurdities which he thinks follow from a purely utilitarian theory. But why is the postulate that *subjects-of-a-life* have inherent value? If the inherent value of a being is completely independent of the value that it or anyone else places upon its experiences, then why does the fact that it has certain sorts of experiences constitute evidence that it has inherent value? If the reason is that subjects-of-a-life have an existence which can go better or worse for them, then why isn't the appropriate conclusion that all sentient beings have inherent value, since they would all seem to meet that condition? Sentient but mentally unsophisticated beings may have a less extensive range of possible satisfactions and frustrations, but why should it follow that they have—or may have—no inherent value at all?

In the absence of a positive account of inherent value, it is also difficult to grasp the connection between being inherently valuable and having moral rights. Intuitively, it seems that value is one thing, and rights are another. It does not seem incoherent to say that some things (e.g., mountains, rivers, redwood trees) are inherently valuable and yet are not the sorts of things which can have moral rights. Nor does it seem incoherent to ascribe inherent value to some things which are not individuals, e.g., plant or animal species, though it may well be incoherent to ascribe moral rights to such things.

In short, the concept of inherent value seems to create at least as many problems as it solves. If inherent value is based on some natural property, then why not try to identify that property and explain its moral significance, without appealing to inherent value? And if it is not based on any natural property, then why should we believe in it? That it may enable us to avoid some of the problems faced by the utilitarian is not a sufficient reason, if it creates other problems which are just as serious.

IS THERE A SHARP LINE?

Perhaps the most serious problems are those that arise when we try to apply the strong animal rights position to animals other than normal, mature mammals. Regan's theory requires us to divide all living things into two categories: those which have the same inherent value and the same basic moral rights that we do, and those which have no inherent value and presumably no moral rights. But wherever we try to draw the line, such a sharp division is implausible.

It would surely be arbitrary to draw such a sharp line between normal, mature mammals and all other living things. Some birds (e.g., crows, magpies, parrots, mynahs) appear to be just as mentally sophisticated as most mammals and thus are equally strong candidates for inclusion under the subject-of-a-life criterion. Regan is not in fact advocating that we draw the line here. His claim is only that normal mature mammals are clear cases, while other cases are less clear. Yet, on his theory, there must be such a sharp line *somewhere,* since there are no degrees of inherent value. But why should we believe that there is a sharp line between creatures that are subjects-of-a-life and creatures that are not? Isn't it more likely that "subjecthood" comes in degrees, that some creatures have only a little self-awareness, and only a little capacity to anticipate the future, while some have a little more, and some a good deal more?

Should we, for instance, regard fish, amphibians, and reptiles as subjects-of-a-life? A simple yes-or-no answer seems inadequate. On the one hand, some of their behavior is difficult to explain without the assumption that they have sensations, beliefs, desires, emotions, and memories; on the other hand, they do not seem to exhibit very much self-awareness or very much conscious anticipation of future events. Do they have enough mental sophistication to count as subjects-of-a-life? Exactly how much is enough?

It is still more unclear what we should say about insects, spiders, octopi, and other invertebrate animals which have brains and sensory organs but whose minds (if they have minds) are even more alien to us than those of fish or reptiles. Such creatures are probably sentient. Some people doubt that they can feel pain, since they lack certain neurological structures which are crucial to the processing of pain impulses in vertebrate animals. But this argument is inconclusive, since their nervous systems might process pain in ways different from ours. When injured, they sometimes act as if they are in pain. On evolutionary grounds, it seems unlikely that highly mobile creatures with complex sensory systems would not have developed a capacity for pain (and pleasure), since such a capacity has obvious survival value. It must, however, be admitted that we do not *know* whether spiders can feel pain (or something very like it), let alone whether they have emotions, memories, beliefs, desires, self-awareness, or a sense of the future.

Even more mysterious are the mental capacities (if any) of mobile microfauna. The brisk and efficient way that paramecia move about in their incessant search for food *might* indicate some kind of sentience, in spite of their lack of eyes, ears, brains, and other organs associated with sentience in more complex organisms. It is conceivable—though not very probable—that they, too, are subjects-of-a-life.

The existence of a few unclear cases need not pose a serious problem for a moral theory, but in this case the unclear cases constitute most of those with which an adequate theory of animal rights would need to deal. The subject-of-a-life criterion can provide us with little or no moral guidance in our interactions with the vast majority of animals. That might be acceptable if it could be supplemented with additional principles which would provide such guidance. However, the radical dualism of the theory precludes supplementing it in this way. We are forced to say that either a spider has the same right to life as you and I do, or it has no right to life whatever—and that only the gods know which of these alternatives is true.

Regan's suggestion for dealing with such unclear cases is to apply the "benefit of the doubt" principle. That is, when dealing with beings that may or may not be subjects-of-a-life, we should act as if they are.[5] But if we try to apply this principle to the entire range of doubtful cases, we will find ourselves with moral obligations which we cannot possibly fulfill. In many climates, it is virtually impossible to live without swatting mosquitoes and exterminating cockroaches, and not all of us can afford to hire someone to sweep the path before we walk, in order to make sure that we do not step on ants. Thus, we are still faced with the daunting task of drawing a sharp line somewhere on the continuum of life forms—this time, a line demarcating the limits of the benefit of the doubt principle.

The weak animal rights theory provides a more plausible way of dealing with this range of cases, in that it allows the rights of animals of different kinds to vary in strength. . . .

WHY ARE ANIMAL RIGHTS WEAKER
THAN HUMAN RIGHTS?

How can we justify regarding the rights of persons as generally stronger than those of sentient beings which are not persons? There are a plethora of bad justifications, based on religious premises or false or unprovable claims about the differences between human and non-human nature. But there is one difference which has a clear moral relevance: people are at least sometimes capable of being moved to action or inaction by the force of reasoned argument. Rationality rests upon other mental capacities, notably those which Regan cites as criteria for being a subject-of-a-life. We share these capacities with many other animals. But it is not just because we are subjects-of-a-life that we are both able and morally compelled to recognize one another as beings with equal basic moral rights. It is also because we are able to "listen to reason" in order to settle our conflicts and cooperate in shared projects. This capacity, unlike the others, may require something like a human language.

Why is rationality morally relevant? It does not make us "better" than other animals or more "perfect." It does not even automatically make us more intelligent. (Bad reasoning reduces our effective intelligence rather than increasing it.) But it is morally relevant insofar as it provides greater possibilities for cooperation and for the nonviolent resolution of problems. It also makes us more dangerous than nonrational beings can ever be. Because we are potentially more dangerous and less predictable than wolves, we need an articulated system of morality to regulate our conduct. Any human morality, to be workable in the long run, must recognize the equal moral status of all persons, whether through the postulate of equal basic moral rights or in some other way. The recognition of the moral equality of other persons is the price we must each pay for their recognition of our moral equality. Without this mutual recognition of moral equality, human society can exist only in a state of chronic and bitter conflict. The war between the sexes will persist so long as there is sexism and male domination; racial conflict will never be eliminated so long as there are racist laws and practices. But, to the extent that we achieve a mutual recognition of equality, we can hope to live together, perhaps as peacefully as wolves, achieving (in part) through explicit moral principles what they do not seem to need explicit moral principles to achieve.

Why not extend this recognition of moral equality to other creatures, even though they cannot do the same for us? The answer is that we cannot. Because we cannot reason with most non-human animals, we cannot always solve the problems which they may cause without harming them—although we are always obligated to try. We cannot negotiate a treaty with the feral cats and foxes, requiring them to stop preying on endangered native species in return for suitable concessions on our part.

> if rats invade our houses . . . we cannot reason with them, hoping to persuade them of the injustice they do us. We can only attempt to get rid of them.[6]

Aristotle was not wrong in claiming that the capacity to alter one's behavior on the basis of reasoned argument is relevant to the full moral status which he accorded to free men. Of course, he was wrong in his other premise, that women and slaves by their nature cannot reason well enough to function as autonomous moral agents. Had that premise been true, so would his conclusion that women and slaves are not quite the moral equals of free men. In the case of most non-human animals, the corresponding premise is true. If, on the other hand, there are animals with whom we can (learn to) reason, then we are obligated to do this and to regard them as our moral equals.

Thus, to distinguish between the rights of persons and those of most other animals on the grounds that only people can alter their behavior on the basis of reasoned argument does not commit us to a perfectionist theory of the sort Aristotle endorsed. There is no excuse for refusing to recognize the moral equality of some people on the grounds that we don't regard them as quite as rational as we are, since it is perfectly clear that most people can reason well enough to determine how to act so as to respect the basic rights of others (if they choose to), and that is enough for moral equality.

But what about people who are clearly not rational? It is often argued that sophisticated mental capacities such as rationality cannot be essential for the possession of equal basic moral rights, since nearly everyone agrees that human infants and mentally incompetent persons have such rights, even though they may lack those sophisticated mental capacities. But this argument is inconclusive, because there are powerful practical and emotional reasons for protecting non-rational human beings, reasons which are absent in the case of most non-human animals. Infancy and mental incompetence are human conditions which all of us either have experienced or are likely to experience at some time. We also protect babies and mentally incompetent people because we care for them. We don't normally care for animals in the same way, and when we do—e.g., in the case of much-loved pets—we may regard them as having special rights by virtue of their relationship to us. We protect them not only for their sake but also for our own, lest we be hurt by harm done to them. Regan holds that such "side-effects" are irrelevant to moral rights, and perhaps they are. But in ordinary usage, there is no sharp line between moral rights and those moral protections which are not rights. The extension of strong moral protections to infants and the mentally impaired in no way proves that non-human animals have the same basic moral rights as people.

WHY SPEAK OF "ANIMAL RIGHTS" AT ALL?

If, as I have argued, reality precludes our treating all animals as our moral equals, then why should we still ascribe rights to them? Everyone agrees that animals are entitled to some protection against human abuse, but why speak of animal *rights* if we are not prepared to accept most animals as our moral equals? The weak animal rights position may seem an unstable compromise between the bold claim that animals have the same basic moral rights that we do and the more common view that animals have no rights at all. . . .

The most plausible alternative to the view that animals have moral rights is that, while they do not have *rights,* we are, nevertheless, obligated not to be cruel to them. Regan argues persuasively that the injunction to avoid being cruel to animals is inadequate to express our obligations towards animals, because it focuses on the mental states of those who cause animal suffering, rather than on the harm done to the animals themselves. . . . Cruelty is inflicting pain or suffering and either taking pleasure in that pain or suffering or being more or less indifferent to it. Thus, to express the demand for the decent treatment of animals in terms of the rejection of cruelty is to invite the too easy response that those who subject animals to suffering are not being cruel because they regret the suffering they cause but sincerely believe that what they do is justified. The injunction to avoid cruelty is also inadequate in that it does not preclude the killing of animals—for any reason, however trivial—so long as it is done relatively painlessly.

The inadequacy of the anti-cruelty view provides one practical reason for speaking of animal rights. Another practical reason is that this is an age in which nearly all significant moral claims tend to be expressed in terms of rights. Thus, the denial that animals have rights, however carefully qualified, is likely to be taken to mean that we may do whatever we like to them, provided that we do not violate any human rights. In such a context, speaking of the rights of animals may be the only way to persuade many people to take seriously protests against the abuse of animals.

Why not extend this line of argument and speak of the rights of trees, mountains, oceans, or anything else which we may wish to see protected from destruction? Some environmentalists have not hesitated to speak in this way, and, given the importance of protecting such elements of the natural world, they cannot be blamed for using this rhetorical device. But, I would argue that moral rights can meaningfully be ascribed only to entities which have some capacity for sentience. This is because moral rights are protections designed to protect rights holders from harms or to provide them with benefits which matter *to them.* Only beings capable of sentience can be harmed or benefited in ways which matter to them, for only such beings can like or dislike what happens to them or prefer some conditions to others. Thus, sentient animals, unlike mountains, rivers, or species, are at least logically possible candidates for moral rights. This fact, together with the need to end current abuses of animals—e.g., in scientific research . . . —provides a plausible case for speaking of animal rights.

CONCLUSION

I have argued that Regan's case for ascribing strong moral rights to all normal, mature mammals is unpersuasive because (1) it rests upon the obscure concept of inherent value, which is defined only in negative terms, and (2) it seems to preclude any plausible answer to questions about the moral status of the vast majority of sentient animals. . . .

The weak animal rights theory asserts that (1) any creature whose natural mode of life includes the pursuit of certain satisfactions has the right not to be forced to exist without the opportunity to pursue those satisfactions; (2) any creature which is capable of pain, suffering, or frustration has the right that such experiences not be deliberately inflicted upon it without some compelling reason; and (3) no sentient being should be killed without good reason. However, moral rights are not an all-or-nothing affair. The strength of the reasons required to override the rights of a non-human organism varies, depending upon—among other things—the probability that it is sentient and (if it is clearly sentient) its probable degree of mental sophistication.

NOTES

1. Tom Regan, *The Case for Animal Rights* (Berkeley: University of California Press, 1983). All page references are to this edition.
2. For instance, Peter Singer, although he does not like to speak of rights, includes all sentient beings under the protection of his basic utilitarian principle of equal respect for like interests. (*Animal Liberation* [New York: Avon Books, 1975], p. 3.)
3. The capacity for sentience, like all of the mental capacities mentioned in what follows, is a disposition. Dispositions do not disappear whenever they are not currently manifested. Thus, sleeping or temporarily unconscious persons or non-human animals are still sentient in the relevant sense (i.e., still capable of sentience), so long as they still have the neurological mechanisms necessary for the occurrence of experiences.
4. It is possible, perhaps probable that some non-human animals—such as cetaceans and anthropoid apes—should be regarded as persons. If so, then the weak animal rights position holds that these animals have the same basic moral rights as human persons.
5. See, for instance, p. 319, where Regan appeals to the benefit of the doubt principle when dealing with infanticide and late-term abortion.
6. Bonnie Steinbock, "Speciesism and the Idea of Equality," *Philosophy* 53 (1978): 253.

STUDY QUESTIONS

1. How does Warren distinguish the strong animal rights position and the weak one?
2. Do all human beings deserve the same rights?
3. Do all nonhuman animals deserve the same rights?
4. According to Warren, why do mountains not have rights?

PART 10

Society

Two Concepts of Citizenship

JEAN HAMPTON

Social and political philosophy focuses on ethical issues related to the structure
of society and the practices of government. A fundamental question about any
society is who is entitled to be a member. In the next selection, Jean Hampton
(1954–1996), who was Professor of Philosophy at the University of Arizona, distinguishes two concepts of citizenship. One, exemplified by Germany and Japan,
is connected with ethnicity; the other, exemplified by Canada and the United
States, is consensual.

....

Citizenship and immigration policies articulate a society's conception of what is
involved in being a member of that society. In our world there are two prominent and competing conceptions of what it means to be a citizen of a country.
I do not mean to suggest that these are the only conceptions of citizenship that
exist or could exist, but I do believe these conceptions are particularly prominent
and important in our world. First, there is the conception of citizenship as analogous to being a (voluntary) member of a club; second, there is the conception of
citizenship as analogous to being one among many organs in a kind of (social)
body.... A review of citizenship policies in various states shows that it is much
easier to gain citizenship rights in a country that conceives of citizenship in the
first way than in a country that conceives of it in the second way....

[T]his nonconsensual conception of membership is ... realized in countries
such as Germany and Japan, explaining why it is very difficult to "become" a
German or Japanese citizen if one emigrates to one of these countries.

Although officially Germany's laws are designed to discourage immigration,
in fact up until recently outsiders have had easy access to Germany because it
has granted admission to any outsider who declared himself a political refugee.[1]
Germany's liberality in this regard is connected to its recent history: Many anti-
Nazis were able to survive World War II because other European countries allowed
them to stay as refugees of political terror.[2] However, the requirements for citizenship in Germany are remarkably stringent and detailed. To review those requirements[3]: All ethnic Germans are granted the right of citizenship regardless of where
they are born or presently live. The attribution of citizenship is based solely on parentage, so that a person born of German citizens anywhere in the world is automatically granted German citizenship upon application, and a person with at least one

Jean Hampton, *Political Philosophy*, Westview, 1997. Reprinted by permission of the
publisher.

German grandparent has the right to apply and be granted German citizenship (this is called being "naturalized by right"). But a person born on German territory to noncitizens is still a foreigner. The acquisition of citizenship is discretionary and requires that the applicant comply with a number of conditions, including ten years of residence (only five for a spouse of a German national), good moral character, knowledge of the German language and the German political order, and integration into a German way of life. Germany has a very low naturalization rate, most likely because of the difficulty in complying with the requirements and because in the final analysis naturalization is discretionary. Moreover, like Britain, Germany makes the renunciation of citizenship difficult and presumes that it is something that the state must grant, not something that the citizen can insist on as her right.

So the German government is essentially requiring that to be a German citizen, one must have the national identity of a German. This involves two things: First, it means being culturally German, so that one must display a mastery of the language, history, social practices, and beliefs of the German culture. Second, and even more important than the cultural requirement, one must have German "blood." No matter where a person is born and no matter the culture in which he is reared, that person has a right to German citizenship if either of his parents or one of his grandparents is German. Moreover, even if his parents or grandparents previously renounced their German citizenship in order to take up the citizenship of another state, the child can apply and be granted German citizenship solely on the basis of the German nationality of his parents or grandparents.[4] So being German involves in general having a certain genetic connection with other members of the state; I refer to this as the "ethnicity" requirement.

Because Germany regards ethnicity as a more important criterion of membership than culture, German rules on citizenship do not grant citizenship automatically to people born in Germany to non-German parents (unless they would otherwise be stateless—a qualification we discuss later). While the rules allow that those of foreign parentage born in Germany may eventually be granted citizenship if they show evidence of "assimilation," in practice that evidence is hard to furnish if their racial and cultural background is perceived as substantially different from that of the traditional German.[5] As one German descendant in the United States has noted about German citizenship rules:

> This writer, who speaks no German, has never lived there, and whose only connection with Germany is that his paternal grandparents left Baden for the United States a century ago, has a better legal claim on German citizenship than the child of a Turkish worker in Germany, born in Germany, educated there, culturally German, and speaking no other language than German.[6]

So to be a German citizen is to be a member of an ethnic, not a cultural nationality. . . .

Another country that exhibits a conception of social membership connected with ethnicity is Japan. Like Germany, Japan grants citizenship on the basis of parentage rather than place of birth: One is automatically granted citizenship if one is a child of Japanese parents, no matter where one is born, whereas a child of non-Japanese parents born in Japan is not an automatic citizen and can only become one through naturalization procedures. The requirements for earning naturalized citizenship *seem* relatively lenient—at least on paper:[7] The would-be citizen must have been continuously domiciled in Japan as a permanent resident for five years, must have upright conduct, and must have sufficient assets not to be a burden on the state. However, the rules also require that making someone a citizen must "accord with the interests of Japan," and that phrase essentially makes the granting of citizenship a largely discretionary matter and in practice remarkably difficult to obtain. Moreover, it turns out that even permanent residency, a necessary condition for citizenship, is granted only at the discretion of the government and is just as difficult to obtain.[8] To become a permanent resident, one must fulfill a vaguely stated assimilation requirement that has been interpreted to involve the taking of a Japanese name (a provision that has offended many of Korean descent in Japan and has been a serious impediment to their becoming citizens). . . .

So not merely the rules but more important the practice of the Japanese government indicates that to be "one of us" in Japan is not only to have a certain kind of cultural identity, which it would be very difficult for anyone to assume unless he had been raised by parents who were thoroughly part of this culture themselves, but also to have (almost always) a certain kind of genetic connection to others in the group—to have a certain "bloodline." And as in Germany, the cultural requirements are not as important as the genetic background, since no matter where a person is born (and subsequently raised), the Japanese government will grant a right of citizenship to a child born of parents who are Japanese citizens.[9] Japan is therefore another example of a country with a nationalist conception of citizenship.

In contrast to this conception of social membership is the *consensual conception of social membership* held in countries such as the United States and Canada (and to an increasing degree Great Britain), by which membership largely rests on a *voluntary* action on the part of the citizen. . . .

Although consent . . . does not make one a citizen of contemporary Germany or Japan, in fact there is a kind of consent that is the foundation of citizenship in countries such as the United States and Canada. If someone is born within the boundaries of these states and/or is born to parents at least one of whom is a citizen, the state will grant that person citizenship, but such a grant is always made with the understanding that this person has the right to *unilaterally* renounce it, if she so chooses, after reaching the age of majority. So it is important that such membership is always understood to be something that a person *can* voluntarily renounce. Hence *it is assumed that if she does not voluntarily and unilaterally renounce it after the age of majority, she has consented to the responsibilities and rights of citizenship.* Let me call this kind of consent by which someone makes herself a member of a society at the age of majority and that she can unilaterally renounce whenever she so chooses in order to join a new political society "membership consent"—it can be either tacitly or expressly given. I understand a citizen to have tacitly consented to membership when she is born into a society that accepts her unilateral right to renounce her membership in it and does not exercise that right after the age of majority. However, this consent is often, sometimes necessarily, expressly given: For example, those who want to become citizens of consensual regimes who have not been born within these countries or born to parents who are already citizens must generally do so by performing a voluntary and *explicit* act of consent and commitment (undertaken in the United States, for example, through a naturalization ceremony).

So the official rules in societies such as the United States and Canada establish that to be a citizen is not to exhibit certain fundamental social or genetic characteristics, nor even to be born within its boundaries, but rather to choose to become a member of the state if given an opportunity to do so, by giving consent, either tacitly (as defined above) or explicitly, to membership. . . .

However, in those regimes that rely on consent to establish membership, an individual's giving such consent is a necessary but not a sufficient condition of membership. In these regimes membership also requires that the individual's consent be solicited and *accepted* by the political society. A country such as the United States or Canada grants all who are born within its borders the right to join it if they choose, and outsiders are granted the right to do so as long as certain conditions are met, which include acceptance of certain political beliefs. This is in part because these countries understand the basis of the unity in their society in a political way. They take it that it is because the citizens of these countries have consented to the same political ideals and institutions that they are part of one political society, even if they have different genetic backgrounds, religions, lifestyles, languages, and social customs. Note that one can choose one's political views in a way that one cannot choose the culture in which one has been raised or the genetics of one's family. So in these societies it is possible to assume voluntarily the defining identity of the society simply by embracing its ruling political conceptions (which one will choose to do as long as one's own ideas are in accord with its institutions and ideals). For all citizens of these countries, then, becoming a citizen is a voluntary act based upon giving the political society one's consent to be part of it. Such a political society has a conception of itself as a community—but a community of a very specific sort. It is not a community defined by a genetic connection among the members nor by a common religion or set of social institutions, but by a common political culture to which one commits oneself when one joins the political society.

Membership is not something that can be unilaterally chosen but depends upon the political society's accepting that consent. Hence the citizenship policies in this kind of society depend on the *mutual* consent of both the would-be member and the rest of the political community, which has to decide whether or not to admit her. So the voluntary consent of the would-be member results in membership only if the rest of the community chooses to accept her. In a very real sense this means that such a society rests upon an ongoing "social contract" between that community and each of its members.[10] . . .

In contrast, a political society such as Germany does not consent to someone's being a member; instead, it *recognizes* the fact of someone's Germanness, after evaluating and tallying up the kind and number of an applicant's characteristics to determine whether they are sufficient for German nationality. Moreover, in societies such as Germany that embrace the nonconsensual, nationalist understanding of citizenship, the nation, defined as above, is conceptually prior both to the individual *and to any political community.* Indeed, this idea was nicely embodied by a 1913 German law (relied upon by West Germany after World War II to establish its laws on citizenship) that states that at bottom the German nation should not be understood as a political entity but rather as an ethnic identity, so that German citizenship was not a purely political matter but an issue that belonged to "the German people." So in Germany the ethnic or national society is understood to be that which defines and authorizes the political society—and surely this idea was one reason so many West and East Germans were eager to unify, despite the profound economic costs to both groups of doing so.

In countries in which political membership is consensually based, the citizenry's genetic backgrounds and cultural identities in matters of custom, dress, religion, or recreation are entirely a function of those who have chosen to constitute it. Hence in social (and nonpolitical) matters the individual member of this type of political society is understood to be conceptually prior to the society itself (so that in general these countries are multicultural in character). If I am a member of such a society, my citizenship does not depend upon whether I have displayed the cultural and genetic characteristics common to the rest of the country's members; instead, the cultural and genetic identity of the country depends upon which individuals (such as myself) have decided to join it. . . .

In an important sense, the histories of political societies explain how each of them has come to embrace one of these two very different conceptions of membership. I once had a conversation with a Chinese citizen whose own ancestors were Chinese for hundreds of generations and who could not conceive of what it was like for me to be an American citizen simply because my very recent forebears happened to turn up here. A nation made up of immigrants cannot have the same strong sense of homogeneous cultural identity as a nation with a long cultural tradition and a long tradition of warding off outsiders. Hence an immigrant nation's sense of citizenship as a voluntary affair is as inevitable a consequence of its history as is other countries' perception of citizenship as a nonconsensual, nonvoluntary fact of social identity.

The consent-based conception of citizenship may also explain why in the United States only a citizen may vote. Because a common commitment to its democratic political culture defines American identity, the act of voting is not only a political act but also an act that indicates one's commitment to the nation's defining political identity. Hence the act of voting becomes one of the most important rights withheld until the society is clear that the person seeking membership is genuinely choosing to belong to and participate in the political culture of that society. . . .

Hence "being American" is *not* manifesting characteristics that are difficult or impossible to assume voluntarily and that mark one out as a lifelong member of a nation; instead, "being American" is belonging to a political "club" (which is perhaps not the only club of which one is a member) after having tacitly or explicitly consented to do so.

NOTES

1. German federal constitution of 1949 (Basic Law), art. 16 (2).
2. William Pfaff, "Neo-Nazi Backlash: Immigration Difficulties Cause Germany to Turn Rightward," *Arizona Daily Star,* April 10, 1992, p. A19.
3. From Jules Coleman and Sarah Harding, "Citizenship, the Demands of Justice, and the Moral Relevance of Political Borders," in Warren Schwartz, ed., *Justice in Immigration* (Cambridge: Cambridge University Press, 1995), pp. 18–62.
4. To state the rules precisely, all people born outside of Germany to German parents or grandparents must accept only German citizenship if they apply for it (and thus renounce any other citizenship they might have at the time of application). Moreover, although such people will be considered "naturalized citizens," they are in the category of citizens "naturalized by right," as opposed to citizens (born of non-German parents) who are "naturalized by discretion" of the German government. For further discussion, see Kay Hailbronner, "Citizenship and Nationhood in Germany," in William R. Brubaker, ed., *Immigration and the Politics of Citizenship in Europe and North America* (New York: University Press of America, 1989), pp. 67–68, 73–74. Cited by Coleman and Harding, "Citizenship."
5. Moreover, oftentimes these immigrants perceive the assimilation requirement as involving changes in their way of life that are disrespectful of their heritage and thus refuse to make them. A very large percentage of German residents of Turkish descent do not wish to apply for citizenship because of the perception that doing so will mean losing all of their Turkish identity. In 1985 only 7.5 percent of Turks in Germany expressed interest in getting German citizenship (see Hailbronner, "Citizenship and Nationhood," p. 75, cited by Coleman and Harding, "Citizenship," n. 122, p. 60).
6. Pfaff, "Neo-Nazi Backlash," p. 19.
7. These requirements are set out in the 1946 Japanese constitution.
8. See Japan's permanent resident act of 1951.
9. The parents must, however, request this within three months of the child's birth.
10. In *Citizenship Without Consent: Illegal Aliens in American Polity* (New Haven: Yale University Press, 1985), Peter Schuck and Rogers Smith argue that citizenship in America is based on "mutual consent."

STUDY QUESTIONS

1. Explain the distinction Hampton draws between two types of citizenship.
2. Do American citizens consent to being Americans?
3. Explain the difference between tacit and explicit consent.
4. According to Hampton, why in the United States may only a citizen vote?

Democracy

JOHN DEWEY

One long-standing area of inquiry in political philosophy is the nature of democracy and its relative advantages or disadvantages compared with alternative
systems. Our next selection is devoted to this subject. The author is John Dewey
(1859–1952), the foremost American philosopher of the first half of the twentieth
century. Born and bred in Burlington, Vermont, his life and thought reflected the
commitment to social equality he found exemplified in the life of his boyhood
New England community. He spent most of his career as Professor of Philosophy
at Columbia University.

Reprinted here is the text of a talk he delivered in 1937 to a meeting of educational administrators. It offers, in brief, his account of democracy.

[D]emocracy is much broader than a special political form, a method of conducting government, of making laws and carrying on governmental administration by
means of popular suffrage and elected officers. It is that of course. But it is something broader and deeper than that.

The political and governmental phase of democracy is a means, the best
means so far found, for realizing ends that lie in the wide domain of human relationships and the development of human personality. It is, as we often say, though
perhaps without appreciating all that is involved in the saying, a way of life, social
and individual. The key-note of democracy as a way of life may be expressed, it
seems to me, as the necessity for the participation of every mature human being in
formation of the values that regulate the living of men together—which is necessary from the standpoint of both the general social welfare and the full development of human beings as individuals.

Universal suffrage, recurring elections, responsibility of those who are in political power to the voters, and the other factors of democratic government are
means that have been found expedient for realizing democracy as the truly human
way of living. They are not a final end and a final value. They are to be judged on
the basis of their contribution to an end. It is a form of idolatry to erect means into
the end which they serve. Democratic political forms are simply the best means
that human wit has devised up to a special time in history. But they rest back upon
the idea that no man or limited set of men is wise enough or good enough to
rule others without their consent; the positive meaning of this statement is that all

those who are affected by social institutions must have a share in producing and managing them. The two facts that each one is influenced in what he does and enjoys and in what he becomes by the institutions under which he lives, and that therefore he shall have, in a democracy, a voice in shaping them, are the passive and active sides of the same fact.

The development of political democracy came about through substitution of the method of mutual consultation and voluntary agreement for the method of subordination of the many to the few enforced from above. Social arrangements which involve fixed subordination are maintained by coercion. The coercion need not be physical. There have existed, for short periods, benevolent despotisms. But coercion of some sort there has been; perhaps economic, certainly psychological and moral. The very fact of exclusion from participation is a subtle form of suppression. It gives individuals no opportunity to reflect and decide upon what is good for them. Others who are supposed to be wiser and who in any case have more power decide the question for them and also decide the methods and means by which subjects may arrive at the enjoyment of what is good for them. This form of coercion and suppression is more subtle and more effective than is overt intimidation and restraint. When it is habitual and embodied in social institutions, it seems the normal and natural state of affairs. The mass usually become unaware that they have a claim to a development of their own powers. Their experience is so restricted that they are not conscious of restriction. It is part of the democratic conception that they as individuals are not the only sufferers, but that the whole social body is deprived of the potential resources that should be at its service. The individuals of the submerged mass may not be very wise. But there is one thing they are wiser about than anybody else can be, and that is where the shoe pinches, the troubles they suffer from.

The foundation of democracy is faith in the capacities of human nature; faith in human intelligence, and in the power of pooled and cooperative experience. It is not belief that these things are complete but that if given a show they will grow and be able to generate progressively the knowledge and wisdom needed to guide collective action. Every autocratic and authoritarian scheme of social action rests on a belief that the needed intelligence is confined to a superior few who because of inherent natural gifts are endowed with the ability and the right to control the conduct of others; laying down principles and rules and directing the ways in which they are carried out. It would be foolish to deny that much can be said for this point of view. It is that which controlled human relations in social groups for much the greater part of human history. The democratic faith has emerged very, very recently in the history of mankind. Even where democracies now exist, men's minds and feelings are still permeated with ideas about leadership imposed from above, ideas that developed in the long early history of mankind. After democratic political institutions were nominally established, beliefs and ways of looking at life and of acting that originated when men and women were externally controlled and subjected to arbitrary power, persisted in the family, the church, business and the school, and experience shows that as long as they persist there, political democracy is not secure.

Belief in equality is an element of the democratic credo. It is not, however, belief in equality of natural endowments. Those who proclaimed the idea of equality did not suppose they were enunciating a psychological doctrine, but a legal and political one. All individuals are entitled to equality of treatment by law and in its administration. Each one is affected equally in quality if not in quantity by the institutions under which he lives and has an equal right to express his judgment, although the weight of his judgment may not be equal in amount when it enters into the pooled result to that of others. In short, each one is equally an individual and entitled to equal opportunity of development of his own capacities, be they large or small in range. Moreover, each has needs of his own, as significant to him as those of others are to them. The very fact of natural and psychological inequality is all the more reason for establishment by law of equality of opportunity, since otherwise the former becomes a means of oppression of the less gifted.

While what we call intelligence be distributed in unequal amounts, it is the democratic faith that it is sufficiently general so that each individual has something to contribute whose value can be assessed only as it enters into the final pooled intelligence constituted by the contributions of all. Every authoritarian scheme, on the contrary assumes that its value may be assessed by some *prior* principle, if not of family and birth or race and color or possession of material wealth, then by the position and rank a person occupies in the existing social scheme. The democratic faith in equality is the faith that each individual shall have the chance and opportunity to contribute whatever he is capable of contributing, and that the value of his contribution be decided by its place and function in the organized total of similar contributions—not on the basis of prior status of any kind whatever.

I have emphasized in what precedes the importance of the effective release of intelligence in connection with personal experience in the democratic way of living. I have done so purposely because democracy is so often and so naturally associated in our minds with freedom of *action,* forgetting the importance of freed intelligence which is necessary to direct and to warrant freedom of action. Unless freedom of individual action has intelligence and informed conviction back of it, its manifestation is almost sure to result in confusion and disorder. The democratic idea of freedom is not the right of each individual to *do* as he pleases, even if it be qualified by adding "provided he does not interfere with the same freedom on the part of others." While the idea is not always, not often enough, expressed in words, the basic freedom is that of freedom of *mind* and of whatever degree of freedom of action and experience is necessary to produce freedom of intelligence. The modes of freedom guaranteed in the Bill of Rights are all of this nature: Freedom of belief and conscience, of expression of opinion, of assembly for discussion and conference, of the press as an organ of communication. They are guaranteed because without them individuals are not free to develop and society is deprived of what they might contribute. . . .

There is some kind of government, of control, wherever affairs that concern a number of persons who act together are engaged in. It is a superficial view that holds government is located in Washington and Albany. There is government in the family, in business, in the church, in every social group. There are regulations, due to custom if not to enactment, that settle how individuals in a group act in connection with one another.

It is a disputed question of theory and practice just how far a democratic political government should go in control of the conditions of action within special groups. At the present time, for example, there are those who think the federal and state governments leave too much freedom of independent action to industrial and financial groups and there are others who think the Government is going altogether too far at the present time. I do not need to discuss this phase of the problem much less to try to settle it. But it must be pointed out that if the methods of regulation and administration in vogue in the conduct of secondary social groups are non-democratic, whether directly or indirectly or both, there is bound to be an unfavorable reaction back into the habits of feeling, thought and action of citizenship in the broadest sense of that word. The way in which any organized social interest is controlled necessarily plays an important part in forming the dispositions and tastes, the attitudes, interests, purposes and desires, of those engaged in carrying on the activities of the group. For illustration, I do not need to do more than point to the moral, emotional, and intellectual effect upon both employers and laborers of the existing industrial system. Just what the effects specifically are is a matter about which we know very little. But I suppose that every one who reflects upon the subject admits that it is impossible that the ways in which activities are carried on for the greater part of the waking hours of the day; and the way in which the shares of individuals are involved in the management of affairs in such a matter as gaining a livelihood and attaining material and social security, can only be a highly important factor in shaping personal dispositions; in short, forming character and intelligence.

In the broad and final sense all institutions are educational in the sense that they operate to form the attitudes, dispositions, abilities, and disabilities that constitute a concrete personality. The principle applies with special force to the school. For it is the main business of the family and the school to influence directly the formation and growth of attitudes and dispositions, emotional, intellectual and moral. Whether this educative process is carried on in a predominantly democratic or non-democratic way becomes therefore a question of transcendent importance not only for education itself but for its final effect upon all the interests and activities of a society that is committed to the democratic way of life. . . .

[T]here are certain corollaries which clarify the meaning of the issue. Absence of participation tends to produce lack of interest and concern on the part of those shut out. The result is a corresponding lack of effective responsibility. Automatically and unconsciously, if not consciously, the feeling develops, "this is none of our affair; it is the business of those at the top; let that particular set of Georges do what needs to be done." The countries in which autocratic government prevails are just those in which there is least public spirit and the greatest indifference to matters of general as distinct from personal concern. . . . Where there is little power, there is correspondingly little sense of positive responsibility—It is enough to do what one is told to do sufficiently well to escape flagrant unfavorable notice. About larger matters a spirit of passivity is engendered. . . .

[I]t still is also true that incapacity to assume the responsibilities involved in having a voice in shaping policies is bred and increased by conditions in which that responsibility is denied. I suppose there has never been an autocrat, big or little, who did not justify his conduct on the ground of the unfitness of his subjects to take part in government. . . . But, as was said earlier, habitual exclusion has the effect of reducing a sense of responsibility for what is done and its consequences. What the argument for democracy implies is that the best way to produce initiative and constructive power is to exercise it. Power, as well as interest, comes by use and practice. . . .

The fundamental beliefs and practices of democracy are now challenged as they never have been before. In some nations they are more than challenged. They are ruthlessly and systematically destroyed. Everywhere there are waves of criticism and doubt as to whether democracy can meet pressing problems of order and security. The causes for the destruction of political democracy in countries where it was nominally established are complex. But of one thing I think we may be sure. Wherever it has fallen it was too exclusively political in nature. It had not become part of the bone and blood of the people in daily conduct of its life. Democratic forms were limited to Parliament, elections, and combats between parties. What is happening proves conclusively, I think, that unless democratic habits of thought and action are part of the fiber of a people, political democracy is insecure. It cannot stand in isolation. It must be buttressed by the presence of democratic methods in all social relationships. The relations that exist in educational institutions are second only in importance in this respect to those which exist in industry and business, perhaps not even to them. . . .

I can think of nothing so important in this country at present as a rethinking of the whole problem of democracy and its implications. Neither the rethinking nor the action it should produce can be brought into being in a day or year. The democratic idea itself demands that the thinking and activity proceed cooperatively.

STUDY QUESTIONS

1. Why does Dewey believe that democracy is much broader than a method of electing officials?
2. According to Dewey, about what are individuals wiser than anyone else can be?
3. According to Dewey, what is the foundation of democracy?
4. How does Dewey connect democracy and education?

What Is a Liberal Education?

SIDNEY HOOK

In the previous selection John Dewey stresses that the welfare of a democratic community depends on the understanding and capability of its citizenry. But what knowledge, skills, and values do we all require to enable us to make a success of our experiment in self-government? That is the question addressed in our next essay, written by Sidney Hook (1902–1989), a leading student of Dewey, who was Professor of Philosophy at New York University.

....

What, concretely, should the modern man know in order to live intelligently in the world today? What should we require that he learn of subject matters and skills in his educational career in order that he may acquire maturity in feeling, in judgment, in action? Can we indicate the minimum indispensables of a liberal education in the modern world? This approach recognizes that no subject per se is inherently liberal at all times and places. But it also recognizes that within a given age in a given culture, the enlightenment and maturity, the freedom and power, which liberal education aims to impart, is more likely to be achieved by mastery of some subject matters and skills than by others. In short, principles must bear fruit in specific programs in specific times. In what follows I shall speak of studies rather than of conventional courses.

1. The liberally educated person should be intellectually at home in the world of physical nature. He should know something about the earth he inhabits and its place in the solar system, about the solar system and its relation to the cosmos. He should know something about mechanics, heat, light, electricity, and magnetism as the universal forces that condition anything he is or may become. He should be just as intimately acquainted with the nature of man as a biological species, his evolution, and the discoveries of experimental genetics. He should know something about the structure of his own body and mind, and the cycle of birth, growth, learning, and decline. To have even a glimmer of understanding of these things, he must go beyond the level of primary description and acquire some grasp of the principles that explain what he observes. Where an intelligent grasp of principles requires a knowledge of mathematics, its fundamental ideas should be presented in such a way that students carry away the sense of mathematics not only as a tool for the solution of problems but as a study of types of order, system, and language.

Such knowledge is important to the individual *not* merely because of its intrinsic fascination. Every subject from numismatics to Sanskrit possesses an intrinsic interest to those who are curious about it. It is important because it helps make everyday experience more intelligible; because it furnishes a continuous exemplification of scientific method in action; because our world is literally being remade by the consequences and applications of science; because the fate of nations and the vocations of men depend upon the use of this knowledge; and because it provides the instruments to reduce our vast helplessness and dependence in an uncertain world.

Such knowledge is no less important because it bears upon the formation of *rational belief* about the place of man in the universe. Whatever views a man professes today about God, human freedom, Cosmic Purpose, and personal survival, he cannot reasonably hold them in ignorance of the scientific account of the world and man.

These are some of the reasons why the study of the natural sciences, and the elementary mathematical notions they involve, should be *required* of everyone. Making such study required imposes a heavy obligation and a difficult task of pedagogical discovery upon those who teach it. It is commonly recognized that the sciences today are taught as if all students enrolled in science courses were preparing to be professional scientists. Most of them are not. Naturally they seek to escape a study whose wider and larger uses they do not see because many of their teachers do not see it. Here is not the place to canvass and evaluate the attempts being made to organize instruction in the sciences. The best experience seems to show that one science should not be taken as the exemplar of all, but that the basic subject matter of astronomy, physics, chemistry, geology, in one group, and biology and psychology in another, should be covered. For when only one science is taught it tends to be treated professionally. Similarly, the best experience indicates that instruction should be interdepartmental—any competent teacher from one of these fields in either group should be able to teach all of them in the group, instead of having a succession of different teachers each representing his own field. This usually destroys both the continuity and the cumulative effect of the teaching as a whole.

2. Every student should be required to become intelligently aware of how the society in which he lives functions, of the great forces molding contemporary civilization, and of the crucial problems of our age which await decision. The studies most appropriate to this awareness have been conventionally separated into history, economics, government, sociology, social psychology, and anthropology. This separation is an intellectual scandal. For it is impossible to have an adequate grasp of the problems of government without a knowledge of economics, and vice versa. Except for some special domains of professional interest, the same is true for the other subjects as well.

The place of the social studies, properly integrated around problems and issues, is fundamental in the curriculum of modern education. It is one of the dividing points between the major conflicting schools of educational thought.

The question of its justification must be sharply distinguished from discussion of the relative merits of this or that mode of approach to the social studies.

The knowledge and insight that the social studies can give are necessary for every student because no matter what his specialized pursuits may later be, the extent to which he can follow them, and the "contextual" developments within these fields, depend upon the total social situation of which they are in some sense a part. An engineer today whose knowledge is restricted only to technical matters of engineering, or a physician whose competence extends only to the subject matter of traditional medical training, is ill-prepared to plan intelligently for a life-career or to understand the basic problems that face his profession. He is often unable to cope adequately with those specific problems in his own domain that involve, as so many problems of social and personal health do, economic and psychological difficulties. No matter what an individual's vocation, the conditions of his effective functioning depend upon pervasive social tendencies which set the occasions for the application of knowledge, provide the opportunities of employment, and not seldom determine even the direction of research.

More important, the whole presupposition of the theory of democracy is that the electorate will be able to make intelligent decisions on the issues before it. These issues are basically political, social, and economic. Their specific character changes from year to year. But their generic form, and the character of the basic problems, do not. Nor, most essential of all, do the proper intellectual habits of meeting them change. It is undeniably true that the world we live in is one marked by greater changes, because of the impact of technology, than ever before. This does not necessitate changing the curriculum daily to catch up with today's newspapers, nor does it justify a concentration on presumably eternal problems as if these problems had significance independent of cultural place–time. The fact that we are living in a world where the rate of cultural change is greater than at any time in the past, together with its ramifications, may itself become a central consideration for analysis. . . .

3. Everyone recognizes a distinction between knowledge and wisdom. This distinction is not clarified by making a mystery of wisdom and speaking of it as if it were begotten by divine inspiration while knowledge had a more lowly source. Wisdom is a kind of knowledge. It is knowledge of the nature, career, and consequences of *human values.* Since these cannot be separated from the human organism and the social scene, the moral ways of man cannot be understood without knowledge of the ways of things and institutions.

To study social affairs without an analysis of policies is to lose oneself in factual minutiae that lack interest and relevance. But knowledge of values is a prerequisite of the intelligent determination of policy. Philosophy, most broadly viewed, is the critical survey of existence from the standpoint of value. This points to the twofold role of philosophy in the curriculum of the college.

The world of physical nature may be studied without reference to human values. But history, art, literature, and particularly the social studies involve problems of value at every turn. A social philosophy whose implications are worked out is a series of proposals that something be *done* in the world. It includes a set of *plans* to conserve or change aspects of social life. Today the community is arrayed under different banners without a clear understanding of the basic issues involved. In the press of controversy, the ideals and values at the heart of every social philosophy are widely affirmed as articles of blind faith. They are partisan commitments justified only by the emotional security they give to believers. They spread by contagion, unchecked by critical safeguards; yet the future of civilization largely depends upon them and how they are held. It is therefore requisite that their study be made an integral part of the liberal arts curriculum. Systematic and critical instruction should be given in the great maps of life—the ways to heaven, hell, and earth—which are being unrolled in the world today.

Ideals and philosophies of life are not parts of the world of nature; but it is a pernicious illusion to imagine that they cannot be studied "scientifically." Their historical origins, their concatenation of doctrine, their controlling assumptions, their means, methods, and consequences in practice, can and should be investigated in a scientific spirit. There are certain social philosophies that would forbid such an investigation for fear of not being able to survive it; but it is one of the great merits of the democratic way of life and one of its strongest claims for acceptance that it can withstand analysis of this sort. It is incumbent upon the liberal arts college to provide for close study of the dominant social and political philosophies, ranging from one end of the color spectrum to the other. Proper study will disclose that these philosophies cannot be narrowly considered in their own terms. They involve an examination of the great ways of life—of the great visions of philosophy which come into play whenever we try to arrange our values in a preference scale in order to choose the better between conflicting goods. Philosophy is best taught when the issues of moral choice arise naturally out of the problems of social life. The effective integration of concrete materials from history, literature, and social studies can easily be achieved within a philosophical perspective.

4. Instruction in the natural, social, and technological forces shaping the world, and in the dominant conflicting ideals in behalf of which these forces are to be controlled, goes a long way. But not far enough. Far more important than knowledge is the method by which it is reached, and the ability to recognize when it constitutes *evidence* and when not; and more important than any particular ideal is the way in which it is held, and the capacity to evaluate it in relation to other ideals. From first to last, in season and out, our educational institutions, especially on the college level, must emphasize *methods* of analysis. They must build up in students a critical sense of evidence, relevance, and validity against which the multitudinous seas of propaganda will wash in vain. They must strengthen the powers of independent reflection, which will enable students to confront the claims of ideals and values by their alternatives and the relative costs of achieving them. . . .

The field of language, of inference and argument, is a broad field but a definite one in which specific training can be given to all students. How to read intelligently, how to recognize good from bad reasoning, how to evaluate evidence, how to distinguish between a definition and a hypothesis and between a hypothesis and a resolution, can be taught in such a way as to build up permanent habits of logic in action. The result of thorough training in "semantic" analysis—using that term in its broadest sense without invidious distinctions between different schools—is an intellectual sophistication without which a man may be learned but not intelligent.

Judging by past and present curricular achievements in developing students with intellectual sophistication and maturity, our colleges must be pronounced, in the main, dismal failures. The main reason for the failure is the absence of serious effort, except in a few institutions, to realize this goal. The necessity of the task is not even recognized. This failure is not only intellectually reprehensible; it is socially dangerous. For the natural susceptibility of youth to enthusiasms, its tendency to glorify action, and its limited experience make it easy recruiting material for all sorts of demagogic movements which flatter its strength and impatience. Recent history furnishes many illustrations of how, in the absence of strong critical sense, youthful strength can lead to cruelty, and youthful impatience to folly. It is true that people who are incapable of thinking cannot be taught how to think, and that the incapacity for thought is not restricted to those who learn. But the first cannot be judged without being exposed to the processes of critical instruction, and the second should be eliminated from the ranks of the teachers. There is considerable evidence to show that students who are capable of completing high school can be so taught that they are aware of *whether* they are thinking or not. There is hope that, with better pedagogic skill and inspiration, they may become capable of grasping the main thought of *what* they are reading or hearing in non-technical fields—of developing a sense of *what validly follows from what,* an accompanying sensitiveness to the dominant types of fallacies, and a habit of weighing evidence for conclusions advanced.

My own experience has led me to the conclusion that this is *not* accomplished by courses in formal logic which, when given in a rigorous and elegant way, accomplish little more than courses in pure mathematics. There is an approach to the study of logic that on an elementary level is much more successful in achieving the ends described above than the traditional course in formal logic. This plunges the student into an analysis of language material around him. By constant use of concrete illustrations drawn from all fields, but especially the fields of politics and social study, insight is developed into the logical principles of definition, the structure of analogies, dilemmas, types of fallacies and the reasons *why* they are fallacies, the criteria of good hypotheses, and related topics. Such training may legitimately be required of all students. Although philosophers are usually best able to give it, any teacher who combines logical capacity with pedagogic skill can make this study a stimulating experience.

5. There is less controversy about the desirability of the study of composition and literature than about any other subject in the traditional or modern curriculum. It is appreciated that among the essentials of clear thought are good

language habits and that, except in the higher strata of philosophic discourse, tortuous obscurities of expression are more likely to be an indication of plain confusion than of stuttering profundity. It is also widely recognized that nothing can take the place of literature in developing the imagination, and in imparting a sense of the inexhaustible richness of human personality. The questions that arise at this point are not of justification, but of method, technique, and scope of comprehensiveness.

If good language habits are to be acquired *only* in order to acquire facility in thinking, little can be said for the conventional courses in English composition. Students cannot acquire facility in clear expression in the space of a year, by developing sundry themes from varied sources, under the tutelage of instructors whose training and interest may not qualify them for sustained critical thought. Clear thinking is best controlled by those who are at home in the field in which thinking is done. If language instruction is to be motivated only by the desire to strengthen the power of organizing ideas in written discourse, it should be left to properly trained instructors in other disciplines.

But there are other justifications for teaching students English composition. The first is that there are certain rules of intelligent reading that are essential to—if they do not constitute—understanding. These rules are very elementary. By themselves they do not tell us how to understand a poem, a mathematical demonstration, a scientific text, or a religious prayer—all of which require special skills. But they make it easier for the student to uncover the nature of the "argument"—what is being said, what is being assumed, what is being presented as evidence—in any piece of prose that is not a narrative or simply informational in content. In a sense these rules are integral to the study of logic in action, but in such an introductory way that they are usually not considered part of logical study which begins its work after basic meanings have been established, or in independence of the meaning of logical symbols.

Another reason for teaching English composition independently is its uses in learning how to write. "Effective writing" is not necessarily the same thing as logical writing. The purpose for which we write determines whether our writing is effective. And there are many situations in which we write not to convince or to prove but to explain, arouse, confess, challenge, or assuage. To write *interestingly* may sometimes be just as important as to write soundly because getting a hearing and keeping attention may depend upon it. How much of the skills of writing can be taught is difficult to say. That it is worth making the effort to teach these skills is indisputable.

The place of language in the curriculum involves not merely our native language but *foreign* languages. Vocational considerations aside, should knowledge of a foreign language be required, and why? . . .

The main reason why students should be requested to learn another language is that it is the most effective medium by which, when properly taught, they can acquire a sensitivity to language, to the subtle tones, undertones, and overtones of words, and to the licit ambiguities of imaginative discourse.

No one who has not translated prose or poetry from one language to another can appreciate both the unique richness and the unique limitations of his own language. This is particularly true where the life of the emotions is concerned; and it is particularly important that it should be realized. For the appreciation of emotions, perhaps even their recognition in certain cases, depends upon their linguistic identification. The spectrum of human emotions is much more dense than the words by which we render them. Knowledge of different languages, and the attempts made to communicate back and forth between them in our own minds, broaden and diversify our own feelings. They multiply points of view, and liberate us from the prejudice that words—*our* words—are the natural signs of things and events. The genius of a culture is exemplified in a preeminent way in the characteristic idioms of its language. In learning another language we enable ourselves to appreciate both the cultural similarities and differences of the Western world. . . .

The place of literature in the curriculum is justified by so many considerations that it is secure against all criticism. Here, too, what is at issue is not whether literature—Greek, Latin, English, European, American—should be read and studied in the schools but what should be read, when, and by what methods. These are details, important details—but outside the scope of our inquiry.

Something should be said about the unique opportunity which the teaching of literature provides, not only in giving delight by heightening perception of the formal values of literary craftsmanship, but in giving insight into people. The opposite of a liberal education, William James somewhere suggests, is a literal education. A literal education is one which equips a person to read formulas and equations, straightforward prose, doggerel verse, and advertising signs. It does not equip one to read the language of metaphor, of paradox, of indirect analogy, of serious fancy in which the emotions and passions and half-believed ideas of human beings express themselves. To read great literature is to read men—their fears and motives, their needs and hopes. Every great novelist is a *Menschenkenner* who opens the hearts of others to us and helps us to read our own hearts as well. The intelligent study of literature should never directly aim to strengthen morals and improve manners. For its natural consequences are a delicacy of perception and an emotional tact that are defeated by preaching and didactic teaching.

A liberal education will impart an awareness of the amazing and precious complexity of human relationships. Since those relationships are violated more often out of insensitiveness than out of deliberate intent, whatever increases sensitiveness of perception and understanding humanizes life. Literature in all its forms is the great humanizing medium of life. It must therefore be representative of life; not only of past life but of our own; not only of our own culture but of different cultures.

6. An unfailing mark of philistinism in education is reference to the study of art and music as "the frills and fads" of schooling. Insofar as those who speak

this way are not tone-deaf or color-blind, they are themselves products of a narrow education, unaware of the profound experiences which are uniquely bound up with the trained perception of color and form. There is no reason to believe that the capacity for the appreciation of art and music shows a markedly different curve of distribution from what is observable in the measurement of capacity of drawing inferences or recalling relevant information. A sufficient justification for making some study of art and music required in modern education is that it provides an unfailing source of delight in personal experience, a certain grace in living, and a variety of dimensions of meaning by which to interpret the world around us. This is a sufficient justification: there are others, quite subsidiary, related to the themes, the occasions, the history and backgrounds of the works studied. Perhaps one should add—although this expresses only a reasonable hope—that a community whose citizens have developed tastes would not tolerate the stridency, the ugliness and squalor which assault us in our factories, our cities, and our countryside.

One of the reasons why the study of art and music has not received as much attention as it should by educators, particularly on the college level, is that instruction in these subjects often suffers from two opposite defects. Sometimes courses in art and music are given as if all students enrolled in them were planning a career as practicing artists or as professional *teachers* of the arts. Sometimes they are given as hours for passive enjoyment or relaxation in which the teacher does the performing or talking and in which there is no call upon the students to make an intelligent response.

The key-stress in courses in art and music should be *discrimination* and *interpretation,* rather than appreciation and cultivation. The latter can take care of themselves, when the student has learned to discriminate and interpret intelligently.

Briefly summarized: the answer to the question *What should we teach?* is selected materials from the fields of mathematics and the natural sciences; social studies, including history; language and literature; philosophy and logic; art and music. The knowledge imparted by such study should be acquired in such a way as to strengthen the skills of reading and writing, of thinking and imaginative interpretation, of criticism and evaluation.

STUDY QUESTIONS

1. What does Hook mean by "a liberal education"?
2. According to Hook, what are the chief components of a liberal education?
3. Would a democratic society be more likely to prosper if its citizens had received a liberal education?
4. How could a faculty ensure that each student who is graduated has mastered the essentials of a liberal education?

Cultivating Humanity

MARTHA NUSSBAUM

Martha Nussbaum is Professor of Law and Ethics in the Philosophy Department, Law School, and Divinity School at the University of Chicago. In this selection she considers how liberal education needs to be adapted to produce citizens in a multicultural, multinational world. She stresses the capacity for critical examination of oneself and one's traditions, the ability to recognize one's ties to all other human beings, and the imaginative power to understand their outlooks.

....

Our campuses are producing citizens, and this means that we must ask what a good citizen of the present day should be and should know. The present-day world is inescapably multicultural and multinational. Many of our most pressing problems require for their intelligent, cooperative solution a dialogue that brings together people from many different national and cultural and religious backgrounds. Even those issues that seem closest to home—issues, for example, about the structure of the family, the regulation of sexuality, the future of children—need to be approached with a broad historical and cross-cultural understanding. A graduate of a U.S. university or college ought to be the sort of citizen who can become an intelligent participant in debates involving these differences, whether professionally or simply as a voter, a juror, a friend. . . .

In most nations students enter a university to pursue a single subject, and that is all they study. The idea of "liberal education"—a higher education that is a cultivation of the whole human being for the functions of citizenship and life generally—has been taken up most fully in the United States. This noble ideal, however, has not yet been fully realized in our colleges and universities. Some, while using the words "liberal education," subordinate the cultivation of the whole person to technical and vocational education. Even where education is ostensibly "liberal," it may not contain all that a citizen really needs to know. We should ask, then, how well our nation is really fulfilling a goal that it has chosen to make its own. What does the "cultivation of humanity" require?

The classical ideal of the "world citizen" can be understood in two ways, and "cultivation of humanity" along with it. The sterner, more exigent version is the ideal of a citizen whose *primary* loyalty is to human beings the world over, and whose national, local, and varied group loyalties are considered distinctly secondary. Its more relaxed version allows a variety of different views about what our priorities should be but says that, however we order our varied loyalties, we should still be sure that we recognize the worth of human life wherever it occurs and see ourselves as bound by common human abilities and problems to people who lie at a great distance from us. . . . Although I do sympathize with the sterner thesis, it is the more relaxed and inclusive thesis that will concern me here. What, then, does this inclusive conception ask us to learn?

Three capacities, above all, are essential to the cultivation of humanity in today's world. First is the capacity for critical examination of oneself and one's traditions—for living what, following Socrates, we may call "the examined life." This means a life that accepts no belief as authoritative simply because it has been handed down by tradition or become familiar through habit, a life that questions all beliefs and accepts only those that survive reason's demand for consistency and for justification. Training this capacity requires developing the capacity to reason logically, to test what one reads or says for consistency of reasoning, correctness of fact, and accuracy of judgment. Testing of this sort frequently produces challenges to tradition, as Socrates knew well when he defended himself against the charge of "corrupting the young." But he defended his activity on the grounds that democracy needs citizens who can think for themselves rather than simply deferring to authority, who can reason together about their choices rather than just trading claims and counterclaims. Like a gadfly on the back of a noble but sluggish horse, he said, he was waking democracy up so that it could conduct its business in a more reflective and reasonable way. Our democracy, like ancient Athens, is prone to hasty and sloppy reasoning, and to the substitution of invective for real deliberation. We need Socratic teaching to fulfill the promise of democratic citizenship.

Citizens who cultivate their humanity need, further, an ability to see themselves not simply as citizens of some local region or group but also, and above all, as human beings bound to all other human beings by ties of recognition and concern. The world around us is inescapably international. Issues from business to agriculture, from human rights to the relief of famine, call our imaginations to venture beyond narrow group loyalties and to consider the reality of distant lives. We very easily think of ourselves in group terms—as Americans first and foremost, as human beings second—or, even more narrowly, as Italian-Americans, or heterosexuals, or African-Americans first, Americans second, and human beings third if at all. We neglect needs and capacities that link us to fellow citizens who live at a distance or who look different from ourselves. This means that we are unaware of many prospects of communication and fellowship with them, and also of responsibilities we may have to them. We also sometimes err by neglect of differences, assuming that lives in distant places must be like ours and lacking curiosity about what they are really like. Cultivating our humanity in a complex, interlocking world involves understanding the ways in which common needs and aims are differently realized in different circumstances. This requires a great deal of knowledge that American college students rarely got in previous eras, knowledge of non-Western cultures, of minorities within their own, of differences of gender and sexuality.

But citizens cannot think well on the basis of factual knowledge alone. The third ability of the citizen, closely related to the first two, can be called the narrative imagination. This means the ability to think what it might be like to be in the shoes of a person different from oneself, to be an intelligent reader of that person's story, and to understand the emotions and wishes and desires that someone so placed might have. The narrative imagination is not uncritical, for we always bring ourselves and our own judgments to the encounter with another; and when we identify with a character in a novel, or with a distant person whose life story we imagine, we inevitably will not merely identify; we will also judge that story in the light of our own goals and aspirations. But the first step of understanding the world from the point of view of the other is essential to any responsible act of judgment, since we do not know what we are judging until we see the meaning of an action as the person intends it, the meaning of a speech as it expresses something of importance in the context of that person's history and social world. The third ability our students should attain is the ability to decipher such meanings through the use of the imagination. . . .

Our campuses educate our citizens. Becoming an educated citizen means learning a lot of facts and mastering techniques of reasoning. But it means something more. It means learning how to be a human being capable of love and imagination. We may continue to produce narrow citizens who have difficulty understanding people different from themselves, whose imaginations rarely venture beyond their local setting. It is all too easy for the moral imagination to become narrow in this way. Think of Charles Dickens' image of bad citizenship in *A Christmas Carol,* in his portrait of the ghost of Jacob Marley, who visits Scrooge to warn him of the dangers of a blunted imagination. Marley's ghost drags through all eternity a chain made of cash boxes, because in life his imagination never ventured outside the walls of his successful business to encounter the lives of the men and women around him, men and women of different social class and background. We produce all too many citizens who are like Marley's ghost, and like Scrooge before he walked out to see what the world around him contained. But we have the opportunity to do better, and now we are beginning to seize that opportunity. That is not "political correctness"; that is the cultivation of humanity.

STUDY QUESTIONS

1. What does Nussbaum mean by "cultivating humanity"?
2. How important to cultivating humanity is the study of foreign language?
3. Can studying certain subjects make more likely the possession of certain attitudes?
4. Is knowledge of certain non-Western cultures more important than knowledge of other non-Western cultures?

Letter from a Birmingham Jail

MARTIN LUTHER KING, JR.

A democracy may pass an unjust law. If citizens of that democracy believe the law is unjust, are they entitled to violate it? Doing so would not be in accord with the principle of majority rule, which is the procedure by which a democracy is supposed to function. But to act in accord with an unjust law would be to act unjustly. Can we find a satisfactory way out of this dilemma?

In 1963 Dr. Martin Luther King, Jr., was imprisoned in Birmingham, Alabama, for participating in a civil rights demonstration. While in jail he writes a letter justifying his actions. He explains that because he believes that the laws that enforced racial segregation are unjust, he refuses to act as the government required but willingly accepts the legal punishment for his actions, thus indicating his respect for democratic procedure. He insists that such civil disobedience be nonviolent, that all laws except the unjust ones be obeyed, and that breaking of the law be resorted to only when fundamental moral principles were at stake.

In 1964 he was awarded the Nobel Peace Prize. In 1968 he was assassinated.

....

My dear Fellow Clergymen,

While confined here in the Birmingham city jail, I came across your recent statement calling our present activities "unwise and untimely." Seldom, if ever, do I pause to answer criticism of my work and ideas. If I sought to answer all of the criticisms that cross my desk, my secretaries would be engaged in little else in the course of the day, and I would have no time for constructive work. But since I feel that you are men of genuine good will and your criticisms are sincerely set forth, I would like to answer your statement in what I hope will be patient and reasonable terms.

I think I should give the reason for my being in Birmingham, since you have been influenced by the argument of "outsiders coming in." I have the honor of serving as president of the Southern Christian Leadership Conference, an organization operating in every southern state, with headquarters in Atlanta, Georgia. We have some eighty-five affiliate organizations all across the South—one being the Alabama Christian Movement for Human Rights. Whenever necessary and possible we share staff, educational and financial resources with our affiliates.

Several months ago our local affiliate here in Birmingham invited us to be on call to engage in a nonviolent direct-action program if such were deemed necessary. We readily consented and when the hour came we lived up to our promises. So I am here, along with several members of my staff, because we were invited here. I am here because I have basic organizational ties here.

Beyond this, I am in Birmingham because injustice is here. Just as the eighth century prophets left their little villages and carried their "thus saith the Lord" far beyond the boundaries of their hometowns; and just as the Apostle Paul left his little village of Tarsus and carried the gospel of Jesus Christ to practically every hamlet and city of the Graeco-Roman world, I too am compelled to carry the gospel of freedom beyond my particular hometown. Like Paul, I must constantly respond to the Macedonian call for aid.

Moreover, I am cognizant of the interrelatedness of all communities and states. I cannot sit idly by in Atlanta and not be concerned about what happens in Birmingham. Injustice anywhere is a threat to justice anywhere. We are caught in an inescapable network of mutuality, tied in a single garment of destiny. Whatever affects one directly affects all indirectly. Never again can we afford to live with the narrow, provincial "outside agitator" idea. Anyone who lives in the United States can never be considered an outsider anywhere in this country.

You deplore the demonstrations that are presently taking place in Birmingham. But I am sorry that your statement did not express a similar concern for the conditions that brought the demonstrations into being. I am sure that each of you would want to go beyond the superficial social analyst who looks merely at effects, and does not grapple with underlying causes. I would not hesitate to say that it is unfortunate that so-called demonstrations are taking place in Birmingham at this time, but I would say in more emphatic terms that it is even more unfortunate that the white power structure of this city left the Negro community with no other alternative.

In any nonviolent campaign there are four basic steps: (1) collection of the facts to determine whether injustices are alive, (2) negotiation, (3) self-purification, and (4) direct action. We have gone through all of these steps in Birmingham. There can be no gainsaying of the fact that racial injustice engulfs this community.

Birmingham is probably the most thoroughly segregated city in the United States. Its ugly record of police brutality is known in every section of this country. Its unjust treatment of Negroes in the courts is a notorious reality. There have been more unsolved bombings of Negro homes and churches in Birmingham than any city in this nation. These are the hard, brutal and unbelievable facts. On the basis of these conditions, Negro leaders sought to negotiate with the city fathers. But the political leaders consistently refused to engage in good faith negotiation.

Then came the opportunity last September to talk with some of the leaders of the economic community. In these negotiating sessions certain promises were made by the merchants—such as the promise to remove the humiliating racial signs from the stores. On the basis of these promises, Rev. Shuttlesworth and the leaders of the Alabama Christian Movement for Human Rights agreed to call a moratorium on any type of demonstrations. As the weeks and months unfolded, we realized that we were the victims of a broken promise. The signs remained. Like so many experiences of the past, we were confronted with blasted hopes, and the dark shadow of a deep disappointment settled upon us. So we had no alternative except that of preparing for direct action, whereby we would present our very bodies as a means of laying our case before the conscience of the local and national community. We were not unmindful of the difficulties involved. So we decided to go through a process of self-purification. We started having workshops on nonviolence and repeatedly asked ourselves the questions, "Are you able to accept blows without retaliating?" "Are you able to endure the ordeals of jail?" We decided to set our direct-action program around the Easter season, realizing that with the exception of Christmas, this was the largest shopping period of the year. Knowing that a strong economic withdrawal program would be the by-product of direct action, we felt that this was the best time to bring pressure on the merchants for the needed changes. Then it occurred to us that the March election was ahead and so we speedily decided to postpone action until after election day. When we discovered that Mr. Connor was in the run-off, we decided again to postpone action so that the demonstrations could not be used to cloud the issues. At this time we agreed to begin our nonviolent witness the day after the run-off.

This reveals that we did not move irresponsibly into direct action. We too wanted to see Mr. Connor defeated; so we went through postponement after postponement to aid in this community need. After this we felt that direct action could be delayed no longer.

You may well ask, "Why direct action? Why sit-ins, marches, etc.? Isn't negotiation a better path?" You are exactly right in your call for negotiation. Indeed, this is the purpose of direct action. Nonviolent direct action seeks to create such a crisis and establish such creative tension that a community that has constantly refused to negotiate is forced to confront the issue. It seeks so to dramatize the issue that it can no longer be ignored. I just referred to the creation of tension as a part of the work of the nonviolent resister. This may sound rather shocking. But I must confess that I am not afraid of the word tension. I have earnestly worked and preached against violent tension, but there is a type of constructive nonviolent tension that is necessary for growth. Just as Socrates felt that it was necessary to create a tension in the mind so that individuals could rise from the bondage of myths and half-truths to the unfettered realm of creative analysis and objective appraisal, we must see the need of having nonviolent gadflies to create the kind of tension in society that will help men to rise from the dark depths of prejudice and racism to the majestic heights of understanding and brotherhood. So the purpose of the direct action is to create a situation so crisis-packed that it will inevitably open the door to negotiation. We, therefore, concur with you in your call for negotiation. Too long has our beloved Southland been bogged down in the tragic attempt to live in monologue rather than dialogue.

One of the basic points in your statement is that our acts are untimely. Some have asked, "Why didn't you give the new administration time to act?" The only answer that I can give to this inquiry is that the new administration must be prod-ded about as much as the outgoing one before it acts. We will be sadly mistaken if we feel that the election of Mr. Boutwell will bring the millennium to Birmingham. While Mr. Boutwell is much more articulate and gentle than Mr. Connor, they are both segregationists, dedicated to the task of maintaining the status quo. The hope I see in Mr. Boutwell is that he will be reasonable enough to see the futility of massive resistance to desegregation. But he will not see this without pressure from the devotees of civil rights. My friends, I must say to you that we have not made a single gain in civil rights without determined legal and nonviolent pressure. His-tory is the long and tragic story of the fact that privileged groups seldom give up their privileges voluntarily. Individuals may see the moral light and voluntarily give up their unjust posture; but as Reinhold Niebuhr has reminded us, groups are more immoral than individuals.

We know through painful experience that freedom is never voluntarily given by the oppressor; it must be demanded by the oppressed. Frankly, I have never yet engaged in a direct action movement that was "well-timed," according to the time-table of those who have not suffered unduly from the disease of segregation. For years now I have heard the words "Wait!" It rings in the ear of every Negro with a piercing familiarity. This "Wait" has almost always meant "Never." It has been a tranquilizing thalidomide, relieving the emotional stress for a moment, only to give birth to an ill-formed infant of frustration. We must come to see with the distin-guished jurist of yesterday that "justice too long delayed is justice denied." We have waited for more than 340 years for our constitutional and God-given rights. The nations of Asia and Africa are moving with jet-like speed toward the goal of politi-cal independence, and we still creep at horse and buggy pace toward the gaining of a cup of coffee at the lunch counter. I guess it is easy for those who have never felt the stinging darts of segregation to say, "Wait." But when you have seen vicious mobs lynch your mothers and fathers at will and drown your sisters and brothers at whim; when you have seen hatefilled policemen curse, kick, brutalize and even kill your black brothers and sisters with impunity; when you see the vast majority of your twenty million Negro brothers smothering in an airtight cage of poverty in the midst of an affluent society; when you suddenly find your tongue twisted and your speech stammering as you seek to explain to your six-year-old daughter why she can't go to the public amusement park that has just been advertised on television, and see tears welling up in her little eyes when she is told that Funtown is closed to colored children, and see the depressing clouds of inferiority begin to form in her little mental sky, and see her begin to distort her little personality by unconsciously developing a bitterness toward white people; when you have to concoct an answer for a five-year-old son asking in agonizing pathos: "Daddy, why do white people treat colored people so mean?"; when you take a crosscountry drive and find it necessary to sleep night after night in the uncomfortable corners of your automobile because no motel will accept you; when you are humiliated day in and day out by nagging signs reading "white" and "colored"; when your first name becomes "nigger" and your middle name becomes "boy" (however old you are) and your last name becomes "John," and when your wife and mother are never given the respected title "Mrs."; when you are harried by day and haunted by night by the fact that you are a Negro, living constantly at tiptoe stance never quite knowing what to expect next, and plagued with inner fears and outer resentments; when you are forever fighting a degenerating sense of "nobodiness"; then you will understand why we find it difficult to wait. There comes a time when the cup of endurance runs over, and men are no longer willing to be plunged into an abyss of injustice where they experience the blackness of corroding despair. I hope, sirs, you can understand our legitimate and unavoidable impatience.

You express a great deal of anxiety over our willingness to break laws. This is certainly a legitimate concern. Since we so diligently urge people to obey the Supreme Court's decision of 1954 outlawing segregation in the public schools, it is rather strange and paradoxical to find us consciously breaking laws. One may well ask, "How can you advocate breaking some laws and obeying others?" The answer is found in the fact that there are two types of laws: there are *just* and there are *unjust* laws. I would agree with Saint Augustine that "An unjust law is no law at all."

Now what is the difference between the two? How does one determine when a law is just or unjust? A just law is a man-made code that squares with the moral law or the law of God. An unjust law is a code that is out of harmony with the moral law. To put it in the terms of Saint Thomas Aquinas, an unjust law is a human law that is not rooted in eternal and natural law. Any law that uplifts human personality is just. Any law that degrades human personality is unjust. All segregation statutes are unjust because segregation distorts the soul and damages the personality. It gives the segregator a false sense of superiority, and the segregated a false sense of inferiority. To use the words of Martin Buber, the great Jewish philosopher, segregation substitutes an "I-it" relationship for the "I-thou" relationship, and ends up relegating persons to the status of things. So segregation is not only politically, economically and sociologically unsound, but it is morally wrong and sinful. Paul Tillich has said that sin is separation. Isn't segregation an existential expression of man's tragic separation, an expression of his awful estrangement, his terrible sinfulness? So I can urge men to disobey segregation ordinances because they are morally wrong.

Let us turn to a more concrete example of just and unjust laws. An unjust law is a code that a majority inflicts on a minority that is not binding on itself. This is difference made legal. On the other hand a just law is a code that a majority compels a minority to follow that it is willing to follow itself. This is sameness made legal.

Let me give another explanation. An unjust law is a code inflicted upon a minority which that minority had no part in enacting or creating because they did not have the unhampered right to vote. Who can say that the legislature of Alabama which set up the segregation laws was democratically elected? Throughout the state of Alabama all types of conniving methods are used to prevent Negroes from becoming registered voters and there are some counties without a single Negro registered to vote despite the fact that the Negro constitutes a majority of the population. Can any law set up in such a state be considered democratically structured?

These are just a few examples of unjust and just laws. There are some instances when a law is just on its face and unjust in its application. For instance, I was arrested Friday on a charge of parading without permit. Now there is nothing wrong with an ordinance which requires a permit for a parade, but when the ordinance is used to preserve segregation and to deny citizens the First Amendment privilege of peaceful assembly and peaceful protest, then it becomes unjust.

I hope you can see the distinction I am trying to point out. In no sense do I advocate evading or defying the law as the rabid segregationist would do. This would lead to anarchy. One who breaks an unjust law must do it *openly, lovingly* (not hatefully as the white mothers did in New Orleans when they were seen on television screaming, "nigger, nigger, nigger"), and with a willingness to accept the penalty. I submit that an individual who breaks law that conscience tells him is unjust, and willingly accepts the penalty by staying in jail to arouse the conscience of the community over its injustice, is in reality expressing the very highest respect for law.

Of course, there is nothing new about this kind of civil disobedience. It was seen sublimely in the refusal of Shadrach, Meshach and Abednego to obey the laws of Nebuchadnezzar because a higher moral law was involved. It was practiced superbly by the early Christians who were willing to face hungry lions and the excruciating pain of chopping blocks, before submitting to certain unjust laws of the Roman Empire. To a degree academic freedom is a reality today because Socrates practiced civil disobedience.

We can never forget that everything Hitler did in Germany was "legal" and everything the Hungarian freedom fighters did in Hungary was "illegal." It was "illegal" to aid and comfort a Jew in Hitler's Germany. But I am sure that if I had lived in Germany during that time I would have aided and comforted my Jewish brothers even though it was illegal. If I lived in a Communist country today where certain principles dear to the Christian faith are suppressed, I believe I would openly advocate disobeying these anti-religious laws. I must make two honest confessions to you, my Christian and Jewish brothers. First, I must confess that over the last few years I have been gravely disappointed with the white moderate. I have almost reached the regrettable conclusion that the Negro's great stumbling block in the stride toward freedom is not the White Citizen's Counciler or the Ku Klux Klanner, but the white moderate who is more devoted to "order" than to justice; who prefers a negative peace which is the absence of tension to a positive peace which is the presence of justice; who constantly says, "I agree with you in the goal you seek, but I can't agree with your methods of direct action"; who paternalistically feels that he can set the timetable for another man's freedom; who lives by the myth of time and who constantly advised the Negro to wait until a "more convenient season." Shallow understanding from people of good will is more frustrating than absolute misunderstanding from people of ill will. Lukewarm acceptance is much more bewildering than outright rejection.

I had hoped that the white moderate would understand that law and order exist for the purpose of establishing justice, and that when they fail to do this they become dangerously structured dams that block the flow of social progress. I had hoped that the white moderate would understand that the present tension of the South is merely a necessary phase of the transition from an obnoxious negative peace, where the Negro passively accepted his unjust plight, to a substance-filled positive peace, where all men will respect the dignity and worth of human personality. Actually, we who engage in nonviolent direct action are not the creators of tension. We merely bring to the surface the hidden tension that is already alive. We bring it out in the open where it can be seen and dealt with. Like a boil that can never be cured as long as it is covered up but must be opened with all its pus-flowing ugliness to the natural medicines of air and light, injustice must likewise be exposed, with all of the tension its exposing creates, to the light of human conscience and the air of national opinion before it can be cured.

In your statement you asserted that our actions, even though peaceful, must be condemned because they precipitate violence. But can this assertion be logically made? Isn't this like condemning the robbed man because his possession of money precipitated the evil act of robbery? Isn't this like condemning Socrates because his unswerving commitment to truth and his philosophical delvings precipitated the misguided popular mind to make him drink the hemlock? Isn't this like condemning Jesus because His unique God-consciousness and never-ceasing devotion to his will precipitated the evil act of crucifixion? We must come to see, as federal courts have consistently affirmed, that it is immoral to urge an individual to withdraw his efforts to gain his basic constitutional rights because the quest precipitates violence. Society must protect the robbed and punish the robber.

I had also hoped that the white moderate would reject the myth of time. I received a letter this morning from a white brother in Texas which said: "All Christians know that the colored people will receive equal rights eventually, but it is possible that you are in too great of a religious hurry. It has taken Christianity almost two thousand years to accomplish what it has. The teachings of Christ take time to come to earth." All that is said here grows out of a tragic misconception of time. It is the strangely irrational notion that there is something in the very flow of time that will inevitably cure all ills. Actually time is neutral. It can be used either destructively or constructively. I am coming to feel that the people of ill will have used time much more effectively than the people of good will. We will have to repent in this generation not merely for the vitriolic words and actions of the bad people, but for the appalling silence of the good people. We must come to see that human progress never rolls in on wheels of inevitability. It comes through the tireless efforts and persistent work of men willing to be co-workers with God, and without this hard work time itself becomes an ally of the forces of social stagnation. We must use time creatively, and forever realize that the time is always ripe to do right. Now is the time to make real the promise of democracy, and transform our pending national elegy into a creative psalm of brotherhood. Now is the time to lift our national policy from the quicksand of racial injustice to the solid rock of human dignity.

You spoke of our activity in Birmingham as extreme. At first I was rather disappointed that fellow clergymen would see my nonviolent efforts as those of the extremist. I started thinking about the fact that I stand in the middle of two opposing forces in the Negro community. One is a force of complacency made up of Negroes who, as a result of long years of oppression, have been so completely drained of self-respect and a sense of "somebodiness" that they have adjusted to segregation, and, of a few Negroes in the middle class who, because of a degree of academic and economic security, and because at points they profit by segregation, have unconsciously become insensitive to the problems of the masses. The other force is one of bitterness and hatred, and comes perilously close to advocating violence. It is expressed in the various black nationalist groups that are springing up over the nation, the largest and best known being Elijah Muhammad's Muslim movement. This movement is nourished by the contemporary frustration over the continued existence of racial discrimination. It is made up of people who have lost faith in America, who have absolutely repudiated Christianity, and who have concluded that the white man is an incurable "devil." I have tried to stand between these two forces, saying that we need not follow the "donothingism" of the complacent or the hatred and despair of the black nationalist. There is the more excellent way of love and nonviolent protest. I'm grateful to God that, through the Negro church, the dimension of nonviolence entered our struggle. If this philosophy had not emerged, I am convinced that by now many streets of the South would be flowing with floods of blood. And I am further convinced that if our white brothers dismiss as "rabble-rousers" and "outside agitators" those of us who are working through the channels of nonviolent direct action and refuse to support our nonviolent efforts, millions of Negroes, out of frustration and despair, will seek solace and security in black nationalist ideologies, a development that will lead inevitably to a frightening racial nightmare.

Oppressed people cannot remain oppressed forever. The urge for freedom will eventually come. This is what happened to the American Negro. Something within has reminded him of his birthright of freedom; something without has reminded him that he can gain it. Consciously and unconsciously, he has been swept in by what the Germans call the *Zeitgeist,* and with his black brothers of Africa, and his brown and yellow brothers of Asia, South America and the Caribbean, he is moving with a sense of cosmic urgency toward the promised land of racial justice. Recognizing this vital urge that has engulfed the Negro community, one should readily understand public demonstrations. The Negro has many pent-up resentments and latent frustrations. He has to get them out. So let him march sometime; let him have his prayer pilgrimages to the city hall; understand why he must have sit-ins and freedom rides. If his repressed emotions do not come out in these nonviolent ways, they will come out in ominous expressions of violence. This is not a threat; it is a fact of history. So I have not said to my people "get rid of your discontent." But I have tried to say that this normal and healthy discontent can be channelized through the creative outlet of nonviolent direct action. Now this approach is being dismissed as extremist. I must admit that I was initially disappointed in being so categorized.

But as I continued to think about the matter I gradually gained a bit of satisfaction from being considered an extremist. Was not Jesus an extremist in love— "Love your enemies, bless them that curse you, pray for them that despitefully use you." Was not Amos an extremist for justice—"Let justice roll down like waters and righteousness like a mighty stream." Was not Paul an extremist for the gospel of Jesus Christ—"I bear in my body the marks of the Lord Jesus." Was not Martin Luther an extremist—"Here I stand; I can do none other so help me God." Was not John Bunyan an extremist—"I will stay in jail to the end of my days before I make a butchery of my conscience." Was not Abraham Lincoln an extremist— "This nation cannot survive half slave and half free." Was not Thomas Jefferson an extremist—"We hold these truths to be self-evident, that all men are created equal." So the question is not whether we will be extremist but what kind of extremist will we be. Will we be extremists for hate or will we be extremists for love? Will we be extremists for the preservation of injustice—or will we be extremists for the cause of justice? In that dramatic scene on Calvary's hill, three men were crucified. We must not forget that all three were crucified for the same crime—the crime of extremism. Two were extremists for immorality, and thusly fell below their environment. The other, Jesus Christ, was an extremist for love, truth and goodness, and thereby rose above his environment. So, after all, maybe the South, the nation and the world are in dire need of creative extremists.

I had hoped that the white moderate would see this. Maybe I was too optimistic. Maybe I expected too much. I guess I should have realized that few members of a race that has oppressed another race can understand or appreciate the deep groans and passionate yearnings of those that have been oppressed and still fewer have the vision to see that injustice must be rooted out by strong, persistent and determined action. I am thankful, however, that some of our white brothers have grasped the meaning of this social revolution and committed themselves to it. They are still all too small in quantity, but they are big in quality. Some like Ralph McGill, Lillian Smith, Harry Golden and James Dabbs have written about our struggle in eloquent, prophetic and understanding terms. Others have marched with us down nameless streets of the South. They have languished in filthy roach-infested jails, suffering the abuse and brutality of angry policemen who see them as "dirty nigger-lovers." They, unlike so many of their moderate brothers and sisters, have recognized the urgency of the moment and sensed the need for powerful "action" antidotes to combat the disease of segregation.

Let me rush on to mention my other disappointment. I have been so greatly disappointed with the white church and its leadership. Of course, there are some notable exceptions. I am not unmindful of the fact that each of you has taken some significant stands on this issue. I commend you, Rev. Stallings, for your Christian stance on this past Sunday, in welcoming Negroes to your worship service on a non-segregated basis. I commend the Catholic leaders of this state for integrating Springhill College several years ago.

But despite these notable exceptions, I must honestly reiterate that I have been disappointed with the church. I do not say that as one of the negative critics who can always find something wrong with the church. I say it as a minister of the gospel, who loves the church; who was nurtured in its bosom; who has been sustained by its spiritual blessings and who will remain true to it as long as the cord of life shall lengthen.

I had the strange feeling when I was suddenly catapulted into the leadership of the bus protest in Montgomery several years ago that we would have the support of the white church. I felt that the white ministers, priests and rabbis of the South would be some of our strongest allies. Instead, some have been outright opponents, refusing to understand the freedom movement and misrepresenting its leaders; all too many others have been more cautious than courageous and have remained silent behind the anesthetizing security of the stained-glass windows.

In spite of my shattered dreams of the past, I came to Birmingham with the hope that the white religious leadership of this community would see the justice of our cause, and with deep moral concern, serve as the channel through which our just grievances would get to the power structure. I had hoped that each of you would understand. But again I have been disappointed. I have heard numerous religious leaders of the South call upon their worshippers to comply with a desegregation decision because it is the *law*, but I have longed to hear white ministers say, "Follow this decree because integration is morally *right* and the Negro is your brother." In the midst of blatant injustices inflicted upon the Negro, I have watched white churches stand on the sideline and merely mouth pious irrelevancies and sanctimonious trivialities. In the midst of a mighty struggle to rid our nation of racial and economic injustice, I have heard so many ministers say, "Those are social issues with which the gospel has no real concern," and I have watched so many churches commit themselves to a completely other-worldly religion which made a strange distinction between body and soul, the sacred and the secular.

So here we are moving toward the exit of the twentieth century with a religious community largely adjusted to the status quo, standing as a taillight behind other community agencies rather than a headlight leading men to higher levels of justice.

I have traveled the length and breadth of Alabama, Mississippi and all the other southern states. On sweltering summer days and crisp autumn mornings I have looked at her beautiful churches with their lofty spires pointing heavenward. I have beheld the impressive outlay of her massive religious education buildings. Over and over again I have found myself asking: "What kind of people worship here? Who is their God? Where were their voices when the lips of Governor Barnett dripped with words of interposition and nullification? Where were they when Governor Wallace gave the clarion call for defiance and hatred? Where were their voices of support when tired, bruised and weary Negro men and women decided to rise from the dark dungeons of complacency to the bright hills of creative protest?"

Yes, these questions are still in my mind. In deep disappointment, I have wept over the laxity of the church. But be assured that my tears have been tears of love. There can be no deep disappointment where there is not deep love. Yes, I love the church; I love her sacred walls. How could I do otherwise? I am in a rather unique position of being the son, the grandson and the great-grandson of preachers. Yes, I see the church as the body of Christ. But, oh! How we have blemished and scarred that body through social neglect and fear of being nonconformists.

There was a time when the church was very powerful. It was during that period when the early Christians rejoiced when they were deemed worthy to suffer for what they believed. In those days the church was not merely a thermometer that recorded the ideas and principles of popular opinion; it was a thermostat that transformed the mores of society. Wherever the early Christians entered a town the power structure got disturbed and immediately sought to convict them for being "disturbers of the peace" and "outside agitators." But they went on with the conviction that they were "a colony of heaven," and had to obey God rather than man. They were small in number but big in commitment. They were too God-intoxicated to be "astronomically intimidated." They brought an end to such ancient evils as infanticide and gladiatorial contest.

Things are different now. The contemporary church is often a weak, ineffectual voice with an uncertain sound. It is so often the arch-supporter of the status quo. Far from being disturbed by the presence of the church, the power structure of the average community is consoled by the church's silent and often vocal sanction of things as they are.

But the judgment of God is upon the church as never before. If the church of today does not recapture the sacrificial spirit of the early church, it will lose its authentic ring, forfeit the loyalty of millions, and be dismissed as an irrelevant social club with no meaning for the twentieth century. I am meeting young people every day whose disappointment with the church has risen to outright disgust.

Maybe again, I have been too optimistic. Is organized religion too inextricably bound to the status quo to save our nation and the world? Maybe I must turn my faith to the inner spiritual church, the church within the church, as the true *ecclesia* and the hope of the world. But again I am thankful to God that some noble souls from the ranks of organized religion have broken loose from the paralyzing chains of conformity and joined us as active partners in the struggle for freedom. They have left their secure congregations and walked the streets of Albany, Georgia, with us. They have gone through the highways of the South on tortuous rides for freedom. Yes, they have gone to jail with us. Some have been kicked out of their churches, and lost support of their bishops and fellow ministers. But they have gone with the faith that right defeated is stronger than evil triumphant. These men have been the leaven in the lump of the race. Their witness has been the spiritual salt that has preserved the true meaning of the gospel in these troubled times. They have carved a tunnel of hope through the dark mountain of disappointment.

I hope the church as a whole will meet the challenge of this decisive hour. But even if the church does not come to the aid of justice, I have no despair about the future. I have no fear about the outcome of our struggle in Birmingham, even if our motives are presently misunderstood. We will reach the goal of freedom in Birmingham and all over the nation, because the goal of America is freedom. Abused and scorned though we may be, our destiny is tied up with the destiny of America. Before the Pilgrims landed at Plymouth we were here. Before the pen of Jefferson etched across the pages of history the majestic words of the Declaration of Independence, we were here. For more than two centuries our foreparents labored in this country without wages; they made cotton king; and they built the homes of their masters in the midst of brutal injustice and shameful humiliation—and yet out of a bottomless vitality they continued to thrive and develop. If the inexpressible cruelties of slavery could not stop us, the opposition we now face will surely fail. We will win our freedom because the sacred heritage of our nation and the eternal will of God are embodied in our echoing demands.

I must close now. But before closing I am impelled to mention one other point in your statement that troubled me profoundly. You warmly commended the Birmingham police force for keeping "order" and "preventing violence." I don't believe you would have so warmly commended the police force if you had seen its angry violent dogs literally biting six unarmed, nonviolent Negroes. I don't believe you would so quickly commend the policemen if you would observe their ugly and inhuman treatment of Negroes here in the city jail; if you would watch them push and curse old Negro women and young Negro girls; if you would see them slap and kick old Negro men and young boys; if you will observe them, as they did on two occasions, refuse to give us food because we wanted to sing our grace together. I'm sorry that I can't join you in your praise for the police department.

It is true that they have been rather disciplined in their public handling of the demonstrators. In this sense they have been rather publicly "nonviolent." But for what purpose? To preserve the evil system of segregation. Over the last few years I have consistently preached that nonviolence demands that the means we use must be as pure as the ends we seek. So I have tried to make it clear that it is wrong to use immoral means to attain moral ends. But now I must affirm that it is just as wrong, or even more so, to use moral means to preserve immoral ends. Maybe Mr. Connor and his policemen have been rather publicly nonviolent, as Chief Pritchett was in Albany, Georgia, but they have used the moral means of nonviolence to maintain the immoral end of flagrant racial injustice. T. S. Eliot has said that there is no greater treason than to do the right deed for the wrong reason.

I wish you had commended the Negro sit-inners and demonstrators of Birmingham for their sublime courage, their willingness to suffer and their amazing discipline in the midst of the most inhuman provocation. One day the South will recognize its real heroes. They will be the James Merediths, courageously and with a majestic sense of purpose facing jeering and hostile mobs and the agonizing loneliness that characterizes the life of the pioneer. They will be old, oppressed, battered Negro women, symbolized in a seventy-two-year-old woman of Montgomery, Alabama, who rose up with a sense of dignity and with her people decided not to ride the segregated buses, and responded to one who inquired about her tiredness with ungrammatical profundity: "My feet is tired, but my soul is rested." They will be the young high school and college students, young ministers of the gospel and a host of their elders courageously and nonviolently sitting-in at lunch counters and willingly going to jail for conscience's sake. One day the South will know that when these disinherited children of God sat down at lunch counters they were in reality standing up for the best in the American dream and the most sacred values in our Judeo-Christian heritage, and thusly, carrying our whole nation back to those great walls of democracy which were dug deep by the Founding Fathers in the formulation of the Constitution and the Declaration of Independence.

Never before have I written a letter this long (or should I say a book?). I'm afraid that it is much too long to take your precious time. I can assure you that it would have been much shorter if I had been writing from a comfortable desk, but what else is there to do when you are alone for days in the dull monotony of a narrow jail cell other than write long letters, think strange thoughts, and pray long prayers?

If I have said anything in this letter that is an overstatement of the truth and is indicative of an unreasonable impatience, I beg you to forgive me. If I have said anything in this letter that is an understatement of the truth and is indicative of my having a patience that makes me patient with anything less than brotherhood, I beg God to forgive me.

I hope this letter finds you strong in the faith. I also hope that circumstances will soon make it possible for me to meet each of you, not as an integrationist or a civil rights leader, but as a fellow clergyman and a Christian brother. Let us all hope that the dark clouds of racial prejudice will soon pass away and the deep fog of misunderstanding will be lifted from our fear-drenched communities and in some not too distant tomorrow the radiant stars of love and brotherhood will shine over our great nation with all of their scintillating beauty.

Yours for the cause of Peace and Brotherhood, Martin Luther King, Jr.

STUDY QUESTIONS

1. What is civil disobedience?
2. How does civil disobedience differ from mere lawbreaking?
3. Is every unjust law an appropriate target for civil disobedience?
4. What is the connection, if any, between Dr. King's religious commitments and his political actions?

Crito

PLATO

The *Crito*, probably written about the time of the *Defence of Socrates*, relates a conversation Socrates has in prison while awaiting death. His lifelong friend Crito urges Socrates to run away, assuring him that his rescue can be arranged. Socrates refuses to try to escape, arguing that he is morally obligated to submit to the sentence of the Court, for he accepts its authority and does not wish to bring the system of laws into disrepute.

A much-discussed issue is whether the view Socrates adopts in the *Crito* coheres with the opinions he espouses in his *Defence*. As our translator, David Gallop, explains the apparent inconsistency:

> To some readers the positions adopted by Socrates in the two works have seemed utterly opposed. In the *Defence* he comes across as a champion of intellectual liberty, an individualist bravely defying the conservative Athenian establishment; whereas in the *Crito* he appears to be advocating the most abject submission of the citizen to state authority.

Gallop believes the supposed conflict is illusory, and many commentators agree. Yet they have not reached consensus as to how the reconciliation is to be achieved. I have a suggestion to offer but urge that you proceed now to the *Crito* and return here after finishing it.

The notes are the translator's. The Index of Names he prepared can be found at the end of the *Defence of Socrates* in Part 1.

In my view the key to recognizing the consistency of Socrates' position is found near the end of the dialogue, where a distinction is drawn, in essence, between unjust laws and unjust application of just laws. Socrates believes his fellow citizens decided his case wrongly, but he accepts the fairness of the laws under which he was tried and convicted. If he believed the laws themselves were unfair, he would break them. As he says in his *Defence*, were a law to be passed banning the study of philosophy, he would disobey it. But he will not evade his death sentence, for he "has been treated unjustly not by us Laws, but by human beings. . . ."

Whether you accept this analysis, you can see why the life of Socrates has so fascinated subsequent generations. He embodies the spirit of philosophical inquiry and the ideal of intellectual integrity.

SOCRATES: Why have you come at this hour, Crito? It's still very early, isn't it?

CRITO: Yes, very.

SOCRATES: About what time?

CRITO: Just before daybreak.

SOCRATES: I'm surprised the prison-warder was willing to answer the door.

CRITO: He knows me by now, Socrates, because I come and go here so often; and besides, I've done him a small favour.

SOCRATES: Have you just arrived, or have you been here for a while?

CRITO: For quite a while.

SOCRATES: Then why didn't you wake me up right away instead of sitting by me in silence?

CRITO: Well *of course* I didn't wake you, Socrates! I only wish I weren't so sleepless and wretched myself. I've been marvelling all this time as I saw how peacefully you were sleeping, and I deliberately kept from waking you, so that you could pass the time as peacefully as possible. I've often admired your disposition in the past, in fact all your life; but more than ever in your present plight, you bear it so easily and patiently.

SOCRATES: Well, Crito, it really would be tiresome for a man of my age to get upset if the time has come when he must end his life.

CRITO: And yet others of your age, Socrates, are overtaken by similar troubles, but their age brings them no relief from being upset at the fate which faces them.

SOCRATES: That's true. But tell me, why *have* you come so early?

CRITO: I bring painful news, Socrates—not painful for you, I suppose, but painful and hard for me and all your friends—and hardest of all for me to bear, I think.

SOCRATES: What news is that? Is it that the ship has come back from Delos,[1] the one on whose return I must die?

CRITO: Well no, it hasn't arrived yet, but I think it will get here today, judging from reports of people who've come from Sunium,[2] where they disembarked. That makes it obvious that it will get here today; and so tomorrow, Socrates, you will have to end your life.

SOCRATES: Well, may that be for the best, Crito. If it so please the gods, so be it. All the same, I don't think it will get here today.

CRITO: What makes you think that?

SOCRATES: I'll tell you. You see, I am to die on the day after the ship arrives, am I not?

CRITO: At least that's what the authorities say.

SOCRATES: Then I don't think it will get here on the day that is just dawning, but on the next one. I infer that from a certain dream I had in the night—a short time ago, so it may be just as well that you didn't wake me.

CRITO: And what was your dream?

SOCRATES: I dreamt that a lovely, handsome woman approached me, robed in white. She called me and said: "Socrates,

Thou shalt reach fertile Phthia upon the third day."[3]

CRITO: What a curious dream, Socrates.

SOCRATES: Yet its meaning is clear, I think, Crito.

CRITO: All too clear, it would seem. But please, Socrates, my dear friend, there is still time to take my advice, and make your escape—because if you die, I shall suffer more than one misfortune: not only shall I lose such a friend as I'll never find again, but it will look to many people, who hardly know you or me, as if I'd abandoned you—since I could have rescued you if I'd been willing to put up the money. And yet what could be more shameful than a reputation for valuing money more highly than friends? Most people won't believe that it was you who refused to leave this place yourself, despite our urging you to do so.

SOCRATES: But why should we care so much, my good Crito, about what most people believe? All the most capable people, whom we should take more seriously, will think the matter has been handled exactly as it has been.

CRITO: Yet surely, Socrates, you can see that one must heed popular opinion too. Your present plight shows by itself that the populace can inflict not the least of evils, but just about the worst, if someone has been slandered in their presence.

SOCRATES: Ah Crito, if only the populace *could* inflict the worst of evils! Then they would also be capable of providing the greatest of goods, and a fine thing that would be. But the fact is that they can do neither: they are unable to give anyone understanding or lack of it, no matter what they do.

CRITO: Well, if you say so. But tell me this, Socrates: can it be that you are worried for me and your other friends, in case the blackmailers[4] give us trouble, if you escape, for having smuggled you out of here? Are you worried that we might be forced to forfeit all our property as well, or pay heavy fines, or even incur some further penalty? If you're afraid of anything like that, put it out of your mind. In rescuing you we are surely justified in taking that risk, or even worse if need be. Come on, listen to me and do as I say.

SOCRATES: Yes, those risks do worry me, Crito—amongst many others.

CRITO: Then put those fears aside—because no great sum is needed to pay people who are willing to rescue you and get you out of here. Besides, you can surely see that those blackmailers are cheap, and it wouldn't take much to buy them off. My own means are available to you and would be ample, I'm sure. Then again, even if—out of concern on my behalf—you think you shouldn't be spending my money, there are visitors here who are ready to spend theirs. One of them, Simmias from Thebes, has actually brought enough money for this very purpose, while Cebes and quite a number of others are also prepared to contribute. So, as I say, you shouldn't hesitate to save yourself on account of those fears.

And don't let it trouble you, as you were saying in court, that you wouldn't know what to do with yourself if you went into exile. There will be people to welcome you anywhere else you may go: if you want to go to Thessaly,[5] I have friends there who will make much of you and give you safe refuge, so that no one from anywhere in Thessaly will trouble you.

Next, Socrates, I don't think that what you propose—giving yourself up, when you could be rescued—is even just. You are actually hastening to bring upon yourself just the sorts of thing which your enemies would hasten to bring upon you—indeed, they have done so—in their wish to destroy you.

What's more, I think you're betraying those sons of yours. You will be deserting them, if you go off when you could be raising and educating them: as far as you're concerned, they will fare as best they may. In all likelihood, they'll meet the sort of fate which usually befalls orphans once they've lost their parents. Surely, one should either not have children at all, or else see the toil and trouble of their upbringing and education through to the end; yet you seem to me to prefer the easiest path. One should rather choose the path that a good and resolute man would choose, particularly if one professes to cultivate goodness all one's life. Frankly, I'm ashamed for you and for us, your friends: it may appear that this whole predicament of yours has been handled with a certain feebleness on our part. What with the bringing of your case to court when that could have been avoided, the actual conduct of the trial, and now, to crown it all, this absurd outcome of the business, it may seem that the problem has eluded us through some fault or feebleness on our part—in that we failed to save you, and you failed to save yourself, when that was quite possible and feasible, if we had been any use at all.

Make sure, Socrates, that all this doesn't turn out badly, and a disgrace to you as well as us. Come now, form a plan—or rather, don't even plan, because the time for that is past, and only a single plan remains. Everything needs to be carried out during the coming night; and if we go on waiting around, it won't be possible or feasible any longer. Come on, Socrates, do all you can to take my advice, and do exactly what I say.

SOCRATES: My dear Crito, your zeal will be invaluable if it should have right on its side; but otherwise, the greater it is, the harder it makes matters. We must therefore consider whether or not the course you urge should be followed—because it is in my nature, not just now for the first time but always, to follow nothing within me but the principle which appears to me, upon reflection, to be best.

I cannot now reject the very principles that I previously adopted, just because this fate has overtaken me; rather, they appear to me much the same as ever, and I respect and honour the same ones that I did before. If we cannot find better ones to maintain in the present situation, you can be sure that I won't agree with you—not even if the power of the populace threatens us, like children, with more bogeymen than it does now, by visiting us with imprisonment, execution, or confiscation of property.

What, then, is the most reasonable way to consider the matter? Suppose we first take up the point you make about what people will think. Was it always an acceptable principle that one should pay heed to some opinions but not to others, or was it not? Or was it acceptable before I had to die, while now it is exposed as an idle assertion made for the sake of talk, when it is really childish nonsense? For my part, Crito, I'm eager to look into this together with you, to see whether the principle is to be viewed any differently, or in the same way, now that I'm in this position, and whether we should disregard or follow it.

As I recall, the following principle always used to be affirmed by people who thought they were talking sense: the principle, as I was just saying, that one should have a high regard for some opinions held by human beings, but not for others. Come now, Crito: don't you think that was a good principle? I ask because you are not, in all foreseeable likelihood, going to die tomorrow, and my present trouble shouldn't impair your judgement. Consider, then: don't you think it a good principle, that one shouldn't respect all human opinions, but only some and not others; or, again, that one shouldn't respect everyone's opinions, but those of some people, and not those of others? What do you say? Isn't that a good principle?

CRITO: It is.

SOCRATES: And one should respect the good ones, but not the bad ones?

CRITO: Yes.

SOCRATES: And good ones are those of people with understanding, whereas bad ones are those of people without it?

CRITO: Of course.

SOCRATES: Now then, once again, how were such points established? When a man is in training, and concentrating upon that, does he pay heed to the praise or censure or opinion of each and every man, or only to those of the individual who happens to be his doctor or trainer?

CRITO: Only to that individual's.

SOCRATES: Then he should fear the censures, and welcome the praises of that individual, but not those of most people.

CRITO: Obviously.

SOCRATES: So he must base his actions and exercises, his eating and drinking, upon the opinion of the individual, the expert supervisor, rather than upon everyone else's.

CRITO: True.

SOCRATES: Very well. If he disobeys that individual and disregards his opinion and his praises, but respects those of most people, who are ignorant, he'll suffer harm, won't he?

CRITO: Of course.

SOCRATES: And what is that harm? What does it affect? What element within the disobedient man?

CRITO: Obviously, it affects his body, because that's what it spoils.

SOCRATES: A good answer. And in other fields too, Crito—we needn't go through them all, but they surely include matters of just and unjust, honourable and dishonourable, good and bad, the subjects of our present deliberation—is it the opinion of most people that we should follow and fear, or is it that of the individual authority—assuming that some expert exists who should be respected and feared above all others? If we don't follow that person, won't we corrupt and impair the element which (as we agreed) is made better by what is just, but is spoilt by what is unjust? Or is there nothing in all that?

CRITO: I accept it myself, Socrates.

SOCRATES: Well now, if we spoil the part of us that is improved by what is healthy but corrupted by what is unhealthy, because it is not expert opinion that we are following, are our lives worth living once it has been corrupted? The part in question is, of course, the body, isn't it?

CRITO: Yes.

SOCRATES: And are our lives worth living with a poor or corrupted body?

CRITO: Definitely not.

SOCRATES: Well then, are they worth living if the element which is impaired by what is unjust and benefited by what is just has been corrupted? Or do we consider the element to which justice or injustice belongs, whichever part of us it is, to be of less value than the body?

CRITO: By no means.

SOCRATES: On the contrary, it is more precious?

CRITO: Far more.

SOCRATES: Then, my good friend, we shouldn't care all that much about what the populace will say of us, but about what the expert on matters of justice and injustice will say, the individual authority, or Truth. In the first place, then, your proposal that we should care about popular opinion regarding just, honourable, or good actions, and their opposites, is mistaken.

"Even so," someone might say, "the populace has the power to put us to death."

CRITO: *That's* certainly clear enough; one might say that, Socrates.

SOCRATES: You're right. But the principle we've rehearsed, my dear friend, still remains as true as it was before—for me at any rate. And now consider this further one, to see whether or not it still holds good for us. We should attach the highest value, shouldn't we, not to living, but to living well?

CRITO: Why yes, that still holds.

SOCRATES: And living well is the same as living honourably or justly? Does that still hold or not?

CRITO: Yes, it does.

SOCRATES: Then in the light of those admissions, we must ask the following question: is it just, or is it not, for me to try to get out of here, when Athenian authorities are unwilling to release me? Then, if it does seem just, let us attempt it; but if it doesn't, let us abandon the idea.

As for the questions you raise about expenses and reputation and bringing up children, I suspect they are the concerns of those who cheerfully put people to death, and would bring them back to life if they could, without any intelligence, namely, the populace. For us, however, because our principle so demands, there is no other question to ask except the one we just raised: shall we be acting justly—we who are rescued as well as the rescuers themselves—if we pay money and do favours to those who would get me out of here? Or shall we in truth be acting unjustly if we do all those things? And if it is clear that we shall be acting unjustly in taking that course, then the question whether we shall have to die through standing firm and holding our peace, or suffer in any other way, ought not to weigh with us in comparison with acting unjustly.

CRITO: I think that's finely *said*, Socrates; but do please consider what we should *do*.

SOCRATES: Let's examine that question together, dear friend; and if you have objections to anything I say, please raise them, and I'll listen to you—otherwise, good fellow, it's time to stop telling me, again and again, that I should leave here against the will of Athens. You see, I set great store upon persuading you as to my course of action, and not acting against your will. Come now, just consider whether you find the starting-point of our inquiry acceptable, and try to answer my questions according to your real beliefs.

CRITO: All right, I'll try.

SOCRATES: Do we maintain that people should on no account whatever do injustice willingly? Or may it be done in some circumstances but not in others? Is acting unjustly in no way good or honourable, as we frequently agreed in the past? Or have all those former agreements been jettisoned during these last few days? Can it be, Crito, that men of our age have long failed to notice, as we earnestly conversed with each other, that we ourselves were no better than children? Or is what we then used to say true above all else? Whether most people say so or not, and whether we must be treated more harshly or more leniently than at present, isn't it a fact, all the same, that acting unjustly is utterly bad and shameful for the agent? Yes or no?

CRITO: Yes.

SOCRATES: So one must not act unjustly at all.

CRITO: Absolutely not.

SOCRATES: Then, even if one is unjustly treated, one should not return injustice, as most people believe—given that one should act not unjustly at all.

CRITO: Apparently not.

SOCRATES: Well now, Crito, should one ever ill-treat anybody or not?

CRITO: Surely not, Socrates.

SOCRATES: And again, when one suffers ill-treatment, is it just to return it, as most people maintain, or isn't it?

CRITO: It is not just at all.

SOCRATES: Because there's no difference, I take it, between ill-treating people and treating them unjustly.

CRITO: Correct.

SOCRATES: Then one shouldn't return injustice or ill-treatment to any human being, no matter how one may be treated by that person. And in making those admissions, Crito, watch out that you're not agreeing to anything contrary to your real beliefs. I say that, because I realize that the belief is held by few people, and always will be. Those who hold it share no common counsel with those who don't; but each group is bound to regard the other with contempt when they observe one another's decisions. You too, therefore, should consider very carefully whether you share that belief with me, and whether we may begin our deliberations from the following premise: neither doing nor returning injustice is ever right, nor should one who is ill-treated defend himself by retaliation. Do you agree? Or do you dissent and not share my belief in that premise? I've long been of that opinion myself, and I still am now; but if you've formed any different view, say so, and explain it. If you stand by our former view, however, then listen to my next point.

CRITO: Well, I do stand by it and share that view, so go ahead.

SOCRATES: All right, I'll make my next point—or rather, ask a question. Should the things one agrees with someone else be done, provided they are just, or should one cheat?

CRITO: They should be done.

SOCRATES: Then consider what follows. If we leave this place without having persuaded our city, are we or are we not ill-treating certain people, indeed people whom we ought least of all to be ill-treating? And would we be abiding by the things we agreed, those things being just, or not?

CRITO: I can't answer your question, Socrates, because I don't understand it.

SOCRATES: Well, look at it this way. Suppose we were on the point of running away from here, or whatever else one should call it. Then the Laws, or the State of Athens, might come and confront us, and they might speak as follows:

"Please tell us, Socrates, what do you have in mind? With this action you are attempting, do you intend anything short of destroying us, the Laws and the city as a whole, to the best of your ability? Do you think that a city can still exist without being overturned, if the legal judgments rendered within it possess no force, but are nullified or invalidated by individuals?"

What shall we say, Crito, in answer to that and other such questions? Because somebody, particularly a legal advocate,[6] might say a great deal on behalf of the law that is being invalidated here, the one requiring that judgments, once rendered, shall have authority. Shall we tell them: "Yes, that is our intention, because the city was treating us unjustly, by not judging our case correctly"? Is that to be our answer, or what?

CRITO: Indeed it is, Socrates.

SOCRATES: And what if the Laws say: "And was that also part of the agreement between you and us, Socrates? Or did you agree to abide by whatever judgments the city rendered?"

Then, if we were surprised by their words, perhaps they might say: "Don't be surprised at what we are saying, Socrates, but answer us, seeing that you like to use question-and-answer. What complaint, pray, do you have against the city and ourselves, that you should now attempt to destroy us? In the first place, was it not we who gave you birth? Did your father not marry your mother and beget you under our auspices? So will you inform those of us here who regulate marriages whether you have any criticism of them as poorly framed?"

"No, I have none," I should say.

"Well then, what of the laws dealing with children's upbringing and education, under which you were educated yourself? Did those of us Laws who are in charge of that area not give proper direction, when they required your father to educate you in the arts and physical training?"[7]

"They did," I should say.

"Very good. In view of your birth, upbringing, and education, can you deny, first, that you belong to us as our offspring and slave, as your forebears also did? And if so, do you imagine that you are on equal terms with us in regard to what is just, and that whatever treatment we may accord to you, it is just for you to do the same thing back to us? You weren't on equal terms with your father, or your master (assuming you had one), making it just for you to return the treatment you received—answering back when you were scolded, or striking back when you were struck, or doing many other things of the same sort. Will you then have licence against your fatherland and its Laws, if we try to destroy you, in the belief that that is just? Will you try to destroy us in return, to the best of your ability? And will you claim that in doing so you are acting justly, you who are genuinely exercised about goodness? Or are you, in your wisdom, unaware that, in comparison with your mother and father and all your other forebears, your fatherland is more precious and venerable, more sacred and held in higher esteem among gods, as well as among human beings who have any sense; and that you should revere your fatherland, deferring to it and appeasing it when it is angry, more than your own father? You must either persuade it, or else do whatever it commands; and if it ordains that you must submit to certain treatment, then you must hold your peace and submit to it: whether that means being beaten or put in bonds, or whether it leads you into war to be wounded or killed, you must act accordingly, and that is what is just; you must neither give way nor retreat, nor leave your position; rather, in warfare, in court, and everywhere else, you must do whatever your city or fatherland commands, or else persuade it as to what is truly just; and if it is sinful to use violence against your mother or father, it is far more so to use it against your fatherland."

What shall we say to that, Crito? That the Laws are right or not?

CRITO: I think they are.

SOCRATES: "Consider then, Socrates," the Laws might go on, "whether the following is also true: in your present undertaking you are not proposing to treat us justly. We gave you birth, upbringing, and education, and a share in all the benefits we could provide for you along with all your fellow citizens. Nevertheless, we proclaim, by the formal granting of permission, that any Athenian who wishes, once he has been admitted to adult status,[8] and has observed the conduct of city business and ourselves, the Laws, may—if he is dissatisfied with us—go wherever he pleases and take his property. Not one of us Laws hinders or forbids that: whether any of you wishes to emigrate to a colony, or to go and live as an alien elsewhere, he may go wherever he pleases and keep his property, if we and the city fail to satisfy him.

"We do say, however, that if any of you remains here after he has observed the system by which we dispense justice and otherwise manage our city, then he has agreed with us by his conduct to obey whatever orders we give him. And thus we claim that anyone who fails to obey is guilty on three counts: he disobeys us as his parents; he disobeys those who nurtured him; and after agreeing to obey us he neither obeys nor persuades us if we are doing anything amiss, even though we offer him a choice, and do not harshly insist that he must do whatever we command. Instead, we give him two options: he must either persuade us or else do as we say; yet he does neither. Those are the charges, Socrates, to which we say you too will be liable if you carry out your intention; and among Athenians, you will be not the least liable, but one of the most."

And if I were to say, "How so?" perhaps they could fairly reproach me, observing that I am actually among those Athenians who have made that agreement with them most emphatically.

"Socrates," they would say, "we have every indication that you were content with us, as well as with our city, because you would never have stayed home here, more than is normal for all other Athenians, unless you were abnormally content. You never left our city for a festival—except once to go to the Isthmus[9]—nor did you go elsewhere for other purposes, apart from military service. You never travelled abroad, as other people do; nor were you eager for acquaintance with a different city or different laws: we and our city sufficed for you. Thus, you emphatically opted for us, and agreed to be a citizen on our terms. In particular, you fathered children in our city, which would suggest that you were content with it.

"Moreover, during your actual trial it was open to you, had you wished, to propose exile as your penalty; thus, what you are now attempting to do without the city's consent, you could then have done with it. On that occasion, you kept priding yourself that it would not trouble you if you had to die: you would choose death ahead of exile, so you said. Yet now you dishonour those words, and show no regard for us, the Laws, in your effort to destroy us. You are acting as the meanest slave would act, by trying to run away in spite of those compacts and agreements you made with us, whereby you agreed to be a citizen on our terms.

"First, then, answer us this question: are we right in claiming that you agreed, by your conduct if not verbally, that you would be a citizen on our terms? Or is that untrue?"

What shall we say in reply to that, Crito? Mustn't we agree?

CRITO: We must, Socrates.

SOCRATES: "Then what does your action amount to," they would say, "except breaking the compacts and agreements you made with us? By your own admission, you were not coerced or tricked into making them, or forced to reach a decision in a short time: you had seventy years in which it was open to you to leave if you were not happy with us, or if you thought those agreements unfair. Yet you preferred neither Lacedaemon nor Crete[10]— places you often say are well governed—nor any other Greek or foreign city: in fact, you went abroad less often than the lame and the blind or other cripples. Obviously, then, amongst Athenians you were exceptionally content with our city and with us, its Laws—because who would care for a city apart from its laws? Won't you, then, abide by your agreements now? Yes you will, if you listen to us, Socrates; and then at least you won't make yourself an object of derision by leaving the city.

"Just consider: if you break those agreements, and commit any of those offences, what good will you do yourself or those friends of yours? Your friends, pretty obviously, will risk being exiled themselves, as well as being disenfranchised or losing their property. As for you, first of all, if you go to one of the nearest cities, Thebes or Megara[11]—they are both well governed—you will arrive as an enemy of their political systems, Socrates: all who are concerned for their own cities will look askance at you, regarding you as a subverter of laws. You will also confirm your jurors in their judgment, making them think they decided your case correctly: any subverter of laws, presumably, might well be thought to be a corrupter of young, unthinking people.

"Will you, then, avoid the best-governed cities and the most respectable of men? And if so, will your life be worth living? Or will you associate with those people, and be shameless enough to converse with them? And what will you say to them, Socrates? The things you used to say here, that goodness and justice are most precious to mankind, along with institutions and laws? Don't you think that the predicament of Socrates will cut an ugly figure? Surely you must.

"Or will you take leave of those spots, and go to stay with those friends of Crito's up in Thessaly? That, of course, is a region of the utmost disorder and licence; so perhaps they would enjoy hearing from you about your comical escape from gaol, when you dressed up in some outfit, wore a leather jerkin or some other runaway's garb, and altered your appearance. Will no one observe that you, an old man with probably only a short time left to live, had the nerve to cling so greedily to life by violating the most important laws? Perhaps not, so long as you don't trouble anyone. Otherwise, Socrates, you will hear a great deal to your own discredit. You will live as every person's toady and lackey; and what will you be doing—apart from living it up in Thessaly, as if you had travelled all the way to Thessaly to have dinner? As for those principles of yours about justice and goodness in general—tell us, where will they be then?

"Well then, is it for your children's sake that you wish to live, in order to bring them up and give them an education? How so? Will you bring them up and educate them by taking them off to Thessaly and making foreigners of them, so that they may gain that advantage too? Or if, instead of that, they are brought up here, will they be better brought up and educated just because you are alive, if you are not with them? Yes, you may say, because those friends of yours will take care of them. Then will they take care of them if you travel to Thessaly, but not take care of them if you travel to Hades? Surely if those professing to be your friends are of any use at all, you must believe that they will.

"No, Socrates, listen to us, your own nurturers: do not place a higher value upon children, upon life, or upon anything else, than upon what is just, so that when you leave for Hades, this may be your whole defence before the authorities there: to take that course seems neither better nor more just or holy, for you or for any of your friends here in this world. Nor will it be better for you when you reach the next. As things stand, you will leave this world (if you do) as one who has been treated unjustly not by us Laws, but by human beings; whereas if you go into exile, thereby shamefully returning injustice for injustice and ill-treatment for ill-treatment, breaking the agreements and compacts you made with us, and inflicting harm upon the people you should least harm—yourself, your friends, your fatherland, and ourselves—then we shall be angry with you in your lifetime; and our brother Laws in Hades will not receive you kindly there, knowing that you tried, to the best of your ability, to destroy us too. Come then, do not let Crito persuade you to take his advice rather than ours."

That, Crito, my dear comrade, is what I seem to hear them saying, I do assure you. I am like the Corybantic revellers[12] who think they are still hearing the music of pipes: the sound of those arguments is ringing loudly in my head, and makes me unable to hear the others. As far as these present thoughts of mine go, then, you may be sure that if you object to them, you will plead in vain. None the less, if you think you will do any good, speak up.

CRITO: No, Socrates, I've nothing to say.

SOCRATES: Then let it be, Crito, and let us act accordingly, because that is the direction in which God is guiding us.

NOTES

1. The small island of Delos was sacred to the god Apollo. A mission sailed there annually from Athens to commemorate her deliverance by Theseus from servitude to King Minos of Crete. No executions could be carried out in Athens until the sacred ship returned.
2. The headland at the south-eastern extremity of Attica, about 50 kilometres from Athens. The winds were unfavourable at the time; so the ship may have been taking shelter at Sunium when the travellers left it there.
3. In Homer's *Iliad* (ix. 363) Achilles says, "on the third day I may return to fertile Phthia," meaning that he can get home in three days.
4. Athens had no public prosecutors. Prosecutions were undertaken by private citizens, who sometimes threatened legal action for personal, political, or financial gain.
5. The region of northern Greece, lying 200–300 kilometres north-west of Attica.
6. It was customary in Athens to appoint a public advocate to defend laws which it was proposed to abrogate.
7. The standard components of traditional Athenian education.
8. Admission to Athenian citizenship was not automatic, but required formal registration by males at the age of 17 or 18, with proof of age and parental citizenship.
9. The Isthmus was the strip of land linking the Peloponnese with the rest of Greece. Socrates may have attended the Isthmian Games, which were held every two years at Corinth.
10. Lacedaemon was the official name for the territory of Sparta. Sparta and Crete were both authoritarian and "closed" societies, which forbade their citizens to live abroad.
11. Thebes was the chief city in Boeotia, the region lying to the north-west of Attica; Megara was on the Isthmus. Both lay within easy reach of Athens.
12. The Corybantes performed orgiastic rites and dances to the sound of pipe and drum music. Their music sometimes induced a state of frenzy in emotionally disordered people, which was followed by a deep sleep from which the patients awoke cured.

STUDY QUESTIONS

1. According to Socrates, must one heed popular opinion about moral matters?
2. If you reside in a country, do you implicitly agree to abide by its laws?
3. Does Socrates accept the fairness of the laws under which he was tried and convicted?
4. Do you believe Socrates would have been wrong to escape?

On Liberty

JOHN STUART MILL

Bring to your mind an opinion so outrageous that it would be repudiated by any sensible person. Now suppose that stating this opinion openly would be an affront to the vast majority of listeners. Under such circumstances, why shouldn't the representatives of the people be empowered to pass a law banning the public expression of this foolishness, thus ensuring that no one is offended by it or tempted to repeat it?

One answer might be that the First Amendment to the Constitution of the United States prohibits any law abridging the freedom of speech. But if an opinion is wrongheaded and repugnant, why does it merit protection?

The most celebrated and eloquent reply is provided in John Stuart Mill's classic work, *On Liberty*. It is dedicated to his wife, Harriet Taylor, "the inspirer, and in part the author, of all that is best in my writings."

What is most surprising about Mill's presentation is that he defends an individual's free speech by appealing not to the majority's kindheartedness but to its own welfare. Yet how can it be in anyone's self-interest to allow blatantly false views to be expressed? Let us consider Mill's argument.

....

CHAPTER I

Introductory

The object of this essay is to assert one very simple principle, as entitled to govern absolutely the dealings of society with the individual in the way of compulsion and control, whether the means used be physical force in the form of legal penalties or the moral coercion of public opinion. That principle is that the sole end for which mankind are warranted, individually or collectively, in interfering with the liberty of action of any of their number is self-protection. That the only purpose for which power can be rightfully exercised over any member of a civilized community, against his will, is to prevent harm to others. His own good, either physical or moral, is not a sufficient warrant. He cannot rightfully be compelled to do or forbear because it will be better for him to do so, because it will make him happier, because, in the opinions of others, to do so would be wise or even right. These are good reasons for remonstrating with him, or reasoning with him, or persuading him, or entreating him, but not for compelling him or visiting him with any evil in case he do otherwise. To justify that, the conduct from which it is desired to deter

From *On Liberty* by John Stuart Mill (1859).

him must be calculated to produce evil to someone else. The only part of the conduct of anyone for which he is amenable to society is that which concerns others. In the part which merely concerns himself, his independence is, of right, absolute. Over himself, over his own body and mind, the individual is sovereign. . . .

This, then, is the appropriate region of human liberty. It comprises, first, the inward domain of consciousness, demanding liberty of conscience in the most comprehensive sense, liberty of thought and feeling, absolute freedom of opinion and sentiment on all subjects, practical or speculative, scientific, moral, or theological. The liberty of expressing and publishing opinions may seem to fall under a different principle, since it belongs to that part of the conduct of an individual which concerns other people, but, being almost of as much importance as the liberty of thought itself and resting in great part on the same reasons, is practically inseparable from it. Secondly, the principle requires liberty of tastes and pursuits, of framing the plan of our life to suit our own character, of doing as we like, subject to such consequences as may follow, without impediment from our fellow creatures, so long as what we do does not harm them, even though they should think our conduct foolish, perverse, or wrong. Thirdly, from this liberty of each individual follows the liberty, within the same limits, of combination among individuals; freedom to unite for any purpose not involving harm to others: the persons combining being supposed to be of full age and not forced or deceived.

No society in which these liberties are not, on the whole, respected is free, whatever may be its form of government; and none is completely free in which they do not exist absolute and unqualified. The only freedom which deserves the name is that of pursuing our own good in our own way, so long as we do not attempt to deprive others of theirs or impede their efforts to obtain it. Each is the proper guardian of his own health, whether bodily *or* mental and spiritual. Mankind are greater gainers by suffering each other to live as seems good to themselves than by compelling each to live as seems good to the rest. . . .

It will be convenient for the argument if, instead of at once entering upon the general thesis, we confine ourselves in the first instance to a single branch of it on which the principle here stated is, if not fully, yet to a certain point, recognized by the current opinions. This one branch is the Liberty of Thought, from which it is impossible to separate the cognate liberty of speaking and of writing. Although these liberties, to some considerable amount, form part of the political morality of all countries which profess religious toleration and free institutions, the grounds, both philosophical and practical, on which they rest are perhaps not so familiar to the general mind, nor so thoroughly appreciated by many, even of the leaders of opinion, as might have been expected. . . .

CHAPTER II

Of the Liberty of Thought and Discussion

The time, it is to be hoped, is gone by when any defense would be necessary of the "liberty of the press" as one of the securities against corrupt or tyrannical government. No argument, we may suppose, can now be needed against permitting a legislature or an executive, not identified in interest with the people, to prescribe opinions to them and determine what doctrines or what arguments they shall be allowed to hear. . . . Let us suppose, therefore, that the government is entirely at one with the people, and never thinks of exerting any power of coercion unless in agreement with what it conceives to be their voice. But I deny the right of the people to exercise such coercion, either by themselves or by their government. The power itself is illegitimate. The best government has no more title to it than the worst. It is as noxious, or more noxious, when exerted in accordance with public opinion than when in opposition to it. If all mankind minus one were of one opinion, and only one person were of the contrary opinion, mankind would be no more justified in silencing that one person than he, if he had the power, would be justified in silencing mankind. Were an opinion a personal possession of no value except to the owner, if to be obstructed in the enjoyment of it were simply a private injury, it would make some difference whether the injury was inflicted only on a few persons or on many. But the peculiar evil of silencing the expression of an opinion is that it is robbing the human race, posterity as well as the existing generation—those who dissent from the opinion, still more than those who hold it. If the opinion is right, they are deprived of the opportunity of exchanging error for truth; if wrong, they lose, what is almost as great a benefit, the clearer perception and livelier impression of truth produced by its collision with error.

It is necessary to consider separately these two hypotheses, each of which has a distinct branch of the argument corresponding to it. We can never be sure that the opinion we are endeavoring to stifle is a false opinion; and if we were sure, stifling it would be an evil still.

First, the opinion which it is attempted to suppress by authority may possibly be true. Those who desire to suppress it, of course, deny its truth; but they are not infallible. They have no authority to decide the question for all mankind and exclude every other person from the means of judging. To refuse a hearing to an opinion because they are sure that it is false is to assume that *their* certainty is the same thing as *absolute* certainty. All silencing of discussion is an assumption of infallibility. Its condemnation may be allowed to rest on this common argument, not the worse for being common.

Unfortunately for the good sense of mankind, the fact of their fallibility is far from carrying the weight in their practical judgment which is always allowed to it in theory; for while everyone well knows himself to be fallible, few think it necessary to take any precautions against their own fallibility, or admit the supposition that any opinion of which they feel very certain may be one of the examples of the error to which they acknowledge themselves to be liable. Absolute princes, or others who are accustomed to unlimited deference, usually feel this complete confidence in their own opinions on nearly all subjects. People more happily situated, who sometimes hear their opinions disputed and are not wholly unused to be set right when they are wrong, place the same unbounded reliance only on such of their opinions as are shared by all who surround them, or to whom they habitually defer; for in proportion to a man's want of confidence in his own solitary judgment does he usually repose, with implicit trust, on the infallibility of "the world" in general. And the world, to each individual, means the part of it with which he comes in contact: his party, his sect, his church, his class of society; the man may be called, by comparison, almost liberal and large-minded to whom it means anything so comprehensive as his own country or his own age. Nor is his faith in this collective authority at all shaken by his being aware that other ages, countries, sects, churches, classes, and parties have thought, and even now think, the exact reverse. He devolves upon his own world the responsibility of being in the right against the dissentient worlds of other people; and it never troubles him that mere accident has decided which of these numerous worlds is the object of his reliance, and that the same causes which make him a churchman in London would have made him a Buddhist or a Confucian in Peking. Yet it is as evident in itself, as any amount of argument can make it, that ages are no more infallible than individuals—every age having held many opinions which subsequent ages have deemed not only false but absurd; and it is as certain that many opinions, now general, will be rejected by future ages, as it is that many, once general, are rejected by the present.

The objection likely to be made to this argument would probably take some such form as the following. There is no greater assumption of infallibility in forbidding the propagation of error than in any other thing which is done by public authority on its own judgment and responsibility. Judgment is given to men that they may use it. Because it may be used erroneously, are men to be told that they ought not to use it at all? To prohibit what they think pernicious is not claiming exemption from error, but fulfilling the duty incumbent on them, although fallible, of acting on their conscientious conviction. If we were never to act on our opinions, because those opinions may be wrong, we should leave all our interests uncared for, and all our duties unperformed. An objection which applies to all conduct can be no valid objection to any conduct in particular. It is the duty of governments, and of individuals, to form the truest opinions they can; to form them carefully, and never impose them upon others unless they are quite sure of being right. But when they are sure (such reasoners may say), it is not conscientiousness but cowardice to shrink from acting on their opinions and allow doctrines which they honestly think dangerous to the welfare of mankind, either in this life or in another, to be scattered abroad without restraint, because other people, in less enlightened times, have persecuted opinions now believed to be true. Let us take care, it may be said, not to make the same mistake; but governments and nations have made mistakes in other things which are not denied to be fit subjects for the exercise of authority: they have laid on bad taxes, made unjust wars. Ought we therefore to lay on no taxes and, under whatever provocation, make no wars? Men and governments must act to the best of their ability. There is no such thing as absolute certainty, but there is assurance sufficient for the purposes of human life. We may, and must, assume our opinion to be true for the guidance of our own conduct; and it is assuming no more when we forbid bad men to pervert society by the propagation of opinions which we regard as false and pernicious.

I answer, that it is assuming very much more. There is the greatest difference between presuming an opinion to be true because, with every opportunity for contesting it, it has not been refuted, and assuming its truth for the purpose of not permitting its refutation. Complete liberty of contradicting and disproving our opinion is the very condition which justifies us in assuming its truth for purposes of action; and on no other terms can a being with human faculties have any rational assurance of being right.

When we consider either the history of opinion or the ordinary conduct of human life, to what is it to be ascribed that the one and the other are no worse than they are? Not certainly to the inherent force of the human understanding, for on any matter not self-evident there are ninety-nine persons totally incapable of judging of it for one who is capable; and the capacity of the hundredth person is only comparative, for the majority of the eminent men of every past generation held many opinions now known to be erroneous, and did or approved numerous things which no one will now justify. Why is it, then, that there is on the whole a preponderance among mankind of rational opinions and rational conduct? If there really is this preponderance—which there must be unless human affairs are, and have always been, in an almost desperate state—it is owing to a quality of the human mind, the source of everything respectable in man either as an intellectual or as a moral being, namely, that his errors are corrigible. He is capable of rectifying his mistakes by discussion and experience. Not by experience alone. There must be discussion to show how experience is to be interpreted. Wrong opinions and practices gradually yield to fact and argument; but facts and arguments, to produce any effect on the mind, must be brought before it. Very few facts are able to tell their own story, without comments to bring out their meaning. The whole strength and value, then, of human judgment depending on the one property, that it can be set right when it is wrong, reliance can be placed on it only when the means of setting it right are kept constantly at hand. In the case of any person whose judgment is really deserving of confidence, how has it become so? Because he has kept his mind open to criticism of his opinions and conduct. Because it has been his practice to listen to all that could be said against him; to profit by as much of it as was just, and to expound to himself, and upon occasion to others, the fallacy of what was fallacious. Because he has felt that the only way in which a human being can make some approach to knowing the whole of a subject is by hearing what can be said about it by persons of every variety of opinion, and studying all modes in which it can be looked at by every character of mind. No wise man ever acquired his wisdom in any mode but this; nor is it in the nature of human intellect to become wise in any other manner. The steady habit of correcting and completing his own opinion by collating it with those of others, so far from causing doubt and hesitation in carrying it into practice, is the only stable foundation for a just reliance on it; for, being cognizant of all that can, at least obviously, be said against him, and having taken up his position against all gainsayers—knowing that he has sought for objections and difficulties instead of avoiding them, and has shut out no light which can be thrown upon the subject from any quarter—he has a right to think his judgment better than that of any person, or any multitude, who have not gone through a similar process. . . .

In order more fully to illustrate the mischief of denying a hearing to opinions because we, in our own judgment, have condemned them, it will be desirable to fix down the discussion to a concrete case; and I choose, by preference, the cases which are least favorable to me—in which the argument against freedom of opinion, both on the score of truth and on that of utility, is considered the strongest. Let the opinions impugned be the belief in a God and in a future state, or any of the commonly received doctrines of morality. To fight the battle on such ground gives a great advantage to an unfair antagonist, since he will be sure to say (and many who have no desire to be unfair will say it internally), Are these the doctrines which you do not deem sufficiently certain to be taken under the protection of law? Is the belief in a God one of the opinions to feel sure of which you hold to be assuming infallibility? But I must be permitted to observe that it is not the feeling sure of a doctrine (be it what it may) which I call an assumption of infallibility. It is the undertaking to decide that question *for others,* without allowing them to hear what can be said on the contrary side. And I denounce and reprobate this pretension not the less if put forth on the side of my most solemn convictions. However positive anyone's persuasion may be, not only of the falsity but of the pernicious consequences—not only of the pernicious consequences, but (to adopt expressions which I altogether condemn) the immorality and impiety of an opinion—yet if, in pursuance of that private judgment, though backed by the public judgment of his country or his contemporaries, he prevents the opinion from being heard in its defense, he assumes infallibility. And so far from the assumption being less objectionable or less dangerous because the opinion is called immoral or impious, this is the case of all others in which it is most fatal. These are exactly the occasions on which the men of one generation commit those dreadful mistakes which excite the astonishment and horror of posterity. It is among such that we find the instances memorable in history, when the arm of the law has been employed to root out the best men and the noblest doctrines; with deplorable success as to the men, though some of the doctrines have survived to be (as if in mockery) invoked in defense of similar conduct toward those who dissent from *them,* or from their received interpretation.

Mankind can hardly be too often reminded that there was once a man called Socrates, between whom and the legal authorities and public opinion of his time there took place a memorable collision. Born in an age and country abounding in individual greatness, this man has been handed down to us by those who best knew both him and the age as the most virtuous man in it. . . . This acknowledged master of all the eminent thinkers who have since lived—whose fame, still growing after more than two thousand years, all but outweighs the whole remainder of the names which make his native city illustrious—was put to death by his countrymen, after a judicial conviction, for impiety and immorality. Impiety, in denying the gods recognized by the State; indeed, his accuser asserted (see the *Apologia*) that he believed in no gods at all. Immorality, in being, by his doctrines and instructions, a "corruptor of youth." Of these charges the tribunal, there is every ground for believing, honestly found him guilty, and condemned the man who probably of all then born had deserved best of mankind to be put to death as a criminal.

To pass from this to the only other instance of judicial iniquity, the mention of which, after the condemnation of Socrates, would not be an anticlimax: the event which took place on Calvary rather more than eighteen hundred years ago. The man who left on the memory of those who witnessed his life and conversation such an impression of his moral grandeur that eighteen subsequent centuries have done homage to him as the Almighty in person, was ignominiously put to death, as what? As a blasphemer. Men did not merely mistake their benefactor, they mistook him for the exact contrary of what he was and treated him as that prodigy of impiety which they themselves are now held to be for their treatment of him. The feelings with which mankind now regard these lamentable transactions, especially the later of the two, render them extremely unjust in their judgment of the unhappy actors. . . . Orthodox Christians who are tempted to think that those who stoned to death the first martyrs must have been worse men than they themselves are ought to remember that one of those persecutors was Saint Paul. . . .

Let us now pass to the second division of the argument, and dismissing the supposition that any of the received opinions may be false, let us assume them to be true and examine into the worth of the manner in which they are likely to be held when their truth is not freely and openly canvassed. However unwillingly a person who has a strong opinion may admit the possibility that his opinion may be false, he ought to be moved by the consideration that, however true it may be, if it is not fully, frequently, and fearlessly discussed, it will be held as a dead dogma, not a living truth.

There is a class of persons (happily not quite so numerous as formerly) who think it enough if a person assents undoubtingly to what they think true, though he has no knowledge whatever of the grounds of the opinion and could not make a tenable defense of it against the most superficial objections. Such persons, if they can once get their creed taught from authority, naturally think that no good, and some harm, comes of its being allowed to be questioned. Where their influence prevails, they make it nearly impossible for the received opinion to be rejected wisely and considerately, though it may still be rejected rashly and ignorantly; for to shut out discussion entirely is seldom possible, and when it once gets in, beliefs not grounded on conviction are apt to give way before the slightest semblance of an argument. Waiving, however, this possibility—assuming that the true opinion abides in the mind, but abides as a prejudice, a belief independent of, and proof against, argument—this is not the way in which truth ought to be held by a rational being. This is not knowing the truth. Truth, thus held, is but one superstition the more, accidentally clinging to the words which enunciate a truth.

If the intellect and judgment of mankind ought to be cultivated, a thing which Protestants at least do not deny, on what can these faculties be more appropriately exercised by anyone than on the things which concern him so much that it is considered necessary for him to hold opinions on them? If the cultivation of the understanding consists in one thing more than in another, it is surely in learning the grounds of one's own opinions. Whatever people believe, on subjects on which it is of the first importance to believe rightly, they ought to be able to defend against at least the common objections. But, someone may say, "Let them be *taught* the grounds of their opinions. It does not follow that opinions must be merely parroted because they are never heard controverted. Persons who learn geometry do not simply commit the theorems to memory, but understand and learn likewise the demonstrations; and it would be absurd to say that they remain ignorant of the grounds of geometrical truths because they never hear anyone deny and attempt to disprove them." Undoubtedly: and such teaching suffices on a subject like mathematics, where there is nothing at all to be said on the wrong side of the question. The peculiarity of the evidence of mathematical truths is that all the argument is on one side. There are no objections, and no answers to objections. But on every subject on which difference of opinion is possible, the truth depends on a balance to be struck between two sets of conflicting reasons. Even in natural philosophy, there is always some other explanation possible of the same facts; some geocentric theory instead of heliocentric, some phlogiston instead of oxygen; and it has to be shown why that other theory cannot be the true one; and until this is shown, and until we know how it is shown, we do not understand the grounds of our opinion. But when we turn to subjects infinitely more complicated, to morals, religion, politics, social relations, and the business of life, three-fourths of the arguments for every disputed opinion consist in dispelling the appearances which favor some opinion different from it. The greatest orator, save one, of antiquity, has left it on record that he always studied his adversary's case with as great, if not still greater, intensity than even his own. What Cicero practiced as the means of forensic success requires to be imitated by all who study any subject in order to arrive at the truth. He who knows only his own side of the case knows little of that. His reasons may be good, and no one may have been able to refute them. But if he is equally unable to refute the reasons on the opposite side, if he does not so much as know what they are, he has no ground for preferring either opinion. The rational position for him would be suspension of judgment, and unless he contents himself with that, he is either led by authority or adopts, like the generality of the world, the side to which he feels most inclination. Nor is it enough that he should hear the arguments of adversaries from his own teachers, presented as they state them, and accompanied by what they offer as refutations. That is not the way to do justice to the arguments or bring them into real contact with his own mind. He must be able to hear them from persons who actually believe them, who defend them in earnest and do their very utmost for them. He must know them in their most plausible and persuasive form; he must feel the whole force of the difficulty which the true view of the subject has to encounter and dispose of, else he will never really possess himself of the portion of truth which meets and removes that difficulty. Ninety-nine in a hundred of what are called educated men are in this condition, even of those who can argue fluently for their opinions. Their conclusion may be true, but it might be false for anything they know; they have never thrown themselves into the mental position of those who think differently from them, and considered what such persons may have to say; and, consequently, they do not, in any proper sense of the word, know the doctrine which they themselves profess. . . .

We have now recognized the necessity to the mental well-being of mankind (on which all their other well-being depends) of freedom of opinion, and freedom of the expression of opinion, on four distinct grounds, which we will now briefly recapitulate:

First, if any opinion is compelled to silence, that opinion may, for aught we can certainly know, be true. To deny this is to assume our own infallibility.

Secondly, though the silenced opinion be an error, it may, and very commonly does, contain a portion of truth; and since the general or prevailing opinion on any subject is rarely or never the whole truth, it is only by the collision of adverse opinions that the remainder of the truth has any chance of being supplied.

Thirdly, even if the received opinion be not only true, but the whole truth; unless it is suffered to be, and actually is, vigorously and earnestly contested, it will, by most of those who receive it, be held in the manner of a prejudice, with little comprehension or feeling of its rational grounds. And not only this, but, fourthly, the meaning of the doctrine itself will be in danger of being lost or enfeebled, and deprived of its vital effect on the character and conduct: the dogma becoming a mere formal profession, inefficacious for good, but cumbering the ground and preventing the growth of any real and heartfelt conviction from reason or personal experience.

STUDY QUESTIONS

1. According to Mill, if we are certain that an opinion is false, would stifling it still be wrong?
2. How does Mill defend his claim that "He who knows only his own side of the case knows little of that"?
3. Do we learn more from listening to those with whom we disagree than from those with whom we agree?
4. How would Mill react to the suggestion that a speaker with views demeaning some members of the student body should be banned from speaking at a university campus?

Economic and Philosophic Manuscripts of 1844

KARL MARX

Karl Marx (1818–1883), who was born in Prussia and earned a doctorate in philosophy, became the founder of revolutionary communism. He considers the key to understanding the social order to be the conflict between those who own property and those who work for them. In his view, labor produces wonderful things, but only for owners. He sees workers as estranged or alienated from the products of their work. The cure, he believes, lies in the creation of a new economic system based on common control of production.

Do not let us go back to a fictitious primordial condition as the political economist does, when he tries to explain. Such a primordial condition explains nothing; it merely pushes the question away into a gray nebulous distance. . . .

We proceed from an economic fact *of the present*. The worker becomes all the poorer the more wealth he produces, the more his production increases in power and size. The worker becomes an ever cheaper commodity the more commodities he creates. With the *increasing value* of the world of things proceeds in direct proportion the *devaluation* of the world of men. Labor produces not only commodities: it produces itself and the worker as a *commodity*—and this in the same general proportion in which it produces commodities.

This fact expresses merely that the object which labor produces—labor's product—confronts it as *something alien*, as a *power independent* of the producer. The product of labor is labor which has been embodied in an object, which has become material: it is the objectification of labor. Labor's realization is its objectification. In the sphere of political economy, this realization of labor appears as loss of *realization* for the workers; objectification as loss of the *object* and *bondage to it*; appropriation as *estrangement*, as *alienation*.

So much does labor's realization appear as loss of realization that the worker loses realization to the point of starving to death. So much does objectification appear as loss of the object that the worker is robbed of the objects most necessary not only for his life but for his work. Indeed, labor itself becomes an object which he can obtain only with the greatest effort and with the most irregular

---

From *Economic and Philosophic Manuscripts of 1844*, translated by Martin Milligan.

interruptions. So much does the appropriation of the object appear as estrangement that the more objects the worker produces the less he can possess and the more he falls under the sway of his product, capital.

All these consequences result from the fact that the worker is related to the *product of his labor* as to an *alien* object. For on this premise it is clear that the more the worker spends himself, the more powerful becomes the alien world of objects which he creates over and against himself, the poorer he himself—his inner world—becomes, the less belongs to him as his own. It is the same in religion. The more man puts into God, the less he retains in himself. The worker puts his life into the object; but now his life no longer belongs to him but to the object. Hence, the greater this activity, the greater is the worker's lack of objects. Whatever the product of his labor is, he is not. Therefore the greater this product, the less is he himself. The *alienation* of the worker in his product means not only that his labor becomes an object, an *external* existence, but that it exists *outside* him, independently, as something alien to him, and that it becomes a power on its own confronting him. It means that the life which he has conferred on the object confronts him as something hostile and alien.

Let us now look more closely at the *objectification*, at the production of the worker; and in it as the *estrangement*, the *loss* of the object, of his product.

The worker can create nothing without *nature*, without the *sensuous external world*. It is the material on which his labor is realized, in which it is active, from which and by means of which it produces.

But just as nature provides labor with the *means of life* in the sense that labor cannot live without objects on which to operate, on the other hand, it also provides the *means of life* in the more restricted sense, i.e., the means for the physical subsistence of the *worker* himself.

Thus the more the worker by his labor *appropriates* the external world, hence sensuous nature, the more he deprives himself of *means of life* in double manner: first, in that the sensuous external world more and more ceases to be an object belonging to his labor—to be his labor's *means of life*; and secondly, in that it more and more ceases to be *means of life* in the immediate sense, means for the physical subsistence of the worker.

In both respects, therefore, the worker becomes a slave of his object, first, in that he receives an *object of labor*, i.e., in that he receives *work*; and secondly, in that he receives *means of subsistence*. Therefore, it enables him to exist, first, as a *worker*, and, second as a *physical subject*. The height of this bondage is that it is only as a *worker* that he continues to maintain himself as a *physical subject*, and that is only as a *physical subject* that he is a *worker*.

(The laws of political economy express the estrangement of the worker in his object thus: the more the worker produces, the less he has to consume; the more values he creates, the more valueless, the more unworthy he becomes; the better formed his product, the more deformed becomes the worker; the more civilized his object, the more barbarous becomes the worker; the more powerful labor becomes, the more powerless becomes the worker; the more ingenious labor becomes, the less ingenious becomes the worker and the more he becomes nature's bondsman.)

Political economy conceals the estrangement inherent in the nature of labor by not considering the direct relationship between the worker (labor) *and production.* It is true that labor produces for the rich wonderful things—but for the worker it produces privation. It produces palaces—but for the worker, hovels. It produces beauty—but for the worker, deformity. It replaces labor by machines, but it throws a section of the workers back to a barbarous type of labor, and turns the other workers into machines. It produces intelligence—but for the worker stupidity, cretinism. . . .

Till now we have been considering the estrangement, the alienation of the worker only in one of its aspects, i.e., the worker's *relationship to the products of his labor.* But the estrangement is manifested not only in the result but in the *act of production*, within the *producing activity*, itself. How would the worker come to face the product of his activity as a stranger, were it not that in the very act of production he was estranging himself from himself? The product is after all but the summary of the activity, of production. If then the product of labor is alienation, production itself must be active alienation, the alienation of activity, the activity of alienation. In the estrangement of the object of labor is merely summarized the estrangement, the alienation, in the activity of labor itself.

What, then, constitutes the alienation of labor?

First, the fact that labor is *external* to the worker, i.e., it does not belong to his essential being; that in his work, therefore, he does not affirm himself but denies himself, does not feel content but unhappy, does not develop freely his physical and mental energy but mortifies his body and ruins his mind. The worker therefore only feels himself outside his work, and in his work feels outside himself. He is at home when he is not working, and when he is working he is not at home. His labor is therefore not voluntary, but coerced; it is *forced labor.* It is therefore not the satisfaction of a need; it is merely a *means* to satisfy needs external to it. Its alien character emerges clearly in the fact that as soon as no physical or other compulsion exists, labor is shunned like the plague. External labor, labor in which man alienates himself, is a labor of self-sacrifice, of mortification. Lastly, the external character of labor for the worker appears in the fact that it is not his own, but someone else's, that it does not belong to him, that in it he belongs, not to himself, but to another. Just as in religion the spontaneous activity of the human imagination, of the human brain and the human heart, operates independently of the individual—that is, operates on him as an alien, divine or diabolical activity—so is the worker's activity not his spontaneous activity. It belongs to another; it is the loss of his self. . . .

We took our departure from a fact of political economy—the estrangement of the worker and his production. We have formulated this fact in conceptual terms as *estranged, alienated* labor. We have analyzed this concept—hence analyzing merely a fact of political economy.

Let us now see, further, how the concept of estranged, alienated labor must express and present itself in real life.

If the product of labor is alien to me, if it confronts me as an alien power, to whom, then, does it belong?

If my own activity does not belong to me, if it is an alien, a coerced activity, to whom, then, does it belong?...

The *alien* being, to whom labor and the product of labor belongs, in whose service labor is done and for whose benefit the product of labor is provided, can only be *man* himself.

If the product of labor does not belong to the worker, if it confronts him as an alien power, then this can only be because it belongs to some *other man than the worker.* If the worker's activity is a torment to him, to another it must be *delight and his life's joy....*

Through *estranged, alienated* labor, then, the worker produces the relationship to this labor of a man alien to labor and standing outside it. The relationship of the worker to labor creates the relation to it of the capitalist (or whatever one chooses to call the master of labor). *Private property* is thus the product, the result, the necessary consequence, of *alienated labor*, of the external relation of the worker to nature and to himself.

Private property thus results by analysis from the concept of *alienated labor*, of *alienated man*, of estranged labor, of estranged life, of estranged man.

True, it is as a result of the *movement of private property* that we have obtained the concept of *alienated labor* (*of alienated life*) from political economy. But on analysis of this concept it becomes clear that though private property appears to be the source, the cause of alienated labor, it is rather its consequence, just as the gods are *originally* not the cause but the effect of man's intellectual confusion. Later this relationship becomes reciprocal.

Only at the last culmination of the development of private property does this, its secret, appear again, namely, that on the one hand it is the *product* of alienated labor, and that on the other it is the *means* by which labor alienates itself, the *realization of this alienation.*

STUDY QUESTIONS

1. According to Marx, why does the worker become all the poorer the more wealth he produces?
2. What does Marx mean by "alienation"?
3. According to Marx, does labor produce beauty?
4. Explain Marx's view of private property.

PART 11

Social Justice

A Theory of Justice

JOHN RAWLS

Under what conditions could a society be properly described as just? An influential answer to this question has been developed by John Rawls (1921–2002),
who was Professor of Philosophy at Harvard University. He contends that the
fairest way to distribute goods is in accord with principles that everyone would
accept, regardless of the abilities they happen to possess, or the social or economic circumstances in which they find themselves.

....

THE MAIN IDEA OF THE THEORY OF JUSTICE

. . . [T]he principles of justice . . . are the principles that free and rational persons
concerned to further their own interests would accept in an initial position of
equality. . . .

[T]he original position of equality corresponds to the state of nature in the
traditional theory of the social contract. This original position is not, of course,
thought of as an actual historical state of affairs, much less as a primitive condition of culture. It is understood as a purely hypothetical situation. . . . Among the
essential features of this situation is that no one knows his place in society, his
class position or social status, nor does any one know his fortune in the distribution of natural assets and abilities, his intelligence, strength, and the like. I shall
even assume that the parties do not know their conceptions of the good or their
special psychological propensities. The principles of justice are chosen behind a
veil of ignorance. This ensures that no one is advantaged or disadvantaged in the
choice of principles by the outcome of natural chance or the contingency of social
circumstances. Since all are similarly situated and no one is able to design principles to favor his particular condition, the principles of justice are the result of a
fair agreement or bargain. For given the circumstances of the original position, the
symmetry of everyone's relations to each other, this initial situation is fair between
individuals as moral persons, that is, as rational beings with their own ends and
capable, I shall assume, of a sense of justice. The original position is, one might say,
the appropriate initial status quo, and thus the fundamental agreements reached in

it are fair. This explains the propriety of the name "justice as fairness": it conveys the idea that the principles of justice are agreed to in an initial situation that is fair. . . .

I shall maintain . . . that the persons in the initial situation would choose two . . . principles: the first requires equality in the assignment of basic rights and duties, while the second holds that social and economic inequalities—for example, inequalities of wealth and authority—are just only if they result in compensating benefits for everyone, and in particular for the least advantaged members of society. These principles rule out justifying institutions on the grounds that the hardships of some are offset by a greater good in the aggregate. It may be expedient but it is not just that some should have less in order that others may prosper. But there is no injustice in the greater benefits earned by a few provided that the situation of persons not so fortunate is thereby improved. The intuitive idea is that since everyone's well-being depends upon a scheme of cooperation without which no one could have a satisfactory life, the division of advantages should be such as to draw forth the willing cooperation of everyone taking part in it, including those less well situated. The two principles mentioned seem to be a fair basis on which those better endowed, or more fortunate in their social position, neither of which we can be said to deserve, could expect the willing cooperation of others when some workable scheme is a necessary condition of the welfare of all. Once we decide to look for a conception of justice that prevents the use of the accidents of natural endowment and the contingencies of social circumstance as counters in a quest of political and economic advantage, we are led to these principles. They express the result of leaving aside those aspects of the social world that seem arbitrary from a moral point of view. . . .

THE ORIGINAL POSITION AND JUSTIFICATION

. . . One should not be misled . . . by the somewhat unusual conditions which characterize the original position. The idea here is simply to make vivid to ourselves the restrictions that it seems reasonable to impose on arguments for principles of justice, and therefore on these principles themselves. Thus it seems reasonable and generally acceptable that no one should be advantaged or disadvantaged by natural fortune or social circumstances in the choice of principles. It also seems widely agreed that it should be impossible to tailor principles to the circumstances of one's own case. We should insure further that particular inclinations and aspirations, and persons' conceptions of their good, do not affect the principles adopted. The aim is to rule out those principles that it would be rational to propose for acceptance, however little the chance of success, only if one knew certain things that are irrelevant from the standpoint of justice. For example, if a man knew that he was wealthy, he might find it rational to advance the principle that various taxes for welfare measures be counted unjust; if he knew that he was poor, he would most likely propose the contrary principle. To represent the desired restrictions, one imagines a situation in which everyone is deprived of this sort of information.

One excludes the knowledge of those contingencies which sets men at odds and allows them to be guided by their prejudices. In this manner the veil of ignorance is arrived at in a natural way. This concept should cause no difficulty if we keep in mind the constraints on arguments that it is meant to express. At any time we can enter the original position, so to speak, simply by following a certain procedure, namely, by arguing for principles of justice in accordance with these restrictions.

It seems reasonable to suppose that the parties in the original position are equal. That is, all have the same rights in the procedure for choosing principles; each can make proposals, submit reasons for their acceptance, and so on. Obviously the purpose of these conditions is to represent equality between human beings as moral persons, as creatures having a conception of their good and capable of a sense of justice. The basis of equality is taken to be similarity in these two respects. Systems of ends are not ranked in value; and each man is presumed to have the requisite ability to understand and to act upon whatever principles are adopted. Together with the veil of ignorance, these conditions define the principles of justice as those which rational persons concerned to advance their interests would consent to as equals when none are known to be advantaged or disadvantaged by social and natural contingencies. . . .

TWO PRINCIPLES OF JUSTICE

I shall now state in a provisional form the two principles of justice that I believe would be chosen in the original position. . . .

The first statement of the two principles reads as follows.

First: each person is to have an equal right to the most extensive scheme of equal basic liberties compatible with a similar scheme of liberties for others.

Second: social and economic inequalities are to be arranged so that they are both (a) reasonably expected to be to everyone's advantage and (b) attached to positions and offices open to all. . . .

These principles primarily apply . . . to the basic structure of society and govern the assignment of rights and duties and regulate the distribution of social and economic advantages. . . . [I]t is essential to observe that the basic liberties are given by a list of such liberties. Important among these are political liberty (the right to vote and to hold public office) and freedom of speech and assembly; liberty of conscience and freedom of thought; freedom of the person, which includes freedom from psychological oppression and physical assault and dismemberment (integrity of the person); the right to hold personal property and freedom from arbitrary arrest and seizure as defined by the concept of the rule of law. These liberties are to be equal by the first principle.

The second principle applies . . . to the distribution of income and wealth and to the design of organizations that make use of differences in authority and responsibility. While the distributions of wealth and income need not be equal, it must be to everyone's advantage, and at the same time, positions of authority and responsibility must be accessible to all. One applies the second principle by holding positions open, and then, subject to this constraint, arranges social and economic inequalities so that everyone benefits.

These principles are to be arranged in a serial order with the first principle prior to the second. This ordering means that infringements of the basic equal liberties protected by the first principle cannot be justified, or compensated for, by greater social and economic advantages. . . .

[I]n regard to the second principle, the distribution of wealth and income, and positions of authority and responsibility, are to be consistent with both the basic liberties and equality of opportunity. . . .

[T]hese principles are a special case of a more general conception of justice that can be expressed as follows.

> All social values—liberty and opportunity, income and wealth, and the social bases of self-respect—are to be distributed equally unless an unequal distribution of any, or all, of these values is to everyone's advantage.

Injustice, then, is simply inequalities that are not to the benefit of all. . . .

THE VEIL OF IGNORANCE

. . . The notion of the veil of ignorance raises several difficulties. Some may object that the exclusion of nearly all particular information makes it difficult to grasp what is meant by the original position. Thus it may be helpful to observe that one or more persons can at any time enter this position, or perhaps better, simulate the deliberations of this hypothetical situation, simply by reasoning in accordance with the appropriate restrictions. . . .

It may be protested that the condition of the veil of ignorance is irrational. Surely, some may object, principles should be chosen in the light of all the knowledge available. There are various replies to this contention. . . . To begin with, it is clear that since the differences among the parties are unknown to them, and everyone is equally rational and similarly situated, each is convinced by the same arguments. Therefore, we can view the agreement in the original position from the standpoint of one person selected at random. If anyone after due reflection prefers a conception of justice to another, then they all do, and a unanimous agreement can be reached. We can, to make the circumstances more vivid, imagine that the parties are required to communicate with each other through a referee as intermediary, and that he is to announce which alternatives have been suggested and the reasons offered in their support. He forbids the attempt to form coalitions, and he informs the parties when they have come to an understanding. But such a referee is actually superfluous, assuming that the deliberations of the parties must be similar.

Thus there follows the very important consequence that the parties have no basis for bargaining in the usual sense. No one knows his situation in society nor his natural assets, and therefore no one is in a position to tailor principles to his advantage. We might imagine that one of the contractees threatens to hold out unless the others agree to principles favorable to him. But how does he know which principles are especially in his interests? The same holds for the formation of coalitions: if a group were to decide to band together to the disadvantage of the others, they would not know how to favor themselves in the choice of principles. Even if they could get everyone to agree to their proposal, they would have no assurance that it was to their advantage, since they cannot identify themselves either by name or description. . . .

The restrictions on particular information in the original position are, then, of fundamental importance. Without them we would not be able to work out any definite theory of justice at all. We would have to be content with a vague formula stating that justice is what would be agreed to without being able to say much, if anything, about the substance of the agreement itself. . . . The veil of ignorance makes possible a unanimous choice of a particular conception of justice. Without these limitations on knowledge the bargaining problem of the original position would be hopelessly complicated.

STUDY QUESTIONS

1. What is "the original position"?
2. What is "the veil of ignorance"?
3. According to Rawls, what are the two principles of justice?
4. Do you agree with Rawls that these two principles would be chosen in the original position?

Distributive Justice

ROBERT NOZICK

Robert Nozick, whose work we read previously, argues that in treating all goods as though they were unowned and distributing them in accord with some preferred scheme, we ignore the source of these goods in the labor and ingenuity of the people who created them. As he sees it, past history plays a crucial role in determining entitlements. If I acquired property appropriately, through my own efforts or by a legal exchange with its rightful owner, then I should not have the property taken away from me in order to satisfy someone's conception of justice.

The term "distributive justice" is not a neutral one. Hearing the term "distribution," most people presume that some thing or mechanism uses some principle or criterion to give out a supply of things. Into this process of distributing shares, some error may have crept. So it is an open question, at least, whether *re*distribution should take place; whether we should do again what has already been done once, though poorly. However, we are not in the position of children who have been given portions of pie by someone who now makes last minute adjustments to rectify careless cutting. There is no *central* distribution, no person or group entitled to control all the resources, jointly deciding how they are to be doled out. What each person gets, he gets from others who give to him in exchange for something, or as a gift. In a free society, diverse persons control different resources, and new holdings arise out of the voluntary exchanges and actions of persons. There is no more a distributing or distribution of shares than there is a distributing of mates in a society in which persons choose whom they shall marry. The total result is the product of many individual decisions which the different individuals involved are entitled to make. . . . We shall speak of people's holdings; a principle of justice in holdings describes (part of) what justice tells us (requires) about holdings. . . .

THE ENTITLEMENT THEORY

The subject of justice in holdings consists of three major topics. The first is the *original acquisition of holdings,* the appropriation of unheld things. This includes the issues of how unheld things may come to be held, the process, or processes, by which unheld things may come to be held, the things that may come to be held by these processes, the extent of what comes to be held by a particular process, and so on. We shall refer to the complicated truth about this topic, which we shall not formulate here, as the principle of justice in acquisition. The second topic concerns the *transfer of holdings* from one person to another. By what processes may a person transfer holdings to another? How may a person acquire a holding from another who holds it? Under this topic come general descriptions of voluntary exchange, and gift and (on the other hand) fraud, as well as reference to particular conventional details fixed upon in a given society. The complicated truth about this subject (with placeholders for conventional details) we shall call the principle of justice in transfer. (And we shall suppose it also includes principles governing how a person may divest himself of a holding, passing it into an unheld state.)

If the world were wholly just, the following inductive definition would exhaustively cover the subject of justice in holdings.

1. A person who acquires a holding in accordance with the principle of justice in acquisition is entitled to that holding.

2. A person who acquires a holding in accordance with the principle of justice in transfer, from someone else entitled to the holding, is entitled to the holding.
3. No one is entitled to a holding except by (repeated) applications of 1 and 2.

The complete principle of distributive justice would say simply that a distribution is just if everyone is entitled to the holdings they possess under the distribution.

A distribution is just if it arises from another just distribution by legitimate means. The legitimate means of moving from one distribution to another are specified by the principle of justice in transfer. The legitimate first "moves" are specified by the principle of justice in acquisition. Whatever arises from a just situation by just steps is itself just. The means of change specified by the principle of justice in transfer preserve justice. As correct rules of inference are truth-preserving, and any conclusion deduced via repeated application of such rules from only true premises is itself true, so the means of transition from one situation to another specified by the principle of justice in transfer are justice-preserving, and any situation actually arising from repeated transitions in accordance with the principle from a just situation is itself just. The parallel between justice-preserving transformations and truth-preserving transformations illuminates where it fails as well as where it holds. That a conclusion could have been deduced by truth-preserving means from premises that are true suffices to show its truth. That from a just situation a situation *could* have arisen via justice-preserving means does *not* suffice to show its justice. The fact that a thief's victims voluntarily *could* have presented him with gifts does not entitle the thief to his ill-gotten gains. Justice in holdings is historical; it depends upon what actually has happened. We shall return to this point later.

Not all actual situations are generated in accordance with the two principles of justice in holdings: the principle of justice in acquisition and the principle of justice in transfer. Some people steal from others, or defraud them, or enslave them, seizing their product and preventing them from living as they choose, or forcibly exclude others from competing in exchanges. None of these are permissible modes of transition from one situation to another. And some persons acquire holdings by means not sanctioned by the principle of justice in acquisition. The existence of past injustice (previous violations of the first two principles of justice in holdings) raises the third major topic under justice in holdings: the rectification of injustice in holdings. If past injustice has shaped present holdings in various ways, some identifiable and some not, what now, if anything, ought to be done to rectify these injustices? What obligations do the performers of injustice have toward those whose position is worse than it would have been had the injustice not been done?

The general outlines of the theory of justice in holdings are that the holdings of a person are just if he is entitled to them by the principles of justice in acquisition and transfer, or by the principle of rectification of injustice (as specified by the first two principles). If each person's holdings are just, then the total set (distribution) of holdings is just. To turn these general outlines into a specific theory, we would have to specify the details of each of the three principles of justice in holdings: the principle of acquisition of holdings, the principle of transfer of holdings, and the principle of rectification of violations of the first two principles. I shall not attempt that task here. . . .

HOW LIBERTY UPSETS PATTERNS

It is not clear how those holding alternative conceptions of distributive justice can reject the entitlement conceptions of justice in holdings. For suppose a distribution favored by one of these nonentitlement conceptions is realized. Let us suppose it is your favorite one and let us call this distribution D_1; perhaps everyone has an equal share, perhaps shares vary in accordance with some dimension you treasure. Now suppose that Wilt Chamberlain is greatly in demand by basketball teams, being a great gate attraction. (Also suppose contracts run only for a year, with players being free agents.) He signs the following sort of contract with a team: In each home game, twenty-five cents from the price of each ticket of admission goes to him. (We ignore the question of whether he is "gouging" the owners, letting them look out for themselves.) The season starts, and people cheerfully attend his team's games; they buy their tickets, each time dropping a separate twenty-five cents of their admission price into a special box with Chamberlain's name on it. They are excited about seeing him play; it is worth the total admission price to them. Let us suppose that in one season one million persons attend his home games, and Wilt Chamberlain winds up with $250,000, a much larger sum than the average income and larger even than anyone else has. Is he entitled to this income? Is this new distribution D_2 unjust? If so, why? There is *no* question about whether each of the people was entitled to the control over the resources they held in D_1; because that was the distribution (your favorite) that (for the purposes of argument) we assumed was acceptable. Each of these persons *chose* to give twenty-five cents of their money to Chamberlain. They could have spent it on going to the movies, or on candy bars, or on copies of *Dissent* magazine, or on *Monthly Review*. But they all, at least one million of them, converged on giving it to Wilt Chamberlain in exchange for watching him play basketball. If D_1 was a just distribution, and people voluntarily moved from it to D_2, transferring parts of their shares they were given under D_1 (what was it for if not to do something with?), isn't D_2 also just? If the people were entitled to dispose of the resources to which they were entitled (under D_1), didn't this include their being entitled to give it to, or exchange it with, Wilt Chamberlain? Can anyone else complain on grounds of justice? Each other person already has his legitimate share under D_1. Under D_1, there is nothing that anyone has that anyone else has a claim of justice against. After someone transfers something to Wilt Chamberlain, third parties *still* have their legitimate shares; *their* shares are not changed. By what process could such a transfer among two persons give rise to a legitimate claim of distributive justice on a portion of what was transferred, by a third party who had no claim of justice on any holding of the others *before* the transfer? . . .

The general point illustrated by the Wilt Chamberlain example . . . is that no end-state principle[1] or distributional patterned principle of justice[2] can be continuously realized without continuous interference with people's lives. Any favored pattern would be transformed into one unfavored by the principle, by people choosing to act in various ways; for example, by people exchanging goods and services with other people, or giving things to other people, things the transferrers are entitled to under the favored distributional pattern. To maintain a pattern, one must either continually interfere to stop people from transferring resources as they wish to, or continually (or periodically) interfere to take from some persons resources that others for some reason chose to transfer to them. (But if some time limit is to be set on how long people may keep resources others voluntarily transfer to them, why let them keep these resources for *any* period of time? Why not have immediate confiscation?) It might be objected that all persons voluntarily will choose to refrain from actions which would upset the pattern. This presupposes unrealistically (1) that all will most want to maintain the pattern (are those who don't, to be "reeducated" or forced to undergo "self-criticism"?), (2) that each can gather enough information about his own actions and the ongoing activities of others to discover which of his actions will upset the pattern, and (3) that diverse and far-flung persons can coordinate their actions to dovetail into the pattern. Compare the manner in which the market is neutral among persons' desires, as it reflects and transmits widely scattered information via prices and it coordinates persons' activities.

NOTES

1. [An "end-state principle" requires that goods be distributed to promote a certain structure of holdings, such as maximizing utility or achieving equality.—S.M.C.]
2. [A "patterned principle" requires that goods be distributed in accord with some feature of persons, such as need or desert.]

STUDY QUESTIONS

1. What does Nozick mean by "justice in acquisition"?
2. What does Nozick mean by "justice in transfer"?
3. What is the general point illustrated by the Wilt Chamberlain example?
4. How is the Wilt Chamberlain example supposed to undermine a theory of justice such as Rawls proposed?

Non-contractual Society:
A Feminist View

Virginia Held

Virginia Held, whose work we read previously, next explores how the relations suitable for mothering persons and children might be used as a social model. Instead of thinking of human relations as a contract between rationally self-interested individuals, she envisions society as a group of persons tied together by ongoing relations of caring and trust.

Contemporary society is in the grip of contractual thinking. Realities are interpreted in contractual terms, and goals are formulated in terms of rational contracts. The leading current conceptions of rationality begin with assumptions that human beings are independent, self-interested or mutually disinterested, individuals; they then typically argue that it is often rational for human beings to enter into contractual relationships with each other. . . .

To see contractual relations between self-interested or mutually disinterested individuals as constituting a paradigm of human relations is to take a certain historically specific conception of "economic man" as representative of humanity. And it is, many feminists are beginning to agree, to overlook or to discount in very fundamental ways the experience of women.

I will try in this paper to look at society from a thoroughly different point of view than that of economic man. I will take the point of view of women, and especially of mothers, as the basis for trying to rethink society and its possible goals. Certainly there is no single point of view of women; the perspectives of women are potentially as diverse as those of men. But since the perspectives of women have all been to a large extent discounted, across the spectrum, I will not try to deal here with diversity among such views, but rather to give voice to one possible feminist outlook. . . .

Since it is the practice of mothering with which I will be concerned in what follows, rather than with women in the biological sense, I will use the term "mothering person" rather than "mother." A "mothering person" can be male or female. . . .

From *Science, Morality, and Feminist Theory*, ed. Marsha Hanen and Kai Nielsen, *Canadian Journal of Philosophy*, Supplementary Volume 13. Calgary: University of Calgary Press, 1987. Reprinted by permission of the publisher with a minor revision by the author.

WOMEN AND FAMILY

A first point to note in trying to imagine society from the point of view of women is that the contractual model was hardly ever applied, as either description or ideal, to women or to relations within the family. The family was imagined to be "outside" the polis and "outside" the market in a "private" domain. This private domain was contrasted with the public domain, and with what, by the time of Hobbes and Locke, was thought of as the contractual domain of citizen and state and tradesman and market. Although women have always worked, and although both women and children were later pressed into work in factories, they were still thought of as outside the domain in which the contractual models of "equal men" were developed. Women were not expected to demand equal rights either in the public domain or at home. Women were not expected to be "economic men." And children were simply excluded from the realm of what was being interpreted in contractual terms as distinctively human.

Women have . . . been thought to be closer to nature than men, to be enmeshed in a biological function involving processes more like those in which other animals are involved than like the rational contracting of distinctively human "economic man." The total or relative exclusion of women from the domain of voluntary contracting has then been thought to be either inevitable or appropriate.

The view that women are more governed by biology than are men is still prevalent. It is as questionable as many other traditional misinterpretations of women's experience. Human mothering is an extremely different activity from the mothering engaged in by other animals. It is as different from the mothering of other animals as is the work and speech of men different from the "work" and "speech" of other animals. Since humans are also animals, one should not exaggerate the differences between humans and other animals. But to whatever extent it is appropriate to recognize a difference between "man" and other animals, so would it be appropriate to recognize a comparable difference between human mothering and the mothering of other animals.

Human mothering shapes language and culture, and forms human social personhood. Human mothering develops morality, it does not merely transmit techniques of survival; impressive as the latter can be, they do not have built into them the aims of morality. Human mothering teaches consideration for others based on moral concern; it does not merely follow and bring the child to follow instinctive tendency. Human mothering creates autonomous persons; it does not merely propagate a species. It can be fully as creative an activity as most other human activities; to create *new* persons, and new types of *persons*, is surely as creative as to make new objects, products, or institutions. Human mothering is no more "natural" than any other human activity. It may include many dull and repetitive tasks, as does farming, industrial production, banking, and work in a laboratory. But degree of dullness has nothing to do with degree of "naturalness." In sum, human mothering is as different from animal mothering as humans are from animals. . . .

FAMILY AND SOCIETY

In recent years, many feminists have demanded that the principles of justice and freedom and equality on which it is claimed that democracy rests be extended to women and the family. They have demanded that women be treated as equals in the polity, in the workplace, and, finally, at home. They have demanded, in short, to be accorded full rights to enter freely the contractual relations of modern society. They have asked that these be extended to take in the family.

But some feminists are now considering whether the arguments should perhaps, instead, run the other way. Instead of importing into the household principles derived from the marketplace, perhaps we should export to the wider society the relations suitable for mothering persons and children. This approach suggests that just as relations between persons within the family should be based on concern and caring, rather than on contracts based on self-interest, so various relations in the wider society should be characterized by more care and concern and openness and trust and human feeling than are the contractual bargains that have developed so far in political and economic life, or even than are aspired to in contractarian prescriptions. Then, the household instead of the marketplace might provide a model for society. Of course what we would mean by the household would not be the patriarchal household which was, before the rise of contractual thinking, also thought of as a model of society. We would now mean the relations between children and mothering persons *without* the patriarch. We would take our conception of the *post*-patriarchal family as a model. . . .

THE MOTHER/CHILD RELATION

Let us examine in more detail the relation between mothering person and child. A first aspect of the relation that we can note is the extent to which it is not voluntary and, for this reason among others, not contractual. The ties that bind child and mothering persons are affectional and solicitous on the one hand, and emotional and dependent on the other. The degree to which bearing and caring for children has been voluntary for most mothers throughout most of history has been extremely limited; it is still quite limited for most mothering persons. The relation *should* be voluntary for the mothering person but it cannot possibly be voluntary for the young child, and it can only become, gradually, slightly more voluntary.

A woman can have decided voluntarily to have a child, but once that decision has been made, she will never again be unaffected by the fact that she has brought this particular child into existence. And even if the decision to have a child is voluntary, the decision to have this particular child, for either parent, cannot be. Technological developments can continue to reduce the uncertainties of childbirth, but unpredictable aspects are likely to remain great for most parents. Unlike that contract where buyer and seller can know what is being exchanged, and which is void if the participants cannot know what they are agreeing to, a parent cannot know what a particular child will be like. And children are totally unable to choose their parents and, for many years, any of their caretakers.

The recognition of how limited are the aspects of voluntariness in the relation between child and mothering person may help us to gain a closer approximation to reality in our understanding of most human relations, especially at a global level, than we can gain from imagining the purely voluntary trades entered into by rational economic contractors to be characteristic of human relations in other domains.

Society may impose certain reciprocal obligations: on parents to care for children when the children are young, and on children to care for parents when the parents are old. But if there is any element of a bargain in the relation between mothering person and child, it is very different from the bargain supposedly characteristic of the marketplace. If a parent thinks, "I'll take care of you now so you'll take care of me when I'm old," it must be based, unlike the contracts of political and economic bargains, on enormous trust and on a virtual absence of enforcement. And few mothering persons have any such exchange in mind when they engage in the activities of mothering. At least the bargain would only be resorted to when the callousness or poverty of the society made the plight of the old person desperate. This is demonstrated in survey after survey: old persons certainly hope not to have to be a burden on their children. And they prefer social arrangements that will allow them to refuse to cash in on any such bargain. So the intention and goal of mothering is to give of one's care without obtaining a return of a self-interested kind. The emotional satisfaction of a mothering person is a satisfaction in the well-being and happiness of another human being, and a satisfaction in the health of the relation between the two persons, not the gain that results from an egoistic bargain. The motive behind the activity of mothering is thus entirely different from that behind a market transaction. And so is, perhaps even more clearly, the motive behind the child's project of growth and development.

A second aspect of the contrast between market relations and relations between mothering person and child is found in the qualities of permanence and non-replaceability. The market makes of everything, even human labor and artistic expression and sexual desire, a commodity to be bought and sold, with one unit of economic value replaceable by any other of equivalent value. To the extent that political life reflects these aspects of the market, politicians are replaceable and political influence is bought and sold. Though rights may be thought of as outside the economic market, in contractual thinking they are seen as inside the wider market of the social contract, and can be traded against each other. But the ties between parents and children are permanent ties, however strained or slack they become at times. And no person within a family should be a commodity to any other. Although various persons may participate in mothering a given child, and a given person may mother many children, still no child and no mothering person is to the other a merely replaceable commodity. The extent to which more of our attitudes, for instance toward our society's cultural productions, should be thought of in these terms rather than in the terms of the marketplace should be considered.

A third aspect of the relation between mothering person and child that may be of interest is the insight it provides for our notions of equality. It shows us unmistakably that equality is not equivalent to having equal legal rights. All feminists are committed to equality and to equal rights in contexts where rights are what are appropriately at issue. But in many contexts, concerns other than rights are more salient and appropriate. And the equality that is at issue in the relation between child and mothering person is the equal consideration of persons, not a legal or contractual notion of equal rights.

Parents and children should not have equal rights in the sense that what they are entitled to decide or to do or to have should be the same. A family of several small children, an adult or two, and an aged parent should not, for instance, make its decisions by majority vote in most cases. But every member of a family is worthy of equal respect and consideration. Each person in a family is as important as a person as every other.

Sometimes the interests of children have been thought in some sense to count for more, justifying "sacrificing for the children." Certainly, the interests of mothers have often counted for less than those of either fathers or children. Increasingly, we may come to think that the interests of all should count equally, but we should recognize that this claim is appropriately invoked only if the issue should be thought of as one of interest. Often, it should not. Much of the time we can see that calculations of interest, and of equal interests, are as out of place as are determinations of equal rights. Both the rights and the interests of individuals seen as separate entities, and equality between them all, should not exhaust our moral concerns. The flourishing of shared joy, of mutual affection, of bonds of trust and hope between mothering persons and children can illustrate this as clearly as anything can. Harmony, love, and cooperation cannot be broken down into individual benefits or burdens. They are goals we ought to share and relations *between* persons. And although the degree of their intensity may be different, many and various relations *between* persons are important also at the level of communities or societies. We can consider, of a society, whether the relations between its members are trusting and mutually supportive, or suspicious and hostile. To focus only on contractual relations and the gains and losses of individuals obscures these often more important relational aspects of societies.

A fourth important feature of the relation between child and mothering person is that we obviously do not fulfil our obligations by merely leaving people alone. If one leaves an infant alone, he will starve. If one leaves a two-year old alone she will rapidly harm herself. The whole tradition that sees respecting others as constituted by non-interference with them is most effectively shown up as inadequate. It assumes that people can fend for themselves and provide through their own initiatives and efforts what they need. This Robinson Crusoe image of "economic man" is false for almost everyone, but it is totally and obviously false in the case of infants and children, and recognizing this can be salutary. It can lead us to see very vividly how unsatisfactory are those prevalent political views according to which we fulfil our obligations merely by refraining from interference. We ought to acknowledge that our fellow citizens, and fellow inhabitants of the globe, have moral rights to what they need to live—to the food, shelter, and medical care that are the necessary conditions of living and growing—and that when the resources exist for honoring such rights, there are few excuses for not doing so. Such rights are not rights to be left to starve unimpeded. Seeing how unsatisfactory rights merely to be left alone are as an interpretation of the rights of children may help us to recognize a similar truth about other persons. And the arguments—though appropriately in a different form—can be repeated for interests as distinct from rights.

A fifth interesting feature of the relation between mothering person and child is the very different view it provides of privacy. We come to see that to be in a position where others are *not* making demands on us is a rare luxury, not a normal state. To be a mothering person is to be subjected to the continual demands and needs of others. And to be a child is to be subjected to the continual demands and expectations of others. Both mothering persons and children need to extricate themselves from the thick and heavy social fabric in which they are entwined in order to enjoy any pockets of privacy at all.

Here the picture we form of our individuality and the concept we form of a "self" is entirely different from the one we get if we start with the self-sufficient individual of the "state of nature." If we begin with the picture of rational contractor entering into agreements with others, the "natural" condition is seen as one of individuality and privacy, and the problem is the building of society and government. From the point of view of the relation between mothering person and child, on the other hand, the problem is the reverse. The starting condition is an enveloping tie, and the problem is individuating oneself. The task is to carve out a gradually increasing measure of privacy in ways appropriate to a constantly shifting independency. For the child, the problem is to become gradually more interdependent. For the mothering person, the problem is to free oneself from an all-consuming involvement. For both, the progression is from society to greater individuality rather than from self-sufficient individuality to contractual ties. . . .

A sixth aspect of the relation between child and mothering person which is noteworthy is the very different view of power it provides. We are accustomed to thinking of power as something that can be wielded by one person over another, as a means by which one person can bend another to his will. An ideal has been to equalize power so that agreements can be forged and conflicts defused. But consider now the very different view of power in the relation between mothering person and child. The superior power of the mothering person over the child is relatively useless for most of what the mothering person aims to achieve in bringing up the child. The mothering person seeks to *empower* the child to act responsibly; she neither wants to "wield" power nor to defend herself against the power "wielded" by the child. The relative powerlessness of the child is largely irrelevant to most of the project of growing up. When the child is physically weakest, as in infancy and illness, the child can "command" the greatest amount of attention and care from the mothering person because of the seriousness of the child's needs.

The mothering person's stance is characteristically one of caring, of being vulnerable to the needs and pains of the child, and of fearing the loss of the child before the child is ready for independence. It is not characteristically a stance of domination. The child's project is one of developing, of gaining ever greater control over his or her own life, of relying on the mothering person rather than of submitting to superior strength. Of course the relation may in a degenerate form be one of domination and submission, but this only indicates that the relation is not what it should be. . . . The power of a mothering person to empower others, to foster transformative growth, is a different sort of power than that of a stronger sword or dominant will. And the power of a child to call forth tenderness and care is perhaps more different still.

MODELS FOR SOCIETY

The relation between child and mothering person seems especially worth exploring to see what implications and insights it might suggest for a transformed society.

There are good reasons to believe that a society resting on no more than bargains between self-interested or mutually disinterested individuals will not be able to withstand the forces of egoism and dissolution pulling such societies apart. Although there may be some limited domains in which rational contracts are the appropriate form of social relations, as a foundation for the fundamental ties which ought to bind human beings together, they are clearly inadequate. Perhaps we can learn from a non-patriarchal household better than from further searching in the marketplace what the sources might be for justifiable trust, cooperation, and caring.

Many persons can imagine human society on the model of "economic man," society built on a contract between rationally self-interested persons, because these are the theories they have been brought up with. But they cannot imagine society resembling a group of persons tied together by on-going relations of caring and trust between persons in positions such as those of mothers and children where, as adults, we would sometimes be one and sometimes the other. Suppose now we ask: in the relation between mothering person and child, who are the contractors? Where is the rational self-interest? The model of "economic man" makes no sense in this context. Anyone in the social contract tradition who has noticed the relation of child and mothering person at all has supposed it to belong to some domain outside the realm of the "free market" and outside the "public" realm of politics and the law. Such theorists have supposed the context of mothering to be of much less significance for human history and of much less relevance for moral theory than the realms of trade and government, or they have imagined mothers and children as somehow outside human society altogether in a region labelled "nature," and engaged wholly in "reproduction." But mothering is at the heart of human society.

If the dynamic relation between child and mothering person is taken as the primary social relation, then it is the model of "economic man" that can be seen to be deficient as a model for society and morality, and unsuitable for all but a special context. A domain such as law, if built on no more than contractual foundations, can then be recognized as one limited domain among others; law protects some moral rights when people are too immoral or weak to respect them without the force of law. But it is hardly a majestic edifice that can serve as a model for morality. Neither can the domain of politics, if built on no more than self-interest or mutual disinterest, provide us with a model with which to understand and improve society and morality. And neither, even more clearly, can the market itself.

When we explore the implications of these speculations we may come to realize that instead of seeing the family as an anomalous island in a sea of rational contracts composing economic and political and social life, perhaps it is instead "economic man" who belongs on a relatively small island surrounded by social ties of a less hostile, cold, and precarious kind.

STUDY QUESTIONS

1. What does Held mean by "contractual thinking"?
2. According to Held, what are the distinctive features of the relation between mothering person and child?
3. According to Held, in what specific ways might the relation between mothering person and child provide a model for society?
4. Does envisioning society as Held proposes suggest support for any particular governmental policies?

HISTORICAL SOURCES

The Republic

PLATO

Plato's *Republic* is a remarkable work that offers a unified account of central issues in metaphysics, epistemology, philosophy of mind, ethics, political philosophy, philosophy of art, and philosophy of education. Due to that book's length, which is more than half as long as this entire collection, space permits only the reprinting of relatively short segments, thereby necessarily omitting crucial materials.

For our purposes, however, I have chosen to highlight Plato's defense of a non-democratic system of government, directed by a small group of philosopher-kings, both men and women, chosen on the basis of their natural aptitudes and specially educated for their roles. A community exhibits justice if the experts rule, supported by those in the military force, while workers and merchants attend to their own trades and businesses.

Note the parable toward the end of the selection in which Plato compares the working of a democratic society to the situation aboard a ship on which the sailors argue over the control of the helm, while none of them has ever learned navigation. And if someone on board happens to possess the needed skills, that person's qualifications are disregarded on the grounds that steering a ship requires no special competence. Plato was no friend of democracy, the system of government that put to death his beloved teacher, Socrates.

This excerpt ends with one of the most famous passages in the history of philosophy, the parable of the cave. This story is intended to reveal why those with knowledge are reviled by others, yet should be compelled to rule so as to promote the good of all. Never has democracy been challenged in a more compelling fashion, and developing a satisfactory response surely tests one's philosophical powers.

In the scenes that follow, Socrates is the first speaker and converses with Glaucon and Adeimantus, Plato's brothers, who are representative of the Athenian aristocracy.

....

[S]uppose we imagine a state coming into being before our eyes. We might then be able to watch the growth of justice or of injustice within it. . . .

Don't waste any more time.

My notion is, said I, that a state comes into existence because no individual is self-sufficing; we all have many needs. But perhaps you can suggest some different origin for the foundation of a community?

No, I agree with you.

So, having all these needs, we call in one another's help to satisfy our various requirements; and when we have collected a number of helpers and associates to live together in one place, we call that settlement a state.

Yes.

So if one man gives another what he has to give in exchange for what he can get, it is because each finds that to do so is for his own advantage.

Certainly.

Very well, said I. Now let us build up our imaginary state from the beginning. Apparently, it will owe its existence to our needs, the first and greatest need being the provision of food to keep us alive. Next we shall want a house; and thirdly, such things as clothing.

True.

How will our state be able to supply all these demands? We shall need at least one man to be a farmer, another a builder, and a third a weaver. Will that do, or shall we add a shoemaker and one or two more to provide for our personal wants?

By all means.

The minimum state, then, will consist of four or five men.

Apparently.

Now here is a further point. Is each one of them to bring the product of his work into a common stock? Should our one farmer, for example, provide food enough for four people and spend the whole of his working time in producing corn, so as to share with the rest; or should he take no notice of them and spend only a quarter of his time on growing just enough corn for himself, and divide the other three-quarters between building his house, weaving his clothes, and making his shoes, so as to save the trouble of sharing with others and attend himself to all his own concerns?

The first plan might be the easier, replied Adeimantus.

That may very well be so, said I; for, as you spoke, it occurred to me, for one thing, that no two people are born exactly alike. There are innate differences which fit them for different occupations.

I agree.

And will a man do better working at many trades, or keeping to one only?

Keeping to one.

And there is another point: obviously work may be ruined, if you let the right time go by. The workman must wait upon the work; it will not wait upon his leisure and allow itself to be done in a spare moment. So the conclusion is that more things will be produced and the work be more easily and better done, when every man is set free from all other occupations to do, at the right time, the one thing for which he is naturally fitted.

That is certainly true.

We shall need more than four citizens, then, to supply all those necessaries we mentioned. You see, Adeimantus, if the farmer is to have a good plough and spade and other tools, he will not make them himself. No more will the builder and weaver and shoemaker make all the many implements they need. So quite a number of carpenters and smiths and other craftsmen must be enlisted. Our miniature state is beginning to grow.

It is.

Still, it will not be very large, even when we have added cowherds and shepherds to provide the farmers with oxen for the plough, and the builders as well as the farmers with draught-animals, and the weavers and shoemakers with wool and leather.

No; but it will not be so very small either.

And yet, again, it will be next to impossible to plant our city in a territory where it will need no imports. So there will have to be still another set of people, to fetch what it needs from other countries.

There will.

Moreover, if these agents take with them nothing that those other countries require in exchange, they will return as empty-handed as they went. So, besides everything wanted for consumption at home, we must produce enough goods of the right kind for the foreigners whom we depend on to supply us. That will mean increasing the number of farmers and craftsmen.

Yes.

And then, there are these agents who are to import and export all kinds of goods—merchants, as we call them. We must have them; and if they are to do business overseas, we shall need quite a number of ship-owners and others who know about that branch of trading.

We shall.

Again, in the city itself how are the various sets of producers to exchange their products? That was our object, you will remember, in forming a community and so laying the foundation of our state.

Obviously, they must buy and sell.

That will mean having a market-place, and a currency to serve as a token for purposes of exchange.

Certainly.

Now suppose a farmer, or an artisan, brings some of his produce to market at a time when no one is there who wants to exchange with him. Is he to sit there idle, when he might be at work?

No, he replied; there are people who have seen an opening here for their services. In well-ordered communities they are generally men not strong enough to be of use in any other occupation. They have to stay where they are in the market-place and take goods for money from those who want to sell, and money for goods from those who want to buy.

That, then, is the reason why our city must include a class of shopkeepers—so we call these people who sit still in the market-place to buy and sell, in contrast with merchants who travel to other countries.

Quite so.

There are also the services of yet another class, who have the physical strength for heavy work, though on intellectual grounds they are hardly worth including in our society—hired labourers, as we call them, because they sell the use of their strength for wages. They will go to make up our population.

Yes.

Well, Adeimantus, has our state now grown to its full size?

Perhaps.

Then, where in it shall we find justice or injustice? If they have come in with one of the elements we have been considering, can you say with which one?

I have no idea, Socrates; unless it be somewhere in their dealings with one another.

You may be right, I answered. Anyhow, it is a question which we shall have to face.

Let us begin, then, with a picture of our citizens' manner of life, with the provision we have made for them. They will be producing corn and wine and making clothes and shoes. When they have built their houses, they will mostly work without their coats or shoes in summer, and in winter be well shod and clothed. For their food, they will prepare flour and barley-meal for kneading and baking, and set out a grand spread of loaves and cakes on rushes or fresh leaves. Then they will lie on beds of myrtle-boughs and bryony and make merry with their children, drinking their wine after the feast with garlands on their heads and singing the praises of the gods. So they will live pleasantly together; and a prudent fear of poverty or war will keep them from begetting children beyond their means.

Here Glaucon interrupted me: You seem to expect your citizens to feast on dry bread.

True, I said; I forgot that they will have something to give it a relish, salt, no doubt, and olives, and cheese, and country stews of roots and vegetables. And for dessert we will give them figs and peas and beans; and they shall roast myrtle-berries and acorns at the fire, while they sip their wine. Leading such a healthy life in peace, they will naturally come to a good old age, and leave their children to live after them in the same manner.

That is just the sort of provender you would supply, Socrates, if you were founding a community of pigs.

Well, how are they to live, then, Glaucon?

With the ordinary comforts. Let them lie on couches and dine off tables on such dishes and sweets as we have nowadays.

Ah, I see, said I; we are to study the growth, not just of a state, but of a luxurious one. Well, there may be no harm in that; the consideration of luxury may help us to discover how justice and injustice take root in society. The community I have described seems to me the ideal one, in sound health as it were: but if you want to see one suffering from inflammation, there is nothing to hinder us. So some people, it seems, will not be satisfied to live in this simple way; they must have couches and tables and furniture of all sorts; and delicacies too, perfumes, unguents, courtesans, sweetmeats, all in plentiful variety. And besides, we must not limit ourselves now to those bare necessaries of house and clothes and shoes; we shall have to set going the arts of embroidery and painting, and collect rich materials, like gold and ivory.

Yes.

Then we must once more enlarge our community. The healthy one will not be big enough now; it must be swollen up with a whole multitude of callings not ministering to any bare necessity: hunters and fishermen, for instance; artists in sculpture, painting, and music; poets with their attendant train of professional reciters, actors, dancers, producers; and makers of all sorts of household gear, including everything for women's adornment. And we shall want more servants: children's nurses and attendants, lady's maids, barbers, cooks and confectioners. And then swineherds—there was no need for them in our original state, but we shall want them now; and a great quantity of sheep and cattle too, if people are going to live on meat.

Of course.

And with this manner of life physicians will be in much greater request.

No doubt.

The country, too, which was large enough to support the original inhabitants, will now be too small. If we are to have enough pasture and plough land, we shall have to cut off a slice of our neighbours' territory; and if they too are not content with necessaries, but give themselves up to getting unlimited wealth, they will want a slice of ours.

That is inevitable, Socrates.

So the next thing will be, Glaucon, that we shall be at war.

No doubt.

We need not say yet whether war does good or harm, but only that we have discovered its origin in desires which are the most fruitful source of evils both to individuals and to states.

Quite true.

This will mean a considerable addition to our community—a whole army, to go out to battle with any invader, in defence of all this property and of the citizens we have been describing.

Why so? Can't they defend themselves?

Not if the principle was right, which we all accepted in framing our society. You remember we agreed that no one man can practise many trades or arts satisfactorily.

True.

Well, is not the conduct of war an art, quite as important as shoemaking?

Yes.

But we would not allow our shoemaker to try to be also a farmer or weaver or builder, because we wanted our shoes well made. We gave each man one trade, for which he was naturally fitted; he would do good work, if he confined himself to that all his life, never letting the right moment slip by. Now in no form of work is efficiency so important as in war; and fighting is not so easy a business that a man can follow another trade, such as farming or shoemaking, and also be an efficient soldier. Why, even a game like draughts or dice must be studied from childhood; no one can become a fine player in his spare moments. Just taking up a shield or other weapon will not make a man capable of fighting that very day in any sort of warfare, any more than taking up a tool or implement of some kind will make a man a craftsman or an athlete, if he does not understand its use and has never been properly trained to handle it.

No; if that were so, tools would indeed be worth having.

These guardians of our state, then, inasmuch as their work is the most important of all, will need the most complete freedom from other occupations and the greatest amount of skill and practice.

I quite agree.

And also a native aptitude for their calling.

Certainly.

So it is our business to define, if we can, the natural gifts that fit men to be guardians of a commonwealth, and to select them accordingly. It will certainly be a formidable task; but we must grapple with it to the best of our power.

Yes.

Don't you think then, said I, that, for the purpose of keeping guard, a young man should have much the same temperament and qualities as a well-bred watchdog? I mean, for instance, that both must have quick senses to detect an enemy, swiftness in pursuing him, and strength, if they have to fight when they have caught him.

Yes, they will need all those qualities.

And also courage, if they are to fight well.

Of course.

And courage, in dog or horse or any other creature, implies a spirited disposition. You must have noticed that a high spirit is unconquerable. Every soul possessed of it is fearless and indomitable in the face of any danger.

Yes, I have noticed that.

So now we know what physical qualities our Guardian must have, and also that he must be of a spirited temper.

Yes.

Then, Glaucon, how are men of that natural disposition to be kept from behaving pugnaciously to one another and to the rest of their countrymen?

It is not at all easy to see.

And yet they must be gentle to their own people and dangerous only to enemies; otherwise they will destroy themselves without waiting till others destroy them.

True.

What are we to do, then? If gentleness and a high temper are contraries, where shall we find a character to combine them? Both are necessary to make a good Guardian, but it seems they are incompatible. So we shall never have a good Guardian.

It looks like it.

Here I was perplexed, but on thinking over what we had been saying, I remarked that we deserved to be puzzled, because we had not followed up the comparison we had just drawn.

What do you mean? he asked.

We never noticed that, after all, there are natures in which these contraries are combined. They are to be found in animals, and not least in the kind we compared to our Guardian. Well-bred dogs, as you know, are by instinct perfectly gentle to people whom they know and are accustomed to, and fierce to strangers. So the combination of qualities we require for our Guardian is, after all, possible and not against nature.

Evidently.

Do you further agree that, besides this spirited temper, he must have a philosophical element in his nature?

I don't see what you mean.

This is another trait you will see in the dog. It is really remarkable how the creature gets angry at the mere sight of a stranger and welcomes anyone he knows, though he may never have been treated unkindly by the one or kindly by the other. Did that never strike you as curious?

I had not thought of it before; but that certainly is how a dog behaves.

Well, but that shows a fine instinct, which is philosophic in the true sense.

How so?

Because the only mark by which he distinguishes a friendly and an unfriendly face is that he knows the one and does not know the other; and if a creature makes that the test of what it finds congenial or otherwise, how can you deny that it has a passion for knowledge and understanding?

Of course, I cannot.

And that passion is the same thing as philosophy—the love of wisdom.[1]

Yes.

Shall we boldly say, then, that the same is true of human beings? If a man is to be gentle towards his own people whom he knows, he must have an instinctive love of wisdom and understanding.

Agreed.

So the nature required to make a really noble Guardian of our commonwealth will be swift and strong, spirited, and philosophic.

Quite so. . . .

[W]hat is the next point to be settled? Is it not the question, which of these Guardians are to be rulers and which are to obey?

No doubt.

Well, it is obvious that the elder must have authority over the young, and that the rulers must be the best.

Yes.

And as among farmers the best are those with a natural turn for farming, so, if we want the best among our Guardians, we must take those naturally fitted to watch over a commonwealth. They must have the right sort of intelligence and ability; and also they must look upon the commonwealth as their special concern—the sort of concern that is felt for something so closely bound up with oneself that its interests and fortunes, for good or ill, are held to be identical with one's own.

Exactly.

So the kind of men we must choose from among the Guardians will be those who, when we look at the whole course of their lives, are found to be full of zeal to do whatever they believe is for the good of the commonwealth and never willing to act against its interest.

Yes, they will be the men we want. . . .

We shall have to watch them from earliest childhood and set them tasks in which they would be most likely to forget or to be beguiled out of this duty. We shall then choose only those whose memory holds firm and who are proof against delusion.

Yes.

We must also subject them to ordeals of toil and pain and watch for the same qualities there. And we must observe them when exposed to the test of yet a third kind of bewitchment. As people lead colts up to alarming noises to see whether they are timid, so these young men must be brought into terrifying situations and then into scenes of pleasure, which will put them to severer proof than gold tried in the furnace. If we find one bearing himself well in all these trials and resisting every enchantment, a true guardian of himself, preserving always that perfect rhythm and harmony of being which he has acquired from his training in music and poetry, such a one will be of the greatest service to the commonwealth as well as to himself. Whenever we find one who has come unscathed through every test in childhood, youth, and manhood, we shall set him as a Ruler to watch over the commonwealth; he will be honoured in life, and after death receive the highest tribute of funeral rites and other memorials. All who do not reach this standard we must reject. And that, I think, my dear Glaucon, may be taken as an outline of the way in which we shall select Guardians to be set in authority as Rulers.

I am very much of your mind.

These, then, may properly be called Guardians in the fullest sense, who will ensure that neither foes without shall have the power, nor friends within the wish, to do harm. Those young men whom up to now we have been speaking of as Guardians, will be better described as Auxiliaries, who will enforce the decisions of the Rulers.

I agree.

Now, said I, can we devise . . . a single bold flight of invention, which we may induce the community in general, and if possible the Rulers themselves, to accept?

What kind of fiction? . . .

Well, here it is; though I hardly know how to find the courage or the words to express it. I shall try to convince, first the Rulers and the soldiers,[2] and then the whole community, that all that nurture and education which we gave them was only something they seemed to experience as it were in a dream. In reality they were the whole time down inside the earth, being moulded and fostered while their arms and all their equipment were being fashioned also; and at last, when they were complete, the earth sent them up from her womb into the light of day. So now they must think of the land they dwell in as a mother and nurse, whom they must take thought for and defend against any attack, and of their fellow citizens as brothers born of the same soil.

You might well be bashful about coming out with your fiction.

No doubt; but still you must hear the rest of the story. It is true, we shall tell our people in this fable, that all of you in this land are brothers; but the god who fashioned you mixed gold in the composition of those among you who are fit to rule, so that they are of the most precious quality; and he put silver in the Auxiliaries, and iron and brass in the farmers and craftsmen. Now, since you are all of one stock, although your children will generally be like their parents, sometimes a golden parent may have a silver child or a silver parent a golden one, and so on with all the other combinations. So the first and chief injunction laid by heaven upon the Rulers is that, among all the things of which they must show themselves good guardians, there is none that needs to be so carefully watched as the mixture of metals in the souls of the children. If a child of their own is born with an alloy of iron or brass, they must, without the smallest pity, assign him the station proper to his nature and thrust him out among the craftsmen or the farmers. If, on the contrary, these classes produce a child with gold or silver in his composition, they will promote him, according to his value, to be a Guardian or an Auxiliary. They will appeal to a prophecy that ruin will come upon the state when it passes into the keeping of a man of iron or brass. Such is the story; can you think of any device to make them believe it?

Not in the first generation; but their sons and descendants might believe it, and finally the rest of mankind.

Well, said I, even so it might have a good effect in making them care more for the commonwealth and for one another; for I think I see what you mean. . . .

Listen, then, and judge whether I am right. You remember how, when we first began to establish our commonwealth and several times since, we have laid down, as a universal principle, that everyone ought to perform the one function in the community for which his nature best suited him. Well, I believe that that principle, or some form of it, is justice.

We certainly laid that down.

Yes, and surely we have often heard people say that justice means minding one's own business and not meddling with other men's concerns; and we have often said so ourselves.

We have. . . .

Again, do you agree with me that no great harm would be done to the community by a general interchange of most forms of work, the carpenter and the cobbler exchanging their positions and their tools and taking on each other's jobs, or even the same man undertaking both?

Yes, there would not be much harm in that.

But I think you will also agree that another kind of interchange would be disastrous. Suppose, for instance, someone whom nature designed to be an artisan or tradesman should be emboldened by some advantage, such as wealth or command of votes or bodily strength, to try to enter the order of fighting men; or some member of that order should aspire, beyond his merits, to a seat in the council-chamber of the Guardians. Such interference and exchange of social positions and tools, or the attempt to combine all these forms of work in the same person, would be fatal to the commonwealth.

Most certainly.

Where there are three orders, then, any plurality of functions or shifting from one order to another is not merely utterly harmful to the community, but one might fairly call it the extreme of wrongdoing. And you will agree that to do the greatest of wrongs to one's own community is injustice.

Surely.

This, then, is injustice. And, conversely, let us repeat that when each order—tradesman, Auxiliary, Guardian—keeps to its own proper business in the commonwealth and does its own work, that is justice and what makes a just society.

I entirely agree. . . .

Then our next attempt, it seems, must be to point out what defect in the working of existing states prevents them from being so organized, and what is the least change that would effect a transformation into this type of government—a single change if possible, or perhaps two; at any rate let us make the changes as few and insignificant as may be.

By all means.

Well, there is one change which, as I believe we can show, would bring about this revolution—not a small change, certainly, nor an easy one, but possible.

What is it? . . .

Unless either philosophers become kings in their countries or those who are now called kings and rulers come to be sufficiently inspired with a genuine desire for wisdom; unless, that is to say, political power and philosophy meet together, while the many natures who now go their several ways in the one or the other direction are forcibly debarred from doing so, there can be no rest from troubles, my dear Glaucon, for states, nor yet, as I believe, for all mankind; nor can this commonwealth which we have imagined ever till then see the light of day and grow to its full stature. . . .

Here Adeimantus interposed. . . . [A]s a matter of plain fact, the votaries of philosophy, when they carry on the study too long, instead of taking it up in youth as a part of general culture and then dropping it, almost always become . . . utterly worthless; while even the most respectable are so far the worse for this pursuit you are praising as to become useless to society.

Well, I replied, do you think that charge is untrue?

I do not know, he answered; I should like to hear your opinion.

You shall; I think it is true.

Then how can it be right to say that there will be no rest from trouble until states are ruled by these philosophers whom we are now admitting to be of no use to them?

That is a question which needs to be answered by means of a parable. . . .

Imagine this state of affairs on board a ship or a number of ships. The master is bigger and burlier than any of the crew, but a little deaf and short-sighted and no less deficient in seamanship. The sailors are quarrelling over the control of the helm; each thinks he ought to be steering the vessel, though he has never learnt navigation and cannot point to any teacher under whom he has served his apprenticeship; what is more, they assert that navigation is a thing that cannot be taught at all, and are ready to tear in pieces anyone who says it can. Meanwhile they besiege the master himself, begging him urgently to trust them with the helm; and sometimes, when others have been more successful in gaining his ear, they kill them or throw them overboard, and, after somehow stupefying the worthy master with strong drink or an opiate, take control of the ship, make free with its stores, and turn the voyage, as might be expected of such a crew, into a drunken carousal. Besides all this, they cry up as a skilled navigator and master of seamanship anyone clever enough to lend a hand in persuading or forcing the master to set them in command. Every other kind of man they condemn as useless. They do not understand that the genuine navigator can only make himself fit to command a ship by studying the seasons of the year, sky, stars, and winds, and all that belongs to his craft; and they have no idea that, along with the science of navigation, it is possible for him to gain, by instruction or practice, the skill to keep control of the helm whether some of them like it or not. If a ship were managed in that way, would not those on board be likely to call the expert in navigation a mere star-gazer, who spent his time in idle talk and was useless to them?

They would indeed.

I think you understand what I mean and do not need to have my parable interpreted in order to see how it illustrates the attitude of existing states towards the true philosopher.

Quite so.

Use it, then, to enlighten that critic whom you spoke of as astonished that philosophers are not held in honour by their country. You may try, in the first place, to convince him that it would be far more astonishing if they were; and you may tell him further that he is right in calling the best sort of philosophers useless to the public; but for that he must rather blame those who make no use of them. It is not in the natural course of things for the pilot to beg the crew to take his orders, any more than for the wise to wait on the doorsteps of the rich; the author of that epigram[3] was mistaken. What is natural is that the sick man, whether rich or poor, should wait at the door of the physician, and that all who need to be governed should seek out the man who can govern them; it is not for him to beg them to accept his rule, if there is really any help in him. But our present rulers may fairly be compared to the sailors in our parable, and the useless visionaries, as the politicians call them, to the real masters of navigation.

Quite true.

Under these conditions, the noblest of pursuits can hardly be thought much of by men whose own way of life runs counter to it. . . .

But what do you mean by the highest kind of knowledge and with what is it concerned? You cannot hope to escape that question. . . .

First we must come to an understanding. Let me remind you of the distinction we drew earlier and have often drawn on other occasions, between the multiplicity of things that we call good or beautiful or whatever it may be and, on the other hand, Goodness itself or Beauty itself and so on. Corresponding to each of these sets of many things, we postulate a single Form or real essence, as we call it.

Yes, that is so.

Further, the many things, we say, can be seen, but are not objects of rational thought; whereas the Forms are objects of thought, but invisible.

Yes, certainly.

And we see things with our eyesight, just as we hear sounds with our ears and, to speak generally, perceive any sensible thing with our sense-faculties.

Of course.

Have you noticed, then, that the artificer who designed the senses has been exceptionally lavish of his materials in making the eyes able to see and their objects visible?

That never occurred to me.

Well, look at it in this way. Hearing and sound do not stand in need of any third thing, without which the ear will not hear nor sound be heard; and I think the same is true of most, not to say all, of the other senses. Can you think of one that does require anything of the sort?

No, I cannot.

But there is this need in the case of sight and its objects. You may have the power of vision in your eyes and try to use it, and colour may be there in the objects; but sight will see nothing and the colours will remain invisible in the absence of a third thing peculiarly constituted to serve this very purpose.

By which you mean—?

Naturally I mean what you call light; and if light is a thing of value, the sense of sight and the power of being visible are linked together by a very precious bond, such as unites no other sense with its object.

No one could say that light is not a precious thing.

And of all the divinities in the skies[4] is there one whose light, above all the rest, is responsible for making our eyes see perfectly and making objects perfectly visible?

There can be no two opinions: of course you mean the Sun.

And how is sight related to this deity? Neither sight nor the eye which contains it is the Sun, but of all the sense-organs it is the most sun-like; and further, the power it possesses is dispensed by the Sun, like a stream flooding the eye. And again, the Sun is not vision, but it is the cause of vision and also is seen by the vision it causes.

Yes.

It was the Sun, then, that I meant when I spoke of that offspring which the Good has created in the visible world, to stand there in the same relation to vision and visible things as that which the Good itself bears in the intelligible world to intelligence and to intelligible objects.

How is that? You must explain further.

You know what happens when the colours of things are no longer irradiated by the daylight, but only by the fainter luminaries of the night: when you look at them, the eyes are dim and seem almost blind, as if there were no unclouded vision in them. But when you look at things on which the Sun is shining, the same eyes see distinctly and it becomes evident that they do contain the power of vision.

Certainly.

Apply this comparison, then, to the soul. When its gaze is fixed upon an object irradiated by truth and reality, the soul gains understanding and knowledge and is manifestly in possession of intelligence. But when it looks towards that twilight world of things that come into existence and pass away, its sight is dim and it has only opinions and beliefs which shift to and fro, and now it seems like a thing that has no intelligence.

That is true.

This, then, which gives to the objects of knowledge their truth and to him who knows them his power of knowing, is the Form or essential nature of Goodness. It is the cause of knowledge and truth; and so, while you may think of it as an object of knowledge, you will do well to regard it as something beyond truth and knowledge and, precious as these both are, of still higher worth. And, just as in our analogy light and vision were to be thought of as like the Sun, but not identical with it, so here both knowledge and truth are to be regarded as like the Good, but to identify either with the Good is wrong. The Good must hold a yet higher place of honour.

You are giving it a position of extraordinary splendour, if it is the source of knowledge and truth and itself surpasses them in worth. You surely cannot mean that it is pleasure.

Heaven forbid, I exclaimed. But I want to follow up our analogy still further. You will agree that the Sun not only makes the things we see visible, but also brings them into existence and gives them growth and nourishment; yet he is not the same thing as existence. And so with the objects of knowledge: these derive from the Good not only their power of being known, but their very being and reality; and Goodness is not the same thing as being, but even beyond being, surpassing it in dignity and power.

Glaucon exclaimed with some amusement at my exalting Goodness in such extravagant terms.

It is your fault, I replied; you forced me to say what I think.

Yes, and you must not stop there. At any rate, complete your comparison with the Sun, if there is any more to be said.

There is a great deal more, I answered.

Let us hear it, then; don't leave anything out.

I am afraid much must be left unspoken. However, I will not, if I can help it, leave out anything that can be said on this occasion.

Please do not.

Conceive, then, that there are these two powers I speak of, the Good reigning over the domain of all that is intelligible, the Sun over the visible world—or the heaven as I might call it; only you would think I was showing off my skill in etymology. At any rate you have these two orders of things clearly before your mind: the visible and the intelligible?

I have.

Now take a line divided into two unequal parts, one to represent the visible order, the other the intelligible; and divide each part again in the same proportion, symbolizing degrees of comparative clearness or obscurity. Then (A) one of the two sections in the visible world will stand for images. By images I mean first *shadows*, and then *reflections in water* or in close-grained, polished surfaces, and everything of that kind, if you understand.

Yes, I understand.

Let the second section (B) stand for the *actual things* of which the first are like-nesses, the living creatures about us and all the works of nature or of human hands.

So be it.

Will you also take the proportion in which the visible world has been divided as corresponding to degrees of reality and truth, so that the likeness shall stand to the original in the same ratio as the sphere of appearances and belief to the sphere of knowledge?

Certainly.

Now consider how we are to divide the part which stands for the intelligible world. There are two sections. In the first (C) the mind uses as images those actual things which themselves had images in the visible world; and it is compelled to pursue its inquiry by starting from assumptions and travelling, not up to a prin-ciple, but down to a conclusion. In the second (D) the mind moves in the other direction, from an assumption up towards a principle which is not hypotheti-cal; and it makes no use of the images employed in the other section, but only of Forms, and conducts its inquiry solely by their means.

I don't quite understand what you mean.

Then we will try again; what I have just said will help you to understand. (C) You know, of course, how students of subjects like geometry and arithmetic begin by postulating odd and even numbers, or the various figures and the three kinds of angle, and other such data in each subject. These data they take as known; and, having adopted them as assumptions, they do not feel called upon to give any account of them to themselves or to anyone else, but treat them as self-evident. Then, starting from these assumptions, they go on until they arrive, by a series of consistent steps, at all the conclusions they set out to investigate.

Yes, I know that.

You also know how they make use of visible figures and discourse about them, though what they really have in mind is the originals of which these figures are images: they are not reasoning, for instance, about this particular square and diagonal which they have drawn, but about *the* Square and *the* Diagonal; and so in all cases. The diagrams they draw and the models they make are actual things, which may have their shadows or images in water; but now they serve in their turn as images, while the student is seeking to behold those realities which only thought can apprehend.

True.

This, then, is the class of things that I spoke of as intelligible, but with two qual-ifications: first, that the mind, in studying them, is compelled to employ assump-tions, and, because it cannot rise above these, does not travel upwards to a first principle; and second, that it uses as images those actual things which have images of their own in the section below them and which, in comparison with those shad-ows and reflections, are reputed to be more palpable and valued accordingly.

I understand: you mean the subject-matter of geometry and of the kindred arts.

(D) Then by the second section of the intelligible world you may understand me to mean all that unaided reasoning apprehends by the power of dialectic, when it treats its assumptions, not as first principles, but as *hypotheses* in the literal sense, things "laid down" like a flight of steps up which it may mount all the way to something that is not hypothetical, the first principle of all; and having grasped this, may turn back and, holding on to the consequences which depend upon it, descend at last to a conclusion, never making use of any sensible object, but only of Forms, moving through Forms from one to another, and ending with Forms.

I understand, he said, though not perfectly; for the procedure you describe sounds like an enormous undertaking. But I see that you mean to distinguish the field of intelligible reality studied by dialectic as having a greater certainty and truth than the subject-matter of the "arts," as they are called, which treat their assumptions as first principles. The students of these arts are, it is true, compelled to exercise thought in contemplating objects which the senses cannot perceive; but because they start from assumptions without going back to a first principle, you do not regard them as gaining true understanding about those objects, although the objects themselves, when connected with a first principle, are intelligible. And I think you would call the state of mind of the students of geometry and other such arts, not intelligence, but thinking, as being something between intelligence and mere acceptance of appearances.

You have understood me quite well enough, I replied. And now you may take, as corresponding to the four sections, these four states of mind: *intelligence* for the highest, *thinking* for the second, *belief* for the third, and for the last *imagining*. These you may arrange as the terms in a proportion, assigning to each a degree of clearness and certainty corresponding to the measure in which their objects possess truth and reality.

I understand and agree with you. I will arrange them as you say.

Next, said I, here is a parable to illustrate the degrees in which our nature may be enlightened or unenlightened. Imagine the condition of men living in a sort of cavernous chamber underground, with an entrance open to the light and a long passage all down the cave.[5] Here they have been from childhood, chained by the leg and also by the neck, so that they cannot move and can see only what is in front of them, because the chains will not let them turn their heads. At some distance higher up is the light of a fire burning behind them; and between the prisoners and the fire is a track[6] with a parapet built along it, like the screen at a puppet-show, which hides the performers while they show their puppets over the top.

I see, said he.

Now behind this parapet imagine persons carrying along various artificial objects, including figures of men and animals in wood or stone or other materials, which project above the parapet. Naturally, some of these persons will be talking, others silent.[7]

It is a strange picture, he said, and a strange sort of prisoners.

Like ourselves, I replied; for in the first place prisoners so confined would have seen nothing of themselves or of one another, except the shadows thrown by the fire-light on the wall of the Cave facing them, would they?

Not if all their lives they had been prevented from moving their heads.

And they would have seen as little of the objects carried past.

Of course.

Now, if they could talk to one another, would they not suppose that their words referred only to those passing shadows which they saw?[8]

Necessarily.

And suppose their prison had an echo from the wall facing them? When one of the people crossing behind them spoke, they could only suppose that the sound came from the shadow passing before their eyes.

No doubt.

In every way, then, such prisoners would recognize as reality nothing but the shadows of those artificial objects.

Inevitably.

Now consider what would happen if their release from the chains and the healing of their unwisdom should come about in this way. Suppose one of them set free and forced suddenly to stand up, turn his head, and walk with eyes lifted to the light; all these movements would be painful, and he would be too dazzled to make out the objects whose shadows he had been used to see. What do you think he would say, if someone told him that what he had formerly seen was meaning-less illusion, but now, being somewhat nearer to reality and turned towards more real objects, he was getting a truer view? Suppose further that he were shown the various objects being carried by and were made to say, in reply to questions, what each of them was. Would he not be perplexed and believe the objects now shown him to be not so real as what he formerly saw?

Yes, not nearly so real.

And if he were forced to look at the fire-light itself, would not his eyes ache, so that he would try to escape and turn back to the things which he could see dis-tinctly, convinced that they really were clearer than these other objects now being shown to him?

Yes.

And suppose someone were to drag him away forcibly up the steep and rug-ged ascent and not let him go until he had hauled him out into the sunlight, would he not suffer pain and vexation at such treatment, and, when he had come out into the light, find his eyes so full of its radiance that he could not see a single one of the things that he was now told were real?

Certainly he would not see them all at once.

He would need, then, to grow accustomed before he could see things in that upper world. At first it would be easiest to make out shadows, and then the images of men and things reflected in water, and later on the things themselves. After that, it would be easier to watch the heavenly bodies and the sky itself by night, looking at the light of the moon and stars rather than the Sun and the Sun's light in the day-time.

Yes, surely.

Last of all, he would be able to look at the Sun and contemplate its nature, not as it appears when reflected in water or any alien medium, but as it is in itself in its own domain.

No doubt.

And now he would begin to draw the conclusion that it is the Sun that produces the seasons and the course of the year and controls everything in the visible world, and moreover is in a way the cause of all that he and his companions used to see.

Clearly he would come at last to that conclusion.

Then if he called to mind his fellow prisoners and what passed for wisdom in his former dwelling-place, he would surely think himself happy in the change and be sorry for them. They may have had a practice of honouring and commending one another, with prizes for the man who had the keenest eye for the passing shadows and the best memory for the order in which they followed or accompanied one another, so that he could make a good guess as to which was going to come next. Would our released prisoner be likely to covet those prizes or to envy the men exalted to honour and power in the Cave? Would he not feel like Homer's Achilles, that he would far sooner "be on earth as a hired servant in the house of a landless man" or endure anything rather than go back to his old beliefs and live in the old way?

Yes, he would prefer any fate to such a life.

Now imagine what would happen if he went down again to take his former seat in the Cave. Coming suddenly out of the sunlight, his eyes would be filled with darkness. He might be required once more to deliver his opinion on those shadows, in competition with the prisoners who had never been released, while his eyesight was still dim and unsteady; and it might take some time to become used to the darkness. They would laugh at him and say that he had gone up only to come back with his sight ruined; it was worth no one's while even to attempt the ascent. If they could lay hands on the man who was trying to set them free and lead them up, they would kill him.[9]

Yes, they would.

Every feature in this parable, my dear Glaucon, is meant to fit our earlier analysis. The prison dwelling corresponds to the region revealed to us through the sense of sight, and the fire-light within it to the power of the Sun. The ascent to see the things in the upper world you may take as standing for the upward journey of the soul into the region of the intelligible; then you will be in possession of what I surmise, since that is what you wish to be told. Heaven knows whether it is true; but this, at any rate, is how it appears to me. In the world of knowledge, the last thing to be perceived and only with great difficulty is the essential Form of Goodness. Once it is perceived, the conclusion must follow that, for all things, this is the cause of whatever is right and good; in the visible world it gives birth to light and to the lord of light, while it is itself sovereign in the intelligible world and the parent of intelligence and truth. Without having had a vision of this Form, no one can act with wisdom, either in his own life or in matters of state.

So far as I can understand, I share your belief.

Then you may also agree that it is no wonder if those who have reached this height are reluctant to manage the affairs of men. Their souls long to spend all their time in that upper world—naturally enough, if here once more our parable holds true. Nor, again, is it at all strange that one who comes from the contemplation of divine things to the miseries of human life should appear awkward and ridiculous when, with eyes still dazed and not yet accustomed to the darkness, he is compelled, in a law-court or elsewhere, to dispute about the shadows of justice or the images that cast those shadows, and to wrangle over the notions of what is right in the minds of men who have never beheld Justice itself.

It is not at all strange. . . .

It is for us, then, as founders of a commonwealth, to bring compulsion to bear on the noblest natures. They . . . must not be allowed, as they now are, to remain on the heights, refusing to come down again to the prisoners or to take any part in their labours and rewards, however much or little these may be worth.

Shall we not be doing them an injustice, if we force on them a worse life than they might have?

You have forgotten again, my friend, that the law is not concerned to make any one class specially happy, but to ensure the welfare of the commonwealth as a whole. By persuasion or constraint it will unite the citizens in harmony, making them share whatever benefits each class can contribute to the common good; and its purpose in forming men of that spirit was not that each should be left to go his own way, but that they should be instrumental in binding the community into one.

True, I had forgotten.

You will see, then, Glaucon, that there will be no real injustice in compelling our philosophers to watch over and care for the other citizens. We can fairly tell them that their compeers in other states may quite reasonably refuse to collaborate: there they have sprung up, like a self-sown plant, in despite of their country's institutions; no one has fostered their growth, and they cannot be expected to show gratitude for a care they have never received. "But," we shall say, "it is not so with you. We have brought you into existence for your country's sake as well as for your own, to be like leaders and king-bees in a hive; you have been better and more thoroughly educated than those others and hence you are more capable of playing your part both as men of thought and as men of action. You must go down, then, each in his turn, to live with the rest and let your eyes grow accustomed to the darkness. You will then see a thousand times better than those who live there always; you will recognize every image for what it is and know what it represents, because you have seen justice, beauty, and goodness in their reality; and so you and we shall find life in our commonwealth no mere dream, as it is in most existing states, where men live fighting one another about shadows and quarrelling for power, as if that were a great prize; whereas in truth government can be at its best and free from dissension only where the destined rulers are least desirous of holding office."

Quite true.

Then will our pupils refuse to listen and to take their turns at sharing in the work of the community, though they may live together for most of their time in a purer air?

No; it is a fair demand, and they are fair-minded men. No doubt, unlike any ruler of the present day, they will think of holding power as an unavoidable necessity.

Yes, my friend; for the truth is that you can have a well-governed society only if you can discover for your future rulers a better way of life than being in office; then only will power be in the hands of men who are rich, not in gold, but in the wealth that brings happiness, a good and wise life. All goes wrong when, starved for lack of anything good in their own lives, men turn to public affairs hoping to snatch from thence the happiness they hunger for. They set about fighting for power, and this internecine conflict ruins them and their country. The life of true philosophy is the only one that looks down upon offices of state; and access to power must be confined to men who are not in love with it; otherwise rivals will start fighting. So whom else can you compel to undertake the guardianship of the commonwealth, if not those who, besides understanding best the principles of government, enjoy a nobler life than the politician's and look for rewards of a different kind?

There is indeed no other choice.

NOTES

1. The ascription of a philosophic element to dogs is not seriously meant. We might regard man's love of knowledge as rooted in an instinct of curiosity to be found in animals; but curiosity has no connexion with gentleness, and for Plato reason is an independent faculty, existing only in man and not developed from any animal instinct.
2. Note that the Guardians themselves are to accept this allegory, if possible. It is not "propaganda" foisted on the masses by the Rulers.
3. Simonides was asked by Hiero's queen whether it was better to be wise (a man of genius) or rich. He replied: Rich; for the wise are to be found at the court of the rich.
4. Plato held that the heavenly bodies are immortal living creatures, i.e, gods.
5. The *length* of the "way in" (*eisodos*) to the chamber where the prisoners sit is an essential feature, explaining why no daylight reaches them.
6. The track crosses the passage into the cave at right angles, and is *above* the parapet built along it.
7. A modern Plato would compare his Cave to an underground cinema, where the audience watch the play of shadows thrown by the film passing before a light at their backs. The film itself is only an image of "real" things and events in the world outside the cinema. For the film Plato has to substitute the clumsier apparatus of a procession of artificial objects carried on their heads by persons who are merely part of the machinery, providing for the movement of the objects and the sounds whose echo the prisoners hear. The parapet prevents these persons' shadows from being cast on the wall of the Cave.
8. . . . The prisoners, having seen nothing but shadows, cannot think their words refer to the objects carried past behind their backs. For them shadows (images) are the only realities.
9. An allusion to the fate of Socrates.

STUDY QUESTIONS

1. How do you defend a system of government in which those who know much about public issues have no more say in the decision process than those who know little?
2. What is the fable of the metals, and does it strengthen or weaken Plato's case against democracy?
3. Do you believe that the parable of the state of affairs on board a ship misrepresents democracy?
4. Do you agree with Plato that the best rulers are found among those not seeking to rule?

Leviathan

THOMAS HOBBES

Thomas Hobbes (1588–1679) was an English philosopher who played a crucial role in the history of social thought. He developed a moral and political theory that views justice and other ethical ideals as resting on an implied agreement among individuals to relinquish the right to do whatever they please in exchange for all others limiting their rights in a similar manner, thus achieving security for all.

OF THE NATURAL CONDITION OF MANKIND AS CONCERNING THEIR FELICITY, AND MISERY

Nature hath made men so equal, in the faculties of body and mind; as that though there be found one man sometimes manifestly stronger in body, or of quicker mind than another; yet when all is reckoned together, the difference between man and man is not so considerable, as that one man can thereupon claim to himself any benefit, to which another may not pretend as well as he. For as to the strength of body, the weakest has strength enough to kill the strongest, either by secret machination or by confederacy with others, that are in the same danger as himself.

And as to the faculties of the mind (setting aside the arts grounded upon words, and especially that skill of proceeding upon general, and infallible rules, called science; which very few have, and but in few things; as being not a native faculty, born with us; nor attained (as prudence) while we look after someone else) I find yet a greater equality amongst men than that of strength. For prudence is but experience; which equal time equally bestows on all men in those things they equally apply themselves unto. That which may perhaps make such equality incredible is but a vain conceit of one's own wisdom, which almost all men think they have in a greater degree than the vulgar; that is, than all men but themselves, and a few others, whom by fame, or for concurring with themselves, they approve. For such is the nature of men, that howsoever they may acknowledge many others to be more witty, or more eloquent, or more learned; yet they will hardly believe there be many so wise as themselves: For they see their own wit at hand, and other men's at a distance. But this proveth rather that men are in that point equal than unequal. For there is not ordinarily a greater sign of the equal distribution of any thing than that every man is contented with his share.

From this equality of ability ariseth equality of hope in the attaining of our ends. And therefore if any two men desire the same thing, which nevertheless they cannot

From Thomas Hobbes, *Leviathan* (1651).

both enjoy, they become enemies; and in the way to their end (which is principally their own conservation, and sometimes their delectation only) endeavour to destroy, or subdue one another. And from hence it comes to pass that where an invader hath no more to fear than another man's single power; if one plant, sow, build, or possess a convenient seat, others may probably be expected to come prepared with forces united to dispossess and deprive him not only of the fruit of his labour but also of his life or liberty. And the invader again is in the like danger of another.

And from this diffidence of one another, there is no way for any man to secure himself, so reasonable, as anticipation; that is, by force, or wiles, to master the persons of all men he can, so long, till he see no other power great enough to endanger him: and this is no more than his own conservation requireth, and is generally allowed. Also because there be some, that taking pleasure in contemplating their own power in the acts of conquest, which they pursue farther than their security requires; if others, that otherwise would be glad to be at ease within modest bounds, should not by invasion increase their power, they would not be able, long time, by standing only on their defence, to subsist. And by consequence, such augmentation of dominion over men, being necessary to a man's conservation, it ought to be allowed him.

Again, men have no pleasure (but on the contrary a great deal of grief) in keeping company, where there is no power able to over-awe them all. For every man looketh that his companion should value him, at the same rate he sets upon himself: and upon all signs of contempt, or undervaluing, naturally endeavours, as far as he dares (which amongst them that have no common power to keep them in quiet, is far enough to make them destroy each other) to extort a greater value from his contemners, by damage; and from others, by the example.

So that in the nature of man, we find three principal causes of quarrel. First, competition; secondly, diffidence; thirdly, glory.

The first, maketh man invade for gain; the second, for safety; and the third, for reputation. The first use violence, to make themselves masters of other men's persons, wives, children, and cattle; the second, to defend them; the third for trifles, as a word, a smile, a different opinion, and any other sign of undervalue, either direct in their persons, or by reflection in their kindred, their friends, their nation, their profession, or their name.

Hereby it is manifest that during the time men live without a common power to keep them all in awe, they are in that condition which is called war; and such a war, as is of every man, against every man. For WAR consisteth not in battle only, or the act of fighting, but in a tract of time, wherein the will to contend by battle is sufficiently known: and therefore the notion of *time* is to be considered in the nature of war, as it is in the nature of weather. For as the nature of foul weather lieth not in a shower or two of rain, but in an inclination thereto of many days together: so the nature of war, consisteth not in actual fighting, but in the known disposition thereto, during all the time there is no assurance to the contrary. All other time is PEACE.

Whatsoever therefore is consequent to a time of war, where every man is enemy to every man; the same is consequent to the time, wherein men live without other security than what their own strength, and their own invention shall furnish them withal. In such condition, there is no place for industry; because the fruit thereof is uncertain: and consequently no culture of the earth; no navigation, nor use of the commodities that may be imported by sea; no commodious building; no instruments of moving, and removing such things as require much force; no knowledge of the face of the earth; no account of time; no arts; no letters; no society; and which is worst of all, continual fear, and danger of violent death; and the life of man, solitary, poor, nasty, brutish, and short.

It may seem strange to some man, that has not well weighed these things; that nature should thus dissociate, and render men apt to invade, and destroy one another: and he may therefore, not trusting to this inference, made from the passions, desire perhaps to have the same confirmed by experience. Let him therefore consider with himself, when taking a journey, he arms himself, and seeks to go well accompanied; when going to sleep, he locks his doors; when even in his house he locks his chests; and this when he knows there be laws, and public officers, armed, to revenge all injuries shall be done him; what opinion he has of his fellow subjects, when he rides armed; of his fellow citizens, when he locks his doors; and of his children, and servants, when he locks his chests. Does he not there as much accuse mankind by his actions as I do by my words? But neither of us accuse man's nature in it. The desires, and other passions of man, are in themselves no sin. No more are the actions that proceed from those passions till they know a law that forbids them: which till laws be made they cannot know: nor can any law be made till they have agreed upon the person that shall make it.

It may peradventure be thought there was never such a time nor condition of war as this; and I believe it was never generally so, over all the world: but there are many places where they live so now. For the savage people in many places of *America*, except the government of small families, the concord whereof dependeth on natural lust, have no government at all: and live at this day in that brutish manner, as I said before. Howsoever, it may be perceived what manner of life there would be, where there were no common power to fear; by the manner of life, which men that have formerly lived under a peacefull government, use to degenerate into a civil war.

But though there had never been any time wherein particular men were in a condition of war one against another; yet in all times, kings and persons of sovereign authority, because of their independency, are in continual jealousies and in the state and posture of gladiators, having their weapons pointing and their eyes fixed on one another; that is, their forts, garrisons, and guns upon the frontiers of their kingdoms; and continual spies upon their neighbours; which is a posture of war. But because they uphold thereby the industry of their subjects there does not follow from it that misery, which accompanies the liberty of particular men.

To this war of every man against every man, this also is consequent that nothing can be unjust. The notions of right and wrong, justice and injustice, have there no place. Where there is no common power, there is no law: where no law, no injustice. Force and fraud are in war the two cardinal virtues. Justice and injustice are none of the faculties neither of the body nor mind. If they were, they might be in a man that were alone in the world, as well as his senses and passions. They are qualities that relate to men in society, not in solitude. It is consequent also to the same condition that there be no propriety, no dominion, no *mine* and *thine* distinct; but only that to be every man's, that he can get; and for so long, as he can keep it. And thus much for the ill condition which many by mere nature is actually placed in; though with a possibility to come out of it, consisting partly in the passions, partly in his reason.

The passions that incline men to peace are fear of death; desire of such things as are necessary to commodious living; and a hope by their industry to obtain them. And reason suggesteth convenient articles of peace, upon which men may be drawn to agreement. These articles are they which otherwise are called the Laws of Nature: whereof I shall speak more particularly, in the two following chapters.

OF THE FIRST AND SECOND NATURAL LAWS, AND OF CONTRACTS

The RIGHT OF NATURE, which writers commonly call *jus naturale,* is the liberty each man hath, to use his own power, as he will himself, for the preservation of his own nature; that is to say, of his own life; and consequently, of doing any thing, which in his own judgment, and reason, he shall conceive to be the aptest means thereunto.

By LIBERTY, is understood, according to the proper signification of the word, the absence of external impediments: which impediments may oft take away part of a man's power to do what he would; but cannot hinder him from using the power left him, according as his judgment, and reason shall dictate to him.

A LAW OF NATURE (*lex naturalis*) is a precept, or general rule, found out by reason, by which a man is forbidden to do that, which is destructive of his life, or taketh away the means of preserving the same; and to omit that, by which he thinketh it may be best preserved. For though they that speak of this subject, use to confound *jus,* and *lex, right* and *law*; yet they ought to be distinguished; because RIGHT, consisteth in liberty to do, or to forbear; whereas LAW, determineth, and bindeth to one of them: so that law, and right, differ as much, as obligation, and liberty, which in one and the same matter are inconsistent.

And because the condition of man (as hath been declared in the precedent chapter) is a condition of war of every one against every one; in which case every one is governed by his own reason; and there is nothing he can make use of, that may not be a help unto him, in preserving his life against his enemies, it followeth, that in such a condition, every man has a right to every thing: even to one another's body. And therefore, as long as this natural right of every man to every thing endureth, there can be no security to any man (how strong or wise soever he be) of living out the time, which nature ordinarily alloweth men to live. And consequently it is a precept, or general rule of reason, *that every man ought to endeavour peace, as far as he has hope of obtaining it; and when he cannot obtain it, that he may seek, and use, all helps and advantages of war.* The first branch of which rule containeth the first and fundamental law of nature; which is *to seek peace and follow it.* The second, the sum of the right of nature, which is, *by all means we can, to defend ourselves.*

From this fundamental law of nature, by which men are commanded to endeavor peace, is derived this second law; *that a man be willing, when others are so too, as farforth, as for peace, and defence of himself he shall think it necessary, to lay down this right to all things, and be contented with so much liberty against other men, as he would allow other men against himself.* For as long as every man holdeth this right of doing any thing he liketh, so long are all men in the condition of war. But if other men will not lay down their right, as well as he, then there is no reason for any one to divest himself of his: for that were to expose himself to prey (which no man is bound to) rather than to dispose himself to peace. This is that law of the Gospel, *whatsoever you require that others should do for you, that do ye to them.* . . .

OF OTHER LAWS OF NATURE

From that law of nature, by which we are obliged to transfer to another, such rights, as being retained, hinder the peace of mankind, there followeth a third; which is this, *that men perform their covenants made*: without which, covenants are in vain and but empty words; and the right of all men to all things remaining, we are still in the condition of war.

And in this law of nature, consisteth the fountain and original of JUSTICE. For where no covenant hath preceded, there hath no right been transferred, and every man has right to every thing; and consequently, no action can be unjust. But when a covenant is made, then to break it is *unjust;* and the definition of INJUSTICE, is no other than *the not performance of covenant.* And whatsoever is not unjust, is *just.*

But because covenants of mutual trust, where there is fear of not performance on either part (as hath been said in the former chapter) are invalid; though the original of justice be the making of covenants; yet injustice actually there can be none, till the cause of such fear be taken away; which while men are in the natural condition of war, cannot be done. Therefore before the names of just and unjust can have place, there must be some coercive power to compel men equally to the performance of their covenants, by the terror of some punishment, greater than the benefit they expect by the breach of their convenant; and to make good that propriety, which by mutual contract men acquire, in recompense of the universal right they abandon: and such power there is none before the erection of a commonwealth. And this is also to be gathered out of the ordinary definition of justice in the Schools: for they say that *justice is the constant will of giving to every man his own.* And therefore where there is no *own,* that is, no propriety, there is no injustice; and where there is no coercive power erected, that is, where there is no commonwealth, there is no propriety; all men having right to all things: therefore where there is no commonwealth, there nothing is unjust. So that the nature of justice, consisteth in keeping of valid covenants: but the validity of covenants begins not but with the constitution of a civil power, sufficient to compel men to keep them: and then it is also that propriety begins.

The fool hath said in his heart, there is no such thing as justice; and sometimes also with his tongue; seriously alleging that every man's conservation and contentment, being committed to his own care, there could be no reason why every man might not do what he thought conduced thereunto: and therefore also to make, or not make: keep, or not keep, covenants was not against reason, when it conduced to one's benefit. He does not therein deny that there be covenants; and that they are sometimes broken, sometimes kept; and that such breach of them may be called injustice, and the observance of them justice: but he questioneth whether injustice, taking away the fear of God (for the same fool hath said in his heart there is no God), may not sometimes stand with that reason, which dictateth to every man his own good; and particularly then, when it conduceth to such a benefit, as shall put a man in a condition to neglect not only the dispraise and reviling, but also the power of other men. . . . This specious reasoning is nevertheless false.

For the question is not of promises mutual, where there is no security of performance on either side; as when there is no civil power erected over the parties promising; for such promises are no covenants: but either where one of the parties has performed already; or where there is a power to make him perform; there is the question whether it be against reason that is against the benefit of the other to perform, or not. And I say it is not against reason. For the manifestation whereof, we are to consider; first, that when a man doth a thing, which notwithstanding any thing can be foreseen, and reckoned on, tendeth to his own destruction, howsoever some accident which he could not expect, arriving may turn it to his benefit; yet such events do not make it reasonably or wisely done. Secondly, that in a condition of war, wherein every man to every man, for want of a common power to keep them all in awe, is an enemy, there is no man can hope by his own strength, or wit, to defend himself from destruction, without the help of confederates; where every one expects the same defence by the confederation that any one else does: and therefore he which declares he thinks it reason to deceive those that help him, can in reason expect no other means of safety than what can be had from his own single power. He therefore that breaketh his covenant, and consequently declareth that he thinks he may with reason do so, cannot be received into any society, that unite themselves for peace and defence, but by the error of them that receive him; nor when he is received, be retained in it, without seeing the danger of their error; which errors a man cannot reasonably reckon upon as the means of his security: and therefore if he be left, or cast out of society, he perisheth; and if he live in society, it is by the errors of other men, which he could not foresee, nor reckon upon; and consequently against the reason of his preservation; and so, as all men that contribute not to his destruction, forbear him only out of ignorance of what is good for themselves.

STUDY QUESTIONS

1. Without government to enforce laws, would life be, as Hobbes says, "nasty, brutish, and short"?
2. What does Hobbes mean by "the right of nature"?
3. What does he mean by a "law of nature"?
4. Why are we obliged to keep our agreements?

Second Treatise of Government

JOHN LOCKE

John Locke is regarded not only as a major figure in the development of British empiricism but also as a leading liberal political philosopher, defending individual freedom against authoritarian power.

In his influential defense of private property, Locke argues that each person is entitled to the holdings that result from that individual's labor being "mixed" with whatever the world contains, so long as what remains is enough and as good for others. Such acquisitions by means of individual effort cannot rightfully be taken away.

OF PROPERTY

25. Whether we consider natural reason, which tells us, that men, being once born, have a right to their preservation, and consequently to meat and drink, and such other things as nature affords for their subsistence: or revelation, which gives us an account of those grants God made of the world to Adam, and to Noah, and his sons, it is very clear, that God, as King David says, Psal. cxv. 16, "has given the earth to the children of men," given it to mankind in common. But this being supposed, it seems to some a very great difficulty how anyone should ever come to have a property in anything: I will not content myself to answer, that if it be difficult to make out property, upon a supposition, that God gave the world to Adam, and his posterity in common; it is impossible that any man, but one universal monarch, should have any property upon a supposition, that God gave the world to Adam, and his heirs in succession, exclusive of all the rest of his posterity. But I shall endeavour to show how men might come to have a property in several parts of that which God gave to mankind in common, and that without any express compact of all the commoners.

26. God, who has given the world to men in common, has also given them reason to make use of it to the best advantage of life, and convenience. The earth, and all that is therein, is given to men for the support and comfort of their being. And though all the fruits it naturally produces, and beasts it feeds, belong to mankind in common, as they are produced by the spontaneous hand of nature; and nobody has originally a private dominion, exclusive of the rest of mankind, in any of them, as they are thus in their natural state: yet being given for the use of men, there must of necessity be a means to appropriate them some way or other, before they can be of any use, or at all beneficial to any particular man. The fruit, or venison, which nourishes the wild Indian, who knows no enclosure and is still a tenant in common, must be his, and so his, i.e. a part of him, that another can no longer have any right to it, before it can do him any good for the support of his life.

From *Second Treatise of Government* by John Locke (1690).

27. Though the earth, and all inferior creatures, be common to all men, yet every man has a property in his own person: this nobody has any right to but himself. The labour of his body and the work of his hands, we may say, are properly his. Whatsoever then he removes out of the state that nature has provided, and left it in, he has mixed his labour with, and joined to it something that is his own, and thereby makes it his property. It being by him removed from the common state nature has placed it in, it has by this labour something annexed to it, that excludes the common right of other men. For this labour being the unquestionable property of the labourer, no man but he can have a right to what that is once joined to, at least where there is enough, and as good, left in common for others.

28. He that is nourished by the acorns he picked up under an oak, or the apples he gathered from the trees in the wood, has certainly appropriated them to himself. Nobody can deny but the nourishment is his, I ask then, when did they begin to be his? When he digested? Or when he eat? Or when he boiled? Or when he brought them home? Or when he picked them up? And it is plain, if the first gathering made them not his, nothing else could. That labour put a distinction between them and common: that added something to them more than nature, the common mother of all, had done; and so they became his private right. And will anyone say he had no right to those acorns or apples he thus appropriated, because he had not the consent of all mankind to make them his? Was it a robbery thus to assume to himself what belonged to all in common? If such a consent as that was necessary, man had starved, notwithstanding the plenty God had given him. We see in commons, which remain so by compact, that it is the taking any part of what is common, and removing it out of the state nature leaves it in, which begins the property; without which the common is of no use. And the taking of this or that part does not depend on the express consent of all the commoners. Thus the grass my horse has bit; the turfs my servant has cut; and the ore I have digged in any place, where I have a right to them in common with others, become my property, without the assignation or consent of anybody. The labour that was mine, removing them out of that common state they were in, has fixed my property in them. . . .

31. It will perhaps be objected to this, that "if gathering the acorns, or other fruits of the earth, &c. makes a right to them, then anyone may engross as much as he will." To which I answer, Not so. The same law of nature, that does by this means give us property, does also bound that property too. "God has given us all things richly," 1 Tim: vi. 17, is the voice of reason confirmed by inspiration. But how far has he given it us? To enjoy. As much as anyone can make use of to any advantage of life before it spoils, so much he may by his labour fix a property in: whatever is beyond this is more than his share and belongs to others. Nothing was made by God for man to spoil or destroy. And thus, considering the plenty of natural provisions there was a long time in the world, and the few spenders; and to how small a part of that provision the industry of one man could extend itself, and engross it to the prejudice of others; especially keeping within the bounds, set by reason, of what might serve for his use; there could be then little room for quarrels or contentions about property so established.

32. But the chief matter of property being now not the fruits of the earth, and the beasts that subsist on it, but the earth it self; as that which takes in, and carries with it all the rest: I think it is plain that property in that too is acquired as the former. As much land as a man tills, plants, improves, cultivates, and can use the product of, so much is his property. He by his labour does, as it were, enclose it from the common. Nor will it invalidate his right to say everybody else has an equal title to it; and therefore he cannot appropriate, he cannot enclose, without the consent of all his fellow commoners, all mankind. God, when he gave the world in common to all mankind, commanded man also to labour, and the penury of his condition required it of him. God and his reason commanded him to subdue the earth, i.e. improve it for the benefit of life, and therein lay out something upon it that was his own, his labour. He that, in obedience to this command of God, subdued, tilled, and sowed any part of it, thereby annexed to it something that was his property, which another had no title to, nor could without injury take from him.

33. Nor was this appropriation of any parcel of land, by improving it, any prejudice to any other man, since there was still enough, and as good left; and more than the yet unprovided could use. So that, in effect, there was never the less left for others because of his enclosure for himself. For he that leaves as much as another can make use of, does as good as take nothing at all. Nobody could think himself injured by the drinking of another man, though he took a good draught, who had a whole river of the same water left him to quench his thirst: And the case of land and water, where there is enough of both, is perfectly the same.

40. Nor is it so strange, as perhaps before consideration it may appear, that the property of labour should be able to over-balance the community of land. For it is labour indeed that puts the difference of value on everything; and let anyone consider what the difference is between an acre of land planted with tobacco or sugar, sown with wheat or barley, and an acre of the same land lying in common, without any husbandry upon it, and he will find that the improvement of labour makes the far greater part of the value. I think it will be but a very modest computation to say that of the products of the earth useful to the life of man, nine-tenths are the effects of labour: nay, if we will rightly estimate things as they come to our use, and cast up the several expenses about them, what in them is purely owing to nature, and what to labour, we shall find that in most of them ninety-nine hundredths are wholly to be put on the account of labour.

46. The greatest part of things really useful to the life of man, and such as the necessity of subsisting made the first commoners of the world look after, as it does the Americans now, are generally things of short duration; such as, if they are not consumed by use, will decay and perish of themselves: gold, silver, and diamonds, are things that fancy or agreement hath put the value on, more than real use, and the necessary support of life. Now of those good things which nature hath provided in common, everyone had a right (as has been said) to as much as he could use, and property in all that he could affect with his labour; all that his industry could extend to, to alter from the state nature had put it in, was his. He that gathered a hundred bushels of acorns or apples had thereby a property in them, they were his goods as

soon as gathered. He was only to look that he used them before they spoiled, else he took more than his share and robbed others. And indeed it was a foolish thing, as well as dishonest, to hoard up more than he could make use of. If he gave away a part to anybody else, so that it perished not uselessly in his possession, these he also made use of. And if he also bartered away plums, that would have rotted in a week, for nuts that would last good for his eating a whole year, he did no injury; he wasted not the common stock; destroyed no part of the portion of goods that belonged to others, so long as nothing perished uselessly in his hands. Again, if he would give his nuts for a piece of metal, pleased with its colour; or exchange his sheep for shells, or wool for a sparkling pebble or a diamond, and keep those by him all his life, he invaded not the right of others, he might heap up as much of these durable things as he pleased; the exceeding of the bounds of his just property not lying in the largeness of his possession, but the perishing of anything uselessly in it.

47.   And thus came in the use of money, some lasting thing that men might keep without spoiling, and that by mutual consent men would take in exchange for the truly useful but perishable supports of life.

48.   And as different degrees of industry were apt to give men possessions in different proportions, so this invention of money gave them the opportunity to continue and enlarge them. For supposing an island, separate from all possible commerce with the rest of the world, wherein there were but an hundred families, but there were sheep, horses, and cows, with other useful animals, wholesome fruits, and land enough for corn for a hundred thousand times as many, but nothing in the island, either because of its commonness, or perishableness, fit to supply the place of money: What reason could any one have there to enlarge his possessions beyond the use of his family and a plentiful supply to its consumption, either in what their own industry produced, or they could barter for like perishable, useful commodities with others? Where there is not something, both lasting and scarce, and so valuable to be hoarded up, there men will not be apt to enlarge their possessions of land, were it never so rich, never so free for them to take. For I ask, what would a man value ten thousand, or an hundred thousand acres of excellent land, ready cultivated and well stocked too with cattle, in the middle of the inland parts of America, where he had no hopes of commerce with other parts of the world, to draw money to him by the sale of the product? It would not be worth the enclosing, and we should see him give up again to the wild common of nature, whatever was more than would supply the conveniences of life to be had there for him and his family.

STUDY QUESTIONS

1. According to Locke, under what conditions is private property consistent with justice?
2. According to Locke, what are the appropriate limits of a person's acquiring property?
3. Does Locke view the introduction of money in a positive light?
4. Is society benefited by each member's having a right to property?

PART 12

Art

The Role of Theory in Aesthetics

MORRIS WEITZ

We turn next to some issues in the philosophical study of the arts, a field known as "aesthetics," from a Greek word for "sense perception." One longtime concern has been the attempt to define art. In this article Morris Weitz (1916–1981), who was Professor of Philosophy at Brandeis University, argues that art is not the sort of concept that can be defined. Using an insight from the influential Austrian philosopher Ludwig Wittgenstein (1889–1951), Weitz contends that works of art do not all share common properties but rather display overlapping similarities.

Theory has been central in aesthetics and is still the preoccupation of the philosophy of art. Its main avowed concern remains the determination of the nature of art which can be formulated into a definition of it. It construes definition as the statement of the necessary and sufficient properties of what is being defined, where the statement purports to be a true or false claim about the essence of art, what characterizes and distinguishes it from everything else. . . . Many theorists contend that their enterprise is no mere intellectual exercise but an absolute necessity for any understanding of art and our proper evaluation of it. Unless we know what art is, they say, what are its necessary and sufficient properties, we cannot begin to respond to it adequately or to say why one work is good or better than another. Aesthetic theory, thus, is important not only in itself but for the foundations of both appreciation and criticism. Philosophers, critics, and even artists who have written on art agree that what is primary in aesthetics is a theory about the nature of art. . . .

In this essay I want to plead for the rejection of this problem. I want to show that theory . . . is *never* forthcoming in aesthetics, and that we would do much better as philosophers to supplant the question, "What is the nature of art?," by other questions, the answers to which will provide us with all the understanding of the arts there can be. I want to show that the inadequacies of the theories are not primarily occasioned by any legitimate difficulty such as, e.g., the vast complexity of art, which might be corrected by further probing and research. Their basic inadequacies reside instead in a fundamental misconception of art. Aesthetic theory— all of it—is wrong in principle in thinking that a correct theory is possible because it radically misconstrues the logic of the concept of art. Its main contention that

From Morris Weitz, "The Role of Theory in Aesthetics," *Journal of Aesthetics and Art Criticism*, 15/1 (1956): 27–35. © 1956. Reprinted by permission of Blackwell Publishing.

"art" is amenable to real or any kind of true definition is false. Its attempt to discover the necessary and sufficient properties of art is logically misbegotten for the very simple reason that such a set and, consequently, such a formula about it, is never forthcoming. Art, as the logic of the concept shows, has no set of necessary and sufficient properties, hence a theory of it is logically impossible and not merely factually difficult. Aesthetic theory tries to define what cannot be defined in its requisite sense. But in recommending the repudiation of aesthetic theory I shall not argue from this, as too many others have done, that its logical confusions render it meaningless or worthless. On the contrary, I wish to reassess its role and its contribution primarily in order to show that it is of the greatest importance to our understanding of the arts. . . .

The problem with which we must begin is not "What is art?," but "What sort of concept is 'art'?" Indeed, the root problem of philosophy itself is to explain the relation between the employment of certain kinds of concepts and the conditions under which they can be correctly applied. If I may paraphrase Wittgenstein, we must not ask, What is the nature of any philosophical x?, or even, according to the semanticist, What does "x" mean?, a transformation that leads to the disastrous interpretation of "art" as a name for some specifiable class of objects; but rather, What is the use or employment of "x"? What does "x" do in the language? This, I take it, is the initial question, the begin-all if not the end-all of any philosophical problem and solution. Thus, in aesthetics, our first problem is the elucidation of the actual employment of the concept of art, to give a logical description of the actual functioning of the concept, including a description of the conditions under which we correctly use it or its correlates.

My model in this type of logical description or philosophy derives from Wittgenstein. It is also he who, in his refutation of philosophical theorizing in the sense of constructing definitions of philosophical entities, has furnished contemporary aesthetics with a starting point for any future progress. In his . . . *Philosophical Investigations*,[1] Wittgenstein raises as an illustrative question. What is a game? The traditional philosophical, theoretical answer would be in terms of some exhaustive set of properties common to all games. To this Wittgenstein says, let us consider what we call "games": "I mean board-games, card-games, ball-games, Olympic games, and so on. What is common to them all?—Don't say: 'there *must* be something common, or they would not be called "games"' but *look and see* whether there is anything common to all.—For if you look at them you will not see something that is common to *all*, but similarities, relationships, and a whole series of them at that. . . ."

Card games are like board games in some respects but not in others. Not all games are amusing, nor is there always winning or losing or competition. Some games resemble others in some respects—that is all. What we find are no necessary and sufficient properties, only "a complicated network of similarities overlapping and crisscrossing," such that we can say of games that they form a family with family resemblances and no common trait. If one asks what a game is, we pick out sample games, describe these, and add, "This and *similar things* are called 'games'."

This is all we need to say and indeed all any of us knows about games. Knowing what a game is is not knowing some real definition or theory but being able to recognize and explain games and to decide which among imaginary and new examples would or would not be called "games."

The problem of the nature of art is like that of the nature of games, at least in these respects: If we actually look and see what it is that we call "art," we will also find no common properties—only strands of similarities. Knowing what art is is not apprehending some manifest or latent essence but being able to recognize, describe, and explain those things we call "art" in virtue of these similarities.

But the basic resemblance between these concepts is their open texture. In elucidating them, certain (paradigm) cases can be given, about which there can be no question as to their being correctly described as "art" or "game," but no exhaustive set of cases can be given. I can list some cases and some conditions under which I can apply correctly the concept of art but I cannot list all of them, for the all-important reason that unforeseeable or novel conditions are always forthcoming or envisageable.

A concept is open if its conditions of application are emendable and corrigible; i.e., if a situation or case can be imagined or secured which would call for some sort of *decision* on our part to extend the use of the concept to cover this, or to close the concept and invent a new one to deal with the new case and its new property. If necessary and sufficient conditions for the application of a concept can be stated, the concept is a closed one. But this can happen only in logic or mathematics where concepts are constructed and completely defined. It cannot occur with empirically descriptive and normative concepts unless we arbitrarily close them by stipulating the ranges of their uses.

I can illustrate this open character of "art" best by examples drawn from its sub-concepts. Consider questions like "Is Dos Passos' *U.S.A.* a novel?," "Is V. Woolf's *To the Lighthouse* a novel?," "Is Joyce's *Finnegan's Wake* a novel?" On the traditional view, these are construed as factual problems to be answered yes or no in accordance with the presence or absence of defining properties. But certainly this is not how any of these questions is answered. Once it arises, as it has many times in the development of the novel from Richardson to Joyce (e.g., "Is Gide's *The School for Wives* a novel or a diary?"), what is at stake is no factual analysis concerning necessary and sufficient properties but a decision as to whether the work under examination is similar in certain respects to other works, already called "novels," and consequently warrants the extension of the concept to cover the new case. The new work is narrative, fictional, contains character delineation and dialogue but (say) it has no regular time-sequence in the plot or is interspersed with actual newspaper reports. It is like recognized novels, A, B, C . . . , in some respects but not like them in others. But then neither were B and C like A in some respects when it was decided to extend the concept applied to A to B and C. Because work N + 1 (the brand new work) is like A, B, C . . . N in certain respects—has strands of similarity to them—the concept is extended and a new phase of the novel engendered. "Is N 1 a novel?," then, is no factual, but rather a decision problem, where the verdict turns on whether or not we enlarge our set of conditions for applying the concept.

What is true of the novel is, I think, true of every sub-concept of art: "tragedy," "comedy," "painting," "opera," etc., of "art" itself. No "Is X a novel, painting, opera, work of art, etc.?" question allows of a definitive answer in the sense of a factual yes or no report. "Is this *collage* a painting or not?" does not rest on any set of necessary and sufficient properties of painting but on whether we decide—as we did!—to extend "painting" to cover this case.

"Art," itself, is an open concept. New conditions (cases) have constantly arisen and will undoubtedly constantly arise; new art forms, new movements will emerge, which will demand decisions on the part of those interested, usually professional critics, as to whether the concept should be extended or not. Aestheticians may lay down similarity conditions but never necessary and sufficient ones for the correct application of the concept. With "art" its conditions of application can never be exhaustively enumerated since new cases can always be envisaged or created by artists, or even nature, which would call for a decision on someone's part to extend or to close the old or to invent a new concept. (E.g., "It's not a sculpture, it's a mobile.")

What I am arguing, then, is that the very expansive, adventurous character of art, its ever-present changes and novel creations, makes it logically impossible to ensure any set of defining properties. We can, of course, choose to close the concept. But to do this with "art" or "tragedy" or "portraiture," etc., is ludicrous since it forecloses on the very conditions of creativity in the arts.

Of course there are legitimate and serviceable closed concepts in art. But these are always those whose boundaries of conditions have been drawn for a *special* purpose. Consider the difference, for example, between "tragedy" and "(extant) Greek tragedy." The first is open and must remain so to allow for the possibility of new conditions, e.g., a play in which the hero is not noble or fallen or in which there is no hero but other elements that are like those of plays we already call "tragedy." The second is closed. The plays it can be applied to, the conditions under which it can be correctly used are all in, once the boundary, "Greek," is drawn. Here the critic can work out a theory or real definition in which he lists the common properties at least of the extant Greek tragedies. Aristotle's definition, false as it is as a theory of all the plays of Aeschylus, Sophocles, and Euripides, since it does not cover some of them[2] properly called "tragedies," can be interpreted as a real (albeit incorrect) definition of this closed concept; although it can also be, as it unfortunately has been, conceived as a purported real definition of "tragedy," in which case it suffers from the logical mistake of trying to define what cannot be defined—of trying to squeeze what is an open concept into an honorific formula for a closed concept.

What is supremely important, if the critic is not to become muddled, is to get absolutely clear about the way in which he conceives his concepts; otherwise he goes from the problem of trying to define "tragedy," etc., to an arbitrary closing of the concept in terms of certain preferred conditions or characteristics which he sums up in some linguistic recommendation that he mistakenly thinks is a real definition of the open concept. Thus, many critics and aestheticians ask, "What is tragedy?," choose a class of samples for which they may give a true account of its common properties, and then go on to construe this account of the chosen closed class as a true definition or theory of the whole open class of tragedy. This, I think, is the logical mechanism of most of the so-called theories of the sub-concepts of art: "tragedy," "comedy," "novel," etc. In effect, this whole procedure, subtly deceptive as it is, amounts to a transformation of correct criteria for *recognizing* members of certain legitimately closed classes of works of art into recommended criteria for *evaluating* any putative member of the class.

The primary task of aesthetics is not to seek a theory but to elucidate the concept of art. Specifically, it is to describe the conditions under which we employ the concept correctly. Definition, reconstruction, patterns of analysis are out of place here since they distort and add nothing to our understanding of art. What, then, is the logic of "X is a work of art"?

As we actually use the concept, "Art" is both descriptive (like "chair") and evaluative (like "good"); i.e., we sometimes say, "This is a work of art," to describe something and we sometimes say it to evaluate something. Neither use surprises anyone.

What, first, is the logic of "X is a work of art," when it is a descriptive utterance? What are the conditions under which we would be making such an utterance correctly? There are no necessary and sufficient conditions but there are the strands of similarity conditions, i.e., bundles of properties, none of which need be present but most of which are, when we describe things as works of art. I shall call these the "criteria of recognition" of works of art. All of these have served as the defining criteria of the individual traditional theories of art. . . . Thus, mostly, when we describe something as a work of art, we do so under the conditions of there being present some sort of artifact, made by human skill, ingenuity, and imagination, which embodies in its sensuous, public medium—stone, wood, sounds, words, etc.—certain distinguishable elements and relations. Special theorists would add conditions like satisfaction of wishes, objectification or expression of emotion, some act of empathy, and so on; but these latter conditions seem to be quite adventitious, present to some but not to other spectators when things are described as works of art. "X is a work of art and contains *no* emotion, expression, act of empathy, satisfaction, etc.," is perfectly good sense and may frequently be true. "X is a work of art and . . . was made by no one," or . . . "exists only in the mind and not in any publicly observable thing," or . . . "was made by accident when he spilled the paint on the canvas," in each case of which a normal condition is denied, are also sensible and capable of being true in certain circumstances. None of the criteria of recognition is a defining one, either necessary or sufficient, because we can sometimes assert of something that it is a work of art and go on to deny any one of these conditions, even the one which has traditionally been taken to be basic, namely, that of being an artifact: Consider, "This piece of driftwood is a lovely piece of sculpture." Thus, to say of anything that it is a work of art is to commit oneself to the presence of *some* of these conditions. One would scarcely describe X as a work of art if X were not an artifact, or a collection of elements sensuously presented in a medium, or a product of human skill, and so on. If none of the conditions were present, if there were no criteria present for recognizing something as a work of art, we would not describe it as one. But, even so, no one of these or any collection of them is either necessary or sufficient.

The elucidation of the descriptive use of "Art" creates little difficulty. But the elucidation of the evaluative use does. For many, especially theorists, "This is a work of art" does more than describe; it also praises. Its conditions of utterance, therefore, include certain preferred properties or characteristics of art. I shall call these "criteria of evaluation." Consider a typical example of this evaluative use, the view according to which to say of something that it is a work of art is to imply that it is a *successful* harmonization of elements. Many of the honorific definitions of art and its sub-concepts are of this form. What is at stake here is that "Art" is construed as an evaluative term which is either identified with its criterion or justified in terms of it. "Art" is defined in terms of its evaluative property, e.g., successful harmonization. On such a view, to say "X is a work of art" is (1) to say something which is taken *to mean* "X is a successful harmonization" (e.g., "Art *is* significant form") or (2) to say something praiseworthy *on the basis* of its successful harmonization. Theorists are never clear whether it is (1) or (2) which is being put forward. Most of them, concerned as they are with this evaluative use, formulate (2), i.e., that feature of art that *makes* it art in the praise-sense, and then go on to state (1), i.e., the definition of "Art" in terms of its art-making feature. And this is clearly to confuse the conditions under which we say something evaluatively with the meaning of what we say. "This is a work of art," said evaluatively, cannot mean "This is a successful harmonization of elements"—except by stipulation—but at most is said in virtue of the art-making property, which is taken as a (the) criterion of "Art," when "Art" is employed to assess. "This is a work of art," used evaluatively, serves to praise and not to affirm the reason why it is said.

The evaluative use of "Art," although distinct from the conditions of its use, relates in a very intimate way to these conditions. For, in every instance of "This is a work of art" (used to praise), what happens is that the criterion of evaluation (e.g., successful harmonization) for the employment of the concept of art is converted into a criterion of recognition. This is why, on its evaluative use, "This is a work of art" implies "This has P," where "P" is some chosen art-making property. Thus, if one chooses to employ "Art" evaluatively, as many do, so that "This is a work of art and not (aesthetically) good" makes no sense, he uses "Art" in such a way that he refuses to *call* anything a work of art unless it embodies his criterion of excellence.

There is nothing wrong with the evaluative use; in fact, there is good reason for using "Art" to praise. But what cannot be maintained is that theories of the evaluative use of "Art" are true and real definitions of the necessary and sufficient properties of art. Instead they are honorific definitions, pure and simple, in which "Art" has been redefined in terms of chosen criteria.

But what makes them—these honorific definitions—so supremely valuable is not their disguised linguistic recommendations; rather it is the *debates* over the reasons for changing the criteria of the concept of art which are built into the definitions. In each of the great theories of art, whether correctly understood as honorific definitions or incorrectly accepted as real definitions, what is of the utmost importance are the reasons proffered in the argument for the respective theory, that is, the reasons given for the chosen or preferred criterion of excellence and evaluation. It is this perennial debate over these criteria of evaluation which makes the history of aesthetic theory the important study it is.

NOTES

1. L. Wittgenstein, *Philosophical Investigations* (Oxford, 1953), tr. by K. Anscombe; see esp. Part I, Sections 65–75. All quotations are from these sections.
2. See H. D. F. Kitto, *Greek Tragedy* (London, 1939), on this point.

STUDY QUESTIONS

1. Can the word "game" be defined?
2. According to Weitz, why is "art" an open concept?
3. What does Weitz mean by his claim that the concept of art is both descriptive and evaluative?
4. According to Weitz, what is the value of offering definitions of art?

Aesthetic Concepts

Frank Sibley

Frank Sibley (1923–1996) was Professor of Philosophy at Lancaster University in England. He distinguishes non-aesthetic properties, such as blue or circular, from aesthetic properties, such as balanced or unified. He maintains that no collection of non-aesthetic properties imply any particular aesthetic property. Thus aesthetic taste cannot be acquired by following rules or generalizations.

The remarks we make about works of art are of many kinds. For the purpose of this paper, I wish to indicate two broad groups. I shall do this by examples. We say that a novel has a great number of characters and deals with life in a manufacturing

From Frank Sibley, "Aesthetic Concepts," *The Philosophical Review* 68 (1959).

town; that a painting uses pale colours, predominantly blues and greens, and has kneeling figures in the foreground; that the theme in a fugue is inverted at such a point and that there is a stretto at the close; that the action of a play takes place in the span of one day and that there is a reconciliation scene in the fifth act. Such remarks may be made by, and such features pointed out to, anyone with normal eyes, ears and intelligence. On the other hand, we also say that a poem is tightly knit or deeply moving; that a picture lacks balance, or has a certain serenity and repose, or that the grouping of the figures sets up an exciting tension; that the characters in a novel never really come to life, or that a certain episode strikes a false note. It would be natural enough to say that the making of such judgements as these requires the exercise of taste, perceptiveness or sensitivity, of aesthetic discrimination or appreciation; one would not say this of my first group. Accordingly, when a word or expression is such that taste or perceptiveness is required in order to apply it, I shall call it an aesthetic term or expression, and I shall correspondingly speak of *aesthetic* concepts or *taste* concepts.

Aesthetic terms span a great range of types and could be grouped into various kinds of sub-species. But it is not my present purpose to attempt any such grouping; I am interested in what they all have in common. Their almost endless variety is adequately displayed in the following list: *unified, balanced, integrated, lifeless, serene, sombre, dynamic, powerful, vivid, delicate, moving, trite, sentimental, tragic.* The list of course is not limited to adjectives; expressions in artistic contexts like *telling contrast, sets up a tension, conveys a sense of* or *holds it together* are equally good illustrations. It includes terms used by both layman and critic alike, as well as some which are mainly the property of professional critics and specialists.

I have gone for my examples of aesthetic expressions in the first place to critical and evaluative discourse about works of art because it is there particularly that they abound. But now I wish to widen the topic; we employ terms the use of which requires an exercise of taste not only when discussing the arts but quite liberally throughout discourse in everyday life. The examples given above are expressions which, appearing in critical contexts, most usually, if not invariably, have an aesthetic use; outside critical discourse the majority of them more frequently have some other use unconnected with taste. But many expressions do double duty even in everyday discourse, sometimes being used as aesthetic expressions and sometimes not. Other words again, whether in artistic or daily discourse, function only or predominantly as aesthetic terms; of this kind are *graceful, delicate, dainty, handsome, comely, elegant, garish.* Finally, to make the contrast with all the preceding examples, there are many words which are seldom used as aesthetic terms at all: *red, noisy, brackish, clammy, square, docile, cured, evanescent, intelligent, faithful, derelict, tardy, freakish.*

Clearly, when we employ words as aesthetic terms we are often making and using metaphors, pressing into service words which do not primarily function in this manner. Certainly also, many words *have come* to be aesthetic terms by some kind of metaphorical transference. This is so with those like 'dynamic', 'melancholy', 'balanced', 'tightly knit', which, except in artistic and critical writings, are not normally aesthetic terms. But the aesthetic vocabulary must not be thought wholly metaphorical. Many words, including the most common (*lovely, pretty, beautiful, dainty, graceful, elegant*), are certainly not being used metaphorically when employed as aesthetic terms, the very good reason being that this is their primary or only use. And though expressions like 'dynamic', 'balanced' and so forth *have come* by a metaphorical shift to be aesthetic terms, their employment in criticism can scarcely be said to be more than quasi-metaphorical. Having entered the language of art description and criticism as metaphors they are now standard vocabulary in that language.

The expressions that I am calling aesthetic terms form no small segment of our discourse. Often, it is true, people with normal intelligence and good eyesight and hearing lack, at least in some measure, the sensitivity required to apply them; a man need not be stupid or have poor eyesight to fail to see that something is graceful. Thus taste or sensitivity is somewhat more rare than certain other human capacities; people who exhibit a sensitivity both wide-ranging and refined are a minority. It is over the application of aesthetic terms too that, notoriously, disputes and differences sometimes go helplessly unsettled. But almost everybody is able to exercise taste to some degree and in some matters. . . .

In order to support our application of an aesthetic term, we often refer to features the mention of which involves other aesthetic terms: 'it has an extraordinary vitality because of its free and vigorous style of drawing', 'graceful in the smooth flow of its lines', 'dainty because of the delicacy and harmony of its colouring'. It is as normal to do this as it is to justify one mental epithet by other epithets of the same general type, *intelligent* by *ingenious, inventive, acute* and so on. But often when we apply aesthetic terms we explain why by referring to features which do *not* depend for their recognition upon an exercise of taste: 'delicate because of its pastel shades and curving lines', or 'it lacks balance because one group of figures is so far off to the left and is so brightly illuminated'. When no explanation of this latter kind is offered, it is legitimate to ask or search for one. Finding a satisfactory answer may sometimes be difficult, but one cannot ordinarily reject the question. When we cannot ourselves quite say what non-aesthetic features make something delicate or unbalanced or powerful or moving, the good critic often puts his finger on something which strikes us as the right explanation. In short, aesthetic terms always ultimately apply because of, and aesthetic qualities always ultimately depend on, the presence of features which, like curving or angular lines, colour contrast, placing of masses or speed of movement, are visible, audible or otherwise discernible without any exercise of taste or sensibility. Whatever kind of dependence this is, and there are various relationships between aesthetic qualities and non-aesthetic features, what I want to make clear in this paper is that there are no non-aesthetic features which serve in *any* circumstances as logically *sufficient conditions* for applying aesthetic terms. Aesthetic or taste concepts are not in this respect condition-governed at all. . . .

Thus an object which is described very fully, but exclusively in terms of qualities characteristic of delicacy, may turn out on inspection to be not delicate at all, but anaemic or insipid. The failures of novices and the artistically inept prove that quite close similarity in point of line, colour or technique gives no assurance of gracefulness or delicacy. . . . A painting which has only the kind of features one would associate with vigour or energy but which even so fails to be vigorous and energetic *need* not have some other character, need not be instead, say, strident or chaotic. It may fail to have any particular character whatever. It may employ bright colours, and the like, without being particularly lively and vigorous at all, but one may feel unable to describe it as chaotic or strident or garish either. It is, rather, simply lacking in character (though of course this too is an aesthetic judgement; taste is exercised also in seeing that the painting has no character).

There are of course many features which do not in these ways characteristically count for (or against) particular aesthetic qualities. One poem has strength and power because of the regularity of its metre and rhyme; another is monotonous and lacks drive and strength because of its regular metre and rhyme. We do not feel the need to switch from 'because of' to 'in spite of'. However, I have concentrated upon features which are characteristically associated with aesthetic qualities because, if a case could be made for the view that taste concepts are in any way governed by sufficient conditions, these would seem to be the most promising candidates for governing conditions. But to say that features are associated only *characteristically* with an aesthetic term *is* to say that they can never amount to sufficient conditions; no description however full, even in terms characteristic of gracefulness, puts it beyond question that something is graceful in the way a description may put it beyond question that someone is lazy or intelligent. . . .

The point I have argued may be reinforced in the following way. A man who failed to realize the nature of aesthetic concepts, or someone who, knowing he lacked sensitivity in aesthetic matters, did not want to reveal this lack might by assiduous application and shrewd observation provide himself with some rules and generalizations; and by inductive procedures and intelligent guessing, he might frequently say the right things. But he could have no great confidence or certainty; a slight change in an object might at any time unpredictably ruin his calculations, and he might as easily have been wrong as right. No matter how careful he has been about working out a set of consistent principles and conditions, he is only in a position to think that the object is very possibly delicate. With concepts like *lazy, intelligent* or *contract,* someone who intelligently formulated rules that led him aright appreciably often *would* thereby show the beginning of a grasp of those concepts; but the person we are considering is not even beginning to show an awareness of what delicacy is. Though he sometimes says the right thing, he has not seen, but guessed, that the object is delicate. However intelligent he might be, we could easily tell him wrongly that something was delicate and explain why without his being able to detect the deception. . . . But if we did the same with, say, 'intelligent' he could at least often uncover some incompatibility or other which would need explaining. In a world of beings like himself he would have no use for concepts like delicacy. As it is, these concepts would play a quite different role in his life. He would, for himself, have no more reason to choose tasteful objects, pictures and so on, than a deaf man would to avoid noisy places. He could not be praised for exercising taste; at best his ingenuity and intelligence might come in for mention. In 'appraising' pictures, statuettes, poems, he would be doing something quite different from what other people do when they exercise taste . . .

One after another, in recent discussions, writers have insisted that aesthetic judgements are not 'mechanical': 'Critics do not formulate general standards and apply these mechanically to all, or to classes of, works of art.' 'Technical points can be settled rapidly, by the application of rules', but aesthetic questions 'cannot be settled by any mechanical method'. Instead these writers on aesthetics have emphasized that there is no 'substitute for individual judgement', with its 'spontaneity and speculation' and that 'The final standard . . . [is] the judgement of personal taste'.[1] What is surprising is that, though such things have been repeated again and again, no one seems to have said what is meant by 'taste' or by the word 'mechanical'. There are many judgements besides those requiring taste which demand 'spontaneity' and 'individual judgement' and are not 'mechanical'. Without a detailed comparison we cannot see in what particular way *aesthetic* judgements are not 'mechanical', or how they differ from those other judgements, nor can we begin to specify what taste is. This I have attempted. It is a characteristic and essential feature of judgements which employ an aesthetic term that they cannot be made by appealing, in the sense explained, to non-aesthetic conditions. This, I believe, is a logical feature of aesthetic or taste judgements in general, though I have argued it here only as regards the more restricted range of judgements which employ aesthetic terms. It is part of what 'taste' means.

NOTE

1. See the articles by Margaret Macdonald and J. Passmore in W. Elton (ed.), *Aesthetics and Language* (Oxford: Oxford University Press, 1954).

STUDY QUESTIONS

1. According to Sibley, into what two groups can we divide remarks about works of art?
2. According to Sibley, how do the two groups of remarks differ?
3. According to Sibley, can either group of remarks be reduced to the other?
4. How does Sibley's account explain the view that issues of taste cannot be settled by any mechanical method?

Speaking in Parables

SALLIE McFAGUE

Sallie McFague was Professor of Theology at Vanderbilt University. She considers a parable by the remarkable German writer Franz Kafka (1883–1924) and emphasizes that the story is an extended metaphor, not translatable into concepts. As she puts it, the parable does not *have* a message; it *is* a message.

....

It was very early in the morning, the streets clean and deserted, I was on my way to the railroad station. As I compared the tower clock with my watch I realized it was already much later than I had thought, I had to hurry, the shock of this discovery made me feel uncertain of my way, I was not very well acquainted with the town as yet, fortunately there was a policeman nearby, I ran to him and breathlessly asked him the way. He smiled and said: "From me you want to learn the way?" "Yes," I said, "since I cannot find it myself." "Give it up, give it up," said he, and turned away with a great sweep, like someone who wants to be alone with his laughter.[1]

This parable by Franz Kafka seems, on a first reading, to invite interpretation—in fact, to insist on it. One can immediately think of autobiographical, psychological, and theological interpretations which might "make sense" out of it. But to attempt such interpretations would be to allegorize it, to treat it as an illustration or embellishment of what we "already know." And all the interpretations do, in fact, fall flat; they are far less interesting than the story itself, and even though they may comfort us for a while with the supposition that we now understand the parable, we find ourselves returning again and again to the story, unsatisfied with *any* interpretation. The parable appears to be more and other than any interpretation.

This is so, I believe, because Kafka's parable is a genuine one—it is not translatable or reducible. . . .

The setting is ostensibly very ordinary: someone, up early in the morning, is rushing through the streets to the railroad station. The sense of haste is heightened by the run-on phrases, punctuated mainly by commas and by the gradual build-up of the person's awareness that "it was already much later than I had thought." A surrealistic note is introduced when the comparison of his watch with the tower clock so shocks him that he is "uncertain of the way." We pause—is that comparison sufficient to make him lose his way? Our credulity is stretched, but not broken. Troubles seem to mount—the person is late, the streets deserted, he is uncertain of the way, and he is apparently new in town—but with "fortunately" we breathe more easily and feel the story will take a turn for the better. Policemen always know their way about town and our credulity is restored completely when the stranger asks the officer "the way" (though we note in passing that he does not add "to the railroad station"). We are, however, unprepared for the answer and even more disturbed—even dumbfounded—by the final reply, "Give it up." The realism of the story has been cracked and through it we glimpse *something*—but what?

This parable is an extended metaphor, and, as a genuine metaphor, it is not translatable into concepts. To be sure, it is shot through with open-endedness, with pregnant silences, with cracks opening into mystery. But it remains profoundly impenetrable. . . . Kafka's parables, like all genuine parables, are themselves actuality—the parables are a figurative representation of an actual, total meaning, so they do not "stand for" anything but *are* life. This means we must make a very careful analysis of all the parts of the parable for they *are* the *meaning* of it. The meaning is not a separate realm, something that can be pointed to; the totality of all the processes of life and thought in the parable *is* its meaning. What this totality of all the processes of life and thought amounted to in Kafka's parables was the incomprehensiblity of the incomprehensible; but this is not an extrinsic meaning—it is *what the story says*.

. . . [T]he aesthetic moment, the moment of new insight, always involves "a felt change of consciousness," which occurs when everyday language is used in an unfamiliar context. Metaphorical language, parabolic language, does not take us out of everyday reality but drives us more deeply into it, de-forming our usual apprehensions in such a way that we see . . . not a new reality but the same reality in a new perspective. The mundane world is transmuted; no new world is created . . . As genuine metaphors, parables could not do other than turn us toward reality, for, as Wallace Stevens says, the purpose of "the symbolic language of metamorphosis" is to intensify one's sense of reality. . . .

Finally . . . we do not interpret the parable, but the parable interprets us. . . . Metaphors cannot be "interpreted"—a metaphor does not *have* a message, it *is* a message. If we have really focused on the parable, if we have let it work on us (rather than working on it to abstract out its "meaning"), we find that we are interpreted.

NOTE

1. Heinz Politzer, *Franz Kafka: Parable and Paradox* (Ithaca: Cornell University Press, 1962), p. 1.

STUDY QUESTIONS

1. Do you agree with McFague that Kafka's story turns us toward reality?
2. How does Kafka's story differ from a factual account?
3. Is Kafka's story beyond interpretation?
4. If someone reads Kafka's story and claims not to draw anything from it, might an appropriate reply be that the issue is not what you draw from the story but what the story draws from you?

Fearing Fictions

KENDALL WALTON

While watching a movie you may become caught up in the action, later telling others about the emotions you felt. But does a horror movie, for example, actually cause you to feel fear? Kendall Walton thinks not, and the reasoning he offers leads him to defend a theory about why fiction is important and why works of art can survive multiple viewings or readings without losing effectiveness. Walton is Professor Emeritus of Philosophy and of Art and Design at the University of Michigan.

··

[T]he plot [of a tragedy] must be structured . . . that the one who is hearing the events unroll shudders with fear and feels pity at what happens: which is what one would experience on hearing the plot of the Oedipus.

Aristotle, Poetics[1]

I

Charles is watching a horror movie about a terrible green slime. He cringes in his seat as the slime oozes slowly but relentlessly over the earth destroying everything in its path. Soon a greasy head emerges from the undulating mass, and two beady eyes roll around, finally fixing on the camera. The slime, picking up speed, oozes on a new course straight toward the viewers. Charles emits a shriek and clutches desperately at his chair. Afterwards, still shaken, Charles confesses that he was "terrified" of the slime. *Was* he?

This question is part of the larger issue of how "remote" fictional worlds are from the real world. There is a definite barrier against *physical* interactions between fictional worlds and the real world. Spectators at a play are prevented from rendering aid to a heroine in distress. There is no way that Charles can dam up the slime, or take a sample for laboratory analysis.[2] But, as Charles's case dramatically illustrates, this barrier appears to be psychologically transparent. It would seem that real people can, and frequently do, have psychological attitudes toward merely fictional entities, despite the impossibility of physical intervention. Readers or spectators detest Iago, worry about Tom Sawyer and Becky lost in the cave, pity Willy Loman, envy Superman—and Charles fears the slime.

Kendall Walton, "Fearing Fictions," *Journal of Philosophy*, 75/1 (1978): 5–27. © 1978 by the *Journal of Philosophy*. Reprinted by permission of the author and the Journal of Philosophy, Inc.

But I am skeptical. We do indeed get "caught up" in stories; we often become "emotionally involved" when we read novels or watch plays or films. But to construe this involvement as consisting of our having psychological attitudes toward fictional entities is, I think, to tolerate mystery and court confusion. I shall offer a different and, in my opinion, a much more illuminating account of it.

This issue is of fundamental importance. It is crucially related to the basic question of why and how fiction is important, why we find it valuable, and why we do not dismiss novels, films, and plays as "mere fiction" and hence unworthy of serious attention. My conclusions in this paper will lead to some tentative suggestions about this basic question.

II

Physical interaction is possible only with what actually exists. That is why Charles cannot dam up the slime, and why in general real people cannot have physical contact with mere fictions. But the nonexistence of the slime does not prevent Charles from fearing it. One may fear a ghost or a burglar even if there is none; one may be afraid of an earthquake that is destined never to occur.

But a person who fears a nonexistent burglar *believes* that there is, or at least might be, one. He believes that he is in danger, that there is a possibility of his being harmed by a burglar. It is *conceivable* that Charles should believe himself to be endangered by the green slime. He might take the film to be a live documentary, a news flash. If he does, naturally he is afraid.

But the situation I have in mind is the more usual and more interesting one in which Charles is not deceived in this straightforward way. Charles knows perfectly well that the slime is not real and that he is in no danger. Is he afraid even so? He says that he is afraid, and he is in a state which is undeniably similar, in some respects, to that of a person who is frightened of a pending real-world disaster. His muscles are tensed, he clutches his chair, his pulse quickens, his adrenalin flows. Let us call this physiological/psychological state "quasi-fear." Whether it is actual fear (or a component of actual fear) is the question at issue.

Charles's state is crucially different from that of a person with an ordinary case of fear. The fact that Charles is fully aware that the slime is fictional is, I think, good reason to deny that what he feels is fear. It seems a principle of common sense, one which ought not to be abandoned if there is any reasonable alternative, that fear[3] must be accompanied by, or must involve, a belief that one is in danger. Charles does not believe that he is in danger; so he is not afraid.

Charles might try to convince us that he was afraid by shuddering and declaring dramatically that he was *"really terrified."* This emphasizes the intensity of his experience. But we need not deny that he had an intense experience. The question is whether his experience, however intense, was one of fear of the slime. The fact that Charles, and others, call it "fear" is not conclusive, even if we grant that in doing so they express a truth. For we need to know whether the statement that Charles was afraid is to be taken literally or not.

More sophisticated defenders of the claim that Charles is afraid may argue that Charles *does* believe that the green slime is real and is a real threat to him. There are, to be sure, strong reasons for allowing that Charles realizes that the slime is only fictional and poses no danger. If he didn't, we should expect him to flee the theater, call the police, warn his family. But perhaps it is *also* true that Charles believes, in some way or "on some level," that the slime is real and really threatens him. It has been said that in cases like this, one "suspends one's disbelief," or that "part" of a person believes something which another part of him disbelieves, or that one finds oneself (almost?) believing something one nevertheless knows to be false. We must see what can be made of these notions.

One possibility is that Charles *half* believes that there is a real danger and that he is, literally, at least half afraid. To half believe something is to be not quite sure that it is true, but also not quite sure that it is not true. But Charles has *no* doubts about whether he is in the presence of an actual slime. If he half believed and were half afraid, we would expect him to have *some* inclination to act on his fear in the normal ways. Even a hesitant belief, a mere suspicion, that the slime is real would induce any normal person seriously to consider calling the police and warning his family. Charles gives no thought whatever to such courses of action. He is not *uncertain* whether the slime is real; he is perfectly sure that it is not.

Moreover, the fear symptoms that Charles does exhibit are not symptoms of a mere suspicion that the slime is real and a queasy feeling of half fear. They are symptoms of the certainty of grave and immediate danger, and sheer terror. Charles's heart pounds violently, he gasps for breath, he grasps the chair until his knuckles are white. This is not the behavior of a man who realizes basically that he is safe but suffers flickers of doubt. If it indicates fear at all, it indicates acute and overwhelming terror. Thus, to compromise on this issue, to say that Charles half believes he is in danger and is half afraid, is not a reasonable alternative.

One might claim that Charles believes he is in danger, but that this is not a hesitant or weak or half belief, but rather a belief of a special kind—a "gut" belief as opposed to an "intellectual" one. Compare a person who hates flying. He realizes, in one sense, that airplanes are (relatively) safe. He says, honestly, that they are, and can quote statistics to prove it. Nevertheless, he avoids traveling by air whenever possible. He is brilliant at devising excuses. And if he must board a plane, he becomes nervous and upset. I grant that this person believes at a "gut" level that flying is dangerous, despite his "intellectual" belief to the contrary. I grant also that he is really afraid of flying.

But Charles is different. The air traveler performs *deliberate* actions that one would expect of someone who thinks flying is dangerous, or at least he is strongly inclined to perform such actions. If he does not actually decide against traveling by air, he has a strong inclination to do so. But Charles does not have even an inclination to leave the theater or call the police. The only signs that he might really believe he is endangered are his more or less automatic, nondeliberate, reactions: his pulse rate, his sweaty palms, his knotted stomach, his spontaneous shriek.[4] This justifies us in treating the two cases differently.

Deliberate actions are done for reasons; they are done because of what the agent wants and what he thinks will bring about what he wants. There is a presumption that such actions are reasonable in light of the agent's beliefs and desires (however unreasonable the beliefs and desires may be). So we postulate beliefs or desires to make sense of them. People also have reasons for doing things that they are inclined to do but, for other reasons, refrain from doing. If the air traveler thinks that flying is dangerous, then, assuming that he wants to live, his actions or tendencies thereto are reasonable. Otherwise, they probably are not. So we legitimately infer that he does believe, at least on a "gut" level, that flying is dangerous. But we don't have to make the same kind of sense of Charles's automatic responses. One doesn't have reasons for things one doesn't *do*, like sweating, increasing one's pulse rate, knotting one's stomach (involuntarily). So there is no need to attribute beliefs (or desires) to Charles which will render these responses reasonable.[5] Thus, we can justifiably infer the air passenger's ("gut") belief in the danger of flying from his deliberate behavior or inclinations, and yet refuse to infer from Charles's automatic responses that he thinks he is in danger.

Someone might reply that at moments of special crisis during the movie—e.g., when the slime first spots Charles—Charles "loses hold of reality" and, *momentarily*, takes the slime to be real and really fears it. These moments are too short for Charles to think about doing anything; so (one might claim) it isn't surprising that his belief and fear are not accompanied by the normal inclinations to act.

This move is unconvincing. In the first place, Charles's quasi-fear responses are not merely momentary; he may have his heart in his throat throughout most of the movie, yet without experiencing the slightest inclination to flee or call the police. These long-term responses, and Charles's propensity to describe them afterwards in terms of "fear," need to be understood even if it is allowed that there are moments of real fear interspersed among them. Furthermore, however tempting the momentary-fear idea might be, comparable views of other psychological states are much less appealing. When we say that someone "pitied" Willy Loman or "admired" Superman, it is unlikely that we have in mind special moments during his experience of the work when he forgot, momentarily, that he was dealing with fiction and felt flashes of actual pity or admiration. The person's "sense of reality" may well have been robust and healthy throughout his experience of the work, uninterrupted by anything like the special moments of crisis Charles experiences during the horror movie. Moreover, it may be appropriate to say that someone "pities" Willy or "admires" Superman even when he is not watching the play or reading the cartoon. The momentary-*fear* theory, even if it were plausible, would not throw much light on cases in which we apparently have other psychological attitudes toward fictions.

Although Charles is not really afraid of the fictional slime depicted in the movie, the movie might nevertheless produce real fear in him. It might cause him to be afraid of something other than the slime it depicts. If Charles is a child, the movie may make him wonder whether there might not be real slimes or other exotic horrors *like* the one depicted in the movie, even if he fully realizes that the movie-slime itself is not real. Charles may well fear these suspected actual dangers; he might have nightmares about them for days afterwards. (*Jaws* caused a lot of people to fear sharks which they thought might really exist. But whether they were afraid of the fictional sharks in the movie is another question.)

If Charles is an older movie-goer with a heart condition, he may be afraid of the movie itself. Perhaps he knows that any excitement could trigger a heart attack, and fears that the movie will cause excitement, e.g., by depicting the slime as being especially aggressive or threatening. This is real fear. But it is fear of the depiction of the slime, not fear of the slime that is depicted.

Why is it so natural to describe Charles as afraid of the slime, if he is not, and how *is* his experience to be characterized? In what follows I shall develop a theory to answer these questions.

IV

[The actor] on a stage plays at being another before a gathering of people who play at taking him for that other person.

Jorge Luis Borges[6]

Compare Charles with a child playing an ordinary game of make-believe with his father. The father, pretending to be a ferocious monster, cunningly stalks the child and, at a crucial moment, lunges viciously at him. The child flees, screaming, to the next room. The scream is more or less involuntary, and so is the flight. But the child has a delighted grin on his face even while he runs, and he unhesitatingly comes back for more. He is perfectly aware that his father is only "playing," that the whole thing is "just a game," and that only make-believedly is there a vicious monster after him. He is not really afraid.

The child obviously belongs to the fictional world of the game of make-believe. It is make-believe that the monster lunges, not into thin air, but at the child. Make-believedly the child is in grave and mortal danger. And when the child screams and runs, make-believedly he knows he is in danger and is afraid. The game is a sort of theatrical event in which the father is an actor portraying a monster and the child is an actor playing himself.

I propose to regard Charles similarly. When the slime raises its head, spies the camera, and begins oozing toward it, it is make-believe that Charles is threatened. And when as a result Charles gasps and grips his chair, make-believedly he is afraid. Charles is playing a game of make-believe in which he uses the images on the screen as props. He too is an actor impersonating himself. . . .

Charles differs in some important respects from an ordinary on-stage, self-portraying actor. One difference has to do with what makes it make-believe that Charles is afraid. Facts about Charles generate . . . make-believe truths about him; in this respect he is like an actor portraying himself on stage. But the sorts of facts about Charles which do the generating are different. Make-believe truths about Charles are generated at least partly by what he thinks and feels, not just by how he acts. It is partly the fact that Charles is in a state of quasi-fear, the fact that he feels his heart pounding, his muscles tensed, etc., which makes it make-believe that he is afraid. It would not be appropriate to describe him as "afraid" if he were not in some such state.[7]

Charles's quasi-fear is not responsible, by itself, for the fact that make-believedly it is the *slime* he fears, nor even for the fact that make-believedly he is afraid rather than angry or excited or merely upset. Here Charles's (actual) beliefs come into play. Charles believes (he knows) that make-believedly the green slime is bearing down on him and he is in danger of being destroyed by it. His quasi-fear results from this belief.[8] What makes it make-believe that Charles is afraid rather than angry or excited or upset is the fact that his quasi-fear is caused by the belief that make-believedly he is in danger. And his belief that make-believedly it is the slime that endangers him is what makes it make-believe that the slime is the object of his fear. In short, my suggestion is this: the fact that Charles is quasi-afraid as a result of realizing that make-believedly the slime threatens him generates the truth that make-believedly he is afraid of the slime.[9]

An on-stage actor, by contrast, generates make-believe truths solely by his acting, by his behavior. Whether it is make-believe that the character portrayed is afraid or not depends just on what the actor says and does and how he contorts his face, regardless of what he actually thinks or feels. It makes no difference whether his actual emotional state is anything like fear. This is just as true when the actor is playing himself as it is when he is portraying some other character. The actor may find that putting himself into a certain frame of mind makes it easier to act in the appropriate ways. Nevertheless, it is how he acts, not his state of mind, that determines whether make-believedly he is afraid.

This is how our conventions for theater work, and it is entirely reasonable that they should work this way. Audiences cannot be expected to have a clear idea of an actor's personal thoughts and feelings while he is performing. That would require knowledge of his off-stage personality and of recent events that may have affected his mood (e.g., an argument with his director or his wife). Moreover, acting involves a certain amount of dissembling; actors hide some aspects of their mental states from the audience. If make-believe truths depended on actors' private thoughts and feelings, it would be awkward and unreasonably difficult for spectators to ascertain what is going on in the fictional world. It is not surprising that the make-believe truths for which actors on stage are responsible are understood to be generated by just what is visible from the galleries.

But Charles is not performing for an audience. It is not his job to get across to anyone else what make-believedly is true of himself. Probably no one but him much cares whether or not make-believedly he is afraid. So there is no reason why his actual state of mind should not have a role in generating make-believe truths about himself.

It is not so clear in the monster game what makes it make-believe that the child is afraid of a monster. The child *might* be performing for the benefit of an audience; he might be *showing* someone, an onlooker, or just his father, that make-believedly he is afraid. If so, perhaps he is like an on-stage actor. Perhaps we should regard his observable behavior as responsible for the fact that make-believedly he is afraid. But there is room for doubt here. The child experiences quasi-fear sensations as Charles does. And his audience probably has much surer access to his mental state than theater audiences have to those of actors. The audience may know him well, and the child does not try so hard or so skillfully to hide his actual mental state as actors do. It may be perfectly evident to the audience that the child has a case of quasi-fear, and also that this is a result of his realization that make-believedly a monster is after him. So it is not unreasonable to regard the child's mental state as helping to generate make-believe truths.

A more definite account of the situation is possible if the child is participating in the game solely for his own amusement, with no thought of an audience. In this case the child himself, at least, almost certainly understands his make-believe fear to depend on his mental state rather than (just) his behavior.[10] In fact, let us suppose that the child is an undemonstrative sort who does not scream or run or betray his "fear" in any other especially overt way. His participation in the game is purely passive. Nevertheless the child does experience quasi-fear when make-believedly the monster attacks him, and he still would describe himself as being "afraid" (although he knows that there is no danger and that his "fear" isn't real). Certainly in this case it is (partly) his quasi-fear that generates the make-believe truth he expresses when he says he is "afraid."

My proposal is to construe Charles on the model of this undemonstrative child. Charles may, of course, exhibit his "fear" in certain observable ways. But his observable behavior is not meant to show anyone else that make-believedly he is afraid. It is likely to go unnoticed by others, and even Charles himself may be unaware of it. No one, least of all Charles, regards his observable behavior as generating the truth that make-believedly he is afraid.

VI

. . . We see, now, how fictional worlds can seem to us almost as "real" as the real world is, even though we know perfectly well that they are not. We have begun to understand what happens when we get emotionally "involved" in a novel or play or film, when we are "caught up in the story."

The theory I have presented is designed to capture intuitions lying behind the traditional ideas that the normal or desired attitude toward fiction involves a "*suspension of disbelief*," or a "*decrease of distance*." These phrases are unfortunate. They strongly suggest that people do not (completely) disbelieve what they read in novels and see on the stage or screen, that, e.g., we somehow accept it as fact that a boy named "Huckleberry Finn" floated down the Mississippi River—at least while we are engrossed in the novel. The normal reader does not accept this as fact, nor should he. Our disbelief is "suspended" only in the sense that it is, in some ways, set aside or ignored. We don't believe that there was a Huck Finn, but what interests us is the fact that *make-believedly* there was one, and that make-believedly he floated down the Mississippi and did various other things. But this hardly accounts for the sense of "decreased distance" between us and fictions. It still has us peering down on fictional worlds from reality above, however fascinated we might be, for some mysterious reason, by what we see.

On my theory we accomplish the "decrease of distance" not by promoting fictions to our level but by descending to theirs. (More accurately, we *extend* ourselves to their level, since we do not stop actually existing when it becomes fictional that we exist.) *Make-believedly* we do believe, we know, that Huck Finn floated down the Mississippi. And make-believedly we have various feelings and attitudes about him and his adventures. Rather than somehow fooling ourselves into thinking fictions are real, we become fictional. So we end up "on the same level" with fictions. And our presence there is accomplished in the extraordinarily realistic manner that I described. This enables us to comprehend our sense of closeness to fictions, without attributing to ourselves patently false beliefs.

We are now in a position to expect progress on the fundamental question of why and how fiction is important. Why don't we dismiss novels, plays, and films as "mere fiction" and hence unworthy of serious attention?

Much has been said about the value and importance of dreams, fantasy, and children's games of make-believe.[11] It has been suggested, variously, that such activities serve to clarify one's feelings, help one to work out conflicts, provide an outlet for the expression of repressed or socially unacceptable feelings, and prepare one emotionally for possible future crises by providing "practice" in facing imaginary crises. It is natural to presume that our experience of representational works of art is valuable for similar reasons. But this presumption is not very plausible, I think, unless something like the theory I have presented is correct.

It is my impression that people are usually, perhaps always, characters in their own dreams and daydreams. We dream and fantasize about ourselves. Sometimes one's role in one's dream-world or fantasy-world is limited to that of observing other goings-on. But to have even this role is to belong to the fictional world. (We must distinguish between being, in one's dream, an observer of certain events and merely "observing," having, a dream about those events.) Similarly, children are nearly always characters in their games of make-believe. To play dolls or school, hobby horses or mud pies is to be an actor portraying oneself.

I suggest that much of the value of dreaming, fantasizing, and making-believe depends crucially on one's thinking of oneself as belonging to a fictional world. It is chiefly by fictionally facing certain situations, engaging in certain activities, and having or expressing certain feelings, I think, that a dreamer, fantasizer, or game player comes to terms with his actual feelings—that he discovers them, learns to accept them, purges himself of them, or whatever exactly it is that he does.

If I am right about this, people can be expected to derive similar benefits from novels, plays, and films only if it is fictional that they themselves exist and participate (if only as observers) in the events portrayed in the works, i.e., only if my theory is on the right track.

I find encouragement for these speculations in the deliberate use of role-playing in educational simulation games, and as a therapeutic technique in certain kinds of psychotherapy (e.g., Gestalt therapy). A therapist may ask his patient to pretend that his mother is present, or that some inanimate object is his mother, and to "talk to her." He may then be asked to "be" the mother, and to say how he feels (when he "is" the mother), how he acts, what he looks like, etc. I will not venture an explanation of how such therapeutic techniques are effective, nor of why simulation games work. But whatever explanation is appropriate will, I suspect, go a long way toward explaining why we are as interested in works of fiction as we are, and clarifying what we get from them. The important place that novels, plays, and films have in our lives appears mysterious only on the supposition that we merely stand outside fictional worlds and look in, pressing our noses against an inviolable barrier. Once our presence within fictional worlds is recognized, suitable explanations seem within reach.

VII

A more immediate benefit of my theory is its capacity to handle puzzles. I conclude with the resolution of two more. First, consider a playgoer who finds happy endings asinine or dull, and hopes that the play he is watching will end tragically. He "wants the heroine to suffer a cruel fate," for only if she does, he thinks, will the play be worth watching. But at the same time he is caught up in the story and "sympathizes with the heroine"; he "wants her to escape." It is obvious that these two apparent desires may perfectly well coexist. Are we to say that the spectator is *torn* between opposite interests, that he wants the heroine to survive and also wants her not to? This does not ring true. Both of the playgoer's "conflicting desires" may be wholehearted. He may hope unreservedly that the work will end with disaster for the heroine, and he may, with equal singlemindedness, "want her to escape such an undeserved fate." Moreover, he may be entirely aware of both "desires," and yet feel no particular conflict between them.

My theory provides a neat explanation. It is merely make-believe that the spectator sympathizes with the heroine and wants her to escape. And he (really) wants it to be make-believe that she suffers a cruel end. He does not have conflicting desires. Nor, for that matter, is it make-believe that he does.

The second puzzle concerns why it is that works last as well as they do, how they can survive multiple readings or viewings without losing their effectiveness.[12]

Suspense of one kind or another is an important ingredient in our experience of most works: Will Jack, of *Jack and the Beanstalk*, succeed in ripping off the giant without being caught? Will Tom and Becky find their way out of the cave? Will Hamlet ever get around to avenging the murder of his father? What is in store for Julius Caesar on the Ides of March? Will Godot come?

But how can there be suspense if we already know how things will turn out? Why, for example, should Tom and Becky's plight concern or even interest a reader who knows, from reading the novel previously, that eventually they will escape from the cave? One might have supposed that, once we have experienced a work often enough to learn thoroughly the relevant features of the plot, it would lose its capacity to create suspense, and that future readings or viewings of it would lack the excitement of the first one. But this frequently is not what happens. *Some* works, to be sure, fade quickly from exposure, and familiarity does alter our experience in certain ways. But the power of many works is remarkably permanent, and the nature of their effectiveness remarkably consistent. In particular, suspense may remain a crucial element in our response to a work almost no matter how familiar we are with it. One may "worry" just as intensely about Tom and Becky while rereading *The Adventures of Tom Sawyer*, despite one's knowledge of the outcome, as would a person reading it for the first time. A child listening to *Jack and the Beanstalk* for the umpteenth time, long after she has memorized it word for word, may feel much the same excitement when the giant discovers Jack and goes after him, the same gripping suspense, that she felt when she first heard the story. Children, far from being bored by familiar stories, often beg to hear the same ones over and over again.

None of this is surprising on my theory. The child hearing *Jack and the Beanstalk* knows that make-believedly Jack will escape, but make-believedly she does *not* know that he will—until the reading of the passage describing his escape. She is engaged in her own game of make-believe during the reading, a game in which make-believedly she learns for the first time about Jack and the giant as she hears about them.[13] It is her make-believe uncertainty (the fact that make-believedly she is uncertain), not any actual uncertainty, that is responsible for the excitement and suspense that she feels. The point of hearing the story is not, or not merely, to learn about Jack's confrontation with the giant, but to play a game of make-believe. One cannot learn, each time one hears the story, what make-believedly Jack and the giant do, unless one always forgets in between times. But one can and does participate each time in a game of make-believe. The point of hearing *Jack and the Beanstalk* is to have the experience of being such that, *make-believedly*, one realizes with trepidation the danger Jack faces, waits breathlessly to see whether the giant will awake, feels sudden terror when he does awake, and finally learns with admiration and relief how Jack chops down the beanstalk, killing the giant.

Why play the same game over and over? In the first place, the game may not be exactly the same each time, even if the readings are the same. On one occasion it may be make-believe that the child is paralyzed by fear for Jack, overwhelmed by the gravity of the situation, and emotionally drained when Jack finally bests the giant. On another occasion it may be make-believe that the child is not very seriously concerned about Jack's safety and that her dominant feelings are admiration for Jack's exploits, the thrill of adventure, and a sense of exhilaration at the final outcome. But even if the game is much the same from reading to reading, one's emotional needs may require the therapy of several or many repetitions.

NOTES

1. Chapter 14. Translated by Gerald F. Else (Ann Arbor: The University of Michigan Press, 1967).

2. I examine this barrier in a companion piece to the present paper, "How Remote Are Fictional Worlds from the Real World?," *Journal of Aesthetics and Art Criticism* [37, 1 (1978): 11–23].

3. By "fear" I mean fear for oneself. Obviously a person can be afraid for someone else without believing that he himself is in danger. One must believe that the person for whom one fears is in danger.

4. Charles *might* scream *deliberately*. But insofar as he does, it is probably clear that he is only pretending to take the slime seriously. . . .

5. Charles's responses are *caused* partly by a belief, though not the belief that he is in danger. (See section IV.) This belief is not a *reason* for responding as he does, and it doesn't make it "reasonable," in the relevant sense, to respond in those ways.

6. From "Everything and Nothing," Borges, *Labyrinths: Selected Stories and Other Writings*, Donald A. Yates and James E. Irby, eds. (New York: New Directions, 1962), p. 248.

7. It is arguable that the purely physiological aspects of quasi-fear, such as the increase of adrenalin in the blood, which Charles could ascertain only by clinical tests, are not part of what makes it make-believe that he is afraid. Thus one might want to understand "quasi-fear" as referring only to the more psychological aspects of Charles's condition: the feelings or sensations that go with increased adrenalin, faster pulse rate, muscular tension, etc.

8. One can't help wondering why Charles's realization that make-believedly he is in danger produces quasi-fear in him, why it brings about a state similar to real fear, even though he knows he is not really in danger. This question is important, but we need not speculate about it here. For now we need only note that Charles's belief does result in quasi-fear, however this fact is to be explained.

9. This, I think, is at least approximately right. It is perhaps equally plausible, however, to say that the fact that Charles *believes* his quasi-fear to be caused by his realization that the slime endangers him is what makes it make-believe that his state is one of fear of the slime. There is no need to choose now between my suggestion and this variant.

10. Observers might, at the same time, understand his behavior alone to be responsible for his make-believe fear. The child and the observers might recognize somewhat different principles of make-believe.

11. A good source concerning make-believe games is Jerome L. Singer, et al., *The Child's World of Make-Believe* (New York: Academic Press, 1973).

12. David Lewis pointed out to me the relevance of my theory to this puzzle.

13. It is probably make-believe that someone (the narrator), whose word the child can trust, is giving her a serious report about a confrontation between a boy named "Jack" and a giant. Cf. my "Points of View in Narrative and Depictive Representation," *Noûs*, x, 1 (March 1976): 49–61.

STUDY QUESTIONS

1. How does fear we feel at a horror movie differ from fear we feel in a situation that actually threatens us?

2. How does Walton explain this difference?

3. Do you read fiction for different reasons than you read nonfiction?

4. Why do some works of art continue to hold our interest after repeated readings or viewings, while other works of art do not?

The Republic

PLATO

We now return to Plato's *Republic* at a point where he explains why in his ideal city he gives such a limited role to artists. While philosophers seek to grasp the Forms, the essences of things, and artisans make copies of the ideals, artists make copies of copies, thus working at the third remove from reality.

To put the point without the metaphysical framework, Plato doubts that artists have any knowledge about the subjects they describe. Instead, they create through inspiration, appealing to our emotions, not our reason, and thus making us vulnerable to strong feelings about matters that should be decided by careful thinking. To use an example of my own, a novel that describes a region beset by poverty may rouse our passions far more than a sociological or economic study of the matter, although the literary work may mischaracterize the situation and its causes.

Plato feared the power of art to lead us away from the truth. The irony is that Plato himself was an artist, the greatest of philosophical stylists. He used his powers as a writer to tell us so movingly of the life of Socrates that many throughout the ages have been led to devote themselves to philosophical inquiry. Plato's attack on art can be seen as an implicit tribute to the extraordinary effects that can be produced by artistic creation.

<hr />

[O]ur commonwealth has many features which make me think it was based on very sound principles, especially our rule not on any account to admit the poetry of dramatic representation. . . .

What makes you say so?

Between ourselves—for you will not denounce me to the tragedians and the other dramatists—poetry of that sort seems to be injurious to minds which do not possess the antidote in a knowledge of its real nature.

What have you in mind?

I must speak out, in spite of a certain affection and reverence I have had from a child for Homer, who seems to have been the original master and guide of all this imposing company of tragic poets.[1] However, no man must be honoured above the truth; so, as I say, I must speak my mind.

Do, by all means.

Listen then, or rather let me ask you a question. Can you tell me what is meant by representation in general? I have no very clear notion myself.

So you expect me to have one!

Why not? It is not always the keenest eye that is the first to see something.

True; but when you are there I should not be very desirous to tell what I saw, however plainly. You must use your own eyes.

Well then, shall we proceed as usual and begin by assuming the existence of a single essential nature or Form for every set of things which we call by the same name? Do you understand?

I do.

Then let us take any set of things you choose. For instance there are any number of beds or of tables, but only two Forms, one of Bed and one of Table.

Yes.

And we are in the habit of saying that the craftsman, when he makes the beds or tables we use or whatever it may be, has before his mind the Form[2] of one or other of these pieces of furniture. The Form itself is, of course, not the work of any craftsman. How could it be?

It could not. . . .

And what of the carpenter? Were you not saying just now that he only makes a particular bed, not what we call the Form or essential nature of Bed?

Yes, I was.

If so, what he makes is not the reality, but only something that resembles it. It would not be right to call the work of a carpenter or of any other handicraftsman a perfectly real thing, would it?

Not in the view of people accustomed to thinking on these lines.[3]

We must not be surprised, then, if even an actual bed is a somewhat shadowy thing as compared with reality.

True.

Now shall we make use of this example to throw light on our question as to the true nature of this artist who represents things? We have here three sorts of bed: one which exists in the nature of things and which, I imagine, we could only describe as a product of divine workmanship; another made by the carpenter; and a third by the painter. So the three kinds of bed belong respectively to the domains of these three: painter, carpenter, and god.

Yes.

Now the god made only one ideal or essential Bed, whether by choice or because he was under some necessity not to make more than one; at any rate two or more were not created, nor could they possibly come into being.

Why not?

Because, if he made even so many as two, then once more a single ideal Bed would make its appearance, whose character those two would share; and that one, not the two, would be the essential Bed. Knowing this, the god, wishing to be the real maker of a real Bed, not a particular manufacturer of one particular bed, created one which is essentially unique.

So it appears.

Shall we call him, then the author of the true nature of Bed, or something of that sort?

Certainly he deserves the name, since all his works constitute the real nature of things.

And we may call the carpenter the manufacturer of a bed?

Yes.

Can we say the same of the painter?

Certainly not.

Then what is he, with reference to a bed?

I think it would be fairest to describe him as the artist who represents the things which the other two make.

Very well, said I; so the work of the artist is at the third remove from the essential nature of the thing?

Exactly. . . .

Then it is now time to consider the tragic poets and their master, Homer, because we are sometimes told that they understand . . . all about human conduct, good or bad, and about religion; for, to write well, a good poet, so they say, must know his subject; otherwise he could not write about it. We must ask whether these people . . . in contemplating the poets' work have failed to see that it is at the third remove from reality, nothing more than semblances, easy to produce with no knowledge of the truth. Or is there something in what they say? Have the good poets a real mastery of the matters on which the public thinks they discourse so well?

It is a question we ought to look into.

Well then, if a man were able actually to do the things he represents as well as to produce images of them, do you believe he would seriously give himself up to making these images and take that as a completely satisfying object in life? I should imagine that, if he had a real understanding of the actions he represents, he would far sooner devote himself to performing them in fact. The memorials he would try to leave after him would be noble deeds, and he would be more eager to be the hero whose praises are sung than the poet who sings them.

Yes, I agree; he would do more good in that way and win a greater name.

Here is a question, then, that we may fairly put to Homer or to any other poet. We will leave out of account all mere matters of technical skill: we will not ask them to explain, for instance, why it is that, if they have a knowledge of medicine and not merely the art of reproducing the way physicians talk, there is no record of any poet, ancient or modern, curing patients and bequeathing his knowledge to a school of medicine, as Asclepius did. But when Homer undertakes to tell us about matters of the highest importance, such as the conduct of war, statesmanship, or education, we have a right to inquire into his competence. "Dear Homer," we shall say, "we have defined the artist as one who produces images at the third remove from reality. If your knowledge of all that concerns human excellence was really such as to raise you above him to the second rank, and you could tell what courses of conduct will make men better or worse as individuals or as citizens, can you name any country which was better governed thanks to your efforts? Many states, great and small, have owed much to a good lawgiver, such as Lycurgus at Sparta, Charondas in Italy and Sicily, and our own Solon. Can you tell us of any that acknowledges a like debt to you?"

I should say not, Glaucon replied. The most devout admirers of Homer make no such claim.

Well, do we hear of any war in Homer's day being won under his command or thanks to his advice?

No.

Or of a number of ingenious inventions and technical contrivances, which would show that he was a man of practical ability like Thales of Miletus or Anacharsis the Scythian?[4]

Nothing of the sort.

Well, if there is no mention of public services, do we hear of Homer in his own lifetime presiding, like Pythagoras, over a band of intimate disciples who loved him for the inspiration of his society and handed down a Homeric way of life, like the way of life which the Pythagoreans called after their founder and which to this day distinguishes them from the rest of the world?

No; on the contrary, Homer's friend with the absurd name, Creophylus,[5] would look even more absurd when considered as a product of the poet's training, if the story is true that he completely neglected Homer during his lifetime.

Yes, so they say. But what do you think, Glaucon? If Homer had really possessed the knowledge qualifying him to educate people and make them better men, instead of merely giving us a poetical representation of such matters, would he not have attracted a host of disciples to love and revere him? After all, any number of private teachers like Protagoras of Abdera and Prodicus of Ceos[6] have succeeded in convincing their contemporaries that they will never be fit to manage affairs of state or their own households unless these masters superintend their education; and for this wisdom they are so passionately admired that their pupils are all but ready to carry them about on their shoulders. Can we suppose that Homer's contemporaries, or Hesiod's, would have left them to wander about reciting their poems, if they had really been capable of helping their hearers to be better men? Surely they would sooner have parted with their money and tried to make the poets settle down at home; or failing that, they would have danced attendance on them wherever they went, until they had learnt from them all they could.

I believe you are quite right, Socrates.

We may conclude, then, that all poetry, from Homer onwards, consists in representing a semblance of its subject, whatever it may be, including any kind of human excellence, with no grasp of the reality. . . . Strip what the poet has to say of its poetical colouring, and I think you must have seen what it comes to in plain prose. It is like a face which was never really handsome, when it has lost the fresh bloom of youth.

Quite so. . . .

We seem, then, so far to be pretty well agreed that the artist knows nothing worth mentioning about the subjects he represents, and that art is a form of play, not to be taken seriously. This description, moreover, applies above all to tragic poetry, whether in epic or dramatic form.

Exactly.

But now look here, said I; the content of this poetical representation is something at the third remove from reality, is it not?

Yes.

On what part of our human nature, then, does it produce its effect?

What sort of part do you mean?

Let me explain by an analogy. An object seen at a distance does not, of course, look the same size as when it is close at hand; a straight stick looks bent when part of it is under water; and the same thing appears concave or convex to an eye misled by colours. Every sort of confusion like these is to be found in our minds; and it is this weakness in our nature that is exploited, with a quite magical effect, by many tricks of illusion, like scene-painting and conjuring.

True.

But satisfactory means have been found for dispelling these illusions by measuring, counting, and weighing. We are no longer at the mercy of apparent differences of size and quantity and weight; the faculty which has done the counting and measuring or weighing takes control instead. And this can only be the work of the calculating or reasoning element in the soul.

True.

And when this faculty has done its measuring and announced that one quantity is greater than, or equal to, another, we often find that there is an appearance which contradicts it. Now, as we have said, it is impossible for the same part of the soul to hold two contradictory beliefs at the same time. Hence the part which agrees with the measurements must be a different part from the one which goes against them; and its confidence in measurement and calculation is a proof of its being the highest part; the other which contradicts it must be an inferior one.

It must.

This, then, was the conclusion I had in view when I said that paintings and works of art in general are far removed from reality, and that the element in our nature which is accessible to art and responds to its advances is equally far from wisdom. The offspring of a connexion thus formed on no true or sound basis must be as inferior as the parents. This will be true not only of visual art, but of art addressed to the ear, poetry as we call it.

Naturally. . . .

But, I continued, the heaviest count in our indictment is still to come. Dramatic poetry has a most formidable power of corrupting even men of high character, with a few exceptions.

Formidable indeed, if it can do that.

Let me put the case for you to judge. When we listen to some hero in Homer or on the tragic stage moaning over his sorrows in a long tirade, or to a chorus beating their breasts as they chant a lament, you know how the best of us enjoy giving ourselves up to follow the performance with eager sympathy. The more a poet can move our feelings in this way, the better we think him. And yet when the sorrow is our own, we pride ourselves on being able to bear it quietly like a man, condemning the behaviour we admired in the theatre as womanish. Can it be right that the spectacle of a man behaving as one would scorn and blush to behave one-self should be admired and enjoyed, instead of filling us with disgust?

No, it really does not seem reasonable.

It does not, if you reflect that the poet ministers to the satisfaction of that very part of our nature whose instinctive hunger to have its fill of tears and lam-entations is forcibly restrained in the case of our own misfortunes. Meanwhile the noblest part of us, insufficiently schooled by reason or habit, has relaxed its watch over these querulous feelings, with the excuse that the sufferings we are contemplating are not our own and it is no shame to us to admire and pity a man with some pretensions to a noble character, though his grief may be excessive. The enjoyment itself seems a clear gain, which we cannot bring ourselves to for-feit by disdaining the whole poem. Few, I believe, are capable of reflecting that to enter into another's feelings must have an effect on our own: the emotions of pity our sympathy has strengthened will not be easy to restrain when we are suffering ourselves.

That is very true.

Does not the same principle apply to humour as well as to pathos? You are doing the same thing if, in listening at a comic performance or in ordinary life to buffooneries which you would be ashamed to indulge in yourself, you thoroughly enjoy them instead of being disgusted with their ribaldry. There is in you an im-pulse to play the clown, which you have held in restraint from a reasonable fear of being set down as a buffoon; but now you have given it rein, and by encouraging its impudence at the theatre you may be unconsciously carried away into playing the comedian in your private life. Similar effects are produced by poetic repre-sentation of love and anger and all those desires and feelings of pleasure or pain which accompany our every action. It waters the growth of passions which should be allowed to wither away and sets them up in control, although the goodness and happiness of our lives depend on their being held in subjection.

I cannot but agree with you.

If so, Glaucon, when you meet with admirers of Homer who tell you that he has been the educator of Hellas and that on questions of human conduct and culture he deserves to be constantly studied as a guide by whom to regulate your whole life, it is well to give a friendly hearing to such people, as entirely well-meaning according to their lights, and you may acknowledge Homer to be the first and greatest of the tragic poets; but you must be quite sure that we can admit into our commonwealth only the poetry which celebrates the praises of the gods and of good men. If you go further and admit the honeyed muse in epic or in lyric verse, then pleasure and pain will usurp the sovereignty of law and of the principles always recognized by common consent as the best.

Quite true.

So now, since we have recurred to the subject of poetry, let this be our defence: it stands to reason that we could not but banish such an influence from our commonwealth. But, lest poetry should convict us of being harsh and unmannerly, let us tell her further that there is a long-standing quarrel between poetry and philosophy. There are countless tokens of this old antagonism, such as the lines which speak of "the cur which at his master yelps," or "one mighty in the vain talk of fools" or "the throng of all-too-sapient heads," or "subtle thinkers all in rags." Nonetheless, be it declared that, if the dramatic poetry whose end is to give pleasure can show good reason why it should exist in a well-governed society, we for our part should welcome it back, being ourselves conscious of its charm; only it would be a sin to betray what we believe to be the truth. You too, my friend, must have felt this charm, above all when poetry speaks through Homer's lips.

I have indeed.

It is fair, then, that before returning from exile poetry should publish her defence in lyric verse or some other measure; and I suppose we should allow her champions who love poetry but are not poets to plead for her in prose, that she is no mere source of pleasure but a benefit to society and to human life. We shall listen favourably; for we shall clearly be the gainers, if that can be proved.

Undoubtedly.

But if it cannot, then we must take a lesson from the lover who renounces at any cost a passion which he finds is doing him no good. The love for poetry of this kind, bred in us by our own much admired institutions, will make us kindly disposed to believe in her genuine worth; but so long as she cannot make good her defence we shall, as we listen, rehearse to ourselves the reasons we have just given, as a counter-charm to save us from relapsing into a passion which most people have never outgrown. We shall reiterate that such poetry has no serious claim to be valued as an apprehension of truth. One who lends an ear to it should rather beware of endangering the order established in his soul, and would do well to accept the view of poetry which we have expressed.

I entirely agree.

Yes, Glaucon; for much is at stake, more than most people suppose: it is a choice between becoming a good man or a bad; and poetry, no more than wealth or power or honours, should tempt us to be careless of justice and virtue.

Your argument has convinced me, as I think it would anyone else.

NOTES

1. The plots of Greek tragedy were normally stories borrowed from epic poetry. Hence Homer was spoken of as the first tragic poet.
2. "Form" does not mean "shape," but the essential properties which constitute what the thing, by definition, is.

3. Familiar with the Platonic doctrine, as opposed to current materialism, which regards the beds we sleep on as real things and the Platonic Form as a mere "abstraction" or notion existing only in our minds.

4. Thales (early sixth cent.) made a fortune out of a corner in oil-mills when his knowledge of the stars enabled him to predict a large olive harvest, thus proving that wise men could be rich if they chose. Anacharsis was said to have invented the anchor and the potter's wheel.

5. Creophylus' name is supposed to be derived from two words meaning "flesh" and "tribe." He is said to have been an epic poet from Chios.

6. Two of the most famous Sophists of the fifth century. Plato's *Protagoras* gives a vivid picture of them on a visit to a rich patron at Athens.

STUDY QUESTIONS

1. According to Plato, why is the work of the artist at the third remove from the essential nature of a thing?

2. Has Plato demonstrated that artists know nothing worth mentioning about their subjects?

3. Can you cite an artistic work which misleads us about the truth?

4. Can you cite an artistic work that arouses passions that should be restrained?

Poetics

ARISTOTLE

Aristotle's influential *Poetics* provides an answer to Plato's criticisms of the artist. Focusing primarily on tragedy, Aristotle views art not as a competitor to philosophy but as a means by which our emotions of pity and fear can be provoked and then purged, a process known as catharsis. Aristotle urges that this end is most effectively achieved by a plot, involving discovery, leading to *peripeteia*, a sudden change in fortune, ideally resulting from the protagonist's own erroneous judgment, and turning happiness into misery. Whereas Plato wished to censor art in an effort to keep our negative emotions under control, Aristotle wished to use art to arouse such feelings, enhance them, and so enable us to be free of them.

6 [L]et us proceed now to the discussion of Tragedy; before doing so, however, we must gather up the definition resulting from what has been said. A tragedy,

From *Aristotle's Theory of Poetry and Fine Art*, translated by S. H. Butcher, New York, Dover Publications, 1951.

then, is the imitation of an action that is serious and also, as having magnitude, complete in itself; in language with pleasurable accessories, each kind brought in separately in the parts of the work; in a dramatic, not in a narrative form; with incidents arousing pity and fear, wherewith to accomplish its catharsis of such emotions. Here by "language with pleasurable accessories" I mean that with rhythm and harmony or song superadded; and by "the kinds separately" I mean that some portions are worked out with verse only, and others in turn with song.

I. As they act the stories, it follows that in the first place the Spectacle (or stage-appearance of the actors) must be some part of the whole; and in the second Melody and Diction, these two being the means of their imitation. Here by "Diction" I mean merely this, the composition of the verses; and by "Melody," what is too completely understood to require explanation. But further: the subject represented also is an action; and the action involves agents, who must necessarily have their distinctive qualities both of character and thought, since it is from these that we ascribe certain qualities to their actions. There are in the natural order of things, therefore, two causes, Thought and Character, of their actions, and consequently of their success or failure in their lives. Now the action (that which was done) is represented in the play by the Fable or Plot. The Fable, in our present sense of the term, is simply this, the combination of the incidents, or things done in the stoɪy; whereas Character is what makes us ascribe certain moral qualities to the agents; and Thought is shown in all they say when proving a particular point or, it may be, enunciating a general truth. There are six parts consequently of every tragedy, as a whole (that is) of such or such quality, viz. a Fable or Plot, Characters, Diction, Thought, Spectacle, and Melody; two of them arising from the means, one from the manner, and three from the objects of the dramatic imitation; and there is nothing else besides these six. Of these, its formative elements, then, not a few of the dramatists have made due use, as every play, one may say, admits of Spectacle, Character, Fable, Diction, Melody and Thought.

II. The most important of the six is the combination of the incidents of the story. Tragedy is essentially an imitation not of persons but of action and life, of happiness and misery. All human happiness or misery takes the form of action; the end for which we live is a certain kind of activity, not a quality. Character gives us qualities, but it is in our actions—what we do—that we are happy or the reverse. In a play accordingly they do not act in order to portray the Characters, they include the Characters for the sake of the action. So that it is the action in it, i.e. its Fable or Plot, that is the end and purpose of the tragedy, and the end is everywhere the chief thing. Besides this, a tragedy is impossible without action, but there may be one without Character. The tragedies of most of the moderns are characterless—a defect common among poets of all kinds, and with its counterpart in painting in Zeuxis as compared with Polygnotus for whereas the latter is strong in character, the work of Zeuxis is devoid of it. And again: one may string together a series of characteristic speeches of the utmost finish as regards Diction and Thought, and yet fail to produce the true tragic effect; but one will have much better success with a tragedy which, however inferior in these respects, has a Plot, a combination of incidents, in it. And again: the most powerful elements of attraction in Tragedy, the Peripeties and Discoveries, are parts of the Plot. A further proof is in the fact that beginners succeed earlier with the Diction and Characters than with the construction of a story; and the same may be said of nearly all the early dramatists. We maintain, therefore, that the first essential, the life and soul, so to speak, of Tragedy is the Plot and that the Characters come second—compare the parallel in painting where the most beautiful colours laid on without order will not give one the same pleasure as a simple black-and-white sketch of a portrait. We maintain that Tragedy is primarily an imitation of action, and that it is mainly for the sake of the action that it imitates the personal agents. Thus comes the element of Thought, i.e. the power of saying whatever can be said, or what is appropriate to the occasion. This is what, in the speech in Tragedy, falls under the arts of Politics and Rhetoric; for the older poets make their personages discourse like statesmen, and the modern like rhetoricians. One must not confuse it with Character. Character in a play is that which reveals the moral purpose of the agents, i.e. the sort of thing they seek or avoid, where that is not obvious—hence there is no room for Character in a speech on a purely indifferent subject. Thought, on the other hand, is shown in all they say when proving or disproving some particular point, or enunciating some universal proposition. Fourth among the literary elements is the Diction of the personages, i.e., as before explained, the expression of their thoughts in words, which is practically the same thing with verse as with prose. As for the two remaining parts, the Melody is the greatest of the pleasurable accessories of Tragedy. The Spectacle, though an attraction, is the least artistic of all the parts, and has least to do with the art of poetry. The tragic effect is quite possible without a public performance and actors; and besides, the getting-up of the Spectacle is more a matter for the costumier than the poet.

9   From what we have said it will be seen that the poet's function is to describe, not the thing that has happened, but a kind of thing that might happen, i.e. what is possible as being probable or necessary. The distinction between historian and poet is not in the one writing prose and the other verse—you might put the work of Herodotus into verse, and it would still be a species of history; it consists really in this, that the one describes the thing that has been, and the other a kind of thing that might be. Hence poetry is something more philosophic and of graver import than history, since its statements are of the nature rather of universals, whereas those of history are singulars. By a universal statement I mean one as to what such or such a kind of man will probably or necessarily say or do—which is the aim of poetry, though it affixes proper names to the characters; by a singular statement, one as to what, say, Alcibiades did or had done to him. In Comedy this has become clear by this time; it is only when their plot is already made up of probable incidents that they give it a basis of proper names, choosing for the purpose any names that may occur to them, instead of writing like the old iambic poets about particular person. In Tragedy, however, they still adhere to the historic names; and for this reason: what convinces is the possible; now whereas we are not yet sure as to the possibility of that which has not happened, that which has happened is manifestly possible, else it would not have come to pass. Nevertheless even

in Tragedy there are some plays with but one or two known names in them, the rest being inventions; and there are some without a single known name, e.g. Agathon's *Antheus*, in which both incidents and names are of the poet's invention; and it is no less delightful on that account. So that one must not aim at a rigid adherence to the traditional stories on which tragedies are based. It would be absurd, in fact, to do so, as even the known stories are only known to a few, though they are a delight nonetheless to all.

It is evident from the above that the poet must be more the poet of his stories or Plots than of his verses, inasmuch as he is a poet by virtue of the imitative element in his work, and it is actions that he imitates. And if he should come to take a subject from actual history, he is nonetheless a poet for that; since some historic occurrences may very well be in the probable and possible order of things; and it is in that aspect of them that he is their poet.

Of simple Plots and actions the episodic are the worst. I call a Plot episodic when there is neither probability nor necessity in the sequence of its episodes. Actions of this sort bad poets construct through their own fault, and good ones on account of the players. His work being for public performance, a good poet often stretches out a Plot beyond its capabilities, and is thus obliged to twist the sequence of incident.

Tragedy, however, is an imitation not only of a complete action, but also of incidents arousing pity and fear. Such incidents have the very greatest effect on the mind when they occur unexpectedly and at the same time in consequence of one another; there is more of the marvellous in them then than if they happened of themselves or by mere chance. Even matters of chance seem most marvellous if there is an appearance of design as it were in them; as for instance the statue of Mitys at Argos killed the author of Mitys' death by falling down on him when a looker-on at a public spectacle; for incidents like that we think to be not without a meaning. A Plot therefore, of this sort is necessarily finer than others.

10   Plots are either simple or complex, since the actions they represent are naturally of this twofold description. The action, proceeding in the way defined, as one continuous whole, I call simple, when the change in the hero's fortunes takes place without Peripety or Discovery; and complex, when it involves one or the other, or both. These should each of them arise out of the structure of the Plot itself, so as to be the consequence, necessary or probable, of the antecedents. . . .

11   A Peripety is the change of the kind described from one state of things within the play to its opposite, and that too in the way we are saying, in the probable or necessary sequence of events; as it is for instance in *Oedipus:* here the opposite state of things is produced by the Messenger, who, coming to gladden Oedipus and to remove his fears as to his mother, reveals the secret of his birth. . . . A Discovery is, as the very word implies, a change from ignorance to knowledge, and thus to either love or hate, in the personages marked for good or evil fortune. The finest form of Discovery is one attended by Peripeties, like that which goes with the Discovery in *Oedipus*. . . . This, with a Peripety, will arouse either pity or fear—actions of that nature being what Tragedy is assumed to represent. . . .

13   The next points after what we have said above will be these: (1) What is the poet to aim at, and what is he to avoid, in constructing his Plots? and (2) What are the conditions on which the tragic effect depends?

We assume that, for the finest form of Tragedy, the Plot must be not simple but complex; and further, that it must imitate actions arousing fear and pity, since that is the distinctive function of this kind of imitation. It follows, therefore, that there are three forms of Plot to be avoided. (1) A good man must not be seen passing from happiness to misery, or (2) a bad man from misery to happiness. The first situation is not fear-inspiring or piteous, but simply odious to us. The second is the most untragic that can be; it has no one of the requisites of Tragedy; it does not appeal either to the human feeling in us, or to our pity, or to our fears. Nor, on the other hand, should (3) an extremely bad man be seen falling from happiness into misery. Such a story may arouse the human feeling in us, but it will not move us to either pity or fear; pity is occasioned by undeserved misfortune, and fear by that of one like ourselves; so that there will be nothing either piteous or fear-inspiring in the situation. There remains, then, the intermediate kind of personage, a man not pre-eminently virtuous and just, whose misfortune, however, is brought upon him not by vice and depravity but by some error of judgement, of the number of those in the enjoyment of great reputation and prosperity; e.g. Oedipus, Thyestes, and the men of note of similar families. The perfect Plot, accordingly, must have a single, and not (as some tell us) a double issue; the change in the hero's fortunes must be not from misery to happiness, but on the contrary from happiness to misery; and the cause of it must lie not in any depravity, but in some great error on his part; the man himself being either such as we have described, or better, not worse, than that. Fact also confirms our theory. Though the poets began by accepting any tragic story that came to hand, in these days the finest tragedies are always on the story of some few houses, on that of Alcmeon, Oedipus, Orestes, Meleager, Thyestes, Telephus, or any others that may have been involved, as either agents or sufferers, in some deed of horror. The theoretically best tragedy, then, has a Plot of this description. The critics, therefore, are wrong who blame Euripides for taking this line in his tragedies, and giving many of them an unhappy ending. It is, as we have said, the right line to take. The best proof is this: on the stage, and in the public performances, such plays, properly worked out, are seen to be the most truly tragic; and Euripides, even if his execution be faulty in every other point, is seen to be nevertheless the most tragic certainly of the dramatists. After this comes the construction of Plot with some rank first, one with a double story (like the *Odyssey*) and an opposite issue for the good and the bad personages. It is ranked as first only through the weakness of the audiences; the poets merely follow their public, writing as its wishes dictate. But the pleasure here is not that of Tragedy. It belongs rather to Comedy, where the bitterest enemies in the piece (e.g., Orestes and Aegisthus) walk off good friends at the end, with no slaying of any one by any one.

14   The tragic fear and pity may be aroused by the Spectacle; but they may also be aroused by the very structure and incidents of the play—which is the better way and shows the better poet. The Plot in fact should be so framed that, even

without seeing the things take place, he who simply hears the account of them shall be filled with horror and pity at the incidents; which is just the effect that the mere recital of the story in *Oedipus* would have on one. To produce this same effect by means of the Spectacle is less artistic, and requires extraneous aid. Those, however, who make use of the Spectacle to put before us that which is merely monstrous and not productive of fear, are wholly out of touch with Tragedy; not every kind of pleasure should be required of a tragedy, but only its own proper pleasure.

STUDY QUESTIONS

1. Do you agree with Aristotle that the first essential of tragedy is plot and that characters come second?
2. According to Aristotle, why is poetry more philosophical and of graver import than history?
3. How does Aristotle differentiate simple and complex plots?
4. Can you offer an example of an important artistic work in which, contrary to Aristotle's principles, an evil person passes from misery to ultimate happiness?

PART 13

Life and Death

The Trolley Problem

JUDITH JARVIS THOMSON

Judith Jarvis Thomson, whose work we read previously, presents a philosophical problem that has become the subject of much recent discussion. Consider the issue for yourself before reading the next selection, in which she offers her latest analysis of the matter.

....

Suppose you are the driver of a trolley. The trolley rounds a bend, and there come into view ahead five track workmen, who have been repairing the track. The track goes through a bit of a valley at that point, and the sides are steep, so you must stop the trolley if you are to avoid running the five men down. You step on the brakes, but alas they don't work. Now you suddenly see a spur of track leading off to the right. You can turn the trolley onto it, and thus save the five men on the straight track ahead. Unfortunately, . . . there is one track workman on that spur of track. He can no more get off the track in time than the five can, so you will kill him if you turn the trolley onto him. Is it morally permissible for you to turn the trolley?

Everybody to whom I have put this hypothetical case says, Yes, it is. Some people say something stronger than that it is morally *permissible* for you to turn the trolley: They say that morally speaking, you must turn it—that morality requires you to do so. Others do not agree that morality requires you to turn the trolley, and even feel a certain discomfort at the idea of turning it. But everybody says that it is true, at a minimum, that you *may* turn it—that it would not be morally wrong for you to do so.

Now consider a second hypothetical case . . .—which I shall call *Fat Man*—in which you are standing on a footbridge over the trolley track. You can see a trolley hurtling down the track, out of control. You turn around to see where the trolley is headed, and there are five workmen on the track where it exits from under the footbridge. What to do? Being an expert on trolleys, you know of one certain way to stop an out-of-control trolley: Drop a really heavy weight in its path. But where to find one? It just so happens that standing next to you on the footbridge is a fat man, a really fat man. He is leaning over the railing, watching the trolley; all you have to do is to give him a little shove, and over the railing he will go, onto the track in the path of the trolley. Would it be permissible for you to do this? Everybody to whom I have put this case says it would not be. But why? . . .

From *The Yale Law Journal, 94* (1985) by permission of The Yale Law Journal and Fred. B. Rothman & Company. The paragraphs are reordered.

In both cases, one will die if the agent acts, but five will live who would otherwise die—a net saving of four lives. What difference in the other facts of these cases explains the moral difference between them? I fancy that the theorists of tort and criminal law will find this problem as interesting as the moral theorist does.

STUDY QUESTIONS

1. Can you imagine another hypothetical case akin to that of the trolley?
2. In what crucial ways, if any, does the case Thomson calls "Fat Man" differ from the original trolley case?
3. Do you believe that turning the trolley is morally permissible?
4. Do you believe that not turning the trolley is morally permissible?

Turning the Trolley

JUDITH JARVIS THOMSON

More than two decades after publishing a lengthy discussion of the trolley problem from which the previous selection was excerpted, Judith Jarvis Thomson returned to the problem. Influenced by the work of a doctoral student, she offered a surprising solution that casts doubt on a widely accepted assumption critical to the case.

I

. . . [L]et us imagine the situation to be as in the case I will call Bystander's Two Options. A bystander happens to be standing by the track, next to a switch that can be used to turn the tram off the straight track, on which five men are working, onto a spur of track to the right on which only one man is working. The bystander therefore has only two options:

Bystander's Two Options: he can
  (i) do nothing, letting five die, or
  (ii) throw the switch to the right, killing one.

Most people say that he may choose option (ii). . . .

From Judith Jarvis Thomson, "Turning the Trolley." *Philosophy & Public Affairs* 36 (2008). Reprinted by permission of John Wiley & Sons. The principles are renumbered.

II

A few years ago, an MIT graduate student, Alexander Friedman, devoted a chapter of his thesis to a discussion of the most interesting solutions to the trolley problem on offer in the literature.[1] He did a very good job: he showed clearly that none of them worked. What was especially interesting, though, was what he concluded. He said: the reason why no adequate solution has been found is that something went wrong at the outset. He said: it just isn't true that the bystander may choose option (ii) in Bystander's Two Options. . . .

Friedman therefore said that we should see the (so-called) trolley problem "for what it really is—a very intriguing, provocative, and eye-opening non-problem."

Well, there's an unsettling idea! But if you mull over Friedman's unsettling idea for a while, then perhaps it can come to seem worth taking very seriously. So let us mull over it.

III

Here is a case that I will call Bystander's Three Options. The switch available to this bystander can be thrown in two ways. If he throws it to the right, then the trolley will turn onto the spur of track to the right, thereby killing one workman. If he throws it to the left, then the trolley will turn onto the spur of track to the left. The bystander himself stands on that left-hand spur of track, and will himself be killed if the trolley turns onto it. Or, of course, he can do nothing, letting five workmen die. In sum,

Bystander's Three Options: he can
  (i) do nothing, letting five die, or
  (ii) throw the switch to the right, killing one, or
  (iii) throw the switch to the left, killing himself.

What is your reaction to the bystander's having the following thought? "Hmm. I want to save those five workmen. I can do that by choosing option (iii), that is by throwing the switch to the left, saving the five but killing myself. I'd prefer not dying today, however, even for the sake of saving five. So I'll choose option (ii), saving the five but killing the one on the right-hand track instead."

I hope you will agree that choosing (ii) would be unacceptable on the bystander's part. If he *can* throw the switch to the left and turn the trolley onto himself, how dare he throw the switch to the right and turn the trolley onto the one workman? The bystander doesn't feel like dying today, even for the sake of saving five, but we can assume, and so let us assume, that the one workman also doesn't feel like dying today, even if the bystander would thereby save five.

Let us get a little clearer about why this bystander must not choose option (ii). He wants to save the five on the straight track ahead. That would be good for them, and his saving them would be a good deed on his part. But his doing that good deed would have a cost: his life or the life of the one workman on the right-hand track. What the bystander does if he turns the trolley onto the one workman is to make the one workman pay the cost of his good deed because he doesn't feel like paying it himself.

Compare the following possibility. I am asked for a donation to Oxfam. I want to send them some money. I am able to send money of my own, but I don't feel like it. So I steal some from someone else and send *that* money to Oxfam. That is pretty bad. But if the bystander proceeds to turn the trolley onto the one on the right-hand track in Bystander's Three Options, then what he does is markedly worse, because the cost in Bystander's Three Options isn't money, it is life.

In sum, if A wants to do a certain good deed, and can pay what doing it would cost, then—other things being equal—A may do that good deed only if A pays the cost himself. In particular, here is a . . . *ceteris paribus* [other things being equal] principle:

> *First Principle:* A must not kill B to save five if he can instead kill himself to save the five.

So the bystander in Bystander's Three Options must not kill the one workman on the right-hand track in furtherance of his good deed of saving the five since he can instead save the five by killing himself. Thus he must not choose option (ii).

On the other hand, morality doesn't require him to choose option (iii). If A wants to do a certain good deed, and discovers that the only permissible means he has of doing the good deed is killing himself, then he may refrain from doing the good deed. In particular, here is a second *ceteris paribus* principle:

> *Second Principle:* A may let five die if the only permissible means he has of saving them is killing himself.

So the bystander in Bystander's Three Options may choose option (i).

Let us now return to Bystander's Two Options. We may imagine that the bystander in this case can see the trolley headed for the five workmen, and wants to save them. He thinks: "Does this switch allow for me to choose option (iii), in which I turn the trolley onto myself? If it does, then I must not choose option (ii), in which I turn the trolley onto the one workman on the right-hand track, for as the *First Principle* says, I must prefer killing myself to killing him. But I don't want to kill myself, and if truth be told, I wouldn't if I could. So if the switch does allow for me to choose option (iii), then I have to forgo my good deed of saving the five: I have to choose option (i)—thus I have to let the five die. As, of course, the *Second Principle* says I may."

As you can imagine, he therefore examines the switch *very* carefully. Lo, he discovers that the switch doesn't allow him to choose option (iii). "What luck," he thinks, "I can't turn the trolley onto myself. So it's perfectly all right for me to choose option (ii)!" His thought is that since he can't himself pay the cost of his good deed, it is perfectly all right for him to make the workman on the right-hand track pay it—despite the fact that he wouldn't himself pay it if he could.

I put it to you that that thought won't do. Since he wouldn't himself pay the cost of his good deed if he could pay it, there is no way in which he can decently regard himself as entitled to make someone else pay it.

Of how many of us is it true that if we could permissibly save five only by killing ourselves, then we would? Doing so would be altruism, for as the *Second Principle* says, nobody is required to do so, and doing so would therefore be altruism; moreover, doing so would be doing something for others at a major cost to oneself, and doing so would therefore be major altruism. Very few of us would. Then very few of us could decently regard ourselves as entitled to choose option (ii) if we were in the bystander's situation in Bystander's Two Options.

NOTE

1. A. W. Friedman. *Minimizing Harm: Three Problems in Moral Theory.* Unpublished doctoral dissertation, Department of Linguistics and Philosophy, Massachusetts Institute of Technology (2002).

STUDY QUESTIONS

1. Do you believe the bystander's turning the trolley is morally acceptable?
2. Do you believe the bystander's not turning the trolley is morally acceptable?
3. Is your judgment affected by which role in the story you imagine yourself playing?
4. Would your judgment be different if turning the trolley saved the lives of thousands of people?

Death

Thomas Nagel

Is death an evil? If so, why? These questions are explored here by Thomas Nagel, whose work we read previously. Note that he does not discuss the value that one person's life or death may have for others, but only the value it has for the person who is its subject.

If death is the unequivocal and permanent end of our existence, the question arises whether it is a bad thing to die.

There is conspicuous disagreement about the matter: some people think death is dreadful; others have no objection to death *per se*, though they hope their own will be neither premature nor painful. Those in the former category tend to think those in the latter are blind to the obvious, while the latter suppose the former to be prey to some sort of confusion. On the one hand it can be said that life is all we have and the loss of it is the greatest loss we can sustain. On the other hand it may be objected that death deprives this supposed loss of its subject, and that if we realize that death is not an unimaginable condition of the persisting person, but a mere blank, we will see that it can have no value whatever, positive or negative.

Since I want to leave aside the question whether we are, or might be, immortal in some form, I shall simply use the word "death" and its cognates in this discussion to mean *permanent* death, unsupplemented by any form of conscious survival. I want to ask whether death is in itself an evil; and how great an evil, and of what kind, it might be. The question should be of interest even to those who believe in some form of immortality, for one's attitude toward immortality must depend in part on one's attitude toward death.

If death is an evil at all, it cannot be because of its positive features, but only because of what it deprives us of. I shall try to deal with the difficulties surrounding the natural view that death is an evil because it brings to an end all the goods that life contains. We need not give an account of these goods here, except to observe that some of them, like perception, desire, activity, and thought, are so general as to be constitutive of human life. They are widely regarded as formidable benefits in themselves, despite the fact that they are conditions of misery as well as of happiness, and that a sufficient quantity of more particular evils can perhaps outweigh them. That is what is meant, I think, by the allegation that it is good simply to be alive, even if one is undergoing terrible experiences. The situation is roughly this: There are elements which, if added to one's experience, make life better; there are other elements which, if added to one's experience, make life worse. But what remains when these are set aside is not merely *neutral*: it is emphatically positive. Therefore life is worth living even when the bad elements of experience are plentiful, and the good ones too meager to outweigh the bad ones on their own. The additional positive weight is supplied by experience itself, rather than by any of its contents.

I shall not discuss the value that one person's life or death may have for others, or its objective value, but only the value it has for the person who is its subject. That seems to me the primary case, and the case which presents the greatest difficulties. Let me add only two observations. First, the value of life and its contents does not attach to mere organic survival: almost everyone would be indifferent (other things equal) between immediate death and immediate coma followed by death twenty years later without reawakening. And second, like most goods, this can be multiplied by time: more is better than less. The added quantities need not be temporally continuous (though continuity has its social advantages).

People are attracted to the possibility of long-term suspended animation or freezing, followed by the resumption of conscious life, because they can regard it from within simply as a *continuation* of their present life. If these techniques are ever perfected, what from outside appeared as a dormant interval of three hundred years could be experienced by the subject as nothing more than a sharp discontinuity in the character of his experiences. I do not deny, of course, that this has its own disadvantages. Family and friends may have died in the meantime; the language may have changed; the comforts of social, geographical, and cultural familiarity would be lacking. Nevertheless these inconveniences would not obliterate the basic advantage of continued, though discontinuous, existence.

If we turn from what is good about life to what is bad about death, the case is completely different. Essentially, though there may be problems about their specification, what we find desirable in life are certain states, conditions, or types of activity. It is *being* alive, *doing* certain things, having certain experiences, that we consider good. But if death is an evil, it is the *loss of life*, rather than the state of being dead, or nonexistent, or unconscious, that is objectionable.[1] This asymmetry is important. If it is good to be alive, that advantage can be attributed to a person at each point of his life. It is a good of which Bach had more than Schubert, simply because he lived longer. Death, however, is not an evil of which Shakespeare has so far received a larger portion than Proust. If death is a disadvantage, it is not easy to say when a man suffers it.

There are two other indications that we do not object to death merely because it involves long periods of nonexistence. First, as has been mentioned, most of us would not regard the *temporary* suspension of life, even for substantial intervals, as in itself a misfortune. If it ever happens that people can be frozen without reduction of the conscious lifespan, it will be inappropriate to pity those who are temporarily out of circulation. Second, none of us existed before we were born (or conceived), but few regard that as a misfortune. I shall have more to say about this later.

The point that death is not regarded as an unfortunate *state* enables us to refute a curious but very common suggestion about the origin of the fear of death. It is often said that those who object to death have made the mistake of trying to imagine what it is like to *be* dead. It is alleged that the failure to realize that this task is logically impossible (for the banal reason that there is nothing to imagine) leads to the conviction that death is a mysterious and therefore terrifying prospective *state*. But this diagnosis is evidently false, for it is just as impossible to imagine being totally unconscious as to imagine being dead (though it is easy enough to imagine oneself, from the outside, in either of those conditions). Yet people who are averse to death are not usually averse to unconsciousness (so long as it does not entail a substantial cut in the total duration of waking life).

If we are to make sense of the view that to die is bad, it must be on the ground that life is a good and death is the corresponding deprivation or loss, bad not because of any positive features but because of the desirability of what it removes. We must now turn to the serious difficulties which this hypothesis raises, difficulties about loss and privation in general and about death in particular.

Essentially, there are three types of problem. First, doubt may be raised whether *anything* can be bad for a man without being positively unpleasant to him: specifically, it may be doubted that there are any evils which consist merely in the deprivation or absence of possible goods and which do not depend on someone's *minding* that deprivation. Second, there are special difficulties, in the case of death, about how the supposed misfortune is to be assigned to a subject at all. There is doubt both as to *who* its subject is and as to *when* he undergoes it. So long as a person exists, he has not yet died, and once he has died, he no longer exists; so there seems to be no time when death, if it is a misfortune, can be ascribed to its unfortunate subject. The third type of difficulty concerns the asymmetry, mentioned above, between our attitudes to posthumous and prenatal nonexistence. How can the former be bad if the latter is not?

It should be recognized that if these are valid objections to counting death as an evil, they will apply to many other supposed evils as well. The first type of objection is expressed in general form by the common remark that what you don't know can't hurt you. It means that even if a man is betrayed by his friends, ridiculed behind his back, and despised by people who treat him politely to his face, none of it can be counted as a misfortune for him so long as he does not suffer as a result. It means that a man is not injured if his wishes are ignored by the executor of his will, or if, after his death, the belief becomes current that all the literary works on which his fame rests were really written by his brother, who died in Mexico at the age of 28. It seems to me worth asking what assumptions about good and evil lead to these drastic restrictions.

All the questions have something to do with time. There certainly are goods and evils of a simple kind (including some pleasures and pains) which a person possesses at a given time simply in virtue of his condition at that time. But this is not true of all the things we regard as good or bad for a man. Often we need to know his history to tell whether something is a misfortune or not; this applies to ills like deterioration, deprivation, and damage. Sometimes his experiential *state* is relatively unimportant—as in the case of a man who wastes his life in the cheerful pursuit of a method of communicating with asparagus plants. Someone who holds that all goods and evils must be temporally assignable states of the person may of course try to bring difficult cases into line by pointing to the pleasure or pain that more complicated goods and evils cause. Loss, betrayal, deception, and ridicule are on this view bad because people suffer when they learn of them. But it should be asked how our ideas of human value would have to be constituted to accommodate these cases directly instead. One advantage of such an account might be that it would enable us to explain *why* the discovery of these misfortunes causes suffering—in a way that makes it reasonable. For the natural view is that the discovery of betrayal makes us unhappy because it is bad to be betrayed—not that betrayal is bad because its discovery makes us unhappy.

It therefore seems to me worth exploring the position that most good and ill fortune has as its subject a person identified by his history and his possibilities, rather than merely by his categorical state of the moment—and that while this subject can be exactly located in a sequence of places and times, the same is not necessarily true of the goods and ills that befall him.[2]

These ideas can be illustrated by an example of deprivation whose severity approaches that of death. Suppose an intelligent person receives a brain injury that reduces him to the mental condition of a contented infant, and that such desires as remain to him can be satisfied by a custodian, so that he is free from care. Such a development would be widely regarded as a severe misfortune, not only for his friends and relations, or for society, but also, and primarily, for the person himself. This does not mean that a contented infant is unfortunate. The intelligent adult who has been *reduced* to this condition is the subject of the misfortune. He is the one we pity, though of course he does not mind his condition—there is some doubt, in fact, whether he can be said to exist any longer.

The view that such a man has suffered a misfortune is open to the same objections which have been raised in regard to death. He does not mind his condition. It is in fact the same condition he was in at the age of three months, except that he is bigger. If we did not pity him then, why pity him now; in any case, who is there to pity? The intelligent adult has disappeared, and for a creature like the one before us, happiness consists in a full stomach and a dry diaper.

If these objections are invalid, it must be because they rest on a mistaken assumption about the temporal relation between the subject of a misfortune and the circumstances which constitute it. If, instead of concentrating exclusively on the oversized baby before us, we consider the person he was, and the person he *could* be now, then his reduction to this state and the cancellation of his natural adult development constitute a perfectly intelligible catastrophe.

This case should convince us that it is arbitrary to restrict the goods and evils that can befall a man to nonrelational properties ascribable to him at particular times. As it stands, that restriction excludes not only such cases of gross degeneration, but also a good deal of what is important about success and failure, and other features of a life that have the character of processes. I believe we can go further, however. There are goods and evils which are irreducibly relational; they are features of the relations between a person, with spatial and temporal boundaries of the usual sort, and circumstances which may not coincide with him either in space or in time. A man's life includes much that does not take place within the boundaries of his body and his mind, and what happens to him can include much that does not take place within the boundaries of his life. These boundaries are commonly crossed by the misfortunes of being deceived, or despised, or betrayed. (If this is correct, there is a simple account of what is wrong with breaking a deathbed promise. It is an injury to the dead man. For certain purposes it is possible to regard time as just another type of distance.) The case of mental degeneration shows us an evil that depends on a contrast between the reality and the possible alternatives. A man is the subject of good and evil as much because he has hopes which may or may not be fulfilled, or possibilities which may or may not be realized, as because of his capacity to suffer and enjoy. If death is an evil, it must be accounted for in these terms, and the impossibility of locating it within life should not trouble us.

When a man dies we are left with his corpse, and while a corpse can suffer the kind of mishap that may occur to an article of furniture, it is not a suitable object for pity. The man, however, is. He has lost his life, and if he had not died, he would have continued to live it and to possess whatever good there is in living. If we apply to death the account suggested for the case of dementia, we shall say that although the spatial and temporal locations of the individual who suffered the loss are clear enough, the misfortune itself cannot be so easily located. One must be content just to state that his life is over and there will never be any more of it. That *fact*, rather than his past or present condition, constitutes his misfortune, if it is one. Nevertheless if there is a loss, someone must suffer it, and *he* must have existence and specific spatial and temporal location even if the loss itself does not. The fact that Beethoven had no children may have been a cause of regret to him, or a sad thing for the world, but it cannot be described as a misfortune for the children that he never had. All of us, I believe, are fortunate to have been born. But unless good and ill can be assigned to an embryo, or even to an unconnected pair of gametes, it cannot be said that not to be born is a misfortune. (That is a factor to be considered in deciding whether abortion and contraception are akin to murder.)

This approach also provides a solution to the problem of temporal asymmetry, pointed out by Lucretius. He observed that no one finds it disturbing to contemplate the eternity preceding his own birth, and he took this to show that it must be irrational to fear death, since death is simply the mirror image of the prior abyss. That is not true, however, and the difference between the two explains why it is reasonable to regard them differently. It is true that both the time before a man's birth and the time after his death are times when he does not exist. But the time after his death is time of which his death deprives him. It is time in which, had he not died then, he would be alive. Therefore any death entails the loss of *some* life that its victim would have led had he not died at that or any earlier point. We know perfectly well what it would be for him to have had it instead of losing it, and there is no difficulty in identifying the loser.

But we cannot say that the time prior to a man's birth is time in which he would have lived had he been born not then but earlier. For aside from the brief margin permitted by premature labor, he *could* not have been born earlier: anyone born substantially earlier than he was would have been someone else. Therefore the time prior to his birth is not time in which his subsequent birth prevents him from living. His birth, when it occurs, does not entail the loss to him of any life whatever.

The direction of time is crucial in assigning possibilities to people or other individuals. Distinct possible lives of a single person can diverge from a common beginning, but they cannot converge to a common conclusion from diverse beginnings. (The latter would represent not a set of different possible lives of one individual, but a set of distinct possible individuals, whose lives have identical conclusions.) Given an identifiable individual, countless possibilities for his continued existence are imaginable, and we can clearly conceive of what it would be for him to go on existing indefinitely. However inevitable it is that this will not come about, its possibility is still that of the continuation of a good for him, if life is the good we take it to be.[3]

We are left, therefore, with the question whether the nonrealization of this possibility is in every case a misfortune, or whether it depends on what can naturally be hoped for. This seems to me the most serious difficulty with the view that death is always an evil. Even if we can dispose of the objections against admitting misfortune that is not experienced, or cannot be assigned to a definite time in the person's life, we still have to set some limits on *how* possible a possibility must be for its nonrealization to be a misfortune (or good fortune, should the possibility be a bad one). The death of Keats at 24 is generally regarded as tragic; that of Tolstoy at 82 is not. Although they will both be dead for ever, Keats' death deprived him of many years of life which were allowed to Tolstoy; so in a clear sense Keats' loss was greater (though not in the sense standardly employed in mathematical comparison between infinite quantities). However, this does not prove that Tolstoy's loss was insignificant. Perhaps we record an objection only to evils which are gratuitously added to the inevitable; the fact that it is worse to die at 24 than at 82 does not imply that it is not a terrible thing to die at 82, or even at 806. The question is whether we can regard as a misfortune any limitation, like mortality, that is normal to the species. Blindness or near-blindness is not a misfortune for a mole, nor would it be for a man if that were the natural condition of the human race.

The trouble is that life familiarizes us with the goods of which death deprives us. We are already able to appreciate them, as a mole is not able to appreciate vision. If we put aside doubts about their status as goods and grant that their quantity is in part a function of their duration, the question remains whether death, no matter when it occurs, can be said to deprive its victim of what is in the relevant sense a possible continuation of life.

The situation is an ambiguous one. Observed from without, human beings obviously have a natural lifespan and cannot live much longer than a hundred years. A man's sense of his own experience, on the other hand, does not embody this idea of a natural limit. His existence defines for him an essentially open-ended possible future, containing the usual mixture of goods and evils that he has found so tolerable in the past. Having been gratuitously introduced to the world by a collection of natural, historical, and social accidents, he finds himself the subject of a *life*, with an indeterminate and not essentially limited future. Viewed in this way, death, no matter how inevitable, is an abrupt cancellation of indefinitely extensive possible goods. Normality seems to have nothing to do with it, for the fact that we will all inevitably die in a few score years cannot by itself imply that it would not be good to live longer. Suppose that we were all inevitably going to die in *agony*— physical agony lasting six months. Would inevitability make *that* prospect any less unpleasant? And why should it be different for a deprivation? If the normal lifespan were a thousand years, death at 80 would be a tragedy. As things are, it may just be a more widespread tragedy. If there is no limit to the amount of life that it would be good to have, then it may be that a bad end is in store for us all.

NOTES

1. It is sometimes suggested that what we really mind is the process of *dying*. But I should not really object to dying if it were not followed by death.
2. It is certainly not true in general of the things that can be said of him. For example, Abraham Lincoln was taller than Louis XIV. But when?
3. I confess to being troubled by the above argument, on the ground that it is too sophisticated to explain the simple difference between our attitudes to prenatal and posthumous nonexistence. For this reason I suspect that something essential is omitted from the account of the badness of death by an analysis which treats it as a deprivation of possibilities. My suspicion is supported by the following suggestion of Robert Nozick. We could imagine discovering that people developed from individual spores that had existed indefinitely far in advance of their birth. In this fantasy, birth never occurs naturally more than a hundred years before the permanent end of the spore's existence. But then we discover a way to trigger the premature batching of these spores, and people are born who have thousands of years of active life before them. Given such a situation, it would be possible to imagine *oneself* having come into existence thousands of years previously. If we put aside the question whether this would really be the same person, even given the identity of the spore, then the consequence appears to be that a person's birth at a given time *could* deprive him of many earlier years of possible life. Now while it would be cause for regret that one had been deprived of all those possible years of life by being born too late, the feeling would differ from that which many people have about death. I conclude that something about the future *prospect* of permanent nothingness is not captured by the analysis in terms of denied possibilities. If so, then Lucretius' argument still awaits an answer. I suspect that it requires a general treatment of the difference between past and future in our attitudes toward our own lives. Our attitudes toward past and future pain are very different, for example. Derek Parfit's unpublished writings on this topic have revealed its difficulty to me.

STUDY QUESTIONS

1. If death is not an evil for a person who dies, is death, therefore, not an evil for anyone?
2. Do you agree with Nagel that a man who devotes himself to cheerful pursuit of a method of communicating with asparagus has wasted his life?
3. Would a life devoted to trying to communicate with beings from another galaxy be wasted?
4. Do you agree with Nagel that all of us are fortunate to have been born?

The Badness of Death

SHELLY KAGAN

Shelly Kagan is Professor of Philosophy at Yale University. He considers a puzzle raised by the Roman thinker Lucretius (c. 94–c. 55 B.C.E.), an Epicurean philosopher and poet. Lucretius asked why we should be concerned about not being alive after the time of our death, although we are unconcerned about not having been alive before the time of our birth.

Let me turn to . . . a puzzle that we get from Lucretius, a Roman philosopher.[1] Lucretius was one of those who thought it a mistake to claim that death could be bad for us. He thinks we are confused when we find the prospect of our death upsetting. He recognizes, of course, that most of us *are* upset at the fact that we're going to die. We think death is bad for us. Why? In my own case, of course, it's because after my death I won't exist. . . . [A]fter my death it will be true that if only I were still alive, I could be enjoying the good things in life.

Fair enough, says Lucretius, but wait a minute. The time after I die isn't the *only* period during which I won't exist. It's not the only period in which it is true that if only I were alive, I could be enjoying the good things in life. There's *another* period of nonexistence: the period before my birth. To be sure, there will be an infinite period after my death in which I won't exist—and realizing that fills me with dismay. But be that all as it may, there was of course also an infinite period *before* I came into existence. Well, says Lucretius, if nonexistence is so bad—and by the deprivation account it seems that we want to say that it is—shouldn't I be upset at the fact that there was also this eternity of nonexistence before I was born?

But, Lucretius suggests, that's silly, right? Nobody is upset about the fact that there was an eternity of nonexistence *before* they were born. In which case, he concludes, it doesn't make any sense to be upset about the eternity of nonexistence *after* you die.

Lucretius doesn't offer this as a puzzle. Rather, he offers it as an argument that we should not be concerned about the fact that we're going to die. Unsurprisingly, however, most philosophers aren't willing to go with Lucretius all the way to this conclusion. They insist, instead, that there must be something wrong with this argument someplace. The challenge is to figure out just where the mistake is.

What are the options here? One possibility, of course, is to simply agree with Lucretius. There is nothing bad about the eternity of nonexistence before I was

From Shelly Kagan, *Death*, Yale University Press, 2012. Reprinted by permission of the publisher.

born. So, similarly, there is nothing bad about the eternity of nonexistence after I die. Despite what most of us think, death is not bad for me. That's certainly one possibility—completely agreeing with Lucretius.

A second possibility is to partly agree with Lucretius. Perhaps we really do need to treat these two eternities of nonexistence on a par; but instead of saying with Lucretius that there was nothing bad about the eternity of nonexistence before birth and so nothing bad about the eternity of nonexistence after death, maybe we should say, instead, that just as there is something bad about the eternity of nonexistence after we die, so too there must be something bad about the eternity of nonexistence before we were born! Maybe we should just stick with the deprivation account and not lose faith in it. The deprivation account tells us that it's bad for us that there's this period after we die, because if only we weren't dead then, we would still be able to enjoy the good things in life. So maybe we should say, similarly, that it *is* bad for us that there's this period before we come into existence. After all, if only we had existed then, we would have been able to enjoy the good things in life. So maybe Lucretius was right when he tells us that we have to treat both periods the same, but for all that he could be wrong in concluding that neither period is bad. Maybe we should think *both* periods are bad. That's a possibility, too.

What other possibilities are there? We might say that although Lucretius is right when he points out that there are two periods of nonexistence, not just one, nonetheless there is a justification for treating them differently. Perhaps there is an important difference between the two periods, a kind of asymmetry that explains why we should care about the one but not the other.

Most philosophers want to take this last way out. They say that there's something that explains why it makes sense, why it's reasonable, to care about the eternity of nonexistence after my death in a way that I don't care about the eternity of nonexistence before my birth. But then the puzzle, of course, is to point to a difference that would *justify* that kind of asymmetrical treatment of the two periods. It's easy to *say* that it's reasonable to treat the two periods differently; the philosophical challenge is to point to something that explains or justifies that asymmetrical treatment.

One very common response is to say something like this. Consider the period after my death. I'm no longer alive. I have *lost* my life. In contrast, during the period before my birth, although I'm not alive, I have not *lost* my life. I have never yet been alive. And, of course, you can't lose something you've never yet had. So what's worse about the period after death is the fact that death involves *loss*, whereas prenatal nonexistence does *not* involve loss. And so (the argument goes), we can see why it's reasonable to care more about the period after death than the period before birth. The one involves loss, while the other does not.

This is, as I say, a very common response. But I am inclined to think that it can't be an adequate answer. It is true, of course, that the period after death involves loss while the period before birth does not. The very definition of "loss," after all, requires that in order to have lost something, it must be true that you don't have something that at an earlier time you did have. Given this definition, it follows trivially that the period after death involves loss, while the period before birth does not. After all, as we just observed, during the period before birth, although I do not *have* life, it is also true that I haven't had life previously. So I haven't *lost* anything.

Of course, there's another thing that's true about this prenatal period, to wit, I don't have life and I'm *going* to get it. So I don't yet have something that's going to come in the future. That's not true about the postlife period. After death I've *lost* life. But it's not true of this postdeath period that I don't have life and I'm going to get it in the future. So this period after death isn't quite like the period before birth: in the period after death, I am not in the state of not yet having something that I am going to get. That's an interesting difference.

As it happens, we don't have a name for this other kind of state—where you don't yet have something that you will get later. It is similar to loss, in one way, but it's not quite like loss. Let's call it "schmoss." When I have *lost* something, then, I don't have it, but I did have it earlier. And when I have *schmost* something, I don't have it yet, but I will get it later.

So here's the deal. During the period after death, there's a loss of life, but no schmoss of life. And during the period before birth, there's no loss of life, but there is a schmoss of life. And now, as philosophers, we need to ask: why do we care more about *loss* of life than *schmoss* of life? What is it about the fact that we don't have something that we used to have, that makes this worse than not having something that we're going to have?

It's easy to overlook the symmetry here, because we've got this nice word "loss," and we don't have the word "schmoss." But that's not really explaining anything, it's just pointing to the thing that needs explaining. Why do we care more about not having what once upon a time we did than about not having what once upon a time we will? That's really quite puzzling.

Various proposals have been made to explain this difference in attitude toward the two periods of nonexistence. One of them comes from Thomas Nagel, a contemporary philosopher.[2] Nagel starts by pointing out how easy it is to imagine the possibility of living longer. Suppose I die at the age of eighty. Perhaps I will get hit by a car. Imagine, though, that if I didn't die then, I would have continued living until I was ninety or even one hundred. That certainly seems possible, even if in fact I am going to die at eighty. The fact that I am going to die at eighty is a *contingent* fact about me. It is not a necessary fact about me that I die at eighty. So it is an easy enough matter to imagine my living longer, by having my death come later. That's why it makes sense to get upset at the fact of my death coming when it does: I could have lived longer, by having death come later.

In contrast, Nagel notes, if I am going to be upset about my nonexistence before my birth, we have to imagine my being born earlier. We have to imagine my living longer by having my birth come sooner. Is this possible? I was born in 1954. Can I be upset about the fact that I was born in 1954 instead of, say, 1944?

Nagel thinks, however, that I shouldn't be upset about the fact that I wasn't born in 1944, because in fact it isn't *possible* for me to have an earlier birth. The date of my *death* is a contingent fact about me. But the date of my *birth* is not a contingent fact about me. Well, that's not quite right. We could change the time of birth slightly, perhaps by having me delivered prematurely, or through Caesarean section, or what have you. Strictly speaking, of course, the crucial moment is the moment at which I come into *existence*. Let's suppose that this is the time when the egg and the sperm join. Nagel's thought is that this is not a contingent moment in my life story. That's an *essential* moment in my life story.

How could that be? Can't we easily imagine my parents having had sex ten years earlier? Sure we can. But remember, if they had had sex ten years earlier, it would have been a different egg and a different sperm coming together, so it wouldn't be *me*. It would be some sibling of mine that, as it happens, never got born. Obviously, there could have been some sibling of mine that came into existence in 1944, but *I* couldn't have come into existence in 1944. The person we are imagining with the earlier birth date wouldn't be *me*. What this means, Nagel suggests, is that although we can *say* the words "if only I had been born earlier," this isn't really pointing to a genuine metaphysical possibility. So there is no point in being upset at the nonexistence before you started to exist, because you couldn't have had a longer life by coming into existence earlier. (In contrast, as we have seen, you could have a longer life by going out of existence later.)

I must say, that's a pretty intriguing suggestion. But I think it can't be quite right. Or rather, it cannot be the complete story about how to answer Lucretius's puzzle. For in some cases, I think, we *can* easily imagine the possibility of having come into existence earlier. Suppose we've got a fertility clinic that has some sperm on hold and has some eggs on hold. Perhaps they keep them there frozen until they're ready to use them. And they thaw a pair out in, say, 2025. They fertilize the egg and eventually the person is born. That person, it seems to me, can correctly say that he could have come into existence earlier. He could look back and say that if only they had put the relevant sperm and egg together ten years earlier, he would have come into existence ten years earlier. It wouldn't be a sibling; it would have been *him*. After all, it would have been the very same sperm and the very same egg, resulting in the very same person. So if only they had combined the sperm and egg ten years earlier, he would have been born ten years earlier.

If that's right—and it does seem to me to be right—then Nagel is wrong in saying it's not possible to imagine being born earlier. In at least some cases it is. Yet, if we imagine somebody like this, somebody who's an offspring of this kind of fertility clinic, and we ask, "Would they be upset that they weren't born earlier?" it still seems as though most people would say, "No, of course not." So Nagel's solution to our puzzle doesn't seem to me to be an adequate one.

Here's another possible answer. This one comes from Fred Feldman, another contemporary philosopher.[3] If I say, "if only I would die later," what am I imagining? Suppose I will get hit by a car in 2034, when I am eighty. We can certainly imagine what would happen if I *didn't* get killed at that point. What do we imagine? Something like this, I suppose: instead of my living a "mere" eighty years, we imagine that I would live to be eighty-five or ninety, or more. We imagine a longer life. When we imagine my dying later, we imagine my having a longer life.

But what do I imagine when I say, "if only I had been born *earlier*"? According to Feldman, you don't actually imagine a longer life, you just *shift* the entire life and start it earlier. After all, suppose I ask you to imagine being born in 1800 instead of the year you were actually born. Nobody thinks, "Why, if I had been born in 1800, I'd still be alive. I would be more than two hundred years old!" Rather, you think, "If I had been born in 1800 I would have died in 1860, or 1870, or some such."

When we imagine being born earlier, we don't imagine a longer life, just an *earlier* life. And of course there is nothing about having a life that takes place earlier that makes it particularly better, according to the deprivation account. So there is no point in bemoaning the fact that you weren't born earlier. But in contrast, when we imagine dying later, it's not as though we shift the life *forward*. We don't imagine being *born* later, keeping the life the same length. No, we imagine a *longer* life. And so, Feldman says, it's no wonder that you care about nonexistence after death in a way that you don't care about nonexistence before birth. When you imagine death coming later, you imagine a longer life, with more of the goods of life. But when you imagine birth coming earlier, you don't imagine more goods in your life, you just imagine them taking place at a different time.

That too is an interesting suggestion, and I imagine it is probably part of a complete answer to Lucretius. But I don't think it can be the complete story. Because we can in fact imagine cases where the person reasonably thinks that if only she had been born earlier she *would* have had a longer life.

Let's suppose that next week astronomers discover the horrible fact that there's an asteroid that's about to land on the Earth and wipe out all life. Suppose that it is going to crash into the Earth on January 1st of next year. Now imagine someone who is currently only thirty years old. It seems to me to be perfectly reasonable for such a person to think to herself that she has only had thirty years of life, and if only she had been born ten years earlier, she would have had forty years before she died, instead of thirty; if she had been born twenty years earlier, she would have had fifty years, instead of thirty. That all seems perfectly intelligible. So it does seem as though, if we work at it, we can think of cases where an earlier birth does result in a longer life and not merely a shifted life. In cases like this, it seems, we can imagine making life longer in the "pre-birth" direction rather than in the "postdeath" direction.

What does that show us? I am not sure. When I think about the asteroid example, I find myself thinking that maybe symmetry is the right way to go here after all. Maybe in a case like this, the relevant bit of prenatal nonexistence *is* just as bad as a corresponding bit of postmortem nonexistence. Maybe Feldman is right when he says that normally, when thinking about an earlier birth, we just shift the life, instead of lengthening it. But for all that, if we are careful to describe a case where an earlier birth would truly mean a longer life for me, maybe it really *is* bad that I didn't get started sooner. (Feldman would probably agree.)

Here's one more answer to Lucretius that's been proposed. This is by yet another contemporary philosopher, Derek Parfit.[4] Recall the fact that even though nonexistence before birth doesn't involve loss, it does involve schmoss. So it would be helpful if we had an explanation of why loss is worse than schmoss. Why should we care more about the former than the latter? Parfit's idea, in effect, is that this is not an arbitrary preference on our part. Rather, it's part of a quite general pattern we have of caring about the future in a way that we don't care about the past. This is a very deep fact about human caring. We are oriented toward the future and concerned about what will happen in it, in a way that we're not oriented toward and concerned about what happened in the past.

Parfit's got a very nice example to bring the point home. He asks you to imagine that you've got some medical condition that will kill you unless you have an operation. So you're going to have the operation. Unfortunately, in order to perform the operation, they can't have you anesthetized. You have to be awake, perhaps in order to tell the surgeon, "Yes, that's where it hurts." You've got to be awake during the operation, and it's a *very* painful operation. Furthermore, we can't give you painkiller, because then you won't be able to tell the surgeon where it hurts. In short, you need to be awake while you are, in effect, being tortured. Of course, it's still worth it, because this will cure your condition, and you can go on to have a nice long life. But during the operation itself, it is going to hurt like hell.

Since we can't give you painkillers and we can't put you out, all we can do is this: after the operation is over, we'll give you this very powerful medication, which will induce a very localized form of amnesia, destroying your very recent memories. You won't remember anything about the operation itself. And in particular, then, you won't ever have to revisit horrible memories of having been tortured. Any such memory will be completely destroyed. Indeed, *all* memories from the preceding twenty-four hours will be completely wiped out. In sum, you are going to have a horrendously painful operation, and you are going to be awake during it. But after the operation you will be given medication that will make you completely forget the pain of the operation, indeed forget everything about the entire day.

So you're in the hospital and you wake up and you ask yourself, "Have I had the operation yet or not?" And of course, you don't know. You certainly don't remember having had it. But that doesn't tell you anything. On the one hand, if you haven't had it yet, it is no wonder you have no memories of having had it. But on the other hand, even if you *have* had the operation, you would have been given the medication afterwards, so would have no memories of it now. So you ask the nurse, "Have I had the operation yet or not?" She answers, "I don't know. We have several patients like you on the floor today, some of whom have already had the procedure, and some of whom are scheduled to have it later today. I don't remember which group you are in. Let me go look at your file. I'll come back in a moment and I'll tell you." So she wanders off. She's going to come back in a minute or two. And as you are waiting for her to come back, you ask yourself, what do you want the answer to be? Do you care which group you're in? Do you prefer to be someone who has *already* had the operation? Someone who *hasn't* had it yet? Or are you indifferent?

Now, if you're like Parfit, and for that matter like me, then you're going to say that *of course* you care. I certainly want it to be the case that I have *already* had the operation. I don't want to be someone who hasn't had the operation yet.

We might ask, how can that make any sense? You are going to have the operation sooner or later. At some point in your life history, that operation is going to have occurred. And so there's going to be the same amount of pain and torture at some point in your life, regardless of whether you're one of the people that had it yesterday or one of the people that are going to have it later today. But for all that, says Parfit, the fact of the matter is perfectly plain: we *do* care. We want the pain to be in the past. We don't want the pain to be in the future. We care more about what's happening in the future than about what's happened in the past.

That being the case, however, it is no surprise that we care about our nonexistence in the future in a way that we don't care about our nonexistence in the past. So perhaps that is the answer that we should give to Lucretius: the future matters in a way that the past does not.

That too is an intriguing suggestion. And it may well provide us with a convincing explanation of our asymmetrical attitudes. But we might still wonder whether it gives us any kind of *justification* for them. The fact that we've got this deep-seated asymmetrical attitude toward time doesn't in any way, as far as I can see, yet tell us whether or not that's a *justified* attitude. Maybe evolution built us to care about the future in a way that we don't care about the past, and this expresses itself in all sorts of places, including Parfit's hospital case and our attitude toward loss versus schmoss, and so forth and so on. But the fact that we've got this attitude doesn't yet show that it's a *rational* attitude.

How could we show that it's a rational attitude? Perhaps we would have to start doing some heavy-duty metaphysics (if what we have been doing so far isn't yet heavy-duty enough). Maybe we need to talk about the metaphysical difference between the past and the future. Intuitively, after all, the past is fixed, while the future is open, and time seems to have a direction, from past to future. Maybe somehow we could bring all these things in and explain why our attitude toward time is a reasonable one. I'm not going to go there. All I want to say is, it's not altogether obvious what the best answer to Lucretius's puzzle is. . . .

But for all that, it seems to me that . . . what's bad about death is that when you're dead, you're not experiencing the good things in life. Death is bad for you precisely because you don't have what life would bring you if only you hadn't died.

NOTES

1. Lucretius, *On the Nature of Things.*
2. Thomas Nagel, "Death," in *Mortal Questions* (Cambridge, 1979).
3. Fred Feldman, *Confrontations with the Reaper* (Oxford, 1992), pp. 154–156.
4. This example comes from Derek Parfit, *Reasons and Persons* (Oxford, 1984), pp. 165–166. I should note, however, that Parfit isn't here explicitly discussing Lucretius. I am simply applying some of his ideas to that puzzle. (Parfit's own discussion of the puzzle can be found in *Reasons and Persons,* pp. 174–177.)

STUDY QUESTIONS

1. Are you concerned about not being alive before the time of your birth?
2. Do you agree with Lucretius that we should be unconcerned about not being alive after the time of our death?
3. How do you assess Nagel's reply to Lucretius?
4. How do you assess Feldman's reply to Lucretius?

HISTORICAL SOURCES

Phaedo

PLATO

The *Phaedo*, one of Plato's greatest and most complex works, is set in the Athenian prison on the day of Socrates' death. The discussion focuses on Plato's attempts to prove the immortality of the soul. Near the end of the dialogue from which this selection is taken, Socrates utters his last thoughts, drinks poison, and dies. What then begins is his enormous influence on the history of Western thought.

When he'd spoken, Crito said: "Very well, Socrates: what instructions have you for these others or for me, about your children or about anything else? What could we do that would be of most service to you?"

"What I'm always telling you, Crito," said he, "and nothing very new: if you take care for yourselves, your actions will be of service to me and mine and to yourselves too, whatever they may be, even if you make no promises now; but if you take no care for yourselves and are unwilling to pursue your lives along the tracks, as it were, marked by our present and earlier discussions, then even if you make many firm promises at this time, you'll do no good at all."

"Then we'll strive to do as you say," he said; "but in what fashion are we to bury you?"

"However you wish," said he; "provided you catch me, that is, and I don't get away from you." And with this he laughed quietly, looked towards us and said: "Friends, I can't persuade Crito that I am Socrates here, the one who is now conversing and arranging each of the things being discussed; but he imagines I'm that dead body he'll see in a little while, so he goes and asks how he's to bury me! But as for the great case I've been arguing all this time, that when I drink the poison,[1] I shall no longer remain with you, but shall go off and depart for some happy state of the blessed, this, I think, I'm putting to him in vain, while comforting you and myself alike. So please stand surety for me with Crito, the opposite surety to that which he stood for me with the judges: his guarantee was that I *would* stay behind, whereas you must guarantee that, when I die, I shall *not* stay behind, but shall go off and depart; then Crito will bear it more easily, and when he sees the burning or interment of my body, he won't be distressed for me, as if I were suffering dreadful things, and won't say at the funeral that it is Socrates they are laying out or bearing to the grave or interring. Because you can be sure, my dear Crito, that misuse of words is not only troublesome in itself, but actually has a bad effect on the soul. Rather, you should have confidence, and say you are burying my body; and bury it however you please, and think most proper."

After saying this, he rose and went into a room to take a bath, and Crito followed him but told us to wait. So we waited, talking among ourselves about what had been said and reviewing it, and then again dwelling on how great a misfortune had befallen us, literally thinking of it as if we were deprived of a father and would lead the rest of our life as orphans. After he'd bathed and his children had been brought to him—he had two little sons and one big one—and those women of his household had come, he talked with them in Crito's presence, and gave certain directions as to his wishes; he then told the women and children to leave, and himself returned to us.

By now it was close to sunset, as he'd spent a long time inside. So he came and sat down, fresh from his bath, and there wasn't much talk after that. Then the prison official came in, stepped up to him and said: "Socrates, I shan't reproach you as I reproach others for being angry with me and cursing, whenever by order of the rulers I direct them to drink the poison. In your time here I've known you for the most generous and gentlest and best of men who have ever come to this place; and now especially, I feel sure it isn't with me that you're angry, but with others, because you know who are responsible. Well now, you know the message I've come to bring: good-bye, then, and try to bear the inevitable as easily as you can." And with this he turned away in tears, and went off.

Socrates looked up at him and said: "Good-bye to you too, and we'll do as you say." And to us he added: "What a civil man he is! Throughout my time here he's been to see me, and sometimes talked with me, and been the best of fellows; and now how generous of him to weep for me! But come on, Crito, let's obey him: let someone bring in the poison, if it has been prepared; if not, let the man prepare it."

Crito said: "But Socrates, I think the sun is still on the mountains and hasn't yet gone down. And besides, I know of others who've taken the draught long after the order had been given them, and after dining well and drinking plenty, and even in some cases enjoying themselves with those they fancied. Be in no hurry, then: there's still time left."

Socrates said: "It's reasonable for those you speak of to do those things—because they think they gain by doing them; for myself, it's reasonable not to do them; because I think I'll gain nothing by taking the draught a little later: I'll only earn my own ridicule by clinging to life, and being sparing when there's nothing more left. Go on now; do as I ask, and nothing else."

Hearing this, Crito nodded to the boy who was standing nearby. The boy went out, and after spending a long time away he returned, bringing the man who was going to administer the poison, and was carrying it ready-pounded in a cup. When he saw the man, Socrates said: "Well, my friend, you're an expert in these things: what must one do?"

"Simply drink it," he said, "and walk about till a heaviness comes over your legs; then lie down, and it will act of itself." And with this he held out the cup to Socrates.

He took it perfectly calmly, Echecrates, without a tremor, or any change of colour or countenance; but looking up at the man, and fixing him with his customary stare, he said: "What do you say to pouring someone a libation from this drink? Is it allowed or not?"

"We only prepare as much as we judge the proper dose, Socrates," he said.

"I understand," he said; "but at least one may pray to the gods, and so one should, that the removal from this world to the next will be a happy one; that is my own prayer: so may it be." With these words he pressed the cup to his lips, and drank it off with good humour and without the least distaste.

Till then most of us had been fairly well able to restrain our tears; but when we saw he was drinking, that he'd actually drunk it, we could do so no longer. In my own case, the tears came pouring out in spite of myself, so that I covered my face and wept for myself—not for him, no, but for my own misfortune in being deprived of such a man for a companion. Even before me, Crito had moved away, when he was unable to restrain his tears. And Apollodorus, who even earlier had been continuously in tears, now burst forth into such a storm of weeping and grieving, that he made everyone present break down except Socrates himself.

But Socrates said: "What a way to behave, my strange friends! Why, it was mainly for this reason that I sent the women away, so that they shouldn't make this sort of trouble; in fact, I've heard one should die in silence. Come now, calm yourselves and have strength."

When we heard this, we were ashamed and checked our tears. He walked about, and when he said that his legs felt heavy he lay down on his back—as the man told him—and then the man, this one who'd given him the poison, felt him, and after an interval examined his feet and legs; he then pinched his foot hard and asked if he could feel it, and Socrates said not. After that he felt his shins once more; and moving upwards in this way, he showed us that he was becoming cold and numb. He went on feeling him, and said that when the coldness reached his heart, he would be gone.

By this time the coldness was somewhere in the region of his abdomen, when he uncovered his face—it had been covered over—and spoke; and this was in fact his last utterance: "Crito," he said, "we owe a cock to Asclepius: please pay the debt, and don't neglect it."[2]

"It shall be done," said Crito; "have you anything else to say?"

To this question he made no answer, but after a short interval he stirred, and when the man uncovered him his eyes were fixed; when he saw this, Crito closed his mouth and his eyes.

And that, Echecrates, was the end of our companion, a man who, among those of his time we knew, was—so we should say—the best, the wisest too, and the most just.

NOTES

1. The poison was hemlock, frequently used in ancient executions.
2. Asclepius was the hero or god of healing. A provocative, but disputed, interpretation of Socrates' final instruction is that he considers death the cure for life and, therefore, wishes to make an offering in gratitude to the god of health.

STUDY QUESTIONS

1. According to Socrates, how could Crito be of most service?
2. Why, according to Socrates, will he have to be caught in order to be buried?
3. What lessons can be drawn from the equanimity with which Socrates faced death?
4. In what ways does the study of philosophy reflect concerns that were espoused by Socrates?

Writings

Epicurus

Epicurus (341–270 B.C.E.) was an influential Greek philosopher who founded a community in Athens called "the Garden," in which men and women as well as free persons and slaves participated on equal terms. He was a prolific author, but few of his writings survive.

His system of thought, known as Epicureanism, stressed that the gods are detached from this world. Its fundamental structure is that of atoms in motion, although persons have free will as a result of uncaused swerves in the atoms. Our knowledge is derived from sense experience. The ultimate aim of philosophy is

From *Epicurus, The Extant Remains*, ed. and trans. Cyril Bailey. Copyright © 1926 Oxford University Press. Used by permission of Oxford University Press, Inc.

to provide a guide to living well, maximizing pleasures and minimizing pains, but accepting such pains as lead to greater pleasures, and rejecting such pleasures as lead to greater pains. The result is a life that avoids extravagance. The virtues, such as temperance or courage, are prized because they lead to a pleasant life. So do friendships, which are, therefore, to be cultivated. Death is not to be feared, because while we exist, death is not present; when death is present, we do not exist.

························

LETTER TO MENOECEUS

Let no one when young delay to study philosophy, nor when he is old grow weary of his study. For no one can come too early or too late to secure the health of his soul. And the man who says that the age for philosophy has either not yet come or has gone by is like the man who says that the age for happiness is not yet come to him, or has passed away. Wherefore both when young and old a man must study philosophy, that as he grows old he may be young in blessings through the grateful recollection of what has been, and that in youth he may be old as well, since he will know no fear of what is to come. We must then meditate on the things that make our happiness, seeing that when that is with us we have all, but when it is absent we do all to win it.

The things which I used unceasingly to commend to you, these do and practice, considering them to be the first principles of the good life. First of all believe that god is a being immortal and blessed, even as the common idea of a god is engraved on men's minds, and do not assign to him anything alien to his immortality or ill-suited to his blessedness: but believe about him everything that can uphold his blessedness and immortality. For gods there are, since the knowledge of them is by clear vision. But they are not such as the many believe them to be: for indeed they do not consistently represent them as they believe them to be. And the impious man is not he who denies the gods of the many, but he who attaches to the gods the beliefs of the many. For the statements of the many about the gods are not conceptions derived from sensation, but false suppositions, according to which the greatest misfortunes befall the wicked and the greatest blessings the good by the gift of the gods. For men being accustomed always to their own virtues welcome those like themselves, but regard all that is not of their nature as alien.

Become accustomed to the belief that death is nothing to us. For all good and evil consists in sensation, but death is deprivation of sensation. And therefore a right understanding that death is nothing to us makes the mortality of life enjoyable, not because it adds to it an infinite span of time, but because it takes away the craving for immortality. For there is nothing terrible in life for the man who has truly comprehended that there is nothing terrible in not living. So that the man speaks but idly who says that he fears death not because it will be painful when it comes, but because it is painful in anticipation. For that which gives no trouble when it comes, is but an empty pain in anticipation.

So death, the most terrifying of ills, is nothing to us, since so long as we exist, death is not with us; but when death comes, then we do not exist. It does not then concern either the living or the dead, since for the former it is not, and the latter are no more.

But the many at one moment shun death as the greatest of evils, at another yearn for it as a respite from the evils in life. But the wise man neither seeks to escape life nor fears the cessation of life, for neither does life offend him nor does the absence of life seem to be any evil. And just as with food he does not seek simply the larger share and nothing else, but rather the most pleasant, so he seeks to enjoy not the longest period of time, but the most pleasant.

And he who counsels the young man to live well, but the old man to make a good end, is foolish, not merely because of the desirability of life, but also because it is the same training which teaches to live well and to die well. Yet much worse still is the man who says it is good not to be born, but

once born make haste to pass the gates of Death.[1]

For if he says this from conviction why does he not pass away out of life? For it is open to him to do so, if he had firmly made up his mind to this. But if he speaks in jest, his words are idle among men who cannot receive them.

We must then bear in mind that the future is neither ours, nor yet wholly not ours, so that we may not altogether expect it as sure to come, nor abandon hope of it, as if it will certainly not come.

We must consider that of desires some are natural, others vain, and of the natural some are necessary and others merely natural; and of the necessary some are necessary for happiness, others for the repose of the body, and others for very life. The right understanding of these facts enables us to refer all choice and avoidance to the health of the body and the soul's freedom from disturbance, since this is the aim of the life of blessedness. For it is to obtain this end that we always act, namely, to avoid pain and fear. And when this is once secured for us, all the tempest of the soul is dispersed, since the living creature has not to wander as though in search of something that is missing, and to look for some other thing by which he can fulfil the good of the soul and the good of the body. For it is then that we have need of pleasure, when we feel pain owing to the absence of pleasure; but when we do not feel pain, we no longer need pleasure. And for this cause we call pleasure the beginning and end of the blessed life. For we recognize pleasure as the first good innate in us, and from pleasure we begin every act of choice and avoidance, and to pleasure we return again, using the feeling as the standard by which we judge every good.

And since pleasure is the first good and natural to us, for this very reason we do not choose every pleasure, but sometimes we pass over many pleasures, when greater discomfort accrues to us as the result of them: and similarly we think many pains better than pleasures, since a greater pleasure comes to us when we have endured pains for a long time. Every pleasure then because of its natural kinship to us is good, yet not every pleasure is to be chosen: even as every pain also is an evil, yet not all are always of a nature to be avoided. Yet by a scale of comparison and by the consideration of advantages and disadvantages we must form our judgement on all these matters. For the good on certain occasions we treat as bad, and conversely the bad as good.

And again independence of desire we think a great good—not that we may at all times enjoy but a few things, but that, if we do not possess many, we may enjoy the few in the genuine persuasion that those have the sweetest pleasure in luxury who least need it, and that all that is natural is easy to be obtained, but that which is superfluous is hard. And so plain savours bring us a pleasure equal to a luxurious diet, when all the pain due to want is removed; and bread and water produce the highest pleasure, when one who needs them puts them to his lips. To grow accustomed therefore to a simple and not luxurious diet gives us health to the full, and makes a man alert for the needful employments of life, and when after long intervals we approach luxuries disposes us better towards them, and fits us to be fearless of fortune.

When, therefore, we maintain that pleasure is the end, we do not mean the pleasures of profligates and those that consist in sensuality, as is supposed by some who are either ignorant or disagree with us or do not understand, but freedom from pain in the body and from trouble in the mind. For it is not continuous drinkings and revellings, nor the satisfaction of lusts, nor the enjoyment of fish and other luxuries of the wealthy table, which produce a pleasant life, but sober reasoning, searching out the motives for all choice and avoidance, and banishing mere opinions, to which are due the greatest disturbance of the spirit.

Of all this the beginning and the greatest good is prudence. Wherefore prudence is a more precious thing even than philosophy: for from prudence are sprung all the other virtues, and it teaches us that it is not possible to live pleasantly without living prudently and honourably and justly, nor, again, to live a life of prudence, honour, and justice without living pleasantly. For the virtues are by nature bound up with the pleasant life, and the pleasant life is inseparable from them. For indeed who, think you, is a better man than he who holds reverent opinions concerning the gods, and is at all times free from fear of death, and has reasoned out the end ordained by nature? He understands that the limit of good things is easy to fulfil and easy to attain, whereas the course of ills is either short in time or slight in pain: he laughs at destiny, whom some have introduced as the mistress of all things. He thinks that with us lies the chief power in determining events, some of which happen by necessity and some by chance, and some are within our control; for while necessity cannot be called to account, he sees that chance is inconstant, but that which is in our control is subject to no master, and to it are naturally attached praise and blame. For, indeed, it were better to follow the myths about the gods than to become a slave to the destiny of the natural philosophers: for the former suggests a hope of placating the gods by worship, whereas the latter involves a necessity which knows no placation. As to chance, he does not regard it as a god as most men do (for in a god's acts there is no disorder), nor as an uncertain cause of all things for he does not believe that good and evil are given by chance to man for the framing of a blessed life, but that opportunities for great good and great evil are afforded by it. He therefore thinks it better to be unfortunate in reasonable action than to prosper in unreason. For it is better in a man's actions that what is well chosen should fail, rather than that what is ill chosen should be successful owing to chance.

Meditate therefore on these things and things akin to them night and day by yourself, and with a companion like to yourself, and never shall you be disturbed waking or asleep, but you shall live like a god among men. For a man who lives among immortal blessings is not like to a mortal being.

PRINCIPLE DOCTRINES

I. The blessed and immortal nature knows no trouble itself nor causes trouble to any other, so that it is never constrained by anger or favour. For all such things exist only in the weak.

II. Death is nothing to us: for that which is dissolved is without sensation; and that which lacks sensation is nothing to us.

III. The limit of quantity in pleasures is the removal of all that is painful. Wherever pleasure is present, as long as it is there, there is neither pain of body nor of mind, nor of both at once.

IV. Pain does not last continuously in the flesh, but the acutest pain is there for a very short time, and even that which just exceeds the pleasure in the flesh does not continue for many days at once. But chronic illnesses permit a predominance of pleasure over pain in the flesh.

V. It is not possible to live pleasantly without living prudently and honourably and justly, [nor again to live a life of prudence, honour, and justice] without living pleasantly. And the man who does not possess the pleasant life is not living prudently and honourably and justly, and the man who does not possess the virtuous life cannot possibly live pleasantly.

VI. To secure protection from men anything is a natural good, by which you may be able to attain this end.

VII. Some men wished to become famous and conspicuous, thinking that they would thus win for themselves safety from other men. Wherefore if the life of such men is safe, they have obtained the good which nature craves; but if it is not safe, they do not possess that for which they strove at first by the instinct of nature.

VIII. No pleasure is a bad thing in itself: but the means which produce some pleasures bring with them disturbances many times greater than the pleasures.

IX. If every pleasure could be intensified so that it lasted and influenced the whole organism or the most essential parts of our nature, pleasures would never differ from one another.

X. If the things that produce the pleasures of profligates could dispel the fears of the mind about the phenomena of the sky and death and its pains, and also teach the limits of desires and of pains, we should never have cause to blame them: for they would be filling themselves full with pleasures from every source and never have pain of body or mind, which is the evil of life.

XI. If we were not troubled by our suspicions of the phenomena of the sky and about death, fearing that it concerns us, and also by our failure to grasp the limits of pains and desires, we should have no need of natural science.

XII. A man cannot dispel his fear about the most important matters if he does not know what is the nature of the universe but suspects the truth of some mythical story. So that without natural science it is not possible to attain our pleasures unalloyed.

XIII. There is no profit in securing protection in relation to men, if things above and things beneath the earth and indeed all in the boundless universe remain matters of suspicion.

XIV. The most unalloyed source of protection from men, which is secured to some extent by a certain force of expulsion, is in fact the immunity which results from a quiet life and the retirement from the world.

XV. The wealth demanded by nature is both limited and easily procured; that demanded by idle imaginings stretches on to infinity.

XVI. In but few things chance hinders a wise man, but the greatest and most important matters reason has ordained and throughout the whole period of life does and will ordain.

XVII. The just man is most free from trouble, the unjust most full of trouble.

XVIII. The pleasure in the flesh is not increased, when once the pain due to want is removed, but is only varied: and the limit as regards pleasure in the mind is begotten by the reasoned understanding of these very pleasures and of the emotions akin to them, which used to cause the greatest fear to the mind.

XIX. Infinite time contains no greater pleasure than limited time, if one measures by reason the limits of pleasure.

XX. The flesh perceives the limits of pleasure as unlimited and unlimited time is required to supply it. But the mind, having attained a reasoned understanding of the ultimate good of the flesh and its limits and having dissipated the fears concerning the time to come, supplies us with the complete life, and we have no further need of infinite time: but neither does the mind shun pleasure, nor, when circumstances begin to bring about the departure from life, does it approach its end as though it fell short in any way of the best life.

XXI. He who has learned the limits of life knows that that which removes the pain due to want and makes the whole of life complete is easy to obtain; so that there is no need of actions which involve competition.

XXII. We must consider both the real purpose and all the evidence of direct perception, to which we always refer the conclusions of opinion; otherwise, all will be full of doubt and confusion.

XXIII. If you fight against all sensations, you will have no standard by which to judge even those of them which you say are false.

XXIV. If you reject any single sensation and fail to distinguish between the conclusion of opinion as to the appearance awaiting confirmation and that which is actually given by the sensation or feeling, or each intuitive apprehension of the mind, you will confound all other sensations as well with the same groundless opinion, so that you will reject every standard of judgement. And if among the mental images created by your opinion you affirm both that which awaits confirmation and that which does not, you will not escape error, since you will have preserved the whole cause of doubt in every judgement between what is right and what is wrong.

XXV. If on each occasion instead of referring your actions to the end of nature, you turn to some other nearer standard when you are making a choice or an avoidance, your actions will not be consistent with your principles.

XXVI. Of desires, all that do not lead to a sense of pain, if they are not satisfied, are not necessary, but involve a craving which is easily dispelled, when the object is hard to procure or they seem likely to produce harm.

XXVII. Of all the things which wisdom acquires to produce the blessedness of the complete life, far the greatest is the possession of friendship.

XXVIII. The same conviction which has given us confidence that there is nothing terrible that lasts for ever or even for long has also seen the protection of friendship most fully completed in the limited evils of this life.

XXIX. Among desires some are natural and necessary, some natural but not necessary, and others neither natural nor necessary, but due to idle imagination.

XXX. Wherever in the case of desires which are physical, but do not lead to a sense of pain, if they are not fulfilled, the effort is intense, such pleasures are due to idle imagination, and it is not owing to their own nature that they fail to be dispelled, but owing to the empty imaginings of the man.

XXXI. The justice which arises from nature is a pledge of mutual advantage to restrain men from harming one another and save them from being harmed.

XXXII. For all living things which have not been able to make compacts not to harm one another or be harmed, nothing ever is either just or unjust; and likewise too for all tribes of men which have been unable or unwilling to make compacts not to harm or be harmed.

NOTE

1. [These words are attributed to the sixth-century B.C.E. Greek poet Theognis—S.M.C.]

STUDY QUESTIONS

1. According to Epicurus, why is death nothing to us?
2. Do you agree with Epicurus that scientific knowledge helps dispel fear?
3. Why, according to Epicurus, can you not fight against all sensations?
4. Do you agree with Epicurus that the pleasant life is a life of virtue?

The Handbook

EPICTETUS

Epictetus (c. 50–c. 130), a freed Roman slave, was an exponent of Stoicism, an influential system of thought founded in Greece soon after the death of Aristotle that offered a unified logical, physical, and moral philosophy. Stoics viewed the world as a completely ordered system but with individuals possessing moral responsibility. How these two aspects of reality are supposed to cohere is one logical problem among many the Stoics explored.

Epictetus was primarily concerned with moral teaching, and like other Stoics believed in living one's life in accord with the natural order, accepting what happens with a tranquility that renders one immune from disappointment and pain. Self-sufficiency is prized, for if you are not dependent on others, their failures cannot harm you. Because happiness can be achieved if events occur as one desires, and one has control over one's desires but not over events, the way to happiness lies in adjusting one's desires so that they are in accord with events.

Note that *The Handbook* ends with quotations from Plato's *Apology* and *Crito*, emphasizing the equanimity of Socrates in the face of death. Such tranquility in the face of tribulation epitomized the outlook on life presented by Epictetus, who had himself endured without complaint the physical abuse that accompanied his slavery.

1

Of all existing things some are in our power, and others are not in our power. In our power are thought, impulse, will to get and will to avoid, and, in a word, everything which is our own doing. Things not in our power include the body,

Epictetus, "Encheiridion." Reprinted from *Epictetus. The Discourses and Manual*, translated by P. E. Matheson (1916), by permission of the Oxford University Press, Oxford.

property, reputation, office, and, in a word, everything which is not our own doing. Things in our power are by nature free, unhindered, untrammelled; things not in our power are weak, servile, subject to hindrance, dependent on others. Remember then that if you imagine that what is naturally slavish is free, and what is naturally another's is your own, you will be hampered, you will mourn, you will be put to confusion, you will blame gods and men; but if you think that only your own belongs to you, and that what is another's is indeed another's, no one will ever put compulsion or hindrance on you, you will blame none, you will accuse none, you will do nothing against your will, no one will harm you, you will have no enemy, for no harm can touch you.

Aiming then at these high matters, you must remember that to attain them requires more than ordinary effort; you will have to give up some things entirely, and put off others for the moment. And if you would have these also—office and wealth—it may be that you will fail to get them, just because your desire is set on the former, and you will certainly fail to attain those things which alone bring freedom and happiness.

Make it your study then to confront every harsh impression with the words, "You are but an impression, and not at all what you seem to be." Then test it by those rules that you possess; and first by this—the chief test of all—"Is it concerned with what is in our power or with what is not in our power?" And if it is concerned with what is not in our power, be ready with the answer that it is nothing to you.

2

Remember that the will to get promises attainment of what you will, and the will to avoid promises escape from what you avoid; and he who fails to get what he wills is unfortunate, and he who does not escape what he wills to avoid is miserable. If then you try to avoid only what is unnatural in the region within your control, you will escape from all that you avoid; but if you try to avoid disease or death or poverty, you will be miserable.

Therefore let your will to avoid have no concern with what is not in man's power; direct it only to things in man's power that are contrary to nature. But for the moment you must utterly remove the will to get; for if you will to get something not in man's power you are bound to be unfortunate; while none of the things in man's power that you could honourably will to get is yet within your reach. Impulse to act and not to act, these are your concern; yet exercise them gently and without strain, and provisionally.

3

When anything, from the meanest thing upwards, is attractive or serviceable or an object of affection, remember always to say to yourself, "What is its nature?" If you are fond of a jug, say you are fond of a jug; then you will not be disturbed if it be broken. If you kiss your child or your wife, say to yourself that you are kissing a human being, for then if death strikes, you will not be disturbed.

4

When you are about to take something in hand, remind yourself what manner of thing it is. If you are going to bathe, put before your mind what happens in the bath—water pouring over some, others being jostled, some reviling, others stealing; and you will set to work more securely if you say to yourself at once: "I want to bathe, and I want to keep my will in harmony with nature," and so in each thing you do; for in this way, if anything turns up to hinder you in your bathing, you will be ready to say, "I did not want only to bathe, but to keep my will in harmony with nature, and I shall not so keep it, if I lose my temper at what happens."

5

What disturbs men's mind is not events but their judgements on events. For instance, death is nothing dreadful, or else Socrates would have thought it so. No, the only dreadful thing about it is men's judgement that it is dreadful. And so when we are hindered, or disturbed, or distressed, let us never lay the blame on others, but on ourselves, that is, on our own judgements. To accuse others for one's own misfortunes is a sign of want of education; to accuse oneself shows that one's education has begun; to accuse neither oneself nor others shows that one's education is complete.

6

Be not elated at an excellence which is not your own. If the horse in his pride were to say, "I am handsome," we could bear with it. But when you say with pride, "I have a handsome horse," know that the good horse is the ground of your pride. You ask then what you can call your own. The answer is—the way you deal with your impressions. Therefore when you deal with your impressions in accord with nature, then you may be proud indeed, for your pride will be in a good which is your own.

7

When you are on a voyage, and your ship is at anchorage, and you disembark to get fresh water, you may pick up a small shellfish or a truffle by the way, but you must keep your attention fixed on the ship, and keep looking towards it constantly, to see if the Helmsman calls you; and if he does, you have to leave everything, or be bundled on board with your legs tied like a sheep. So it is in life. If you have a dear wife or child given you, they are like the shellfish or the truffle, they are very well in their way. Only, if the Helmsman call, run back to your ship, leave all else, and do not look behind you. And if you are old, never go far from the ship, so that when you are called you may not fail to appear.

8

Ask not that events should happen as you will, but let your will be that events should happen as they do, and you shall have peace.

9

Sickness is a hindrance to the body, but not to the will, unless the will consent. Lameness is a hindrance to the leg, but not to the will. Say this to yourself at each event that happens, for you shall find that though it hinders something else it will not hinder you.

10

When anything happens to you, always remember to turn to yourself and ask what faculty you have to deal with it. If you see a beautiful boy or a beautiful woman, you will find continence the faculty to exercise there; if trouble is laid on you, you will find endurance; if ribaldry, you will find patience. And if you train yourself in this habit, your impressions will not carry you away.

11

Never say of anything, "I lost it," but say, "I gave it back." Has your child died? It was given back. Has your wife died? She was given back. Has your estate been taken from you? Was not this also given back? But you say, "He who took it from me is wicked." What does it matter to you through whom the Giver asked it back? As long as He gives it you, take care of it, but not as your own; treat it as passers-by treat an inn.

12

If you wish to make progress, abandon reasonings of this sort: "If I neglect my affairs I shall have nothing to live on"; "If I do not punish my son, he will be wicked." For it is better to die of hunger, so that you be free from pain and free from fear, than to live in plenty and be troubled in mind. It is better for your son to be wicked than for you to be miserable. Wherefore begin with little things. Is your drop of oil spilt? Is your sup of wine stolen? Say to yourself, "This is the price paid for freedom from passion, this is the price of a quiet mind." Nothing can be had without a price. When you call your slave-boy, reflect that he may not be able to hear you, and if he hears you, he may not be able to do anything you want. But he is not so well off that it rests with him to give you peace of mind.

13

If you wish to make progress, you must be content in external matters to seem a fool and a simpleton; do not wish men to think you know anything, and if any should think you to be somebody, distrust yourself. For know that it is not easy to keep your will in accord with nature and at the same time keep outward things; if you attend to one, you must neglect the other.

14

It is silly to want your children and your wife and your friends to live for ever, for that means that you want what is not in your control to be in your control, and what is not your own to be yours. In the same way if you want your servant to make no mistakes, you are a fool, for you want vice not to be vice but something different. But if you want not to be disappointed in your will to get, you can attain to that.

Exercise yourself then in what lies in your power. Each man's master is the man who has authority over what he wishes or does not wish, to secure the one or to take away the other. Let him then who wishes to be free not wish for anything or avoid anything that depends on others; or else he is bound to be a slave.

15

Remember that you must behave in life as you would at a banquet. A dish is handed round and comes to you; put out your hand and take it politely. It passes you; do not stop it. It has not reached you; do not be impatient to get it, but wait till your turn comes. Bear yourself thus towards children, wife, office, wealth, and one day you will be worthy to banquet with the gods. But if when they are set before you, you do not take them but despise them, then you shall not only share the gods' banquet, but shall share their rule. For by so doing Diogenes[1] and Heraclitus and men like them were called divine and deserved the name.

16

When you see a man shedding tears in sorrow for a child abroad or dead, or for loss of property, beware that you are not carried away by the impression that it is outward ills that make him miserable. Keep this thought by you; "What distresses him is not the event, for that does not distress another, but his judgement on the event." Therefore do not hesitate to sympathize with him so far as words go, and if it so chance, even to groan with him; but take heed that you do not also groan in your inner being.

17

Remember that you are an actor in a play, and the Playwright chooses the manner of it: if he wants it short, it is short; if long, it is long. If he wants you to act a poor man, you must act the part with all your powers; and so if your part be a cripple or a magistrate or a plain man. For your business is to act the character that is given you and act it well; the choice of the cast is Another's.

18

When a raven croaks with evil omen, let not the impression carry you away, but straightway distinguish in your own mind and say, "These portents mean nothing to me; but only to my bit of a body or my bit of property or name, or my children or my wife. But for me all omens are favourable if I will, for, whatever the issue may be, it is in my power to get benefit therefrom."

19

You can be invincible, if you never enter on a contest where victory is not in your power. Beware then that when you see a man raised to honour or great power or high repute you do not let your impression carry you away. For if the reality of good lies in what is in our power, there is no room for envy or jealousy. And you will not wish to be praetor, or prefect or consul, but to be free; and there is but one way to freedom—to despise what is not in our power.

20

Remember that foul words or blows in themselves are no outrage, but your judgement that they are so. So when anyone makes you angry, know that it is your own thought that has angered you. Wherefore make it your first endeavour not to let your impressions carry you away. For if once you gain time and delay, you will find it easier to control yourself.

21

Keep before your eyes from day to day death and exile and all things that seem terrible, but death most of all, and then you will never set your thoughts on what is low and will never desire anything beyond measure.

22

If you set your desire on philosophy, you must at once prepare to meet with ridicule and the jeers of many who will say, "Here he is again, turned philosopher.

Where has he got these proud looks?" Nay, put on no proud looks, but hold fast to what seems best to you, in confidence that God has set you at this post. And remember that if you abide where you are, those who first laugh at you will one day admire you, and that if you give way to them, you will get doubly laughed at.

23

If it ever happen to you to be diverted to things outside, so that you desire to please another, know that you have lost your life's plan. Be content then always to be a philosopher; if you wish to be regarded as one too, show yourself that you are one and you will be able to achieve it.

24

Let not reflections such as these afflict you: "I shall live without honour, and never be of any account"; for if lack of honour is an evil, no one but yourself can involve you in evil any more than in shame. Is it your business to get office or to be invited to an entertainment?

Certainly not.

Where then is the dishonour you talk of? How can you be "of no account any-where," when you ought to count for something in those matters only which are in your power, where you may achieve the highest worth?

"But my friends," you say, "will lack assistance."

What do you mean by "lack assistance"? They will not have cash from you and you will not make them Roman citizens. Who told you that to do these things is in our power, and not dependent upon others? Who can give to another what is not his to give?

"Get them then," says he, "that we may have them."

If I can get them and keep my self-respect, honour, magnanimity, show the way and I will get them. But if you call on me to lose the good things that are mine, in order that you may win things that are not good, look how unfair and thoughtless you are. And which do you really prefer? Money, or a faithful, modest friend? Therefore help me rather to keep these qualities, and do not expect from me actions which will make me lose them.

"But my country," says he, "will lack assistance, so far as lies in me."

Once more I ask, What assistance do you mean? It will not owe colonnades or baths to you. What of that? It does not owe shoes to the blacksmith or arms to the shoemaker; it is sufficient if each man fulfils his own function. Would you do it no good if you secured to it another faithful and modest citizen?

"Yes."

Well, then, you would not be useless to it.

"What place then shall I have in the city?"

Whatever place you can hold while you keep your character for honour and self-respect. But if you are going to lose these qualities in trying to benefit your city, what benefit, I ask, would you have done her when you attain to the perfection of being lost to shame and honour?

25

Has some one had precedence of you at an entertainment or a levee or been called in before you to give advice? If these things are good you ought to be glad that he got them; if they are evil, do not be angry that you did not get them yourself. Remember that if you want to get what is not in your power, you cannot earn the same reward as others unless you act as they do. How is it possible for one who does not haunt the great man's door to have equal shares with one who does, or one who does not go in his train equality with one who does; or one who does not praise him with one who does? You will be unjust then and insatiable if you wish to get these privileges for nothing, without paying their price. What is the price of a lettuce? An obol perhaps. If then a man pays his obol and gets his lettuces, and you do not pay and do not get them, do not think you are defrauded. For as he has the lettuces so you have the obol you did not give. The same principle holds good too in conduct. You were not invited to some one's entertainment? Because you did not give the host the price for which he sells his dinner. He sells it for compliments, he sells it for attentions. Pay him the price then, if it is to your profit. But if you wish to get the one and yet not give up the other, nothing can satisfy you in your folly.

What! you say, you have nothing instead of the dinner?

Nay, you have this, you have not praised the man you did not want to praise, you have not had to bear with the insults of his doorstep.

26

It is in our power to discover the will of Nature from those matters on which we have no difference of opinion. For instance, when another man's slave has broken the wine-cup we are very ready to say at once, "Such things must happen." Know then that when your own cup is broken, you ought to behave in the same way as when your neighbour's was broken. Apply the same principle to higher matters. Is another's child or wife dead? Not one of us but would say, "Such is the lot of man"; but when one's own dies, straightway one cries, "Alas! miserable am I." But we ought to remember what our feelings are when we hear it of another.

27

As a mark is not set up for men to miss it, so there is nothing intrinsically evil in the world.

28

If any one trusted your body to the first man he met, you would be indignant, but yet you trust your mind to the chance comer, and allow it to be disturbed and confounded if he revile you; are you not ashamed to do so?

29

In everything you do consider what comes first and what follows, and so approach it. Otherwise you will come to it with a good heart at first because you have not reflected on any of the consequences, and afterwards, when difficulties have appeared, you will desist to your shame. Do you wish to win at Olympia? So do I, by the gods, for it is a fine thing. But consider the first steps to it, and the consequences, and so lay your hand to the work. You must submit to discipline, eat to order, touch no sweets, train under compulsion, at a fixed hour, in heat and cold, drink no cold water, nor wine, except by order; you must hand yourself over completely to your trainer as you would to a physician, and then when the contest comes you must risk getting hacked, and sometimes dislocate your hand, twist your ankle, swallow plenty of sand; sometimes get a flogging, and with all this suffer defeat. When you have considered all this well, then enter on the athlete's course, if you still wish it. If you act without thought, you will be behaving like children, who one day play at wrestlers, another day at gladiators, now sound the trumpet, and next strut the stage. Like them you will be now an athlete, now a gladiator, then orator; then philosopher, but nothing with all your soul. Like an ape, you imitate every sight you see, and one thing after another takes your fancy. When you undertake a thing you do it casually and half-heartedly, instead of considering it and looking at it all round. In the same way some people, when they see a philosopher and hear a man speaking like Euphrates (and indeed who can speak as he can?), wish to be philosophers themselves.

Man, consider first what it is you are undertaking; then look at your own powers and see if you can bear it. Do you want to compete in the pentathlon or in wrestling? Look to your arms, your thighs, see what your loins are like. For different men are born for different tasks. Do you suppose that if you do this you can live as you do now—eat and drink as you do now, indulge desire and discontent just as before? Nay, you must sit up late, work hard, abandon your own people, be looked down on by a mere slave, be ridiculed by those who meet you, get the worst of it in everything—in honour, in office, in justice, in every possible thing. This is what you have to consider: whether you are willing to pay this price for peace of mind, freedom, tranquility. If not, do not come near; do not be, like the children, first a philosopher, then a tax-collector, then an orator, then one of Caesar's procurators. These callings do not agree. You must be one man, good or bad; you must develop either your

Governing Principle or your outward endowments; you must study either your inner man or outward things—in a word, you must choose between the position of a philosopher and that of a mere outsider.

30

Appropriate acts are in general measured by the relations they are concerned with. "He is your father." This means you are called on to take care of him, give way to him in all things, bear with him if he reviles or strikes you.

"But he is a bad father."

Well, have you any natural claim to a good father? No, only to a father.

"My brother wrongs me."

Be careful then to maintain the relation you hold to him, and do not consider what he does, but what you must do if your purpose is to keep in accord with nature. For no one shall harm you, without your consent; you will only be harmed, when you think you are harmed. You will only discover what is proper to expect from neighbour, citizen, or praetor, if you get into the habit of looking at the relations implied by each.

31

For piety towards the gods know that the most important thing is this: to have right opinions about them—that they exist, and that they govern the universe well and justify—and to have set yourself to obey them, and to give way to all that happens, following events with a free will, in the belief that they are fulfilled by the highest mind. For thus you will never blame the gods, nor accuse them of neglecting you. But this you cannot achieve, unless you apply your conception of good and evil to those things only which are in our power, and not to those which are out of our power. For if you apply your notion of good or evil to the latter, then, as soon as you fail to get what you will to get or fail to avoid what you will to avoid, you will be bound to blame and hate those you hold responsible. For every living creature has a natural tendency to avoid and shun what seems harmful and all that causes it, and to pursue and admire what is helpful and all that causes it. It is not possible then for one who thinks he is harmed to take pleasure in what he thinks is the author of the harm, any more than to take pleasure in the harm itself. That is why a father is reviled by his son, when he does not give his son a share of what the son regards as good things; thus Polynices and Eteocles were set at enmity with one another by thinking that a king's throne was a good thing.[2] That is why the farmer, and the sailor, and the merchant, and those who lose wife or children revile the gods. For men's religion is bound up with their interest. Therefore he who makes it his concern rightly to direct his will to get and his will to avoid, is thereby making piety his concern. But it is proper on each occasion to make libation and sacrifice and to offer first-fruits according to the custom of our fathers, with purity and not in slovenly or careless fashion, without meanness and without extravagance.

32

When you make use of prophecy remember that while you know not what the issue will be, but are come to learn it from the prophet, you do know before you come what manner of thing it is, if you are really a philosopher. For if the event is not in our control, it cannot be either good or evil. Therefore do not bring with you to the prophet the will to get or the will to avoid, and do not approach him with trembling, but with your mind made up, that the whole issue is indifferent and does not affect you and that, whatever it be, it will be in your power to make good use of it, and no one shall hinder this. With confidence then approach the gods as counsellors, and further, when the counsel is given you, remember whose counsel it is, and whom you will be disregarding if you disobey. And consult the oracle, as Socrates thought men should, only when the whole question turns upon the issue of events, and neither reason nor any art of man provides opportunities for discovering what lies before you. Therefore, when it is your duty to risk your life with friend or country, do not ask the oracle whether you should risk your life. For if the prophet warns you that the sacrifice is unfavourable, though it is plain that this means death or exile or injury to some part of your body, yet reason requires that even at this cost you must stand by your friend and share your country's danger. Wherefore pay heed to the greater prophet, Pythian Apollo, who cast out of his temple the man who did not help his friend when he was being killed.[3]

33

Lay down for yourself from the first a definite stamp and style of conduct, which you will maintain when you are alone and also in the society of men. Be silent for the most part, or, if you speak, say only what is necessary and in a few words. Talk, but rarely, if occasion calls you, but do not talk of ordinary things—of gladiators, or horseraces, or athletes, or of meats or drinks—these are topics that arise everywhere—but above all do not talk about men in blame or compliment or comparison. If you can, turn the conversation of your company by your talk to some fitting subject; but if you should chance to be isolated among strangers, be silent. Do not laugh much, not at many things, nor without restraint.

Refuse to take oaths, altogether if that be possible, but if not, as far as circumstances allow.

Refuse the entertainments of strangers and the vulgar. But if occasion arise to accept them, then strain every nerve to avoid lapsing into the state of the vulgar. For know that, if your comrade have a stain on him, he that associates with him must needs share the stain, even though he be clean in himself.

For your body, take just so much as your bare need requires, such as food, drink, clothing, house, servants, but cut down all that tends to luxury and outward show.

Avoid impurity to the utmost of your power before marriage, and if you indulge your passion, let it be done lawfully. But do not be offensive or censorious to those who indulge it, and do not be always bringing up your own chastity. If someone tells you that so and so speaks ill of you, do not defend yourself against what he says, but answer, "He did not know my other faults, or he would not have mentioned these alone."

It is not necessary for the most part to go to the games; but if you should have occasion to go, show that your first concern is for yourself; that is, wish that only to happen which does happen, and him only to win who does win, for so you will suffer no hindrance. But refrain entirely from applause, or ridicule, or prolonged excitement. And when you go away do not talk much of what happened there, except so far as it tends to your improvement. For to talk about it implies that the spectacle excited your wonder.

Do not go lightly or casually to hear lectures; but if you do go, maintain your gravity and dignity and do not make yourself offensive. When you are going to meet any one, and particularly some man of reputed eminence, set before your mind the thought, "What would Socrates or Zeno[4] have done?" and you will not fail to make proper use of the occasion.

When you go to visit some great man, prepare your mind by thinking that you will not find him in, that you will be shut out, that the doors will be slammed in your face, that he will pay no heed to you. And if in spite of all this you find it fitting for you to go, go and bear what happens and never say to yourself, "It was not worth all this"; for that shows a vulgar mind and one at odds with outward things.

In your conversation avoid frequent and disproportionate mention of your own doings or adventures; for other people do not take the same pleasure in hearing what has happened to you as you take in recounting your adventures.

Avoid raising men's laughter; for it is a habit that easily slips into vulgarity, and it may well suffice to lessen your neighbour's respect.

It is dangerous too to lapse into foul language; when anything of the kind occurs, rebuke the offender, if the occasion allow, and if not, make it plain to him by your silence, or a blush or a frown, that you are angry at his words.

34

When you imagine some pleasure, beware that it does not carry you away, like other imaginations. Wait a while, and give yourself pause. Next remember two things: how long you will enjoy the pleasure, and also how long you will afterwards repent and revile yourself. And set on the other side the joy and self-satisfaction you will feel if you refrain. And if the moment seems come to realize it, take heed that you be not overcome by the winning sweetness and attraction of it; set in the other scale the thought how much better is the consciousness of having vanquished it.

35

When you do a thing because you have determined that it ought to be done, never avoid being seen doing it, even if the opinion of the multitude is going to condemn you. For if your action is wrong, then avoid doing it altogether, but if it is right, why do you fear those who will rebuke you wrongly?

36

The phrases "It is day" and "It is night" mean a great deal if taken separately, but have no meaning if combined. In the same way, to choose the larger portion at a banquet may be worth while for your body, but if you want to maintain social decencies it is worthless. Therefore, when you are at meat with another, remember not only to consider the value of what is set before you for the body, but also to maintain your self-respect before your host.

37

If you try to act a part beyond your powers, you not only disgrace yourself in it, but you neglect the part which you could have filled with success.

38

As in walking, you take care not to tread on a nail or to twist your foot, so take care that you do not harm your Governing Principle. And if we guard this in everything we do, we shall set to work more securely.

39

Every man's body is a measure for his property, as the foot is the measure for his shoe. If you stick to this limit, you will keep the right measure; if you go beyond it, you are bound to be carried away down a precipice in the end; just as with the shoe, if you once go beyond the foot, your shoe puts on gilding, and soon purple and embroidery. For when once you go beyond the measure there is no limit.

40

Women from fourteen years upwards are called "madam" by men. Wherefore, when they see that the only advantage they have got is to be marriageable, they begin to make themselves smart and to set all their hopes on this. We must take pains then to make them understand that they are really honoured for nothing but a modest and decorous life.

41

It is a sign of a dull mind to dwell upon the cares of the body, to prolong exercise, eating, drinking, and other bodily functions. These things are to be done by the way; all your attention must be given to the mind.

42

When a man speaks evil or does evil to you, remember that he does or says it because he thinks it is fitting for him. It is not possible for him to follow what seems good to you, but only what seems good to him, so that, if his opinion is wrong, he suffers, in that he is the victim of deception. In the same way, if a composite judgement which is true is thought to be false, it is not the judgement that suffers, but the man who is deluded about it. If you act on this principle, you will be gentle to him who reviles you, saying to yourself on each occasion, "He thought it right."

43

Everything has two handles, one by which you can carry it, the other by which you cannot. If your brother wrongs you, do not take it by that handle, the handle of his wrong, for you cannot carry it by that, but rather by the other handle—that he is a brother, brought up with you, and then you will take it by the handle that you can carry by.

44

It is illogical to reason thus, "I am richer than you, therefore I am superior to you," "I am more eloquent than you, therefore I am superior to you." It is more logical to reason, "I am richer than you, therefore my property is superior to yours," "I am more eloquent than you, therefore my speech is superior to yours." You are something more than property or speech.

45

If a man wash quickly, do not say that he washes badly, but that he washes quickly. If a man drink much wine, do not say that he drinks badly, but that he drinks much. For till you have decided what judgement prompts him, how do you know that he acts badly? If you do as I say, you will assent to your apprehensive impressions and to none other.

46

On no occasion call yourself a philosopher, nor talk at large of your principles among the multitude, but act on your principles. For instance, at a banquet do not say how one ought to eat, but eat as you ought. Remember that Socrates had so completely got rid of the thought of display that when men came and wanted an introduction to philosophers he took them to be introduced; so patient of neglect was he. And if a discussion arise among the multitude on some principle, keep silent for the most part; for you are in great danger of blurting out some undigested thought. And when some one says to you, "You know nothing," and you do not let it provoke you, then know that you are really on the right road. For sheep do not bring grass to their shepherds and show them how much they have eaten, but they digest their fodder and then produce it in the form of wool and milk. Do the same yourself; instead of displaying your principles to the multitude, show them the results of the principles you have digested.

47

When you have adopted the simple life, do not pride yourself upon it, and if you are a water-drinker do not say on every occasion, "I am a water-drinker." And if you ever want to train laboriously, keep it to yourself and do not make a show of it. Do not embrace statues. If you are very thirsty, take a good draught of cold water, and rinse your mouth and tell no one.

48

The ignorant man's position and character is this: he never looks to himself for benefit or harm, but to the world outside him. The philosopher's position and character is that he always look to himself for benefit and harm.

The signs of one who is making progress are: he blames none, praises none, complains of none, accuses none, never speaks of himself as if he were somebody, or as if he knew anything. And if anyone compliments him he laughs in himself at his compliment; and if one blames him, he makes no defence. He goes about like a convalescent, careful not to disturb his constitution on its road to recovery, until it has got firm hold. He has got rid of the will to get, and his will to avoid is directed no longer to what is beyond our power but only to what is in our power and contrary to nature. In all things he exercises his will without strain. If men regard him as foolish or ignorant he pays no heed. In one word, he keeps watch and guard on himself as his own enemy, lying in wait for him.

49

When a man prides himself on being able to understand and interpret the books of Chrysippus,[5] say to yourself, "If Chrysippus had not written obscurely this man would have had nothing on which to pride himself."

What is my object? To understand Nature and follow her. I look then for someone who interprets her, and having heard that Chrysippus does I come to him. But I do not understand his writings, so I seek an interpreter. So far there is nothing to be proud of. But when I have found the interpreter it remains for me to act on his precepts; that and that alone is a thing to be proud of. But if I admire the mere power of exposition, it comes to this—that I am turned into a grammarian instead of a philosopher, except that I interpret Chrysippus in place of Homer. Therefore, when some one says to me, "Read me Chrysippus," when I cannot point to actions which are in harmony and correspondence with his teaching, I am rather inclined to blush.

50

Whatever principles you put before you, hold fast to them as laws which it will be impious to transgress. But pay no heed to what any one says of you; for this is something beyond your own control.

51

How long will you wait to think yourself worthy of the highest and transgress in nothing the clear pronouncement of reason? You have received the precepts which you ought to accept, and you have accepted them. Why then do you still wait for a master, that you may delay the amendment of yourself till he comes? You are a youth no longer, you are now a full-grown man. If now you are careless and indolent and are always putting off, fixing one day after another as the limit when you mean to begin attending to yourself, then, living or dying, you will make no progress but will continue unawares in ignorance. Therefore make up your mind before it is too late to live as one who is mature and proficient, and let all that seems best to you be a law that you cannot transgress. And if you encounter anything troublesome or pleasant or glorious or inglorious, remember that the hour of struggle is come, the Olympic contest is here and you may put off no longer, and that one day and one action determines whether the progress you have achieved is lost or maintained.

This was how Socrates attained perfection, paying heed to nothing but reason, in all that he encountered. And if you are not yet Socrates, yet ought you to live as one who would wish to be a Socrates.

52

The first and most necessary department of philosophy deals with the application of principles; for instance, "not to lie." The second deals with demonstrations; for instance, "How comes it that one ought not to lie?" The third is concerned with establishing and analysing these processes; for instance, "How comes it that this is a demonstration? What is demonstration, what is consequence, what is

contradiction, what is true, what is false?" It follows then that the third department is necessary because of the second, and the second because of the first. The
first is the most necessary part, and that in which we must rest. But we reverse the
order: we occupy ourselves with the third, and make that our whole concern, and
the first we completely neglect. Wherefore we lie, but are ready enough with the
demonstration that lying is wrong.

<h1 style="text-align:center">53</h1>

On every occasion we must have these thoughts at hand,

> "Lead me, O Zeus, and lead me, Destiny,
> Whither ordained is by your decree.
> I'll follow, doubting not, or if with will
> Recreant I falter, I shall follow still."[6]

> "Who rightly with necessity complies
> In things divine we count him skilled and wise."[7]

> "Well, Crito, if this be the gods' will, so be it."[8]

> "Anytus and Meletus have power to put me to death, but not to harm me."[9]

NOTES

1. [Diogenes (c. 412–323 B.C.), a Greek philosopher of the Cynic (doggish) school, taught that the virtuous life was the simple life. He flouted custom, living in a tub and discarding all his possessions. When Alexander the Great reportedly visited him and in admiration offered to fulfill any request, Diogenes is said to have replied, "Just step out of my sunlight."—S.M.C.]
2. [According to Greek mythology, Polynices and Eteocles were the sons of Oedipus. After his blinding they insulted him, and he therefore cursed them. The curse was fulfilled when, the two having agreed to reign in alternate years, Eteocles would not relinquish the throne, and the brothers entered into combat and killed each other.]
3. [Reference is to a story about three men sent to Delphi, site of the Oracle housed in the Temple of Apollo. When attacked by robbers, one fled and a second, in attempting to defend the third, accidentally killed him. The Oracle rejected the runaway and absolved the homicide.]
4. [Zeno of Citium (c. 334–c. 262 B.C.), a Greek philosopher who had studied under the Cynics, was the founder of Stoicism. He is not to be confused with Zeno of Elea (c. 490–430 B.C.), creator of the immortal paradoxes.]
5. [Chrysippus (c. 279–200 B.C.), third leader of the Stoic school, is said to have been one of the greatest logicians of ancient times.]
6. [This quotation is from Cleanthes (c. 331–232 B.C.), who headed the Stoic school following Zeno and whose most famous work is the poem *Hymn to Zeus*.]

7. [These lines are from a fragment by the Greek tragic dramatist Euripides (c. 480–406 B.C.)]
8. [The reference is to Plato's *Crito*.]
9. [The reference is to Plato's *Apology*.]

STUDY QUESTIONS

1. How does Epictetus recommend that we deal with loss?
2. According to Epictetus, why is the desire to live forever silly?
3. How much control do we have over our desires?
4. Would you be able to go through even one day maintaining the outlook on life and death recommended by Epictetus?

PART 14

The Meaning of Life

The Meaning of Life

RICHARD TAYLOR

Those who begin the study of philosophy often assume the subject will focus on the meaning of life. This supposedly crucial topic, however, is rarely mentioned. Yet philosophers do occasionally consider the issue, as witness our next selection. Its author is Richard Taylor, whose work we read previously. He concludes that the meaning of life comes from within us and is not bestowed from without.

The question whether life has any meaning is difficult to interpret, and the more you concentrate your critical faculty on it the more it seems to elude you, or to evaporate as any intelligible question. You want to turn it aside, as a source of embarrassment, as something that, if it cannot be abolished, should at least be decently covered. And yet I think any reflective person recognizes that the question it raises is important, and that it ought to have a significant answer.

If the idea of meaningfulness is difficult to grasp in this context, so that we are unsure what sort of thing would amount to answering the question, the idea of meaninglessness is perhaps less so. If, then, we can bring before our minds a clear image of meaningless existence, then perhaps we can take a step toward coping with our original question by seeing to what extent our lives, as we actually find them, resemble that image, and draw such lessons as we are able to from the comparison.

MEANINGLESS EXISTENCE

A perfect image of meaninglessness, of the kind we are seeking, is found in the ancient myth of Sisyphus. Sisyphus, it will be remembered, betrayed divine secrets to mortals, and for this he was condemned by the gods to roll a stone to the top of a hill, the stone then immediately to roll back down, again to be pushed to the top by Sisyphus, to roll down once more, and so on again and again, *forever*. Now in this we have the picture of meaningless, pointless toil, of a meaningless existence that is absolutely *never* redeemed. It is not even redeemed by a death that, if it were to accomplish nothing more, would at least bring this idiotic cycle to a close.

From *Good and Evil*, revised edition, by Richard Taylor (Amherst, NY: Prometheus Books, 2000), pp. 319–334. Copyright © 2000 by Richard Taylor. All rights reserved. Reprinted with permission of the publisher.

If we were invited to imagine Sisyphus struggling for a while and accomplishing nothing, perhaps eventually falling from exhaustion, so that we might suppose him then eventually turning to something having some sort of promise, then the meaninglessness of that chapter of his life would not be so stark. It would be a dark and dreadful dream, from which he eventually awakens to sunlight and reality. But he does not awaken, for there is nothing for him to awaken to. His repetitive toil is his life and reality, and it goes on forever, and it is without any meaning whatever. Nothing ever comes of what he is doing, except simply, more of the same. Not by one step, nor by a thousand, nor by ten thousand does he even expiate by the smallest token the sin against the gods that led him into this fate. Nothing comes of it, nothing at all.

This ancient myth has always enchanted people, for countless meanings can be read into it. Some of the ancients apparently thought it symbolized the perpetual rising and setting of the sun, and others the repetitious crashing of the waves upon the shore. Probably the commonest interpretation is that it symbolizes our eternal struggle and unquenchable spirit, our determination always to try once more in the face of overwhelming discouragement. This interpretation is further supported by that version of the myth according to which Sisyphus was commanded to roll the stone *over* the hill, so that it would finally roll down the other side, but was never quite able to make it.

I am not concerned with rendering or defending any interpretation of this myth, however. I have cited it only for the one element it does unmistakably contain, namely, that of a repetitious, cyclic activity that never comes to anything. We could contrive other images of this that would serve just as well, and no mythmakers are needed to supply the materials of it. Thus, we can imagine two persons transporting a stone—or even a precious gem, it does not matter—back and forth, relay style. One carries it to a near or distant point where it is received by the other; it is returned to its starting point, there to be recovered by the first, and the process is repeated over and over. Except in this relay nothing counts as winning, and nothing brings the contest to any close, each step only leads to a repetition of itself. Or we can imagine two groups of prisoners, one of them engaged in digging a prodigious hole in the ground that is no sooner finished than it is filled in again by the other group, the latter then digging a new hole that is at once filled in by the first group, and so on and on endlessly.

Now what stands out in all such pictures as oppressive and dejecting is not that the beings who enact these roles suffer any torture or pain, for it need not be assumed that they do. Nor is it that their labors are great, for they are no greater than the labors commonly undertaken by most people most of the time. According to the original myth, the stone is so large that Sisyphus never quite gets it to the top and must groan under every step, so that his enormous labor is all for nought. But this is not what appalls. It is not that his great struggle comes to nothing, but that his existence itself is without meaning. Even if we suppose, for example, that the stone is but a pebble that can be carried effortlessly, or that the holes dug by the prisoners are but small ones, not the slightest meaning is introduced into their lives. The stone that Sisyphus moves to the top of the hill, whether we think of it as large or small, still rolls back every time, and the process is repeated forever. Nothing comes of it, and the work is simply pointless. That is the element of the myth that I wish to capture.

Again, it is not the fact that the labors of Sisyphus continue forever that deprives them of meaning. It is, rather, the implication of this: that they come to nothing. The image would not be changed by our supposing him to push a different stone up every time, each to roll down again. But if we supposed that these stones, instead of rolling back to their places as if they had never been moved, were assembled at the top of the hill and there incorporated, say, in a beautiful and enduring temple, then the aspect of meaninglessness would disappear. His labors would then have a point, something would come of them all, and although one could perhaps still say it was not worth it, one could not say that the life of Sisyphus was devoid of meaning altogether. Meaningfulness would at least have made an appearance, and we could see what it was.

That point will need remembering. But in the meantime, let us note another way in which the image of meaninglessness can be altered by making only a very slight change. Let us suppose that the gods, while condemning Sisyphus to the fate just described, at the same time, as an afterthought, waxed perversely merciful by implanting in him a strange and irrational impulse; namely, a compulsive impulse to roll stones. We may if we like, to make this more graphic, suppose they accomplish this by implanting in him some substance that has this effect on his character and drives. I call this perverse, because from our point of view there is clearly no reason why anyone should have a persistent and insatiable desire to do something so pointless as that. Nevertheless, suppose that is Sisyphus' condition. He has but one obsession, which is to roll stones, and it is an obsession that is only for the moment appeased by his rolling them—he no sooner gets a stone rolled to the top of the hill than he is restless to roll up another.

Now it can be seen why this little afterthought of the gods, which I called perverse, was also in fact merciful. For they have by this device managed to give Sisyphus precisely what he wants—by making him want precisely what they inflict on him. However it may appear to us, Sisyphus' fate now does not appear to him as a condemnation, but the very reverse. His one desire in life is to roll stones, and he is absolutely guaranteed its endless fulfillment. Where otherwise he might profoundly have wished surcease, and even welcomed the quiet of death to release him from endless boredom and meaninglessness, his life is now filled with mission and meaning, and he seems to himself to have been given an entry to heaven. Nor need he even fear death, for the gods have promised him an endless opportunity to indulge his single purpose, without concern or frustration. He will be able to roll stones *forever*.

What we need to mark most carefully at this point is that the picture with which we began has not really been changed in the least by adding this supposition. Exactly the same things happen as before. The only change is in Sisyphus' view of them. The picture before was the image of meaningless activity and existence.

It was created precisely to be an image of that. It has not lost that meaninglessness, it has now gained not the least shred of meaningfulness. The stones still roll back as before, each phase of Sisyphus' life still exactly resembles all the others, the task is never completed, nothing comes of it, no temple ever begins to rise, and all this cycle of the same pointless thing over and over goes on forever in this picture as in the other. The *only* thing that has happened is this: Sisyphus has been reconciled to it, and indeed more, he has been led to embrace it. Not, however, by reason or persuasion, but by nothing more rational than the potency of a new substance in his veins.

THE MEANINGLESSNESS OF LIFE

I believe the foregoing provides a fairly clear content to the idea of meaninglessness and, through it, some hint of what meaningfulness, in this sense, might be. Meaninglessness is essentially endless pointlessness, and meaningfulness is therefore the opposite. Activity, and even long, drawn out and repetitive activity, has a meaning if it has some significant culmination, some more or less lasting end that can be considered to have been the direction and purpose of the activity. But the descriptions so far also provide something else; namely, the suggestion of how an existence that is objectively meaningless, in this sense, can nevertheless acquire a meaning for him whose existence it is.

Now let us ask: Which of these pictures does life in fact resemble? And let us not begin with our own lives, for here both our prejudices and wishes are great, but with the life in general that we share with the rest of creation. We shall find, I think, that it all has a certain pattern and that this pattern is by now easily recognized.

We can begin anywhere, only saving human existence for our last consideration. We can, for example, begin with any animal. It does not matter where we begin, because the result is going to be exactly the same.

Thus, for example, there are caves in New Zealand, deep and dark, whose floors are quiet pools and whose walls and ceilings are covered with soft light. As you gaze in wonder in the stillness of these caves, it seems that the Creator has reproduced there in microcosm the heavens themselves, until you scarcely remember the enclosing presence of the walls. As you look more closely, however, the scene is explained. Each dot of light identifies an ugly worm, whose luminous tail is meant to attract insects from the surrounding darkness. As from time to time one of these insects draws near it becomes entangled in a sticky thread lowered by the worm, and is eaten. This goes on month after month, the blind worm lying there in the barren stillness waiting to entrap an occasional bit of nourishment that will only sustain it to another bit of nourishment until.... Until what? What great thing awaits all this long and repetitious effort and makes it worthwhile? Really nothing. The larva just transforms itself finally to a tiny winged adult that lacks even mouth parts to feed and lives only a day or two. These adults, as soon as they have mated and laid eggs, are themselves caught in the threads and are devoured by the cannibalist worms, often without having ventured into the day, the only point to their existence having now been fulfilled. This has been going on for millions of years, and to no end other than that the same meaningless cycle may continue for another millions of years.

All living things present essentially the same spectacle. The larva of a certain cicada burrows in the darkness of the earth for seventeen years, through season after season, to emerge finally into the daylight for a brief flight, lay its eggs, and die—this all to repeat itself during the next seventeen years, and so on to eternity. We have already noted, in another connection, the struggles of fish, made only that others may do the same after them and that this cycle, having no other point than itself, may never cease. Some birds span an entire side of the globe each year and then return, only to insure that others may follow the same incredibly long path again and again. One is led to wonder what the point of it all is, with what great triumph this ceaseless effort, repeating itself through millions of years, might finally culminate, and why it should go on and on for so long, accomplishing nothing, getting nowhere. But then you realize that there is no point to it at all, that it really culminates in nothing, that each of these cycles, so filled with toil, is to be followed only by more of the same. The point of any living thing's life is, evidently, nothing but life itself.

This life of the world thus presents itself to our eyes as a vast machine, feeding on itself, running on and on forever to nothing. And we are part of that life. To be sure, we are not just the same, but the differences are not so great as we like to think; many are merely invented, and none really cancels the kind of meaning-lessness that we found in Sisyphus and that we find all around, wherever anything lives. We are conscious of our activity. Our goals, whether in any significant sense we choose them or not, are things of which we are at least partly aware and can therefore in some sense appraise. More significantly, perhaps, we have a history, as other animals do not, such that each generation does not precisely resemble all those before. Still, if we can in imagination disengage our wills from our lives and disregard the deep interest we all have in our own existence, we shall find that they do not so little resemble the existence of Sisyphus. We toil after goals, most of them—indeed every single one of them—of transitory significance and, hav-ing gained one of them, we immediately set forth for the next, as if that one had never been, with this next one being essentially more of the same. Look at a busy street any day, and observe the throng going hither and thither. To what? Some office or shop, where the same things will be done today as were done yesterday, and are done now so they may be repeated tomorrow. And if we think that, unlike Sisyphus, these labors do have a point, that they culminate in something lasting and, independently of our own deep interests in them, very worthwhile, then we simply have not considered the thing closely enough. Most such effort is directed only to the establishment and perpetuation of home and family; that is, to the begetting of others who will follow in our steps to do more of the same. Everyone's life thus resembles one of Sisyphus's climbs to the summit of his hill, and each day of it one of his steps; the difference is that whereas Sisyphus himself returns to push the stone up again, we leave this to our children. We at one point imag-ined that the labors of Sisyphus finally culminated in the creation of a temple, but for this to make any difference it had to be a temple that would at least endure, adding beauty to the world for the remainder of time. Our achievements, even though they are often beautiful, are mostly bubbles; and those that do last, like the sand-swept pyramids, soon become mere curiosities while around them the rest of humankind continues its perpetual toting of rocks, only to see them roll down. Nations are built upon the bones of their founders and pioneers, but only to decay and crumble before long, their rubble then becoming the foundation for others directed to exactly the same fate. The picture of Sisyphus is the picture of existence of the individual man, great or unknown, of nations, of the human race, and of the very life of the world.

On a country road one sometimes comes upon the ruined hulks of a house and once extensive buildings, all in collapse and spread over with weeds. A curious eye can in imagination reconstruct from what is left a once warm and thriving life, filled with purpose. There was the hearth, where a family once talked, sang, and made plans; there were the rooms, where people loved, and babes were born to a rejoicing mother; there are the musty remains of a sofa, infested with bugs, once bought at a dear price to enhance an ever-growing comfort, beauty, and warmth. Every small piece of junk fills the mind with what once, not long ago, was utterly real, with children's voices, plans made, and enterprises embarked upon. That is how these stones of Sisyphus were rolled up, and that is how they became incorporated into a beautiful temple, and that temple is what now lies before you. Meanwhile other buildings, institutions, nations, and civilizations spring up all around, only to share the same fate before long. And if the question "What for?" is now asked, the answer is clear: so that just this may go on forever.

The two pictures—of Sisyphus and of our own lives, if we look at them from a distance—are in outline the same and convey to the mind the same image. It is not surprising, then, that we invent ways of denying it, our religions proclaiming a heaven that does not crumble, their hymnals and prayer books declaring a significance to life of which our eyes provide no hint whatever.[1] Even our philosophies portray some permanent and lasting good at which all may aim, from the changeless forms invented by Plato to the beatific vision of St. Thomas and the ideals of permanence contrived by the moderns. When these fail to convince, then earthly ideals such as universal justice and brotherhood are conjured up to take their places and give meaning to our seemingly endless pilgrimage, some final state that will be ushered in when the last obstacle is removed and the last stone pushed to the hilltop. No one believes, of course, that any such state will be final, or even wants it to be in case it means that human existence would then cease to be a struggle; but in the meantime such ideas serve a very real need.

THE MEANING OF LIFE

We noted that Sisyphus' existence would have meaning if there were some point to his labors, if his efforts ever culminated in something that was not just an occasion for fresh labors of the same kind. But that is precisely the meaning it lacks.

And human existence resembles his in that respect. We do achieve things—we scale our towers and raise our stones to the hilltops—but every such accomplishment fades, providing only an occasion for renewed labors of the same kind.

But here we need to note something else that has been mentioned, but its significance not explored, and that is the state of mind and feeling with which such labors are undertaken. We noted that if Sisyphus had a keen and unappeasable desire to be doing just what he found himself doing, then, although his life would in no way be changed, it would nevertheless have a meaning for him. It would be an irrational one, no doubt, because the desire itself would be only the product of the substance in his veins, and not any that reason could discover, but a meaning nevertheless.

And would it not, in fact, be a meaning incomparably better than the other? For let us examine again the first kind of meaning it could have. Let us suppose that, without having any interest in rolling stones, as such, and finding this, in fact, a galling toil, Sisyphus did nevertheless have a deep interest in raising a temple, one that would be beautiful and lasting. And let us suppose he succeeded in this, that after ages of dreadful toil, all directed at this final result, he did at last complete his temple, such that now he could say his work was done, and he could rest and forever enjoy the result. Now what? What picture now presents itself to our minds? It is precisely the picture of infinite boredom! Of Sisyphus doing nothing ever again, but contemplating what he has already wrought and can no longer add anything to, and contemplating it for an eternity! Now in this picture we have a meaning for Sisyphus' existence, a point for his prodigious labor, because we have put it there; yet, at the same time, that which is really worthwhile seems to have slipped away entirely. Where before we were presented with the nightmare of eternal and pointless activity, we are now confronted with the hell of its eternal absence.

Our second picture, then, wherein we imagined Sisyphus to have had inflicted on him the irrational desire to be doing just what he found himself doing, should not have been dismissed so abruptly. The meaning that picture lacked was no meaning that he or anyone could crave, and the strange meaning it had was perhaps just what we were seeking.

At this point, then, we can reintroduce what has been until now, it is hoped, resolutely pushed aside in an effort to view our lives and human existence with objectivity; namely, our own wills, our deep interest in what we find ourselves doing. If we do this, we find that our lives do indeed still resemble that of Sisyphus, but that the meaningfulness they thus lack is precisely the meaningfulness of infinite boredom. At the same time, the strange meaningfulness they possess is that of the inner compulsion to be doing just what we were put here to do, and to go on doing it forever. This is the nearest we may hope to get to heaven, but the redeeming side of that fact is that we do thereby avoid a genuine hell.

If the builders of a great and flourishing ancient civilization could somehow return now to see archaeologists unearthing the trivial remnants of what they had once accomplished with such effort—see the fragments of pots and vases, a few broken statues, and such tokens of another age and greatness—they could indeed ask themselves what the point of it all was, if this is all it finally came to. Yet, it did not seem so to them then, for it was just the building, and not what was finally built, that gave their life meaning. Similarly, if the builders of the ruined home and farm that I described a short while ago could be brought back to see what is left, they would have the same feelings. What we construct in our imaginations as we look over these decayed and rusting pieces would reconstruct itself in their very memories, and certainly with unspeakable sadness. The piece of a sled at our feet would revive in them a warm Christmas. And what rich memories would there be in the broken crib? And the weed-covered remains of a fence would reproduce the scene of a great herd of livestock, so laboriously built up over so many years. What was it all worth, if this is the final result? Yet, again, it did not seem so to them through those many years of struggle and toil, and they did not imagine they were building a Gibraltar. The things to which they bent their backs day after day, real-izing one by one their ephemeral plans, were precisely the things in which their wills were deeply involved, precisely the things in which their interests lay, and there was no need then to ask questions. There is no more need of them now—the day was sufficient to itself, and so was the life.

This is surely the way to look at all of life—at one's own life, and each day and moment it contains; of the life of a nation; of the species; of the life of the world; and of everything that breathes. Even the glow worms I described, whose cycles of existence over the millions of years seem so pointless when looked at by us, will seem entirely different to us if we can somehow try to view their existence from within. Their endless activity, which gets nowhere, is just what it is their will to pursue. This is its whole justification and meaning. Nor would it be any salvation to the birds who span the globe every year, back and forth, to have a home made for them in a cage with plenty of food and protection, so that they would not have to migrate anymore. It would be their condemnation, for it is the doing that counts for them, and not what they hope to win by it. Flying these prodigious distances, never ending, is what it is in their veins to do, exactly as it was in Sisyphus's veins to roll stones, without end, after the gods had waxed merciful and implanted this in him.

You no sooner drew your first breath than you responded to the will that was in you to live. You no more ask whether it will be worthwhile, or whether any-thing of significance will come of it, than the worms and the birds. The point of living is simply to be living, in the manner that it is your nature to be living. You go through life building your castles, each of these beginning to fade into time as the next is begun; yet it would be no salvation to rest from all this. It would be a condemnation, and one that would in no way be redeemed were you able to gaze upon the things you have done, even if these were beautiful and absolutely per-manent, as they never are. What counts is that you should be able to begin a new task, a new castle, a new bubble. It counts only because it is there to be done and you have the will to do it. The same will be the life of your children, and of theirs; and if the philosopher is apt to see in this a pattern similar to the unending cycles of the existence of Sisyphus, and to despair, then it is indeed because the meaning and point he is seeking is not there—but mercifully so. The meaning of life is from within us, it is not bestowed from without, and it far exceeds in both its beauty and permanence any heaven of which men have ever dreamed or yearned for.

NOTE

1. A popular Christian hymn, sung often at funerals and typical of many hymns, expresses this thought:

> Swift to its close ebbs out life's little day;
> Earth's joys grow dim, its glories pass away;
> Change and decay in all around I see:
> O thou who changest not, abide with me.

STUDY QUESTIONS

1. Can a life be enjoyed yet meaningless?
2. Can a life be immoral yet meaningful?
3. If you find meaning in a task, can you be mistaken?
4. If you don't find meaning in a task, can you be mistaken?

Meaning in Life

SUSAN WOLF

Susan Wolf, Professor of Philosophy at the University of North Carolina, at Chapel Hill, defends the view that not all lives are meaningful but only those in which a person actively engages in projects of worth. Thus, unlike Taylor, Wolf would not find meaning in the life of Sisyphus, even if his fondest desire was to roll stones up hills.

A meaningful life is, first of all, one that has within it the basis for an affirmative answer to the needs or longings that are characteristically described as needs for meaning. I have in mind, for example, the sort of questions people ask on their

From "Happiness and Meaning: Two Aspects of the Good Life," *Social Philosophy & Policy*, Vol. 24, 1997. Reprinted with the permission of Cambridge University Press.

deathbeds, or simply in contemplation of their eventual deaths, about whether their lives have been (or are) worth living, whether they have had any point, and the sort of questions one asks when considering suicide and wondering whether one has any reason to go on. These questions are familiar from Russian novels and existentialist philosophy, if not from personal experience. Though they arise most poignantly in times of crisis and intense emotion, they also have their place in moments of calm reflection, when considering important life choices. Moreover, paradigms of what are taken to be meaningful and meaningless lives in our culture are readily available. Lives of great moral or intellectual accomplishment—Gandhi, Mother Teresa, Albert Einstein—come to mind as unquestionably meaningful lives (if any are); lives of waste and isolation—Thoreau's "lives of quiet desperation," typically anonymous to the rest of us, and the mythical figure of Sisyphus—represent meaninglessness.

To what general characteristics of meaningfulness do these images lead us and how do they provide an answer to the longings mentioned above? Roughly, I would say that meaningful lives are lives of active engagement in projects of worth. Of course, a good deal needs to be said in elaboration of this statement. Let me begin by discussing the two key phrases, "active engagement" and "projects of worth."

A person is actively engaged by something if she is gripped, excited, involved by it. Most obviously, we are actively engaged by the things and people about which and whom we are passionate. Opposites of active engagement are boredom and alienation. To be actively engaged in something is not always pleasant in the ordinary sense of the word. Activities in which people are actively engaged frequently involve stress, danger, exertion, or sorrow (consider, for example: writing a book, climbing a mountain, training for a marathon, caring for an ailing friend). However, there is something good about the feeling of engagement: one feels (typically without thinking about it) especially alive.

That a meaningful life must involve "projects of worth" will, I expect, be more controversial, for the phrase hints of a commitment to some sort of objective value. This is not accidental, for I believe that the idea of meaningfulness, along with the concern that our lives possess it, is conceptually linked to such a commitment.[1] Indeed, it is this linkage that I want to defend, for I have neither a philosophical theory of what objective value is nor a substantive theory about what has this sort of value. What is clear to me is that there can be no sense to the idea of meaningfulness without a distinction between more and less worthwhile ways to spend one's time, where the test of worth is at least partly independent of a subject's ungrounded preferences or enjoyment.

Consider first the longings or concerns about meaning that people have, their wondering whether their lives are meaningful, their vows to add more meaning to their lives. The sense of these concerns and resolves cannot fully be captured by an account in which what one does with one's life doesn't matter, as long as one enjoys or prefers it. Sometimes people have concerns about meaning despite their knowledge that their lives to date have been satisfying. Indeed, their enjoyment and "active engagement" with activities and values they now see as shallow seems only to heighten the sense of meaninglessness that comes to afflict them. Their sense that their lives so far have been meaningless cannot be a sense that their activities have not been chosen or fun. When they look for sources of meaning or ways to add meaning to their lives, they are searching for projects whose justifications lie elsewhere.

Second, we need an explanation for why certain sorts of activities and involvements come to mind as contributors to meaningfulness while others seem intuitively inappropriate. Think about what gives meaning to your own life and the lives of your friends and acquaintances. Among the things that tend to come up on such lists, I have already mentioned moral and intellectual accomplishments and the ongoing activities that lead to them. Relationships with friends and relatives are perhaps even more important for most of us. Aesthetic enterprises (both creative and appreciative), the cultivation of personal virtues, and religious practices frequently loom large. By contrast, it would be odd, if not bizarre, to think of crossword puzzles, sitcoms, or the kind of computer games to which I am fighting off addiction as providing meaning in our lives, though there is no question that they afford a sort of satisfaction and that they are the objects of choice. Some things, such as chocolate and aerobics class, I choose even at considerable cost to myself (it is irrelevant that these particular choices may be related); so I must find them worthwhile in a sense. But they are not the sorts of things that make life worth living.[2]

"Active engagement in projects of worth," I suggest, answers to the needs an account of meaningfulness in life must meet. If a person is or has been thus actively engaged, then she does have an answer to the question of whether her life is or has been worthwhile, whether it has or has had a point. When someone looks for ways to add meaning to her life, she is looking (though perhaps not under this description) for worthwhile projects about which she can get enthused. The account also explains why some activities and projects but not others come to mind as contributors to meaning in life. Some projects, or at any rate, particular acts, are worthwhile but too boring or mechanical to be sources of meaning. People do not get meaning from recycling or from writing checks to Oxfam and the ACLU. Other acts and activities, though highly pleasurable and deeply involving, like riding a roller coaster or meeting a movie star, do not seem to have the right kind of value to contribute to meaning.

Bernard Williams once distinguished categorical desires from the rest. Categorical desires give us reasons for living—they are not premised on the assumption that we will live. The sorts of things that give meaning to life tend to be objects of categorical desire. We desire them, at least so I would suggest, because we think them worthwhile. They are not worthwhile simply because we desire them or simply because they make our lives more pleasant.

Roughly, then, according to my proposal, a meaningful life must satisfy two criteria, suitably linked. First, there must be active engagement, and second, it must be engagement in (or with) projects of worth. A life is meaningless if it lacks active engagement with anything. A person who is bored or alienated from most of what she spends her life doing is one whose life can be said to lack meaning. Note that she may in fact be performing functions of worth. A housewife and mother, a doctor, or a busdriver may be competently doing a socially valuable job, but because she is not engaged by her work (or, as we are assuming, by anything else in her life), she has no categorical desires that give her a reason to live. At the same time, someone who is actively engaged may also live a meaningless life, if the objects of her involvement are utterly worthless. It is difficult to come up with examples of such lives that will be uncontroversial without being bizarre. But both bizarre and controversial examples have their place. In the bizarre category, we might consider pathological cases: someone whose sole passion in life is collecting rubber bands, or memorizing the dictionary, or making handwritten copies of *War and Peace*. Controversial cases will include the corporate lawyer who sacrifices her private life and health for success along the professional ladder, the devotee of a religious cult, or—an example offered by Wiggins[3]—the pig farmer who buys more land to grow more corn to feed more pigs to buy more land to grow more corn to feed more pigs.

We may summarize my proposal in terms of a slogan: "Meaning arises when subjective attraction meets objective attractiveness." The idea is that in a world in which some things are more worthwhile than others, meaning arises when a subject discovers or develops an affinity for one or typically several of the more worthwhile things and has and makes use of the opportunity to engage with it or them in a positive way.

NOTES

1. This point is made by David Wiggins in his brilliant but difficult essay "Truth, Invention, and the Meaning of Life," *Proceedings of the British Academy*, vol. 62 (1976).
2. Woody Allen appears to have a different view. His list of the things that make life worth living at the end of *Manhattan* includes, for example "the crabs at Sam Woo's," which would seem to be on the level of chocolates. On the other hand, the crabs' appearance on the list may be taken to show that he regards the dish as an accomplishment meriting aesthetic appreciation, where such appreciation is a worthy activity in itself; in this respect, the crabs might be akin to other items on his list such as the second movement of the *Jupiter Symphony*, Louis Armstrong's recording of "Potatohead Blues," and "those apples and pears of Cézanne." Strictly speaking, the appreciation of great chocolate might also qualify as such an activity.
3. See Wiggins, "Truth, Invention, and the Meaning of Life," p. 342.

STUDY QUESTIONS

1. Based on the examples Wolf provides, what does she mean by "a project of worth"?
2. How would Wolf decide whether some activity was a project of worth?
3. In your view, are the lives of a college professor, a professional golfer, a janitor, and a hobo equally meaningful?
4. Would studying certain subjects add more meaning to life than studying other subjects?

Meaningful Lives

CHRISTINE VITRANO

Christine Vitrano, whose work we read previously, considers the views of a meaningful life offered by Richard Taylor and Susan Wolf. Vitrano finds neither convincing and goes on to offer her own view of a meaningful life as one in which a person finds satisfaction while displaying due regard for others.

Richard Taylor and Susan Wolf offer contrasting visions of a meaningful life. I find each account partially persuasive, but neither by itself entirely satisfactory.

For Wolf, a meaningful life is one in which you are actively engaged in projects of worth. To be engaged is to be "gripped, excited, involved." If you find your life dreary, then it is not meaningful.

Enjoying activities, however, does not by itself render them meaningful; they also need to be worthwhile. As she says, "When someone looks for ways to add meaning to her life, she is looking . . . for worthwhile projects about which she can get enthused" and "whose justifications lie elsewhere," specifically in "objective value."

According to Wolf, worthwhile activities include "[r]elationships with friends and relatives . . . [a]esthetic enterprises (both creative and appreciative), the cultivation of personal virtues, and religious practices." Specific examples include "writing a book, climbing a mountain, training for a marathon." Among the activities that lack such worth are solving crossword puzzles, watching sitcoms, playing computer games, and eating chocolate, as well as "collecting rubber bands, or memorizing the dictionary, or making handwritten copies of *War and Peace*." Controversial cases are the paths of the "corporate lawyer who sacrifices her private life and health for success along the professional ladder, the devotee of a religious cult, or . . . the pig farmer who buys more land to grow more corn to feed more pigs, to buy more land to grow more corn to feed more pigs."

An obvious problem with Wolf's position is that by her own admission she has "neither a philosophical theory of what objective value is nor a substantive theory about what has that sort of value." She relies on supposedly shared intuitions regarding the worth of various activities, but to assume such agreement is unjustified. Some people appreciate an activity Wolf disparages, yet dismiss one she values highly. For example, spending thousands of hours training for a marathon strikes many as wearisome; they may be far more engaged by computer games. On the other hand, grappling with a *New York Times* Sunday Magazine crossword puzzle is a popular intellectual challenge, holding far more appeal for most than reading an article on meta-ethics, a subject Wolf finds fascinating.

She might respond to these observations by claiming that the problem with crossword puzzles lies not in their essential unimportance but in their use as mere pastimes. In other words, even those who enjoy solving them don't take them seriously.

This reply, however, only deepens Wolf's difficulty, because the same activity could be judged as meaningful or meaningless depending on why a person engages in it. Consider, for instance, a physicist who does scientific research because of the enjoyment it brings but is devoted to chess problems for their intellectual challenge. For that scholar, pursuing physics would be meaningless, but composing and solving chess problems would be meaningful—hardly the conclusion Wolf is seeking.

Furthermore, suppose that in order to distract myself from the monotony of caring for my two children, I read an article on metaphysics. Why should the motive affect the worthiness of the activity?

Because Wolf's position is weakened by her commitment to an objective value that she cannot explain, we might drop that aspect of her position and accept Richard Taylor's view that a meaningful life is one that affords you long-term satisfaction, regardless of the activities you choose. Thus the life of Sisyphus would be meaningful if Sisyphus relished rolling stones up hills.

Yet even if a person's life is enjoyable, if it is morally unworthy, displaying no concern for the welfare of others, then such a life does not deserve to be judged positively by anyone with moral compunctions.

I would suggest, however, that by combining insights from Taylor and Wolf, we can understand the nature of a meaningful life. It is one in which an individual acts morally while achieving happiness.

To be happy is to be satisfied with one's life, content with one's lot, not suffering excessively from anxiety, alienation, frustration, disappointment, or depression. Satisfied people may face problems but view their lives overall more positively than negatively.

The crucial point is that how satisfaction may be achieved differs from person to person. One individual may be satisfied only by earning ten million dollars. Another may be satisfied by going each day with friends to a favorite club to swim, eat lunch, and play cards. Another may be satisfied by acting in community theatre productions. Their paths to contentment are different, yet their degree of satisfaction may be the same.

Some may be poor, yet satisfied. Others may be alone, yet satisfied. Still others may find satisfaction regardless of the depth of their learning or self-knowledge and irrespective of whatever illness or disability they may face. In any case, the judgment of satisfaction is the individual's, not anyone else's.

Does satisfaction depend on achieving one's goals? Not necessarily. You may achieve your aims only to find that doing so does not provide the satisfaction for which you had hoped. For example, you might eagerly seek and gain admission to a prestigious college only to find that its rural location, which seemed an advantage when you applied, turns out to be a disadvantage when you develop interests better pursued in an urban environment.

Furthermore, some people don't have specific goals. They can happily live here or there, engage in a variety of hobbies, or even pursue various careers. They find delight in spontaneity. Perhaps that approach doesn't appeal to you, but so what? If it works for others, why not let them have their enjoyment without derogating it?

How do you achieve satisfaction, considering that it has eluded so many? The key lies within yourself, because you cannot control the events outside you. If your satisfaction depends on whether others praise you, then they control how satisfied you will be with your life. If you wish to avoid being subject to the power of others, then you have to free yourself from dependence on their judgments.

Some warn against a life spent in "childish pursuits."[1] But which pursuits are childish? How about collecting dolls, telling jokes, planting vegetables, selling cookies, running races, recounting adventures, or singing songs? While children engage in all these activities, so do adults, who may thereby find satisfaction in their lives. Assuming they meet their moral obligations, why disparage them or their interests?

An obituary provides information about an individual's life, detailing accomplishments. What we don't learn therein, however, is whether that individual found satisfaction. If so, and assuming the person displayed due regard for others, then that person's life was meaningful.[2]

NOTES

1. Philippa Foot, *Natural Goodness* (Oxford: Clarendon Press, 2001), p. 86.
2. This theory is developed at length in Steven M. Cahn and Christine Vitrano, *Happiness and Goodness: Philosophical Reflections on Living Well* (New York: Columbia University Press, 2015).

STUDY QUESTIONS

1. What is Vitrano's objection to Wolf's account of a meaningful life?
2. What is Vitrano's objection to Taylor's account of a meaningful life?
3. Do you believe that some activities are more conducive to a meaningful life than others?
4. Can a person who is without friends and without any appreciation for beauty nevertheless live a meaningful life?

PART 15

Asian Outlooks

The Buddha's Message

CHRISTOPHER W. GOWANS

Up to this point we have focused our attention on major themes and thinkers in Western philosophy. But philosophical thought has also been pursued in various Asian traditions, and, before concluding, we would do well to consider some of these. Let us begin with Buddhism.

The Buddha sought to enlighten people on the problem of suffering in life: its pervasiveness, cause, cure, and cessation. Wisdom is found in moral conduct and mental discipline. This teaching is explored in our next selection authored by Christopher W. Gowans, Professor of Philosophy at Fordham University.

....

The person we know as the Buddha was born . . . near the present-day border of India and Nepal, sometime between the seventh and the fifth centuries B.C.E. He was called Siddhattha Gotama (Siddhārtha Gautama in Sanskrit). . . .

His father was determined that [Siddhattha] should become a ruler, and to ensure this outcome he protected [Siddhattha] from everything unpleasant in life. . . . Eventually, [Siddhattha] discovered what everyone comes to know— that . . . aging, illness, and death are facts of every human life. . . . He wondered: What is the meaning of human suffering? What is its cause? Can it be overcome? . . .

SUFFERING AND ITS CAUSE

The Buddha's teaching is primarily practical rather than theoretical in its orientation. The aim is to show persons how to overcome suffering and attain *Nibbāna*.[1] The purpose is not to persuade them to accept certain doctrines as such. This practical approach is famously illustrated by a story the Buddha told Mālunkyāputta, a skeptically minded disciple, when he persisted in demanding answers to a series of philosophical questions the Buddha refused to answer. The Buddha described someone wounded by a poison arrow who would not allow a surgeon to treat him until he knew the name and class of the man who wounded him, his height and complexion, where he lived, and so on. The Buddha pointed out that the man would die before finding out the answers to all his questions, and that he did not need these answers in order for the surgeon to operate successfully to save his life. For the practical purpose of healing his wound, there was no reason to answer the questions. The point of the story is that the Buddha had not declared

---

answers to Mālunkyāputta's questions because there was no practical need to do so. Answering these questions would have been 'unbeneficial' and would not have led 'to peace, to direct knowledge, to enlightenment, to *Nibbāna*.' The teaching of the Buddha does not consist of answers to any and all philosophical questions that might occur to us. Rather, it consists of answers that are needed for a practical purpose. The Buddha then gave the moral of the story: 'And what have I declared? "This is suffering"—I have declared. "This is the origin of suffering"—I have declared. "This is the cessation of suffering"—I have declared. "This is the way leading to the cessation of suffering"—I have declared.' The Buddha put forward these answers—the Four Noble Truths—because they were 'beneficial,' because they did lead 'to peace, to direct knowledge, to enlightenment, to *Nibbāna*'. The practical orientation of the Buddha's teaching does not mean it includes no theoretical doctrines, nor that it is unconcerned with the truth of these doctrines. It plainly contains such doctrines, and they are put forward as true and known to be true. Nonetheless, the Buddha would not have taught these doctrines unless they served the practical aim of overcoming human suffering. . . .

The Buddha's central teaching has the form of a medical diagnosis and plan of treatment: it describes a disease and its symptoms, identifies its cause, outlines what freedom from this disease would be like, and prescribes the course of treatment required to attain this healthy state. The story of the wounded man should be read in this light. We are to think of the Buddha as a physician who cures not strictly physical ailments, but broadly psychological ones, who shows 'wounded' human beings the way to the highest form of happiness. . . .

Here is the description of the disease and its symptoms:

> *First Noble Truth.* Now this, *bhikkhus,*[2] is the noble truth of suffering: birth is suffering, aging is suffering, illness is suffering, death is suffering; union with what is displeasing is suffering; separation from what is pleasing is suffering; not to get what one wants is suffering . . .

The key term here and throughout is *dukkha*. It is ordinarily translated into English as 'suffering'. This is correct in part, but it is misleading. The description above features aging, sickness and death (the observation of which first led Siddhattha to seek enlightenment) and we naturally associate these with suffering. But for the other items listed—union with what is displeasing, separation from what is pleasing, and not getting what one wants—'suffering' sometimes is the right term and sometimes seems too strong. The Buddha clearly has in mind a broad range of ways in which our lives may be unsatisfactory. For the time being, we may summarize the first Noble Truth as the claim that human lives regularly lack contentment, fulfillment, perfection, security, and the like.

Stream-observers[3] might regard this as a rather pessimistic diagnosis. They might be inclined to think that many (if not most) human lives are not so bad, that the positive aspects of life outweigh the negative ones. The Buddha would not have been surprised by this response and did not deny that many persons would question his analysis. His point may be illustrated by an analogy: if an alcoholic is told his life is in bad shape, he will probably point out, perhaps correctly, that he has lots of good times; nonetheless, he has a serious problem and could have a far better life without alcohol and the 'good times' it brings. Similarly, the Buddha thought, most of us can point to some positive features of life: he is not saying we are miserable all the time. However, there is something not fully satisfactory about the lives most of us live. We seek enduring happiness by trying to attach ourselves to things that are in constant change. This sometimes brings temporary and partial fulfillment, but the long-term result is frustration and anxiety. Because of the impermanence of the world, we do not achieve the real happiness we implicitly seek. The Buddha thought we could all sense the truth of this with a moderate amount of honest reflection on the realities of human life, but he also believed that full understanding of the first Truth was difficult to achieve and would require significant progress towards enlightenment.

The next Noble Truth is a claim about the cause of discontentment in human life. Here is how the Buddha explained it:

> *Second Noble Truth.* Now this, *bhikkhus*, is the noble truth of the origin of suffering: it is this craving which leads to renewed existence, accompanied by delight and lust, seeking delight here and there; that is, craving for sensual pleasures, craving for existence, craving for extermination.

There is much in this passage that is likely to perplex us. For now, what is important is the contention that suffering and other forms of distress have a cause associated with various kinds of desire—craving, clinging, attachment, impulse, greed, lust, thirst, and so on are terms frequently employed in this connection. The Second Noble Truth states that the source of our discontentment is found not simply in our desires, but in the connection we forge between desires and happiness. In its simplest form, it asserts that we are typically unhappy because we do not get what we desire to have, or we do get what we desire not to have. We do not get the promotion we wanted, and we do get the disease we feared. Outcomes such as these are common in human life. These outcomes, and the anxieties their prospect produces, are causes of our discontentment. . . .

NIBBĀNA

Many people would agree that suffering or unhappiness is rooted in desire, that it consists of not getting what we want and getting what we do not want. It may seem natural to infer from this that happiness consists of the opposite, in getting what we want and not getting what we do not want. Happiness, in this view, is acquisition of all that we try to gain and security from all that we seek to avoid.

The Buddha taught that this understanding of happiness is a mistake. We can never achieve true and complete happiness in these terms, and there is another, far better form of happiness that we can achieve. To revert to our earlier analogy, someone who holds the first view is like an alcoholic who reasons that, since he is unhappy when he is not drinking, he will be truly happy only if he is always drinking. However, what will really make him happy is to find a way to stop the obsessive craving to drink, to stop looking for happiness in drinking. The Buddha's striking assertion is a similar but broader claim. Obtaining what we are hoping to gain and safety from what we are trying to avoid will not bring us real happiness. This can only be achieved by a radical transformation of our desires and aversions—and especially of our attitudes towards them. We have arrived at the next Truth:

> Third Noble Truth. Now this, *bhikkhus*, is the noble truth of the cessation of suffering: it is the remainderless fading away and cessation of that same craving, the giving up and relinquishing of it, freedom from it, nonreliance on it.

True happiness in life, the opposite of suffering, is brought about by reaching a state in which, on my reading, we eliminate many of our desires and stop clinging or attaching ourselves to all of them. The Buddha referred to this state with the term 'Nibbāna'.

Why not seek happiness in the fulfillment of our desires, in striving to get what we want and to avoid what we do not want? The Buddha did not deny that a measure of happiness may be obtained from such striving, but he believed it would always be unsatisfactory in some respects. In part, the reason is that a life seeking such happiness will always be precarious because of the impermanent nature of the universe. What would fulfill our typical desires—for status, power, wealth, friends, and so on—is always subject to change. Even if we were fortunate and got all that we wanted (and can anyone truthfully say this?), old age, disease, and death would always stand ready to take these things from us. No matter what we have, we can never be secure that we will continue to possess it, and so we will never be truly happy. Another reason is that fulfilling our desires does not always make us happy. 'In this world there are only two tragedies,' said Oscar Wilde. 'One is not getting what one wants, and the other is getting it' (*Lady Windermere's Fan*: act 3).

For the Buddha, a better strategy than seeking to fulfill desires would be to live a morally good life: on account of *kamma*,[4] this would eventually produce greater happiness. However, the Buddha thought such happiness still would be temporary and imperfect, and he thought it would always be a struggle to live a truly good life as long as the belief that one is a self persisted. At best, this strategy might bring improvement, but ultimately it would only perpetuate the cycle of rebirth and its inherent suffering.

Considerations of this sort might be taken to show that these are inadequate roads to real happiness. But why suppose there is another form of happiness—Nibbāna—that is not only possible to achieve but better? The answer is the key to the Buddha's teaching and it involves the not-self doctrine. Sometimes it sounds as if *Nibbāna* involves the complete cessation of all desires (the word 'nibbāna' literally means extinction or cessation), but this is not generally true of a person who has achieved enlightenment. This person does eliminate many desires, specifically all those that presuppose the belief that oneself has primary importance. This belief gives rise to an orientation to life in terms of what is mine and hence is more valuable, in contrast to what is not mine and hence is less valuable. The resulting thoughts and desires are the source of hatred, intolerance, anger, pride, greed, thirst for power and fame, and so on. These states bring unhappiness not only to others, but to those who possess them: a person full of hate does not have a happy life. On the other hand, full realization that I am not a distinct self would undermine the tendency to think myself has primary importance. The Buddha thought this would put an end to all desires associated with hatred and the like, and in fact would release my capacity for universal compassion. The result would be increased happiness for all concerned.

However, enlightenment does not mean the elimination of all desires—at least, not in a sustained way during this life (during meditative experiences of *Nibbāna*, and with the attainment of *Nibbāna* beyond death, desires are absent). For one thing, compassion clearly involves desire in some sense—namely, the desire that others fare well. Moreover, no human life is possible that does not involve some elementary desires such as for food or sleep. Surely the Buddha did not mean to deny this (in fact, the extreme asceticism he rejected would seem to have been an endeavor to achieve freedom from any desires in this life). But the Buddha did think the realization that we are not selves would bring about a fundamental change in our attitude towards those desires that would remain. This realization would eliminate clinging or attachment to the satisfaction of these desires, and it would thereby cut through the bond we ordinarily forge between this satisfaction and happiness.

On my interpretation, there are at least two aspects of this difficult idea. First, in the absence of the belief that I am a self distinct from other selves, I would no longer think of some desires as mine, as things with which I deeply identify and so need to satisfy to achieve my well-being. As a result, there would no longer be an unhealthy drive or obsession to fulfill these desires. Second, in the absence of the belief that I am a self with identity, a substance persisting through time in some respects unchanged, I would no longer be preoccupied with regrets about the past unfulfillment of my desires and worries about the prospects for their future fulfillment. Liberated in these ways from attachment to desires as mine, from pinning my happiness on their satisfaction, there would be freedom to focus attention on the present moment at all times. The implicit message of the Buddha is that, in this state of awareness, no matter what happened, there would always be something of value, something good, in what was experienced. Not clinging to the fulfillment of our desires would release a capacity for joy at each moment in our lives.

For a person who has attained *Nibbāna*, life is a process of living selflessly in which, unencumbered by the false belief that we are selves, we are enabled to live compassionate and joyful lives. To this it may be added that our lives would also possess great peace and tranquility. They would be lives of perfect contentment and true happiness.

In addition to *Nibbāna* in this life, the Buddha described *Nibbāna* as a state beyond this life and the entire cycle of rebirth (henceforth, when it is important to distinguish these, I will refer to them respectively as *Nibbāna*-in-life and

Nibbāna-after-death). Though he thought it could not be described adequately in our concepts, we may say by way of a preliminary that he believed *Nibbāna*-after-death is neither a state in which one exists as a self nor a state of absolute nothingness. It is a form of selfless existence in which there is realization of some union with *Nibbāna* understood as ultimate reality beyond change and conditioning. This is a state in which suffering, and all that causes suffering, is entirely absent. *Nibbāna* both in this life and beyond is a state of perfect well-being and tranquility, one that all conscious beings have reason to seek.

WISDOM, VIRTUE, AND CONCENTRATION

Even if we were convinced that *Nibbāna* would be the ultimate happiness, we might well wonder whether it would be possible for us to attain it. The Buddha's practical orientation made this a primary concern. He believed it is possible to achieve *Nibbāna*, but very difficult to do so. We have come to the final Truth:

> *Fourth Noble Truth.* Now this, *bhikkhus,* is the noble truth of the way leading to the cessation of suffering. It is this Noble Eightfold Path; that is right view, right intention, right speech, right action, right livelihood, right effort, right mindfulness, right concentration.

In the first discourse, addressed to the ascetic *samanas*,[5] the Buddha described the Eightfold Path as a 'middle way' that avoids two extremes: 'The pursuit of sensual happiness in sensual pleasures, which is low, vulgar, the way of worldlings, ignoble, unbeneficial; and the pursuit of self-mortification, which is painful, ignoble, unbeneficial.' Though the Buddha portrayed the Eightfold Path as a middle way between seeking sensual happiness and undergoing self-mortification, it clearly involves a rigorous regime that is supposed to radically transform us. This path, the Buddha said, 'leads to peace, to direct knowledge, to enlightenment, to *Nibbāna*.'

The eight steps of the path are to be pursued not in sequence, but all together, with each step reinforcing the others (though the last two, right mindfulness and right concentration, are the culmination). The Buddha divided these steps into three parts: *wisdom* pertains primarily to intellectual development and conviction (right view and intention), *virtue* concerns moral or ethical training (right speech, action, and livelihood), and *concentration*—often rendered as 'meditation'—involves a set of mental disciplines (right effort, mindfulness, and concentration).

The first part, wisdom, instructs us to acquire a thorough comprehension of the Four Noble Truths and all that they involve. However, it does not require us to answer philosophical questions unrelated to attaining *Nibbāna*. In fact, this is discouraged, as we saw in the story of the man wounded by the arrow. Mālunkyāputta wanted the Buddha to tell him whether the world is eternal, whether it is finite, whether body and soul are one, and whether the *Tathāgata*[6] exists after death. The Buddha refused to answer these questions on the ground that attempts to do so would only hinder efforts to understand the Four Noble Truths.

Comprehension of the Four Noble Truths requires more than intellectual cultivation. We also need a fundamental commitment to understanding them, and our emotions and desires must be disciplined so that they do not distract us or lead us astray. Hence, the Buddha said we must renounce sensual desire, ill will, and cruelty. In this respect, he thought thinking and feeling, the mind and the heart, were closely connected.

The second part of the path concerns morality or ethics. Enlightenment requires moral as well as intellectual and emotional preparation. The Buddha spoke of morality at length, and he expected much more of members of the *Sangha*[7] than of lay followers. But there are basic precepts that apply to all persons. These fall into three categories. Right speech requires that we speak in ways that are truthful, friendly, useful, and productive of harmony. Right action dictates that we do not kill any living beings (human or animal), nor steal, nor have illegitimate sexual relations. Right livelihood says we should not earn our living by harming others (for example, by selling arms). Violation of these precepts, the Buddha thought, would only reinforce self-centered desires and would hinder attainment of *Nibbāna*.

The third part of the path—concentration, or meditation—is the least familiar to persons in the West, but the most significant for the Buddha. . . . Though the Buddha taught many forms of meditation, the general aim of these mental disciplines is twofold: first, to purify the mind of disturbances so as to bring about a peaceful, concentrated, attentive and mindful mental state; and second, to know reality as it actually is by observing that all things in our ordinary experience are impermanent, involve suffering, and are empty of any self. The ultimate aim is not to escape from the world nor to acquire special powers: it is to attain *Nibbāna*.

NOTES

1. [Sanskrit, *Nirvana*.—S.M.C.]
2. [Monks.]
3. [Those who are culturally part of the contemporary Western world and have no Buddhist upbringing.]
4. [Sanskrit, *Karma*.]
5. [Spiritual wanderers.]
6. [Truthfinder; Buddha's title for himself.]
7. [Fully enlightened ones; the Buddha's first followers.]

STUDY QUESTIONS

1. What are the Four Noble Truths?
2. How does Gowans distinguish "*Nibbāna*-in-life" and "*Nibbāna*-after-death"?
3. What is the Eightfold Path?
4. How does Buddhism link thought and action?

The Confucian Way

HENRY ROSEMONT, JR.

A Confucian stresses our obligations toward those with whom we stand in distinctive relationships. In particular, rituals are central to the moral life, for by performing them sincerely we cultivate our selves, show respect for others, and contribute to a better society. The Confucian outlook is explored in our next selection, authored by Henry Rosemont, Jr., Visiting Professor of Religious Studies at Brown University.

....

Confucius (551–479 B.C.E.) may well be the most influential thinker in human history, if influence is determined by the sheer number of people who have lived their lives in accord with that thinker's vision of how people ought to live, and die.

Long recognized and described as China's "First (or Premier) Teacher," [Confucius'] ideas have been the fertile soil in which the Chinese cultural tradition has been cultivated, although at the same time a number of the views and practices he championed were already evidenced in China centuries before his birth. Like many other epochal figures of the ancient world—Buddha, Socrates, Jesus—Confucius does not seem to have written anything that is clearly attributable to him; all that we know of his vision directly must be pieced together from the several accounts of his teachings and his activities, found in the little work known as the *Analects*.

Beginning shortly after he died, a few of the disciples of Confucius began setting down what they remember the Master saying to them . . . Some disciples of the disciples continued this process for the next 75 years or so, and an additional dozen little "books" were composed by we-know-not-whom during the following century, and it was to be still another century before a number of these little "books" were gathered together to make up the *Analects* as we have it today.

Thus it is not at all surprising that the text does not seem to form a coherent whole. Worse, if we take the writings of, say, Aristotle, or Spinoza, or Kant, as exemplary of philosophical texts, then the *Analects* does not seem to be properly philosophical, for it contains precious little metaphysics, puts forth no first principles, is not systematic, and the "sayings" which comprise it are not set down in a hypotheticodeductive mode of discourse.

On the other hand, if the New Testament—or the Hebrew scriptures, or the *Quran*—are taken as religious texts *par excellence*, then it would appear that the

From *Living Well: Introductory Readings in Ethics*, ed. Steven Luper, Harcourt Brace, 2000. Reprinted by permission of the author.

Analects isn't a religious text either, for it speaks not of God, nor of creation, salvation, or a transcendental realm of being; and no prophecies will be found in its pages.

However, if we are willing to construe philosophy and religion more broadly— i.e., as those domains that address the question "What kind of life should I live?"— then the *Analects* is both philosophical and religious, for it does indeed address this question; it does proffer models of what is right and what is good, models that are perhaps no less important and relevant today in the post-modern, post-industrial West than they were in pre-modern, pre-industrial China over two millennia ago. This is not at all to suggest that Confucius and his disciples were "just like us"; manifestly they were not. Hence, before coming to appreciate what they nevertheless may have to say to us today, we must first focus on how different they really were. . . .

. . . [W]e must first appreciate that for Confucius, we are fundamentally relational, not individual selves. The life of a hermit could not be a human life for him:

> *I cannot flock with the birds and beasts.*
> *If I am not to a person in the midst of others,*
> *what am I to be?*

In other words, Confucian selves are first and foremost sons and daughters; then siblings, friends, neighbors, students, teachers, lovers, spouses, and perhaps much else; but not autonomous individuals. In the contemporary West, these relationships are described in terms of roles, which we first consciously (i.e., rationally) choose, and thereafter "play"; just as actors and actresses play different roles on the theater stage, so do autonomous individuals play roles on the stage of life. These roles may be important for our lives, but are not of our essence.

Confucian selves, on the other hand, are the sum of the roles they *live*, not play, and when all the specific roles one lives have been specified, then that person has been fully accounted for as a unique person, with no remainder with which to construct a free, autonomous, individual self. Consider how Confucius would respond to the "identity crisis" so many undergraduate students undergo at some point during their college career. When Mary Smith asks "Who am I?" the Master will first respond straightforwardly "You are obviously the daughter of Mr. & Mrs. Smith, and the sister of Tom Smith; you are the friend of x, y, and z, the roommate of w, the student of professors a, b, c, and d," and so forth. To which Mary will undoubtedly reply "I don't mean *that*. I'm searching for the *real* me." To which Confucius could only respond sadly, shaking his head: "No wonder you call it a 'crisis,' for you have taken away everything that could possibly count as answers to your question."

This view of a fully relational rather than autonomous self has a number of immediate implications for moral philosophy. In Western thought the basis for moral analysis and evaluation is the *agent* and the *action*. "What did *you* do?" and "why did you do it?" are the central questions. But whereas the first question remains the same in a Confucian framework, the second becomes "with whom did you do it?" followed by a third, "When?" Put another way, Confucius focuses on interactions, not actions, and on specific, not general, interactors. Individual selves are agents who perform actions. Relational selves are always dynamically interacting in highly specific ways.

The roles we live are reciprocal and at the abstract level can be seen to hold between benefactors and beneficiaries. Thus we are, when young, beneficiaries of our parents, and when they age, become their benefactors; the converse holds with respect to our children. We are beneficiaries of our teachers, benefactors of our students, and are, at different times, benefactors and beneficiaries of and to our friends, spouses, neighbors, colleagues, lovers, and so on.

It is for these reasons that there can be no *general* answer to the question "What should I do?" except "Do what is *appropriate* (not "right") under the specific circumstances." Fairly careful readers of the *Analects* will note that Confucius sometimes gives a different answer to the same question asked by one of his disciples. But *very* careful readers of the text will also note that it is *different* disciples who ask the question, and the Master gives an answer appropriate for each questioner. To do this is neither dissembling, nor wrong. For example, your roommate asks you to read and comment on a paper she has just written for a course. You are not impressed with it. What do you say? Well, if your roommate is fairly intelligent, but having troubles at home right now, is experiencing her identity crisis, and is thinking of quitting school, your answer might run something like "There are problems with this paper, but you have a really good potential thesis here, and argument there, which you can develop along thus-and-such lines. And when you've done so, I'll be happy to read it again." But now suppose that your roommate is different. He has just received a few As on exams he didn't really study for; and while he is basically a good person, he is showing signs of arrogance and pomposity, in which case you might well be inclined to say "This paper is junk from start to finish. Why did you have me waste my time reading it?"

For a Confucian, these differing responses are not at all either inconsistent or hypocritical, but are both altogether appropriate responses with respect to the second Confucian moral question: "With whom did you do it?" The third question, "When?," is equally significant, because the benefactor–beneficiary relationships are not static. Having just failed an examination yourself, you schedule an appointment with your instructor to go over it, your basic question being "How can I improve next time?" But upon arriving at the appointed time, you find that your instructor—who does not drive—has just learned that his wife has had a heart attack and been taken to the emergency room at the hospital. Not at all surprisingly, you do not ask your original question, but instead say "Please let me drive you to the hospital."

All of these little examples appear simple, everyday, common-sensical at best, perhaps even trivial when compared to these moral issues focused on in the West: abortion, euthanasia, draft resistance, suicide, and so forth. But . . . they are the basic "stuff" of our human interactions, and Confucius seems to be telling us that if we learn to get the little things right on a day-in and day-out basis, the "big" things will take care of themselves.

And we start out on the path of getting the little things right by focusing on our first, most important, and lifelong role: that of son or daughter. . . .

We did not ask to come into this world, we did not choose to be offspring, but we nevertheless have manifold responsibilities toward our parents; we are responsible for their well-being even though we have not freely chosen to assume those responsibilities. . . .

Confucius insists that we cannot merely rest content with seeing to the material needs of our parents: filial piety is "something much more than that." We must not only meet our familial obligations, we must have the proper attitude toward them, we must *want* to meet our responsibilities; we must have feelings appropriate to the situation. This is why Confucius "could not bear to see the rituals of mourning conducted purely formally, without genuine grief." This point is brought home forcefully when it is seen that our obligations to our parents do not cease when they die; we must continue to show respect for them, and honor their memory. Only then will we know and show the extent of our true filiality.

By cultivating filial piety in our relational roles to our parents—as both beneficiaries and benefactors—we are on the way (better: the Confucian Way) to achieving *ren*, which is the highest excellence, or virtue, for Confucius. . . . Usually translated as "goodness," or "benevolence," it is perhaps best captured in English by "authoritativeness," which signifies having to do with both authoring and authority. On the one hand, *ren* is easy, because we are human. On the other hand, it can be difficult to achieve in practice owing to our more basic—i.e., biological—desires. But once we set out on the path of *ren*, it is with us forever. . . .

In order to achieve ren one must submit to *li*. This term has been variously translated as "rituals," "rites," "etiquette," "ceremony," "mores," "customs," "propriety," and "worship." . . . "Rituals" and "rites" are the two most common translations, and are acceptable so long as it is appreciated that the *li* are not only to be thought of in terms of a solemn high mass, wedding, bar mitzvah, or funeral; the *li* pertain equally to our manner of greeting, leave-taking, sharing food, and most other everyday interpersonal activities as well.

It is through rituals, custom, and tradition that one's roles are properly effected. There are customary rituals, large and small, by means of which we interact with our parents, grandparents, relatives, young children, neighbors, officials, friends. These rituals are different for the different people with whom we are relating, and they may differ across time as well (we wouldn't hug friends we saw every day, but probably would if we hadn't seen them for some time). It is through the rituals that we express our filial piety toward our parents, respect for elders, care and affection for the young, and love and friendship for lovers and friends. We cannot simply "go through the motions" of performing the rituals, for this would show both a lack of concern for the other(s) and a lack of sincerity as well. It is through rituals, properly performed, that our true attitudes and feelings shine forth, and we more nearly approach *ren*.

Consider meeting someone for the first time. Your right hand automatically is raised, as is theirs; then you clasp it. Your clasp can be such that your hand feels like a dead fish, or you can show off your strength by attempting to crack the other's knuckles, and in either case you can utter a flat "How do you do?" Or you can present a warm hand, squeezing only an appropriate amount; perhaps you will put your left hand over the handshake, after which you say "I'm very pleased to meet you," looking at the other directly. In short, it is not the case that when we've seen one introduction we've seen them all.

Rituals, and the proper performance thereof, have been largely neglected in developing theories of the right and the good in the Western philosophical tradition. Worse, the contemporary West is virtually anti-ritualistic. Rituals are seen as purely formal, empty, dead weights of the past, and detrimental to the full expression of individuality.

They are, however, absolutely central in Confucianism, and without an understanding of their potential for enriching human life, the *Analects* cannot come alive for the modern reader. We can only become fully human, for Confucius, by learning to restrain our impulses to accord with the prescriptions of rituals. Rituals are the templates within which we interact with our fellows: there are proper (customary) ways of being a father, a sister, a neighbor, a student, a teacher. These ways are constrained by rituals but, once mastered, are liberating and are the vehicle by means of which we express our uniqueness.

But unless we have guidelines (the rituals) our behaviors can only be random. (Listen to Beethoven's Fifth Symphony, first as conducted by Toscanini, then by Bernstein, then by Rostropovich; is it not easy to distinguish them despite the severe constraints imposed on them all by the score?) There are many ways to be a good parent, teacher, friend, etc.; if Confucian selves aren't autonomous, they are certainly not automatons either.

So, then, it is through ritual that we cultivate and enhance our authoritativeness, but this can only be done as we become full participants in the rituals, expressing our feelings thereby, and thereby in turn investing them—and consequently ourselves—with significance. If someone you know is getting married, the ritual tradition dictates the giving of a gift. But if you merely purchase the first thing you see—or worse, have someone else buy it for you—you may be "going through the ritual," but are not participating in it, and it will thus be largely devoid of meaning. You must, first, *want* to buy the betrothed a gift (evidenced even in the modern Western expression "It's the thought that counts"), but in order to be a full participant in the ritual, and express yourself relationally, you must devote the time and effort to secure a gift that is appropriate for that person. This is what Confucius is telling us when he says "Ritual, ritual! Is it no more than giving gifts of jade and silk?"

It must also be noted that for Confucius, the significance of rituals is not confined to our interpersonal relations, rituals can also serve as the glue of a society. A people who accept and follow ritual prescriptions will not need much in the way of laws or punishments to achieve harmony, and no government that fails to submit to rituals will long endure; indeed, he even suggests that rituals can be sufficient for regulating a society. And true rulers, having a full measure of authoritativeness and submitting to ritual, will rule by personal example, not coercion; their formal duties are minimal.

Excepting the sages and sage kings, Confucius gives his highest praise to the *jun zi*, usually rendered as "Gentleman," which can be highly misleading. The *jun zi* have traveled a goodly distance along the Confucian way, and live a goodly number of roles. Benefactors to many, they are still beneficiaries of others like themselves. While still capable of anger in the presence of wrongdoing, they are in their persons tranquil. They know many rituals (and much music) and perform all of their roles not only with skill, but with grace, dignity, and beauty, and they take delight in the performances. Still filial toward parents and elders, they now endeavor to take "All under heaven"—i.e., the world—as their province. Always proper in the conduct of their roles, that conduct is not forced, but rather effortless, spontaneous, creative.

Thus the best way to understand Confucius' concept of the *jun zi* is to render the term as "exemplary person." Having learned, submitted to, and mastered the rituals of the past, the *jun zi* re-authorizes them by making them his or her own, thus becoming their author, who can speak with authority in the present. The *jun zi* fully exemplify authoritativeness, and are content with it, no longer worrying about wealth, fame, or glory.

Against the background of the authoritative person as an ideal, we can appreciate that even though Confucianism is highly particularistic in defining our conduct in specific relational roles, it nevertheless bespeaks a universalistic vision. The one exception to the lack of general principles . . . is the negative formulation of the Golden Rule: "Do not do unto others as you would not have them do unto you."

But more than that, it should be clear that Confucius had a strong sense of, empathy with, and concept of humanity writ large. All of the specific human relations of which we are a part, interacting with the dead as well as the living, will be mediated by the *li*, i.e., the rituals, customs, and traditions we come to share as our inextricably linked histories unfold, and by fulfilling the obligations defined by these relationships, we are, for Confucius, following the human way (*dao*).

It is a comprehensive way. By the manner in which we interact with others, our lives will clearly have a moral dimension infusing *all*, not just some, of our conduct. By the ways in which this ethical interpersonal conduct is effected, with reciprocity, and governed by courtesy, respect, affection, custom, ritual, and tradition, our lives will also have an aesthetic dimension for ourselves and others. And by specifically meeting our defining traditional obligations to our parents, elders, and ancestors on the one hand, and to our contemporaries and descendants on the other, Confucius proffers an uncommon, but nevertheless spiritually authentic form of transcendence, a human capacity to go beyond the specific spatiotemporal circumstances in which we live, giving our personhood the sense of humanity shared in common and thereby a strong sense of continuity with what has gone before and what will come later. In the cosmic sense, Confucius never addresses the question of the meaning of life; he probably wouldn't even have understood it. But his vision of what it is to be a human being provided for everyone to find meaning *in* life, a not inconsiderable accomplishment.

STUDY QUESTIONS

1. According to Rosemont, how does a Confucian differentiate between a relational and an autonomous self?
2. What is meant by *ren*?
3. How do rituals acquire meaning?
4. Does performing rituals play a significant part in your own life?

The Tao

RAY BILLINGTON

Along with Confucianism and Zen Buddhism, Taoism stands as one of the three major traditions of thought in China. The focus is "the Tao," the first principle of the universe, which is unknowable. Nevertheless, the central precept of Taoism is to live in harmony with the Tao. In our next selection Ray Billington (1930–2012) offers a brief exposition of the Taoist outlook. He was a Methodist minister who turned against Christianity, became an exponent of Eastern philosophy, and headed the Philosophy Department at the University of West Bristol, England.

What . . . does 'Tao' mean? To be able to give a direct answer to this seemingly straightforward question would, paradoxically, be to fall into error, since, as the opening verse of the most famous of all Taoist classics states unambiguously,

> *The tao that can be told is not the eternal Tao;*
> *The name that can be named is not the eternal*
> *Name.*

This couplet is from the *Tao Te Ching*, the 'classic of the way and its power'. According to Chinese tradition, it was written by Lao Tzu, a famous teacher and mystic of the sixth century BCE, just before he removed himself from civilisation in order to become a recluse. It is now generally agreed by sinologists that the work is the product of many hands (Lao Tzu means 'great master', which is more a title than a name); that it was compiled over some centuries; and that it was finalised in its present form around the second century BCE.

From *Religion Without God*, Routledge, 2002. Reprinted by permission of Taylor & Francis.

According to the *Tao Te Ching*, the Tao is *the first principle of the universe, the all-embracing reality from which everything else arises*. Although the Tao remains eternally unknowable, its power (Te) can enter into every human being, so that the test of one's commitment to Taoism is viewed as the extent to which one's life is in harmony with the Tao. (The Chinese hieroglyphic for 'philosophy' depicts a hand and a mouth, symbolising a condition where words are consistent with deeds.) . . . Taoism does not proceed to make any case for God, or gods, as divine powers operating under the Tao's auspices, so to speak. Section 42 of the *Tao Te Ching* puts the matter rather differently:

> The Tao gives birth to One.
> One gives birth to Two.
> Two gives birth to Three.
> Three gives birth to all things.

The 'One' to which the Tao gives birth . . . is Ch'i, or primordial breath (wind, spirit, energy, like the Hebrew word *Ruach* as used in Genesis 1: 2: 'The spirit of God moved upon the face of the waters'). It is the life-force that pervades and vitalises all things, the cosmic energy which brought the universe into being and continues to sustain it. . . .

For Taoists even the Ch'i remains remote. It can be experienced, but only with time and dedication. If the Te, the power of the Tao in each individual life, is to be evinced, a force is needed which can be experienced more immediately. It is here that Taoists turn to the 'Two' to which the Ch'i gives birth. These are the twin forces of yin and yang, the polar opposites by which the universe functions, such as negative and positive, cold and heat, darkness and light, intuition and rationality, femininity and masculinity, earth and heaven. Neither of these can be without the other, and neither has any meaning without the other. We know the meaning of 'hot' only in relation to 'cold', of 'wet' to 'dry', of 'tall' to 'short', of 'dark' to 'light', of 'life' to 'death'. (We know that we are alive only because we know that we were once, and shall again be, dead. If we were eternal, there would be no word either for 'eternal' or for 'living'.) . . .

[N]either yin nor yang is ever motionless; each is continuously moving into the other, which means that one must learn to recognise when to apply yin, and when yang, energies. This again means allowing the intuition to exert itself: to know when to speak out and when to remain quiet; when to be gentle and when to be violent; when to be active and when to stand and stare. Both the workaholic and the playboy are, according to the yin–yang doctrine, living distorted and incomplete lives because only half of their natures is being allowed expression. Neither the ant nor the grasshopper in Aesop's fable would receive Taoism's stamp of approval.

The 'Three' to which the Two give birth are heaven, earth and humanity. [I]t is when there is harmony between these three—the yang of heaven, the yin of earth, and the human occupants of the arena which between them they bring into being—that the Te can be identified in people's lives. The final stage is the creation of 'all things' which we encounter and experience, for which 'the Three' are responsible.

The important consideration with Taoism, however, . . . is not to speculate on the meaning of the idea of the Tao, but to find out how to respond to its power (Te) in one's own life. The aim . . . is to be natural, and the *Tao Te Ching* gives many hints about how this state may be achieved. One way is to practise *wu-wei*. This is often translated as living a life of 'non-action', but a more accurate translation would be not to take any *inappropriate* action. The most famous exponent of Taoism who was unquestionably a historical figure was the teacher of the third century BCE, Chuang-Tzu (Master Chuang). He argued that many of the things we do and the words we speak are simply a waste of time and breath, since the situation we are discussing or trying to affect cannot be changed by our efforts: all we're actually doing, he said, was 'flaying the air'. Or worse: our frenetic efforts may actually lead to the loss of what was wholesome and acceptable in itself. We destroy a lily by gilding it; a snake is no longer a snake if we paint legs on it; we shall not help young wheat to grow by tugging at it. We must practise patience . . . acting only at the right time and with the minimum amount of effort. In fact, if we learn how to wait, we shall frequently find that no action is necessary in any case. The *Tao Te Ching* states:

> Do you have the patience to wait
> till your mud settles and the water is clear?
> Can you remain unmoving
> till the right action arises by itself?

* * *

Wu-wei means striking only when the iron is hot, sowing one's seed—whether in deed or word—and leaving it time to burgeon. Where disagreement with another person occurs, its approach is to present one's viewpoint unambiguously, then leave it time to germinate—if there is any worth in the idea—in the mind of the other, rather than to overcome the other with decibels or, worse, to force him to accept a viewpoint or an activity against either his will or his personal assessment of the situation. Wu-wei is the way of the diplomat, not the dictator; of the philosopher, not the proselytiser.

Another concept in Taoism with which wu-wei is linked is *fu*, meaning 'returning'. This could be interpreted as aligning oneself with the yin and yang by understanding that seasons, whether in nature or in a nation's culture and values, arrive and pass, only to return again and pass away again, so that the wise person will accommodate his living to the eternal process of change. More basically Taoism is the concept of fu as returning, or, at any rate, remaining loyal, to one's roots:

> If you let yourself be blown to and fro, you lose
> touch with your root.
> If you let restlessness move you, you lose touch
> with who you are.

* * *

[A]nother Taoist virtue . . . is *p'u* literally an unhewn block, and is an image used to denote simplicity, even innocence: not arising from ignorance, but from a backcloth of full awareness of the human condition: childlikeness without being childish. . . . To live according to p'u is to speak as one feels, to behave according to the person one is, or has become; in other words, to act naturally. The *Tao Te Ching* states:

> Man follows the earth.
> Earth follows the universe.
> The universe follows the Tao.
> The Tao follows only itself.

That final phrase has also been translated as 'suchness', the spontaneous and intuitive state of *tzu-yan*, meaning 'being such of itself', 'being natural'. In human beings, it includes everything which is free of human intention or external influences: that which is in harmony with itself. It may therefore be linked with wu-wei with its call for action only when it is appropriate—that is, when it is the natural action for those particular circumstances. When a person achieves this condition (which is not easy), he or she can be described as being at one with the Tao. It will not be achieved by academic research, or the study of sacred texts, or through a correct observance of ritual: . . . Taoism relegates all these activities to a low ranking on the scale of spiritual aids. It will be gained by living one's life in accordance with the natural forces of the universe, expressed both in nature itself and in human nature.

STUDY QUESTIONS

1. What does Taoism mean by "*wu-wei*"?
2. What does Billington mean by "childlikeness without being childish"?
3. Does Taoism, like Confucianism, stress correct observance of ritual?
4. Can we knowingly act in accord with an unknowable principle?

Twelve Zen Stories

Buddhism was introduced in China in the first century. After hundreds of years Buddhist and Taoist ideas blended to yield Zen Buddhism, which more than a millennium later spread to Japan. Zen places comparatively little emphasis on ritual, morality, or book learning. Rather, Zen finds enlightenment in spontaneous experience and challenges adherents with koans, puzzles that seek to force respondents to abandon reason.

From *Zen Flesh/Zen Bones*, compiled by Paul Reps and Nyogen Senzaki, Tuttle Publishing, 1957.

Our final selection contains a dozen Zen stories that illustrate how paradox is supposed to provide a path to understanding. The ultimate lesson is supposed to be the elimination of all dualities, including any separation between consciousness and the object of meditation.

....

A CUP OF TEA

Nan-in, a Japanese master during the Meiji era (1868–1912), received a university professor who came to inquire about Zen.

Nan-in served tea. He poured his visitor's cup full, and then kept on pouring.

The professor watched the overflow until he no longer could restrain himself. "It is overfull. No more will go in!"

"Like this cup," Nan-in said, "you are full of your own opinions and speculations. How can I show you Zen unless you first empty your cup?"

IS THAT SO?

The Zen master Hakuin was praised by his neighbors as one living a pure life.

A beautiful Japanese girl whose parents owned a food store lived near him. Suddenly, without any warning, her parents discovered she was with child.

This made her parents angry. She would not confess who the man was, but after much harassment at last named Hakuin.

In great anger the parents went to the master. "Is that so?" was all he would say.

After the child was born, it was brought to Hakuin. By this time he had lost his reputation, which did not trouble him, but he took very good care of the child. He obtained milk from his neighbors and everything else the little one needed.

A year later the girl-mother could stand it no longer. She told her parents the truth—that the real father of the child was a young man who worked in the fishmarket.

The mother and father of the girl at once went to Hakuin to ask his forgiveness, to apologize at length, and to get the child back again.

Hakuin was willing. In yielding the child, all he said was: "Is that so?"

THE MOON CANNOT BE STOLEN

Ryokan, a Zen master, lived the simplest kind of life in a little hut at the foot of a mountain. One evening a thief visited the hut only to discover there was nothing in it to steal.

Ryokan returned and caught him. "You may have come a long way to visit me," he told the prowler, "and you should not return empty-handed. Please take my clothes as a gift."

The thief was bewildered. He took the clothes and slunk away.

Ryokan sat naked, watching the moon. "Poor fellow," he mused, "I wish I could give him this beautiful moon."

HAPPY CHINAMAN

Anyone walking about Chinatowns in America will observe statues of a stout fellow carrying a linen sack. Chinese merchants call him Happy Chinaman or Laughing Buddha.

This Hotei [sage] lived in the T'ang dynasty. He had no desire to call himself a Zen master or to gather many disciples about him. Instead he walked the streets with a big sack into which he would put gifts of candy, fruit, or doughnuts. These he would give to children who gathered around him in play. He established a kindergarten of the streets.

Whenever he met a Zen devotee he would extend his hand and say: "Give me one penny." And if anyone asked him to return to a temple to teach others, again he would reply: "Give me one penny."

Once as he was about his play-work another Zen master happened along and inquired: "What is the significance of Zen?"

Hotei immediately plopped his sack down on the ground in silent answer.

"Then," asked the other, "what is the actualization of Zen?"

At once the Happy Chinaman swung the sack over his shoulder and continued on his way.

MUDDY ROAD

Tanzan and Ekido were once traveling together down a muddy road. A heavy rain was still falling.

Coming around a bend, they met a lovely girl in a silk kimono and sash, unable to cross the intersection.

"Come on, girl," said Tanzan at once. Lifting her in his arms, he carried her over the mud.

Ekido did not speak again until that night when they reached a lodging temple. Then he no longer could restrain himself. "We monks don't go near females," he told Tanzan, "especially not young and lovely ones. It is dangerous. Why did you do that?"

"I left the girl there," said Tanzan. "Are you still carrying her?"

THE SOUND OF ONE HAND

The master of Kennin temple was Mokurai, Silent Thunder. He had a little protégé named Toyo who was only twelve years old. Toyo saw the older disciples visit the master's room each morning and evening to receive instruction in sanzen or personal guidance in which they were given koans to stop mind-wandering.

Toyo wished to do sanzen also.

"Wait a while," said Mokurai. "You are too young."

But the child insisted, so the teacher finally consented.

In the evening little Toyo went at the proper time to the threshold of Mokurai's sanzen room. He struck the gong to announce his presence, bowed respectfully three times outside the door, and went to sit before the master in respectful silence.

"You can hear the sound of two hands when they clap together," said Mokurai. "Now show me the sound of one hand."

Toyo bowed and went to his room to consider this problem. From his window he could hear the music of the geishas. "Ah, I have it!" he proclaimed.

The next evening, when his teacher asked him to illustrate the sound of one hand, Toyo began to play the music of the geishas.

"No, no," said Mokurai. "That will never do. That is not the sound of one hand. You've not got it at all."

Thinking that such music might interrupt, Toyo moved his abode to a quiet place. He meditated again. "What can the sound of one hand be?" He happened to hear some water dripping. "I have it," imagined Toyo.

When he next appeared before his teacher, Toyo imitated dripping water.

"What is that?" asked Mokurai. "That is the sound of dripping water, but not the sound of one hand. Try again."

In vain Toyo meditated to hear the sound of one hand. He heard the sighing of the wind. But the sound was rejected.

He heard the cry of an owl. This also was refused.

The sound of one hand was not the locusts.

For more than ten times Toyo visited Mokurai with different sounds. All were wrong. For almost a year he pondered what the sound of one hand might be.

At last little Toyo entered true meditation and transcended all sounds. "I could collect no more," he explained later, "so I reached the soundless sound."

Toyo had realized the sound of one hand.

EVERY-MINUTE ZEN

Zen students are with their masters at least ten years before they presume to teach others. Nan-in was visited by Tenno, who, having passed his apprenticeship, had become a teacher. The day happened to be rainy, so Tenno wore wooden clogs and carried an umbrella. After greeting him, Nanin remarked: "I suppose you left your wooden clogs in the vestibule. I want to know if your umbrella is on the right or left side of the clogs."

Tenno, confused, had no instant answer. He realized that he was unable to carry his Zen every minute. He became Nan-in's pupil, and he studied six more years to accomplish his every-minute Zen.

IN THE HANDS OF DESTINY

A great Japanese warrior named Nobunaga decided to attack the enemy although he had only one-tenth the number of men the opposition commanded. He knew that he would win, but his soldiers were in doubt.

On the way he stopped at a Shinto shrine and told his men: "After I visit the shrine I will toss a coin. If heads comes, we will win; if tails, we will lose. Destiny holds us in her hand."

Nobunaga entered the shrine and offered a silent prayer. He came forth and tossed a coin. Heads appeared. His soldiers were so eager to fight that they won their battle easily.

"No one can change the hand of destiny," his attendant told him after the battle.

"Indeed not," said Nobunaga, showing a coin which had been doubled, with heads facing either way.

THE SUBJUGATION OF A GHOST

A young wife fell sick and was about to die. "I love you so much," she told her husband, "I do not want to leave you. Do not go from me to any other woman. If you do, I will return as a ghost and cause you endless trouble."

Soon the wife passed away. The husband respected her last wish for the first three months, but then he met another woman and fell in love with her. They became engaged to be married.

Immediately after the engagement a ghost appeared every night to the man, blaming him for not keeping his promise. The ghost was clever too. She told him exactly what had transpired between himself and his new sweetheart. Whenever he gave his fiancée a present, the ghost would describe it in detail. She would even repeat conversations, and it so annoyed the man that he could not sleep. Someone advised him to take his problem to a Zen master who lived close to the village. At length, in despair, the poor man went to him for help.

"Your former wife became a ghost and knows everything you do," commented the master. "Whatever you do or say, whatever you give your beloved, she knows. She must be a very wise ghost. Really you should admire such a ghost. The next time she appears, bargain with her. Tell her that she knows so much you can hide nothing from her, and that if she will answer you one question, you promise to break your engagement and remain single."

"What is the question I must ask her?" inquired the man.

The master replied: "Take a large handful of soy beans and ask her exactly how many beans you hold in your hand. If she cannot tell you, you will know she is only a figment of your imagination and will trouble you no longer."

The next night, when the ghost appeared the man flattered her and told her that she knew everything.

"Indeed," replied the ghost, "and I know you went to see that Zen master today."

"And since you know so much," demanded the man, "tell me how many beans I hold in this hand!"

There was no longer any ghost to answer the question.

ONE NOTE OF ZEN

After Kakua visited the emperor, he disappeared and no one knew what became of him. He was the first Japanese to study Zen in China, but since he showed nothing of it, save one note, he is not remembered for having brought Zen into his country.

Kakua visited China and accepted the true teaching. He did not travel while he was there. Meditating constantly, he lived on a remote part of a mountain. Whenever people found him and asked him to preach, he would say a few words and then move to another part of the mountain where he could be found less easily.

The emperor heard about Kakua when he returned to Japan and asked him to preach Zen for his edification and that of his subjects.

Kakua stood before the emperor in silence. He then produced a flute from the folds of his robe, and blew one short note. Bowing politely, he disappeared.

REAL PROSPERITY

A rich man asked Sengai to write something for the continued prosperity of his family so that it might be treasured from generation to generation.

Sengai obtained a large sheet of paper and wrote: "Father dies, son dies, grandson dies."

The rich man became angry. "I asked you to write something for the happiness of my family! Why do you make such a joke as this?"

"No joke is intended," explained Sengai. "If before you yourself die your son should die, this would grieve you greatly. If your grandson should pass away before your son, both of you would be broken-hearted. If your family, generation after generation, passes away in the order I have named, it will be the natural course of life. I call this real prosperity."

A LETTER TO A DYING MAN

Bassui wrote the following letter to one of his disciples who was about to die:

"The essence of your mind is not born, so it will never die. It is not an existence, which is perishable. It is not an emptiness, which is a mere void. It has neither color nor form. It enjoys no pleasures and suffers no pains.

"I know you are very ill. Like a good Zen student, you are facing that sickness squarely. You may not know exactly who is suffering, but question yourself: What is the essence of this mind? Think only of this. You will need no more. Covet nothing. Your end which is endless is as a snowflake dissolving in the pure air."

STUDY QUESTIONS

1. Do you have to empty your cup of opinions in order to learn?
2. What do you take to be the lesson of "Muddy Road"?
3. What is meant by the action of blowing one short note on a flute?
4. What significance do you find in "A Letter to a Dying Man"?

Bibliographical Note

To learn more about any aspect of philosophy, an excellent source to consult is the ten-volume *Routledge Encyclopedia of Philosophy* (London and New York: Routledge, 1998), edited by Edward Craig, which contains detailed entries with bibliographies on every significant topic in the field. Reliable, single-volume guides to the entire subject are Ted Honderich, ed., *The Oxford Companion to Philosophy, New Edition* (Oxford and New York: Oxford University Press, 2005); Robert Audi, ed., *The Cambridge Dictionary of Philosophy*, 2d ed. (Cambridge and New York: Cambridge University Press, 1999); and a shorter single-authored work, Simon Blackburn, *The Oxford Dictionary of Philosophy, New Edition* (Oxford and New York: Oxford University Press, 2007).

An accessible one-volume history of philosophy is Anthony Kenny, *An Illustrated Brief History of Philosophy* (Oxford and Malden, MA: Blackwell, 2006). A convenient collection of major writings in the history of philosophy is Steven M. Cahn, ed., *Classics of Western Philosophy*, 8th ed. (Indianapolis and Cambridge, MA: Hackett, 2012). An advanced, comprehensive anthology of historical and contemporary work in philosophy is Tamar Szabó Gendler, Susanna Siegel, and Steven M. Cahn, eds., *The Elements of Philosophy: Readings from Past and Present* (Oxford and New York: Oxford University Press, 2008).

Index